Robbie

Photo: Max Koot, The Hague, NL.

Robbie

The life of
Sir Robert Jennings
1913-2004

Whewell Professor of International Law
Fellow of Jesus College, Cambridge
Judge of the International Court of Justice

A personal account by
Christine Jennings

Matador
9 Priory Business Park,
Wistow Road, Kibworth Beauchamp,
Leicestershire, LE8 0RX
Tel: 0116 279 2299
Email: books@troubador.co.uk
Web: www.troubador.co.uk/matador
Twitter: @matadorbooks

ISBN 978 1789018 134

British Library Cataloguing in Publication Data.
A catalogue record for this book is available from the British Library.

Printed and bound in the UK by T J International, Padstow, Cornwall
Typeset in 11pt Adobe Garamond Pro by Troubador Publishing Ltd, Leicester, UK

Matador is an imprint of Troubador Publishing Ltd

For our children and grandchildren,

&

the multitude of
Robbie's former pupils and friends

In his book on 'The International Court of Justice (1946-1996*)', the Librarian (Arthur Eyffinger) wrote: 'few judges carried their knowledge and wisdom, that rich harvest of a lifetime, so lightly and with such comfort and ease'. He was writing, of course, of Sir Robert Jennings ... who felt no need to impress, never sought to impose his ideas: Sir Robert was content quietly to be as he was. And yet his qualities were such that he was famous the world over and received every conceivable accolade.*

More than most, his life was 'all of a piece'. The Robbie Jennings who allowed himself to be button-holed by a thrilled student was the same Robbie Jennings who dined with the Queen of the Netherlands ... He never felt the need to choose between the world he came from – the unpretentious world of mills, manufacturing and Methodism in Yorkshire – and the decidedly grand world stage on which he came to be seen as an influential player. It all sat comfortably together, and he liked it all.

Extract from the address given by HE Dame Rosalyn Higgins at the Memorial Service for Sir Robert Jennings in Great St Mary's Church. Cambridge, 11 December 2004

Contents

Origins & Childhood

1913-32

Robert Yewdall Jennings was born on 19th October 1913 at Idle, near Bradford, in the West Riding of Yorkshire, a place whose character was essential in forming his own. There, as a toddler watching eggs in an incubator crack open to release chicks that dried out, cheeping, he made his first coherent comment: *'Flooffy little booggers, aren't they?'*

Idle was an industrial village in the Airedale valley, its rows of stone cottages blackened with soot from the chimneys of big woollen mills. His home, Hawthorn Cottage, was uphill on Highfield Road and had its own small field behind, with a splendid view across the valley to the countryside around. Over the previous century or so the village had grown and was now at the height of its busyness and prosperity. Most of the community worked in the woollen industry, yet there were still a few small farms, and nearby was Idle Moor. A Wesleyan Methodist chapel provided most of the Jennings's social life.

Robbie's father, Arthur Jennings, was the middle child of a family of nine; his mother, Edith (née Brotherton), was second in a family of five. A piece written by Robbie to amuse our own children gives a flavour of those two strands of his inheritance, first describing Grandpa Jennings, who lived in Eccleshill, a slight but significant distance from Idle itself. Tea at that household began with Grandpa Jennings '– slight, beady eyes and grey pointed beard –'rapping the table for grace. The meal was austere, the conversation sometimes interesting but terminated by one of the sons being required "to return thanks"'. Afterwards, there might be music in the parlour, with the uncles and aunts singing around the piano. Finally, there would be a bible-reading and prayers by the paterfamilias.

'Looking back [Robbie wrote] I can see that Grandpa Jennings was a good, gentle if puritanical soul, who, with the help of chapel, somehow managed, in spite of real poverty, to earn and protect a great degree of respectability for

1

his very large family. But he meant little to me, I'm afraid. It never occurred to me ask whether I liked him or not. The question didn't arise.

'Now Grandpa [Brotherton] was another thing altogether. Again rather small, but with a biggish bald head, blue kind and stupid eyes, and a ginger moustache, he always wore a country-type tweed suit which had once been some sort of dark green check. I cannot remember that he had any other garment. To go out for a walk he would add an old, shapeless hat of the same sort of tweed, with a feather stuck in the band, brown leather leggings over his heavy boots, and an ash walking stick which he called for some reason an "ash-plant"...'

Set down in longhand on a wet holiday in Eskdale sometime in the late 1970s, this description was part of an affectionate and whimsical tale about that Grandpa's pride in his small flock of hens, kept on the Hawthorn Cottage small field in rivalry to Robbie's own cluster of Leghorns.

The two sides of his family were clearly different. The more stuffy-seeming Jenningses were staunch Methodists and proud of the part they had played in the development of the local Wesleyan chapels. Grandpa Jennings died when Robbie was only ten, and his wife just three years later. An obituary in the local newspaper describes Thomas Yewdall Jennings as an *Eccleshill Wesleyan Stalwart,* one who 'for 49 years laboured assiduously for the good of the Sunday School'. (One has to recognize the importance of the Sunday School in the Methodist churches at that time and the influence of its Superintendent.) Moreover, while Mr Jennings 'was a zealous Wesleyan, there was nothing narrow in his sympathies, for he took a lively interest in noble causes outside the scope of his own church' – the local Free Church Council, the National Children's Home and Orphanage, the Liberal Club and so on. For a man whose wage as a Warehouse Manager would have been modest, there was no room for luxuries at home.

Grandma Jennings had been born Annie Harland, and her family, too, were staunch Methodists – they could, indeed, claim descent from a John Harland who had been a contemporary and friend of John Wesley. Her grandfather had run a prosperous painting and decorating firm, and her father followed in that trade.

The worthy Thomas Yewdall Jennings himself was the son of a handloom weaver, John Jennings, noted for the excellent white flannel he produced. This would have been a solitary business carried out on the top floor of one of those high terrace cottages on the Long Row, with a good light from large windows. As the years went by, such work was taken over by the mills. John Jennings' wife was Betty Yewdall, herself daughter of a 'clothier', George Yewdall. Both had signed their marriage certificate with an 'X', as had their parents. But though Betty was illiterate, the Yewdall[1] family commanded respect in the local community. A chapter in the small book by Wright Watson, *Wesleyan Methodism in Idle*, begins:

> 'Of all the families connected with local Methodism there is not one which claims so high a place as that of the Yewdalls. . . the name can be traced back for nearly four hundred years in the annals of Idle township'[2]. [Later he tells how] 'The third preaching house erected in the Bradford district' was provided at Eccleshill in 1775, 'largely due to the labours of two of the members, Zachariah and Thomas Yewdall', and a few months later 'Mr [John] Wesley paid a visit to Eccleshill and preached in the new chapel, "to a people", he says, "just sprung out of the dust, exceeding artless, and exceeding earnest; many of whom seemed to be already saved from sin…"'

By 1781 the Eccleshill congregation of Methodists numbered 105, while at Idle there were just 33. But presently more chapels were built, each representing a mighty effort of fund-raising by folk who had little to spare. A family recollection is of

> '… a big Family Pew with a door on at Eccleshill Methodist Chapel and Grandfather [i.e. John Jennings] and Father [T.Y. Jennings] always wore Silk Hats and morning coats down to the knees. Grandpa sat at the front of the pew with Father, and we children all sat behind in ages. We were the most important family at the Chapel and we always had to take the Minister home to Sunday dinner if he came a distance … I was the only one who was never in the Choir of all the family.'

Aunt Kitty, who wrote that, could also remember a special tea set, cherished because it had been used to entertain John Wesley.

---

[1] The name has been carried down successive generations. Robbie's second name was Yewdall; our son is Richard David Yewdall; and his son is Thomas William Yewdall.

[2] The 'township' was made up of several villages, Idle being the principal one. It included Windhill, Calverley and Thackley, each with distinct variations of the local dialect. Eccleshill was close by.

Up on the moor, in Westfield Lane, there is a small Quaker burial ground, established in 1690 by a Thomas Yewdall. Here lie the remains of ten of the Yewdall family – one, Zechariah Yewdall, was a pioneer Wesleyan itinerant minister, and another, David Yewdall (whose portrait shows a strong similarity to RYJ's own appearance) became a successful business man. One of the great woollen mills was leased by John and David and was for years, even after they had left, referred to as Yewdall Mill, in loyalty to the memory of good employers. The Jenningses were proud of that connection.

Robbie's mother's family, as already indicated, were of more wayward stock and took life a little less seriously than the sober Jenningses. Her father, Robert (known as Bob) Brotherton, who could never read or write, worked as a slaughterman. For Robbie, he seemed 'the most contented man I ever knew', and their house always offered a warm welcome. Grandma's daily newspaper, after she had read it, served as a cover for their table except on Sundays, when a white cloth was laid. She must have exerted some authority in that household, raising two daughters and three sons. Yet money was short, and so the children could not stay at school any longer than the law required, all five leaving and starting work at the age of 12 or 13. Minnie, the eldest, and Edith, Robbie's mother, became millworkers, and acquired the skill for promotion to weaver. The three sons all became butchers, with stalls in the big covered market in Bradford. Minnie (Amelia Ann) was to marry fairly late in life. Teddy (George Edwin) and Albert became skilled and respected in their trade. The middle son, Arty (Arthur Cavendish) was a rascal, selling his inferior meat through sheer charm and always being forgiven for misdemeanours by his doting mother. (That name *Cavendish* was intriguing: might the family have had an injection of blue blood?[3])

Tracing the Brotherton line we find that Bob the slaughterman was the son of Michael, who in 1851 married Mary Bradley (or Broadley) of Ellingstring, daughter of a gardener. Michael appears variously as a quarryman and later a 'cloth tenterer'. Family tradition spoke of burials in the churchyard at Kirkby Malham, near the source of the River Aire. Wanting to see for ourselves, one day Robbie and I found time to explore that churchyard. It is a bewilderingly large one, grazed by sheep, and most of its gravestones are hidden by ivy and moss. Just as we were despairing, though, we came upon a large flat stone,

---

3   'Aunt Liza' used to tell that her mother had been a servant at Holker Hall, a seat of the Cavendish family.

raised like a table, which bore the names of John Brotherton and his wife Sarah, besides several children. We read their dates with awe, for John, farmer of High Trenhouse, had died in 1841 at the age of 97, and Sarah a few years later aged 91. Survival to such a great age high on the moor by Malham Tarn meant a robust constitution! And it was not surprising that although John's son William seems to have carried on the farm, there was no livelihood up there for all nine of the Brotherton children of that generation. Down the valley there were limestone quarries, and so a fit young man could find employment there. That is what William's son Michael seems to have done, before following the river eastwards, where great woollen mills were being developed further along the Aire Valley at Saltaire and Idle, to find steady work to support his own five children.

In a passage about the one-time great mills of Idle, Wright Watson[4] tells how 'Yewdall Mill' was burned down three times. The second of these fires, he says, occurred in 1864.

> 'Michael Brotherton's last remaining daughter, Sarah Ann … says that her father was then working at the Albion Mill, but drawn by the glare and the need for help he was soon among those who were hurrying to salvage what cloth they could from the burning building. It was while thus engaged and carrying a rather heavy piece over his shoulder along the narrow path by the dam side that he fell, piece and all, into the dam. To those who still remember Michael and his ever-ready fund of humour and flow of language it will not be difficult to imagine how he took his ducking, nor his opening remarks when he emerged from his unwelcome bath.
>
> This second fire was definitely at Yewdall Mill, for the Yewdalls were then in occupation of the whole of the Mills, and either in part or wholly owned them.'

This anecdote oddly links the family names of Robbie's forbears from both father and mother: the once-prosperous Yewdalls, and a cheerfully improvident Brotherton prepared to take a chance on any kind of labour.

———

Quite probably Arthur Jennings and Edith Brotherton met at work. Already, in the Census of 1901, we find Arthur Jennings, aged 14, described as

---

4   *Idlethorp*, p.312

'accountant's clerk', while Edith Brotherton was at 15 a 'worsted spinner', both perhaps working in the same mill. The fellowship of chapel membership would have provided a gently respectable social life for them. Although her parents did not bother with church attendance Edith, having a pretty singing voice, had joined the choir. At the time of their wedding, in July 1912, the groom was described as 'paper tube maker's cashier', and the bride as 'worsted weaver'. By October 1913, when registering the birth of Robbie, Arthur had become 'paper tube maker's manager' and the young family were at 25 Sherborne Villas, Town Lane, Idle. It was a house Robbie scarcely remembered, for within his first year they moved into the place where he grew up – Hawthorn Cottage on Highfield Road.

Robbie always loved to talk about Idle, reciting the names of its streets and lanes, the shops and farms and chapels, and the quirky characters to be met there. The place had indeed been proud of its distinctive character. In his early years it had its own railway station, through which LMS and LNER trains ran; it was the junction of the Bradford and the Leeds and Liverpool Canals; Jowett motor vehicles were built in the village, and later Wharfedale loudspeakers. But after the death of his mother in 1961 he had no wish to return: by then Idle had already changed, and there were to be reports of even more drastic changes over the following years. The great Thorp Methodist Chapel where his family had worshipped was closed and converted into a YMCA hall while the (evidently diminished) congregation moved into a small brick-and-glass building. Even that is now gone, and there is no trace left of either building, or of the huge Sunday School that he had attended. The village had once been at one with its landscape, almost every house built from the local stone. Now, it seems, the 'improvements' of the 1970s meant that its mills have gone, many of its picturesque houses have gone, the railway and canal have gone, and a new road system obliterates much of the layout that would have been familiar to RYJ.

Miraculously, his beloved Hawthorn Cottage survives. There had been a moment just before the 1939-45 war when it looked as though it must be demolished to make way for road-widening, but it turned out that the sacrifice of its front garden satisfied that need. It was that threat, though, which prompted Arthur and Edith to move into a modern semi-detached house with up-to-date fittings on the Idle Road, a place that Robbie never quite warmed to. It was their old home with all its awkwardness that he said –

6

'…I loved exceedingly, and I was secretly very distressed when just before the war my parents felt they had to move to an easier house. Hawthorn Cottage was a quite modest house. It was built of what is now called York stone but which came from a sandstone quarry actually in Idle, so it was very local. The house was a "semi-bungalow". There were two storeys and a rather nice staircase in two flights of stairs with a "landing" (mezzanine) half-way up. But there were only two bedrooms and a small windowless "box room" upstairs. The bedroom ceilings were the insides of the sloping roofs of the house … what tends to happen in the attic rooms of larger houses.'

His own bedroom looked out onto part of the 'field' area of their acre-plus back garden, where once quite ambitious poultry-keeping had been attempted.

'… The great quality of the garden was the view from it and from the house windows on that north side. We were above Idle village and almost on top of a range of hills and moors forming the south side of a wide stretch of the valley of the River Aire. So we looked down to Idle and then beyond and down to the valley floor where were both the river and a canal. Beyond that, and forming the main part of the view, was what must have been a 20 miles wide stretch of the slope forming the north side of the valley. This view extended as far as the eye could see both to the left and to the right. It was mainly fields and woods. But there were also villages, some like Rawdon part way up the slope and others like Horsforth, near the top. And halfway up that slope and running along the line of the valley, and I suppose some 15 or so miles away as the crow flies, was a part of the Midland Railway main line between St Pancras and Carlisle. So on a fine day one could see main line expresses with their busy plumes of steam and smoke going straight across our view, and on the left-hand side of the view, watch them coming out of, or disappearing into Thackley tunnel. On a clear day one might also sometimes make out the smoke trail of a local "slow train" that had left the main line to climb up the hilly branch line to Guiseley, which was just out of view over the top of the hill; after Guiseley the train would be running down the other side into Wharfedale at Otley. Much nearer and down below, at Idle village, one could see the Great Northern Railway branch line trains that then ran through Idle on the branch line between Bradford and Shipley. When we were first at Hawthorn Cottage, my father used to go to his work, at Thornbury, south east of Bradford, by taking the train from Idle station. But then it became easier to take the tram to Bolton and then change to a "trackless car" (trolleybus) which went through Thornbury to places south of the City. The tram, after all, passed by our own house, where there was a "stop"; but Idle station was nearly 15 minutes walk…'

He went on to describe the house, room by room, ending with –

'The loo was an earth toilet next to the coalplace, and to reach it you had to go out by the front door. At some time we got an inside WC in the bathroom, much to the disgust of my grandpa, who thought an inside loo a very unpleasant idea. The lighting had at first been gas, though one went to bed by candlelight; but electricity was installed later.'

It must have been when Robbie was aged about two that, as he hazily remembered, he was taken to spend a few weeks with a relative's family – because, he was told, his mother was unwell. What was really happening was never revealed to him, or at least he had no memory of it. Edith had borne a second baby, a girl, who was either stillborn or died after just a few days. (In a rare intimate disclosure shortly before her death, she told me of this, revealing that the child's name was Christine like my own.) There were to be no more children. As he once commented[5] 'I was an only child and so you learn to be a loner and you learn to do things on your own and be different'.

Never troubled by the lack of playmates, his great companion in early years was Rock, a big Airedale terrier. Rock would tolerate almost anything from the small boy, who could even ride on his back, though any hint of a threat to his charge made him ferociously protective – once obliging the Jennings parents to make amends when a neighbour had the back of his trousers torn through what Robbie called 'a doggie misunderstanding'.

Their own small field provided space for both Grandpa Brotherton's hens and the young Robbie's.

'I took over from my father the hen business, having bought a poultry keeper's account book and balance sheets. I bought the food for my six hens and one cock. And I charged my mother the market price for the eggs. I even made a paper profit, but of course I paid nothing for the field so it was not really profit.

---

[5] in an interview for the student law magazine *Per Incuriam* in 2002

'I actually made a new hen place. My father's works used to get paper rolled onto centres made from 8ft long 3" x ½" soft wood planks. We could have any number of these sent to Hawthorn Cottage. I made panels of these planks using two others as battens secured with 1½ inch nails…

'I had White Leghorns (one of those became very tame and would fly onto my hand to be fed); or Rhode Island Reds. I also experimented with some pretty Leghorns with black stripes. And I was much taken by a so-called 'Exchequer Leghorn' bred and advertised by a man at Falkirk in Scotland, and with whom I had some correspondence, as he was anxious to help me to restock my poultry farm. I was a bit of a menace generally about writing to firms. I complained to Spillers Oil and Cake Company at Hull that I was quite unable to get supplies of their 'balanced mash' in Idle. They sent a representative to get my 'contract'! Fortunately I was at school, and my mother had to deal with him. He was quite nice about it and did go to see Walter Wade, our Idle grocer, who did then stock just enough for my six hens and the cock…'

A part of that field, mown and rolled by his father, was reserved for cricket practice where the aspiring young cricketer might practise the sort of strokes made by his heroes, Wilfred Rhodes or George Macauley, seen at Bradford Park Avenue cricket ground. In those years the Yorkshire team could meet the Australian touring team on almost equal terms, and the game would forever be for Robbie 'more than a game – a religion'. A rare memento is the score card he preserved from a Test Match played at Headingley in 1930 at which only one full innings was played by each side because rain stopped play. But he had watched Don Bradman score 334 for Australia, and Hammond 113 for England, and seen Hobbs, Sutcliffe, Hammond, Duleepsinhji, Tate, Larwood and other legendary figures in action.

A childhood running through the First World War and into the 1920s provided him with memories of the village lamplighter with his ladder tramping from one gas lamp to the next, the muffin man with a basket filled with muffins and large soft oatcakes, and a village policeman patrolling the streets three times a day. There were great gatherings at Whitsuntide, when all the village's nonconformist congregations (Methodist, Baptist and Congregationalist) joined together to sing hymns and tramp over the moors, and the performances of *Messiah* in Bradford with fierce rivalry between choral societies. (Later and most memorable of all had been the performance, accompanied by organ, in their own Thorp Wesleyan Church when Kathleen Ferrier[6] had been one of the soloists.)

And so, when in those early days Robbie took up another hobby making wireless sets, it was at first with crystal sets consisting of a piece of crystal in a glass cylinder with a coiled and springy copper wire (the 'cat's whisker') controlled by a handle outside the cylinder container. A faint radio signal might be received by tweaking this until one found the sensitive spot, while listening on a single pair of headphones. (The miracle needed a long and high outside aerial, too.) When a relay station was established in Leeds,

> '… I made a crystal set and finished it in time for the opening of 2 LS (Leeds) and on the opening day it worked. Big Ben was to be broadcast at 6 pm and I ran down to my Grandpa Brotherton, and though he had already been up to feed his hens, I had him walk all the way back again to hear Big Ben. He was suitably impressed, though I'm not sure he knew what Big Ben was …'

From there he progressed to valve sets, making a loudspeaker from stiff paper formed into a cone. It became an obsession that was to persist: haunting the new wireless shop in Hall Ings in Bradford would lead, decades later, to his frequent calls at the University Audio shop in Cambridge.

Robbie first went to Idle Board School, where the pupils sat at long desks arranged in tiers. Discipline was firm, and the children were expected to sit with their hands behind their backs while listening to the teacher, unless told to write on their slates with a squeaky slate pencil. He had a vivid memory of the moment when he learnt to read:

> 'Miss Walker put the letters of the alphabet onto the blackboard with her piece of chalk and told us what sound they each stood for, and had us then repeat the sound after her, and in unison. There was, what seemed like, only a few lessons like that. Then one day – and I remember it vividly and just where I was sitting – she put **C A T** on the board and it dawned on me that this was the word for the name of that animal my grandma Brotherton had, usually

---

[6] – though at this time scarcely heard of, Kathleen Ferrier was to become the greatest British contralto of her time.

on the rug in front of the fire. It was a revelation that this was opening a new door on a whole world of being able to read books and newspapers. There was still a long way to go…'

And for him, 'the only boring part of the infants' school was playtime' when they had to go out into the tar-macadam school yard. To Robbie this enforced interval seemed a waste of time, and he avoided joining in the rushing-about of the others, preferring to talk with friends. But on the whole in those first years he found the grown-ups around him more interesting than his contemporaries, especially funny old Grandpa Bob Brotherton, with no book-learning but plenty of country wisdom. It was worth missing a day's school to ride with him in his trap up the dale to call at a farm and haggle over the sale of a beast for slaughter. The bargain would be sealed with a handshake and a good farm tea, and home they would trot behind Kitty the pony.

He was selective about sport. He had no interest in football, but the handsome young Sunday School supervisor at Thorp Wesleyan Church, Dick Sargent, who played for the Yorkshire team confirmed his passion for cricket.

After a year or two in the 'mixed infants' at Thorp, one would normally move into the upper school that had Mr Wright Watson as its headmaster. Like most Board School teachers of that time, Mr Watson had received only the minimal training needed for 'certification'. Yet he was highly respected, both as a prominent figure in the Wesleyan chapel and for his unpaid labours as local historian. He compiled at least two books, *Wesleyan Methodism in Idle* and *Idlethorp,* in which he gathered all the archival material and reminiscences available about the district. Robbie was not actually taught by this 'mild, kind man' with a 'trim little beard' at Thorp School, but he learnt a good deal from Mr Watson as they went for walks together in the Dales. Robbie always walked home for the midday meal…

'… except on Wednesdays, when I went to Grandma Brotherton's, which was quite near the school, and had dinner with her and with Auntie Minnie, my mother's sister, who came from the mill where she was a weaver (and sometimes called for fish and chips for all three of us at the shop next to the mill) and had to return for the afternoon shift when the buzzer went. Each mill had a buzzer (rather like a ship's siren) on a different note. So you straight away knew whether it was the "Fisher's mill" buzzer, or "t' New Mill". or "Ben's mill" or "Castle mills". My auntie was at New Mill. Sometimes she would take me to see the weaving shed. It was very noisy, the looms being driven by pulleys and belts connected to the main big steam engine on the lower floor, next to the boiler house making the steam. And then there was the noise of the shuttle going back and forth on each loom. So all weavers tended to shout a bit even in conversation outside the mill. They were quite well paid. What they feared was being on "slack time" when trade was bad. Sometimes, of course, people were off ill, and that was called "being on Lloyd George" (the Prime Minister who had brought in some sort of sickness benefit).'

His memories of those schooldays, as written in old age for his grandchildren, give many details of important influences at that stage. They also reveal the odd prejudices and stubborn nonconformity that erupted from time to time. He acknowledged this awkwardness when he wrote:

'I believe I could have gone on to the Bradford Grammar School, which was a very good and even famous school. But my friends round where we lived were going to Belle Vue, a quite good secondary school, so I just insisted on going there ... I don't know how I always got my own way in such matters. I suppose it was largely because an only child tends to be spoiled and rather assumes that he can get his own way.'

The new school meant taking a tram from the 'top road' into Bradford, and another to Belle Vue, sometimes reducing the fare by taking a short cut of 1½ miles by foot. And being Robbie, he still insisted on returning for the midday meal because 'I had a sort of horror of eating somewhere other than home or at one of my own relations'.

Robbie's parents took him for summer holidays, though necessarily limited to the second-week-of-August that all Bradford working people shared. In the early years before his father had a car, they went by train, and it was naturally supposed that a little boy would want the seaside. So an early holiday was to Colwyn Bay, where his boredom was slightly relieved by the railway that ran along the seafront; another, to Bridlington, by 'an orchestra on the pier with a show-off conductor'; another tedious stay at Morecombe; and then one at Arnside further up the west coast, where there was a magnificent viaduct over the estuary for the Furness Railway to Grange-over-Sands. In the distance the Lake District beckoned, and they took one charabanc trip into the nearest part.

At last his parents realised that he was simply not a bucket-and-spade child – 'And then came the greatest holiday of all when we went to stay at Fieldside Farm near Keswick', where they made great friends with the farmer Mr Hawkrigg and his wife and their twin son and daughter. He loved jolting along on the farm cart, 'helping' with the cows, sheep, hens and turkeys, and playing with Tom and Betty. The highlight of that holiday – 'the most wonderful day of all days' – was an outing right into the fells.

It must have been one of the last rides on a horse-drawn 'four-in-hand' coach run by Papes of Keswick, and they went on a gloriously fine day. They sat up high, ranged three in a row, with the coachman up on the front

… 'And off clip-clop up Borrowdale, stopping to water the horses and rest them outside the Scafell Inn at Rosthwaite. It was very quiet: a kind of quietness now utterly lost… no traffic. And someone inside the hotel was playing a piano very nicely. What more could one ask? This was very heaven!

'Then to Seatoller at the head of the valley and the foot of the Honister Pass. It was then free of cars because it was still a very rough shale road, and cars could not get up it. There we all had to dismount because the horses could not be expected to pull us all up the pass. So we had, I suppose, about the best part of two miles to walk up the pass, and the horses with their empty carriages went a roundabout alternative route not quite so steep. At the top of the hill they were waiting for us, but we could ride only a few hundred yards along the top of the pass, for the horses could not take us down the very steep Honister road to Buttermere, or the weight of the coaches would have overrun the horses. So slipper brakes were put on, which made the empty coaches dig deep ruts into the loose surface as they went down the steep road. The coachman led the horses from the front. We walked behind all the way down into the Buttermere valley, where we could again mount up to our high seats and ride. There were lots of gates, and at each local lads would be waiting with the gate opened, expecting a copper or two from the passengers.

'At the far end of the valley and on the strip of land separating Buttermere from Crummock Water, we stopped for a good lunch at the Fish Inn. There was an hour or more to spare for a good walk around that most lovely part of the world. Then up on our high seats again for the journey back to Keswick by Buttermere Hause and the Newlands Valley. The horses could manage Buttermere Hause both up and down, for even then it was a made road. And so back home to supper after a tour which belonged to another world soon about to end. When we next visited Keswick, Papes had had to sell their horses and had gone over to motor coaches. Nobody will ever again be able to enjoy that incomparable tour on the hard high seats on a coach with four horses, the jangling harness and a coachman with whip and cloak straight out of an illustration of Pickwick Papers!

'It was that holiday that started me off on my Lake District madness. After that I really did not want to go anywhere else much. The Hawkriggs had a few books, and one of them was the book on the Lake District by Canon Rawnsley, the founder of the National Trust. I read it every word … I learned that Wordsworth was the poet to know …'

All this, like music and cricket, became essential to Robbie's wellbeing and remained with him until his last days.

The small factory under Arthur Jennings' management grew less profitable as some manufacturers ceased to use their paper tubes, and it looked as though the workforce of six men might have to be dismissed and the firm shut down. To avoid this he touted for custom, persuading Bowaters to roll their paper on these tubes. An even more enterprising – and successful – effort was to travel up to Dundee to sell these strong cardboard tubes[7] as the core for the rolls of linoleum that were produced there. On more than one such trip young Robbie went with him, going by cargo ship from Hull up the North Sea coast. He admired his father's determination to keep that small enterprise going, and he regarded his religious and political views with respect: Dad was a class leader in chapel and a Liberal.

—•—

Once he moved into Belle Vue Secondary School, Robbie encountered some interesting teachers. One was the deputy head, a marvellous mathematics teacher who communicated his own enthusiasm for the subject. Another was the German master. Robbie had chosen that language with no thought that he might later need Latin (the alternative) for admission to Oxford or Cambridge. At that stage, he recalled, 'I assumed I would want to go into the

---

[7]   The paper tubes were a cheaper substitute for the heavy poles formerly used.

textile business, which all really sound Bradford men wanted to do'. Thus he acquired decent German, with the ability to write the *Schrift* still in use at that period. Mr Turner, who was 'soppy' about the Swiss Alps, also loved opera. He hauled his massive gramophone into the school and introduced the boys to *The Barber of Seville*, after which they were taken to a matinée performance given by Sir Thomas Beecham's opera company.

The history master, Tommy Dunwell, was a less effective teacher but became a friend and companion to the older boys, taking three or four for all-day walks over the moors or in the dales of the West Riding.

'He was a Methodist of course, and even a local preacher … not a very interesting man. But he was a very nice and kind man. I took to law as a change from the boring history which I offered in the scholarship examinations and oddly enough it was the Cambridge university law teachers who taught me to enjoy at any rate legal history, and to wish that I had worked harder at my school history.

'Then there was Russell Clegg, another Methodist [i.e. approved] but from a rather suspect chapel in Manningham where they had a robed choir and other deplorable high church practices. I believe they actually had a cross on the communion table. But they were at least Wesleyan Methodists and not Primitive Methodists. Clegg taught geography. But he took little notice of the official syllabus. One morning he came in and said "Forget about geography this morning. I have decided that as future citizens of our country you ought to learn about our legal system and the courts, the differences between solicitors and barristers, how magistrates are appointed" and so on. And we had a fascinating lesson, for which I have always been grateful. Another day he told us about different universities (he was from Liverpool University, having been brought up in Birkenhead) and details like the differences between BA and MA gowns. He was an MA, and wanted us of course to realise that in this way at least he was superior to some other teachers. For he was not without a certain vanity, was Mr Clegg.

'Clegg was also a walker, and he and two other masters once took most of our class on an official school outing (during a weekday, I think) for a really long walk. We went to Bell Busk on the Midland Railway line to the north from Forster Square Station. From Bell Busk (near to Coniston Cold) we walked to Malham village, then out to Gordale Scar, climbed up the side of the scar by the path that involves some rock scrambling, and out on the tops to Malham Tarn, where we had our picnic lunch… (Little did I know then that one of the lonely farms on the moor had been farmed by my Great Great Grandfather Brotherton, who was buried in Kirkby Malham churchyard.) Then from the Tarn we went back over the limestone pavements to the descent to Malham Cove and thence by country road to Bell Busk Station for the train to Bradford; and then for me the tram to Idle. It was a memorable day…

'Mr Large was our sixth form English master. I owe him a lot. He taught me how to enjoy good writing, and above all how to enjoy poetry…Large had been at Birmingham University, but he was madly in love with Oxford and talked a great deal about it. It was he who gave me the ambition to get to Oxford or at least Cambridge; something which nobody else at Belle Vue had ever done, and we had no teacher who had belonged to either.'

Robbie must already have been aware of one inspiring example: Professor Joseph Wright the great Oxford philologist had recently died, and those in Idle knew his story– how he, from the Windhill district of their parish and as a six-year-old had earned his first pennies to help his widowed mother to support her three young boys, then moved to hard regular work in the mill at Saltaire a year later. There, he had learnt a little from evening classes but never attended a regular school. It was not until he was fifteen that he mastered reading, and after that it was by late-night poring over books bought from saved earnings that he steadily increased his knowledge. Every penny and every minute had been devoted to self-education, until a little extra money could be obtained by teaching. At last, having acquired sufficient German, he 'walked to Heidelberg', as Robbie would say. After studying philology there, his later work at Oxford culminated in the publication of the great Oxford Dialect Dictionary and academic honours.[8] 'I have been an Idle man all my life' he had boasted, 'and shall remain an Idle man till I die'.

In this account of his schooldays, Robbie went on to write of the music master under whom he had, in Form IV, sung in choir practices, and who could be persuaded to play some Bach on the poor classroom piano. The art master found Robbie's contrariness led to a refusal to take the Art paper in the matriculation exam, preferring to try metal work. When even the Head Master

---

[8] At some time Robbie bought both the biography of this hero and his *Grammar of the Dialect of Windhill in the West Riding of Yorkshire.*

failed to persuade him, he did his metal work, 'which I found messy and very boring, and serve me right…'

[Finally, he says] 'I must not forget Loseby, who rather late in the day taught me sufficient Latin in his spare time alongside another class of those who had taken Latin instead of German all along. Loseby I greatly admired. He had one glass eye (result of the 1914-18 war), so you were never sure whether he was seeing you or not, so his classes were always orderly. He managed to teach enough, mainly by giving me a good introductory grammar to read in a corner by myself. But when I knew enough to join in the class it was wonderful. We had to do set passages of Cicero for the examination. He greatly admired Cicero, which was a great help in teaching it. But he adored Horace, which was not in the official syllabus, and he took the view that to omit at least an introduction to Horace would have been wicked. So he spent whole lessons reciting his favourite Odes to us and conveying something of his own enthusiasm and joy at least to some of us. I still have a copy of an excellent book with selected readings that he wrote and gave to me. I got the Latin prize that year! Not because I really had any Latin, but then you see there was just no competition.'

Looking back, Robbie acknowledged his own contrariness – enjoying gymnastics but declining to take part in a team display; or in inter-school races when he knew that he could run faster than his friend Harold Holdsworth, the school's champion. Somehow this was understood and accepted, and he was elected Head Prefect. He was in fact devoted to the school and his record had been consistent: conscientious work, regular attendance … At the end of his final term Russell Clegg, his form master, wrote:

'He is completing a School career in which he has made distinguished contributions to the general life of the School. His full use of the opportunities provided by the School has assisted him to make remarkable intellectual, and, especially, cultural progress. He has adorned the office of Senior Prefect with exceptional gifts of character and leadership and his influence has been a power for good in the School. I look forward confidently to his achieving a future of public service and personal success.'

Downing

1932-36

Inspired by Mr Large's enthusiasm, Robbie resolved to get a place at Oxford University. With no-one else to advise him, he browsed through a booklet about the colleges. Trinity was said to have a handsome lime avenue, and he liked the sound of that, so he applied there and took their entrance examination. At the subsequent interview he was told that he had done quite well but was not up to Scholarship standard. They were nevertheless prepared to offer him a place. He felt he could not possibly accept, since he would never be able to afford the fees.[9]

Financial help was essential. Turning to Cambridge, he noticed that Downing was the cheapest college, so in April 1932 he wrote, asking whether a sizarship[10] might be available and whether he might be offered a provisional place while waiting for his Higher School Certificate exam results. At his interview the Senior Tutor jotted some notes on his application form: RYJ was evidently not much of a sportsman – though he had mentioned an interest in cricket, claimed to play a little tennis, took part in the school debating society and played the piano. His references from his Headmaster and the English master Mr Large were, however, glowing: in the Debating Society:

'his impromptu speeches reveal a mind that quickly grasps the essentials of a subject and works logically ... His manner in conversation is marked by frankness, ease, judgement, and a constant play of wit and humour ...'

He was told that a vacancy had occured in time for him to be offered a place as Pensioner (the Cambridge name for Commoner) the following

---

9 Years later he realised that Trinity, one of the richest Oxford colleges, would surely have found some sort of bursary to see him through his first year.

10 The status of sizar (whereby one's fees could be offset by taking menial jobs such as serving meals) had become obsolete well before 1932.

Michaelmas Term. On arrival, the Senior Tutor explained that Downing was a poor college and would be unable to provide any money to help with fees: Robbie had reached Scholarship standard in his English History paper 'but you did not reach Exhibition Standard in the examination as a whole'. The stately Old-Etonian Mr Whalley-Tooker must have seemed rather forbidding at that moment, though he was to show wonderful sympathy and support in the following terms.

Idle and Cambridge were different worlds. The Bradford City Council Education Committee would have been prepared to make a grant had Robbie intended to study at the University of Leeds, which seemed the obvious place for a Yorkshireman, but they were not ready to support his extravagant notion of going to Cambridge. His father eventually agreed to scrape up just enough to pay for his first year, after which he must depend on whatever funds he could obtain through examination success.

That first year was remembered for its acute misery. His lodging-house in Mawson Road turned out to confirm his worst prejudice about the slovenly ways of the South. As he later realised, his landlady was struggling bravely to make ends meet while her drunken husband wasted much of her effort. On his Heffers calendar Robbie marked off the days until the blessed end of term when he could return home. While still a rather bewildered freshman, another undergraduate from Bradford – in his second year and worldly-wise – undertook to give him good advice. 'You should have a blind', he said. Robbie thought his curtains were adequate. Having scarcely, if ever, tasted alcohol he had no idea what the man was talking about.

In a speech to the Law Faculty at his retirement, in 1981, he recalled the lectures given in those days (in what later became the Marshall building occupied by the Faculty of Economics, on the Downing site):

'… the lectures put on by the faculty in the early '30s had a far greater range than would even be thought possible today. They ranged from Winfield's and McNair's superb lectures, through the whole spectrum right down to Hazeltine's lectures, which were so bad you wouldn't believe it unless you had actually been there. But he was a sweet man. And it was almost worth attending in order to see his look of genuine puzzlement as he turned to yet another page of his bundle of disordered and tattered notes. One could almost see him saying to himself: "I wonder what *this* page will turn out to be about?"

'Of course, there were some very good lectures too. I have mentioned McNair and Winfield. Another excellent course in the first year was Meredith Jackson's on the English Legal System. There was then no "book of the subject". But by the end of it most of us had read a good deal of Holdsworth Vol.I, Maitland on Equity, and had at least dipped into classics like Maine's Ancient Law. I wonder how many undergraduates today have made an acquaintance with some of the legal classics, even by the end of their courses?

'Another happy recollection was the C.L.J. case notes that those who had done reasonably well in the Tripos were asked to write, with the careful guidance of Winfield. That meant preparing a draft, and taking it to Winfield's rooms in St John's to be discussed over tea and hot crumpets before a blazing fire. The passing of this system of lessons in practical drafting was a great loss to the education of our undergraduates.'

Robbie was spotted by the Downing Boat Club as a light, wiry chap to cox their third boat, and would in his second and third years cox the second. Although at that time their performance was ignominious, he did enjoy the comradeship of the Boat Club. And at the end of the year he passed the Law Qualifying Examination with a very respectable Second (and was told by Whalley-Tooker that it was at 2i level).

Once again he appealed to the Bradford Education Committee, and was now supported by a letter from Whalley-Tooker, saying, 'He is a man of very considerable promise. His character is excellent and he is an active member of the College Boat Club'. This yielded a grant of £20 a year, and he moved into a room in the college's newest range of buildings designed by Sir Herbert Baker.

Things improved generally. He was being supervised by Ellis Lewis of Trinity Hall and by Meredith Jackson as well as Whalley-Tooker[11], and it was probably at this stage that, besides the occasional lecture from the Whewell Professor, Pierce Higgins, he began to attend the lectures of Dr McNair of Caius. Everything was falling into place: McNair was a fascinating speaker who convinced him that it was International Law that should become his specialist subject.

By the end of his second year, in June 1934, having achieved a 1st Class in Part I of the Law Tripos, a college Exhibition of £30 as well as £15 from the Sir Richard Stapley Educational Trust were added to his grant of £20 from

---

[11] Whalley-Tooker was known in the college as 'W-T'.

Bradford. Money, however, was still tight, and Robbie wrote to W-T to say that he would not be coming up for the Long Vacation term (a useful period in residence for concentrated study) because 'in spite of its obvious advantages I ought to try to do without it in view of my financial position'. That was eased further, though, by a prize of two guineas-worth of books (to be chosen at Deighton Bell & Co.) and a Squire Scholarship from the Law Faculty of £60 p.a.

By his third year he was enjoying Cambridge fully – President of the college's Cranworth Law Society, successively Secretary, Vice-President and President of the Debating Society, as well as coxing the Downing Second Boat. And he ended that academic year with a 'distinction' added to his First in Part II of the Law Tripos.

It was not just college life that suited him. Throughout those three years and the one to follow, he was a member of '*Methsoc*', the Methodist Society for students which met at Wesley Church. There they discussed deep matters and made friends, and – a wonderful bonus – were offered hospitality by church members. Robbie and his close friend Russell Walton were often invited to cycle out to Impington after morning service to share Sunday lunch with the Lamb family. Mr Lamb, as manager for Chivers' great jam factory at Histon, seemed very prosperous to the hungry students who ate his generous meals. The family atmosphere soothed their homesickness too, with a son and three daughters with whom to play games or go for punting picnics in summer. (The son would be lost in the Second World War, but friendship with the 'girls' lasted for many years.) Methsoc provided friendships and a spiritual commitment which occasionally led him to serve as a lay preacher, cycling out to small village chapels to take an evening service. He was to remain a member for many years.

By the beginning of his fourth academic year Robbie's various awards seemed sufficient for his expenses, and he was now a Scholar although the college seemed hesitant in raising its own grant to the £60 p.a. to which his scholarship would normally have entitled him, marking his success instead with a prize of £5.5/- worth of books.

Arnold McNair was now Whewell Professor of International Law, and Robbie started reading for the LL.B. in that subject. In McNair he had found the ideal mentor, who would continue, by example and in discreet advice, to inspire his work for years to come. In a piece written for the *Cambridge Law Journal* in 1975 Robbie describes McNair's lecturing style:

'He entered wearing cap and gown, opened all windows within reach, and then placed his square carefully and exactly on the right-hand top corner of the lectern. This was the signal for silence. He had a pleasant, clear and well-inflected voice but always a quiet one. The audience was already provided with a fairly elaborate printed syllabus with all needful references. The reading list advised candidates to read "the latest editions of the text-books of Oppenheim *or* Hall *or* Lawrence according to the time they can devote to the subject and their preference as to the style and method of the respective authors". He begged his audience, with the aid of the syllabus, to make their own notes before coming to the lecture. One of his lecture syllabuses began with the warning: "… no attempt will be made to cover the ground outlined in this syllabus…"

'His delivery was deliberate, polished and lucid. A master of dry, even sardonic humour, he did not hesitate to enliven the facts of a case to make them more memorable. Once, he even had one party in a complicated case having lunched off "perhaps chops and tomato sauce" – this with the lightest suspicion of a smile which saved one from searching the report for so unusual a reference. Having posed a problem with exemplary clarity, he offered the solution with an actor's sense of timing, after a nicely calculated pause, leaning forward over the lectern, finger upraised, and in an almost hushed and confidential manner which suggested that the answer was being shared as both a revelation and a privilege…

'For … graduates he ran a seminar in international law: not a seminar in the American sense, with its organisation and documentation, but something very like a supervision; and, like a supervision, it was not in the law school but in his keeping room in Caius. We sat round the fire in easy chairs, McNair sat on the right of the fireplace, the usual position of the senior in any kind of college gathering, and we talked quite informally and rather generally about some topic of international law for an hour. There was also the international law club which he founded – an example since followed in Oxford and Harvard – which also met in his keeping room after hall, when discussion could go on to a late hour. This assembly would include other dons interested in international law, such as Patrick Duff, Emlyn Wade and Bryan King and … J. Mervyn Jones.

A crisis at home delayed Robbie's arrival at Cambridge for Lent Term 1936. His mother was having to undergo a hysterectomy, and so he asked permission '…to see her completely out of danger before I leave …' This was allowed. He was working hard and seems to have tried applications for a Cholmeley Studentship and a Henry Fellowship without success; but in the Easter Term he so impressed Harry Hollond with his performance in a Moot[12] that he was urged to try for the Joseph Hodges Choate Memorial Fellowship at Harvard University. For the Moot Robbie had been called upon to stand in for someone else at the last moment, yet succeeded in arguing his case fluently and convincingly. Professor H.A. Hollond's recommendation was most valuable.

The date for applications for the Choate was already passed. W-T in his letter of support told the Vice-Chancellor that 'it was only yesterday that any question of Jennings' application arose' and went on to say 'He is an extremely level headed, sensible man who should make a very good impression at Harvard. I know him very well and it is seldom that I have been able to recommend a man with more confidence'. That was on 6th June, and for the following weeks Robbie grew anxious about the next stage of his career. But he had again, in the LL.B., achieved a 1st Class with distinction and won the Whewell Scholarship. On 9th July he heard that he had been chosen for the Choate, and on the 31st that Lincoln's Inn had elected him to a Cassel Scholarship.

He wrote to Whalley-Tooker with warm thanks for the 'pleasure and privilege [of having been his pupil, and also] for the promise of teaching work when I return to Cambridge. I shall be very glad of it'.

---

[12]   A 'moot' is an imitation of a court of law, in which a mock hearing is conducted to test students' proficiency as would-be barristers.

A Year at Harvard

1936-37

Robbie was determined to make the most of the coming academic year. Before boarding the *Queen Mary* at Southampton he asked his parents to save all the letters describing this great adventure. From the resulting archive (which when tanscribed runs to some 90 pp of A4) extracts can be quoted verbatim to convey some of the range and value of his experience.

The day of his departure became a family occasion. Both his parents accompanied him to Southampton, and an uncle and aunt joined them to see him off from the quayside.

On arrival he sent home a letter of 24 smallish pages, describing the voyage and his first impressions of Manhattan. The Atlantic crossing had actually been speeded by a tremendous gale, and during the passage Robbie had got on well with his companions at mealtimes and with two of the three who had shared the Tourist Class cabin. One of these, John Sellman, turned up at the Harvard Club in his Ford V8 and straightway took him to see some of the sights. They dined together at International House, a club for graduates of all nationalities, and then drove round Harlem, where

'everybody is coloured … and all the shops and theatres are run by them. We got out to listen to a negro speaker at an open air Presidential Election meeting … We were the only white men in the crowd. I rather like the negroes, but I'm afraid the majority of Americans don't very much. At least they want to keep them apart and the coloured people want to mix …'

The Secretary of the Harvard Club was not only welcoming but arranged some useful introductions. There was Governor Forbes – 'Ambassador Extraordinary to the Chinese Government, and former Governor of the Philippines. A Republican of Republicans', whom Robbie did not much like. The other was Ralph Foss, 'a very interesting fellow who is a Democrat. . . He says he wants me to see more of America than the pompous side that we see at the Harvard Club and is going to put me onto the books to read and the people to meet – the most interesting "contact" so far. [Next morning, accordingly, Robbie] went to see New York west of 8ᵗʰ Avenue … and saw what must be some of the most appalling slums in the world. The Republicans had told me that prosperity had, in a large measure, returned to America. It may have returned to the sort of people who frequent the Harvard Club, but I'm afraid the people who live around the Docks and "down town" would have a different story to tell.'

He had walked on his own around Central Park and been dazzled by the Rockefeller Centre, and on the train journey up the 250 miles of coast to Boston he viewed countryside and small townships, including a tiny one called Bradford.

Home was never to be far from his thoughts during that year; he was to find, indeed, how many connections there were in that part of New England, soon leading to an invitation from someone actually from his own village. To make that visit he took a train to Worcester, north of Boston, and then was taken by Mr Saville, his host, to Barre, 'a small town with no station and regularly out in the wilds'. There he found that Jack Saville, who was related to a number of family friends, had retained his Yorkshire accent and could point out houses saying 'that man comes from Bingley, Shipley, Idle etc.' – having brought their expertise to Barre Mills, where wool was combed. The warm hospitality he received there would later include a traditional Thanksgiving celebration.

Another invitation came from the Rev. Ambler Garnett of Salem Methodist Church. Again the Idle link was strong, and his host was distantly related to Edith Jennings. Robbie found that the Methodist Church in the U.S. had an episcopal organisation with Bishops, and none of the circuit system he was used to. Moreover, the minister was himself responsible for the church's finances, 'and if they fall short the treasurer may decide to pay other bills and the minister has to wait for his salary … Tell that to some of our ministers at home!'

Those home connections were, of course, a small part of the wonderful range of experiences provided by that year at Harvard, one after another dispelling the early tendency to express generalisations about 'the Americans'. Very soon he was noticing variations in the origins and attitudes of the people he met. A totally different sort of election meeting was witnessed in Boston, for instance, when he and a friend took a 'very respectable' English solicitor to a meeting in support of Governor Curley of Massachusetts, who was standing for Senator, 'the crook of all crooks'. They enjoyed that meeting very much: 'There was not a thing American about it. Everybody spoke in broad Irish, and the speakers, when they were not quite unashamedly boosting themselves, told funny stories about Irishmen and priests ...'

He and his friends in Winthrop House took an intense interest in the actual Presidential election. One of them had a wireless set, on which they heard F.D. Roosevelt speak – 'a wonderful orator [with] a really beautiful voice. I am all for him anyhow. – I wish we had a democratic leader with his courage and wisdom.' And one day he went to see the President pass through Harvard Square on his final election tour –

'It was an amazing sight. First came two police on motorbikes, clearing the way and making an awful row with those sirens that you will have heard in American talkies. There followed a car full of detectives, all, of course, with revolvers slung from their belts. Two more police on motorbikes, and then the President's car, an open tourer. He sat at the back. There were three detectives standing on each running board and three hanging onto the back, making nine in all, not to speak of those who had seats in the car. Two more cars full of detectives followed and some more police and then cars full of local candidates and supporters.'

Descriptions and comments such as these were principally for his father's benefit. His mother, he knew, wanted all the details of his domestic arrangements, so he told about the fine set of rooms provided for him as Choate Fellow in Winthrop House, and the astonishingly cheap and convenient cafeteria meals he could get. At home they would be reassured to hear that he had quickly acquired several friends – one, Arnold Kean, already known in Cambridge (England), another an Emmanuel man from South Africa, as well as a Dane and a Belgian.

It was going to be a year full of interesting experiences, but threatened to be a disappointment in his principal aim – advanced study in international law. At Harvard the star attraction in that subject was Professor Manley Hudson, about to become a judge at the Permanent Court of International Justice at The Hague. Without him, the only teaching available seemed second-rate. Robbie tried attending the regular Harvard Law School lectures that would lead to a further degree, and decided they were a waste of time. Instead, he might perhaps

'do Administrative Law under Professor Felix Frankfurter, who is acknowledged to be the world's expert on the subject. He is rather notorious here as being Roosevelt's right hand man, having advised him and really designed almost the whole of the New Deal legislation …'

A few days later he could write:

'I am feeling ever so much happier about my work now. I went to see Professor Frankfurter today to see if he would let me take his course in administrative law, now that Hudson's course is definitely off, but instead of that he gave me some most excellent advice. He thought it was very foolish to take a degree and far better to spend my time as I please, making the most of the really marvellous library and going to the Dons just when I thought they could help me instead of sitting in on a course simply for the purposes of another blessed examination. I had rather thought all along that this was what I ought to be doing, but the faculty board had put me down right away as a candidate for the LL.M …

'Of course I'm awfully bucked about this as it means that I shall be able to spend a much more useful year from every point of view. The amazing thing was how the attitude of these people changed immediately it was decided that I was not to be a candidate for a degree …'

His first impression of the Law Faculty had been distinctly off-putting:

'The thing that struck me about the great men at Cambridge [England] was how very humble and friendly they are. The opposite is the case here. They each have an "office" with their name over the door. There is a secretary, though goodness knows how they find enough work for her to do. Winfield[13] hasn't even a typewriter and he gets through more than most people here. Of

---

13   Sir Percy Winfield, Rouse Ball Professor of English Law at Cambridge.

course, they are very decent and polite but one feels exactly as if one were going to see the manager of a departmental store to ask for 6 month's credit.'

But the suggestion that he should opt out of the regular LL.M. course changed all that. From this point onwards he was receiving invitations from senior academics, and as for Frankfurter himself – he was

'a grand dapper little fellow. He was most friendly right away, and has promised to introduce me to a local Unitarian who comes from Bradford.'

To equip himself for his new style of work he took advice from his South African friend Dr Van Heyningen, and bought a typewriter. Since this had cost $57 he felt he must justify its purchase to his parents. It was a 'Remington deluxe noiseless portable, a very heavy machine and one that will stand a lot of racket. It has every gadget that one could wish for, including such things as tabulators, and very heavy levers that one can knock about'. He got an instruction manual and practised touch-typing, though he promised his parents that after the first demonstration-letter he would, as usual, write to them by hand. That typewriter was indeed durable: he managed to bring it back to England without an export tax, as a 'tool of his trade,' and it continued in use for more than 50 years. The ability to touch-type, moreover, would stay with him to the end as he moved on to electric word-processor and finally computer.

Dr 'Kits' Van Heyningen, who was at Harvard on a Commonwealth Scholarship, told him about the medical research he was pursuing and later invited Robbie to watch the tedious process in his laboratory. It seemed wonderfully promising: 'It appears that now they are beginning to make real progress in the study of cancer. The theses and ideas are beginning to fit together and he thinks that it will not be very long before they have a cure …'[14]

At the beginning of October Robbie's Belgian friend, M. Verplatse, had taken him in his car for a long drive northwards up the coast through Massachusetts, New Hampshire and Maine with autumnal trees in all their glory. A few weeks later he would ride in Van Heyningen's car to Providence,

---

[14]   – But W.E. van Heyningen would be diverted into quite different work during the Second World War and eventually be made the founding Master of St Cross College, Oxford, carrying on his research on bacterial toxins at the Sir William Dunn Laboratory.

Rhode Island, to see Brown University; and soon he went with two other friends to visit Yale, which pleased him more, its architecture almost resembling Oxford.

There were constant political comments for his father. 7 Nov. 1936:

'Was so glad to hear that English public opinion is rallying round the Jarrow men. You have really no idea how English prestige has gone down under this government. Since the climbing down over Abyssinia we have come to be regarded everywhere in America as a C3 nation. The national govt. is despised. But the Americans were very much impressed with the outcry over the Hoare-Laval plan but can't understand how such a public were induced at the election to send back the national govt. with a large majority. And neither can I!' [Later] 'I don't see much to choose between Communism and Fascism...'

He tussled with the dilemmas presented by the recently published book by Sir Norman Angell[15] that his father had been reading, with its criticism of 'George Lansbury & Co.', pacifists. This was in a typewritten letter unusually addressed 'Dear Dad'. Refusing to commit himself to any one generalisation, he comments:

'In spite of the fact that more and more I seem to make my friends among the most rabid communists and anti-religious people, their lives and the way they live them only serve to make me more and more convinced that the Christian way is ultimately the only way that life works ...'

Although he describes himself as 'never a full-blooded pacifist – only a conscientious objector, if you see the difference', he does acknowledge the 'tremendous power' of pacifism –

'Gandhi managed to give the British Government far more trouble than any of the militant nationalists have ever succeeded in doing ... the only

---

15   Norman Angell, later made Nobel Laureate. The book referred to may have been *Preface to Peace*, which Robbie had bought the previous year, or possibly *The Great Illusion*. George Lansbury, a Christian pacifist, had shifted from the Liberal to the Labour Party and denounced the suggested use of force against Italy at this time.

opposition which has so far completely baffled Hitler is an insignificantly small group of parsons who make up the Confessional Church and whose attitude so far has been completely pacifist.'

In his abhorrence of war and his belief in Christian love as the only possible remedy for dissension, he suggests that a way to eliminate the belligerence of Hitler and Mussolini would be to give away some of our own Empire to appease their sense of injustice – an attempt by the earnest 23-year-old to reconcile ethics with pragmatism.

—

He was revealing a strong sympathy, consistent with his upbringing as a Liberal and Methodist, with the socialist outlook. In a long letter at the end of November he told more about the side of American life it was impossible to admire.

> 'America is a wonderful place but something seems to have gone rotten at the core. All you have heard or read or saw at the pictures about gangsters and rackets are quite true … [and he describes various corrupt practices.] The only people who genuinely want to alter all this are the communists. Perhaps that is why I get on so well with them. Believe me, our worst politicians are angels with wings compared with the ones here and the Bradford Corporation is a monument of integrity. There is one exception, and that is Roosevelt …'
>
> [On 6th December he could write]: 'Yesterday I went to hear a lecture on the new Soviet Constitution. It seems very democratic and altogether good … I imagine that this is the civilisation of the future.'

A week later he was commenting on the news from England of the abdication of King Edward VIII. He had already mentioned something revealed in the American newspapers '– for instance one gets to know about Mrs Simpson, an American lady who is King Edward's wife in all but name'. By now the Hearst papers were full of the story: and while he felt that Baldwin had dealt with the constitutional crisis 'magnificently', the attitude across the Atlantic was largely indignant.

He had joined the criminology class one day for an interesting experience, visiting the headquarters of the Boston Police. They were shown all sorts of details of methods and procedures – 'I was surprised to learn that it is much easier to track a typewritten letter than a handwritten one' – and 'I was amused to see that in the files they have a special file for communists'.

And now came a major experience. His friend Arnold Kean had bought 'a really beautiful second-hand Ford – last year's model – eight cylinders, 20-40 h.p., 5– seater.' Since Kean had not yet learnt to drive, Robbie and his co-driver the Dane, Axel Serup, made up a trio venturing on a great Christmas excursion all the way down to Florida. First, Robbie had to take the Massachusetts driving test (something not yet required in England). After a little practice with this large car with left-hand drive and on the right side of the road, that was accomplished.

A long letter dated 20th December 1936, written in pencil on both sides of very thin paper ('this is not toilet paper but air mail paper') describes the early stages of their journey. They had arrived at 'Something Swamp[16]' to sleep in a little wooden hotel surrounded by humid tropical swamp. On their way there had been wonders galore:

'… It was most thrilling to drive down Broadway, New York, and then over the magnificent George Washington Bridge which is a swing bridge about 1 mile long and spanning the Hudson River. Then came the second thrill of the Jersey City Skyway …'

Axel had relatives in Jersey City and friends a little further on, and was the sort of charming young man (with big blue eyes, Robbie would recall) who had a number of girlfriends along their route whose families were happy to offer hospitality to the three of them. Thus they progressed to Washington, where 'we drove round and round till almost midnight … the floodlit Capitol looked great …'

After a night in a tourist cabin 'we awoke to find the car half buried in snow. For the first hour or so one had to keep melting the ice on the windscreen by holding a lighted candle to it on the inside …' and so they went on to a warmer climate, first with tobacco and cotton fields on either side then, towards South Carolina, 'the country turned into pure desert …' before reaching the swamp whose name he had forgotten. 'It is all like a strange dream' he writes, 'I still

---

[16]   Santee Swamp

can't believe that I, from Idle, have been driving between tropical swamps in S. Carolina.' He found that references to 'the war' down there meant the Civil War, and the war memorials were to those fallen in the war of 1862-7.

On they went, to Charleston (very Spanish in style) then into Georgia, where it was very hot and they stayed at the John Wesley Hotel, Savannah – the place 'where John Wesley proved such a failure as a missionary' (something his Methodist parents knew all about).

> 'Both here and Charleston, they have a dialect of their own called Gashie, which sounds very negro. Many of the older negroes in Georgia were once slaves. We examined the negroes' quarter in Savannah and were horrified by what we saw. They live in filthy wooden shacks and it is quite evident that their position is very little better than it was in slavery days. The only difference is that they are theoretically able to change masters. There are still periodic lynchings in Georgia, and the whole of G. & S. Carolina is barbarous in many ways. They still have negroes working in chain gangs, but we have not seen one yet. The negroes work chained together and sing their spirituals all the while.'

The next stop was Jacksonville, where they stayed with relatives of Kean but they did not think much of the place – 'terribly provincial'. They were taken for Yankees, but didn't mind, feeling that by now they belonged to Massachusetts and were actually flying a Union Jack on the car. He had to explain that not *all* southerners, after all, were charming: there were the

> 'altogether lovable people of Virginia and North Carolina … Then there is the barbaric and primitive S. Carolina and Georgia, where the whites are all virtual slave owners – the country is beautiful but in an exotic way. It consists mainly of swamps covered with jungle growth. The trees are all covered with Spanish moss, which is like grey beards hanging from the branches.'
>
> [On southwards, stopping at St Augustine, then past Daytona Beach] 'where Sir Malcolm Campbell broke the speed record. The beaches here are wonderful. They are very long and consist in beautiful white sand. By now we were getting into really warm country [and spent the night in Melbourne]. Many of the men here wear real American dress. They have these big cowboys' hats, sloppy leather trousers with frills, and embroidered jackets. They look just like Buffalo Bill. The coloured people here are not chocolate like the ones further north, but quite black.

'Christmas Eve we have spent mainly on the beach on the edge of the Atlantic. The beach here is on an island about 1 mile out to sea (there is a long wooden bridge across the sound). It was a moonlit night, with the wind blowing a slight gale with scurrying clouds. The Atlantic breakers down here are wonderful. The air is soft and balmy. It was almost uncanny to spend Christmas Eve on the Florida coast watching the Atlantic in the moonlight and being perfectly warm with no coat. There was no other person in sight on the coast, and we just sat there and talked and thought.'

On Christmas Day itself they went on the extra 70 miles to Miami, then to Miami Beach – very garish, 'still more snooty and still more expensive' than Miami itself. It is hot, 'at about the same latitude as Sierra Leone in Africa', with palm trees, coconuts, oranges and grapefruits growing wild.

'We found a little British cargo boat in the harbour, and the captain promised to take us to the Bahamas (British West Indies) for $17. But, unfortunately, we discovered that we would have had difficulty in getting back into the U.S.A. without paying for another visa. We could have solved the difficulty by signing on as part of the crew, but we could not find the U.S. immigration officer although we chased all over the town for him.'

From Miami they went to Matacombe, the most southerly point to which the road goes, 'the first part of the journey … through swamp, home of alligators and large vultures. The swamps stink something awful. Then came the part with the sea on both sides. That was very beautiful.' Their other excursion was to Fort Myers on the west coast, where they saw several Indian villages and bought some souvenirs.

'On New Year's Eve we listened to Big Ben chiming in the New Year. That was at 7 pm by Eastern Standard Time. Then we went to the cinema. Earlier in the day we had had some Chili Concarne which is a hot Chilean dish and which proved to have much the same effect as Beecham's Pills only more so. The result was that I was compelled to usher in the American New Year in a manner wholly inappropriate. After 12 o'clock we careered round the streets of Miami blowing our horn incessantly. Hundreds of cars did likewise. In Europe we celebrate the New Year with church bells. In the U.S. they do it with motor horns, which is somehow symbolic. There was also a ceaseless firing of blank cartridges from innumerable guns. This went on most of the night but we went to bed at about 2 am.'

The next letter, 10th January 1937, comes from Winthrop House. They had returned through Lynchburg and the Shenandoah Valley, and over the skyline drive for about 70 miles along the ridge of the Alleghany Mountains of Virginia. There was a night in New York, with Robbie thrilled once more to be driving along 5th Avenue and Broadway.

'By that time', he says, 'I was just about broke and it was a good thing I could stay at the Harvard Club free of charge. As I sat in the magnificent dining hall consuming a perfect dinner, surrounded by waiters and successful business men, I wondered what they would all have thought of me if they had known that I had just 40 cents in my pocket!

'On the way from New York we ran into fog and successively almost everything that can go wrong with a car went wrong with our car. We limped into Cambridge at 3.30 am. It finally gave up the ghost almost 10 yards short of the parking place and we had to push it in.'

Thus ended a memorable trip, which he found had cost him just £13.10/– – 'Pretty good, don't you think, for over 4,000 miles!'

He had returned, needing extra sleep, to a heap of Christmas greetings and presents from home, especially appreciative of calendars with pictures of the Lake District. He had 'rather missed having no Xmas, for we all soon gave up the idea of trying to be Xmassy in the midst of palm trees and eating ice-cream under a tropical sun and even the policemen wearing white sun helmets. Besides, we failed to find any Plum Pudding …' Something he found he had missed while being away was the chance to have spent Christmas with some people from Bradford, which Professor Frankfurter would have kindly arranged for him. Again he says 'Frankfurter is a name repeated with awe over here.'

Music, as ever, was important for him. He revelled in the series of Boston Symphony Orchestra concerts, the organ and choir of the University Church, and the collection of gramophone records available to Winthrop House members. He enjoyed, too, the company at meals there, talking with men from a wide range of disciplines.

At the end of January 1937 it was time to let his Downing tutor know how he was getting on. After saying how happy he was both with the country and the people, he wrote about the Law School. 'In some ways the Law School has exceeded expectations. The library, especially the international law section, is a lawyer's dream come true…' But he found the teaching strictly vocational, with no encouragement to widen cultural reading. The lecturers seemed lacking in commitment, simply drilling their pupils to 'soak up vast quantities of material without having time to meditate upon it' and being unavailable for discussion. He missed 'the cosy atmosphere of the Squire, where one may work at a table with McNair on one side and Winfield on the other, [which] is quite inconceivable in the H.L.S.' Those were the conditions for normal undergraduates –

'For my own part, I am working here entirely as a free-lance and using the magnificent library to the full. I began by putting myself down as a candidate for the LL.M. but Professor Frankfurter advised me not to tie myself down to an examination syllabus but to direct myself in whatever work attracted me most. I took his advice and I think it was very sound…'

And although he felt the Harvard lawyers lacked a fully rounded education, he himself was taking every opportunity to listen to good music, see good plays and films, and read a wide range of books. He had discovered in the library records of Messiah choruses conducted by Malcolm Sargent (familiar to him from live performances at home) and of Schweitzer playing Bach organ preludes. He was, too, practising a little public speaking, addressing a W.P.A. (Works Progress Administration) meeting on 'The position of Great Britain in foreign affairs,' and some young League of Nations sympathisers on 'The Machinery of Peace'.

An interlude in the infirmary with 'flu provided a chance to enjoy some cosseting and read Scott's *Heart of Midlothian.* But soon, back at work, he was commenting on recent Russian trials – 'if anybody deserved capital punishment, Trotzky & Co. did' – and the proposal of Roosevelt to increase the membership of the Supreme Court. Then, on 21st February, 'I had the peculiar experience last week of reading a book by a Norwegian international lawyer called Hambro and then meeting him almost immediately afterwards. Almost as soon as I had finished the book, in walked my Danish friend and introduced me to his companion who turned out to be Hambro.' This was Eddi Hambro, who would become the first Registrar of the new International Court of Justice after the war.

Robbie needed to make plans if possible for the next stage in his career, and he consulted his parents about a Research Studentship at Corpus Christi College for which he might apply. W-T's advice was that while it just might lead to a Fellowship, Corpus was hardly the place for Robbie: he felt 'doubtful whether you would find it a congenial atmosphere'. And by the time his father replied, Robbie had already decided to reject the idea, partly because he might be breaking faith with Lincoln's Inn while receiving his Cassel Scholarship money.

Manley Hudson had been over from the Netherlands, and before returning had kindly read through 'some stuff' that Robbie had written that he 'had been good enough to pronounce "swell" and which I shall, accordingly, send to the *American Journal of International Law* to see if they would like to have it, since Hudson (who is one of the editors) thinks they would. But you never know'. In fact, it was accepted for publication in 1938 as an article (*The Caroline and McLeod Cases*, which appears in the second volume of his Collected Writings).

Also at the end of February, he 'had the privilege of meeting a very interesting and charming Arabian Christian whose home is in Jerusalem. We talked quite a lot about the Jew and Arab problem in Palestine but the only conclusion we could reach was that, at present, no solution seems to be possible'. This man had described 'a charming game known as "baiting the British"', teasing a nervous British occupying force by setting up small bursts of gunfire from one hilltop after another, merely as a protest against the Jewish immigration. Neither the established Jewish population nor the Arabs liked the newcomers.

He found time to attend some lectures given 'by Professor Whitehead, an old Cambridge man, who lectures on the function of reason. He is a great mathematician and his lectures are a combination of mathematics, logic and philosophy. Of course, that has nothing to do with the law school, but it seems a pity to miss probably the greatest man that Harvard has'.[17] Apart from that he had really settled down to work and become 'a man of very regular habits'. In mid-March he 'invested $2.50 (10/-) in a set of *International Conciliations* from 1927-36 … Also, I have subscribed to future numbers for 5 years, which only costs a dollar'.

---

[17] Robbie was not to know that the last 43 years of his life would be spent in Grantchester, a village where in the first decade of the 20th century A.N. Whitehead had lived together with Bertrand Russell in the Mill House while they collaborated on their *Principia Mathematica*.

Early in April he could write with promising news. H.A. Hollond had written to tip him off that a junior post at the London School of Economics was likely to be vacant soon, for which 'a person of [his] age and record might well be a suitable candidate'. Even if it would bring in less money than supervising in Cambridge, this might be a much better qualification.

> 'The L.S.E. [he tells his parents] is world famous for its law school – it has Lauterpacht, probably the greatest international lawyer in the world today, and my namesake, W. Ivor Jennings, probably the best English constitutional lawyer, besides political science men of the calibre of Harold Laski, who left Oxford to go there – all this supposing I could get the job. Hollond, knowing nothing of my plans, simply asked me to let him know what I planned to do on my return … That Oxford-Cambridge moot whereby I was able to impress Hollond was a good thing, wasn't it!'
>
> … And indeed it had led to his Cassel award, and now a suggestion that appeared to be 'infinitely more promising than the Studentship at Corpus'. 'Both McNair and Gutteridge' he adds 'started their teaching careers at the L.S.E. (and also old Pearce-Higgins, who was Whewell Professor before McNair)'.

Next day his letter was headed 'ON BOARD STEAMSHIP'. The short Easter Vacation allowed him to take a trip to New York on board the *S.S. Boston*, travelling overnight in a 'most excellent cabin' that cost a dollar, and greatly enjoying the thrilling passage through the Cape Cod Canal. He linked with Van Heyningen (and entertained him to a luxurious dinner at the Harvard Club without having to pay), went to a play with a largely English cast, dined with the family of a Harvard friend, saw films, Macy's, caught a glimpse of Prince Chichibu of Japan (on his way to the Coronation in London), and was hugely impressed by opera and ballet performances, before sailing back to Boston.

Accounts of these and other delights are punctuated with comments on the political situation. Then towards the end of April he could write of a 'welcome surprise … It seems that the 'Varsity has decided, in a generous mood, to give me a "room scholarship" in with the Choate'. This paid for his expensive rooms in Winthrop House and left him with a bank balance of over $500. And this, I suspect, is what allowed him to buy a good number of secondhand books which became a valuable part of his personal library.

With the next week's letter came enclosures – several copies of the programme of the Winthrop House Play, a hilarious version of *East Lynne* performed entirely by men. As an Entr'acte 'Mr Jennings [had favored them] with *Albert and the Lion*', which went down so well that he was urged to repeat the performance again and again during the final weeks of his stay in America. 'I seem to have discovered, quite by accident, a histrionic gift, which I had no idea that I possessed,' he commented.

On 9th May he enclosed a newspaper cutting with photographs of 'the tragic news of the disaster to the *Hindenburg*', the great zeppelin which had passed over Boston only a few days earlier and had now crashed and been consumed by fire.

The Coronation of King George VI had excited great interest in the States, and on 16th May he could say 'I imagine I had far more *Coronation* than you had at home.' A group at Winthrop had woken early to hear the whole ceremony and procession on the radio, and in the evening attended a great Promenade Concert and Ball. The newspapers, too, were full of the Coronation – and the Hearst press achieved a tremendous scoop by publishing pictures in a special supplement for the *New York Times* by sending 'Merrill and his co-pilot' over to England and back on a record-breaking 'ping pong flight' of just over 24 hours.

There were just a few final excursions. One, up into New Hampshire, was to give an after-dinner speech followed by the inevitable *Albert and the Lion*, which included a trip into wonderful mountain county. Another was to a friend's home at Newton where he was captivated by the house and company. 'They also had a coloured butler from the West Indies who was very glad to talk about cricket …' After a night there, he went on for a last visit to the Savilles, hugely enjoying two car rides – one 'to the summit of Mt. Wachusett, about 2,500 ft high, from which you look down on mile after mile of untouched virgin forest …' and the other in the evening through forests and typical neat New England towns. Barre itself was delightful, too, with lilacs in full blossom.

As May advanced he was advising his parents about arrangements for his return voyage, although there were still a few notable events to fit in before sailing; but as he himself would be likely to arrive as soon as any letters, he would write no more. He had by now been promised publication of his article on the Carolina case, and he had had a valuable talk with Professor Baxter, 'famous historian, specialising in C19 diplomacy'.

There was just one more talk to give, to a Kiwani club '(rather like freemasons, but not quite so swanky'). Then he would sail from New York and, 'All being well, I will see you on the Quay at Southampton, about noon, 14th June'.

Cambridge and the L.S.E.

1937-39

From the *Queen Mary* Robbie returned to family and friends at Idle. Some typewritten scraps are evidence of a talk that he gave, either at Thorp Methodist Church or the local Liberal association – probably both – about his impressions of America; he seems, too, to have taken a holiday with his parents in the Lake District. He was eager to move on to the next stage of his career, and had already undertaken to supervise a few men at Jesus in the Long Vacation.

His plan was to return to Cambridge, where he was allowed to keep his college rooms at Downing, and there to combine supervision work with preparing a thesis on 'The Law of Estoppel' for a Ph.D., while trying for the Yorke Prize in December 1938. His days were full, for there were pupils at Downing, as well as St Catherine's and Jesus (where eight are listed for the Michaelmas Term).

He was persuaded to reconsider this plan by one of his own former supervisors, Emlyn Wade[18], whom he met by chance in the Cambridge market place. Wade, on hearing what Robbie was doing, advised him that his proposed course would get him nowhere: if he wanted to advance his career he should leave Cambridge for a while, even if it meant sacrificing the decent fees he was earning from supervision.

And so in December 1937 Robbie applied for the post at the London School of Economics, with a testimonial from Whaley-Tooker in support. The success of his interview for that post at the LSE he attributed to the fact that, besides the Principal, his inquisitor was Professor Chorley, an authority on banking law. Chorley happened to be 'a fanatical fell walker' and co-founder of a society called *The Friends of the Lake District*. Robbie could say that he was already a member – and was accepted forthwith.

Starting his Assistant Lectureship early in 1938, he was able to commute to London for the two or three days' duty there while continuing to fulfil his

---

[18] E.C.S. Wade, Professor of English Law

commitments as supervisor at Cambridge. Enrolment as a Research Student, though, limited his hours of supervision to ten hours only, which meant that he needed special permission to continue taking a few Jesus men – where in January 1938 Henry Barnes[19] was still asking him to teach History of Contract and Tort and/or Personal Property to two pupils. Once fully committed to his work at the L.S.E., it was advice from the ever-helpful McNair[20] which persuaded him to abandon the idea of a PhD and to prepare instead for practical experience at the bar.

From the beginning of the next academic year he ceased to commute to London, and instead shared lodgings in Barnes with his old friend Russell Walton. They went to concerts and theatrical performances together, and Robbie could spend occasional Sundays with his Uncle Fred and his wife at their suburban home. He now entered chambers at Lincoln's Inn as well, having abandoned his earlier plan of preparing to become a solicitor.

That experience as Assistant Lecturer at the L.S.E. was a time he never regretted: he always said it was the liveliest Common Room he ever encountered.

There were R.H. Tawney, Lionel Robbins, Eileen Power, Anstey, Chorley and some who had taken refuge from spreading fascism on the Continent.[21] It was an immensely stimulating time: among those from abroad were not only Lauterpacht (Polish), Laski (Austrian), Michael Postan (Russian) and Malinowski (Polish) but Friedrich von Hayek (Austrian), Otto Kahn-Freund (German), and Meyer Fortes (South African). Discussions with Laski, the fierce advocate of Fabian Socialism, were special wit-challenging fun.

Those months (February 1938 – July 1939) at the L.S.E. were a wonderful preparation for the next stage of his career. Lecturing, with intensive preparation beforehand, was valuable experience. He had to teach Jurisprudence & Legal Theory as assistant to Professor D.H. Parry (Professor of English Law), and International Law (Disputes, War, and Neutrality) with Professor Herbert A.

---

[19] Law Fellow at Jesus – an eccentric character who later adopted an Irish form of his name as O'Bierne

[20] by now Vice-Chancellor of the University of Liverpool

[21] R.H. Tawney, economic historian; Harold Laski, economist and political theorist; Lionel Robbins, economist; Eileen Power, economic historian, medievalist – married Michael Postan, also economic historian, medievalist; Bronislaw Malinowski, anthropologist; Vera Anstey, economist mainly on India; Theodore (Lord) Chorley, commercial and industrial law.

Smith. He also took a class in Legal System. And it was during this year that his first major article, *The Caroline and McLeod Cases,*[22] was published.

The academic year had not run its course before he was invited to take up a Fellowship at Jesus College, Cambridge. The supervising he had already done there had stood him in good stead, for on 19th June 1939 the College Council decided 'to terminate Barnes's Fellowship and R.Y. Jennings was pre-elected in his place.'[23] (Henry Barnes's behaviour had been growing erratic through alcoholism. He withdrew to Ireland and overcame this trouble in his last years.)

Sooner than he might have expected, Robbie was to return to Cambridge. And the response from one of the uncles at Idle was 'Well, that's very nice I suppose; but when are you going to get a *job?*'

---

[22] AJTIL, vol.32

[23] Quoted from *Fifty Years at Jesus: the Diaries of Frederick Brittain, LLit.D., Fellow of Jesus College, Cambridge*

Jesus College

1939-40

Before acceptance of the Jesus College Fellowship, Robbie had had an embarrassing moment of indecision, for he had already accepted an appointment at the University of Leeds and needed to extricate himself. Recalling this years later, he said,[24] '... they were delighted to let me go because they realized that this would enable them instead to appoint Trevor Thomas; and how right they were!'

The Jesus College appointment he attributed, once more, to

'Hollond of Trinity, former Secretary of the mid-twenties Oxford & Cambridge Commission, perpetual chairman of the Faculty Board of Law – who at that period virtually appointed to all faculty posts and all law fellowships of colleges. Of course I was "looked at" over dinner by the Fellows first, staying in the old, splendid and worthy Fellows' Guest Room on C Staircase. Combination Room was easy, for Arthur Gray, very deaf, never stopped talking; so all one had to do was to listen.'[25]

Gray, the Master, was in his late eighties and the senior Head of House in the University, in robust health and seemingly indestructible. He was a classical lecturer and antiquarian: among his writings were a history of the college and some ghost stories set in the older part of its buildings. As Robbie found, it was no ordeal to listen to his tales, and wonderful to have this link with a man who had come up to the college in 1870.

The Second World War broke out just before Robbie's actual arrival at the college as a Fellow. He must have been with his parents at Idle at the time of

---

[24]   in an address to the Law Faculty at his retirement from the Whewell Chair in 1981

[25]   Quoted from an address given by RYJ at the celebration in college of his 80th birthday

that momentous announcement on the wireless at 11 am on 3rd September, for he recalled overhearing one old man in Bradford commenting to another 'Tha' knows, John, we could 'ave done very well without this' – typical Yorkshire ironic understatement.

His first set of rooms in Jesus was in North House (now replaced by North Court): quite pleasant, though conditions were the normal ones for that time: a good 'keeping room', a bedroom, and a 'gyp-room' in which was just a cold tap. His bedmaker would bring hot water for shaving and a tray of breakfast from the college kitchen. The only heating was from a coal fire in the keeping room, and in winter both he and the undergraduates wore their overcoats during supervisions. (These, unlike Oxford tutorials, were not a matter of listening to pupils' essays, but of going through topics and moot cases, discussing them and arguing about them. 'One's pupils would also bring along written essays but the supervisors in law always marked those in their own time and returned them, sometimes with longish comments added in writing.'

Although he did not have to traipse across the college courts in a dressing-gown in order to take a bath (as was common at that time), the bath in North House yielded only tepid water, since the small coke boiler also heated a radiator in an outside garage which kept Duckworth's Daimler from freezing in winter.

It was W.L.H. Duckworth who, after the death of Arthur Gray in April 1940, succeeded him as Master. Robbie described him as…

'…the dominant personality of the College … a medical man and specialist in anatomy with anthropology as a hobby. He was a meticulous scholar with a fascinatingly circumlocutory way of speaking. … He had become Master under the wartime emergency statutes (he was too old in the ordinary statutes) … He was already the Bursar (in charge of the finances of the College), and Steward (in charge of the meals and of all the staff of College servants). So he had managed to combine within himself all the major College offices except for Senior Tutor.'

A character such as Duckworth provided plenty of anecdotes. As war threatened he had got the college to make a large underground air raid shelter, fully equipped. At the first alarms Robbie had gone down there, finding Bernard Manning, Freddie Brittain and Sir Arthur Quiller Couch also taking shelter. Manning, Senior Tutor, had amused the others by 'reading a passage from

Fielding's *Tom Jones* which was a statement by a medical man using language just like Duckworth's'; but soon they all gave up leaving their beds during air raids. Duckworth, though, was a very kind man, and while making his pompous circumlocutions always had a humorous glint in the eye.

It was clear that Robbie had settled in at Jesus very happily. The fellowship at that time was far smaller than it is now, and it formed a close community. In addition to those already mentioned there were Gardner-Smith, Dean; W.H. Mills the chemist; C.H. Dodd, theologian who was destined to become C.H. Dodd, C.H.[26]; A.L. Pars, mathematician; E.M.W. Tillyard, English scholar; Robert Gittings, literary biographer and poet; C.H. Wilson, economic historian; and A.L. Percival, engineer, whom Robbie had already encountered in Cambridge, Mass., when he was studying at M.I.T.

Having been elected a 'Fellow of Class II', Robbie became a member of the College Council – a small enough body, at that time, to be able to meet around a table in the Conference Room of the Master's Lodge. By the Lent Term 1940 he had 27 pupils for whom he did 12 hours of teaching a week. The subjects he had to cover were: Roman Law, International Relations, Jurisprudence, Property, Constitutional Law and Contract. Later he was to comment that his supervision class 'seemed to be rowing Blues to a man, for it was the golden age of the Jesus Boat Club. But they were friendly and courteous and prepared to take a polite interest in law.' He also fulfilled his university duties as Lecturer, apparently having to speak on Constitutional Law as well as International Law.

But it was wartime. The college magazine *Chanticlere*[27] declared, in October 1939, that admissions and the daily routine of college life would continue as normally as possible, as they had in the 1914-18 war; it welcomed (in the whimsical stye customary at that time) Mr R.Y. Jennings as a new Fellow and gave a resumé of his achievements: '... Despite this somewhat alarming record of academical distinction Mr Jennings has already taught us not to be scared of him; and despite his almost cosmopolitan background it is clear that he has always been one of Nature's Jesus men...'

By the next term (Lent 1940) the first of the Fellows is reported to have 'joined up': in February, 'Mr Sinker left us for work more directly connected with Herr Hitler than that which he has been doing here...', and others were

---

[26]   C.H. Dodd was chairman of the committee which produced the *New English Bible*.

[27]   Named, in Chaucer's spelling, after the college emblem: a *rebus* of a cockerel upon an orb, which recalls the name of its founder (in 1496), Bishop John Alcock.

deployed to replace him as Tutor, with his teaching in Classics being taken over by Mr Balme. Mr Jennings, meanwhile, was forming a Law Society, with the great H.A. Hollond delivering its first talk.

By the summer, with undergraduate numbers dropping as young men were recruited into the services, Robbie, by then aged 26, felt there might be some advantage in volunteering himself instead of waiting to be conscripted. His first idea was to go into the Royal Navy (and found the local recruiting officer was a gate porter at Jesus). But as it turned out, the perils of service as a naval rating were spared him.

He was asked by Professor Wordie[28] whether he might be interested in joining the Intelligence Corps. 'I thought no more about it', he recalled, 'until I received one morning in the post an "Order" to "proceed" on a certain day "to a particular barracks … at Aldershot"'. Thus it was that Robbie found himself in an infantry officers' training unit attached to the Queen's Regiment.

—

[28] Later Sir James Wordie, Master of St John's College, Cambridge. He was a geologist and polar explorer (with Shackleton in the Antarctic), and responsible for the Naval Intelligence Handbooks, half of which were produced in Cambridge and half in Oxford.

Military Service

1940-46

Concerned about abandoning his supervision pupils, on 19th August 1940 Robbie wrote to the Senior Tutor, explaining the situation and apologising. A month later he wrote again, agreeing that Ellis Lewis might not be a suitable substitute as supervisor because of the animosity between him and Henry Barnes; but he suggested that '... If help is needed, Glanville Williams[29] of St John's is a brilliant young man who would probably be glad of the work ...' or possibly Meredith Jackson.

In that same letter he describes his introduction to the Army. It seemed that he would probably be commissioned as an infantry officer at the end of the four months course.

'The first month has been a hard one ... The training is rather old fashioned. A great deal of stress is still laid on bayonet fighting, and the only anti-tank rifles we see are useless against heavy tanks. I have become an expert on the various ways of polishing brass and shining leather, and I am not convinced that that is the most profitable contribution I could make to the war effort. The life has its compensations, however. I am fitter than I have ever been before and have learned how to get sufficient sleep in the minimum of time. It is, of course, very different from life at Jesus, but I am really quite happy....'

A long description, written many years later, of his wartime experiences acknowledged its better moments as well as the arduous and occasionally humiliating ones. He learnt to ride a motorbike. Even though he was not good at drill, he 'did rather enjoy it. It was satisfying to be doing things together and in time, and somehow helped the comradeship, which was important...' Early rising was eased by 'the distant and romantic sound of a bugle' sounding the

---

[29]   Professor Glanville Williams later came to the college in 1956 as one of its most distinguished lawyers.

reveille – 'a delight to anyone with some sort of a musical ear…' As a Methodist, he and two others avoided the spit-and-polish of the Anglican church parade: they went instead to a tiny Methodist chapel, where the accompanying sergeant exclaimed 'You're not going in, are you?' and left them to themselves.

After some home leave in October, he continued training at Droitwich. As an officer cadet there he was expected to drill a group of men; and he loved to recall his ineptitude in this exercise, when he had set his troops marching straight ahead towards a brick wall and could not for the life of him remember the command to halt them. As collision loomed he shouted 'Left turn!', and turned them again as they approached another barrier … until at last, sweating, he managed to call 'Halt!' The sergeant major and senior officers, he found, were doubled up in laughter. The hardship of those weeks was lessened by his appreciation of the landscape.

> 'It was near the River Severn and we had some wonderful early spring mornings crawling on our bellies, and pushing our rifles in front of us in the meadows near the river. Infantry training is tough but it has its appeal to anyone who loves open country.' [One night exercise was especially memorable:] '… very sad, for we were not far from Coventry and it was the night of the devastating German bombing raid … It was I suppose about 20 miles or so from us crawling in the fields. But we could see well enough what was happening.'

After being commissioned as a second lieutenant from the 168 OCTU at Droitwich, he then found himself 'proceeding' to Oxford, where the Intelligence Corps HQ was in Oriel College. There was further training in Pembroke College, and in both places he met and got on well with elderly dons who were still in residence. His first posting, surprisingly, took him back to Cambridge for a course at Trinity College preparing people to govern Germany after the war was over. This can be dated as taking place in January 1941. 'Looking back', he commented, 'it seems remarkable that in 1941 the confidence of the country should have been so strong. But it was, and it did not in the least strike me as odd at the time.'

Among the lecturers was Ernest Barker[30], who became quite a friend; and among his Intelligence Corps companions were

---

30 Sir Ernest Barker was Professor of Political Science at Cambridge at the time.

'Hans Keller, the German refugee musical expert, with whom I spent quite a bit of time; there was Winton Dean the great Handel Opera expert (a useful and stubborn batsman in one cricket match we managed to have); and also David Hinks, then Bursar of Trinity who later became a very distinguished soldier and a Brigadier General. He had his own rooms in New Court with a wonderful (for those days) Murphy wireless and record player. He made me listen to Wanda Landowska playing Bach on a harpsichord, a revelation to me who did not even know what a harpsichord was. That was a very rewarding friendship, but it came to an end with the war when he returned to Trinity, only to get fatal blood poisoning from pruning a rose bush.'

It was probably while spending these weeks in Trinity, Cambridge, that he was able to turn up at debates with the LSE (evacuated from London to Peterhouse) organised by the Alcock Society at Jesus. *Chanticlere* reported that '… An aircraftsman, second class, dimly recognisable as Mr Balme, Fellow of Jesus, spoke attractively …; and from beneath a second lieutenant's uniform Mr Jennings … used his lawyer's skill to drive his points home.'

But now, having (he felt) made a poor impression on senior officers during the course, he was directed to the work that was to occupy him for the duration. Back he went to Oxford.

'There was an organisation just beginning which was later called ISTD – the Inter Services Topographical Department. It was the result of the disastrous attempt at an invasion in Norway at Narvik, [when] the invading force knew nothing about Narvik; nothing even about the climate and the weather to be expected, for this was in the far north of Norway. So Admiral Godfrey, the Director of Naval Intelligence[31], determined to set up a unit to make sure this lack of basic information would never happen again. It began as a few people working in the ground floor of the University Geographical School in Mansfield Road. The CO was a marine colonel called Bassett, and the Naval side was under a Commander Hughes, RN. Being an inter-service unit, the Royal Navy was in overall command.'

Robbie was at first given a humble rôle, assisting a nice Lt Col. of First World War vintage nicknamed 'Old Pigsticker'. But soon things livened up,

---

[31]   Admiral Sir John Godfrey's *Naval Memoirs* are preserved at Churchill College.

when Commander Hugo Hughes – 'handsome and smart and tough' – took over. Robbie admired him and they worked well together, becoming 'quite close friends'.

The unit moved into Manchester College, where their work entailed the close scrutiny of maps and marine charts together with the aerial photographs (later stereoscopic[32]) obtained by daring young pilots in low-flying Spitfires.[33] The centre for the intensive interpretation of photographs as they came in was the RAF station at Medmenham. Sworn to secrecy as all intelligence personnel were, little could be told of their activities. But I did hear that detailed information was gathered and recorded about many sites along the Channel coast that might have been intended for Allied invasion, although those doing all this preparatory work had no idea which spot might be actually chosen. They were also probably studying the areas around the Mediterranean where conflict might occur. One of those joining in the work was a young woman Oxford geographer, Mary Marshall, who was producing detailed information for the Admiralty about those places. Another woman contributing to their work was Flight Lieut. Constance Babington-Smith, interpreting aerial photographs which later in the war identified secret German installations such as the launching-sites for the dreaded V1 and V2 weapons. (Many years later a BBC documentary programme, *Operation Crossbow*, has revealed more fully how important that intensive work had been.)

What Robbie did enjoy recalling was the range of new friendships made at that time. He was fortunate in being adopted by Jesus College, Oxford as an honorary member of their Senior Common Room and there he lived for the whole of his Oxford posting. He made friends with the Bursar, Baker, a geographer who was in the RAF; Seymour the classicist who, on retiring, sold him his college furniture; Cross ('Holy Cross') the chaplain who would drive him, with Commander Hughes, in his big Daimler to a shoot in the country

---

[32] The double image produced by twin cameras gave depth to what was otherwise seen as a flat surface.

[33] In the book *Most Secret War* R.V. Jones describes (p.226) how, with a camera mounted so that it 'pointed sideways and looking somewhat aft from the fuselage of a Spitfire just behind the pilot's seat' the pilot had to 'dive and fly past the object to be photographed; the object would disappear under his wing, and he had to guess when it would reappear behind the wing and fire the shutter accordingly. Since all this had to take place when he was flying at fifty feet and three hundred miles an hour, with quite possibly a light anti-aircraft gun firing at him, it is not surprising that he found it difficult'.

west of Oxford; Woodward the chemist, in whose house he frequently lunched or dined; and Geronwy Edwards, the distinguished medieval historian.

His promotion was described thus: 'At some time I became a captain and after a bit longer I became a major, which was rather nice and about right for me. I did not have very high ambitions in the Army'. He quite often had to go to London, 'usually to see somebody in MI6, then in the War Office. One just walked into the War Office; there was no great scare about security. Sometimes I had to go to argue about staff we required and so on.' It may be that on these visits he was able to eat dinners at Lincoln's Inn, for he was called to the Bar in 1943, having been exempted from the Bar Final '…on the ground of existing qualifications and war service'.

Some contact with Jesus College, Cambridge, was maintained by appearing at the Rustat Feast. By Michaelmas Term 1943 *Chanticlere* reported that D.M. Balme had been awarded the DFC, and that 'Mr Sinker, Mr Guy, Mr Wilson and Captain Jennings' had all paid visits during the term. Next term Robbie had attended the Audit Feast, and David Balme had added a DSO to his DFC.

Now came the order to start an ISTD in India as part of Mountbatten's South East Asia Command. Cmdr. Hughes was chosen to lead it, and selected Robbie as second in command, taking an RAF Officer from their section in Oxford and a Wren from another section, 'a very capable girl, the daughter of a sea captain whose home was in Fowey' – a place familiar to Robbie from 'Q's descriptions. This must have been in March 1944; and after several false starts, they were off: –

'We began our journey to India in a slow train to Bournemouth. We arrived there in the early evening … The sea front then was lined with barbed wire and there were gun emplacements all along the promenade – after all, we were still preparing for a German invasion. After dark we were taken to Poole Harbour, where a rowing boat took us out to the Short's flying boat that was to take us to Karachi. It was not very comfortable. We sat on steel forms along the side of the aircraft. There were no seat belts, of course, and no cushions. We spent a long night nodding off when we could, but only in a sitting position on steel. In those days this discomfort did not matter at all!

'Our journey on the first leg, which was to Gibraltar, was long because the Germans still occupied France. So we had to go well out westward over the Atlantic before turning to the south and then back eastward to make the harbour at Gibraltar by early morning. It was a beautiful morning. A rowing boat fetched us into the quay and we had breakfast I can't remember where, but somewhere in the middle of the town. Then a brief walk around and back into our flying boat for the next leg, which was along the north coast of Africa well inland with fine views, for we went quite slowly by modern standards and at only 7 or 8 thousand feet. There was no pressurised cabin, of course. The desert fight had already been won by the Eighth Army, so we could just steer for our next destination, which was on an island off the coast of Tunisia. There we found a marquee in which we were given a very pleasant supper by silent Berbers in Arab dress. Hughes and I went to bed in another marquee quite soon, but the others went in search of a French colonial hotel on the mainland and had some very bad wine, which meant they were sick all over the plane next morning. H. and I were not best pleased.

'Next day a rather boring long journey over the western desert, but ending in some excitement because, having only floats instead of wheels, we had to 'land' on the Nile and there was a cross wind, which made it a bit chancy and rather difficult. The pilot had three goes at it, but in the end it was well done. Then Cairo for one night at the famous Shepherd's Hotel (which was burned down sometime after the war, but which I believe has re-opened). Cairo was a bit of a culture shock to most of us, but not of course to Hughes. The east is different. Very different. And we were still west of Suez!

'In the morning we joined our flying boat again, and taking off along the Nile really was a rather splendid adventure. Then over the desert again and right over Jerusalem, following the road through the hills to Jericho and seeing the Jordan flowing into the Dead Sea. Then the empty deserts of Arabia all day, to arrive on the Lake at Habbaniya in Iraq. Habbaniya was then a British military outpost on the Euphrates some ?30 miles west of Baghdad. There we had a short rest and a meal, and talked to the homesick troops who would have given anything to get even to Baghdad. At Habbaniya there was nothing but this large lake near the Euphrates. It was the lake which was important for the British, in providing water on which a flying boat could land. We had our little rest and tea there with the garrison of fed-up British soldiers. There was nothing there but the lake, and nothing ever happened except for the occasional short visits of flying boats.

'Then another night flight east over the desert and the dramatic mountains of Arabia, and Oman, then over the Persian Gulf to arrive after a very long leg at the harbour in Karachi. We had two or three days in Karachi, lodging at a posting station called Somerset House. This was, relatively speaking, very comfortable. In the street there was again culture shock – beggars everywhere, easily spotting the new arrivals and beginners. Appalling poverty. But Somerset House was a haven. I had arrived, of course, in English battle dress. I was taken off by a splendid bearer, elderly and bearded and turbaned (a bearer is an Indian Army batman in a way, but also something on his own and very special to India) to be kitted out with tropical clothes: cotton shorts and a light linen jacket. When he took my battle dress off he was appalled at its coarseness and said 'You must never wear that again, Sahib'.

'Then on with our journey again, this time still in a flying boat but a very comfortable one that was really part of the civilian fleet of the Imperial Airways. It was very fine flying quite low and ensconced in a sort of armchair with a good view in front as well as at the side. There is no lake at Delhi. So this was a Calcutta-bound plane, and we were with it as far as the lake at Gwalior, then a native state ruled by a principal Maharajah. Again an even bigger culture shock as our Army vehicle took us from the lake into the middle of the town, teeming thousands of natives noisily thronging the streets. We passed a railway station with big Stead locomotives obviously built in England. We passed the Palace with its extraordinary display of wealth and power right in the very midst of extreme poverty. It really was a very great culture shock for me, and for the others, except for Hughes who, as a regular Naval officer, had spent a lot of time at Rangoon before the war.

'And so to an ordinary plane on an ordinary airfield for the last leg of the journey to Delhi. It was a small RAF plane. And the pilot, knowing we were new to India, was kind enough to go via Agra, miles from Delhi, and fly low over the Taj Mahal. From the Delhi airport we were taken to our temporary living quarters, which was bell tents in a field …'

After this memorable journey, Robbie sent home 28 airletters – his writing even smaller than usual because of the limited space. The sights, sounds and daily routine of life in Delhi were described, though never the actual work of their unit there. Under Mountbatten's command, they were presumably making detailed study of maps and marine charts to assist his plans for landings on the mainland coast and many islands occupied by the Japanese in South-East Asia. Robbie was engaged in this work from April until October 1944.

Some of his experiences were enjoyable, others not. They were soon moved from tents to better quarters in Jaipur House, a town palace belonging to the Maharaja of Jaipur, with a pleasant morning walk to the great Lutyens Secretariat Building where their offices were.

> 'We had plenty of good staff in our section, but their morale was sometimes a bit under the weather. Most of them were exiles who fled from the Japanese in Malaya, from Burma on the famous and dangerous long jungle trail from Burma to India if you were very lucky, and from Singapore. They were naturally rather fed up with the concentration of the war effort on the Germans in Europe and felt they had been let down by home. And in many ways they had. The futile defences of Singapore were a disgrace resulting largely from complacency …'

But while he sympathised with their anger, the increasing heat and humidity of New Delhi made him realise how much effort was needed to maintain efficiency during long hours of work. A temperature of 117° F with high humidity might be replaced by a bitter hot wind from the desert. It helped that some of his fellow officers were good company. One was Glyn Daniel,[34] who had already before the war been scrutinising aerial photographs of archaeological sites. They were amused to find, while themselves keeping as cool as possible in thin bush shirts and shorts, Lt Col. Enoch Powell[35] at his desk 'stiffly wearing his mess jacket and his Sam Browne (the officer's belt and shoulder strap) throughout the hot weather.' Powell's later recollections of their Delhi period were inaccurate, denying that he had ever met Major-General Orde Wingate. But, said Daniel in a letter to RYJ, 'Stuart Piggott and I well remember meetings in his rooms in the Secretariat with Wingate and Peter Fleming[36] planning the mock-invasion of Akijab!' (So it was not only in the European sector that MI6 created false rumours to mislead the enemy.)

Robbie was attending the Methodist chapel fairly regularly and enjoyed its mixed congregation. He tried the Anglican Cathedral just once and couldn't stand it.

---

34   Fellow of St John's College, Cambridge, later Professor of Archaeology and popular entertainer on a television programme, *Animal, Vegetable, Mineral* as well as author of several detective novels.

35   Classical scholar and later prominent Conservative MP.

36   Stuart Piggott, archaeologist; Peter Fleming, described as 'adventurer and travel writer', the elder brother of Ian Fleming.

But that Methodist connection stood him in good stead: a missionary, the Rev. J.W. Sweetman, from his own Idle circuit at home was working at Benares and wrote to invite him to join his little group at the house they rented in the hot weather in the Himalayan foothills above Mussouri. He accepted, and took a night train from Delhi up to Dehra Dun.

It made a wonderfully refreshing break. He had at first been shocked by the English missionaries he encountered in Delhi, thinking of the sacrifices made by hard-up people in Idle for 'brave missionaries living amongst very poor natives in the villages' since those in India seemed to be living in luxury – but later realised that

> even a poorly-paid missionary in this country was obliged to employ the full complement of native house servants by the caste system, which limited specific tasks to each caste.

Once he reached Mr Sweetman's retreat, he rose at dawn to climb a little higher and really see the Himalayas.

> '– there they were. Mile after mile of them, in a long line from left as far as the eye could see, to right as far as the eye could see, of wonderful peaks and chains of peaks, the highest mountains in the world. That was one of the greatest sights that the world can offer … I have never since seen anything like that view of, I suppose, something approaching 100 miles of the Himalayan chain with the sun shining on the snow peaks.'

After a three-day trek with some young missionaries further up into the hills, he spent some happy days with the Sweetmans, with plenty of chat not only about home, but also about the Moslem religion, which Sweetman was studying. At an afternoon of home-produced entertainment in the local community centre he even found himself reciting *Albert and the Lion*.

Early in May he was saddened to hear news from Cambridge from Freddie Brittain of the death of 'Q'.

> 'I shall greatly miss that visit to his rooms after dinner when I return to college, and the sound of his cheery "Ah, come in my boy". I shall always treasure the memory of his beautifully furnished rooms, profuse with flowers (red and yellow roses whenever possible), his neat writing desk with the old-

fashioned quill pen, and the blotting paper always salmon-pink. We shall never see anybody like him again. As he used to say himself, he was a "period piece – from a good period".'

If Robbie had decided to join the regular Indian Army rather than remain merely 'seconded', his pay would have been higher and probably his rank. He was already doing the work of a Lt Colonel, and was tempted. But he was sure he wanted to get home as soon as possible and felt an obligation to return to Cambridge.[37] It was a difficult decision and he wondered whether he might regret it. In the meantime he had asked his geographer friend at Oxford, Mary Marshall, to post some books on international law; and Professor Hollond had helpfully written,

'… discussing what lines of law I ought to take up when I return to Cambridge … This has set me all of a dither to get back to my civilian job. I feel that after 5 years in the Army I have so much more that I can put into my proper job. The experience in the Army has, I feel, been by no means wasted even from the academic point of view…'

Those weekly letters home included many small incidents. He had found himself singled out at a gathering with General Auchinleck[38] for drinks after dinner 'in the garden in front of the Vice-Roy's Palace right at the heart of the great Lutyens scheme of New Delhi,' where he was introduced to the Vice-Roy himself. He visited a Hindu temple built at vast expense by a Hindu industrialist millionaire, brand new and excessively vulgar, where he nevertheless appreciated the warm welcome given.

On 18th August he comments on the progress of the war: 'I don't know whether people at home realize what astonishing feats are being performed by the 14th Army in Burma', and says he is following the news of the Allied advance on the European continent. While working hard, he was also finding time to read: 'I have almost finished the 600 page law textbook[39] I had sent out to me'.

---

[37]   Jesus College had been paying his 'dividends' while he was away on service.

[38]   'the commander who had made possible the desert triumphs of Montgomery'

[39]   Possibly the latest edition of *Oppenheim Vol.II,* on Disputes, War & Neutrality, ed. Hersch Lauterpacht.

Glyn Daniel, he recorded, 'did me good by making me go and see things like the Qutb Minar, a remarkable ancient tower some miles outside Delhi' – an interesting if rather exhausting day, climbing its 300+ steps in the heat. But they

> '…were part of Mountbatten's South East Asia Command, and Mountbatten could not wait to get away from the stifling and stuffy atmosphere of GHQ India. So we were all to go to Ceylon – present day Sri Lanka – to huts being built in the Botanic Gardens of Peradenia, a mile or two outside the famous and beautiful hill town of Kandy, with its great lake and temples.'

Once the great task of packing up all their papers and equipment was complete, Cmdr Hughes and 'the Wren' (never named) left by air; the main party had an exhausting train journey southwards via Madras; and then Robbie and one other officer, who stayed to close down their office in Delhi, had an easier journey, since they were carrying the most secret and important papers – 'by RAF Dakota aeroplane via Bangalore to Colombo. From Colombo we caught the wonderful train – with steam locomotives made by Kitsons of Leeds – up through the mountains to Kandy …' And his first letter home from there, dated 14th September 1944, starts 'I am delighted with Ceylon. It is quite the most beautiful country I have ever seen …'

His work, very intensive, was now to organise the new branch of the ISTD. A pleasant diversion occurred when he got in touch with his namesake, Ivor Jennings, known from his LSE days and now Principal (later Vice Chancellor) of the emerging University of Ceylon, who was living in a hotel close to Colombo[40], and gave Robbie a day of sight-seeing. Another memorable break was to go with other members of their group on an excursion to Sigiriya – 'the extraordinary rock outcrop you see in miniature on the 10 cent postage stamps'. He could now feel that he had seen some of the most notable sights of the island, as well as the occasional snake, scorpion and plenty of elephants.

He admired their commander, Mountbatten:

---

[40] – probably at that time waiting for the arrival of his wife and children. While he, after delay, had been permitted to fly from Britain, they had set off by sea and their ship had been bombed and sunk. Although rescued, one daughter had been injured, so the journey was not attempted again immediately.

'Every so often there was a meeting of the whole company with all ranks to hear him address us. The talks were excellent. He told us all frankly what the military position was, what the problems were that we had to tackle and just how he proposed we set about it. He did not shirk difficult matters, e.g. home leave, which was on many people's minds. He said that the prospects were dim or non-existent; but at least he showed that the matter was being thought about and the problems of the ranks were not being altogether forgotten. Of course he liked talking and had a very good opinion of himself. But that is what you want in wartime. And we were a very large company of people and these talks were in the open air, but nobody had the least difficulty in hearing what he said.'

But now the moment had come for his promised return to Oxford, to be in charge of the section there working on the war against the Japanese. In spite of Hughes' attempt to dissuade him, he had held to his decision and was allowed to return. He first flew by Lancaster bomber to Karachi…

'… then a night in a dreadful place on the Shatt-al-Arab (Basra); the Western Desert in Egypt with one night in a hut in the Army Depot west of Cairo; Malta for breakfast and then over France (by then liberated except for the Channel Islands!), and landing finally, after several days, at Lynam RAF airport.'

For that last leg he was the only passenger, so on arrival was treated with great suspicion; but at last he was released and made his way 'back to a surprised Jesus College, Oxford, and reported in the morning to Colonel Bassett'.

Back in Oxford he was still unsure whether he had made the right decision. But this last phase of his Intelligence service was once again busy and interesting: at one point he had to stand in for the major who was normally in charge at Manchester College, and quite enjoyed it. And again he 'came across some very interesting people, especially Jim Butler[41], historian of Trinity, Cambridge … also Toby Milsom[42] who later became our best legal historian since Maitland; and Peter Carter, lawyer of Wadham College, Oxford'.

He also became friends with Tony Bridge, an officer in the School of Military Intelligence at Matlock – a handsome, hard-drinking, hard-swearing artist, emphatically atheist, 'painting away in his spare time at the Derbyshire

---

[41] J.R.M. Butler – later Sir James Butler
[42] Professor S.F.C. Milsom, of St John's College, Cambridge

scenery.'[43] They were demobilized together, and after collecting their 'demob' suits had lunch before the Bridges kindly saw him off at King's Cross for Cambridge. Many years later Robbie received a letter from the Very Reverend Antony Bridge, Dean of Guildford, reminding him of that moment. As the train taking him back to Jesus College, Cambridge was starting to move, Bridge had called out that he had no address to keep in touch. And Robbie, raising his voice above the chuffing and clanking, shouted from the window, 'JESUS WILL ALWAYS FIND ME!' – a moment Bridge would always remember.

Robbie's own college certainly wanted him back. Having kept in contact throughout the war and received his share of 'dividends', in May 1945 the Master, Duckworth, applied for his early release. Thus it was that the Senior Tutor, Tillyard, was able to write on 22nd December 1945, 'Dear Robbie – It is very good to feel that you will be properly in residence next term'.

Had his diversion into military service been a waste of his time? For a career that was to be dedicated to international law, those years were of value to him later. He had enjoyed the comradeship of military life, and developed his aptitude for administration and an expertise in the study of maps and naval charts that would be an advantage in understanding the complexities of boundary disputes in his later career. Besides this, he had managed to read more fully in his chosen subject and been called to the Bar. He had even found time during the last year or so to write some articles for the British Yearbook. *Open Towns* appeared as a note in 1945; *International Civil Aviation and the Law* in the same volume of *BYIL*; *Government in Commission* in 1946, as well as a note, *International Civil Aviation 1945-46*. It is remarkable that he should have found time to develop such a comprehensive knowledge of Air Law while still completing his military service; but of course the full range of his contacts and activities during the war remain secret. It is quite likely that he had read an article by Daan Goedhuis published in the *British Aeronautical Journal* in January 1943, 'Changes in Approaches to International Air Agreements' – and may indeed have met this influential Dutchman who, after his adventurous escape from the Nazis, was able to set up a temporary office of his organisation, *IATA*[44], in London.

---

43   One of Bridge's paintings still hangs at home.

44   *IATA* – the International Air Traffic Association, of which Goedhuis was Secretary-General.

As Robbie said in an 80th birthday speech, 'I was fortunate, having a relatively very comfortable war compared with some [other members of Jesus College]. … but looking back, the Army seems to me to have been at least as good a preparation for an academic career as the present alternative of spending those young years accumulating a thesis for a Ph.D.'

—

After the war Robbie remained on the list of reserve officers. He never applied for the service medals that were his due, feeling that, unobtrusive as his contribution had been, it was better that it should remain so. Outstanding heroism, he knew, had been shown in daring RAF bombing raids over Germany by his cousin Group Captain Geoffrey Womersley, who was awarded two DSOs and a DFC.

—

Back to Jesus College, Cambridge

1946

By the beginning of Lent Term 1946 Robbie was installed in a set of rooms on N Staircase in Jesus, Cambridge. He found the college buildings showing some effects of the war years – a general shabbiness, and the best of its stained-glass, the ancient cockerel emblems in the Old Library and the Burne-Jones windows in the Chapel not yet restored after their removal for safekeeping. Three great figures from his earlier time there had gone – Arthur Gray, Bernard Manning and 'Q' – but all the Fellows except Wilkinson were now back from National Service. David Balme had added a bar to his DSO, Vivien Fisher had been badly wounded, and Laurence Picken had been working in China. All must have been affected by their experiences.

This was true of a large proportion of the undergraduates, too. Those coming straight from school must have felt very young compared with those either returning or entering the college as veterans. In that first term Robbie had only four supervision pupils, but that number would increase until in 1951 there were 30. Before the war his pupils had been largely rowing men with little real interest in the law; now the men he was to teach were, like him, 'back from the war, very much of an age, and very rusty; and it was perfectly understood that the teachers could do no more than try to keep in front of the taught, and might not always succeed'. At his nervous first lecture –

> 'The room was full of colonels and brigadiers. After the lecture two or three, knowing full well that I was on trial, came up to me and the highest-ranking one said: "Well done, Sir. Really quite good. If you carry on like that I'm sure you'll be all right, Sir".'

His university duties now involved giving a course of 20 lectures on International Law for the LL.B. candidates and 40 classes on the subject for the Law Tripos Part I. The Law Faculty minute book records his part in organising meetings for the conference in the Long Vacation of the International Law

Association that had taken place in Cambridge, with special thanks 'for all the hard work he put in to make the meeting so successful'. (Some 300 had attended, staying in various colleges.) Later he was appointed to examine Law Tripos Pt I candidates in Constitutional Law, and to assist Lauterpacht with International Law for the LL.B.

He was also making a home for himself in those spacious rooms in the Waterhouse Building. N Staircase, unlike most, rises in a spiral up a tower. Robbie's set comprised a large dining room, a large 'keeping room' or study, a bedroom and a lavatory and a 'gyp room'[45]. The main rooms look eastwards across the cricket field towards Jesus Green, and the bedroom and offices overlooked Pump Court, as did a small room that would later accommodate a secretary. At a time when the only new furniture available was the standard 'Utility' design, he had fortunately been able to buy some handsome pieces from his Oxford friend Seymour for his main rooms. Tony Bridge's painting hung on the wall, to be joined by landscapes of Yorkshire and the Lake District as time went by, as well as his baby grand piano, his gramophone and record collection.

Before long, the Master and Fellows of Jesus College, Oxford, were invited to a dinner at Jesus, Cambridge, in return for their hospitality at 'the other place'. This link – established through Robbie's wartime residence there – is still maintained in the exchange of privileges and friendly cricket matches. (Eustace Tillyard is said to have startled the Porter at Jesus, Oxford by turning up on a bicycle with a rucksack and announcing himself as the Master of Jesus, Cambridge.)

In an encouraging letter dated 30 December 1947 Arnold McNair congratulated Robbie on his British Yearbook article, *Government in Commission* – 'a most lucid and convincing piece of reasoning' – and suggested it might be extended and published as a short monograph as *the Legal Status of Germany & the Control Commission*. A few days later Professor Sir Percy Winfield[46] commented on the same article –

'… the importance and attraction of which you modestly underrate. A point of special importance for every student of International Law is "III The Allied Occupation and International Law", and indeed the whole article is of such conspicuous interest on a topic that crops up in the daily papers that I should recommend any intelligent layman, as well as every lawyer, to read it.'

---

[45] The pantry where the bedmaker could boil a kettle and store cleaning materials.
[46] Winfield was a Fellow of St John's, specialising in the Law of Torts.

Belle Vue High School for Boys now also recognised RYJ as one of its Distinguished Old Boys, inviting him to deliver an address and present the prizes at their Speech Day. This he did, and must have felt especially pleased that since his time a number of boys had entered Oxbridge colleges and done well – one at Oxford, nine at Cambridge, several as scholars or exhibitioners.

College life suited Robbie well. The routines of meals in Hall, meetings of the college council, frivolous society meetings such as those of the Roosters, pedalling perilously along the towpath in support of the triumphant college boats and listening to records played on W.H. Thorpe's magnificent gramophone[47] ... these were enough to fill any gaps in between study and teaching.

But there were also visits to London to serve his pupillage at Lincoln's Inn in the Chambers of Tom Strangman, 13 Old Square.[48] He remembered that –

'...thanks to a bomb that hit Lincoln's Inn near to there, the doors did not fit, and some windows were cracked, and there was no coal. It was very cold. I was fortunate in my pupil-Master ... who died unfairly young, soon after he had been able to retire to his beloved orchids and ducks. Generous and kind, but highly strung and terribly nervous before appearing in Court, he was very good once he got on his feet, was one of the few good cross-examiners at the Chancery Bar, and did have that quality essential to a successful barrister, a way of winning cases. This he did not by great learning but by an acute sensitivity that enabled him to see far more than was actually said in a bundle of papers. It was sheer accident and good luck that gave me the chance to be Tom's pupil – the first he had ever had – for he was not an obvious choice for an academic.'

The winter of 1946-47 was, indeed, quite exceptionally cold, and there was little heating in those spacious rooms on N Staircase.

At the end of that academic year he took part in the organising of the first post-war May Ball, and it was reported in *Chanticlere* that 'Mr Jennings proved a wizard of finance'. He was to become a Tutor next term as well as Financial Tutor, and found that a wizard might have been useful in procuring essential equipment. He had to plead for the installation of a telephone in his

---

47   Dr W.H. Thorpe, zoologist, whose slowed-down recordings of the song of chaffinches revealed much about their behaviour

48   13 Old Square, Robbie's chambers for the rest of his life, in May 2004 joined 9 Old Square to become Maitland Chambers.

rooms, long delayed. There were negotiations with the Bursar[49] about furniture provided by the college, for which he was charged rent: might, for instance, one of the two bookcases used for textbooks be considered 'for use in connection with College duties?' [Yes.] After the payment for furniture, bedmaker, gas and electricity (total £46.0s.5d) his net dividend, before tax, came to £336.5.7. It was not until 1953 that his accommodation was rearranged slightly to allow for a bathroom and more convenient gyp room.

Having a car,[50] Robbie would make the 4½-hour journey up to Idle to see and assist his parents; and whenever possible he drove on to the Lake District.

Another Jesus fellow with a passion for the Lakes was A.P. Rossiter, English scholar, whose qualities were described[51] as 'energy, brilliance, humour always astringent, sometimes biting, a rare humaneness'. After a career ranging from Natural Science to Basic English, and including a 5-year lectureship at a Naval College in Japan and 10 years at Durham, he had arrived at Jesus in 1945, by this time engrossed in Medieval and Elizabethan Drama.

Robbie admired this complex character, and was himself to add a note to the obituary in *The Times* about 'A.P.' as supervisor and Tutor –

'The suave manner, the decanter of sherry on the sideboard, and the invitation to tea were not his line at all. His manner towards his pupils when they called on him was kindly, though businesslike; and could, when occasion required, be brusque. He was always ready with frank, wise advice for any who really needed it. Much of his best work as tutor, however, was done in the late evenings after his men had gone, and as often as not without their knowledge: the anxious and careful thinking about their characters and needs; the extraordinary care he devoted to his beautifully written, brilliantly penetrating terminal reports on each man's progress, the immense energy spent absolutely without limit in protecting any man who suffered hurt or injustice. In such matters "A.P." always made the rest of us seem slipshod in comparison…'

---

49   At that time it was Charles Wilson
50   His first car was a much-travelled Vauxhall, bought secondhand from Alan Pars in c1948.
51   – by Graham Storey, in an obituary for the *Cambridge Review* of 2nd February 1957.

A.P. was now married to his second wife, Barbara Bloch,[52] and it was with this pair that Robbie was introduced to a farm guest house in Wasdale from where one could spend days on some of the area's most challenging fells and crags. The farm was run by two slightly eccentric ladies, Rosalind and Rosamund – the 'Rosaceae' – tenants of Bowderdale,[53] close by Yewbarrow, where they tended Herdwick sheep and offered hospitality to suitable academics, including the economists Richard Kahn and Joan Robinson. Robbie found he fitted into this curious ménage, and would spend one vacation after another there walking his beloved fells. While he, as a romantic Wordsworthian, revelled simply in the place and its atmosphere, A.P. concentrated fiercely on rock-climbing: his pioneering ascents were categorised by The Fell & Rock Climbing Club as 'difficult' or 'extreme'. A.P. wanted Robbie to take up this sport, and nailed a pair of his boots with climbing nails (knowing that the noise of hammering on the last he had in his rooms annoyed Picken, living in the set below).

Though not a natural rock-climber, Robbie did get some experience, when he

'...overlapped at Bowderdale with Jan Lochmatter, a Swiss guide from Zermatt. Rosamund had climbed with him in Switzerland, and was giving him a free holiday in the Lake District. He was a good guide. I did some rock climbs with him, including some quite exposed ones like the Needle ridge on Gable, i.e. the ridge of the main mountain behind the Napes Needle and leading up to the summit. Also a rather strenuous chimney climb on Kern Knotts (also on Great Gable). But it was easy with Lochmatter. I don't know quite why. Of course it was very safe because he could easily dangle me on a rope if he wanted to. On the other hand I found rock climbing with A.P. quite the opposite. I was scared stiff, even though the climbs were much easier. Of course I believe A.P. rather enjoyed intentionally taking grave risks and scaring himself. He was very odd indeed. But I was very fond of him.

'Later I did forsake the Lakes on one holiday and went climbing with Lochmatter in the Alps. We met at Chamonix and then went into Switzerland by train to the southern Alps; and eventually to Arrolla...'

And from there he did some quite severe climbs, including the Pigne d'Arrolla, which included glacier and crevasse work. Rising at 4 a.m., using an ice axe

---

52   daughter of the German Expressionist painter, Martin Bloch

53   afterwards taken by a true Cumbrian, Joss Naylor, who won fame as champion fell-runner.

on a steep ice slope, and taking longer trips with overnight stays in mountain huts … it was a great experience though troubled by anxiety about cost, since in those austere times the British were allowed to take so little currency abroad.

But Wasdale and 'the two ladies of Bowderdale' were of great importance. Rosalind Beach-Thomas was the daughter of a well-known journalist and writer on country matters, and was herself thoroughly well-read. Rosamund Crichton, with an M.Litt from a year or two at Girton, was less stable, haunted by two failed marriages and unfulfilled literary ambitions. They both loved their tough Cumberland neighbours as well as the conversation of their academic visitors. And a special memory for Robbie, normally a solitary walker, was of a walk with them up Yewbarrow on a cold, moonlit night with snow on the hills, to look across to Scafell: 'very beautiful'.

He was introduced by Tony Roberts, the Jesus medical fellow, to Glyndebourne. _Figaro_[54] was for him a revelation: 'Mozart "comic" opera was in an entirely different class from all the rest. It was up there in a league of its own as one of the greatest art forms of all time …' As an Associate Member of the Glyndebourne Festival Society he would attend as many operas there as possible in later years.

Yet another of his bachelor vacation sorties was to act as crew on _Clothilde_. This happened by accident. At a noisy gathering with drinks at Downing, he was asked 'And are you a Yorkshireman too?' 'Yes' said Robbie warmly … and found during the ensuing conversation that the question had been whether he was a _yachtsman_. By then it was too late to back out – he was being recruited by Jim Grantham, the college Bursar, for the next voyage in his yacht, together with Clive Parry, Downing law fellow. On that first trip all Robbie's land-lubberly prejudices were confirmed. Sailing down the estuary on a falling tide, the boat went aground. They lay askew as night fell, anxiously waiting for the next tide to lift them off. Then in darkness they wound their way through the narrow channel into the shallow but turbulent North Sea. The novice had to learn the ropes and acquire sea legs in the nastiest of conditions until the owner-skipper safely got them into port. And then Robbie, who had for hours been thinking 'Never again!' experienced the joy of drinking Dutch beer and eating a hearty meal with close companions. Next time Jim Grantham proposed a

---

[54] That performance – _The Marriage of Figaro_ with Sena Jurinac as the Countess – is recalled on Glyndbourne's DVD _On Such a Night_.

trip on '*Clottie*' he was eager to join him, even though they had some pretty scary moments battling through the fierce currents around Alderney.

———

These were diversions in a life that was seriously dedicated to his work as a don. In the summer of 1948 David Balme, the classicist whose career in the RAF had been so splendid, was recruited to become the first Principal of the new University College of the Gold Coast (now Ghana) and resigned his Fellowship. Robbie was appointed Senior Tutor in his stead.

The duties of Senior Tutor were combined with those of Tutor for Admissions and Financial Tutor. Balme had kindly left some notes of advice for his successor, and there were always the college's Chief Clerk, Mr Lenoir, and the disciplinarian Head Porter, Capt. Austin, to make sure that nothing went too badly wrong. McNair, congratulating him, warned –

'… But it is very difficult, while carrying that burden, to maintain a lively interest in one's work. I sincerely hope that you will … compartmentalize your tutorial and your legal work so that the latter will not be submerged.'

To be able to cope with it all, Robbie eventually asked the College Council whether he might be allowed some secretarial assistance. The Master, Duckworth, and the Council considered this innovation and finally conceded the appointment of a secretary, provided she would be available to all five Tutors. The post of Tutors' Secretary was duly advertised through the University Women's Appointment Board. That small room beside the entrance to his set on N Staircase would serve as her office, but he must himself find any furniture and equipment that was needed. He bought an inexpensive desk for the trusty Remington typewriter, a filing cabinet and found an old chair.

Captain Austin, MBE, a veteran of the First World War and a warrant officer in the second, made sure that the new Senior Tutor knew the name of every undergraduate: Robbie would be tested by reciting each name as Austin pointed to the faces on the freshmen's photograph. Moreover, as a bachelor living in college, he might be wakened by the unrelenting Head Porter if there was any disturbance or sudden illness among his charges during the night. This once happened even in vacation, when there was a conference of the Coal Board on the premises. Nervously, he had to knock on the door and enter, to interrupt a gathering of boozy miners shouting and singing. When he asked them to be quiet since it was past midnight, one challenged him: 'Why should we? Who are you?' all he could say was 'Because I say so, and because I am the Senior Tutor.' To his amazement, instead of flinging him downstairs they accepted this and calmed down!

Slight in build and never loud, he always carried a certain authority. It was recognised by people of all sorts, and so there was rarely need for an unpleasant confrontation.

⸻

That first Tutors' Secretary was a Miss B— (whose name I was told but have forgotten) who had for a while during the war worked for Winston Churchill – a nerve-racking experience, taking dictation straight onto a typewriter at random moments and always with urgency. I do not know how long she stayed in her new and very different job, but she was succeeded by another Miss B— who must have been a homely character, since she liked to knit woollen socks for Robbie, producing knee-length ones that he liked for fell-walking. (Two pairs of long crimson ones were laid aside unworn; and they, much later, became the family's stockings hung out each year for Father Christmas to fill.)

⸻

International law is a wide and ever-expanding subject. At this time Robbie was particularly engaged in the study of Air Law. It provided work in the form of occasional Opinions, (advice to clients on difficult points); and in 1949 he was invited to lecture on the subject at that summer's course at The Hague Academy. *Some Aspects of the International Law of the Air* may be found in the *Recueil des Cours* for that year.[55] It marked a growing recognition of his significance as a scholar.

A preserved letter reveals that in 1950 Robbie was offered a Chair at the University of London but declined it. He is likely to have felt that his work at Cambridge, though complicated in all its different aspects, was going well: he was getting into his stride as Senior Tutor, as Lecturer and Director of Studies, as a member of the General Board of the University, and had made friendships too valuable to be disturbed. London, moreover, was so much further from Idle and Cumberland.

The Whewell Professor of International Law was now Hersch Lauterpacht, who had arrived in Cambridge in 1938. Lauterpacht was an acknowledged

---

[55]   It is also included in *The Collected Writings,* pp1124-1186.

authority on the subject, with an impressive output of published work. He had initiated the *Annual Digest of International Law*; was editing the *British Yearbook of International Law* and successive editions of *Oppenheim*, the major textbook on the subject; and had, during the war, advised on foreign policy both in Britain and the U.S.A. He had also played an important part in the early stage of the Nuremburg trials after the war – something which must for him have brought searing memories of his own family's sufferings, for he was a Polish Jew who had progressed from the University of Lvov to Vienna, and then to the London School of Economics in 1923. His parents and all close relatives except one niece had perished in the concentration camps organised by the men under trial.

Lauterpacht's style of lecturing was very different from McNair's but very effective; particularly admired was his occasional intervention during the weekly seminars, when a student might make a confident assertion only to find Professor Lauterpacht, after a telling pause, quietly ask: 'Is that *so*?' The young man's confidence would crumble, and the group would then have to set about considering the whole matter more searchingly.

———

In 1952 I, Christine Bennett, became the third Miss B— to be appointed Tutors' Secretary. I had, after an undistinguished degree in English at Oxford, taken a concentrated secretarial course and then worked in the office of the Academic Registrar at the University College of the South-West of England (later Exeter University). Among possible second jobs suggested by the University Women's Appointments Board I had chosen to apply to Jesus College, Cambridge, encouraged by the Registrar at Exeter who was himself a Jesuan.

It was not until October that I – emerging from a bath and wrapped in a towel – took a telephone call from the Senior Tutor. When, having travelled from South Devon to Cambridge, I met Mr Jennings in his keeping room, the interview was less of an ordeal than I had expected. He had probably checked that my secretarial skills were adequate, and needed to know whether I could fit into this rather unusual post. We talked a little about music and art, and when he showed me the small office I was to occupy if appointed, he suddenly pointed across the court and asked 'What period would you say those buildings are?' '16ᵗʰ century' I guessed, 'except for the obviously Victorian Gothic part over there', pointing to Small Hall (later demolished). The inquisition seemed to have gone well, but I was told that he could not give an outright answer since it was for the College Council to agree to the appointment. I returned to Exmouth, where my father challenged me: 'Didn't you tell him that your brothers had been at Christ's and your uncle was a Fellow of St John's?' 'No, it didn't arise.' And after a few days I heard that the job was mine and that I should start as soon as possible.

When I arrived at the college, on a Saturday morning in November, I was 'introduced to everything and everybody at Jesus – the Chief Clerk, the Buttery Steward, the Manciple, the Kitchens, the Head Porter, the Library and the filing system'; the Fellows I would come to know as time went on.

We began as I had expected, with Mr J dictating letters. I think he found it tiresome, and I now and then came to an abrupt halt when he used a mystifying expression such as 'give backword'. Had I misheard? No, it was a Yorkshirism, meaning 'to give apologies or decline an invitation'. Similarly, 'back end' was 'autumn' or what Americans call 'the fall'. I learnt to interpret these and modify the wording a little. We got on better if he said 'Tell him that ...', leaving me to take down important phrases verbatim but composing the letters myself for his signature. In that way, right at the start, I had to find suitable wording for a letter to the Countess of Rosse, explaining that, since he had passed none of his university exams in architecture during his two years at the college, her son Anthony Armstrong-Jones[56] simply could not be allowed to return for another year. (He had been one of those gifted undergraduates whose time had been spent producing photographs for the magazine *Varsity*, or on the river coxing the University Boat. But rules were rules ...)

Towards Christmas the work intensified, with examinations for admission candidates, some to qualify for scholarships or exhibitions, most for entry as Pensioners (known as Commoners elsewhere). It was at that time easier for men to get a place than women; and unlike the two women's colleges, Jesus could afford to welcome a few men on their sporting merits, provided they seemed genuinely able to cope with a degree course. There was certainly no preference given to public school boys over grammar school ones.

Interviewing those candidates continued late into the evening for several days, in addition to Robbie's regular meetings and correspondence. To remind himself later when sorting out their applications he, like the other Tutors, would jot down cryptic notes. These might include remarks on appearance – a big muscular chap looked a promising oarsman or likely member of the

---

[56]   who became, after marriage to HRH Princess Margaret, the Earl of Snowdon

First XV – or some particular interest. On one rather adenoidal young man from the Midlands: 'Thought he said he was member of Poultry Club. Asked intimate questions about hens, and then found it was *Poetry* Club'.

It was the easy relationship with Mr Jennings that made my job bearable. As I soon found, my position was very isolated, neither a college servant nor a member of High Table, and seldom encountering either. As I passed through the entrance gateway each morning I at first felt an intruder – for it would be many years before women (apart from the early bedmakers and one or two typists) were allowed to enter until the afternoon. Once in my small office I might meet nobody face to face all day up there except a porter bringing mail or Mr J himself. At first I fetched my lunch each day from the college kitchen, carrying it on a cloth-covered tray up to my eyrie to consume on my own; but soon I walked instead into the town to eat a cheaper meal with a friend, Joyce Baird, from my old school.

I lived in the attic of a house off Mill Road – spartan and at first filthy, but once thoroughly purged of dirt and smells it suited quite well. Below were a young family with whom I shared the bathroom, Dick Matthews, a New Zealand biochemist, his American wife Lois and their young baby Sue. They became friends and introduced me to a bohemian world of research scientists.[57] I also joined the CUMS[58] chorus, and a life-drawing group.

At times there was little for me to do at work, though my presence was needed each weekday from 9.30 am to 6 pm or later and on Saturdays until 1 pm, to answer the telephone and receive the occasional caller who had ascended N staircase. Mr J, sympathising, might lend an interesting book; and he even suggested that when he was away during the Long Vacation I might practice on his piano – which I did, although was interrupted once by a deeply shocked Captain Austin. May Week allowed me to have some light-hearted contact with undergraduates when I took minor parts in plays in the college cloisters, or in the Miracle Plays performed at Christmas in the chapel. On 7th June 1953 Mr J himself went up to London to watch the Coronation procession from a raised seat in the Mall, a privilege which, in spite of pouring rain, he enjoyed.

---

[57] Among those remarkable people were Francis Crick and James Watson just at this particularly exciting time of their DNA breakthrough. The Cricks made me welcome at their home.

[58] Cambridge University Musical Society, in which I sang under Boris Ord, David Willcocks, Philip Ledger and Stephen Cleobury.

Occasionally there might be something else to fill those days when I had little to do as Tutors' Secretary, a request to type something entirely unrelated to my regular work – an article on medicine for Dr Roberts, or a piece of satire for the Master, Tillyard. It was when I had tackled a longish legal Opinion for Robbie that the question of a suitable payment arose. Would I like a modest fee, or a 'nice surprise'? And it turned out that the Nice Surprise was a ticket for Glyndebourne, far more generous but presenting several problems. How to get there? What to wear? I somehow managed to go, solo and very modestly dressed, and of course loved it.

In the summer Robbie would find time to practice in the nets for the annual cricket match between Fellows and Servants (later called Staff) that he and Derek Taunt had started, a friendly family occasion. The teams were fairly evenly matched: some very fit gardeners and porters, and some young academics, as well as oddities from both sides devoted to the game but past their prime. I remember relishing the sight of the Master, Eustace Tillyard, who had been athletic in his younger days and still had a good eye, standings at the crease wearing sandals and behind him, stout Mr Day the Head Cook, in ancient cricket boots held together with string, keeping wicket.

Cricket and music: evidence of Robbie's love of both are still there in his study – the volumes of *Wisden* and Yorkshire Cricket Club annals, and a collection of records which was that of a man who took his listening very seriously – the entire opera *Don Giovanni*, for instance, with accompanying booklets of libretto and commentary.[59]

Summoned by the college chapel bell, he might attend evensong to hear Gardner-Smith's sermons. But he was still a loyal Methodist, keeping up his connection with Wesley Church and serving as Trustee of Wesley House, the theological college. And in October 1953, when his old Thorp Methodist Sunday School at Idle celebrated its half-century, he was there to chair one of their special gatherings and join in the service taken by his old friend the Rev. Philip Watson.

---

59 Many years later when LP records had become the norm, he gave his earlier collection to Judith Weir, the composer, who was appreciative and was able to get some of the rarities transposed to tape.

During those years as Senior Tutor, Robbie was offered at least two other appointments. His efficiency as an administrator and ability to get on with all manner of colleagues might well have led to his becoming Secretary General of the Faculties, a senior post and one with powerful influence in the University; yet, though tempted, he decided that he preferred to teach, and declined. A few years later a different opportunity arose – to become Vice-Chancellor of the University of Witwatersrand, in South Africa. This appealed in several ways: he knew how fulfilling David Balme had found his work in Africa, and he wanted to support an institution that accepted students of all races, with no *apartheid.* Yet again, enticing as the challenge might be, he enjoyed his work at Cambridge and could not move so far from his parents, who were increasingly relying on him for support.

There were further reasons for choosing to stay where he was, ones he would not feel able to explain when rejecting those offers. Many years later, when preparing a volume[60] which was to be a *Festschrift* in his honour, Vaughan Lowe asked me 'Would you say Robbie was an ambitious man?' and I found the question difficult to answer. I could remember Robbie at this time telling me, in his quiet way, that there were certain aspirations for an international lawyer: membership of the *Institut de Droit International*, the Whewell Chair at Cambridge, and to become a Judge of the International Court. But a Yorkshireman 'never lets on' – never reveals an ambition lest he look a fool for having supposed himself better than others and then failed. But most certainly, and understandably, he was aware of those goals and worked towards them, just as he had – quietly, persistently – got himself into Cambridge. (The same attitude had caused him, when handed a bicycle and told to ride along the Cam towpath with the rowing coaches, not to 'let on' that he had never sat on a bike before but simply to set off, terrified, with the river close by and other cyclists rushing past with their megaphones ... and to find that it had, perhaps, been the best way to learn to ride!)

Another reason, cherished even more privately, was that he longed to settle down as a married man with a home of his own. His days were filled with work and there was still deep satisfaction in roaming the Lake District fells during vacations entirely free of company ... yet he did not intend to forego family life for ever.

---

60   *Fifty Years of the International Court of Justice*, edited by Vaughan Lowe & Malgosia Fitzmaurice

He was an eligible bachelor; he was particular about his appearance, wearing good tailor-made suits (examining samples of cloth with the eye of one who had been brought up to recognize good worsted) and handmade shoes. He liked a car with style, too. His loyalty to Idle might have led to a Jowett; but that small firm, where Uncle Herbert had once made their timber chassis, was now closing down. Instead, he appeared one day in something which was indeed distinctive – an AC saloon,[61] black, low and slinky. Having grown up with brothers talking about cars, I accepted his invitation for a ride without hesitation.

That first outing was, I think, to dine at The Bridge at Clayhithe. Another time we walked together along the Roman Road to Horseheath; another drive to the churches of Lavenham, Clare and Long Melford; another was to Bedford for lunch at The Swan (when, to his embarrassment, he found he had left his wallet behind and was relieved that I had just enough to pay the bill); another, an intended visit to the tulip fields, was overtaken by dusk and so ended under moon and stars wandering around the precincts of Peterborough cathedral, with a supper of fish and chips eaten out of newspaper. All these outings took us a safe distance from Cambridge and allowed us to talk rather less formally than at work: 'Mr Jennings' and 'Miss Bennett' became, shyly, 'Robbie' and 'Christine.'

Although we got on so well together, it was a shock to me when, at the end of a working day in April 1954, he sat down opposite me in my small office and spoke directly and earnestly: 'I want to say something that you may need to consider very carefully – would you be prepared to become my wife?' The large gap in our ages (I being then 26 and he 40) might well, if I were his tutorial pupil, cause him to warn against it, so he would quite understand if I felt unable to answer immediately... He then withdrew, leaving me stunned – but popped his head around the door and added '– By the way, I would want to have children.' 'So would I', I found myself replying.

My thoughts were in turmoil: I knew and admired this man, but had scarcely seen him among other company, and knew nothing about his family. My situation was vulnerable in that I was earning so little, and so wondered whether the attraction was largely one of status and a more comfortable way of life. I had my pride, and was wary of the rather restricted life expected of a don's wife in those days... And so in June I said 'No'.

---

[61] The AC (Autocarriage) firm had been making vehicles since 1904 but not in great quantity. They boasted that by 1950 five were produced each week.

We carried on as before, strongly aware of the growing attraction. The tension contributed to persistent back pain and headache for which, on Robbie's recommendation, I went to the Rev. Conrad Skinner, a Jesus man and retired Methodist minister who was treating people with pain. Conrad's newly-discovered healing power[62] was effective, as were his sympathetic words. Was something worrying me, he wondered? I revealed the situation that was obsessing me. 'Oh, I know Jennings' he said, 'He is a *good* man.' And that helped to resolve my doubts.

By completing all the work on college scholarships and admissions by the end of Christmas Eve, Robbie was able to drive northwards to join his parents, and I could get my packing done in time to join a group at the bus station early on Boxing Day to set off for a fortnight's skiing in Austria, as I had done the year before. But on this trip I injured a knee right at the start and returned bandaged and limping. Back in Cambridge in January 1955, more settled in mind, our extreme shyness dissolved, we were talking more freely, and both felt ready for full commitment.

In February Robbie heard that the Law Faculty's appointment committee had (unanimously, he was told) elected him to the Whewell Chair of International Law in succession to Hersch Lauterpacht, who was now himself succeeding Arnold McNair at the International Court at The Hague. One effect of that was that Professor Jennings could no longer be Senior Tutor. And, while the new Senior Tutor, Vivian Fisher, hoped I would stay on for some time, we decided that it would be best for me to resign at the end of the Lent Term and withdraw home to Devon 'to apply the acid test' to our relationship, as Robbie put it.

As newly-elected Whewell Professor he had many adjustments to make, lectures to prepare and committees to attend while at the same time smoothing the transition for the incoming Senior Tutor – and also dealing with a new Tutors' Secretary. On top of that, his promotion had created a vacancy in the college, and a new Director of Studies in Law was needed.

We exchanged letters, and I find that 28 of his have survived. They express the turbulence of the weeks between the beginning of April and August as we approached marriage. It was hard on my mother and father, who must have found our continuing uncertainty bewildering. It was not easy for me,

---

62   Known as *Odic force*, it consisted of hand movements over, but not touching, the affected region.

when I supposed the resolution of my own doubts had cleared the way. And, as I gradually discovered, there was anguish for Robbie as he fought his way through barriers I had never suspected.

First, in April, he came down to Littleham, on the outskirts of Exmouth, to stay for a few days at my home. He travelled by train, having absent-mindedly damaged the black AC by backing it into a garage door. My parents welcomed him warmly. He could now understand more of my background, and relax a little with me in the Devon countryside.

Those letters to me were a mixture of college news, reports of his own activities and hints of his excitement at the prospect of our making a home together. The 25 applications for admission he found on his return were no longer his responsibility and could be dismissed as simply 'a bore'. He was doing a BBC talk, and after making the recording in London he had paid a call on Sir Gerald Fitzmaurice at the Foreign Office.

'What a fine room he has! Very large, with fine armchairs separated by at least 3 yards of floor, and an enormous long table for conferences away in the distance. Imagine an extremely handsome, grey-haired man, superbly dressed, with a cravatty sort of tie and diamond tie pin, sitting most elegantly in one of the arm chairs, and you have the scene. Of course it was mainly polite small talk but every here and there a casual reference to the fact that we might be useful to each other. An awfully nice man; but I can see why foreigners like and are frightened of him at the same time. How odd that he and Lauterpacht should have got on so well together – both great men but so different.'

'It's going to be tremendously exciting buying furniture and things' he wrote, wondering which style I most favoured – Chippendale, Sheraton ...? and revealing that he had on impulse bought a small painting by Philip le Bas (son of Edward) called 'Umpires and Coaches' for seven guineas, but unsure of his own taste in choosing such things. It is in fact a splendid picture that I have always enjoyed; but that, and the Chelsea blue-and-white mug that he had also bought, could hardly be described as furniture. ('Where are you going to live?' asked my father. Good question ...)

At the beginning of May he at last drove me up to Yorkshire to meet his own parents. At their neat three-bedroom semi-detached he found the back door locked, and had to ring the front-door bell and parlay with the person who opened it and let him in, before returning to invite me to follow.

I found the atmosphere strange. Everything was tidy, clean, of good quality but somehow lacking in warmth. His father's appearance echoed his own in a slightly shrunken form, and his voice was faint and husky. Mrs Jennings, too, seemed rather colourless – once attractive but faded. We both behaved in as gentle and friendly way as possible, and I tried to be helpful. We stayed two nights, the day between being spent together driving through Wharfedale and Wensleydale, lovely in gusty sun-and-shower weather. I wondered whether the senior Jenningses might feel hurt that they had been left out but Robbie was, I think, just anxious to escape and show me the places he loved. After the second breakfast we left, and of course I thanked my hosts. But I sensed that they were deeply offended and I wondered just what I had done.

Driving southwards Robbie was silent until he drew into a lay-by. I think I was weeping and shaking as he turned to me. 'Now' he said 'you see why I have taken so long in getting married!' He had been conscious of the chilly atmosphere and had indeed been dreading it, for it was not the first time. Years before, in his twenties, he had got engaged and written 'Rejoice with me!' to his parents, and taken the girl home. But Arthur and Edith Jennings had made it so clear that they disapproved of her and were furious with him for deserting them that she, realizing that she could not face such opposition, had broken the engagement off. Even a Bradford girl with whom he had been friendly for years was rejected in the same way; so he fully expected to lose me, too. But I felt that we had by then been through so much heart-searching and become so close that it simply could not be allowed to happen.

Fearing their disapproval, he had not yet actually told his parents that we intended to marry. When he did so, by letter, the reply was every bit as bad as he feared – his father writing 'a shocking letter'. Late at night after a busy day of calls, meetings, teaching and more, he poured out his distress to me:

'I think they must be going mad up there, living alone. It's nothing but complaints about me. I'm afraid I'm not very good at handling them; but when this only-child, anti-marriage neurosis takes hold of them I just dry up and behave like a stick of wood. I can't help it. But the worst of it is that they refuse to say they approve; and actually say it would be better if I did not take you there again, and that if that means that I don't go home again myself they can't help it – painful as it is for them to say so and so on and so forth…'

I could only respond with assurances of support: we should carry out our plans and do our utmost to make them not only accept but gradually find contentment in gaining an enlarged family.

Letter after letter followed, as Professor Jennings, aged now 41, brought himself to be firm with his parents, and disclosed the torment this situation had caused for so many years. In the meantime he was busy. On 17th May he wrote that…

'…Yesterday I had the candidate [for the Law Fellowship] till 11.30 pm after three meetings. This morning I had a lecture, and this afternoon an applications committee. Saturday was the long arranged Parsian[63] evening when I had to go up to "Liberty Hall", try "not to be shy" and be taken to Henry IV Pt I at the Old Vic. As it turned out, it was quite a pleasant tonic, just at the right time. The production was good, Falstaff extremely good, the Prince very good, and Hotspur unspeakably bad. The only thing that marred the proceedings was that on return to Liberty Hall at about 11.30 pm there was waiting to be faced and dealt with an immense cold supper of three courses and a bottle of wine. And of course the "old nurse" of 75 or whatever it is, obediently bringing in the second course at the ringing of the bell sometime just before midnight. I was exhausted, but Pars ("never really well this term at all") was chirping like an excited sparrow.

'Today we discovered at lunch time that this stalwart invalid arose at 4 am this morning to listen to the big fight on the wireless!'

(This needs some interpretation. Alan Pars was an elderly unmarried mathematics Fellow of Jesus, who maintained his old family home in Acton. There his sister Dora lived, and both were cared for by Leitha, their one-time Nanny. Pars was an enthusiastic theatre-goer and loved to entertain young men, both in his college rooms and for trips to the London theatres.)

The letter continues with more of his Easter Term activities: entertaining Arthur Armitage[64] at dinner, with the aim of procuring a fellowship at Queens' for a former tutorial pupil if possible; next day dining at Downing as 'new professor' guest; Thursday dining at Trinity Ascension Day Feast to meet Sir

---

[63]   i.e. entertainment by Dr Alan Pars at his London home

[64]   Law Fellow of Queens' College, later President, and then, as Sir Arthur, Vice Chancellor of Manchester University.

Hartley Shawcross[65] and the chief legal adviser to Shell Oil[66]; Friday the 'Club' dinner, to listen to Malcolm Muggeridge[67]; Saturday interview another law candidate … And the candidate the previous night had been good:

'Very nice chap, already a Reader at L.S.E.[68] I had forgotten that he was once mercilessly castigated by George Schwarz in the Sunday Times for an article he wrote about control of administrative authorities. It was pleasant to find him reminding one of this, evidently bearing George no ill will at all, and feeling that the castigation was richly deserved. That is a good sign. I always think the sign of a good scholar is to be grateful for criticism and not angry at it.'

After more interviews and meetings, the College Council reached an impasse; and it was just then that Glanville Williams, already Professor of Jurisprudence at UCL, chose to return to Cambridge where his home was, and asked to be considered as a candidate. Robbie felt how fortunate the college was to acquire someone of such outstanding ability – who would indeed become Rouse Ball Professor in 1968. He was duly appointed by the college.

By 20th May Robbie could write, 'I now do a fair amount of work in my new room (ex-Lauterpacht) at the Squire [Law Library]. It's rather easier to work if one has to *go* to work and to a place where one does nothing but work'. Four days later he wrote 'I have been asked to become editor of the International Law Quarterly; but I have said that I couldn't take on anything this summer and that if they really want me they will have to wait till the autumn and manage somehow or other in the meantime'. As term drew to an end he was able to vary his activities:

'This afternoon I am going on an excursion to King's Lynn for a change, to help Grantham ship the mast of his yacht … [and he had] played cricket with the M.A.s, getting my usual score of 0. It was very enjoyable and a good game – but now I can't even sit down without pain! And I walk very slowly about the place rather like Duckworth.'

---

65   Distinguished lawyer, formerly Attorney General and M.P.
66   This was John Blair: a valuable introduction.
67   Popular satirical journalist and television personality.
68   This was John Griffith, later made Professor at the LSE and highly regarded.

He had at last received a letter from his father, rather grudgingly accepting his decision to go ahead with his engagement but saying that he should not bring me to Idle again. It took courage for him to come again to Devon (this time surprising me with a different, jade-green, AC), and on 4th June take me to Exeter to buy a ring. Once he was back in Cambridge he still felt the need to apologise for his behaviour, writing eight pages on 12th June to try to pour out all the turmoil that had afflicted him even at that moment of formal engagement.

'I have never before managed to get to the stage of buying a ring, because I felt that to be crucial and virtually impossible. One found that one was simply incapable – physically incapable – of taking the necessary action of going into the shop and so on. And yet last weekend I managed it quite happily. It was your victory as well as mine…' [After further outpouring, in which he revealed the unfair and demented accusations made by his parents, and the anxiety that had at one time driven him to consult a psychiatrist, he commented…] 'Of course, everything has its compensations. All these years of struggle and fundamental unhappiness or at any rate discontent has enabled me to be a good tutor simply because I knew all the chaps' difficulties almost before they tried to hint at them!'

The jitters were not quite over, and despite wanting, now, to be married without further delay, it was thought best to defer the ceremony until early August and simply announce that we were to be married 'quietly' at Littleham Church, to give his parents more time to adjust to the idea.

By now he felt able to tell people at Cambridge – and found

'the position seems to be not altogether unknown … The Dean [Gardner-Smith] asked me – with an incredulous note in his voice – if it were true that I was to marry shortly. I said it might well turn out to be not untrue (one Yorkshireman to another), whereupon he said he was very glad – again managing to convey in his voice that it was surprising, a very serious step, but not blameworthy. A wonderful man, the Dean.'

Although one might at first find the Dean's sepulchral voice and grim humour rather alarming, he was a generous friend.

In early June, Robbie managed to go northwards and take his parents for a short stay at Dent, a favourite place close to the Lake District. Before leaving Idle he wrote:

'Things began unpromisingly here at first but then there was a sudden change. Dad & Mother *are* coming [to the wedding] and it would be a good thing to book their room if possible for a day or two afterwards so that they can have a holiday. Mother is now running around wondering what she can give us …'

It was a huge relief, and Dent restored some serenity, expressed in a postcard:

'A magic valley: at least for me. Little cobbled village-town in midst of lush meadows, rich hedges & woods, a river, and behind on every side the wide sweep of soft fell. Other countrysides I like to see & admire & even wonder at; but this I am part of… The belt of country from Cumberland across to Yorkshire is my home – much more so than Bradford…'

A letter written 27th June was sent from Poole Harbour, where he was about to set off for the last time on board *Clothilde*. 'Have told the Skipper I can't complete the voyage… Sail for Alderney at 4.30 a.m. so up about 3 a.m.!' And the skipper, Jim Grantham, had told him of a ground floor flat in one of the Downing houses near the Catholic Church which we could rent for a while. When, a fortnight before our wedding day, I went to Cambridge to see this temporary accommodation I was not thrilled; and it was even later that a Jesus College house became vacant and suited us better and which we decided to take.

By 18th July, kind letters and gifts were arriving. Phyllis Tillyard, the Master's wife, had sent 'a most charming note … saying that she can't imagine two people better suited and that you will be a real asset to the College and most warmly welcomed back. How nice of her!' Clive Parry, characteristically, asked 'what present, useful or useless?' – and Robbie, knowing Clive's taste, said 'useless please'. On 31st July he sent me a list of presents received. He had been especially touched by a box of pastry forks 'from a very poor little Methodist spinster who used to keep a tiny shop in her house; sheer saintliness and goodness that makes her spend so much. In proportion to income I would say it is far the most valuable present we are getting'. And his excitement at the approaching event is expressed in suggestions for hymns, largely by Charles Wesley (although some only in the Methodist hymnbook and not in the 'bad' *Hymns A & M*).

Arrangements were finally falling into place, although at my home they were proving stressful. 4th August had been announced as the wedding date before we realised that it fell in Bank Holiday week, when Exmouth could provide no catering and Robbie's plan for our honeymoon encountered difficulties in booking a hotel room in the Lake District. More seriously, my 92-year-old grandmother, who had spent the past year in a nearby nursing home, had a massive stroke and clung on for several agonising days before dying, and her funeral took place while I was away in Cambridge. It was thanks to helpful friends that my mother was later able to provide refreshments for our modest wedding reception.

On the eve of the wedding Robbie drove his mother and father down to Devon, to stay in a pleasant guest house near to our family home, where he spent that night with them. My Uncle Donald and Aunt Marjorie Miller (missionaries with years of service in India) stayed there too, and helped to make the Jenningses welcome. My own part in the preparations was to arrange flowers in the church; and it was while setting pots of blue scabious before the roodscreen that I heard the door open. There was Robbie, just arrived, and we chatted and walked together back to the house. When it was time for him to leave, he paused at the back gate and said 'Goodnight, Miss Bennett.'

—

Marriage and the Whewell Chair

1955-1956

4th August, 1955 was sunny. We were married in Littleham's ancient parish church, with its choir of men and boys. Joyce Baird was my bridesmaid, and Alan Pars had been chosen as Robbie's best man. To spare any embarrassment to Arthur Jennings, morning coats were not worn. The group of family and close friends then gathered for refreshment up the road at my home, wandering and chatting in the garden. We were relieved to hear, later, that Edith Jennings had declared 'I'm very pleased'. She had found that she was among people of similar outlook – my parents, my missionary uncle and aunt, my solicitor uncle, all 'chapel folk' – and was charmed by their kindness in afterwards driving the pair of them around South Devon for a few days before their return to Yorkshire.

The new Professor & Mrs Jennings drove off in the jade-green AC to spend our first night together at Gloucester. Next day we carried on up to the Lodore Hotel in Borrowdale, stopping on the way to send home a picture-postcard of Wigan Pier with a message of heartfelt thanks to my mother and father.

There followed a pretty active honeymoon in a heatwave, Robbie eager to show me the places he loved. First, gently, to Watendlath and up Cat Bells. Another day it was Sty Head to look down on Wasdale, with a glimpse of Bowderdale, his haunt during so many university vacations; then across the traverse and a scramble up up Great Gable. Next day, in rain, we visited Keswick and Windermere antique shops. Then a drive to Crummock Water and Buttermere, to climb Red Pike and High Stile, with a refreshing swim (naked) for me in a small tarn halfway down (and looking upwards as I did backstroke in its chill water, I saw distant male figures on the skyline, pausing to use their binoculars). On the long, long walk round the other side of the lake and back to the car I learnt how Robbie would lengthen his stride as the end came in sight. Next day was Grasmere and Ambleside; then a day with a skiff on Derwentwater … and the following day he drove me to Cockermouth, where we looked at Wordsworth's birthplace and bought five 'country Chippendale' dining chairs from an antique shop (£40, including carriage to Cambridge) and drove back singing Gilbert & Sullivan songs. The final day was the most strenuous: up Grain Ghyll to Scafell Pike (shrouded in mist), Mickeldore, Sty Head and down to Seathwaite.

———

With a call on the Jennings parents on the way, we drove to our temporary first home in Cambridge, at the end of Cranmer Road. The house was a rare example of postwar architecture belonging to James Winny[69] and his wife Doris, who were spending some weeks with her family in Switzerland, which we were lucky to be able to rent while they were away. Our plans for a permanent residence had been left so late that it was only now that we heard that a Jesus College house had become vacant. We would move into No.3 Claremont, Hills Road as soon as some refurbishment had been completed.

After three weeks in the Winnys' house the Claremont one was not yet ready; so the Lauterpachts came to the rescue with the offer of a flat in the top storey of their house at 6 Cranmer Road – another temporary solution while they were in The Hague, giving us time to see our eventual home made ready. In the meantime, having absorbed some useful ideas about furniture and fittings from the Winnys' modern home, we shopped in London at Heals, Maples and Sandersons, and locally at Eaden Lilley. We still found beautiful things hard to resist (a silk Persian rug which we really could not afford) but were at last thinking about practical kitchen equipment and curtains as well. One day, though, visiting an auction at Much Hadham (two more items not strictly necessary), we met a former pupil of Robbie's and joined him and his wife for tea at his house, a part of the old Bishop's Palace. There under the kitchen table was a basket containing a cat nursing a litter of enchanting kittens … and we agreed to have one of them.

The arrival of a small kitten at a house undergoing refurbishment complicates matters. Little Puffin had to be provided with a bed and bowls of water and food to survive lonely nights until workmen arrived to continue their labour on electric points, telephone installation, plumbing and resurfacing the scullery floor. We redecorated the kitchen ourselves, brightening its gloom with white walls and blue paintwork. But painting the top of a door with a sleepy kitten on my shoulder one day, I jerked my arm as I felt her begin

---

[69] A young Fellow of Jesus in the English Faculty.

to slip, and a thin streak of blue appeared down a white wall. And Robbie, standing on top of a stepladder as he applied emulsion to the ceiling, found a frantic kitten climbing up the frame and then the *inside* of a trouser-leg. The only way to extricate her was to undress while perched aloft.

At last, at the end of many busy weeks, on 9th October the house was sufficiently furnished for us to move in. As I wrote to my parents, 'The Lauterpachts are quite extraordinarily lavish in every way: the other evening we asked them here for sherry and savouries, and the evening ended with our having a huge dinner with them in their kitchen!' A few days later Hersch and Rachel took us, together with the Parrys, out for a country treat – first lunch at Coton, then to a friend's farm to picnic in an orchard and be shown the modern milking parlour there. It was characteristic of their generosity; and it also revealed Hersch's naivety about country matters when he asked, on being shown the cooler in the farm's dairy, 'But is milk *warm* when it comes from the cow?'

Robbie had started his tenure of the Whewell Chair, not in October but back in the Trinity Term; and, having already deputised several times when Lauterpacht had been involved in other matters such as the opening session of the Nuremburg trials of war criminals, he was already fairly familiar with the course to be given. But as the new academic year approached there was nervous tension as he attended to the preparation of his own course of lectures and seminars, meetings and correspondence. There were more invitations, too. University society was a good deal more formal in those days: there were 'At Home' cards to which one responded in the third person; a woman wore a hat for a luncheon, a dress of the appropriate length for a sherry party or dinner, and so on. Somehow it all had to be fitted in around our home-making activities.

Soon it became evident that I was pregnant, and feeling sick and faint at inconvenient moments – even having to withdraw from High Table at a Downing College Ladies Night. Nevertheless, I found all the people to whom I was being introduced were much less intimidating than their titles suggested. A lunch given by the Lauterpachts introduced me to the McNairs; and both Arnold (now Lord McNair) and Marjorie made the occasion wonderfully easy, as did their other guests, Wilfred Jenks[70] and his wife. Rather stickier was

---

[70]   Wilfred Jenks, Director General of the International Labour Organisation and distinguished international lawyer – author of many important books.

the Vice Chancellor's dinner at Christ's, with Brian Downs, Master, as host: absolutely formal, with the ladies withdrawing to allow the men to enjoy their port while we were supposed to sip coffee and 'powder our noses'.

As Whewell Professor, Robbie was entitled to most of the privileges of a Fellow of Trinity College – something he greatly enjoyed. Early in our marriage, accordingly, we found ourselves attending the ceremonial opening of the new Veterinary School building in Madingley Road by Queen Elizabeth II, and the great luncheon in Hall which followed. Rather less dazzling was the awkward dinner given at Jesus for the wives of fellows by Freddy Brittain, who was college Steward at that time, and still a bachelor. Jesus College could not yet permit such a thing as a 'Ladies Night', yet there was this unacknowledged society of wives who saw little of the college to which their husbands were attached. Dr Brittain's gesture was to invite us all to a private dinner (at which he wore white tie) in the Prioress' Room. We came in long dresses, and found at each place-setting a carnation. At the end of the evening we emerged, to be taken home by husbands who, for once, had eaten a slightly less good meal in hall. (After some years, 'Freddy's dinner' would be replaced by a Ladies Night which managed still to be awkward, and then by a President's Evening each term which is less formal and more fun.)

We settled into life at Claremont, finding that our neighbours had young families. No.1 was the home of Denys Wilkinson[71] and his French wife Christiane. Next door, at no.2, was Stanley Mitchell, a schoolmaster from Robbie's own village and school, and his German wife Martha. Across the courtyard, which had a little lawn and flowerbeds, were rather older but very friendly people. There was, however, no garage, so the AC was kept in college. We were not yet fully furnished, and Robbie still kept some of his clothes in his old rooms ... which was occasionally awkward. Once, when off to a white-tie dinner, he had to dash to Jesus on his bike wearing tails and the obligatory stiff shirt fastened with cheap laundry studs, a khaki woollen scarf around his neck, to collect a wing collar, white tie and decent studs and cufflinks, before heading to St Catherine's for a feast.

---

[71]   Sir Denys Wilkinson, nuclear physicist, was a Fellow of Jesus and later Nobel Laureate and Vice Chancellor of the University of Sussex.

Another great re-arrangement was his change of rooms. It had been back in July that he had written to tell me that he was to move out of the large set on N Staircase. As he wrote to me:

'Have looked at several smaller, including Mathias'[72] room; but decided on the 'Ghost Room', one of the loveliest in any college. Very nice to be able to move into one of the best rooms in College, though not suitable for continuous living in. Lovely timbered roof, superb proportions, fine old fireplace, and four elegant windows on Chapel Court. Very exciting.'

And so now there was the removal of furniture – some very bulky – up the precipitous staircase known as 'Cow Lane'[73] to this cavernous set at the top of the oldest range of buildings. By regularly climbing that staircase he could with ease ascend Cumbrian fells into a quite advanced age; and it would amuse him to see how badly puffed some of his pupils and visitors were on arriving at the top. (Although Robbie never felt a ghostly presence, his successor did; and Mr West, Head Porter 1956-77, claimed to have seen the apparition of Charles Bellasis, Fellow and Secretary of the legendary Everlasting Club, who had died in 1766.)

We spent our first Christmas down in Devon with my parents, accompanied by the disruptive kitten. By January some boarding arrangement must have been made, since we managed to take another short break. Robbie wanted to entice A.P. Rossiter and his wife Barbara up to Cumberland. As I wrote to my parents,

'[A.P's] invitation had to be put in the form of a request to teach me climbing, in order to budge him at all! Once in the Lakes, though, he goes off a good deal on his own to enjoy the luxury of frightening himself on difficult climbs.'

---

[72]   Peter Mathias, from his Research Fellowship at Jesus, was moving to a Fellowship at Queens'. He later became Chichele Professor of Economic History at Oxford; then Master of Downing College.

[73]   The staircase got its name not, as undergraduates like to imagine, from a cow having been coaxed up to the top, but because down below were the medieval lavatories. The actual room was the setting for a ghost story by the former Master, Arthur Gray, *The Everlasting Club*, in which an annual dinner was laid for the full membership, whose numbers dwindled year by year as they died.

So far, my impression of this brilliant but unpredictable don had been intriguing, even alarming: there were his exhilarating Third Programme talks and his notes on tutorial pupils. But when, as Tutors' Secretary, I had to telephone him I evidently caught him at a bad moment – his response being blistering rage which reduced me to tears. I was glad to get to know him and Barbara properly.

We had supposed that accommodation would be available at one of the homelier inns or guest houses – only to find them closed. Instead, we stayed once more at the luxurious Lodore Hotel, aware that at dinner we looked like tramps in our tweeds and rough shoes. I did indeed climb a rockface or two – Robbie watching anxiously from below, as I was by now 4½ months pregnant – and we all climbed Blencathra. This was in snow and ice, and in our descent of its dramatic Sharp Edge we encountered a small group stuck there, unable to persuade an elderly man paralysed by vertigo to cross its 'bad step'. In such freezing conditions their situation was dangerous. With sudden ferocity A.P. took charge, extending a hand and barking at the ditherer to stride straight across – which he did, to the relief of his companions.

In February Robbie had to take a few days off his university commitments to undergo an operation to clear a blockage of his sinus. I was shocked to see him afterwards in Addenbrooke's Hospital, looking as though he had been in a bad car crash – his head swathed in bandages, what was visible swollen and bruised, and with two black eyes. Convalescing at home, he was visited by Alan Pars, who 'started a long rigmarole about his own sufferings with toothache' and had to be gently coaxed away before long. But the operation had been effective, relieving a trouble which had persisted for years.

The following month he was to give a Third Programme talk. It had taken many hours of preparation and I had typed successive drafts for him. I went with him up to London, the plan being for me to do some shopping while he made the recording, and then spend the late afternoon and evening together enjoying ourselves. We parted as arranged. When I turned up at Broadcasting House with a large carrier bag labelled *Maternally Yours*, there was no Robbie. Instead, the producer, P.H. Newby[74], appeared, wringing his hands. He was most terribly sorry: they had run through the talk and he had taken Robbie out to lunch, but when they got back to the studio he found the precious

---

[74] Newby was charming but a little vague, and told Robbie he never listened to the wireless at home. He was, however, a successful novelist, the first winner of the Booker prize.

typescript was lost – slipped out of his pocket somewhere! The only solution was for Robbie to use an earlier draft and scribble in all the amendments he could remember. I was led upstairs to a small office, where I sat down and retyped the whole script[75]. By the time the recording was successfully made, evening was drawing on. We returned to Cambridge in a rather giggly state, eating railway sandwiches.

Increasing in bulk, I was by now in no state for us to accept an invitation from Meredith Jackson and his wife Lenli to join them on their yacht for a voyage to Norway – a pity, since I loved sailing as much as Robbie did. Instead, we took a short Easter holiday at Aldeburgh, memorable for the bitter wind off the North Sea (which meant that, as we heard later, the Jacksons had had a difficult voyage in foul seas). Again, we found some entertainment in buying oddities which were not strictly 'furniture': an old elmwood flourbin, a handsome portrait of a Victorian lady, Mrs Garrett Anderson (first woman mayor of Aldeburgh, mother of the formidable Dr Elizabeth) and a wrought-iron firescreen.

The house was by now looking presentable, and so it was time for a housewarming party. To assist in serving the delicious Pimms fruit cup we had prepared, a waiter was recruited from Jesus. But he was a tall and doleful one, who thrust a tray at guests saying 'Sherry sir – or *cup*? Sherry madam – or *cup*?' in such an ominous way that almost everyone chose the safer sherry. For long minutes it seemed a disastrously sticky gathering; but then the atmosphere changed with the arrival of Professor and Mrs Hollond, accompanied by an interesting figure. Harry Hollond had rung me that morning in some embarrassment: 'Would you mind very much if we brought along an artist? He is painting Marjorie's portrait, and we don't know what to do with him in the evenings'. I did not mind at all, for their companion was Stanley Spencer, at that time painting both the Bursar (Marjorie) and the Mistress (Dame Mary Cartwright) of Girton. Cheerfully scruffy, he soon gathered a cluster around him. I mentioned the self-portrait that hangs in the Fitzwilliam Museum. 'Ah, goggles, goggles!' he said, twirling his hand beneath his eyes to imitate the shadow of his glasses: 'I painted that by electric light'.

I was already finding that marriage to a don meant endless adaptation to his way of life. Terrified at the prospect of feeding someone who had always been provided

---

75   The talk, one of the *Law in Action* series, was published in *The Listener* (5.4.56 'International Monopolies & International Law'). Three others, in 1958, 1960 & 1961 also appeared there.

with regular and excellent meals, I had bought a Good Housekeeping Cookery Book from which to learn basic skills. He was, however, dining in Hall about five evenings a week during termtime, so the challenge arose mainly at weekends. On Sundays we soon dispensed with *The Observer*, which frittered too much time with its many pages, and instead high-mindedly embarked on reading aloud – Wordsworth's *Prelude*, Dickens's *Martin Chuzzlewit*, George Eliot's *Middlemarch* … until the arrival of children made such tranquil evenings impossible.

Life did indeed become very different after 4th June 1956, when our son was born. The Maternity Hospital in Mill Road was a former Workhouse, had few of the facilities one would expect nowadays, and it was overcrowded. There, after a long labour, Richard (soon to be generally known as Dicky) was born just after midnight.

Fathers were allowed in to see their babies for one hour in the evening, and at the head of the troop was Robbie, who had spent the long hours of Sunday, he said, shifting furniture around and cleaning the drains. My stay there was protracted by illness, so we were thankful for my mother's help in settling into the new routine. But she found that life with Robbie was never quite 'routine'. As she wrote to my father: 'Robbie just brought her [CDJ] home and then went off to a luncheon engagement, so he doesn't yet know what a baby in the house means!' and when he was as usual out to one engagement after another, she commented 'How glad I am that I didn't marry a don!' And the eminent don himself soon found that his preferred steady routine of meals and a good night's sleep could no longer be relied upon.

Four months later, Robbie brought his parents down to meet their grandson. I could not help finding such visits an ordeal, knowing that any shortcomings in my housekeeping would be noted, and finding their long silences unnerving. They were, though, thoroughly pleased with Dicky.

On 12th November 1956 I wrote of Robbie's fury over Prime Minister Eden's invasion of Suez, and of his contact with an Important Person (presumably Sir Gerald Fitzmaurice) at the Foreign Office which revealed that 'the legal advisers are worried and impotent'. Sleepless with indignation, and occasionally helping to walk a wailing baby in the night when I was exhausted, Robbie could give little practical help with housework; so in the New Year we welcomed a young Swiss woman, Loni Kleiner, as an *au pair*. (The arrangement had its drawbacks, but we got on pretty well.)

The baptism of Richard David Yewdall Jennings took place in the chapel of Wesley House, the theological college of which Robbie was a Trustee. That fitted well, accommodating the gathering of 20 or 30 (not, alas, including grandparents, who were unable to be present) in a pleasant building in Jesus Lane. The Principal of Wesley House was the Rev. W.F. Flemington whom Robbie had known from his undergraduate days, and the Vice-Principal, Dr Philip Watson, was an even older friend from his schooldays at Idle.

By now we were house-hunting. Although we liked our neighbours at Claremont (four of the six houses occupied by people from Yorkshire), our dream was to have somewhere with a real garden, preferably in the country. The Bursar[76] of Jesus helped us in our search, sending Mr Robinson, the college's very experienced man in charge of buildings, to inspect any likely properties. But there were always drawbacks, not least the cost.

Money had become rather important. The professorial salary had made it possible for many of his plans to be carried out, but fatherhood had increased his commitments, and Robbie was glad to be offered occasional extra work from his chambers at Lincoln's Inn.

——

The Whewell Chair of International Law was, however, his principal responsibility. That Professorial Chair had been founded in 1866 by the Will of the great Dr Whewell[77] of Trinity College who,

> '… moved by the Christian and noble wish of diminishing the evils of war when it happens, lessening the chances of its happening, and finally extinguishing it, so far as lies within the reach of man's foresight, [had] devised and bequeathed to the master, fellows and scholars of Trinity College means for founding in the University [this professorship, together with] scholarships for students [attending] its teaching.'[78] [It was a branch of law which had been] 'regarded more as an accomplishment beyond the range of ordinary men, than as a fitting part of a gentleman's education'; [and henceforth it was hoped that the Whewell foundation would remedy this deficiency].
>
> '… The Professor of International Law must give twelve lectures in the year, and must make his teaching worthy of an audience. For Dr Whewell,

---

76   At that time, Alan Percival, Fellow in Engineering

77   Dr William Whewell, polymath Master of Trinity, provided the endowment of both the Whewell Chair and Whewell Scholarships in International Law.

78   Quoted from *The Law Times* of 27th October 1866.

well aware of the tendency of all professorships which do not contribute to the solid academical preferment of the disciple to sink into a spiritless routine with a few chance hearers, has made the salary of the Professor of International Law dependent on the success of his lectures. At the end of every year he must produce to the master and seniors of Trinity College a certificate signed by at least ten resident members of the University, graduates and undergraduates, that they have each of them attended ten at least of the lectures given in the preceding year...'

I do not know whether this requirement is still observed; but certainly Robbie took his role very seriously, and was particularly mindful of the high reputation of his recent predecessors, Arnold McNair and Hersch Lauterpacht (and also of the Chichele Professor at Oxford, James Brierly). McNair's approach he admired for the breadth of its vision, Lauterpacht's for its sheer scholarship and firm judgment. His own attitude can, I think, be glimpsed in some remarks made by him many years later in a confidential reference for a candidate for the Chichele Chair, in which he makes it clear that, 'If they [the electors] want a hermit scholar who will disappear into the Law Library and write great tomes on the subject', then this – highly recommended – man would not be such a one; but that he understands the art and value of *teaching*. In support of another candidate he says:

'... He is very good at anticipating where there might be difficulties of understanding and one can almost hear him pausing to explain the problem and the way through it. In short, it seems to me that here is a man who can teach and loves teaching. This is a quality that I rate very highly; not least in relation to the needs for the teaching of international law in Oxford ... the next Chichele Professor should be someone who regards the straight university work of teaching and research, and perhaps some administration, as his or her primary occupation.'

With those remarks in mind, one can see how his attitude matched that of McNair in believing that experience of working at the Bar could actually enhance and enrich the teaching he provided. To be immersed in the fascinating intricacies of legal theory was one thing; but to find how a legal dispute was apt to run into practical and political complications which affected its conduct and outcome was another. And for those listening, to hear a practitioner speaking of his experience made a lecture far more interesting. Like the topics discussed in seminars or debated in moots, it trained students to consider wider aspects of problems than the purely legal. Robbie was constantly enlarging his own knowledge of history, geography and scientific matters in an ever-changing world.

Work and Family Both Increase

1957-58

1957 began with a terrible shock. A.P. Rossiter, with whom we had shared that memorable break in the Lake District the previous January, crashed his motorbike and was killed instantly. He had again been testing himself on the crags in Wasdale and was driving down the A1 on his return journey. Barbara, at home in Cambridge, was in advanced pregnancy, and so to spare her the trauma of visiting the mortuary Robbie drove north to identify the body, and attended the inquest. It was a grievous loss, and her friends gave Barbara all the assistance they could.

Teaching took most of Robbie's time, now in the form of lectures, seminars, supervision of LL.B. and doctoral candidates preparing theses, with the addition of meetings of the International Law Club that McNair had founded. His style was highly effective and was to be remembered gratefully by many pupils from all over the world. As Rosalyn Higgins wrote[79]:

> 'His teaching [was always] popular – he gave the impression of merely chatting with his lecture class, and the students would be surprised at the end of the agreeable hour to discover how much well-structured information had been imparted to them …'

Others spoke of his 'lucidity and incisiveness', 'a style devoid of pomposity or showiness' and his 'gift for plain expression'.

The minutes of the Faculty Board of Law reveal how assiduous he was in attending its meetings. One topic of discussion which first arose in February 1946, and was to grind on and on for years, was the reform of the Law Tripos

---

[79] This came from her obituary for *The Times*. She also delivered the address at his Memorial Service.

syllabus. Robbie's contribution, as a member of that committee, was to deplore the decision to make International Law an optional subject. He also became the Cambridge representative on the General Committee of the Society of Public Teachers of Law; and, as a member of the university's General Board, their external member of the Faculty of Economics, whose meetings – more lively and fractious than the lawyers' – he rather enjoyed. The Council of the Senate made him for a while their representative on the City Council as well, and soon Councillor Jennings was serving on its Education Committee. His Methodist attachment was maintained in his trusteeship of Wesley House and as Governor of Culford School. He became chairman of the newly-founded Jesus College Housing Society, planning the provision of affordable first homes on some sites belonging to the college. Meetings of all these bodies took up much of his time. Besides these, there was membership of several college clubs. One was The Roosters[80], whose silly rituals and debates, filled with 'gallinaceous' puns, were all derived from the college's emblem of a cock. Robbie stayed with that out of loyalty to Freddy Brittain; but he preferred the rival group started by Alan Pars, The Club, whose meetings were altogether more dignified and interesting. And a summer diversion was the annual Fellows v Servants cricket match that he and Derek Taunt had established.

———

I think it was in the spring of 1957 that we went up to Wilmslow, to stay for a night or two with Professor Ben Wortley and his wife Peggy (gentle and charming hosts), while Robbie delivered some lectures at the University of Manchester – something that was possible while Dicky was still easily portable.

There were other commitments away from Cambridge, too but what I think was his first intended trip abroad after our marriage was aborted at the last moment by a sudden and mysterious affliction. He was actually at the station, about to take the train, when he confessed that he could not go. Back at home he took to his bed, and I called the doctor. But – while he was clearly suffering, pale and shaky – Dr Simpson could find no physical symptoms, and diagnosed the trouble as 'hysteria.' Robbie accepted this, and so did I: it seemed to be a recurrence of that extreme attachment to

---

[80]   The Roosters was the invention of Freddy Brittain, who taught medieval French, edited the
        Cambridge Review for some years and cultivated a slightly clownish character.

home (as manifest in the inability to break away from his parents earlier) – something to be conquered by an effort of will. The syndrome was genuine, and after a day or two of rest he recovered. Next time he had to make such a journey we approached it with steady determination and once the barrier was overcome it never presented quite such a problem again.

A rare outing to Grantchester is recorded in snapshots of the nine-month-old Dicky crawling on the grass by the millpond. We may have been there to look at a house, always hoping for something in Grantchester if possible. Robbie tended to favour grand old houses with mature gardens, not noticing the back regions that I would have to inhabit – the echoing dimly-lit kitchens with ancient ranges, sculleries, butlers' pantries and steep staircases intended for servants. Such properties tended to be 'good value' simply because, without those servants, they were a nightmare for a housewife with small children and so, despite admiring the fine panelling and plasterwork of their reception rooms, I discouraged the idea.

Something which did excite both of us at this time was the suggestion of creating a home at Wandlebury, on the Gog Magog hills. Up there, plans had been drawn by an architect, Mr Crompton, for the conversion of a neglected stable block, the sole remnant of a once-great mansion standing within an iron-age circular fort and surrounded by woodland. There were to be three dwellings, one of which the Cromptons themselves intended to occupy, and we dreamt of taking another – actually taking Robbie's parents up to see the stable yard, where heaps of bricks and planks were assembled for the building work. But just as a more realistic assessment of this idyllic place's suitability was raising doubts, news came of the sudden death of both Mr and Mrs Crompton in a car crash, and the project was dropped.

We drove up to Westmorland (now 'Cumbria') that summer. There we spent a week or so in the topfloor holiday flat of Barbon Manor, a shooting lodge amidst the woods and fells of the Shuttleworth family estate, where our hosts were Mr and Mrs. Roger Fulford[81]. This was country familiar to Robbie: the little town of Dent, birthplace of Adam Sedgwick,[82] lay in one direction and Kirkby Lonsdale in another, with Arnside on the coast not far away.

---

[81]   Roger Fulford, historian and author, was married to the widow of Lord Shuttleworth.

[82]   Adam Sedgwick, 1785-73, the pioneering geologist after whom the Sedgwick Museum in Cambridge was named.

After this Robbie did go abroad, over to the Netherlands for a meeting of the Curatorium of The Hague Academy.[83] A photograph taken in the Peace Palace shows him with that group of leading international lawyers: Friedman, Oda, Dupuy, Boutros-Ghali and van Panhuys, all men with whom he was to associate on many other occasions in the coming years.

While his own work was so fascinatingly varied, he was aware that my life was far more humdrum. Since university wives were at that time still excluded from the intellectual and most of the social life enjoyed by their menfolk, he was entirely supportive when in February 1957 I became a founding-member of a women's literary group, The Cambridge Reading Circle[84], the dreamchild of Marjorie McNair and Rachel Lauterpacht. I was also singing in the Cambridge University Musical Society choir and doing a little drawing and painting.

But even these escapes from tedious domestic duties could not have been managed without the succession of *au pair* girls who stayed with us during our early years of family life. The Swiss Loni was followed by Lisbeth, who was succeeded, in January 1958 by Dutch Marijke (who was happy to adopt the nickname Tiddle provided by our toddler). All these girls and their successors became friends with whom we kept in touch ever after and the children, we hoped, would learn to feel comfortable with people of slightly different cultures as they were followed by Danish, Icelandic, German, Austrian and French.

After Christmas Robbie drove up to Bradford, having undertaken to speak to an audience that he feared might be difficult: opinionated local councillors, political activists and high-minded chapel dignitaries. But his main purpose was to support his parents, since his father was recovering from illness and still poorly.

He had accepted an invitation to give a lecture in the Easter vacation of 1958 at the University of Grenoble, an opportunity for a trip abroad that I might share. It called for more than usually meticulous preparation, since the lecture was to be delivered in French. M. Derôme, who supervised Jesus undergraduates in Modern Languages, made a translation of the text and coached him in reading it with an

---

[83]   The Hague Academy, founded in 1923, has its own building within the premises of the Peace Palace. Its annual course of lectures attracts students of international law from all over the world.

[84]   Nick-named the Learned Ladies, the group has now passed its 60th anniversary.

acceptable accent. Although rather nerve-racking, his performance went well and there was time to meet faculty members and see a little of our surroundings, being even taken up to Chamrousse, a ski station high in the Savoy alps.

By this time Robbie was also advising the Anglo-Iranian Oil Company and was involved in the background preparation for an arbitration between Aramco and Saudi Arabia. The development of oil-drilling in the Middle East was producing new territorial complications for resolution by international lawyers, and so he was recruited as a regular legal consultant by Shell. The head of their legal department was John Blair, a man for whom Robbie developed both respect and affection: an Austrian Jewish refugee who had in the first year of the 1939-45 war been interned in the Isle of Man, but who then enlisted in the Pioneer Corps of the British Army and anglicised his original name. As an insight into global economics and an introduction to practising lawyers in the Netherlands and further afield, this work for Shell would turn out to be valuable for Robbie's teaching.

The influence of Hersch Lauterpacht was strong. I found that Robbie had sought his guidance in venturing to propose marriage to me (which HL, having encountered me in my office or on the phone, had approved). and then about the conduct expected of a Whewell Professor and his spouse. Hersch and Rachel were glad to give advice but their concept of our rôles was modelled more on continental behaviour than the manner of other Cambridge dons, and introduced an awkwardness to some aspects of our first married year or two. I kept careful account of every penny of housekeeping-money, dressed as was expected and even pinned my hair up, just as Rachel would expect – though feeling that a young woman educated at a good school and Oxford might have been trusted to behave without quite so many restraints.

It was a curious situation, explained perhaps by the Lauterpachts' own awkwardness. Many years later, Robbie was to describe his relationship with Hersch to Martti Koskenniemi:[85]

'... Although I, in my approach to international law was, and still am, much more a McNair man than a Lauterpacht man, Lauterpacht was a much closer friend; indeed I think probably the closest friend I ever had. I spent a lot

---

[85] Professor of International Law at the University of Helsinki.

of my time at Lauterpacht's house, and enjoyed many lunches there, always with very interesting company. It was thus that I first met Wilfred Jenks, and S.W.D. Rowson (as Shabtai Rosenne then was) and Alona Evans and indeed it was in the Lauterpacht house that I got to know Fitzmaurice much better than I had previously known him. For of course Fitzmaurice was a great admirer of Lauterpacht, and indeed also of McNair.

'Lauterpacht would sometimes summon me for an afternoon walk in the country round Cambridge. I knew very well that the walking would not be very serious but the talking would be: sometimes it was something that I must do, such as to write another article for the British Year Book of International Law ... At other times Lauterpacht would want to talk about quite other things: faculty politics and its members, family, music, especially some new records he had bought, his plans for lectures or publications, and so on...

'Great and learned scholar that he was, he still had complete sympathy with beginners and their difficulties. He *liked* young people. He demanded complete attention in his lectures, for international law for him was a very serious matter indeed. One did not expect any of the sly, pawky jokes that lightened McNair's also distinguished but very different lectures ...'

Elsewhere he was to add that Hersch's apparent stuffiness arose from the anxiety of a naturally warm-hearted and fun-loving man to conform.

Our own wedding had taken place in the same week as their son Eli's, and Rachel became almost overwhelming in her generous attention to the newly-marrieds. It did not really help in settling into our own private ways but gradually we relaxed and shed some of our compliance with their more continental style. There were plenty of social demands in the academic life, anyway – mostly enjoyable (May Week particularly) but hard to fit in with Robbie's work commitments and my childcare.

In the Long Vacation of 1958 Robbie must have missed the ILA conference in New York. Instead, calling to give some attention to his own parents on the way, he drove up to the Lake District to stretch his legs. His companion was Shackleton Bailey,[86] one of the more curious fellows of Jesus, a classics scholar

---

[86]   D.R. Shackleton Bailey was Director in Classics at Jesus 1955-64, while also University Lecturer in Tibetan. He later became Professor at Harvard. His *magnum opus* was a 10-volume edition of the Letters of Cicero to Atticus. Some impression of his character may be found in his obituaries.

who was also learned in Tibetan (and was annoyed when a student in the Faculty of Oriental Languages actually wanted to be taught the subject).

They met in Borrowdale and stayed at the Scafell Hotel, from where I received rapturous descriptions:

'It was a long journey (261 miles) but a glorious day to arrive in the hills. I could have wept for joy when I saw the high hills again. And now here I am in bed at the Scafell, with the beck rushing by under my window, feeling tremendously happy and wondering how one manages to survive in Cambridge.

'The magic worked again for the umpteenth time. The mountains and lakes this evening surprised me all over again with their presence and I got something of the sheer joy I remember when first I saw them as a boy. It isn't just any mountains that will do, either. There is a friendliness about these hills that uplifts the spirit in a way the more sombre though grander Alps can fail to do. I wish we could get a cottage hereabouts. Like A.P., I feel a different person up here...

[Next day] 'Lovely morning with pale blue sky, frosty grass, air like a fine chilled hock, and the sun suddenly rising above the hill and flooding the valley with gold.

'We made first up Grain Ghyll to Esk Hause, then up Bowfell. By the time we got to the summit for lunch it had clouded over but the clouds were high and the views extensive. Then I would have turned, but Shackleton wanted more so we went along the ridge to climb the Crinkles. When we got to the rise to Bowfell again Sh. wanted to avoid it (very rough) and wanted to go round and down to Langdale (bump of direction not very good). I said it was going to be much harder than going over Bowfell as we should lose all our height, end in the wrong valley and then have to climb over to our valley again. However, I thought it politic to let him have his head. So we traversed Bowfell and then climbed Rossett Ghyll (the roughest pass in the Lakes) and Sh. was nearly paid out and nearly lost his sense of humour. Then we had to climb Esk Hause, the highest pass in the Lakes. Then we had to traverse Grain Ghyll, the wettest pass. In all I think just about 24 miles of mountain, and in all we must have ascended about 8000 rough feet. I was never so tired. But I'm glad to say I finished stronger than Sh. and backed the car to meet him at Seathwaite. I ran the last part down Grain Ghyll, not because I was full of energy, but because I was just too tired to walk it. However, I have just had a glass of Younger's bitter and feel much better. Sh. had a glass of soda water and is still a little morose…'

After that they had an easier day, walking through fields, up Dalehead and down to the summit of Honister Pass and back to Rosthwaite for tea. Then they drove to Buttermere

'… and walked right out to Crummock Water edge. There is a lovely spot. A very still, quiet lake. Water like glass. A solitary rowing boat in the distance. A grove of oaks on the bank. And a lovely shingle beach rolled by the gales into a perfectly even curve. A perfect place for throwstoneswhewsplosh.[87] I could see why Bill Wade likes this place for children for, as he says, there is something for all ages.

'After contemplation of this scene we called on the Provost of Eton,[88] who was very pleasant and gave us some beer…'

And so, after a lazier day or two, they returned to Cambridge and for Robbie it was an end to tranquillity for a while.

Our second child was born on 27ᵗʰ September 1958. (She had nearly arrived while I was down in Devon with Dicky, visiting my parents; and my mother had accompanied us on the homeward train journey, just in case I gave birth on the way.) She was delivered at home by an aged midwife, and so Robbie became more aware than before of what was involved. We named her Philippa Mary (Pippa), and Clive Parry immediately coined a telegraphic address for Robbie, *Pippaspoppa*.

---

[87] One of the phrases in Dicky-language: the toddler loved throwing stones into water.

[88] This was Sir Claud Elliott, senior fellow of Jesus, whose house, Gatesgarth, was a centre for Cambridge fell-walkers.

More Developments

JANUARY 1959–MAY 1961

It was time for Robbie, as recently-appointed Whewell Professor, to deliver the public Inaugural Lecture he had spent so much time in preparing. It was an awesome occasion, chaired by the Vice-Chancellor, Lord Adrian, and before an audience which included Lord McNair, Sir Hersch Lauterpacht and five Heads of Houses. He had chosen *The Development of International Law* as his title – a large subject to be condensed into 45 minutes' talk – and it was delivered in January 1959.[89] It went well, and the Lauterpachts gave a party in his honour at Cranmer Road afterwards.

Robbie had amassed far more material than could be covered in this talk, which was largely a discussion of the problems entailed in developing universally accepted legislation. All this could have been worked up into a book if only his busy life had allowed time for extended writing. Its theme was one of importance, and he was to deplore the removal from the syllabus, at Cambridge and the Inns of Court, of the course on the history of international law that he himself had valued. His later writings would be permeated by his understanding of the historical development and further evolution of international law – discussed in articles such as *An Internatiional Lawyer Takes Stock (1990)* and *International Lawyers and the Progressive Development of International Law (1996.)*[90]

Although Claremont was an agreeable little enclave, conveniently close to the station, it left us longing to be in the countryside. I took the children into the nearby Botanic Gardens every day, where each during those years underwent a minor drama – Dicky falling and cutting his head in the rockery one Sunday,

---

[89] The lecture appeared in print (*BYIL* and p.271 in *Collected Writings*) incorrectly dated 1958.

[90] Both articles are published in his *Collected Writings*.

and later, a tiny Pippa having to be rescued from Hobson's Brook. But it was the nearest thing to the country life we craved.

Robbie's relaxation at home was largely in the form of Hi-Fi. I noted…

'…a great do-it-yourself effort [in which he] erected a V.H.F. aerial (brass curtain rod cut into lengths, and scraps of wood) on our extremely perilous kitchen roof. He then hacked another hole in our long-suffering cabinet and installed a tuner; and now we have a very good wireless indeed. He sits and listens to it with all the gratified wonder of a cat's-whisker-twiddler.'

That Easter vacation he gave some lectures in Madrid. His first letter home, dated 4th April 1959, began 'I think I shall like Spain very much', and was a detailed description of the journey and the wonders he had already seen.

'… Then I saw a funeral of a bigwig. Priests in special, sumptuous black velvet embroidered in gold, with black birettas and silver maces, leading the way. Then the hearse – and what a hearse! About 1922 'Chev.' with a black oblong Albert Memorial built onto it. Even the bonnet had very heavy black carving. The coffin was again in ebony lavishly plated with what looked uncommonly like deeply carved silver. The mourners (and some young American sight-seers) walked after the hearse. Excited police stopped all traffic….'

He found the late-evening habits of the Spanish rather trying – going out to dinner at 10 pm, and being taken to a ballet performance which began at 10.45 pm. He enjoyed the Prado Museum and being taken to Toledo. But the '*escuela*' he found odd:

'Splendid premises, lots of money but very few students. My audience so far has been 5, 9 and 16: from which I gather the lectures are not a failure … An amazing feature of their system is that when the hour is nearly up, a beadle comes in and announces in a loud voice that the hour has come. According to de Luna one visiting lecturer died of heart failure because he thought it was the Last Judgment…'

We all went down to Devon for a stay with my parents. Then, leaving me there, Robbie returned to Cambridge for the new term. It was for him an uncomfortable time, revealed in a series of letters. Dr Eustace Tillyard was retiring as Master of Jesus, and Robbie had allowed himself to be nominated as possible successor. The election was to be made between four candidates, all fellows of the college. By 5th May, when he wrote to me, there had already been more than one vote taken, and he reported that…

> '…a large party … now want to go outside and have enforced consideration of outside candidates by rather naughtily (at this stage) returning blank papers. So in the voting I was easily top this time but well short of an absolute majority. It is clear that the seniors will do almost anything rather than have a Master much younger than themselves …'

He had, meanwhile, made another BBC broadcast – and had found that the producer this time turned out to be '(a) a man I interviewed at the scholarships in 1950 and offered a place to …; (b) from Bradford Grammar School; (c) from Idle; (d) from Thorp Council School, Idle, and (e) a cousin of Stanley Mitchell [our next-door neighbour at Claremont].'

And with the election still unresolved, he passed the time with his favourite activities:

> 'The Indian touring team is at Fenners so I have been spending a good deal of these lovely sunny days watching some good cricket. I have been going to bed rather late, owing to very loud gramophone recitals I have been giving myself (mainly Britten, over and over), and last night I actually played the piano as well…
>
> 'The house is getting filthy, but I am leaving it all for you and Annette, I'm afraid.
>
> 'I had a rise out of the assembled fellows at lunch yesterday. I knew they had had a confabulation the previous evening, so I said to Vivian [Fisher], "Well, Vivian, and what is the position now?" Shocked amazement from junior fellows surprised at this example of bad taste. But I knew Vivian would rise to it, and he did. Without even waiting to think, he replied "70 for 2, with India batting". General laughter.'

I knew how proud Robbie would have been to be chosen as Master of his college, but, as he understood, for me the prospect was alarming. Although it would put an end to our house-hunting, how could we give our young family a normal childhood? And how could I cope with all the entertaining demanded of a Head of House?

The classics dons, headed by Moses Finley,[91] canvassed an alternative choice: Denys Page, Regius Professor of Greek and Fellow of Trinity College. On 7th May Robbie warned me – 'But don't yet build too much on Page or somebody getting it. My chances, are, I'm afraid, still quite strong.' It was not just ourselves becoming edgy: as a P.S. he added that Peppercorn, the butler at the Lodge, was anxious and wondering whether he should perhaps be looking for another job – 'So would we want him if I were elected? I have said we certainly would want the Peppercorns to stay and would feel like throwing our hand in if they did not.'

His next two letters made no mention of the debate going on within the college, except to say how kind his friends, such as the Percivals, were being. And he had been to a party in Trinity of Lincoln's Inn members.

'One of my lecture audience, a Maugham grandchild, was saying that he dare not go to the bar because he could not think on his feet. But the Lord Chief Justice said that for years he had to write out the first 20 minutes of his speech, including the name of his client, because otherwise he would have been unable to stammer a word. And he said his father (who also became a Judge) was so nervous that he vomited every morning of his life before standing up in Court!'

The Fellowship eventually achieved a clear decision, and Professor D.L. Page was admitted as Master in October 1959. I had read C.P. Snow's novel, *The Masters*, and had thought it wildly unrealistic. But now his tale of rivalry and intrigue over a Mastership election did not seem so far-fetched.

———

As an Associate of the *Institut de Droit International*, Robbie attended its biennial conference that September. He spent a few days in Devon with the family before travelling to Neuchatel, where he found assembled the most eminent international lawyers of the time – Lauterpacht, Jessup, Jenks and Hambro among them. The opening session of the conference was tedious and he would find it was indeed the established routine of this august society...

---

91   Later to become Professor Sir Moses Finley, Master of Darwin College. Ancient Historian and extremely left-wing, he was American but had moved to England in 1955 to escape the attention of Senator McCarthy's anti-Communist campaign.

'... speeches and speeches and then speeches. A local minister (political kind), then the President, then the Secretary General – all Swiss, all prosy and totally devoid of humour and all very long. Then, by way of "entertainment" a lecture of *1½ hours* on the details of the history of Neuchatel from 900 to the present day....

'After all this Jenks was to have brought me back by car but he missed me. So I accepted an invitation ... to dine ... At 9.30 I left [my hosts] and decided, as it was a fine evening, to walk the 7 km. back. But I allowed myself, with incredible folly, to attempt to find the more direct path I knew there must be, up through the pine woods. You can imagine what happened. I found myself in a maze of paths with steep, branch strewn, rocky pitches, completely black tunnels, infinite cross-paths and variations, and no possibility of reading any signpost for it was long after dark. About 11 pm I wondered whether to prepare to spend the night somehow in the wood and wait for first light. But I decided to make the attempt to get back to Neuchatel by keeping going down, made it by midnight and got an expensive taxi to the Hotel. Now you may laugh!'

He later learnt the route and walked both up and down ('1½ hours quite hard going'), and found the excursions delightful – the unspoilt countryside and small towns, and the singing and dancing of young people in their cantonal costumes. And, as he was always to say of his best experiences, he wished I could be there with him.

On his return he went up to Bradford to be with his parents for a few days. His father had been unwell, and he found him poorly still and completely lacking in energy. A car ride up to the moors revived Arthur a good deal. Next day they went further, and he rejoiced in the country, not seen for many years, where he used to walk as a boy.

'... the attractiveness fairly took my breath away. It *is* a wonderful bit of wide country, with its wonderful air, rolling moors and wooded hills and deep valleys, and Yorkshire stone houses with their unmistakable style. And it was interesting to find that roads that I remembered as gently rolling have dramatic ups and downs and furious corners. After living in Cambridge one forgets how hilly, hills are...'

We were engrossed once more in the events of a new academic year. There were lunches and dinners to attend – with the new Master and Mrs Page, with the Vice-Chancellor Herbert Butterfield[92] (Master of Peterhouse and a man after Robbie's own heart, a Methodist from Yorkshire) – as well as less formal meals with friends.

At one party at Trinity Robbie found a connection of special significance. In chatting with the wife of the University Registrary, Monica Rattenbury,[93] he mentioned our search for a house, wishing we might live, like them, in Grantchester, where properties were so seldom available. She told him of their neighbour, Dr Banister, who had recently suffered a stroke and was considering reducing the size of his large garden. It suggested an opportunity to build a house for ourselves.

When my parents came to stay, shortly before Christmas 1959, we took them to Grantchester for a peep at the house at the end of the Bridle Way, where a section of the front garden was to be separated. Attractive as the position was, we found the proposed building plot rather cramped for a family house. Soon, however, the Banisters were persuaded by their son to alter their plans: it was they who should build a bungalow to suit their declining years, and offer us the house and remaining (almost an acre) garden. And we were very glad to accept this plan and pay the price estimated by an estate agent.

For Christmas that year we entertained one of Robbie's students – a Czech, Zdenek Cervenka and his wife. Because their country was behind the Iron Curtain they had been obliged to leave their own little son behind with his grandparents, to ensure that they would not defect to the West. They brought gifts for our children and ourselves, and we felt concern for them after Cervenka had completed his course and went to work in Nigeria, when after a while we lost contact.[94]

The year ended with parties: for Robbie and Dicky the wonderful fireworks party held each year by the Bicknells[95] in their garden at Finella, on Queens'

---

92 Later Sir Herbert Butterfield, Regius Professor of Modern History

93 The Rattenbury name was also significant for Robbie, since they were related to a famous Yorkshire Methodist minister of that name.

94 … but Cervenka seems to be continuously active in African affairs and is published by S.O.A.S.

95 Peter Bicknell, 'renaissance man', who had studied at Jesus and later became a Fellow of Downing, was an architect as well as a mountaineer, both in the Alps and the Lake District.

Road. I meanwhile attended one given by Hugo Jones[96], a donnish gathering at which we were challenged with word-and-drawing games and charades. And on New Year's Day 1960 we entertained Robbie's wartime senior intelligence officer, Commander Hughes and his wife and son.

———

Needing some northern air, Robbie spent a few days walking, this time with Maurice Cowling,[97] before calling at Bradford to be with his parents for a while. His father was not strong, and the following month developed pneumonia. Although seeming better, he died on 4th March. Now it was Robbie's task to make arrangements for the funeral, comfort his mother, and look into his father's financial situation.

The funeral was conducted by 'as nice a parson as [he had] come across for a long time,' and the cremation was at Nab Wood, 'beyond Shipley, in the Aire valley, surrounded by trees, and within sight of the moors'. And – a further consolation – 'it is on our side of Bradford. The other crematorium is on the south side of Bradford which still strikes me as alien, unfriendly, and depressing!'

Arthur Jennings' money affairs were in a hopeless muddle. Robbie was shocked to find that he, who had in earlier years kept meticulous accounts, had recently been scribbling 'extraordinary calculations … which are detailed but make no kind of sense …' Edith was devastated by his death and could only sit weeping helplessly. But fortunately 'Auntie' – Alice, widow of Albert Brotherton, who was now married again – was endlessly kind, helping Robbie to set things to some sort of order.

When Robbie returned home, he brought his mother with him. She was still bewildered, and the arrival of a buff envelope containing an official form concerning her Widow's Pension so shocked her that, retreating upstairs, she nearly fell in a faint. I supported her to the sofa, where she was able to rest under a rug with feet up, and wondered what else might restore her. Brandy, perhaps? So, remembering that some foreign visitor had given us a bottle (unused, gathering dust) I poured a generous glassful of the stuff. It did seem to cheer her up – and Robbie, when I told him what I had done, was astonished. It was, it seemed, a rather strong dose, especially for a lifetime teetotaller!

---

[96]   A.H.M. Jones, Professor of Classical Antiquity, Fellow of Jesus
[97]   Cowling was a Research Fellow at Jesus before settling into a Fellowship at Peterhouse. A famous Conservative and historian.

But the incident helped my relationship with my mother-in-law, who now understood that my intentions were good; and 'Mrs Jennings' could now be addressed as 'Grandma'. She was of course delighted with the children, and accompanied us on our daily walk through the Botanic Gardens. Once back in Idle, though, she felt lonely: the exchange of pleasantries with the few neighbours who thought to call in was a relief but no real comfort.

By now Robbie was feeling the need for additional income and had taken the post of Reader in International Law to the Inns of Court Council of Legal Education, which entailed regular trips to London to lecture there. He was also co-editing the *British Yearbook of International Law* with Professor Humphrey Waldock[98] as well. Concerned for his mother, he made the journey north to spend weekends with her whenever he could; and I knew how stressful this division of loyalties between Idle and Cambridge was for him. It was certainly difficult for me.

We shared that Easter vacation with Grandma up in Wharfedale, in a small farmhouse at Grassington – a holiday she enjoyed.

In May came an unforeseen death. Hersch Lauterpacht, who had seemed restored after a heart attack the previous autumn, had been rushed to hospital for an operation and died under the anaesthetic. It was a great loss. We attended his funeral in the Thompson's Lane synagogue and the burial, where I saw Arnold McNair moved to tears over his old friend's grave. The vacancy at the International Court was to be filled by Sir Gerald Fitzmaurice.

All that year, tantalisingly, arrangements for the acquisition of our Grantchester house moved slowly. The legal transaction was completed by September, but the building of the Banisters' new bungalow took longer than expected. That was not unusual, and Dr Banister wrote with charming apologies; but it meant that we could not begin to have work done on the house itself. When completed, their bungalow suited them very well, having been designed by the young architect, Peter Hall, who lived next door.

In the midst of his varied teaching commitments that summer Robbie brought his mother for another stay with us in Cambridge, and in the Long Vacation went with me and the children down to Exmouth for a week. After, for his leg-stretching holiday he went off with Alan Pars; and later in September

---

98   Chichele Professor at Oxford, later (as Sir Humphrey Waldock) Judge at the I.C.J.

we all again took a Yorkshire holiday at Grassington. There, once more in Mrs Nicholl's farmhouse (Grandma in a room of her own, the rest of us together in a big room, half-smothered in old-fashioned feather beds) we took small excursions to favourite places around, such as Arncliffe in Littondale.

We were all longing to move to Grantchester – a need that had become more urgent as the children developed. The small shared garden of Claremont had no gate to keep children from straying. At 18 months Pippa had trotted off alone down Hills Road one day and was caught by me just about to step off the pavement into the traffic; and some months later her liveliness had plunged her off the Botanic Garden bridge into Hobson's Brook on a cold November afternoon (from which, waist-deep, I rescued her).

Besides his regular weekend visits to help his mother, Robbie brought her to spend a month with us over Christmas. On 27th February 1961 I wrote in my diary: 'BANISTERS MOVE (at last!)'. It meant that renovation work could now be begun on our Grantchester house – a happy prospect only clouded by the feeling that Edith Jennings must be invited to share it.

But suddenly the situation changed: on 13th April, while workmen were still busy at Grantchester, Grandma had a stroke while scrubbing her front doorstep, and died.[99] My own mother at once offered to come and look after the children, allowing me to join Robbie for the funeral. Thus it was that I stayed once more in that house on Idle Road, and was helped in setting out a proper funeral tea by Robbie's kind Aunt Alice, someone who completely sympathised with the awkwardness of my relationship with poor shut-in, lonely Edith.

The day after the funeral Robbie walked me around Idle – the first and only time he could show me the places that meant so much to him from his childhood. I saw the huge Wesleyan chapel and Sunday School, the village school, the woollen mills, the rows of cottages and shops and their setting in the Aire valley. It made a deep impression, as did those fleeting glimpses of his Uncles and Aunties and the real warmth of his family background.

Then it was time to return to our totally different life at Cambridge – a life which was so alien to all that Grandma had known, and in which we knew she would never have felt at home if, as duty urged, we had taken her to live with us.

---

[99] Edith's death echoed her own mother's, toiling over a washtub.

When Robbie came to clear up the last of his parents' estate, there was little to claim as inheritance. A few pieces of furniture and oddments of sentimental value were added to our possessions, and the sale of the house raised £2,850. Much of that money had been contributed by Robbie himself over the years.

The removal to Grantchester took place in June. First, as soon as term ended, we drove down to Exmouth. While Robbie returned to Cambridge, the children and I went on with Granny and Grandad to north Cornwall, to our cousins' holiday house at Trevone. There, after overseeing the removal of our furniture from Claremont to Grantchester, Robbie joined us all for a splendid holiday – enjoying cliff walks and games on the sands though never actually swimming or surfing. Having delivered us back to Littlecot, he then drove off to spend his first nights at Grantchester on his own. I followed by train with the children after a day or two, and from Cambridge he brought us to our new home.

[Our successor at no. 3 Claremont was Tresillian Nicholas, a geologist who spent most of his long career as Bursar of Trinity College. He was followed by Christopher Hogwood, conductor, keyboard player and musicologist.]

Grantchester

JUNE 1961–DECEMBER 1962

Robbie's few days ahead of us had been spent in arranging and re-arranging furniture in our new home. When I arrived with the children, we could settle in without delay.

Standing at the far end of the Bridle Way, the house now has a number, 61 (confusing to visitors). It had been built in 1925[100] by Dr Harry Banister, a Fellow of St John's, at the centre of a furlong-length piece of land alongside a matching plot containing some other dwellings. One pair of cottages had been converted into a single house for Robert Rattenbury, classics don and University Registrary; and in place of a small tumbledown one there was now a bright new house designed and occupied by a young architect Peter Hall, and his family.

Dr Banister had named his original house *Alfordesweye,*[101] and the bungalow *Alfordesweye Cottage.* Robbie preferred a modern version, *Alfordsway.* Besides having to replace all the electric wiring and antiquated plumbing, we found some peculiarities in the house. Until 1954 it had had no mains water supply, which accounted for a curious 'engine room' containing the mechanism (a large iron wheel, rods and a sort of bicycle arrangement) by which Dr Banister had pumped each day's supply of water from an artesian well into a tank in the roof. This room had to be dismantled and the wall separating it from the study removed. But the enlarged study had thin outer walls and a flat roof, so for many years, despite all efforts at insulation with bookshelves and panelling, it was a cold place in winter. Another idiosyncrasy of the Banister years was the arrangement of double doors between study and sitting room to ensure complete privacy while he, as a psychiatrist, was being consulted by a patient.[102]

---

[100] It was designed by Harold Tomlinson, first Head of the University's School of Architecture.

[101] Having consulted John Saltmarsh, local historian and Fellow of King's, he adopted an ancient name for the Bridle Way, which had once continued through the village and down to a ford across the Cam.

[102] Dr Banister's career had taken him from a mathematics degree to a commission in the Indian Army, in which he served for some years on the North-west Frontier; then back to Cambridge to study medicine, eventually specialising in psychology.

The back garden, too, was characteristic of its former owner. He had been a keen golfer, and his son an accomplished cricketer, so the large lawn was left completely open for them to practise their sports. Our own planting of trees would change this rather barren look.

For all its slight oddities and defects, we settled into Alfordsway very happily. Robbie had found that the agreed price, £8,000, needed the addition of nearly another £2,000 for alterations and a garage, and was glad to be given a loan by my parents.

We soon discovered that our neighbours had children whose ages matched our own. The Halls' elder child, Lucy, and our own Dicky were both just five years old and were welcomed at once into the village school, a school at that time perilously short of pupils. It made a good introduction to village life – meeting other mothers at the school gate and shopping for food across the road in one of the two shops (since gone.) Not far away was the church, and so this area was the acknowledged centre of the village, whose population at that time was less than 300.

We had barely established our new way of life when Robbie was off abroad for the biennial *Institut* conference, this time in Salzburg. His first letter home described a rather trying journey, during which 'a jarring note, as always, was the pretty little village of Dachau[103] on the main line'. The 'very beautiful baroque town' and agreeable hotel are mentioned, and 'I have already invited the very nice Quincy Wright from Chicago to come and stay at Grantchester when they are in Cambridge' – alarming for a wife with two young children and now pregnant with a third.

In his next letter he says, 'I suppose I am enjoying myself as much as might be expected with the international situation such as it is' – a reference to heightened tensions in the Cold War, following the Bay of Pigs episode in Cuba. He found the Austrians very agreeable and courteous, if rather slow. Their food, though, was not to his taste:

---

[103] Dachau, where in 1933 the first of Hitler's notorious concentration camps had been built.

'That abominable Wiener-Schnitzel appears at every meal, and even the potatoes are flavoured till they no longer taste like potatoes. I long for decent meat (I mean grown-up animals) honestly cooked…'

The *Institut* sessions were always valuable as an opportunity to renew contacts. He spoke of sharing entertainments with Humphrey Waldock[104] and with Eddi and Elizabeth Hambro,[105] and going for a drive with Ben and Peggy Wortley. He also hoped to go to a performance of *Fidelio*. And, typically, he mentioned his disappointment that his return would be too late for a demonstration of his latest hi-fi purchase, a big Wharfedale loudspeaker – bought partly from loyalty to his place of origin,[106] to a friend leaving Cambridge.

The furnishing of Alfordsway was almost complete when my intended colour-scheme for the sitting room was unexpectedly capsized. Robbie had done some advisory work for the Iranian government. His chambers clerk had not been involved, and so he had no idea of an appropriate fee. 'Well, do you like Persian rugs?' he was asked – Yes, he had become interested in fine rugs during his time in India. The result was the arrival of an enormous parcel 'by diplomatic bag'. We cut the stitching that held together its hessian wrapping, and unrolled what turned out to be an immense 'rug', 13ft 3ins by 9ft 5ins (4.05 metres x 2.88 metres) with a ground of bright crimson. This splendid item has dominated the room ever since.

1962 was another eventful year. On 1st March our third baby was born, and this time Robbie was present and giving a hand. Thanks to our nearby farmer, a tractor with a snowplough had cleared drifts so that the midwife could arrive in time, and a healthy second daughter was delivered. We named her Joanna, soon shortened to Joey.

---

[104] Sir Humphrey Waldock, Chichele Professor at Oxford, who later succeeded Sir Gerald Fitzmaurice at the International Court.

[105] Hambro, a Norwegian, was now Registrar of the International Court. His wife was English, daughter of Jacques and Gwen Raverat.

[106] The Wharfedale, and later Quad speakers were designed by Briggs of Ilkley, Yorks. His firm was to set up its main factory in Highfield Road, Idle.

The following month Robbie was lecturing in Iceland. A former pupil, Gunnar Schram, had arranged it all, and was there to meet his delayed plane at 3 am.

He liked all he saw of Reykjavik, and as a special treat was flown up to Akureyri for an impression of the coast and country in the north. And he returned with gifts he had chosen for the children and me and was also loaded with a sheepskin (long, silky white fleece) and a smelly parcel wrapped in newspaper: a whole side of smoked salmon.

It had become clear to us that, regretfully, we must change our beloved AC for something more practical. Robbie still, though, hankered for a car of distinction. After dismissing an aged Rolls-Royce offered by the Vicar of Grantchester, we actually test-drove a slightly more recent one belonging to Ashton-Cross, a friend in the Law Faculty. Then Robbie tried a 1936 Bentley saloon, a purring giant which barely fitted into our large garage, had a rather limited boot, and seemed an incongruously stately vehicle for village life. It, too, had to be rejected. Urged by my sister, he drove all the way down to Romney Marsh and returned with another Bentley, a 1934 monster touring car. This one was exciting to drive: at 35 miles an hour it gave an impression of hectic speed. Its steering veered to the left, and its great lamps shone straight at any opposing traffic, so driving home in the dark along a narrow country road after college dinner tended to intimidate other cars and call for concentration and muscle-power from its driver.

Another form of transport acquired that spring was a new bicycle. Ashton-Cross introduced us to his friend Alex Moulton, who had just designed a new form of suspension which allowed the production of a bicycle with small wheels.[107] Robbie was asked to try out a prototype, and happily agreed. Soon a photograph appeared in *Varsity*, the undergraduate magazine, of an unnamed man in a Burberry raincoat cycling down Trinity Street on this strange machine – someone very recognizable to university lawyers.

After about three months of Bentley No.2 we realised that we must think again. This time Robbie changed the characterful Bentley for a sensible Volvo, and it was in that car that we drove down to Cornwall for our summer holiday at Trevone with my parents, another wonderful adventure for the children.

---

[107] Moulton had designed the suspension for the popular Minicar. His bicycle would be introduced to the public in October of that year. The only other example being tried-out in Cambridge was one being ridden by Lord Rothschild.

Thanks, probably, to his friendship with Professor Ben Wortley, Robbie was invited to deliver the Melland Schill Lectures at Manchester that December. They were well received and later published as a hardback book, *The Acquisition of Territory in International Law*.[108] Although slim, it is regarded as a 'seminal work'. Malcolm Shaw[109] wrote in *The Times Higher Education* in 1995 that he had come across the book while studying for the LL.M. at the Hebrew University of Jerusalem at the time before the Yom Kippur War, when there was much discussion of title to territory; and Georges Abi-Saab[110] regards it as 'the foremost synthesis of one of the most complicated topics of international law; a model of its kind ...'; and even Tony Blair, when we encountered him momentarily years later, claimed to have read it!

Everything now seemed to have settled into exactly the sort of life we had envisaged. But then an alternative was proposed, forcing Robbie to make a difficult decision. He was invited to submit his name for the Vice-Chancellorship of the University of Leeds, with a strong indication that he would be the preferred choice. I dreaded the uprooting, though was determined to obey the call to duty ... But it turned out that Robbie, too, felt that the time was not right for him to undertake this position. The dilemma was for him a real one: Yorkshire meant so much to him, and he knew he was an able administrator. The position of Vice-Chancellor would, moreover, be one with influence in the City of Leeds, not just its university. He had seen the spacious stone-built house with the dales beckoning beyond, an attraction in harmony with his boyhood dreams, and he evidently expressed these feelings in declining the post. The chairman of the appointing board, Noel Tetley, replied (from The Brewery) with understanding, saying that 'if you consider there is work which you must do in your own field, it would be quite impossible to pursue it here'.

Cambridge had won – the work he had yet to do as Whewell Professor, the daily cycle ride or drive to his college room, the house and garden and three young children at Grantchester.

---

[108] See *Collected Writings* pp 933-1003.

[109] Sir Robert Jennings Professor of International Law at the University of Leicester.

[110] Professor of International Law at the University of Cairo and at the Graduate Institute of International and Development Studies in Geneva.

Work and Family

1963-65

The winter of 1962-63 was ferocious. We all – including Ingrid, our German *au pair* – developed infections in turn, our water tank froze and our neighbour Dr Banister died. It became so cold that it was possible for another neighbour, Angus Macpherson,[111] to skate along the river to his daily work in the Old Schools.

By this time *work* had become ever more demanding, and *family*, though precious, must somehow be there for Robbie to enjoy whenever possible. His children never found him remote, but they understood some unwritten rules. When Daddy was shut in his study you tapped on the door as you went in, then paused until he looked up, a finger laid at the point of the text he was reading, and gave you his attention. The request might be for some 'clean-on-one-side' paper on which to draw or scribble stories, and of which there was an endless supply provided by old examination scripts or discarded letters. The Daddy who was in playful mood at bedtime or on Sundays was likely to put on gramophone records of noisy music, including French *chansons* or the sound of Dutch street organs as well as *Peter and the Wolf* or Britten's *Child's Guide to the Orchestra*.

But it was work that filled his days: teaching, in its several modes (now in London at the Inns of Court as well as in Cambridge), the regular meetings of the University Council of the Senate, the General Board of the Faculties and its committees; and also, from 1962 to 1965, as university representative on the City Council, where Councillor Jennings served on its Education Committee.

He was regularly being consulted by John Blair, head of the legal department at Shell, too: advisory work that led to his attending a conference at Athens in July 1963 – one that he called in his first letter home 'World Peace Through Back-slapping'. Athens was undergoing a stifling heatwave, so he was able to see a little of his surroundings only late in the evenings. His second letter describes his impressions more fully:

---

[111] R.E. Macpherson, University Registrary and Fellow of King's

'... the conference stinks in many ways. It is vulgar and crude, elementary in the extreme, and very much that combination of back-slapping and ruthlessness that is characteristic of Americans at their worst. They say the two aims are (1) to get Rhein, the organiser, the Nobel Peace Prize, and (2) to get him nominated as Republican candidate for President of the U.S.A. I can well believe it, and from what I have seen he will succeed in both endeavours!

'Yet there is another side. There *are* some very good people here (all very restive) and it is a chance to talk to the kind of lawyer who does not attend purely academic bodies. For example, the South African who beautifully summed up the discussion this morning is the barrister who defended the prisoners in the treason trial.[112] There is Aron Broches of the Netherlands, who is legal advisor to the World Bank. And many others who are both nice and very good.

'I said my piece this morning and from comments it went down very well. I could say that it was one of the best speeches so far at the Conference, but I'm afraid that would mean merely that it was coherent, more or less! But I am satisfied with the discussion on this particular topic. It was quite good.

'11.50 pm. Have just returned from a very fine fishy supper with Shell manager and wife, and British Embassy commercial counsellor and wife, followed by view of Athens and Acropolis from Philopapus, a magical hill with marble ruined steps and cyprus trees commanding a view of all Athens and the sea, with the moonlit Parthenon in the foreground.'

Once he was home, we took the children down to Devon. We all loved my parents' house, Littlecot. Its garden provided a variety of delights, and there were beaches of all kinds along that coast, with red sandstone cliffs at Exmouth or large pebbles at Budleigh Salterton. Back at home for the new term Dicky, aged seven, started at St Faith's, a preparatory school. I took him there and heard him give his name to a 'big' boy as Jennings. But we were not prepared for the sensation it caused – the other boys clustering around, having all read popular schoolboy tales of *Jennings at School*, which he had not. He survived, and settled in well. Pippa, and in due course Joey, followed him at the village school.

Late that year there was a British Institute of International and Comparative Law conference at Edinburgh. The text of the talk Robbie gave there, on

---

112 This must refer to the notorious arrest of 156 S. Africans in 1956, all charged with treason. Among them was Nelson Mandela, and the trial ran on until 1961.

'Recent Developments in the International Law Commission: its Relation to the Sources of International Law', appears in his *Collected Papers.*[113] In it, he speaks of some matters where codification might be beyond the powers of the Commission.

> '...problems such as that of what lawyers call outer space and what astronomers call inner space ... [something which might] probably be taken on in the not too far distant future... Another new problem of the greatest possible importance is the regulation of experiments which are calculated or, judging by experience so far, miscalculated to change the earth's environment ... irresponsibility on an Olympian scale [which] the Commission is not likely to touch with a barge-pole for obvious reasons ... and which call for *political* action.'

Air Law had been an interest for some years and was the subject of one of his earliest papers.[114] His friendship with Arnold Kean, whose car he had driven down to Florida during his Harvard year, may have influenced him, since Kean had after the war become Legal Adviser to the Civil Aviation Authority and visiting Professor at the Institute of Air and Space Law, whose correspondence might well have included discussion of ongoing developments. But Space Law was a topic which the great authority Hersch Lauterpacht could not at first contemplate. When his friend C.W. Jenks had submitted an article for the *International & Comparative Law Quarterly* daring to raise this brand-new topic, he was horrified. 'Robbie' he exclaimed, 'we can't possibly publish this – it's sheer fantasy!' But Robbie, as assistant editor, recognised the importance of the piece and included it, as *'International Law and Activities in Space',* in the 1956 number. It would not be until 1961, after Sir Hersch's death, that the first cosmonaut circled the earth, but already the need for regulation had indeed become urgent.

Edinburgh left Robbie pretty tired and he was glad of a respite. It was a wonderful Christmas, with the three children at an age to revel in all its excitements. And their father had given himself a real treat, a second loudspeaker to enable the enjoyment of the new stereophonic records. 'He

---

[113]   *Collected Writings* p.679

[114]   See *International Civil Aviation & the Law (1945* p.1097) and *Some Aspects of the International Law of the Air (1949)* p.1124.

has been screwing and soldering at odd moments all yesterday and today; and tomorrow, perhaps, we may be able to hear the stereo records of *The Wind in the Willows* bought last Christmas!' I wrote to my parents.

———

In April 1964 Robbie went to Istanbul to address a conference, most of which was conducted in Turkish. They were worked hard: '...we left the hotel at 9 am and got back at 11 pm – this after a supper in a lovely spot by the Bosphorus, but of course nobody wanted any supper because we were too tired to eat but had to make the attempt in order to be polite,' an experience he would encounter again and again over the years. But he appreciated his surroundings:

> '...an extraordinary mixture of squalor and bygone splendour' [– and was able to see St Sofia and the Blue Mosque, and later] 'an exquisitely beautiful Byzantine church covered with frescoes, mosaics and murals of breath-taking beauty. Unusually, they showed movement and liveliness, evidently coming at a period when religious painting was getting less formal and the artists allowed more freedom'.

His next trip abroad was to Brussels, from where he reported on a postcard: 'Have been kept very busy and worked till 1am drafting last night. But the meetings are well worth while' – this again, I think, being work for Shell.

In July he had to address a meeting in Dallas, Texas, glad of the company of his increasingly close friend John Blair, the Shell lawyer whose skill was to operate effectively behind the scenes without attracting any fame for himself. Robbie knew he was likely to be back with me before his letter arrived, but liked to chronicle events while they were fresh. It told how he spent the flight – taking a route northwards over Greenland because of head winds – lying down with a fever...

> '... but the temperature eased in time for me to see all the Great Lakes from the air. At Chicago I was feeling not too bad and spent part of the time calling up Philip Watson[115] and had a very pleasant chat....
>
> 'By the time we got to Dallas of course my temp. was up again and we got a doctor straight away who, seeing I had to lecture next day, gave me

---

115 – his friend from Idle, now head of a Methodist training college.

antibiotics with instructions that the receptionist call me every 4 hours to take them, with sleeping pills in between so that I could get some rest! Result was that I was able to read my paper yesterday and to take the seminar and I gathered it went very well. A New York attorney, who is interested in getting a liberalising bill through Congress about a certain somewhat technical matter, asked me if I could spend a weekend in New York in November to run a seminar to help him in his propaganda. We will see if anything comes of it.

'Well, all my task being over, I am now spending a luxurious day in bed to have a really good rest… John B[lair] is a marvellous companion. The first night he insisted that he was used to waking and sleeping just any time and I must call him if I felt unwell or even just wanted a chat. Actually I had quite a comfortable night.

'Dallas – big, noisy, garish, aggressive – but better than one might expect. Hotel is superb. Service is quietly efficient and polite. The people are enormously friendly. I mean, a taxi driver chats all the way and is most anxious that an Englishman should get a good impression of the place. In fact I must confess I like USA and find it a most easy and friendly and generally helpful country to visit.

'The Southeastern Legal Foundation is part of the Southern *Methodist* University in Dallas! Now you see here an example of the kind of leaven that is found everywhere in the States. Dallas, and Texas generally, are frankly reactionary and isolationist to a degree. But here we find a man called Storey (a friend of Shawcross and a Republican) getting an enormous sum of oil money and other money, to found an institute for the study of international law *in Dallas* and to get foreigners to come here and build up some kind of international consciousness. So here we are, in part to study a very technical problem that happens to be of interest to oil men, but in part also (and possibly the main task) to act as missionaries. And that is, I must say, a very pleasant task when the natives are so friendly and hospitable!

'During such time on the plane as my temp. was normal I was made to work very hard by J.B. and we considered every word of my talk, which really was pretty good by the time we had finished. I had, under Win [Haight's] influence, made it fairly tactful – but J.B. insisted that I should say exactly what I thought, and explained that, under Shawcross, Shell had got a reputation for liberal thinking. So I put back all my original stuff about the *right* of States to nationalize under certain conditions if they wanted to. This plainly scandalized one of the organizers (who, tho' very nice, is recognized by the oil companies to be so "right" as to be a menace to their interests) but delighted the New York attorneys and more than delighted a large group of able youngsters from India, Pakistan, Egypt and so on. I am grateful to J.B. for encouraging me to say what I thought, not least because it went down much better with most of the audience. Shell is a curious concern. In both Shawcross and J.B. you get a strong streak of idealism which, with great shrewdness, they recognize to be also good business. Thus the fact is that they alone have made a very good secret settlement with Indonesia just by refraining from screaming and letting it be known that they entirely understand the aims and difficulties of the government.

'My talk was, I gather, especially welcome to the two Swiss who are here, because they expected to be alone in expressing liberal ideas, so now they can just follow me and were fulsome in their thanks.'

Home he came, and next month was off to Tokyo, this time for the I.L.A.[116] conference. Besides meeting colleagues there from all over the world, he took part in a televised discussion with Dick Baxter[117] and Shigeru Oda.[118] The climate being more than usually hot and humid, he had not managed to write home; but he knew how to cope with these conditions by missing lunch and lying down at midday, and his own contribution to the conference had evidently been a resounding success, defeating the American rulings against all monopolies. An overwrought Swiss had afterwards said to him 'Sir, you have saved Switzerland!' since that country depends on a big monopolistic combine in order to market their clocks and watches abroad.

Besides hearing his traveller's tales, there were again gifts for all of us at home: a pearl brooch for me; a paper Japanese lantern; kimonos for each of the girls; fans; a model express train for Dicky; a little drum; and a recording of part of a Noh play. Listening to its weird sounds, together with a collection of colour slides, conjured up for us an impression of that faraway land.

We ended the summer with a Lake District holiday based in a farm guesthouse at Satterthwaite, from where we ranged around much of the eastern part.

---

[116] International Law Association, which held conferences every second year, alternating with the Institut de Droit International (the senior body).

[117] Professor Richard Baxter of Harvard University, who had studied international law at Jesus.

[118] Professor at Tohoku University, Sendai, Japan.

In October I wrote to my parents:

'Robbie is becoming steadily more busy with examination scripts, Chairman of the Law Faculty work, City Council meetings, and all the usual beginning-of-term work. But on Friday evening, at the college's Society meeting, another responsibility was added. He has been elected President of the College,[119] and will probably remain in office for three years. It is a comparatively new office [created in 1926, really as a continuation of the older position of Senior Tutor] and involves acting as shop steward or go-between in the relationship between the Fellows and Master – also as Master's deputy on many occasions. He says it is one of the few offices he has held which involve only duties and no privileges, emoluments or benefits, and gives him the greatest pleasure of anything which has happened to him in his life ... – and then, guiltily glancing at his wife, he adds "in *college*, of course."'

Among those many duties was a brief but welcome visit by James Fawcett[120], who was in Cambridge to address a meeting. He played our piano, and was captivated by the strange sounds of that Japanese Noh play recording, vowing to procure a copy for himself. Years later, Robbie was to write his entry in the *Dictionary of National Biography.*

———

1965 began for Robbie with a visit to New York. He was attending a 'Forum' of evident importance to Shell, for there was detailed preparatory work with both John Blair and Win Haight, an American lawyer, before the main event. After delivering his own important speech there, Robbie had another assignment. Professor Richard Baxter had invited him to speak to the International Law Club at Harvard; and this, he told me, was his 'nicest trip ever.' He had taken the train northwards along the eastern seaboard, with sparkling snow around, passing through fishing ports on the way. He found Boston and Cambridge, Mass, after 30 years, even more attractive than he had remembered. And he returned with, among other presents, the poems of Robert Frost – bought

---

[119]   The President, originally appointed by the Master as his deputy for an indefinite period, was from 1926 elected by the Fellows for a two-year term.

[120]   James Fawcett, QC, was later knighted. Professor of International Law at King's College, London 1976-80, member of the European Commission on Human Rights – and grandfather of Boris Johnson.

partly because the poet had lived in the house opposite Dick Baxter's, along a street where Longfellow's granddaughter, aged 90, was still a resident.

But while that part of the US was reassuringly recognisable, Grantchester was undergoing change. Our end of the village was disturbed by bulldozers and lorries engaged in building an estate of council houses which would double the population and lead to the enlargement of the village school.

———

The first Hersch Lauterpacht Memorial Lecture[121] was delivered by the distinguished Judge Jessup,[122] someone we entertained afterwards. As Chairman of the Faculty, Robbie also edited a volume of *Cambridge Essays on International Law* in honour of McNair's 80th birthday, including his own piece on 'Nullity and Effectiveness in International Law.'[123]

———

His next trip abroad was to Vienna in May, once more combining work for Shell with a lecture at the University. There, his host was Dr Stefan Verosta,[124] who himself seems to have been involved in advising the Shell lawyers. Robbie's stay was, he wrote to me, 'really hard work'. And as he tried to make the most of all the cultural offerings in this great city, it became more strenuous still as Verosta took him home for dinner –

'… V. talked and talked! Trying to find something polite to say to the daughter, I said, hypocritically, that I must learn German. They took me up on that and spoke thereafter for the most part in German, very clearly and slowly. Very good for me. I found by last night – V. talks at such length – that I could understand most of what was said. They speak English in the hotel but I am insisting on practising my German instead. V. has a theory that English people don't speak foreign languages because they are "perfectionists" – which is a polite way of saying the truth, i.e. that we are scared of making mistakes…'

---

[121] Eli Lauterpacht was keen to ensure that his father's name was not forgotten, and was the moving force in creating the Lauterpacht Research Centre for International Law some years later.

[122] Judge Philip C. Jessup was currently the US judge at the International Court.

[123] See *Collected Writings* p. 692

[124] Stefan Verosta, a former Austrian Ambassador, was Professor of International Law at Vienna.

His second letter spoke again about how exhausting he was finding this visit. He was from habit getting up at 7 am and keeping active until midnight, growing stiff from walking for miles on pavements to learn the layout of the city, and persisting in improving his (already fairly competent) German. Verosta took him...

'... – great privilege – to see the Chancellory, which was opened up specially. More particularly it was fascinating to see the room where the Congress of Vienna met – fine but quite small room, for this was Metternich's private palace. I also saw the corner of the entrance room, where Dolfuss was shot by the Nazis when they occupied. These people make no secret of their dislike of North Germans!'

'Then ... out to the Opera at 7 pm. Rather disappointing in a way, because the show was *Katherina Michailova [sic]*[125] by Shostakovich – music very good and interesting but there is such a lot of brass and drums and noise that it becomes rather monotonous in a three hour performance. The story was very Russian, and violent and repulsive. But the leading soprano was quite remarkable (a Russian called Dvorakova). And of course the opera house itself was fine and the orchestra was fine. But there is *no* Mozart at all this week. There is some Wagner but it is booked up. For the rest there is stuff like Cav. & Pag.!

'After the opera, to supper with the Vs at a late hour. Very nice, very kind – but exhausting trying to follow Austrian dialect after a long day...

[Next day] – 'I spent the morning looking at pictures. Wonderful collection indeed. Far too many, of course. Every school is here. Lots of fine Flemish, esp. the two Breughels. I was particularly excited by Holbein, and especially "Jane Seymour" – very well known, of course, and I bought a reproduction. But it is one of those pictures where the reproduction somehow sheds all the magic. Then Rembrandts galore ... Came out exhausted and stiff.

'Then formal lunch – very pleasant, with the Dean (awfully nice), V. and Zemanek, who is also a Professor of International Law and educated at Balliol and wore a Balliol tie and has a very Balliol manner.

'Then back for a bath and so out to the Burg Theater to see a performance of Goethe's *Urfaust*. Very well done – but of course a bit heavy and very

---

[125]   This was surely *Katerina Ismailova* or *Lady Macbeth of Mtsensk*.

German, with its sententious preaching, relieved not by humour but by heavy clowning, after the German manner. Very exhausting, I found.'

After his lecture, which went well – 'At least they were a pleasant, kind and appreciative audience' – he lunched with the Assistant in International Law, Ginther, who had been at Trinity a few years before: a charming wife, a small baby, a splendid apartment, altogether 'a very pleasant occasion indeed.' Then he went to see 'a Norwegian international lawyer at the Atomic Energy Agency'. And after that there was 'a four-hour marathon at the Opera – Wieland Wagner's new production of *Lohengrin*.

'I had one of the best seats in the Opera, though seats have been booked for months. I gather V. got them via the F.O. The performance was very impressive and the sound at times quite out of this world. The brass of the orchestra is tremendous. At the opera I again chanced to meet John Havard[126] and we later had some supper together.'

And there was a final excursion next day, before he returned home, bringing gifts for us all.

In June we, together with Jack and Isabella Hamson[127], attended the grand service in St Paul's Cathedral celebrating the 750th anniversary of the Magna Carta. The pomp and circumstance, the dazzling colours of military uniforms, heralds and clergy were unforgettable. Robbie, though, was back in London next day for a new commitment – preparatory work on a boundary dispute between Argentina and Chile.

Even the rare tranquillity of our Sunday morning was interrupted by some unexpected callers, an Indian who wished to bid adieu after taking his LL.D. the day before. It was Nagendra Singh[128] and his wife, this time bringing extravagant gifts; and it was only now that we learnt that he was a Maharaja, and that we were urged to accept the use of the Owner's Suite on one of his cargo boats plying around the Mediterranean ports sometime … an invitation we were never free to accept.

---

[126] Dr John Havard, a former law pupil of Robbie's at Jesus, had then trained in Medicine and had a distinguished career as a barrister with medical expertise.

[127] C.J. Hamson, Professor of Comparative Law and Fellow of Trinity.

[128] Nagendra Singh would become a Judge of the International Court, 1974-88, and was its President for the last three years.

May Week, with its bump races and tea at Fen Ditton,[129] college plays and the Fellows v. Servants cricket match, actually saw us – for the first and only time – at the May Ball, Robbie as President having been urged to attend since it was thought that the presence of a number of senior Fellows would discourage any unseemly behaviour by the young. We reached home at 4 a.m. to relieve our baby-sitter, and were up again at 7 am to get the children off to school. But we had enjoyed it, as spectators since Robbie was no dancer.

It was, I think, during these years that the Law Faculty, to their indignation, were evicted from one of their best lecture rooms. The Faculty was housed in the range of buildings opposite the University Church, with the Squire Law Library at the end overlooking Senate House Passage. But the University Registry and Treasurers' offices were in the nearby Old Schools building (the original King's College) and needed to expand. The law lecture room was sacrificed in order to house a *computer*, an apparatus whose bulk demanded a room of that size. All the records of the University's business can nowadays probably be fitted onto something quite tiny.

At about this time, too, a Congregation of the university's Regent House debated whether it was acceptable for those appointed to university teaching posts to engage also in professional activities earning additional fees? – a question particularly relevant to subjects such as Medicine, Engineering and Law. A robust case for allowing these earnings was mounted by the Professor of Physiology, Sir Bryan Matthews; and Robbie, citing McNair's view that professional practice contributed much to the value of one's teaching, spoke in support.

---

[129]   Gardner-Smith had started a tradition of inviting Jesuans to Ditton Hall for refreshments between races, carried on by his successors Hugo and Freda Jones.

Argentina-Chile Frontier Case: 'Rio Encuentro'

1965-66

I t was Tim Tyler of Coward Chance[130] who must have noticed Robbie's work for Shell, and who recruited him to join the team representing Argentina in a dispute with its neighbour, Chile.

On 1st April 1965 the two countries made their formal application to Her Majesty Queen Elizabeth II, '… for the arbitration of a controversy between the Argentine Republic and the Republic of Chile concerning certain parts of the boundary between their territories.' The British Government was responsible for resolving the matter because King Edward VII had in 1902 signed an Award 'containing decisions upon certain parts of the boundary between the territories of the Parties'. The dispute was, accordingly, to be heard before an all-British tribunal, with Lord McNair as its President. The Argentine agent was Jose Maria Ruda, and counsel were Maurice Bathurst QC, Mervyn Heald and (before long) Robbie himself. Counsel on the Chilean side were Humphrey Waldock, supported by Eli Lauterpacht and a Chilean lawyer.

By December that year, a good deal of preliminary work had been done on the case, and we had enjoyed a good family Christmas. But on 28th December the first 'interlocutary' hearing began, and Robbie stayed with Alan Pars in Acton to take part. On the 30th *The Guardian* published a starry-eyed impression of this arbitration:

Frontier clash – the civilised way

By Norman Shrapnel

Ask the way to the Argentina-Chile frontier clash, and they point to a tall, sedate building in Kingsway, London. Seek out the 40-mile sector of the Andes which is in dispute, and your guide sends you up in a lift.

---

[130] Coward Chance would in 1987 amalgamate with Clifford Turner to become 'Clifford Chance'.

This looks like the final solution, the ultimate sanity. The lift deposits you at a range of high, windswept offices normally occupied by the Performing Rights Trinbunal, now taken over by the arbitration court set up by the British Government to sort out the frontier tangle between Boundary Posts 16 and 17.

Britain is accepted as umpire under a treaty of 1902, and yesterday there was a short public session, abounding in sweetness and light, before Argentina and Chile got down to their word war. Seekers after violence had clearly to look elsewhere.

Instead of the real mountains, all those thousands of miles away, there was a contour model. Instead of cowled figures cracking rifles (or worse) at each other from behind crags as is the habit of less civilised States, we had the amiable drone of voice against voice – one demonstrably Argentine, the other firmly Chilean.

The friendly hostilities were held up for a time by a tremendous barrage of camera-firing in the light of which could be seen Lord McNair, the president, with the Argentine forces ranged on his right and those of Chile on his left. No doubt the pictures will be object lessons for less happy communities up and down the world.

These preliminaries over, the tone of the engagement was at once set by His Excellency Dr Jose-Maria Ruda, Ambassador Extraordinary Plenipotentiary, legal adviser to the Argentine Ministry of Foreign Affairs, appearing as agent for the Argentine Republic. "One of the most characteristic features of the foreign policy of the Argentine Republic," he told us "has always been the peaceful settlement of her international controversies, even of those which refer to her territorial boundaries".

And never let it be said that nobody listens to us any more. Both Ambassador Ruda and his Chilean counterpart, His Excellency Senor Don Victor Santa Cruz, expressed their confidence that Britain would arrive at a just solution of their dispute.

Up in the real mountains, a field mission is at work, with aerial photography and ground reconnaissance going on just as it does around and across other disputed frontiers. The difference is that in this sector of the Andes, apparently, everybody cooperates with everybody else.

And before the whole heartening affair sinks below the horizon of public admiration, let us fade out to some more exemplary words from the rival Ambassadors.

"When nearly a century ago at the end of our last armed conflict we emerged victorious, we pointed out that victory gives no rights to the victor", said Ambassador Ruda. Their present policy implied a determination "to find the way whereby these two fraternal countries, born together to independent life, may find a common purpose." And Ambassador Santa Cruz called the 1902 treaty "a great and good example".

Other countries please copy.

Those days of intensive work followed a pattern that was to become familiar over the years. It had been only on Christmas Eve that Ruda had appointed Robbie as counsel and for the meetings that followed, the team were likely to be hard at work in one room (with lunchtime sandwiches), until late in the evening, or else attending diplomatic receptions.

After days of this, it was noble of him to make yet another trip to London on his weekend of rest, this time to take the children, now aged 9, 7 and 3, for their first visit to the city, to see Bernard Miles' production of *Treasure Island:* proof of his devotion to the family. He took me to Ladies' Night at Jesus, too. This had replaced the annual 'Freddy's dinner' for college wives – for the 65-year-old bachelor Brittain had in 1959 amazed everyone by marrying Muriel Cunningham[131], and a new, still not-quite-comfortable, form of entertainment, a rich meal followed by sedate dancing, was substituted.

A greater relaxation for him was, as always, playing with hi-fi. For Christmas he had given me a reel-to-reel tape recorder, something which encouraged lots of experiments in home-produced music, stories and interviews. (I resisted the offer of a larger and more complicated machine; but over the years he would make many more purchases from University Audio to indulge his passion.)

Although the *Encuentro* case involved days and late nights of hard work for Robbie, it was all fascinating. In what seems to be the text of an informal talk delivered some time later to an audience including non-lawyers – quite probably to members of The Club – he conveyed something of the complexities of the two major Argentine/Chile cases in which he was to take part. This script is rather clumsily typed, with scribbled corrections and cryptic notes, on

---

[131] Muriel, a pharmacist, came from his own village of South Mimms and had been known to him since girlhood. She would later, as widow, become the college's Keeper of the Records.

'clean-on-one-side' old examination scripts. Its subject is *'What it is like to be an international lawyer'* –

'... Law is not one of those subjects where there is just one correct answer to a question if only you are clever enough to find it. It involves policy at nearly every stage. It is an art and not a science. This of course is why it is such fun to do...

'It is of the nature of a lawyer's job that one is involved mainly in disputes. There are any number of ways of settling them or of leaving them unsettled according to taste. The way of settlement dear to the heart of any lawyer is of course the great public drama of the day in court: a formal disputation conducted according to strict rules. And at the end of the day, Judgment: a judgment by which usually one party is seen clearly to have won and the other to have lost. The layman's instinctive question, and rightly so, is, "Who won?"

'It does not need a very powerful mind to discern that this is not always the best way of settling international disputes ... There are some disputes where some justice can be done to the strength of the argument on either side. And a good example is the kind of case where a court is asked to determine, what is the proper course of a boundary line?'

He then goes on to describe the situation which needed to be clarified in the *Rio Encuentro* arbitration. It had been assumed, at the time of the 1881 treaty which laid down the boundary between Argentina and Chile, that the boundaries of the colonies established by Spain in the colonial period were sufficiently defined. But...

'They... had frequently been left very vague because, since all were under the same rule ultimately, it was not a matter of great importance.

'But between Argentina and Chile there is a formidable boundary provided by nature. The great chain or cordillera of the Andes traces almost the whole of this very long frontier: one of the longest in the world, extending from near the Tropic of Capricorn to within a hundred miles of the Antarctic ice barrier...

[In 1899 it was found that the wording of the 1881 treaty was ambiguous, and a tribunal was appointed by the British Crown – the arbitrators – to examine the region in more detail.]

'The key member of the tribunal … was a remarkable geographer and military man, Colonel Sir Thomas Holdich, then Vice President and later President of the Royal Geographical Society.

'His first task was to collect such maps as he could find, mainly Argentinian, for that country already had a flourishing Geographical Society … This Argentinian paramountcy in surveying and mapping was later, as we shall see, to become something of an embarrassment.

'Holdich then went to look at the country, travelling the length of the frontier in a journey which would be difficult and arduous today, but at the turn of the century seems to us remarkable, were it not that those remarkable late Victorians were doing that sort of thing all the time. He later described his journeys in a very readable book called *The Countries of the King's Award…*

'It was this settlement (1902) that inspired the two nations jointly to erect the famous "Christ of the Andes" statue over the tunnel of the Trans Andean Railway…'

[He then describes the disputed territory] '…a sector of some 60 miles only in the Patagonian Andes, in an extremely remote area having even now only difficult and intermittent communications with the more developed parts of either country.

'The area consists of snow mountains and very rough pasture won by burning the forests. A small population of cowboys with sombrero and poncho manages to survive but little more. The climate is abominable, rain, fogs and high winds being the predominant features. It is an alpine economy – *verenadas* – with cattle on the hoof.

'The burnt dead trees mostly lie where they fell, strewn over the valley floors, making only movement by horses possible. "But many are still standing, grey and stark on the green slopes of the cloud-wreathed mountains. They lend a melancholy air to the countryside."

[And in answer to the obvious question: 'Why bother with such a useless area?' he explains:] 'Any territorial question is important to those who live there. Clearly it matters in which country your home may be. And who shall say that these poor but proud people are less important than the nonentities who people our cities?'

He then goes on more fully to convey the passion and romance which sustains the lawyer investigating the details of such a case and constructing its arguments.

The people involved in the case were an interesting group: agents, counsel, diplomats, geographers and solicitors. The British lawyers on the Argentine side were from Caius, Jesus and Magdalene; for Chile, from All Souls and Trinity, Cambridge. (If he met colleagues or opponents on the train to London on a Sunday evening their chat would avoid discussion of the case.)

Over the long months of preparation the teams immersed themselves in half a century of local history: land surveys and titles; births, marriages and deaths; animal brand marks; military service; electoral rolls; crime; courts; police activity; hospitals and health; census; religion ... And of course the geographers had to make close inspection on the ground for comparison with aerial photographs.

The formal hearing at Lancaster House, Robbie wrote, presented the 'fascinating and highly civilized atmosphere of a law court with its elaborate courtesy and discipline. It was moving to hear differences that have led to violence the subject of not always dispassionate, but always courteous and dignified, argument.' And in the close proximity of this court, one could watch the faces around.

> [It was] 'very strenuous work, taking notes when not talking, arranging materials, making subtle changes of emphasis and refining the argument – perhaps dropping an argument; and finally conducting a post mortem after each day.'
>
> [And once the Award had been read, he noted] '...the cathartic effect of procedure which surprised me. Emptied of intellectual effort and passion. Everything has been said, and said at full length. The Award is it. It is the end of the matter. Quite impossible to question it. (But both governments did.)'

Because the disputed area was so inaccessible otherwise, it was on horseback that members of the opposing sides had made their inspection – Eli Lauterpacht for Chile, and the Coward Chance solicitor Nigel Fox-Bassett for Argentina.

⎯⎯

Two unrelated items preserved in the Jesus College files from this time are of interest. One, dated 8th February, 1966, is a newspaper cutting headed '*No question of moon claim*'. It reads:

'There was no question that the first country landing a man on the Moon or any other celestial body could claim sovereignty to it, Prof. R.Y. Jennings, of Jesus College, Cambridge, professor of International Law, said yesterday.

'He said that most nations agreed that celestial bodies could only be exploited by nations in common for peaceful purposes. If man managed to inhabit the Moon, there would likely be an international regime similar to that in operation in Antarctica. There, expeditions can go anywhere and observe any other expeditions.

'The apparent success of Luna 9, the Russian Moon vehicle, could mean a man would land on the Moon in 1969, said Dr R.A. Lyttleton, of St John's College, Cambridge, a reader in Theoretical Astronomy …'

The other item is a handwritten letter from Robbie to the college Bursar, Derek Taunt, describing the spartan conditions still endured by some Fellows:

'Dear Derek,

I have been asked to edit what is still (tho'? whether it will remain) the principal English text book on Intl. Law – a very considerable work of some 1,200 pp packed with stuff. This means setting up a biggish system of files &c because there is a very great deal of information and sources to get, and keep in usable form. The only way I can do this is to use my College room as my main working room whilst this job lasts. And, of course, it will make a most attractive room to work in *but* there are two snags that will make themselves felt next winter: (i) there is no present possibility for arranging a reading lamp near the work table – the lighting is 50 volt and poor in illumination and the only wall plug on the lighting system is an old 2-pin that has not produced any juice for many years; (ii) the room gets impossibly cold.

'There is one 200 volt socket at the *far* end of the room and it is possible to use this to help the lighting with the aid of a length of flex that would distress the fire brigade; but I *could* manage thus.

'But the heating worries me. I can use an electric convector, again at the far end – but I am very short of adequate warmth at the working end near the fire place. The now rather old gas fire makes almost no difference in cold weather and I have been in the habit of fleeing to the combination room even to read letters.

'Would there be hope of getting a modern, convector gas fire installed – which I think would probably solve the problem? I would happily contribute towards the cost by paying a rent.

'Sorry to trouble you with this. I make no claims because I fully realize that I am more than fortunate to have a room at all.

'P.S. – I should explain that I can't use my room in the law library because this is perforce merely a part of the library and there is no room even for my own books.'

A year later, although Taunt had agreed to help, the work had not begun and so Robbie suggested that

'… conversion to 240 volts is the first thing to do. Any extra heat put in goes straight out through the vast roof; and the electricity bills for the College would simply go up without very much benefit to me.

'Would it be possible to insulate the roof? …'

He was about to start his long, painstaking labour on the 9th edition of *Oppenheim* in that fine but chilly 16th century room.

———

By the Easter vacation we felt badly in need of a break. Robbie had so many things going on – a discussion with someone from the David Davies Institute of International Relations about the drafting of a treaty about settlement on the moon is mentioned, and a Hague Academy Curatorium meeting in Italy that he ought to have attended – that only two days could be spared, so we decided to spend them at Budleigh Salterton, close to my parents' former home in Devon. We stayed in a hotel, a wild extravagance, where the children enjoyed television: altogether a refreshment –

'For the first time ever, I think, Robbie took *no* work, and dealt with only one or two letters; so we felt a little sore when one of our two days was wiped out pretty much by the gale. He was, however, returning home to redoubled labours, and we were surprised to find no mail and no newspapers. I popped over to Bannie [Mrs Banister, our octogenarian neighbour] to collect the key we had left with her "for emergencies only". (We had emphasized again and again that we were to be away for so short a spell that we didn't want her to do a thing – the cat was being fed, etc....)

'"Oh, my dear" said Bannie as she opened the door, "Are you back so *soon*? Did something happen? I was *sure* you would stay over Easter. And there were several important-looking letters this morning – one, a big long one, marked

URGENT – so of course I forwarded them on to you." Somehow I managed not to say, "You SILLY old thing!" and instead smiled and thanked her effusively. What about all the newspapers we had expected to find accumulated? Oh yes, she had killed them dead too …

> 'Ah me, it was so very kind of her. We haven't quite managed to restore the full delivery of papers yet, and some are lost irretrievably. And perhaps if he is lucky, Robbie will on Tuesday receive the urgent & important & confidential mail which should have been waiting here on Thursday!'

Such plans as we were able to make seldom worked out quite as intended.

In a relatively quiet Easter Term he could carry on his regular activities, although as college President he had some curious extra ones – welcoming a group of visiting Russians and an international conference of ornithologists; or, as Chairman of the Law Faculty, attending the National Conference on Criminology dinner. That term, too, he dined at New Hall[132] with a young international law fellow, Gillian White[133], and also took his distinguished senior colleague as counsel for Argentina, Maurice Bathurst, to the Rustat Feast.

It was also in 1966 that Robbie became Chairman of the King Street Housing Association, a Jesus College project for which Derek Taunt, the Bursar, was a prime mover and Alan Percival another. Their aim was to develop some college land as attractive small homes for young people starting their ascent of the housing ladder. With advice from Leslie Martin[134], Professor of Architecture, two sets of accommodation were built on King Street, and the scheme would grow over the years, eventually becoming the independent *King Street Housing Society*.

Family holiday arrangements were again uncertain. Chile was asking for the next *Encuentro* hearings to be delayed, and (as I wrote to my parents) –

---

[132]   Now named Murray Edwards College. Its buildings had only just been opened, in 1965

[133]   She succeeded Professor Ben Wortley at the University of Manchester, and after marriage became Gillian Fraser

[134]   Sir Leslie Martin, Fellow of Jesus, famed particularly for the Festival Hall on London's South Bank.

'… of course the latest complication is that (as the solicitors, anxious about fees, had been fearing for some time) the Argentine president has been overthrown and nobody is quite certain of continued employment under the new government!'

———

Late in July Robbie did go to The Hague for a meeting of the Hague Academy curatorium. He wrote to me that –

'The work has not been very hard so far. Most questions of principle have been decided and it seems a little absurd that we should have been gathered from the ends of the earth (Oda has come from Tokyo) for this. But it represents a tiny invisible export for U.K. so one mustn't grumble. The American was glad to escape from New York, where the temperature is 103°F.

'Last evening I had dinner with Friedmann – quite pleasant. This evening I had a really enjoyable time. I gathered the two I particularly like – the Japanese, Oda, and the Egyptian, Boutros-Ghali[135] – and we went by tramcar to Scheveningen. Very like Blackpool now, with a great pier you pay to walk on, and lights and people. But a marvellous rather angry, brown (deep brown) sea, and a splendid sunset behind piled blue-black clouds. After walking about we went into a seaside restaurant and had raw herrings and beer and a long, long talk. Then back by tramcar…'

He now made a visit to Helsinki, to speak on Anti-Trust matters at the ILA conference before we got away for our Lake District holiday, this time staying on the Bowness side of Windermere at Storrs Hall Hotel. Even now he could not relax entirely, having some 'heavy reading' to get through and the possibility of having to go to London for a day of meetings. He was being consulted, too, about a dispute concerning Japanese fishing limits; but it turned out that the two people (one of them his friend Shigeru Oda) with whom the matter was to be discussed were quite willing to travel up to Windermere to meet him there. We have some happy snapshots from their brief visit. For the rest of our stay we walked and scrambled as usual, and on one wet day visited Eskdale, where with our friends the Johnsons,[136] we rode on the miniature

---

[135] Boutros Boutros-Ghali would many years later become Secretary-General of the UN.

[136] Professor Ken Johnson, FRS, an engineering Fellow of Jesus, had a cottage at Ravenglass.

railway up the valley. A slight diversion on the way home allowed us to call on Mrs Holdsworth – a tiny, indomitable person, widowed early in the First World War and left to raise her baby son Harold without assistance. She was a last link with Robbie's boyhood and had introduced him to many books and the gramophone records of classical music that meant so much to him, and a generous friend to the end.

Back at home, he was toiling away on the final preparation of his arguments for the next *Encuentro* hearing. Once it got under way I wrote –

'the Argentine case seems to have dominated our lives lately: each day it has been impossible to know when [Robbie] would be home, and whether fed or hungry. On Friday we were to have attended a Vice-Chancellor's luncheon for the Lord Chief Justice of Malta; but that morning I had to ring up with apologies and explain that Robbie *must,* after all, go to London for last-minute discussions ...'

All I could do was to try to supply moral support for my nervous and excited husband. The pressure continued; I managed to join him for a Foreign Office reception at Carlton Gardens; he made his speech before Lord McNair at Lancaster House (and got home just before the children's bedtime on Pippa's tenth birthday), and there was still more to do. But I had now met some of the people connected with the case:

'Mme. Santa Cruz (wife of the Chilean Ambassador), Lord Walston, and – a wish granted – Eric Shipton, the mountaineer and explorer used by Chile for their geographical survey. He is an impressive man: faraway blue eyes and a wild restless look – he was fed up to be shut in Lancaster House for weeks during the hearing, having been dragged home from an expedition in Alaska. Finally, we got talking to Dingle Foot and his wife ...'

And, of course, probably like every other woman – I fell headlong in love with the great explorer, to Robbie's amusement. It was my first experience of arriving at such a reception, feeling stiff and crumpled from the train journey, and having on my own to ascend a grand staircase (red carpet, chandelier, tapestries) with a uniformed butler watching from above.

By early October the case had reached its final stage.

'Argentina said their say, for about a week and a half; and Chile have spent the next week-and-a-half with their case. Now – possibly all weekend, although R. does hope to get home for Saturday night (he'll need to collect some clean clothes!) – they are plotting replies. There is just this final week to go, in which (as Eli Lauterpacht explained to me,) Argentina will do another Ding and Chile a final Dong. It should all end next Friday, October 14.'

The Award was in fact signed and delivered on 24th November 1966. It was a process which was to become familiar as the years went by. For now it meant a great break-through for Robbie. Having once addressed an arbitration court, he was accepted among the elite band of counsel employed for hearings of international disputes. It had gone well, and thanks to the wisdom of McNair and his colleagues, both Argentina and Chile were content to accept their revised boundary line.

———

The Hague Academy General Course

1967

R obbie took sabbatical leave from his university work for the Lent and Easter terms of 1967 to allow him to concentrate on an important new commitment. He had agreed to give the General Course – a series of 13 lectures – for The Hague Academy. His audience would be advanced students of international law from all over the world, and the lectures would later appear in print, in the annual *Recueil des cours/Collected Courses,* described as 'the most rewarding treasure-trove of contemporary international law,'[137] with an added quotation from Robbie's own assessment in its 1973 Jubilee Book:

> "The *Recueil* was the first and is still the major international work on international law ... not only a unique record of the development of international law during the last half-century; it has also itself made a formidable contribution towards that development."

It was a task that scarcely allowed time for other activities. He did find time that January, though, for a visit to London to lecture on North Sea Gas to the Royal Geographical Society. As I wrote to my parents –

> 'He went off feeling rather nervous, never having attempted anything of quite this sort before, and wondering how he was going to fit in with the eminent Kent[138] who was to give the technical and descriptive part of the lecture, with slides. Yesterday evening he rang up sounding more cheerful, and saying what a pity it was that I hadn't managed to come up for the lecture ...'

... because he found that Kent's wife Betty had known me when I was a little girl, and indeed it was at her parents' wedding that my own parents had met each other.

---

[137]   Quoted from his book on *The Peace Palace* by Arthur Eyffinger, 1988.
[138]   Sir Peter Kent, geologist, later to become President of the Royal Geological Society

He was still giving his regular Bar lectures[139] – after which, one day, he travelled to Oxford to talk to Humphrey Waldock's group of young international lawyers. A month later he was off to Reading, to talk to the Political Science Society at the University. And now he had been consulted, too, by the States of Jersey and would make a short visit there to 'advise about Common Market problems' (my rather vague description of a commitment that would increasingly occupy him for the next 16 years).

Work on *Oppenheim* was itself a challenge, and slow work. The General Course, though, called for a different approach from the necessarily dry tone of the great textbook. In his years of experience at both Cambridge and the Inns of Court, Robbie had developed his own manner of teaching; and Professor Georges Abi-Saab, introducing the two volumes he later edited of Robbie's *Collected Writings*,[140] says that he included the text of the General Course…

> '…because it reflects the pedagogic style of Sir Robert and conveys some of the flavour of his oral lectures to successive generations of students in Cambridge and elsewhere.'

And indeed McNair, in one of his friendly notes, wrote in 1969 that he had just received the newly-published Academy *Recueil* of Robbie's General Course and, having reached his chapters on Treaties, commented:

> 'I … am very pleased by its practical and unsophisticated (using sophisticate in the bad sense) outlook – debunking even. It is most important that international law should from time to time get a good drench from the spirit of the common law. I feel that our attitudes are very close – probably because we both come from somewhere north of a line connecting the Humber and the Mersey.'

In April Robbie broke off to join his colleagues on The Hague Academy Curatorium at Villa Serbelloni in Bellagio, a wonderful spot on Lake Como.

139　Robbie was Reader in International Law for the Council of Legal Education, 1959-70.

140　*Collected Writings of Sir Robert Jennings,* published in 1998, was edited by Prof. Abi-Saab, who made the selection of lectures and articles. The General Course runs from p.1-267.

He was thrilled with his first impressions of Italy, and described them in letters home. Travelling from Milan airport by car, he and Friedmann…

'…did the journey in remarkable time with skilled but hair-raising driving, with much light-flashing, sighs, exclamations and groans from the driver… This is not a country house at all. It is a palace. The rooms are vast and very beautifully furnished … painted furniture decorated with stencils, an all-marble bathroom … and a view for the Gods. One knows roughly what to expect; but it takes one's breath away all the same. Garden runs steeply down from the windows, past straight groups of cypress to lake on the left and lake on the right. Straight ahead, between the arms of lake, is a wooded hillside with farms and villas. Round the whole thing is a fantastic backcloth of snow mountain – not distant-looking, but just like a backcloth of gigantic proportions suspended immediately behind our view.'

He found to his dismay that he had failed to bring a tweed jacket, and that their host, Marshall, was dressed in that style:

'American – must be Bostonian I think – for his accent is very English, with drooping moustaches and a slightly drooping gait, is dressed this morning in an ancient tweed jacket and striped guardsie-looking tie. No Englishman could do it quite so accurately… [And he carries on with excited descriptions of his surroundings.]

'… It seems that Dupuy, the French colleague, almost became a professional singer. Friedmann is a good pianist. So this evening we are to have Schubert after dinner. There is of course a splendid Bechstein grand in the drawing room…'

It had been an exhilarating few days, but he and Oda had to miss the final one in order to attend a conference on the Continental Shelf at Cambridge.

———

Among our Jesus friends, Laurence Picken must have been one of the most interesting Fellows in the college's history. Having at first taught Zoology, he then moved to Oriental Musicology and was fluent in all the languages needed on his travels from Turkey to Japan. Although a shy man, he had an instant rapport with children; and after a happy Sunday visit to Grantchester there was later an unforgettable occasion when he in turn invited us all to lunch in his college rooms – a double set needed to accommodate the musical instruments he had collected from many countries and periods. I had warned the children that they should not touch these precious objects, but Laurence urged them to take up and sound the great hunting-horn from the Forest of Versailles, the strings of a Chinese zither-like instrument, the Turkish cymbals, or sit at the chamber organ and try its keys … And after that he showed them how to write an approximation of their names in Chinese characters, using brush and a tablet of ink. It was a very special experience. On his solitary travels he, with his sensitive ear for language, could communicate in the most remote regions of Turkey or Mongolia.

While the college had its remarkable characters, so did Grantchester. We made new friends at the lower end of the village that year. One was Peter Ward[141] at the Old Vicarage, who devised and constructed scientific instruments. The other was Sandy Cockerell[142] at Riversdale, whose bindery workshop was full of ingenious tools for bookbinding and restoration, appealing to Robbie's love of craftsmanship. There our children could watch the production of Cockerell marbled papers, too.

All three children were developing individual interests; and when the Headmaster of St Faith's proposed grooming Dick as a possible scholarship candidate for Westminster or Winchester Robbie demurred, sure that he would respond best to being allowed to follow his own, very varied and very earnest, activities: 'A *happy* boy comes first'.

The whole family went over to The Hague for the beginning of the Academy course. It was a huge thrill for the children, taking the overnight boat from Harwich and then staying at the Parkhotel in Molenstraat. Everything – the street organs, the carillon from the Grote Kerk, tram rides to the seafront at

---

[141]   Peter Ward was the son of Dudley Ward, friend of Rupert Brooke, to whom Brooke's mother had entrusted the greatly-loved Old Vicarage after the First World War. At first making exquisite musical boxes and automata, he later, in partnership with Cecil Chapman, set up a firm, Grant Instruments, now making scientific apparatus in Shepreth.

[142]   S.M. Cockerell, son of Douglas Cockerell, both leading bookbinders. His uncle was Sir Douglas Cockerell, one-time Director of the Fitzwilliam Museum; his cousin was Sir Christopher Cockerell, inventor of the hoverboat.

Scheveningen – was exciting. They saw the Peace Palace[143] and, in its grounds, the Hague Academy building where Robbie was to deliver his course.

Once he had given his first lecture, getting the feel of his elite 200-strong audience, he settled down to several hours' work completely recasting the second ('I see how to do it now'). It would all have to be rewritten and typed anew in its revised form, and the completed series[144] is an impressive work, bringing his audience up to date with latest developments, including Space Law. The following, taken at random, conveys something of his approach:

'The need to invent a law to govern the extra-terrestrial activities of man presents peculiar problems; but it also exhibits familiar complications such as the unremitting pressure of technological advances, and tensions between civilian and military uses and aims. Even in so novel a situation as the exploration of space and celestial bodies the lawyer does not begin with an entirely clean slate. Man cannot escape from law any more than he can escape from moral obligations merely by projecting his activities beyond the limits of the global system. For much international law is not territorial or even terrestrial in that sense …'

Whenever he was free, Robbie accompanied us on our visits to Madurodam, Delft, the Mauritshuis, the Panorama Mesdag and to the wonderful zoo (no longer there) at Wassenaar. We took a canal trip in Amsterdam, and visited the family of 'Tiddle', our loyal former *au pair*. At a reception given by the Burgomaster and Aldermen of the The Hague I saw how 'the students crowded around Robbie – American, Polish, Ghanaian, Hungarian, Brazilian, Ceylonese, &c., in a great hot scrum.' After ten days I took the children home, leaving Robbie to complete his course.

He had little chance of relaxation. Writing to me after my return, he said –

'Today I had a lecture, lunch with the Columbia University party, and then a seminar – so I feel pretty tired. But I must spend this evening preparing both a lecture and to talk to Movahed[145] tomorrow.

---

[143] – described by Mark Greenberg as 'a hulking neo-Gothic structure of no particular architectural distinction but great symbolic significance'

[144] – published both in the *Recuiel* and in *The Collected Writings*.

[145] Movahed was a representative, I think, of the Anglo-Iranian Oil Company.

'I have done 2/3 of the actual lectures now – and I must say I shall be glad when it is over. One every day (including Sat. now) is a bit much. But I am doing so many extra seminars, which are paid for now and not later, that there should be plenty of guilders in the end. I very much enjoy the seminars and especially two extremely good Frenchmen who ask very good questions and ask them very well. I used the translator at first but their French is so clear I soon found it actually easier just to listen to the French. Trouble is that one must have the earpiece to tune to the translator handy because some of these French-speaking Africans from the Cameroons might decide to ask a question and I find their French impossible. The translator tells me he has difficulty too…'

Amidst all this pressure, a stomach infection added to the stress of his final days. His Shell contacts – Diephuis, the head lawyer, Jan Jitta and Ellis – had arranged for him an 'exquisite meal' at which he fasted, but also took him to Gouda, and then along …

'…narrow lanes on dykes, with great avenues of willows; soft meadows with trees all over in rows; water everywhere, much of it bright green with algae or whatever it is; farms and houses and barns all matching.

'Then Schoonhoven (nice little town,) over the very fine and wide River Lek (part of Rhine system) by ferry; and back via Kinderdyk (windmills galore) and Rotterdam.

'Jitta and Ellis were, as you will have gathered, most kind. But of course I was pretty tired…'

His British Shell contact and friend John Blair now came up with a completely new proposal, 'probably of no practical importance but pleasing':

'There is an old agreement for setting up an arbitration tribunal between a clutch of oil companies and Iraq. It has never met because Iraq has always stonewalled by refusing to nominate her arbitrator. But the Oil Companies long ago nominated Arnold [McNair]. Now he has withdrawn and they want to nominate me. J.B. thinks I had better ask the Persians first and not accept if they find it awkward – tho' I don't think they will. In all probability it will in any case be no more than nominal because the tribunal is most unlikely ever to meet. Still it is pleasing even to be thought of to succeed Arnold. And not the least pleasing part is that the solicitor of this oil group (6 or 7 of the leaders) is Bischoff, who is senior partner in the firm that acted for Chile in the Arbitration. So they must have thought I had made a little dent in their case…

'Sunday

'Had a somewhat busy day yesterday. Movahed arrived at 9.30 with a lot more work and we talked till my lecture time. He attended my lecture. Then I gave him lunch at the hotel (very simple man: wanted water and some fish without sauces or anything fancy and nothing further.) After lunch we walked round the Mauritshuis, which clearly impressed him very much indeed. Then he went off to Amsterdam. He flies to Tehran today…

'This morning I went to the service at the Grote Kerk and enjoyed it very much. There was a reasonable congregation – perhaps 150. The minister wore a velvet gown, wing collar and bands. There was much psalm-singing and hymn-singing (the latter mostly familiar) but that is done sitting down, which makes a change. No choir. Congregational singing quite hearty but swamped by very loud organ. Finally there was a sermon of nearer ½ hour than 25 minutes! After the sermon there was an organ voluntary – presumably to get people properly awake again. The collection was a surprise. There were 2 collections – this much I gathered from the announcement but, of course, could not understand what they were for, tho' we were told. Then the sidesmen came round with two bags each, one red and one blue. This part did catch me off guard and I had to fish for a 2nd coin.

'The sidesmen all wore black suits with striped trousers, hard white collars and light grey ties. For the collection they put on black gloves and took them off again when it was safely gathered in! The collection was very nonconformist. They marched up to the communion table with it – very much like Wesley Church – and then retired, pulling their black gloves off.

'I had a hymn book with tunes, but my Dutch numbers not going above about 7, I was unable to find the right ones because there is no hymn board and one must therefore understand the announcement.

'The apostles' creed is recited in the service but only by the minister. I gathered from the hymn book that the church is the Dutch-Reformed Church – I think a kind of Lutheran. There were Lutheran Evangelical papers at the bookstall. A sidesman told me that the infant prince will be "baptismed" in that church next week …'

Once his lecture course was completed, Robbie did not stay for the examinations but flew home.

— ✦ —

Now in need of a break, we took what I described afterwards as 'the perfect holiday to restore Robbie's wellbeing'. We simply drove northwards to Arncliffe, a small village in Littondale we had enjoyed before. This time we were not in the Falcon Inn itself but at Bridge End, an old house run by Marmaduke and Mary Miller – he being an artist who had formerly run the inn. To the children's delight their garden ran down to the beck, caramel-coloured and sparkling, where they could throw sticks and stones for the two house dogs; and the house itself was said to be where Charles Kingsley had conceived the idea for his *Water Babies*. The weather was at first poor; but it provided a great thrill. We had arrived on a Thursday evening when there were shafts of sunlight between big clouds. Then it began to rain, and continued all Friday, mostly in torrents.

'… In the afternoon we tired of sitting indoors and went gently by car up the dale, seeing the white spates all along the fellsides. By the time we came back, about half an hour later, the car could only just get through a flood on the road. And the rain went on. We listened to fishermen's yarns in the inn, and got drenched every time we went out.

'When we came over to [Bridge End] to change for dinner that evening, we found the sittingroom and diningroom carpets being taken up, and the men of the house trying to reckon up how far the beck might rise. Later, when the children should have been asleep in bed, the drama began, for waves of brown water began to spread across the lawn. The level rose and rose, and the children, standing in the stone porch wrapped in odd coats over their pyjamas, had the thrill of seeing it about 8 inches above ground level, held back only by a wall of earth sods across the entrance. In the diningroom we looked beneath the floorboards – and there, at last, there was rushing brown water. This rose and swamped a part of the floor, and threatened to spring through the cracks of the rest. But at that point the rain stopped and the flood held for a while, then quite rapidly began to fall.

'… the beck had risen about 10 or 12 feet on Friday evening – something which happens about only every 10 years – so the children had an experience they won't forget.'

Next morning there were fresh trout for breakfast. As it grew fine, the children and I swam in a pool beneath a waterfall in Cowside Beck. We listened to Marmaduke Miller's tales and bought one of his delightful watercolours.

Once back home, Robbie was tormented by indecision about the impending conference of the *Institut de Droit International* in Nice. After his alarming experience at The Hague, where he had passed out all alone one night, he needed me to be with him, and nobody was available to look after the children. He had started work on a new Opinion; time was running out … So in the end he decided to cancel the project altogether. That left him with calm days in autumn sunshine, working in the Squire Law Library, catching up with college gossip, and eventually indulging in a three-day break at Overy Staithe in Norfolk.

In December, at the end of a busy term, he was happy to take a train up to Bradford after lecturing in London, to address the United Nations Association there on 'Human Rights'. He stayed with Aunt Alice at Wibsey and called on his few remaining friends and relations thereabouts. Another link was renewed when his old schoolfriend Harold Holdsworth called on us, home in England on leave from Dar-es-Salaam, where he was University Librarian.

That busy year culminated in a very happy Christmas and the Bicknell party, with rockets, hot-air balloons, and a number of great set-pieces such as *Don Quixote & the Windmill, The Battle of Trafalgar* and – highly topical this year – *The Sinking of the Torrey Canyon*. What a privilege, and what fun!

Beagle Channel and Jersey

1968

1968 brought new challenges to add to his many other commitments. The Opinion mentioned some months earlier was on a major case concerning a territorial dispute between Argentina and Chile of a totally new kind. The disputed territory this time consisted of three islands lying in the southern channel between the South Atlantic and the Pacific across Tierra del Fuego. The islands – Picton, Nueva and Lennox – were claimed by both Argentina and Chile, and although in a desolate area close to Cape Horn, they were of strategic significance. Very careful and complicated preparation was needed before presenting a 'Memorial' to the Court of Arbitration. As with the *Encuentro* case, the original definition of the division between the two territories had been vague, since it was laid down before a detailed survey had been made of an area so remote. The *Treaty of Arbitration* of 1902 had, indeed, been 'a treaty without a map',[146] merely saying 'to the east' or 'to the south'. The solution would require close examination on the spot.

Robbie was now advising, too, on a quite different matter, 'the relationship of the States of Jersey with the Common Market'. That is the way I referred to the matter of his first visit to the island in February 1968 for consultations principally in preparation, with the UK Foreign Office, for the *English Channel* case (the Arbitration between the UK and the French Republic on the Delimitation of the Continental Shelf, eventually to be settled in March 1978). As we were to learn, the Channel Islands' relationship with mainland Britain is unique – as 'British crown dependencies' they are at once independent and yet firmly linked.

Both cases were to take much of Robbie's attention for years to come. But our ordinary life went on, with many colourful events added. Right at the

---

[146] – as described by one of the arbitration tribunal, Professor André Gros

beginning of January an unexpected visitor arrived. This was 'the caravan lady', as the children called her – Rosamund,[147] whose car had broken down. One of the 'Rosaceae' who had run Bowderdale Farm in Wasdale, Robbie knew her well so we took her in and fed her, though she and her sheepdog slept in the caravan. She was to become a significant figure in our lives over the next few years.

We subscribed to the excellent Thursday Concerts given in the University Music School, hearing many up-and-coming quartets and soloists. (On one occasion I noticed Prince Charles in the audience – 'a very nice shy earnest young man: I believe he plays the 'cello in the Trinity orchestra'.) And in February we at last acquired a small television set, and were glad of it when the children had to take to their beds. Home life did not always go smoothly –

'Dear Granny,
On Monday the Dokter came and fond out that Dicky had got mesles. Then when they had finisht they went to the kitchin and fond that Mummy had left the tap on and in the sculary ther was a flud, about 2 & ½ inches high, so Mummy scoped it up in a dustpan. Today Daddy loked the car keys in-side the car.
        Love from Pippa.'

On 9th March 1968 Robbie set off to Argentina to see for himself the disputed islands in the Beagle Channel. Expecting rough weather at the southernmost tip of South America, he was equipped (reluctantly, as one normally dressed in a three-piece-suit or tweed-jacket-and-flannels) with an Arran sweater, thick trousers and a heavy cagoule. His letters to me described the adventure – his excited response, first to Buenos Aires and then to Patagonia and Tierra del Fuego, where he was shown the Beagle Channel and the three islands at its eastern end that were the subject of the dispute with Chile. The following are passages from those letters:

---

[147] Originally Rosamund Frere, she had married Tom Crichton, a barrister. That marriage had failed, and she was at this stage rather shakily married to a retired naval officer, Jim Templer.

*Sitting in aircraft on
airfield at Comodoro Rivadavia.*

We started this morning from Buenos Aires on the 9 am ordinary plane to this extraordinary place on the coast of Patagonia – wild, empty, volcanic landscape, but rather beautiful brown and yellow colours, especially when there is a momentary glimpse of the sun, which seems to be very seldom. The only asset here is a certain amount of oil.

The main feature here, however, is already wind. It was exceedingly bumpy coming in – and the children on the plane were sick. The next leg of the journey is to continue in the same 'plane to Gallegos, the most southerly point served by ordinary, civilian, services. But we are held up [… and were delayed by bad weather until nightfall.]

…Then it was decided that the 'plane would not go at all. So we are in the hotel of this town – a kind of frontier town. There is oil on the bare hills around. There is a fine ocean. But for the rest it is just like the frontier towns of the cowboys. In fact that is what it is. It serves the big Estancias in the country. There are saddle shops. And walking around we saw some very tough-looking sun-browned men in wide trousers like bloomers who are, I suppose, real cowboys. Alas I did not have the camera handy.

Well, there it is. The first day of the great adventure has had its interesting moments but rather a lot of boredom. Very like being back in the Army – just waiting. [Late in the evening the passengers were to be taken 20 km out of town for a meal. But by then it was 9.30 pm – 1.30 am for Robbie: so he declined, and went to bed in the hotel.]

Tuesday 12 March
Ushuaia

We started at 8 am from the hotel at Comodoro Rividavia in a bus for the airport (5 kms). There we waited and then waited. At 11 am we were off in a Caravelle for Gallegos. Gallegos is a real frontier shanty town with dusty gravel roads and streets. But some fine looking children and the very poor seem to be clean.

Then we were taken to the Naval Base at Gallegos and had a good but interminable lunch in the mess, presided over by a Captain of the Naval Air Wing. After every delay – they are great ones for standing around talking

– we were allotted to our next conveyances, for two of their planes were needed for our party – besides me, de la Guardia who is legal advisor, Captain Rio (Navy), a Mr Lima (Foreign Office), Professor Daus (geographer), Mrs Gibourg (F.O.) and a young woman whose name I have not yet caught. (F.O.)

I was allotted to the small plane – a Beechcraft. It was a dear little 2-engined propeller affair with old-fashioned piston engines, and room for 3 passengers besides crew. I was astonished to find that the Captain who was station commander was to be our pilot. It seemed absurd to have so much gold braid to drive that tiny little aircraft.

Of course it was a joy because this is the true flying – quite different from jet flying in pressurised cabins. You fly underneath the clouds, you feel the movement of the air, and you can see every detail beneath. Besides, you really are flying instead of being hurled through the sky.

At first there was more of the unspeakably melancholy wastes of waterless Patagonia – empty and sandy but showing fine browns and yellows in the sun. There are almost no people for stretches of hundreds of miles.

Next we crossed over the eastern end of the Straits of Magellan – not very exciting but of course a magic name. Gradually the landscape changed, and areas of vegetation appeared as we got further along the eastern part of Tierra del Fuego. Then mountains in the distance. Then a lake and after that wooded hills, followed by mountains rather like the Lake mountains, but wooded on their lower slopes, then mountains with snow. It was a splendid and exhilarating experience to weave in and out of the mountains in our tiny plane, marvellously piloted. We were lucky too in having a perfect day, with plenty of cloud but clear of the tops except little bunches of cotton wool clouds clinging to the summits here and there. This was certainly a great experience worth coming all this way for.

Having woven in and out of these mountains and hills – very like the Highlands of Scotland but quite quite empty – we turned towards the coast again and approached the Beagle from the sea, quite low down. What a romantic place it is. The mountains here are more like the Alps, with sheer rock faces. And the channel runs straight as a die, and quite narrow, towards the massive glaciers and snow peaks of the Chilean Andes – and through them is the Pacific.

We landed at Ushuaia and found ourselves eventually here in the Albatross Hotel – very new, very fine hotel, with spacious rooms and wooden floors with rugs, rather like the best kind of Swiss mountain hotel. The town is again a shanty town of rusty corrugated iron and dusty roads. It is, after all, the most southerly town in the world by a very big margin. B.A. is 3100 kms northward. And the Antarctic Continent is not so very far to the southward.

It is odd to traverse those miles of desert in Patagonia and find this breathtakingly beautiful place at the last stop before Antarctica.

It is not really very cold – a pleasant nip in the air which I like very much. The hotel is overwarm and I had to open the window.

Curious interview with the Governor of Tierra del Fuego. Ushered past a sentry, we entered a wooden house and found him in a large, old-fashioned room with an Argentine flag stuck in a wooden base dominating the room. We were sat down at a green baize table and given an aimiable lecture on the elements of the Beagle problem. I think he must have forgotten that his audience was almost the whole legal staff of the Foreign Office!

Tomorrow we board a naval frigate at 6 am! We shall be in the charge of the Commanding Officer of this naval base – a delightful, fresh-faced, bullet-headed, pipe-smoking man, who looks more like a don than an Admiral.

Well, there have been long periods of wretched waiting and frustration this two days past, with everybody restless and anxious. But what a reward! And what a privilege to see this country – for except for some excursion steamers in the summer, there is *no* means of getting here except by grace of the Navy. But it surely will become a tourist show place in the next 20 years, when I suppose they will have to run a sort of steamer service connecting with the jets at Gallegos. For there is no room for an airstrip for jets at Ushuaia.

Wednesday 13 March
Ushuaia

Up at 5 am in the dark to be piped (or rather to tag along with the piping of El Capitan Rio) aboard the frigate, as I suppose she would be. This was a great experience. We had the complete freedom of the bridge and one learnt a great deal about the management of a ship by watching and listening. We had to pass through the Paso MacKinley, which is narrow and difficult, and one was able to partake of the tenseness and concentration and even anxiety of such a manoeuvre. The complication of checks and counter-checks is surprising. The commander of the watch stands at a porthole with a windscreen wiper and receives shouted information from watches at direction finders on both sides of the ship, the chart table, the radar, the depth-echo-finder, the engine control and the helm. Sometimes this is in response to his shouted questions. And all the time he is giving commands in the Paso, changing the bearing every few seconds. Clearly the room for human error is still very great. But it was fascinating to watch.

It was a pearl day, with low cloud – but almost windless, raining sometimes but at others almost bright. We went right out to the Atlantic, where there was a tremendous swell, and back up the channel by another course. In all we sailed for 12 hours from 6 am to 7 pm or a little more. One ought to have been very tired after standing most of the day – but it was so stimulating that it did not seem to tire one.

We were very well fed in the ward room at meal times – there was a constant flow of coffee and soups to the Bridge anyway.

The scenery was for all the world like the Highland lochs – perhaps even kinder than that at the eastern end – more like the Lake District. But almost empty of human beings, and with a fresh nip in the air (tho' it was not cold) that is almost a special smell of countries near the Poles.

Apparently the massive Antarctic Continent has a much more powerful influence than the northern 'iced-water' Polar regions. So this is, as it were, even further south than appears from its latitude, remote as that is. Today we were once within about 10 miles of Cape Horn and the Polar ice is not very much further – especially, apparently, this year.

The proof of the nature of the climate we saw, most excitingly. On the way out we saw a school of 3 small whales, swimming and wallowing most beautifully. And on the way back we passed a small island and there was the scene one has so often seen in illustrations to polar expeditions – hundreds of penguins just standing around with, it seemed, no more than inches between them, as if they had so multiplied that there was no longer room to sit down. And for anyone who knows about duck this must be a wonderful place – obviously they are present in great variety.

… We have completed our task here but there is no possibility of getting a plane tomorrow so we are stuck for another day, and I gather we are to have an excursion by car to some beauty spot in Tierra del Fuego. But I wonder about the weather. It has already been kind for two days and that seems to be a good ration for many days. It is raining hard tonight.

Wet first thing – went shopping for postcards to send to the children – no light task with my Spanish!

About 11 am it began to lift a little and a Navy Land Rover turned up to take us to Mount Olivia – a very attractive little excursion past rocky, sheer mountains reminiscent of Chamonix. The night's rain had fallen as snow on the tops, and now the sun filtered through the clouds to make the scene one to uplift the spirits. In the valley a clear stream meandered through meadow and woods. No pines here. All the trees are hardwood (mainly 'linga'), so it looks very like the Lake District except that the mountains are higher, more ragged and have snow a good deal of the time. Back to the hotel for lunch.

After lunch another excursion to Lapataia (Indian name) which lies westward, near the Chilean frontier, in an Argentine National Park. Over dirt roads with splendid views of the Beagle Channel, then inland a little along the Rio Lapataia. Then suddenly the road stopped at the edge of the most heavenly lake I have ever seen. Clouds were still low, but lit by sun from time to time, and constantly, rapidly shifting colour and shadow. In the background the glacier mountains, framed on either side by intricate folds of kinder hills. The lake quite still – not even a ripple on the bank – the only sound from the abundant bird life. It was a moment of great happiness and I ran about taking photo after photo trying to capture for you the changes of colour and shape as mist and rain formed different atmospheres. Today at least the lake was so beautiful that it was impossible to be other than joyful just being there.

The frontier crosses the lake here, so really we were standing in Argentina but looking at Chile.

Then back a little way to a very attractive new hotel for tea. There was a fine, very large dining room with splendid views; and a log quite six feet long burning in a vast grate. ... In front of the hotel was a sleigh straight out of a Christmas card – used for getting about in winter, I suppose.

I am somewhat embarrassed by being under-dressed for this trip. Taking Enrique's concern about cold far too seriously, I packed as for an expedition in the wilds and never thought of the social life in Ushuaia. So I have no jacket with me – and this evening we are bidden to dine with the Commadore of the Naval Station at his home. Having confessed my embarrassment, however, my good Argentine friends have rallied round, and Professor Daus, who is pure gold, has found a spare jacket which really fits me very well. So I shall feel reasonably happy tonight instead of conspicuous.

The Navy has treated us splendidly – everything very efficient and everybody most friendly. I forgot to say that on the ship yesterday I talked with one officer – very efficient one too – whose English was obviously the real thing. No, he was Argentine bred and born – but had an English nurse! One of the midshipmen had been to Portsmouth in his training ship and was anxious to practise his English. He it was who pointed out the school of penguins to me when I would have missed them, being at the time on the other side of the ship.

———

Friday, 15 March
Hotel Plaza, Buenos Aires

Conveyed by service Jeeps to the Commandant's House. Rather Spanish in assembling about 9.30 pm, when we were expected to drink neat whisky on very empty stomachs, beginning to eat about 10 pm. And we certainly ate very well when the time came.

… After dinner came the most delightful surprise (the party, by the way, included the captain of the ship we sailed in). One expected the usual desultory conversation over coffee. But the Commandant took a beautiful Paraguayan Harp (smaller than ours) from a corner and played tangos in a most accomplished manner for perhaps ½ hour. Then he put it back in its corner and emerged with a guitar and played that most beautifully. Next he wanted to sing but could only do so with the lights out. The light being out had a magic effect, for through the big windows one now saw the backcloth of Ushuaia Bay, the lights of Ushuaia on the far shore, and behind that, great snow mountains silhouetted against a cloudy sky made silver by moonlight. And so the Commandant took his guitar again and sang to it in a fine, powerful voice produced Spanish style – sad, melancholy, tender tunes. Then a change that made me wish I had more Spanish. It sounded just the same to me, but the company were shouting with laughter every other line. Some parodies I suppose. I gathered one was about a countryman who saw a motor for the first time and went back and described what a car does with the aid of a pre-car set of images and ideas. One can see the possibilities. Finally some rousing songs with refrains in which the company could join. I tried to imagine an English Naval Commander singing to a guitar after dinner, and the Foreign Office legal staff, led by Fitzmaurice, joining in the chorus with beaming faces and clapping hands!

Then the C. put his guitar firmly away, stood up, and we all went home. Perfect evening and another wonderful slice of life.

Bed at 1.30 am. Up at 5.30 am to catch a plane.

Friday morning we went in two lots. I was assigned to the Governor's plane lent to us for the occasion – a dear little 4-seater piloted by a huge, flowing, elderly man with whiskers and a patient smile. No uniform this time – just a very old jersey. To climb we had to circle southward and saw the great bay which extends behind the circle of islands almost to Cape Horn – in fact the end of the bay is the 'Falso' Cape Horn, easily mistaken for the true one. Then, having gained height, we headed northward to the great snow peaks. It seemed we had not enough height to clear them, but of course we did, and there we were in this tiny 1920 type plane dancing just above cruel sheer peaks of ice and snow. I shot the camera right and left and all round through the Perspex with little hope of success but just because it seemed criminal not to try.

Then a dull flight, comparatively, over the flat part of Tierra del Fuego, the Straits of Magellan, and part of Santa Cruz to land at Rio Gallegos, where we caught the Caravelle jet via Comodoro Rivadavia to B.A. Beautiful weather.

So ended my most exciting journey bar none.

———

Plaza Hotel, B.A. Sat.

Meeting all morning with de la Guardia[148] and all the staff working on this problem. The Minister breezed in at one point, made polite conversation for 2 minutes and breezed out.

Then lunch at a restaurant along the River Plate with the de la Guardias. The Plate is the widest river in the world – looks like sea most of the time but it is just possible to see the Uruguayan shore from a high building. It brings down so much clay silt that it looks red-brown in colour. But I believe the water is quite clear and clean and there are many bathing places along the spacious promenades.

Then sightseeing in B.A, by taxi. An attractive city – though the colonial buildings are, I'm afraid, rapidly coming down. I am told that to see a colonial

---

[148] HE Senor Ernesto de la Guardia, 'Ambassador Extraordinary & Plenipotentiary', was the senior Agent on the Argentine team for this case.

type capital still one must go to Montevideo, which, though on the northern bank of the Plate, is actually south from B.A. because the river bends southward and Montevideo is nearer to the mouth.

Weather very pleasant with sunshine but getting quite cool. The summer is over, they keep saying.

Sunday Plaza Hotel, B.A

Easy day. Walked in morning along Avenida Santa Fe, the B.A. Bond St. Then read and wrote. Nice lunch of cold turkey and a salad made of fresh sliced apple and pineapple and lettuce. Siesta. Tea with ham sandwiches, cakes and very good tea (clearly the English tradition is strong here, but it is now directed towards scores of rich Americans who throng the hotel – the most revolting I find are the so prosperous looking American parsons – 'have another cake, Father' – tucking into this luxury…).

This evening the Gibourgs are to take me to the Ballet – at the San Martin theatre: the 'Colon' Opera House is closed, for the 'season' is winter, i.e. June, July, August.

Plaza Hotel B.A. 18.iii.68

Ballet was in a very fine theatre finished 10 years ago – indeed there are 2 theatres in the same building as well as a large cinema, cafes, etc. An atmosphere of great spaciousness and good taste. *Constanza* (Chopin) was a bore; *House of Usher* – Poe & Morilljo – was beautiful but also rather a bore; *Bolero* – Ravel – was vulgar but exciting for the music. The Gibourgs refused even to clap for the *Bolero* for they said the choreography was more suited to an American musical. Valid comment: but I found excitement in something like 60 dancers at 3 levels on a huge stage all dancing at the same time, and enjoyed it most of all.

Then to La Cabana, a famous restaurant, for supper. We talked and talked about every conceivable subject including religion and whether or not to have children (the Gibourgs so far have not). Then I was made to walk the streets – especially Corrientes, the lively theatre street, to taste night liveliness in B.A. Then coffee at an Italian bar on the ground that the coffee at la Cabana was not good. To bed about 2 am. Up at 7.30 am. The after-lunch siesta makes this possible.

'Plane between B.A. & Rio

7.15 pm Tuesday 19th

Yesterday had a meeting all morning with the legal people and the naval people. Then lunch with the Minister for Foreign Affairs at the Jockey Club – charming person with perfect English – a great admirer of George Brown,[149] whose resignation he much regretted. Brown seems to appeal very much to the sophisticated type of person one would expect to react unfavourably. As expected – most charming, but I was grilled all the time – not a comfortable situation with his own legal adviser there silent and staring at the ceiling (he is far from talkative in any situation and has long periods of complete silence, but a most kind man all the same). The others present at the lunch were Lastra, who *was* Ambassador in London before the revolution, the present Ambassador to Chile and a former Ambassador to Chile. Nice lunch.

Then shopping. Then work till late writing a tentative report on my conclusions.

Today – meeting all morning to discuss my paper. Then great lunch at La Cabana of all the people who were on the Ushuaian team – a sort of farewell lunch for me. Then two young men saw me to the airport, looked after my luggage and tickets and saw me on to the 'plane.

Altogether a very satisfactory visit for me and I hope for them. They seemed pleased. The Foreign Minister had wanted to see me again this morning but he never sent for me, and then we discovered that the President had sent for him! The visit was certainly worthwhile. Quite apart from seeing the area, they were able to tell me things that could not have been put into letters. I think I won their complete confidence and I don't think there was anything they kept back at our final meeting. They could not have been kinder.

Towards the end I was glad to find myself just beginning to pick up the drift of conversations.

Now for Rio de Janeiro, then 9 hours of sea, Madrid, Paris & London.

---

[149] George Brown was Foreign Minister and Deputy Prime Minister in the Labour Government at the time, but known for his love of alcohol.

A week after his returns from Argentina Robbie turned his attention to Jersey. For the family it provided an Easter holiday; for him, an opportunity for consultations with his clients. From a farmhouse at Grève de Lecq, in the north, we explored the island in an open-topped Triumph Herald, getting repeatedly lost in the maze of narrow lanes inland. Robbie's discussions were with Senator Ralph Vibert, President of the States committee on the Constitution and Common Market, the Greffier and the Bailiff, and were at this stage concerned with fishing limits. A warm friendship developed with the Vibert family, and our children were to have great fun with them on each of our visits to the island.

But even while enjoying our stay in Jersey, Robbie could never concentrate exclusively on one matter. I wrote:

> 'Robbie is reading a Spanish article about the Beagle Channel just now: he has been hopping about *such* a lot in the last month! Last Wednesday he gave a little talk to the older children in the village school about his Argentine trip, illustrated with some of the slides he took'. [And a few days later I was saying] '... there are two new interesting projects. One is further work for Persia, which may mean a trip to Tehran in September; and the other – a continuation of his previous work on Space Law – is the chairmanship of a committee considering the international control and conservation of the environment. This includes control of pollution of air, sea and land, and of things like large-scale increase or decrease of human or animal populations, or the creation of artificial lakes or manipulation of weather, which can alter ecology. It's a most fascinating and enormous field of study; and one of the people who has agreed to serve on the committee is, I gather, the Duke of Edinburgh.'

The suggested committee under his chairmanship did not materialise, and he did not visit Tehran. But he was increasingly aware of potential developments affecting the environment which would need international regulation.

———

Our ever-expanding circle of friends included a wide range of nationalities and interests. One who turned up at our house was Dick Matthews[150], 'a strange scruffy character for the children to encounter, with his smelly pipe and torn

---

[150] Later to become Professor R.E.F. Matthews, FRS of the University of Auckland, New Zealand.

flapping shirt over a singlet …' the New Zealander who, with his American wife, had occupied rooms below mine when I was a secretary on meagre pay. It was typical of Robbie that he was drawn to this outlandish biochemist and found him an amusing companion.

One of our stranger evenings out was with Meredith Jackson[151] and his wife. She was an ethnic Chinese from Jamaica – its first woman barrister. Their other guests that evening were Dr Joseph Needham[152] and his wife, and a woman friend, Dr Lu. We ate a succession of Chinese dishes in their courtyard – the rather dreamy atmosphere enhanced by the passage of a hot-air balloon across the moon – and then went inside to hear Lenli Jackson playing the piano.

Dinner with Alan Pars was quite different. We had to present ourselves, formally dressed, at 7 pm (regardless of baby-sitting complications) for a sumptuous meal served from the Jesus College kitchen. Women guests must withdraw for coffee and 'to powder their noses' while the men made merry over port for some time. The suggestion that Dame Mary Cartwright[153], another Girton don and I should meanwhile chat about the latest fashions left us simmering with indignation.

In that summer we managed to take two family holidays. The first was in Cornwall, staying in a cottage belonging to Miss Stocker, my first teacher. Its joys included 'motorail' from London, exploring coves on both south and north coasts, and chugging along creeks in the Fal in our aged hostess's small boat (and Robbie as usual attending to some of his casework in quiet intervals).

The second break was up north to Rosthwaite, in Borrowdale. As we walked and climbed I found the high fells, coated with heather, under broken skies, irresistible for a photographer, and so those holidays are preserved on colour slides. But my husband did not believe in total holidays, especially when there was an impending International Law Association conference:

'Robbie has been working hard in the evenings, preparing for his Buenos Aires conference. Once or twice each day there have been long telephone calls from London to discuss material for the meetings – the Shell legal man

---

[151] Jackson had in 1966 become Downing Professor of the Laws of England.

[152] Master of Gonville & Caius at that time, Dr Joseph Needham, CH, FRS, FRA was immensely distinguished both as biochemist and sinologist. He wrote a massive history of Chinese science.

[153] Mistress of Girton, and mathematician.

has been in between ringing New York and Curaçao for contributions to the discussion!

'...All through our stay in Borrowdale he was working on a draft, which was telexed to various places, and comments on which were received by long telephone calls each evening from London and, finally, a two-page cable from New York. What with those and the Special Delivery packages, it was fortunate that Rose Cottage is in fact the Post Office for Rosthwaite!'

After one day at home, he was off to Buenos Aires for the ILA conference[154], returning eight days later.

And so his busy life continued, with meetings with Shell lawyers and consultations over Jersey's sea boundaries fitted between academic commitments. He found time, too, to write an article for the *International & Comparative Law Quarterly* on 'The Limits of Continental Shelf Jurisdiction,'[155] which considers questions of general principal thrown up by current UN discussions about deep sea resources. Without mentioning his advisory work for Jersey, it examines problems in defining *continental shelf* – the matter which was to come to arbitration in the *English Channel* case some years later.

---

[154] The 1968 conference was chiefly concerned with Diplomatic & Territorial Asylum.

[155] The article, 'The Limits of Continental Shelf Jurisdiction: some possible implications of the North Sea Case Judgment', appears on p.1042 of his *Collected Writings*.

Advancement

1969-70

The occasional fees that Robbie was now receiving for his bar practice helped but did not entirely dispel his anxiety over planning a secure future for his family. At 55, and at a time when the Wilson government was imposing ferocious taxes, he was anxious lest premature death leave his wife with insufficient provision for the education of three young children. It was time to apply for promotion to QC:[156]

That application to the Lord Chancellor summarizes his position:

'Alongside my purely academic work I have for some years had a steady practice in international law, and am at present under instructions from the Shell International Oil Company, Imperial Chemical Industries Ltd, the Argentine Government and the Government of the Sudan and I have recently completed work for the Japanese Government. The work is mainly advisory but I have pleaded as junior counsel before the Arbitrators in the Argentine/ Chile Frontier case. It is my intention to continue in this practice whether or not my present request be successful.'

His sponsors were The Rt Hon Lord Wilberforce, PC, CMG, OBE, QC and Professor Sir Humphrey Waldock, CMG, OBE, QC.

It was one of those fierce winters: a blizzard created snowdrifts 4 ft high along most of the Bridle Way, and by the end of a busy Lent Term we were ready for our break in Jersey. Robbie expected something in the post that morning, but nothing was delivered at Grantchester, so before the arrival of the car to take us to the airport, he made a dash into college – where, to his

---

[156]   The first I heard of this was when the clerk of his chambers, David, rang and asked to speak to Robbie '– It's about his application for silk, Madam'. I knew that R. was a 'junior' barrister, and that there was a higher rank, Queen's Counsel; but as always, he had kept quiet about his aspirations.

relief, the important letter had arrived, and it confirmed his appointment as Queen's Counsel.

We were once more based at Lecq Farm and were treated by the Viberts to a grand beach picnic; and this time a dinner was given for Robbie and Stanley de Smith[157] in recognition of their work for the States of Jersey. That stay was followed for Robbie by a meeting in Utrecht. I then (leaving the children with their grandparents in Kent) joined him in London to spend the evening at a performance of *The Barber of Seville*.

He 'took silk' on 15th April 1969, having received detailed instructions beforehand about the ceremonial and dress. Glanville Williams had offered to lend some items from his own set of these bizarre garments;[158] but in the event, it was Peter Oliver, head of 13 Old Square chambers, who, with 'characteristic kindness … lent [him] his whole outfit, from wig to buckle shoes.'[159] Robbie had to set off early to his chambers to dress, then, with his clerk, proceeded to the House of Lords where, in the Moses Room, each of the candidates in turn read their declaration before the Lord Chancellor that they would 'well and truly serve the Queen as one of Her Counsel learned in the Law…' After a break for glasses of champagne, they were introduced to the Royal Courts of Justice. Entering a court (interrupting a trial – whether divorce, burglary, fraud …), these quaint figures 'took their seats within the Bar' after bowing to the judge, bowing to the left, bowing to the right and turning to bow to Junior Bar. The judge then says '… Do you move?' The QC rises, bows to the judge and leaves. This strange procedure is repeated in each court; and I was amused to notice one or two, when traipsing along the corridors between courts, limping with the agony of their borrowed shoes.

Finally, having received his Letters Patent, been photographed and then refreshed with coffee and smoked salmon sandwiches in Thirteen Old Square, Robbie could change into normal dress, and we returned to Lydd for a quiet evening with the children and grandparents. Home we came next morning, to a heap of congratulatory letters. McNair's said:

---

[157] S.A. de Smith was at that time Professor of Constitutional and Administrative Law at the LSE, but moved to Cambridge as Downing Professor. Robbie was distressed by his death, aged 51, in 1974.

[158] There is a superabundance of buttons – 24 on the jacket, 10 on the waistcoat; and the full costume includes knee breeches and silk stockings, besides wig, ruffles, buckle shoes and silk gown.

[159] Quoted from a speech RYJ gave to the Law Faculty many years later.

'I am very glad that you have taken silk. It is most important for international law that those who profess it should be identified in the public mind with the practising profession, therein differentiating us from those who profess English law.'

And old Mrs Holdsworth, having been sent a photograph of the new QC in his borrowed finery, said it made her feel 'all happy within'.

He had now reached a new stage in his career. Although he had no intention of reducing his commitment to his Cambridge academic work, his increased professional fees allowed him to give up the regular lectures he had been delivering in London to the Inns of Court School of Law.

A new custom at Jesus was the series of Evening Talks given each term by one of the Fellows about some topic he – and it was still 'he' – was working on. These talks could be fascinating. Laurence Picken recruited sixteen musicians (undergraduates and fellows) to perform some pieces of ancient Chinese music that he had transcribed from old manuscripts; Alan Percival showed the Hercules aircraft engine that he had designed during the war; the young John Adkins taught us about 'superconductivity'. The elderly Pars, after explaining a very elementary concept quite successfully, would then jot down at great speed a few "amusing" or "elegant" proofs expressed in algebra, leaving many of us baffled.

It was not easy to interest an audience of both fellows and wives, and when in April Robbie took his turn he was at first nervous. But once settled down, he spoke with his usual clarity and humour about the Argentina v Chile boundary disputes, illustrating the current one with some of the slides he had taken in Tierra del Fuego.

The next time Rosamund turned up with her dogs, the children began begging us for one of their own. Oh dear, surely life was already complicated enough! But once shown some young outcasts kept in a shed on a remote farmstead in Essex, we all fell for the shaggiest one, Rags, and brought him home. Robbie was as delighted as the children to have this messy, disruptive addition to the family.

Among other diversions, at the end of May Robbie had to open a Methodist garden fête at the small church[160] on the Newmarket Road for which he had

---

[160]   Called Meadowlands, it merged with an Anglican church next door in 2004 to become the Church of Christ the Redeemer.

laid the foundation stone in the 1950s. We enjoyed dining with the Argentine Ambassador, where we learned that their government was secure for some more years. And at a less formal dinner with our friends the Fishers,[161] we found the other guests were

'... a young bachelor history don, Edward Norman,[162] and the Regius Professor of History (Master of Selwyn, soon to be Vice-Chancellor) Owen Chadwick[163] and his wife. A good deal of discussion of the direction of undergraduate demands: Cambridge hopes, by a certain slow-moving magnanimity, to weather present storms.'

It was the period when 'revolting students' were emulating the disturbances in Paris and elsewhere. Their rebellious attitude manifested itself largely in deliberately sloppy dress, long unwashed hair and even bare feet. A new Students' Union was formed (quite unlike the Union Society) which was allowed to send a representative to attend meetings of the Council of the Senate. (My nephew Jonathan Bennett,[164] an undergraduate at Christ's College, was one of the first of these spokesmen.) At Trinity, Lord Butler ('Rab'), the Master, defused potential trouble by inviting the student body to make their complaints known to him over refreshments with wine, and was so affable that they were unable to behave disagreeably.

There was a general relaxation of formality, even at Trinity Ladies' Night –

'... Robbie, finding himself [in the seating plan] next to Lady Butler, had crammed himself into boiled shirt and white tie – and I broke my thumbnail extracting him from it afterwards! – the shirt is now in the dustbin and he is resolved to get a soft pleated one next time he has to be ultra-formal. I was very lucky in my neighbours: on my right I had Mr Nicholas, ex-Bursar of Trinity and our successor at 3 Claremont, by now an old friend; and on my

---

[161] D.J.V. Fisher, medieval historian and Fellow of Jesus.

[162] Dr Edward Norman was, after his time as Chaplain at Jesus, to hold successive senior appointments as an academic and in the church. As historian he was of 'the Peterhouse school of history', and gave a series of Reith lectures. Later in life, he converted to the Roman Catholic church.

[163] The Rev. Dr Owen Chadwick, of the utmost distinction, would later receive the honour of KBE and become a member of the Order of Merit.

[164] Now Professor Jonathan Bennett, Associate Dean for Students, Hull York Medical School.

left Sir Lawrence Bragg, the great physicist (and opposite him his old friend Sir George Thomson – both giants of the Cavendish Lab.[165]) Bragg was a dear, friendly and amusing.

'But there was an unexpected clamour suddenly in the middle of dinner, when long-haired demonstrators from King's broke in shouting, and distributed leaflets around the hall before being hustled out by waiters. It was the presence of Enoch Powell, who generally comes to these dinners (he is, I think, an Honorary Fellow) which was being protested about.'

Robbie's law students generally dressed tidily. And while some undergraduate members of CUMS might turn up to rehearsals looking grubby and dishevelled, for concerts they appeared in black ties and dinner-jackets: singing and playing music was *important*. But many displayed their indignation about perceived injustice in demonstrations against apartheid in South Africa and other matters: the protest which attracted greatest publicity was to occur in February 1970 – the 'Garden House Riot' about the situation in Greece, when a number of undergraduates were arrested and one of the Proctors was injured. (That Proctor was Dr C.B. Goodhart of Caius, years later to become Pippa's father-in-law.)

Good college tutors were prepared to listen to their charges, and had a steadying effect. Robbie maintained a close relationship with the pupils he supervised and who attended his seminars, and in most cases the link was sustained for years after. Like his hero McNair, he would suggest topics for theses; would discuss the development of their careers and support their applications for jobs; and in his later travels he was often to be rewarded with invitations to their homes, or sent books and offprints acknowledging his helpful influence.

Several examples of that close relationship occurred in July 1969. First, he became concerned about the mental breakdown of a brilliant young woman ex-pupil, patiently responding to her frantic night-time telephone calls from hospital. Another, Delbert Smith, American, was now working with NASA and had a special gift for us, a photograph of Earth taken by an Apollo spacecraft. The date on which we received this awesome image was 21st July 1969 – the day after Neil Armstrong and Buzz Aldrin had stepped onto the

---

[165]   Both Bragg and Thomson were Nobel Laureates. Bragg said he regarded my uncle, G.M. Bennett, as one of his 'star pupils' in crystallography.

Moon's surface for the first time – so a memento to be cherished. Some well-meant gifts were consigned to a cupboard, but most of them could be seen in Robbie's study, where one might notice an Australian boomerang, a carved head from Nigeria, the heavy ornamental walking-stick of a Somali tribal chief or a box containing a silk scroll from Japan. He never liked to dispose of things with interesting associations.

Another former pupil who called was Chai Fook Loong, with wife and young daughter. He was from Singapore, and eternally grateful to his former Tutor for having devised a way of admitting him to Jesus, where he took a 'Special' degree in Chinese and gained a Half-Blue in badminton. The prosperous business career he later developed enabled him to give generously to his old college.

It was in July 1969, too, that Lord McNair wrote to Robbie, thanking him for his letter on a proposed Bill of Rights, adding –

'… We had quite a good debate [in the House of Lords] and were alerted to many new kinds of abuse of human rights – "bugging", long-distance telephonic communication, telephoto lenses, &c – particularly by Ritchie-Calder who made our blood curdle. One interesting thing he said is that in 1939 when Nils Bohr the great Danish physicist escaped from Denmark to London for the purpose of helping the Allies, the only way he could safely converse with Sir Henry Dole, President of the Royal Society, was for them to sit on two chairs in a remote part of Hyde Park!'

That August we spent a fortnight at Arncliffe, staying at the Falcon Inn once more. The village was utterly quiet[166] and had enticing tracks leading to remoter hamlets. It rained, of course, but there were gloriously fine days; and the children revelled as much as we did in those limestone hills and becks, with unfamiliar birds and wild flowers. One day we took the car up to Malham Moor and wandered around Malham Tarn and down to Gordale Scar. Then, at Kirkby Malham, we admired the splendid church and spent some time

---

[166] – and we recommended it, later, as a good place for the artists Angela Taunt and her mentor, Ben Nicholson. For our Silver Wedding, Angela gave us a cherished watercolour of Littondale.

searching for some trace of Robbie's forebears. It was a large churchyard, with sheep grazing; its many gravestones were covered with ivy and moss, and we had no real idea what we were looking for – it was just a tale that 'Aunt Liza'[167] used to tell, of family burials in that churchyard. Finding nothing, we gave up the quest.

———

The *Institut* meeting that year was held in Edinburgh. After attending the greater part of its conference, Robbie was straightway thrust into the world of Shell once more. John Blair came to spend hours of Deep Sea discussion – preparation for a weekend conference at Ditchley Park[168] on *The Resources of the Ocean Bed.*

———

Grantchester presented us with a completely new concern when, taking Rags for his usual walk in the fields one day, I found a young man installing a large yellow concrete cross by the corner of our garden. It marked, I was told, the edge of a new road. We had been told nothing of this, and nor had anyone else in the village. My indignant letter to the *Cambridge Evening News* led to Robbie being shown the outline plans for what was called 'the Western Bypass', a projected dual-carriageway road (indeed, a motorway.) Robbie attended the next Parish Council meeting to rouse support for some sort of opposition to this outrageous scheme, and set up the *Grantchester Protection Association* consisting of three QCs – himself, Martin Nourse[169] and Professor Glanville Williams (who lived in Trumpington;) also two or three architects, and two solicitors from the village. It was a formidable group; and to protect his Lord's Bridge Radio Telescope on the Barton side against radio emissions from passing traffic, Professor Martin Ryle[170] raised his own objections.

Robbie's committee held a series of meetings to prepare their case, which was played out in a long-running Enquiry held at the Cambridgeshire Shire Hall. Eventually the route of the M11 was altered, to run equidistant between Grantchester and Barton and be lowered between banks planted with trees; also

---

[167]   Sister of RYJ's grandfather, Bob Brotherton

[168]   The Ditchley Foundation runs two-day conferences on international relations.

[169]   The Rt Hon Sir Martin Nourse, as he later became, rose to be a Lord Justice of Appeal. He lived in Grantchester at the time.

[170]   Later Sir Martin Ryle, Nobel laureate and Astronomer Royal.

with a metal fence as extra protection for the Lords Bridge Radio Telescope. Although a distraction from their other work, the group had all found the battle quite fun.

After some harsh wintry weeks, the 1970 New Year saw Robbie back in action. On 2nd January he attended the funeral of Jim Grantham, the Downing friend who had introduced him to sailing on his yacht 'Clottie' (*Clothilde*). Straight after, he caught a train to London to see the Iranian Ambassador. Next day he was in London again, taking the family for their Christmas treat, a children's opera, *Lucky Peter's Journey*, based on a fairytale by Strindberg and composed by the Master of the Queen's Music, Malcolm Williamson. It was a disappointment – managing, in Robbie's words, to be 'both heavy and shallow' – though the sight of Trafalgar Square's Christmas tree almost made the trip worthwhile for the children. At home, he planted 17 trees and shrubs in the back garden to provide a sound-barrier against the threatened motorway.

At Easter we were again in Jersey, where he combined his advisory work with fun provided by the Vibert family. This time the highlight was a visit to Corbière lighthouse, where the lighthouse-keeper set the foghorn lowing – a shattering noise from close to. (It carried for 17 miles, so we hoped it caused no confusion to shipping that sunny day.) There followed winkle-picking from the rocks, a treasure-hunt, tea and mad cricket amid the sand-dunes of St Ouen's.

After the children and I left, Robbie stayed on for more serious work with the Crowther Commission.[171] He was delighted to find that two members of that Commission actually came from Idle. (One was Norman Hunt,[172] economist and frequent broadcaster, who lived just down the road from his own house. And the other was the Principal of St Anne's, Oxford, who instantly recognized him, as she was the daughter of his old headmaster.) The Commission's work must have been in preparation for negotiations with the French Government over fishing boundaries: not a straightforward matter, since there were rocky outcrops – the Ecréhou and the Minquiers – claimed by the States of Jersey,

---

[171] This was, I think, the Royal Commission, a group preparing for British negotiations with France about the continental shelf boundary in the English Channel.

[172] Later Lord Crowther-Hunt, who headed the Royal Commission on the Constitution, or *Crowther Commission*, which eventually produced the Kilbrandon Report, on which he dissented.

and a tiny archipelago, the Isles Chausèy, by France. When Robbie rejoined us at home he revealed that the Royal Commission had been given a jaunt in one of the States launches over to the Normandy coast to land on the main Chausèy island, where they had eaten a delicious eight-course lunch.

But that trip had not, of course, been entirely for fun. In determining the true 'median line' between the French and British[173] coasts, there had to be close technical examination of any small islands or rocky outcrops between them. The whole matter of 'territorial waters' was becoming one of increasing complexity, no longer entirely resolved by rules proposed in Grotius' *Mare Liberum* of 1609. The great areas of 'continental shelf' were now being exploited in ways never contemplated before. And in Malcolm Shaw's words,[174] 'The vital fact about the continental shelves is that they are rich in oil and gas resources and quite often are host to extensive fishing grounds.' One case after another would reflect the rival claims of neighbouring states to these resources.

Once back from from Jersey, Robbie was plunged immediately into discussion of a new case with an American counsel, Northcutt ('Mike') Ely[175], engaged by Sharjah[176] for negotiations with *Buttes Gas & Oil Co.* in the search for oil beneath its coastal seabed, a field in which Robbie had by now some expertise.[177] His work for *Buttes*, which later became *Crescent Petroleum*, would enable their offshore seismic explorations to identify the Mubarek Field where on 31st July 1974, after 'wildcat' drilling, a rich oil well was opened. (That precise date is celebrated on one of Robbie's odder mementoes, still on a shelf in his study: a small phial containing a sample of oil, the first fruit of their legal work.)

This was yet another major concern to be fitted into Robbie's congested timetable as he settled back into the routine of the university term with all its commitments. Typically, one Saturday was spent in Cambridge discussing Sharjah in the morning and the Beagle Channel in the evening.

---

173 The Channel Islands, being a 'crown dependency', are regarded as part of the UK.
174 *International Law*, 5th edition.
175 Northcutt Ely, of the Watergate Building, Washington DC, was a lawyer with expertise on seabed mining for oil and other valuable resources.
176 Sharjah, one of the Trucial States on the Persian Gulf, is mentioned here at the inception of the *Buttes Gas & Oil* case. Robbie would later take part in its border dispute with the neighbouring Dubai.
177 See his article, *The Limits of Continental Shelf Jurisdiction: Some Possible Implications of the North Sea Case Judgment*, 1969, pub. in ICLQ and p. 1024 of *Collected Writings*.

He was not the only international law don to lead such a life. From Cambridge, Derek Bowett who had just been elected President of Queens' College[178] was involved in practice, as was Eli Lauterpacht (and, later, Christopher Greenwood, David Lloyd Jones, James Crawford and others); and successive Chichele Professors at Oxford, Humphrey Waldock and Ian Brownlie were as well.

———

Dicky's 14th birthday was notable, not only for his acquisition of an Albion press and a range of printing apparatus from our neighbour Miss Clay,[179] but for the delivery of our second car, a Triumph Herald for my use. That June, we actually attended a Royal Garden Party, too. It was a hot, hot day, heavy and humid – made memorable by the almighty thunderstorm that broke just as we wandered in the grounds by a small lake enlivened by flamingos. As the downpour began the whole scene changed as all those in morning suits, fluttering dresses and hats, oriental and African robes or military uniforms dashed in a genteel stampede for the shelter of marquees. Once home, we were glad to peel off our sticky clothes and resume our normal (though never tranquil) life.

Before we took off for the Lake District that summer, Robbie heard that he had been elected an Honorary Bencher of Lincoln's Inn, another pleasing advancement. The holiday itself, because of late booking for a family of five, had to be in two parts: the first week at Yew Tree Farm in Rosthwaite,[180] with a range of walks in mixed weather; and the second in the annexe of the Lodore Hotel. There we arrived on the Swiss National Day, celebrated with a sumptuous buffet. They had a record of our honeymoon stay exactly 15 years before, so Robbie and I drank claret with our dinner that night. The sun shone, we rowed across the lake, I swam with the children in the swimming pool … Then, on our final day, I was called to the telephone at breakfast, to hear that my mother, after a decline of many weeks, had died.

Robbie (fitting in a meeting at Coward Chance on the way) and I went down to join the rest of my family in Kent for the funeral.

---

178 The Heads of Houses (colleges) have a variety of titles. At Queens', the President is the Master, whereas at Jesus the President is Vice-Master.

179 A retired art mistress, Miss Clay came from the family of Richard Clay, printers in Suffolk.

180 – recommended by John & Cherry Hopkins, themselves keen fell-walkers. John became Senior Tutor of Downing; and Cherry, a Fellow of Girton, assisted Robbie in editing the *BYIL*.

In August 1970 the biennial conference of the International Law Association was held in The Hague, and once again we all crossed to the Netherlands, this time staying in the Kurhaus[181] on the seafront at Scheveningen. Its rooms were vast, its corridors wide enough for a coach, and at its centre was a concert hall. There were, moreover, other young families attending the conference and so the special excursions were suited to all ages. The children went with us to Amsterdam for a visit to the Rijksmuseum and a boatride along the canals; to Gouda and to Rotterdam and by boat to Schoonhavn. Finally, there was a huge informal party held in the Fish Hall (its concrete floor slightly slippery with fish scales), ending with the entry of a noisy brass band played by fishermen in blue smocks and wooden clogs – and a winding conga dance of delegates and families.

For Robbie, of course, the proceedings had its serious purpose. John Blair was there, and also Joyce Gutteridge,[182] probably presenting the conclusions of their 'ocean bed' committee at one of the sessions. In this huge gathering were people from all over the world with whom he had been corresponding, or whose articles he had read. And for me it was an introduction to many whose names and faces would become increasingly familiar (and increasingly important) in the years ahead.

Among the general junkettings we managed to fit in a dinner for the Stork family; and it was through an introduction by 'Tiddle' (Marijke Stork) that we visited Sijthoff's printing works, where Dicky, keen printer and typographer, was able to watch the production of a variety of printed matter, from newspapers to bank notes.

Our exchange of Christmas presents that year reflected our private interests. Robbie had found for me a good Nikon camera; and I gave him a workbench for the carpentry that he dreamt of doing in his spare time and on retirement. But while I would make great use of my camera, his 'spare time' and 'retirement' remained pretty much a dream. Work, in its fascinating variety, absorbed most of his time, and when he needed to rest, the gramophone or televised cricket provided refreshment.

---

181 The Kurhaus was still in its original 1887 state, lavish and eccentric.

182 Joyce Gutteridge, daughter of H.C. Gutteridge, Professor of Comparative Law at Cambridge, was in the office of the Legal Adviser to HM Government, specialising in 'ocean bed' matters.

Arment House: A Dream Fulfilled

1971

A sudden distraction arose when, in March 1971, Robbie quietly asked me how I felt about the possibility of his being a candidate for the Mastership of Corpus Christi College in succession to Sir Frank Lee. A law Fellow of the college[183] had made the suggestion, but we needed to think carefully about its implications. A week later he dined at Corpus, and a little after that we were shown around the Lodge. It was difficult to balance the sense of excitement at being considered for a fine and ancient college with dismay at the extra complication to already action-packed lives ... and eventually Robbie asked for his name to be dropped. Sir Duncan Wilson was elected Master.

Once again the Easter vacation took us all to Jersey, and this year the highlight, arranged by Ralph Vibert, was a visit to the Isles de Chausèy – a trip taken on the States launch since its purpose for the lawyers was to see again those disputed small outcrops, the Minquiers and Ecrehos, on the way. The wind was Force 5, the sky grey, the Corbière foghorn hooting, and one or two members of the group felt seasick; but the weather brightened and it became for our family a delightful adventure. The main island was so small that we could walk all around it (though the skipper of the launch had to stay nearby, adjusting its moorings as the tide rose and fell – a range of 40 feet.)

Rosamund, the Caravan Lady, had called in on us quite often in the past year *en route* between Cumberland and Norfolk, where her ancient uncle was ending his days in a nursing home.[184] She now had no real home: Bowderdale had been let to a Cumbrian farmer;[185] a second marriage had failed and she had

---

[183] This was Chancellor the Rev. Garth Moore, great authority on canon and ecclesiastical law.

[184] The uncle, a retired cleric, and his late wife had taken responsibility for bringing her up – the unwanted child of a successful barrister.

[185] Joss Naylor, famous as a champion fell-runner.

only temporary use of a friend's cottage. Having got wind of a property for sale in Eskdale, she realised that it might offer a solution. Robbie, she knew, loved the Lakes so dearly that the thought of a holiday cottage would appeal, so she suggested he should look at the place.

It was term-time, but off he went one Saturday on an overnight train to Barrow-in-Furness, changing to the stopping-train that meandered up the coast to Carlisle. Thus it was that, early on the morning of 1st May, from Ravenglass he took the narrow-gauge railway to Boot in Eskdale. He walked along the road and up the narrow track (known as a 'lonning') in mounting excitement, and reached Arment House[186]. The 'Particulars' of the property, as provided by the estate agents, were as follows:

> Set amidst unspoilt panoramic mountain scenery "ARMONT HOUSE" occupies a superb tranquil position approximately 1 mile from the Village of Boot which is situated at the head of the Ravenglass and Eskdale narrow-gauge railway. It stands on a strategic site at the head of an occupation Lane leading from the Boot to Hardknott Pass roadway and looks on to Birker Fell and Hardknott with Scafell in the near background.
>
> This typical example of Lakeland Property is beautifully constructed of colourful local Eskdale Stone under slated roofs and retains all its old-world character. It comprises an extremely comfortable Dwelling-house with a loft Barn and other Buildings adjoining; a separate Range of similarly constructed Out-Buildings which have the possibility of Planning Consent (see Lot 2), together with Garden Ground, Orchard and Pasture Land belonging thereto, the whole containing 1.6 acres or thereabouts.
>
> The property will be offered either as a whole or in two Lots as may be decided at the time of Sale which provides a rare opportunity for those wishing to reside in a unique Lakeland setting.

The owner, who received him and showed him inside, was Mrs Whattam-Ward, a sweet widowed lady, formerly an art teacher. She was quite severely lame and had decided, sadly, that she was no longer able to live in such isolation. Rosamund had called at the house but been refused admission, but Robbie she seems to have instantly trusted. By the time he found his way out

---

[186]   We decided to adopt the spelling used on the Ordnance Survey map, one of many alternative versions used over the centuries.

by the back lonning and down a narrow track to the Esk, his enchantment was complete. He had taken a camera with him, and took just a few shots to give the family a glimpse of what he had seen that heavenly morning.

The sale was to be by auction in nearby Gosforth a month later, but he could not possibly attend, nor did he like to entrust Rosamund with the bidding for the property. He therefore appointed an agent to do his best to get it at a reasonable price. On 10th June, a day of pouring rain, the auction took place at The Globe Hotel. Lot 2 (barn buildings across the yard from the small farmhouse) did not attract bids, so the two lots were combined. And our agent acquired the whole property for us at £12,600. At the sale of furniture, Rosamund bought just an oak table and a small oak corner-cupboard.

For the next two months, until the end of the university and school terms, the Jennings family had to remain at home. When Rosamund spent a night with us in Grantchester we arranged that she should occupy and look after Arment House free of charge, so that it was well-kept in readiness for our own visits whenever we could manage to make them. Her excited letters in spidery writing arrived almost daily, telling us how she had furnished it cheaply from the auction room in Whitehaven; how she planned to grow vegetables in the small upper garden; and how meat, bread, milk and other provisions could be found …

At last we were able to make our own first visit – Robbie, with Dick, in a car loaded with luggage (cutlery, folding bed, sleeping bags and such), and I taking the girls by train. After changing at Ely, Nuneaton and Barrow-in-Furness, we eventually arrived at Ravenglass to be met by Rosamund, who drove us up the valley to Arment House.

Our first impression was astonishing. One entered the lonning by an opening in the drystone wall along the road so unobtrusive that it might easily be missed. There were three gates to be opened and closed as one made one's way up the overgrown and rutted track. At the final gate one was confronted with a range of granite barn buildings, at the end of which was the modest farmhouse with its whitewashed front. Across the yard was another massive range of barns and a small granite outhouse, intended as washhouse below and hen loft above. There were small fields, ash trees and sycamore; and set beneath a sheltering wall was a stone pump. Looking back, the view was a great panorama of hills – the Scafell range to the left, Hardnott Pass in the distance ahead, and to the right Harter Fell and the looming mass of Birker Moor across the Esk valley, with a high waterfall down its rocky front.

Robbie later described his own first impression on entering the house.

'Why do Lake District farm houses – at least the older ones – have a pleasant, distinctive smell, quite different from the smell of other houses? And what makes the smell so distinctive? Old timber, or flag floors, or acid soil, or what is it?

'When Dicky and I first arrived at Arment House it was empty, because Rosamund had gone to meet the others at the station. So we let ourselves in and had the house for a brief time all to ourselves. And that wonderful smell – very strong – met us in the entrance hall. For me it brought back keen memories of Lake District farm holidays when I was Dicky's age and younger. That smell made me happy with the house from that moment...'

We found that Rosamund's cheap furniture included a shabby large sofa in the main kitchen (known locally as 'the house', the place where most of one's time indoors was spent) and that her two shotguns were resting across the hooks on the beams above our heads. Now and then she might take a gun outside to try to pot a rabbit. She had, that first evening, prepared a good meal for us. Despite increasing rain on the first few days, we sorted our belongings, ate lunch at the Woolpack Inn, shopped for food at Boot and Gosforth, drove into Wasdale to have tea with Rosalind at Mill Place, her own very attractive cottage, and the day after took tea with our nearest neighbour at Christcliff half a mile away, Dr Marca Burns, an expert in animal husbandry. Next day, in fine weather, we walked up the valley – through Penny Hill farm, on to Brotherikeld and on into Upper Eskdale to the waterfalls of Throstle Garth. And this, a fulfilment of Robbie's dream, was enjoyed by us all.

As the days passed, though, there was a growing unease about our relationship with Rosamund. Robbie, having known her for some years and understood something of her troubled background, wanted to help her in her latest difficulties. But while providing a rent-free home, her exact status must be made clear. He took a piece of paper and on it wrote a brief statement that she was required to sign, acknowledging that she was a 'bare licensee'.

Once this thoroughly unpleasant confrontation was disposed of, we spent the rest of our stay exploring further, one day climbing Harter Fell, another revisiting Throstle Garth, Robbie and Dick striding further on and to the top of Bowfell. On a day when Rosamund was in Whitehaven, the children discovered two ancient bicycles in one of the barns and joyfully clattered about the yard on them. Every other day one or two of us walked down to Boot to collect 7 pints of milk and bring them back in rucksacks; Dick and I took a long hot walk up onto Birker Moor, blundering through bog, rocks and miles of purple heather to Green Crag... And at the end of our stay, our Grantchester neighbour, the architect Peter Hall, joined us, to make drawings, take measurements, and discuss the possible conversion we thought of making to one of the big barns.

That first stay set the pattern of our spells at Arment House for years to come: walking when the weather invited, cutting bracken and grass with a sickle or scythe, mending gaps in drystone walls where Herdwick sheep had knocked down the lumps of granite, and getting provisions as far as possible on foot. On a soaking wet day the girls and I 'sewed toy creatures out of old socks' – it was a great place for learning to improvise, with no radio or television by way of entertainment! And on Sundays we would walk down beside the Esk to St Catherine's church, where we enjoyed the unaccompanied singing of hymns.

Arment House meant a huge amount to Robbie. He had only recently earned enough money to buy it, and it must not be spoilt by our tenant's behaviour. His dream was of spending every possible break up there among his beloved fells, but one obstacle after another was to present itself in our complicated lives. Over the years we fitted in visits whenever possible, and the children and their friends did so too.

Part of our original Arment project was to make an imaginative barn conversion of the high granite range alongside the old farmhouse. Peter Hall produced architectural drawings for us. But the cost estimated by Alan Tyson, the local builder, exceeded what had been paid for the whole property, and we hesitated. Then Tyson himself suddenly died, and the scheme was abandoned.

―――

Having to visit London so often, Robbie felt he should join a club where he might stay the night, and was made a member of the Atheneum. There he stayed when, in October 1971, he addressed the Jesus Old Boys at their annual dinner at Simpson's, and on one or two other occasions. But it did not really suit him, this grandiose hushed place, and at some point he joined the Oxford & Cambridge Club instead. There he felt at home, and – although at that time a wife (even an Oxford graduate) could not ascend the main staircase or venture into its bar or library – it was possible for us to spend a night together there on the rare occasions when I accompanied him to some evening event in London.

In addition to his other commitments he was now advising the state of Brunei and since both the Argentine and Chilean teams had set up offices in Geneva to make their preparations for the *Beagle Channel* case, he needed to make visits there, too. By December I could write to my father that 'the Sharjah [case][187] is now very satisfactorily concluded, and it remains to be seen whether he will ever be paid for the 18 months' work he put into it!' ... following, in January 1972 with the remark 'I expect you will have noticed that Robbie's Sheik of Sharjah has been shot ...'

I was hoping my father might enjoy hearing about some of our social events, such as a Sunday lunch with the Radzinowiczes.[188] One with a Cornish connection I knew would interest him:

'... A group of the senior dons and wives at Jesus were invited to dinner to meet Miss Quiller-Couch, who was here for a visit. It really *was* fun. She must be in her 60s or 70s, and is astonishingly like 'Q' in appearance[189]; and she talked with me quite a bit, so that I'm now nostalging for Cornwall terribly. Her first name is "Foy". She left Fowey because the house, I think, became uninhabitable – coastal erosion was eating into the garden, anyway. So she went to the Lizard peninsula and lived there for years. And now she has just moved into a part of the big house at Lanhydrock. Alan Pars talked to her about the du Mauriers, and mentioned Gerald du Maurier's performance in *Dear Brutus* ... and we found that J.M. Barrie was her godfather. She's a wonderfully friendly and enthusiastic person ...

'—and that party went straight on to the next event, which was the termly talk by one of the fellows. It was by a maths don [Derek Taunt[190]], explaining the mathematical fun involved in ringing the 40,320 changes for

---

[187] This antitrust case, *Occidental Petroleum Corp. v Buttes Gas & Oil Co.*, was of great importance and led to further work for Robbie on sea boundaries.

[188] Sir Leon Radzinowicz, Professor of Criminology, had recently married his second wife, Mary-Ann, a distinguished American academic.

[189] We were all familiar with Q's appearance. In Robbie's case, there was a vivid memory of the man himself – also known to my father from his prominence in his native Cornwall, where he had for some years inspected his taxes.

[190] Derek Taunt's speciality was in 'group theory'. He had worked during the war on the Enigma codebreaking at Bletchley Park.

a Grandsire Triple. Miss Q seemed to enjoy it, and by luck was able to be introduced to the artist Ben Nicholson, whose father Sir William Nicholson had painted the portrait of her father hanging there in the Upper Hall. A proper "name-dropping" evening!'

———

At this time university business was sometimes disturbed by student unrest. As I reported,

'... Cambridge had one of these minor but unpleasant and carefully-publicized "sit-ins" last week. The pretext was a "demand" to see the Vice-Chancellor and extract from him promises to change the regulations for the Economics Tripos Pt.I, something which is currently being considered but has not yet been pronounced upon; but also absurd requirements – e.g. that cleaners and porters be represented on academic bodies discussing courses of study, &c ... Their manifesto was quite childish. The young people (our paper says "600 students" – the movement itself claims "some 2,000" – but there were certainly far fewer and a great many were probably the usual "extras" imported from the Technical College and Essex University, and hippy hangers-on whose numbers grow) got into the Old Schools building and then persuaded the Proctors to let them have some keys so that they could use the lavatories. Then they broke the promise they had given to come out at a certain time, and were only evicted a day later by a High Court injunction. And of course the lovely University Combination Room and other fine rooms, including the Squire Law Library, had suffered a good deal from their presence – irreplaceable carpets damaged with cigarette-burns, the Council Chamber broken open with a crowbar, and so on. The place was so filthy that it could not be used for several days, and so Robbie on Monday lectured in the University Church. He found it an excellent place for lecturing; and his own students (he gets an audience of 200 or more, of all sorts and nationalities) were particularly nice and courteous!'

This was a difficult winter, for we were contending with frequent power cuts arising from the miners' strike at that time. A dinner in the Master's Lodge at Jesus, perfect as usual, was made memorable by being entirely by candlelight. But the extra effort in contriving that perfection must have led to the Master's wife, Katie Page, suffering heart trouble soon after. We all in turn went down with 'flu as well; and Robbie,

> '...feeling that Satan might find work for idle hands to do, occupied himself very agreeably by writing down for the children a description of his Grandfather Brotherton. ... As part of the exercise, he wrote down memories of all the shops in Idle, working along both sides of the street.'

As March progressed he spent many precious hours at the motorway enquiry, most of which was slow-moving and tiring. But it included, on the 15th March, a moment of glory as he conducted the first cross-examination of his career, pressing the Landscaping Engineer to divulge details of the road's planned line between Grantchester and Barton. After years of discussion and protest, preparations for the section of the M11 motorway (not fully to 'motorway' standard) passing Cambridge would be begun in late 1976 with the fencing-off of fields full of potatoes (gathered by eager neighbours, who arrived in cars with forks and buckets). It would be completed at last in 1980.

In early April 1972 we spent a fortnight at Arment House. Days of rain meant that the hilltops were scarcely visible though spectacular floods, and cataracts added interest to our sorties for food supplies, occasional breaks in the cloud revealing Eskdale in its full glory. Robbie laboured in the lonning with pick and shovel, and we managed just one good family walk up Harter Fell – halfway in hot sunshine, then slogging through wet snow in thickish cloud.

An overnight break at Casterton on our way home exorcised any feelings of depression about Arment House problems. We spotted a poster announcing a performance of *The Gondoliers* in the Village Hall, and went along. It was a triumph: the local operatic society, accompanied by an energetic elderly lady pianist, put heart and soul into the choruses – hefty folk with rich local accents – and the Duke of Plaza-Toro had the ripest accent of all. Robbie and family never forgot the joy of that evening.

When it came to the next half-term there was no chance of going north, since Robbie was examining 210 Tripos scripts and many LL.B. ones, some in almost indecipherable handwriting. It happens that some extra-large pads of clean-on-one-side paper kept for family drawings are really the charts of Tripos marking. Some typical RYJ comments, added to those of his co-examiner Cherry Hopkins, on candidates identified only by numbers – are:

'Fascinating! Quite incredibly pompous and plausible rubbish. Says "I quote". Should go into politics.'

'Shows shrewd comprehension of the true problems. *I* would raise. The 1ˢᵗ class marks are mine

'Reread – I perhaps overdid it but there *are* good answers and 11 is one of the best on this subject and very full.'

He was anxious to give what credit he could. An example he would enjoy quoting was the dim candidate who wrote '*Grotius was*' ... and then dried up. He thought it only fair to allot one mark for the existential truth of the statement.

In July Robbie spent a few days in Heidelberg, taking part in a small conference discussing the future of the International Court. He wrote to me:

'Frightening turn-up. Select body and all the best people. Had I seen the list first I would never have accepted to talk to them about a matter they all know more about than I do...'

His address went well, though, and he was able to enjoy the later part of their work.

At last we managed to take the family up to Arment House for our summer holiday. We found that Rosamund had moved out with her caravan, having done some rough-and-ready tidying but leaving us to set to, the moment we arrived, to clean decayed crusts and mouse-droppings and plain grime before feeling able to prepare meals or sit down. Her complete indifference to her obligations as a 'licensee' left us hurt and bewildered, our dream of an idyllic retreat almost ruined.

But we cleaned up, and Pippa's friend Eleanor Huxley joined us. The girls decorated their bedroom with cut-out silhouettes of horses and fantastic coloured birds, and went riding together from the farm just up the valley.

Robbie and I had been invited to lunch with Sir Claude Elliott[191] at his home by Buttermere. He had explained that, now aged 84 and dependent on the help of an elderly housekeeper, it would not be possible to offer a proper meal for the children. So for us, after driving through Egremont and past Loweswater, there was a superb luncheon and stimulating conversation, while the children were provided with sandwiches (and a bottle of cider for a startled Dicky) and left to wander in the garden. Elliott was, or at least had been, a passionate mountaineer, fellwalking regularly with his Trinity College contemporaries, Lord Adrian and Sir James Butler. Although he had a dignified presence, he was modest and he amused us with his recollection of his last visit to Eton on the Fourth of June. A dreadful realisation had grown that he, former Provost, was now a totally forgotten figure. He had slunk off to hide in the lavatories, and soon took himself away.

Everything at Arment had to be done the hard way. I found it difficult to cater for holiday appetites since Rosamund had left no provisions and we had no refrigerator, relying on the cool dairy/larder for storage. To collect milk (and on this occasion 9½lb meat) we walked down to Boot and carried it all uphill in rucksacks. When my brother rang up and announced that they (three of them) would like to join us, it strained my hospitality. We could not offer beds, but they arrived for supper and next day after sharing a long walk with us returned for supper again. After I had had to cook a third large supper for nine, Robbie felt this must be enough. The weather was so fine and hot that our shallow well was getting low. Explaining about the shortage of water, he rang the Lodore Hotel, where we escaped for two nights. And there we ate delicious hotel meals, did some shopping in Keswick, and rowed on Derwentwater.

Refreshed, we returned to welcome Dick's schoolfriend, an easy guest. His stocky build made him a splendid worker in the lonning, though less suited to fell-climbing. And he was clearly smitten with the beauty of Eskdale.

Among other callers that August, we had a brief visit by Mrs Whattam-Ward, whose nephew drove her up to view once more the place which she had owned for nearly forty years. She did not ask to see inside the house, but was delighted simply to gaze at the great familiar panorama and sense our own enchantment with the place. On selling the house, she had indeed tried

---

[191]   Sir Claude Elliott, fellow emeritus of Jesus College, former Headmaster and then Provost of Eton.

to convey her feelings to Robbie, writing of 'the freedom and peace' and of 'a sense of belonging to the wholeness of experience'.

In her first years at Arment House she, wearing callipers on her legs due to polio as a child, had to get water from the pump in the yard, and with no electricity had depended on oil lamps. By the time we bought the house, electric power had already been installed for lighting and for a night-storage radiator. An electric pump drew water from that shallow well. But the spring which in earlier times had evidently provided a plentiful supply no longer did so, and Robbie summoned a 'boring engineer' to examine the problem. He turned out to be full of amusing anecdotes, so was not too boring; but his best advice was to install storage tanks in the big barn above the pump-house, so that there would be a reserve when the well dried up. This was done, and it was also understood that as little water as possible should be used in the house. The privy in the small wash-house building across the yard must be used and Robbie himself actually enjoyed standing out in the yard each morning to wash with cold rainwater drained into a tub.

A dream house seldom visited does present problems: grass and bracken grows, Herdwick sheep knock down boulders as they leap over walls, woodwork flakes and rots, and one finds that mice have made nests in the row of walking boots on a high shelf in the hall. Since the original dream of creating a second holiday house was never carried through, the barns (and owls) were left undisturbed. The awkward entrance to the lonning, owned by Marca Burns, was widened, though, and we were amused to find that she, who was a committed Communist and whose first name derived from her father's admiration for Karl Marx, had set a notice by the gate: *PRIVATE. No admission.*

The Tyson family of builders were connected to former owners of Arment House. There were, indeed, all sorts of names, drawings and rhymes on the walls of the old granary and the hen-house – incised, too, on the capstone of the pump in the yard; and we found a lovely scratched signature on our bedroom window.

J & S TYSON

1837

Henry Tyson

Another Tyson (of a different family) was the young farmer from Wha House, up the valley, who ran his sheep and grew hay in fields around our land. Gordon Tyson became a good neighbour, as did his successors as tenants of that National Trust farm.

———

Once we had the place to ourselves we decided to prolong our stay a little. Pippa and Joey cleared out old flaky limewash and hen-droppings from the stoutly-built 'wash-house' across the yard to make their own playhouse; and Dick, who had been earnestly pursuing a geography project, wanted to stay behind to continue his research. It was a challenge for a 16-year-old, but we eventually agreed. He spent five days on his own, walking about surveying field-patterns and setting himself some private adventures which must have secretly alarmed him … but he survived, cleared up, and managed a difficult journey back to Cambridge safely.

The *Institut* meeting that year was to take place in Rome, but with dire reports of stifling heat and an outbreak of cholera in southern Italy, Robbie decided to miss the conference. Soon we were back to the congested routine of termtime: Dick as a day-boarder at The Leys, Pippa at Impington Village College, Joey at the village school, and Robbie attending to a bewildering range of responsibilities all at the same time.

———

All Manner of Experiences

1972

On top of his other commitments, Robbie was now being consulted by the Government of Venezuela. As the search for oil and gas beneath coastal waters grew more competitive and urgent, so too did the need for the resolution of national claims over those waters, and Venezuela had been found to have rich reserves. It was also in 1972 that his article on 'A Changing International Law of the Sea' was published in the *Cambridge Law Journal* – a subject on which he was now considered a leading authority.

The varied demands of his practice, interesting as they were, had to be kept in place, though: he was first and foremost an academic, and the College had elected him to serve once more as President. This time it was to be a more demanding appointment, as Sir Denys Page had announced his intention to retire as Master at the end of the academic year and that meant that Robbie must now organise the election of a successor.

He was obliged, too, to attend more college events, such as the long weekend celebration of the bicentenary of S.T. Coleridge, which attracted a starry gathering of English dons. Although preferring to join me in a village buffet supper given by the Huxleys, he attended some of its events on the Sunday morning, making sure to be in the college chapel for evensong to hear Gardner-Smith (retired Dean, now about 83) give a fascinating sermon on our regard for animal life, based on Coleridge's *Ancient Mariner* (Gardner-Smith being firmly of the belief that animals have souls and are as likely to go to heaven as we are).

We felt that we really ought to entertain all the college Fellows, by now such a large number. A meal for eleven of them at home went well, but entailed so much work that we could scarcely contemplate entertaining them all.

Eli Lauterpacht, two days later, had an easier time. I wrote that

'The new Oxford Professor of International Law[192] was here to take his LL.D., and so Eli Lauterpacht arranged a big buffet luncheon [in Trinity College] for his family (5 children) and all the Cambridge international lawyers and families. There were 14 youngish children in all; and when we decided it was time to leave, they had all disappeared. Robbie and I hunted all over the place – I found the O'Connell children with their mother in the gallery of the Senate House, but where were the others? Eventually they were found: after chasing around the Backs and in and out of Trinity, they were playing ball in the Old Kitchen, being offered more food by the butler!'

For us, Sunday lunch, always the most elaborate meal of the week, was a relatively easy way to invite two or three extra people at a time. And we gave occasiomal dinners – one for Professor Louis Henkin[193] and his wife – in the Fellows' Guest Room in college.

On 24th November we went shopping to prepare Robbie for another journey to the furthest tip of South America, and brought home a large cagoule, a glaring orange colour which horrified him. 'He is going to be encumbered with an awful lot of luggage for air travel', I wrote, 'because in Buenos Aires the temperature will be 90° and humidity high, while far south on a ship in the Beagle Channel he must wear wool and windproof clothes … and be sure to have a dinner jacket with him, too!'

Second expedition to Tierra del Fuego

Once again each party in the dispute needed to submit to the arbitration court a *Memorial* setting out the legal argument for its claim – while, at the initial stage, having little idea exactly which points their opponent may have chosen as the crux of the argument. This *Beagle Channel Case* involved an ill-defined boundary[194] which left uncertainty as to the ownership of three islands, Picton, Nueva and Lennox. An agreement of 1871 between the two countries had laid down that the islands south of the Beagle Channel belonged to Chile

---

[192]   Dan O'Connell, successor to Sir Humphrey Waldock in the Chichele Chair.

[193]   Henkin was Professor of International Law at Columbia University, NY.

[194]   The wording of Article III of the Treaty was ambiguous: '*to Chile shall belong all the islands to the south of Beagle Channel up to Cape Horn, and those there may be to the west of Tierra del Fuego*'. A useful summary of the case, together with maps and photographs, may be found on the internet.

and those to the north, to Argentina. But what, exactly, was the course of the Beagle Channel at its eastern end?

The Argentine team decided that if it could be proved that a branch of the channel (south of Navarino Island and then northwards along '*Paso Goree/ Goree Road*') had been the original course of *HMS Beagle* as it had sailed under the command of Capt. Fitzroy in 1831, then the three disputed islands, lying to the north of that channel, might be claimed by Argentina. This led to intensive historical research – a scrutiny of many fascinating charts, drawings and logbook entries, and the purchase by Robbie of his own copy of the four volumes of Fitzroy and Darwin's *Narrative of the Voyage of The Beagle.* Now, after anxious packing and repacking of luggage, on 25th November he set off to see the actual territory in more detail.

The following is his diary, sent as letters to me, in small scribbled writing: –

[He was received at Heathrow and seen off by someone from the Argentine Embassy, then had a very bumpy flight to Paris. On to Madrid, where, in bitter cold, they had an hour's stop. 'Gendarmes have long, loose capes down to the ankles like a Dickens coachman.' [The 10-hour flight meant a long uncomfortable night] '…So the morning is very welcome and, just as welcome, the iced-orange juice that comes first thing.'

… And there is the coast of northern Brazil, somewhere just south of the equator, forested and covered with a tropical haze. Put watches back 3 hrs on English time, or 4 hrs on Paris/Madrid time; so we find that it is still only very early morning after all, and still quite a way to Rio.

The view of Rio not so impressive this time. We came in rather away from the mountains, which therefore did not seem to embrace the 'plane as they did on previous occasions. The terrible shanty town up the hill very evident from the air. Not *very* far from Copacabana Beach!

Whatever Brazil is like as a country, the airport is dreadful – untidy, unbeautiful, unfinished. Even at 7 am there was a foetid, damp heat, with low cloud, and the effort to air-condition the transit lounge made no impression whatever. Everybody fanning their faces with their transit tickets. Staff lethargic and sullen. A depressing and sinister place. Have always been glad to see the back of the Rio transit lounge. It makes the aircraft seem like home by contrast.

Off in a rainstorm to Sao Paulo. A surprise. No sign of any city. Must be miles away. But the country here is green and forested. And the airport staff look more alive. Still heavy rain.

Off again for Buenos Aires. As we cross the River Plate and enter Argentine territory (north of the river is Uruguay), all the Argentines look round, smiling, and nod to me as much as to say, "Ah! We're all right now!" Oddly enough I feel much the same, rather to my surprise. But of course the atmosphere in a small plane load, cooped up together for nigh on 24 hours, is very catching.

But it *is* a sort of home for me as I quickly find. For even as I emerge from the plane I see friendly faces smiling broadly with real welcome and not just courtesy. It's nice to find people obviously delighted that you've come. Again VIP lounge whilst my passport and luggage are seen to, then by car to the hotel. Actually newsmen waiting!

Surprised again by the friendly beauty of the City. Broad avenues with lawns, massive forest trees, and the jacarandas now a mass of brilliant blue. Hot but not unpleasantly so. Sort of very hot English summer day. I don't mind that. And it seems luxurious after that oven at Rio.

Relieved to learn that we do not go south till Tuesday. We start 5 am from the hotel on Tuesday. And – to make Dick green with envy – they have decided that the little minesweeper we had last time won't quite do, so their Antarctic ice-breaker is being sent to the Beagle to meet us. We shall start in the minesweeper and rendezvous with the ice-breaker in the little cove on Picton Island where Thomas Bridges[195] first landed, and which he called Banner Cove. Since Picton is claimed by Chile, we feel that a rendezvous of two warships in the harbour, transferring counsel from the one to the other, will be more telling than sending letters with Picton postmarks.

The plan is that we return to B.A. on Sunday.

[At this point I should introduce Jeremy Carver[196], the very able young solicitor from Coward Chance who would accompany him throughout this trip, and who had made a thorough study of all the historical records concerning the first discovery and settlement of the Beagle area. Jeremy – tall, with ginger curly hair, a deep voice and rich sense of humour – proved the perfect companion for Robbie, and has remained a family friend.]

---

[195]   The English missionary, Bridges, settled in Tierra del Fuego in 1859, at the age of 18. He mastered the Fuegian Indians' language, and became enormously important to them and to later settlers. His son, Lucas Bridges (described as 'uncrowned King of Patagonia') wrote an account of the early settlement in a book called *Uttermost Part of the Earth*. The old Mrs Bridges referred to later is the granddaughter of the original settler.

[196]   Now Jeremy Carver CBE, he is a senior adviser for *Transparency International*, having been involved since its inception.

Monday

This afternoon, just before beginning this letter, I had a little sleep after a good bath. But yesterday evening was a typical Argentine evening. Knowing I would be tired, there was to be "just a simple supper at a quiet restaurant quite early". We (Carver and I) were to be collected at 6.30. We were finally collected at nearly 8.0! Admittedly it was partly because a Peronist demonstration had created great traffic jams. Of course it was then rather elaborate food which I didn't want at all and I got back not long before 11 pm, which was 2 am to me. But this morning I seem all right and plan a quiet day, resting as much as possible, before going south tomorrow.

It *is* rather warmer here perhaps than I thought. I'm glad of my tropical suit. In bed one is on a gentle sweat all the time. But it is a very pleasant warmth – not at all humid. It was nice having my continental breakfast by an open window with jacaranda trees just outside. The size and age of the trees in these city squares is a constant surprise and delight.

There are to be *two* professional photographers with the expedition: Jeremy told me that he tried very hard to get both you and Anthea [his wife] onto the expedition but I think they were afraid that they would be open to criticism for wasting public money (though none *would* have been: one could have travelled 2ⁿᵈ class and this is an enormous room with twin beds anyway!). However, perhaps one day the opportunity will arise. I should think by that time I could plead that I'm too old to travel alone!

I learn now that the main role of the ice-breaker will be to provide a helicopter with which to land on the islands, etc. We are likely to be shadowed all the time by the Chilean Navy, so it promises to be a curious little drama. Perhaps Dicky could put it on tape!

———

Really hot, after all, this morning – I suppose well up in the 80s. Spent morning reading documents, then had excellent lunch with Jeremy in the Plaza grill room. Very good food and very pleasant service.

After lunch we were taken to see the Commander-in-Chief of the Navy. Biggest building, I should think, in B.A. Up great bank of steps commanded from all sides by sentries with machine guns and even some on the entrance roof. But the sergeant signalled that we might approach. Met at the door by Captain Ornstein, who is coming with us on the trip. Then lifts and corridors getting ever grander, finally one with portraits of Admirals on all the walls.

This led to a pleasant room where we were received very pleasantly and simply by the Admiral and given tea and iced water. 10 minutes or so of courteous chat, everybody obviously trying to think of a suitable remark. Then very pleasantly dismissed.

On way out we were shown some of the treasures of the library. One was the First Edition of Fitzroy's "Sailing Directions" for Patagonia and Tierra del Fuego. On the fly leaf the following inscription: "Cmdr. Robert Fitzroy, presented by the Hydrographer" and below in a different hand, "This is Bob's book but he asked me to take care of it for him. Laura Fitzroy" (F's wife). Also the bookseller's note of the price: £1!

After Navy we went to Foreign Office and were pleasantly received by our old friend José Maria Ruda, now the Under-Secretary. Then to archives to look at some papers. Then a series of rather Argentine interludes. Learnt at F.O. that they had not booked any hotel rooms for us on return from the South. So we hared back to the hotel determined to do that for ourselves only to find that they had in fact been booked all along. Then telephone rang and we were told a man would come to collect our return UK tickets to confirm the flights. I had already done that for myself, but they insisted they must have the tickets. Both very loath to part with that little life-line of paper. However, we did get them back. Heaven knows why they suddenly got excited about them at 8 o'clock in the evening. Possibly because the official itinerary showed me as returning on the wrong day on a flight that does not exist on any day! However, this is all part of the atmosphere and one just learns to expect that someone will give all the arrangements a great undirected stir-up every so often. Rather reminds me of life in the Army.

Tuesday 28*th*

Up at 4.15 am. No trouble at all in getting breakfast brought to the room at 4.30! (24 hr service and very good too.) Decided that F.O. should be taken over by Plaza Hotel!

Rainy and humid. Off by jet 6.30. First stop at Trelew, the 1865 Welsh settlement. Had been heavy rain: rare in these parts. Then Commodoro Rivadavia. Very pleasant weather here, fresh and sunny. Temp. coming down. It was 75º at Trelew and 65º at Commodoro. Next stop at Rio Gallegos at the southern tip of Patagonia. Beautiful weather. Now c55º. Two-hour wait and change of planes to a "Fokker Friendship" – nice old machine, with old-fashioned propellers and RR engines. Pleasant flight to Rio Grande.

Introduced to pilot and saw the flight deck of a quite biggish aircraft. One-hour wait at Rio Grande. Still sunny and fine. Then over the mountains in thick cloud to Beagle Channel, overshooting it to lose height, then turned to approach Ushuaia from the south.

Ushuaia looking really most beautiful. It seems there was new snow last night and the mountains are white over. But now it is sunny and not a bit cold.

Met by Captain of ship we are to go on. No ice-breaker after all. Another Argentine "arrangement". Actually we find she is in B.A.!! But this is a nice-looking little ship, judging from the view we had of her as the plane came in to land.

The Argentine party will be at the Naval base, but Jeremy and I have a set of rooms in the "Albatross Hotel". What a terrible, terrible waste! We each have a large double room, the two rooms communicating as a sort of separate suite with a kind of lobby for the two. If only the Argentines could have felt able to let you and Anthea come! Seems awful having a spare bed to waste every night both in B.A. and here.

Really very nice room with view over Ushuaia Bay.

(Later) Most exciting evening. At 6 pm we started in a naval seaplane (an Albatross) to survey the area. Noisy, but wonderful pilots who would fly very low or high, and right over islands, just as we wanted. A superb evening, with the sun still shining when we got back at 8 pm. We looked at the whole area very closely. We went out as far as Evout (see chart) [– c30 nautical miles NNE of Cape Horn] to take a close look at a beacon the Chileans have put there. Then south again to Terhaltan, where Jeremy thought he saw something peculiar but it turned out to be hundreds of penguins. Very fascinating flying very low over these remote, stormy, uninhabitable little islands in the Cape Horn region, on a superb, calm summer's evening such as can rarely be encountered hereabouts. On one tiny islet we disturbed not only penguins but also a colony of seals.

Then we flew up the Beagle again and westward, took a very close look at the Bridges' place at Harberton, where they came out and waved to us. Then to look at the Murray Narrows, the wonderful mountains on Hoste, and the frontier at Lapataia. Then a great thrill. The navigator had kindly let me have his seat, with a superb view and the pilot let me sit there for the landing. Quite an experience landing on a little strip on the sea, between mountains, with a perfect view of what is happening.

It looks as if there will be sunshine most of the night. So far south and nearly at mid-summer, the daylight must be very long.

Dinner at 9 pm, then to bed. We do it by ship tomorrow but start only at 10 *pm* and sail all night and all the next day.

Wednesday 29th

Lay abed till 8.45 then continental breakfast. Hotel food a bit rough but all right. Place quite full with a sort of medical congress – whole families of them. They've all gone off on a sea-excursion this morning. Ushuaia much developed since 5 years ago. Clearly saw it just in time. There are now several properly-made roads, and they are trying to get some very young trees going along the seafront.

P.M. – Excursion to Lapataia and Lago Rocca. Superb afternoon. Sunny, very warm but fresh, snow on the mountains, high cloud, very clear. Able to see Sarmiento (the highest mountain hereabouts) from Lago Rocca with ease. Magnificent. Must have been too distant in the haze on my last visit. Tea at Alkushla Hotel, then back to Ushuaia.

7.30 pm. Piped aboard "Commodoro Somellera". Nice little ship. Poor officers have given up their bunks for us. Left Ushuaia in evening light. Surely most wonderful views in the world in all directions. Sea, islands, mountains of all kinds, all magnificent: glacier, snows – everything.

Long meeting till midnight about our programme of landings tomorrow. Expect to be off Evout about 6 am. So to bed.

Thurs. 30th

Up at 4.45 am to see sun rise behind the Island of Evout – very splendid sight. Fine, very clear, morning. Turn into Nassau Bay, a huge sea with snow and ice mountains and islands on all sides. Good sight of "Deceit" – an island that is in front of Cape Horn and hides it from us.

Then we follow Fitzroy's course, tacking east and then west, and at each extremity stop engines to allow the photographers to take a panorama of the horizons.

9.30 Approach Caleta Lennox where Fitzroy landed. Anchor about ¾ mile offshore. Jeremy, I, and Captain Ornstein are to land, by rubber dinghy with outboard motor. Don life jackets and go through drill, then over the side to dinghy, manned by two men in diving suits. Notice the life boat is swung out on its davits. The captain says it is "in case there are problems". I wish the young officer in charge of the dinghy did not look so nervous. Captain explains that it is a "difficult" landing.

However, we make it all right. Really rather pleasant. The idea is to see Fitzroy's view from his landing place. A Chilean runs up. He has not heard of our permission to land, so we prepare to go. On way back we see an albatross – very clear through the glasses.

Not easy to climb aboard from a dinghy that is bobbing up and down but not in phase with the ship. But gratified when the First Officer who hauls me aboard says "Muy Buen".

10.45 Given hot soup as a reward.

11.00 Chilean patrol MB seen making for bay we just landed at! Told a storm is on its way from south.

11.30 Excellent lunch: centolla (sort of lobster) soup, meat, rice and milk. Served by ratings who put on whites to do it. Nice to see these clean young men with smart, short haircuts.

12.00 On deck again. Squally, some sleet, changing cloud, hard horizons, shocking, incomparable beauty all around. Skuas(?) – an enormous brown gull – have followed the ship day and night. Magnificent, powerful birds. Seem very daring, even perhaps friendly.

12.30 Went for lie down and must have gone straight to sleep, for awakened by sound of anchor chain going down and realized it must be Porto Toro in undoubted Chile, which was Fitzroy and Darwin's "portrait cove". Landed this time in the launch with full party as this is quite a little port. Recd. by senior Chilean Naval Officer, 2 guardsmen, the port commandant and one Chilean civilian; with great courtesy and pleasantness. Walked about in very heavy rain getting soaked immediately. But found Fitzroy's sketches true in detail still. Chilean Naval Officer (very nice and impressive) said he would see us again at the next landing. Evidently sent down by Santiago.

Sailed up Channel in squalls and cross-wind. Passed by Chilean in his very fast motor torpedo boat, going to the next place to wait for us.

Weather suddenly changed again to a peaceful, sunny, warm evening. Made rubber-dinghy landing at Porto Eugenie in Chilean island of Navarino, on south side of B.Ch. 4.30 Received by same Chilean officer and the men of the village – seven of them. 5 houses of wood, all same (? Government) pattern. One horse with woolly saddle and stirrups of wood, like clogs. That is their communication with the tiny port of Porto Williams (1½ hrs on horseback).

Climbed hill to see Channel. Breathtakingly beautiful. Miles of snow mountains on either side of Beagle Channel east and west, glaciers gleaming in the sun miles away in the entrances from the Pacific, perfectly still blue water, green turf under foot. One could cry at the sheer joy of the scene.

Geese of many kinds. Some large, with long curved beaks and gorgeous gold and red colouring like a cock pheasant, and a peculiar croaking cry. And many others. Also cormorants in the bay.

Lots of dogs and some children. Odd how the feel of the place is quite different from Argentina.

How lucky we are. No tourist could get here at any price – only someone like Shipton. And to be here on a perfect evening!

Sailed then to Harberton: the Bridges' present farm (named after Harberton in Devon whence Mrs Bridges came), where we were to stay the night. Very pretty, sheltered harbour.

"Tommy Goodall", the present incumbent, arrived on board and had dinner on ship with us. His mother was a Bridges, the Rev. Thomas B. being his great-grandfather. Rosy-cheeked youngish man with strong features, face not unlike Rosalind Beach Thomas, and made of muscle. He farms 50,000 acres, on which only 9,000 sheep can run, however. They still speak English "at home". Old Mrs B., his mother, away just now but she is only 70 and still rides horseback. Now nr. Rio Grande because she feels she might need medical attention sometimes.

The house is home-made but very pleasant and large. Rather old-fashioned. Oil cloth on floors except for rugs. Flowered wallpapers. Big wood-burning stoves. Large radio communications set dominates the large sitting room, seems to be permanently on, tuned to BBC. He can transmit as well. Link now with Ushuaia is by small plane. Otherwise it has to be launch. (In winter this can take 3 days with helmsman lashed on deck!) No telephone.

Lovely Indian bow hanging on wall. Family photographs, &c. All very pleasant. Odd period things about, like a trouser press of the sort I used to have. Quite nice simple garden, but not much to look at till January, he says. Vegetables almost impossible to grow because any night can be frosty even at mid-summer. Otherwise climate in Channel is equable. Never below 22°F, and 80°F is record highest. Normally a range of only about 30° winter and summer.

Got to bed at last after a very long day and slept very well indeed, being quite oblivious till 6.30, when I woke quite fresh and ready to get up. This "sea" life, with loads of fresh air, tasks to do, and quite a lot of exercise getting into and out of these landing craft, is pretty healthy.

Friday 1ˢᵗ December

Taken by launch at 8 am back to ship for a trip eastward again to examine the Atlantic mouths of the Channel. Breakfast aboard, then up comes the anchor and we start down Channel in a heavy squall from the north. See a seal swimming in opposite direction.

10.00 Weather improves and the northerly wind moderates.

11.00 Making for Atlantic. Weather squally again. Very cold even with vest, shirt, sweater, tweed jacket and windproof. But clear, with fine views.

11.15 Excellent lunch. Has to be early because there will be at least one more tableful later, depending on changes of the watch.

1.00 Chilean escort appears; evidently been looking for us.

2.00 Small landing in cove in New Island. Did not go as Captain advised against it. Jeremy went and found nothing. Chilean captain, who had somehow to get in first in order to receive the party, said as far as he knew nobody had ever set foot on it before.

Weather not very pleasant but sea moderating quite a lot – mainly because we are turning back into the Channel and away from the open sea. All agree that in really bad weather the sea outside the islands is impossible and one just has to run for it.

This morning we had very clear views of the Cape Horn group.

This afternoon we saw two more albatross.

3.30 Landing party in rubber dinghy (I did not join this one) at Puerto Paballon in Picton Island (Banner Cove of the English days). After they had made land a sudden storm arose and the ship began to drag her anchor. So we had to go backwards and forwards across the B.Ch. until the storm quietened. Then the dinghy was able to return. The weather here is clearly very local and never to be trusted.

c 5.30 Sailed for Harberton again and landed after a late dinner which Tommy Goodall again joined. We (J. and I) then went ashore to sleep in the house again.

Harberton, with its 50,000 acres and only 9,000 sheep, is subsistence farming indeed. The house is corrugated iron outside, with nice, large windows and a red roof, as have all the farm buildings. But looks nice and is very pleasant inside. It has a very powerful relaxing and welcoming effect inside, even though the wind rattles the stovepipe.

There is a "road" part way to Ushuaia but T.G. said the other day when he tried to take a truck along, he had to winch himself out 3 times.

Presented him with Xerox of his great grandfather's description of Tierra del Fuego, now in the Royal Geographical Society, and he showed us his g.g's diary – very detailed and beautifully written for pretty well whole time he was at Ushuaia and then Harberton. Jeremy dutifully stayed up till 2.30 reading it. We need to get a copy somehow.

Learned the brown 'goose' with curved bill we saw in Puerto Eugenie is the brown Ibis.

Sat. 2nd Dec.

Up at 6.30 to join ship. Plan to be put in rubber dinghy east of Gable Island and explore northern passage, while ship goes round main southerly passage and waits for us in Bahia Valiente Brown, at the west end of Gable. I did go on this one after borrowing waterproof trousers from the ship. Very rough journey at first with waves coming over the front, so had to bale. When we got into smoother water behind the island, however, there was a lot of kelp which got tangled in the propeller of the little outboard motor. So we rowed ashore, left two officers in charge of the dinghy and started to walk the 3 or 4 miles over pathless country to where we supposed the ship would be. No joke with waterproof trousers and life jacket, so had to carry these.

Wonderful walk. Place alive with geese of all kinds. Twice we put up a sitting bird and almost stumbled into the beautiful downy nest, one with five large eggs and one with 4. Also lots of ibis, with their sad, conversational piping. Very attractive.

When we saw the ship I was glad of my startling orange windproof. We put it on a stick and waved it, and almost immediately got an answering toot from the siren, though she was quite a mile out in the bay.

Then a series of little disasters. They sent the spare rubber dinghy, which reached us; but attempting to take us off, it destroyed its propeller on a rock.

Then they sent the launch which couldn't get near. So we had to drag the dinghy round to a better spot. Wonderful beach on way – saw duck's nest with eggs on the beach, probably hardly trodden by man since the Yaghan Indians succumbed. Then we launched the dinghy and started to row to the launch. But in the ensuing confusion (far too many people talking – an

Argentine weakness) the dinghy's warp got tangled in the launch propeller. So we were stranded again! Getting it untangled was cold hard work for two officers who had to stand in the water in their clothes and work at it – a wet nylon rope is resistant to a knife. The crew lit a fire of brushwood, and the two chaps working at the propeller took it in turns to go for a warm up.

At last it was freed and we were "rescued" and clambered aboard the ship. It would hardly have been possible to row to her because the current and the wind were strong onto the shore.

Meanwhile the other two officers had managed to get the other dinghy going and they got back to the ship also. After all that, lunch was very welcome. Yet had it not been for the chapter of accidents we (Jeremy Carver, Federico Mirré, Captain Olstein and I) would not have had the great privilege of walking that superb, almost untouched country, teeming with wild life and grasses and flowers.

4.00 Reached Ushuaia and settled down to a good bath and a good dinner. We meant to do a bit more flying, but weather was turbulent and the pilot advised against it. Met Tommy Goodall again and had tea with him. He had flown to Ushuaia for the day in his little plane.

Sunday 3rd Dec.

After night at "Albatross" at Ushuaia, got up at 6.15 am to get down to naval-base airstrip to do our last survey flight. Nice little Beachcraft 4-seater. Still very turbulent so not a comfortable journey. In fact the pilot said it was the worst he had ever experienced. But we saw what we wanted to see at the eastern end. We then turned to go towards the west but then the pilot rather went on strike and said it was really too turbulent for a tiny machine and we must be satisfied.

Breakfast at officers' mess in airbase, then wait for our civilian flight to B.A. – Fokker "Friendship" to Rio Gallegos then Boeing 707 to Commodoro Rivadavia and B.A. Landed at B.A. at 6.00, completing almost the 12 hours of flying or waiting in airports. Got to Plaza Hotel 7.30. Same rooms as before. Got shoes, white with salt spray, cleaned inside 10 minutes. Good dinner sent up to rooms and beautifully served. Wonderful hotel.

Pretty hot here but not as big a contrast as it could have been, because there was some rain this morning, it seems.

Mon. 4ᵗʰ Dec.

Worked on drafts a.m. with Jeremy. Lunch at La Cabana given by Ruda – delicious ham and pineapple with a rich toffee sauce. Then more work. Then walk round shops with Jeremy and Federico. Rather hot but not too bad. Wonderful shops and large shopping streets with no cars. Dinner in the Plaza Grill with Jeremy. Then to bed. Have meeting at F.O. at 10 am tomorrow morning.'

And there his blow-by-blow account ends. He arrived home on 6ᵗʰ December, after a journey 'delayed by floods' (where?). It had been a great adventure for a 59-year-old academic, and characteristic of him to have been so moved by his wild surroundings. On his return, though, there was just an hour or two for him to present us with gifts and tell a little of his exploits before he went out to a dinner given by Eli Lauterpacht.

Robbie was back to Cambridge life, with a two-day visit to Geneva for *Beagle* work. Christmas itself was quiet, at home among neighbours. With Robbie 'full of yawns' and freezing fog outside, we decided not to attempt a visit to Arment House (– tantalizing to hear about the marvellous four days my godson and seven young friends had spent there before Christmas). I experimented with developing and printing my photographs. Dicky, who had saved up hard-earned money for his printing hobby, was writing a play, *The Hermit of Arment*[197] in mock-Shakespearian verse which we tried to perform, with lots of elaborate sound-effects, for the tape-recorder. Pippa and Joey spent their Christmas money on stilts, and 'P. walked about Robbie's college room on hers'.

We had a riotous evening on Boxing Day. Having embarked on a game of charades, there was knocking at the door – just as Robbie was doing a vivid impersonation of Rosamund, dressed in a voluminous nightdress of mine pulled over his shirt, a large hat on his head, a stick in his hand and a pipe in his mouth … so it was a relief to find that our unexpected callers entered into the spirit of the evening at once. An old school friend of mine, only recently

---

[197] *Place Names of Cumberland & Westmorland* suggests that the name 'Arment' probably derives from the Scandinavian word for 'Hermit'; and Mary Fair's *Bygone Eskdale* says that Arment House 'was also written Harmit Hows with variations, and may have originally alluded to the cell of some hermit who may have been connected with the holy well just over the hill'.

rediscovered after years apart, had arrived with a dotty artist friend and bearing wonderful homemade gifts.

For my birthday, at the end of December, Robbie had cleverly chosen to give me a silver fountain-pen exactly like his own, except with the initials CJ incised on the end. Altogether, with family fun and a few gentle outside entertainments, it was a restorative Twelve Days of Christmas.

—

Ever More Diverse

1973

After playing the fool at Christmas, Robbie now had some sobering matters to deal with. On 19th January 1973 he returned from another two-day session with the Argentine team in Geneva, to refocus on developments at Jesus College.

'R. home from Geneva – and to Society meeting. Question of possible Mastership looms' is my diary entry for that day. Being responsible, as President, for organising the forthcoming election, it would be uncomfortable to be at the same time a candidate for the post. In any case, everything was to be managed with the utmost discretion, and we did not mention it even to our children.

The question had evidently been 'looming' for some time. On 11th November 1972 the 84-year-old Gardner-Smith had written –

'Dear Robbie,
'About the Mastership: I hope you will allow yourself to be nominated, though you may have other fish in the fryingpan.

'The proceedings in connexion with the election are of course (and happily) in your hands and I have no wish to interfere, but I do hope we may avoid the weary succession of meetings we endured in 1959. We have had one meeting to consider the problem *in vacuo* and I do not see that anything is to be gained by holding further meetings of the same kind.

'Glanville Williams has asked for a debate on possible outsiders at which many names will presumably be suggested. That may be a lengthy business and will give an opportunity to those who enjoy talking, but I doubt whether anything will come of it. Various names will be brought forward without the slightest probability of their being elected. We did something of the sort last time and it fell to my lot to approach several distinguished persons to ask whether, *if* they were offered the Mastership, they would accept it. I had to admit that their chances were somewhat remote, and understandably they said No.

'This time I feel pretty sure that the Society will choose one of its own members and long consideration of outsiders will prove a waste of time. On the other hand, a debate on the merits and demerits of this or that Fellow would prove impossibly embarrassing at a Society meeting, and if nominees were asked to withdraw in turn hopes would be aroused only to be disappointed with consequent resentment.

'Is there any alternative? Could you not simply request nominations and then allow some sort of confidential straw vote to eliminate those who have obviously no chance of success? Probability suggests that two or three would be outstanding and these could be voted on in the Chapel according to the Statutes. It might still be possible that no one individual would secure a majority, and then we must try again; but actual names need not be mentioned until the final stage. If it seems hopeless to get a majority, then we may have to go outside…'

Robbie's response to this letter may be inferred from P. G-S's letter of 15th:

'I am glad to get your letter and I quite understand your hesitations: I have been in similar dilemmas in other fields. Particularly I sympathise with your unwillingness to leave your rural retreat:

"How blest is he who leads a country life,
  Unvexed with anxious cares, and void of strife."
Not always, perhaps.

'The immediate question concerns "strong and widely-based support". I have not much doubt that it would be forthcoming, but I doubt whether I am the one to organize it. I do not know many of the Fellows, and I might be met with the question What has it to do with you? The last meeting showed that some will want to plan for radical 'reform' and they may do a good deal of intriguing. They might point to me as just the sort of person to stand in the way. There is another difficulty: if one were to approach A and ask him to support B one would be conscious that A might himself wish to be a candidate. The position would be embarrassing.

'As to procedure, I am sure we can rely on you to deliver us from endless meetings, but your own position will not be easy.'

Indeed it was not. Robbie could remember all too well the protracted agonising over the choice of Master in 1959, when the Fellows, unable to choose between four inside candidates, had brought in Page from Trinity.

A circular was sent out to Fellows, inviting contributions to a leaving present for Sir Denys Page on his retirement as Master, and on 10th January Sir Claude Elliott, as Senior Fellow, wrote to Robbie apologising for delay – 'I had … clean forgotten about it (I forget everything nowadays – latterly articles of clothing, so far nothing of importance, but I hope it never comes to trousers) …' and enclosing a cheque. He said he hoped to come to Cambridge, combining a meeting about the Mastership with a visit to Jim Butler at Trinity. Robbie evidently wrote back to bring him up-to-date on the situation. In reply, Elliott wrote –

'I can readily understand your dilemma about the Mastership – you must indeed be pulled in opposite directions. I certainly hope that you will let your name go forward (even tho' this would mean that Pars would preside at the meetings!) …

'I know very little of Sharpe but I have heard excellent things of him. In fact my lack of knowledge of the Fellows (50 of them instead of the 16 when I became a Fellow) makes me begin to wonder if my attendance might be resented, just as we used to resent Foakes Jackson[198] when he came over from Columbia University and took an active part in our discussions on things of which he knew very little.'

Elliott, like Gardner-Smith, was 84 years old. In a note of 1st March he confessed that his planned visit to Cambridge was delayed, since he had…

'…been so idiotic that I am beside myself with sheer rage. I was coming down some fairly steep scree on Robinson just behind the house when I tripped up and slid head first down the scree. This was due to sheer carelessness, probably induced by senility. I don't know how many thousands of feet I must have descended in my day without any fall at all…' [And later –] 'I am touched by what you say of my knowledge of what the College stands for [he had, after all, been a Fellow since 1910 and served as Senior Tutor], but sometimes a Rip van Winkel such as I would be can do more harm than good…' [And he was again urging Robbie to stand.]

The Jesus College 1973 Annual Report said:

---

[198]   F. Foakes Jackson, church historian, had been a Fellow of Jesus for 34 years, and Dean, before moving to New York.

'The election of a Master is not one of the happiest occasions in the life of a College. The Statutes require the Fellows to meet in the Chapel and every Fellow must give his vote in favour of one particular person ...

'That sounds simple enough, but if three or more names have been put forward it is not very likely that one will have an absolute majority and the Fellows must vote again. The process may go on indefinitely ...'

In May I did mention our strange preoccupation in a letter to my father, saying it was a matter about which 'one keeps strictly quiet until an appointment is actually published', feeling that he was unlikely to meet anyone on Romney Marsh with whom to share gossip in any case. I wrote –

'The Fellows will assemble in chapel and make their votes [on Thursday]; but as there are three candidates and an overall majority is needed, they may quite well fail to reach a decision on this occasion. We ourselves just look forward to *knowing*. As I have just said to Robbie, "It makes it so difficult to know how to plan the garden"; and he replied, "Yes, and I can't decide about *loudspeakers*." Agony!'

And it was not to be until October that the election was finally made.

All this was, of course, in the background to a year that was full of other developments.

Robbie was spending a good deal of time with the Argentine team in Geneva, so the children's half-term in February gave us a brief stay with Sami Shubber[199] and his wife Suzie, during which we crammed in visits to the WHO, the Palais des Nations and the old town, and were driven up to the mountains at the far end of the lake. (In this peaceful place it was startling to read that one of the chief Argentine naval commanders whom Robbie had met was shot dead in the street a few weeks later.)

At home our hospitality was mainly for the children's friends, but one Sunday lunch was made memorable when Laurence Picken came, fresh from a tour of Afghanistan, Korea, Taiwan and Japan. As the children developed, so

---

199   Dr Sami Shubber, an Iraqi, was working at the World Health Organisation in Geneva. He was a devoted former pupil of Robbie's.

did an interest in family history, and – having failed to make notes of some of my mother's and her parents' stories before their death – I was keen to record what memories could still be attached to old photographs while my father was alive. Robbie too realised how much might be lost as his last few relatives disappeared, so he started jotting pencilled notes of the backs of photographs of his own family members: something for which we are now grateful.

A novelty for me at this time was to attend a rather grand embassy reception, which I described for my father:

'[Arriving in London by train] … we took the Underground (not the best way to keep fresh-looking in evening dress) and then walked – delightfully – through Green Park. The Mall had flags for the State Visit of the President of the Sudan. We wandered around the back of St James's, and then arrived for the reception just as the President and his entourage did – with police outriders and a certain kowtowing as they stepped out of their Rollses onto the red carpet. But the Embassy is inside not particularly attractive and the arrangements were very much the usual jobbing caterers' affair. One joined the line of guests, was announced, shook hands, bowed slightly and said "Excellencey" to the Ambassador – who kept Robbie chatting for a moment – and then on into a thronged room where there was another line; and this time, rather bewildered, one smiled and nodded to various handsome African ladies in colourful draperies, shook hands with a dusky man, slightly bowed respectfully to a very tall grim-looking one … and after running the gauntlet of them all wondered just *which* had been President Numeiri. (It turned out that he had been the affable one whose hand one had shaken.) After that we stayed rather trapped at the far end of the room, and after a little got talking to an extremely nice Englishman who also had no-one nearby whom he recognized. He was, he said, "a sailor": quite a distinguished one, I would guess, now stuck "in the Ministry". The room was filling more and more, with a large number of photographers flashing, clicking and filming the arrivals of all the more notable – such as the Lord Mayor, the Sheriff, the Esquire (all in court dress, with lace ruffs and chains of office) and others less picturesque, including Mr Heath. He was standing close by us … and seems very fit and beaming and pleasant. What a chore it must be to such people to have to put in an appearance at such functions so frequently. But he was soon gone; and then we chatted with the Sheriff, who was arranging for Robbie to attend one of the Judges' luncheons at the Old Bailey. We talked also with the Sudanese Minister of Information, who then went off and fetched their Foreign Minister – both impressive and charming chaps. They are pleased with Robbie, whose advice recently helped them to win a boundary dispute with Ethiopia,[200] and who has helped a number of Sudanese students. And we had a word with Dingle Foot, whom we had met before … and then we left. So, to make more of the evening and fill in time before catching our train back, we went to a madly-expensive and beautiful restaurant (Overton's) in St James's. To pay so much for a lobster salad and glass of wine and a cup of coffee is absurd; but since it has only happened once before, when R. took silk, we deemed it not *too* extravagant!'

(That long passage may, I hope, be excused on the grounds that it describes the sort of event to which we would become thoroughly accustomed a decade later.)

That Easter we did get away to Cumberland. We called on Aunt Kitty, eager to welcome us with home-baked cakes and a display of family photographs (now 91, she was to live for 10 years more). Of Robbie's Brotherton relatives we learnt that Uncle Teddy, in his 80s, was still able to get up at 6.30 am to work as a butcher, and was still singing in the local Glee Club.

Then, driving up Wharfedale, we ran into a blizzard and were glad to reach the Falcon Inn at Arncliffe, stamp our feet, and warm up by their blazing fire. I wrote:

'After our very good dinner we felt loath to leave the fire; yet the snow had stopped, so we resolved to poke our noses out. Sheer magic: the glimmering evening light (a small moon and some stars) on the snow, and the baa-ing and bleating of sheep and newborn lambs. We walked up the hillside and looked down on the snug little stone village with its few lights and the dramatic fells behind …'

On to Eskdale, where sunshine allowed me to spread the Arment bedding out to air before making up the beds. Conditions lovely, people friendly – yet Robbie, with a return to Geneva imminent, could allow us only a short stay this time. Still, it was a good stay: Marca Burns took Pippa and Joey on as slave labour to help her catch, inoculate and dip her few sheep, while Robbie and Dicky were as usual at work navvying and mending walls in the lonning. Our

---

[200]   Although I cannot trace this consultation, it may have been connected with the *Addis Ababa Agreement* concluded at this time, ending the First Sudanese Civil War.

Grantchester neighbours, the Halls, joined us with two young boys and a dog; and we went again over to Buttermere for lunch with Sir Claude Elliott.

In May Week that summer it was our turn to run the usual President's Garden Party in the Fellows' Garden. While I sailed over to Belgium with members of CUMS for the Society's first-ever overseas trip, (a grand farewell to our retiring conductor, David Willcocks),[201] Robbie and the children coped at home and attended our final performance of Tallis's 40-part *Spem in Alium* and other motets in King's.

His own varied activities included taking part in a televised *Today* programme to discuss with a Labour M.P. the exploitation of the high seas, and *firmly and politely completing what he had to say* – the last worth remarking. The day after that he was off at 6 am for a journey to Utrecht to discuss a 'feasibility study' for the construction of an artificial island in the North Sea as a base for unpleasant activities like oil refining, away from residential areas. A very tired Robbie reached home at 1.30 next morning, and the discussions on this topic would be resumed at Heidelberg.

The Mastership election was still in progress. On 1st July, while another inconclusive vote was taken, Robbie stayed away and instead received a former pupil, Myron Nordquist,[202] for a chat in the garden at home about Deep Sea Law. By this time it seemed clear that an external candidate would become Master, and we could relax a little. Robbie enjoyed making the promised visit to the Old Bailey for a Judges' luncheon and...

'By way of entertainment/instruction afterwards he sat for most of the afternoon in the main Criminal Court, listening to the very unedifying case of a Soho gang who twice tried to kill a man with knives. Horrible characters, all of them, R. said, and all seeming to go about in Rolls-Royces and Bentleys!'

We got ourselves up to Arment House in the Long Vacation, Robbie and Dick making the journey in a heavily-laden car while I took the girls and Rags by train. This time Pippa had a bright idea: a magazine to be produced by everyone there. I wrote that...

---

[201] Later Sir David Willcocks, he was about to become Principal of the Royal College of Music and devote more time to the Bach Choir. But before he left, members of the chorus made a recording of this programme. It was an experiment with *quadraphonic* sound, involving 16 microphones. I noted that 'Robbie would have drooled over the recording equipment!'

[202] – now Professor at the University of Virginia, and leading authority on Sea Law.

'… Certainly the first has proved well worth doing – with amusing stories, drawings and "compotitions" by Pippa and Joey, rhymes by Dicky, a delightful illustrated story by Eleanor Huxley who is with us again …; a little gem from Robbie – a description of his grandfather buying a cow – and from me Rags's diary of his journey and first days here.'

Several of these 'magazines' have survived, happy mementoes of rainy spells when we needed to provide our own entertainment. Fortunately this holiday included some fine days for walking, the Gosforth Show, the Eskdale Fête and a unique display of stunt flying, as a small plane skimmed over the hillocks and fellside to spray bracken – a dangerous and only slightly effective effort to curb the growth which we regularly attacked with scythes.

We came back to an unresolved Mastership election; and having chosen not to attend that summer's *Institut* conference, we spent two days in a hotel in Aldeburgh on the Suffolk coast, with nice harmless meals and a chance to swim in the sea – both appreciated by the children. We had the appealingly scruffy Rags with us; and one morning Pippa took him onto the beach and came back all aglow, having been talking to Imogen Holst and Benjamin Britten! That little break allowed us to draw breath before Robbie was off to Heidelberg again.

———

By 14th October we knew the result of the Jesus Mastership election, which was announced in the press a few days later. The 'outside' candidate chosen as new Master was Professor Sir Alan Cottrell[203], a metallurgist fellow of Christ's (my nephew Jonathan's college, where one of his friends was Cottrell's son). Claude Elliott, in what turned out to be the month before his death, wrote:

'I am dreadfully disappointed, as all your many friends must be, that you have not been elected to the Mastership. I only hope that you both do not feel it too deeply…'

Indeed we did not. Robbie was able to play with new loudspeakers, and we soon made friends with Alan Cottrell and his wife Jean, both music-lovers and fell-walkers. Alan's years as Master would include service as Vice-Chancellor and the period while Prince Edward was in residence as an undergraduate.

———

[203]   Sir Alan Cottrell was also Chief Scientific Adviser to the Government at this time.

Sabbatical leave for the academic year 1973-74 relieved Robbie of university and college responsibilities. The college granted him continued use of his rooms so that he could work there when in Cambridge, although he was expecting to be abroad for much of the year – he would certainly be needed in Geneva by the Argentine team working on their submissions in the *Beagle Channel* case. He was also being asked when he could visit Tehran to give further advice on the setting up of a School of International Studies, a project that suggested a really exciting family journey, perhaps in the spring holidays.

Dealings with foreign states certainly brought extra variety to all our lives. An evening was spent with the Argentine ambassador, who urged Robbie to continue working for them even though most of the other British team members had been dropped. Then we stayed for a memorable dinner. It was an intimate and wholly delightful occasion – just Ambassador Barbosa, Federico Mirré (who had gone with Robbie down to Tierra del Fuego) and wife, and, besides ourselves, one other guest, a young woman pianist. She was Sylvia Kersenbaum, who played for us a variety of pieces – Schubert and others – with formidable technique and delicacy. Next day Robbie bought one of her records to remind us of that evening.

Some clients could be less easy to deal with. In a letter to my father that October, Robbie wrote:

> '… the last few weeks have been to quite an extent spent in trying quite vainly to keep up with Colonel Gadaffi. Every time a draft letter or some such was complete he would go and do something different. It would be easier in some ways if he marched steadily on his course all the time, as he *seems* to be doing in his speeches. But in fact he sometimes darts sideways, and not infrequently takes several smart steps backward along the paths he seemed already to have progressed along. But this, I am told, is the Libyan way; and it is a typical western fatuity to suppose that what is said and what is in fact done need conform more than marginally. Being an Arabist must make a man into a quite different sort of person.'[204]

---

[204] This must refer to advisory work concerning oil-drilling that Robbie was doing on behalf of Texaco Overseas Petroleum Company and California Asiatic Oil Company in a dispute with The Government of the Libyan Arab Republic which would finally be resolved in 1977, with René-Jean Dupuy as Sole Arbitrator. (See *Five Masters of International Law – The Texaco Case*.)

And we were again reminded how differently they do things abroad when, the following January, I wrote about his relations with Iran:

> 'Robbie is popping with frustration. What he wants is a letter of full instructions about the work he is to do for the Persians. And they reply by a string of charming courtesies ("How we look forward to having your assistance … and now, to mark the festive season, we are sending you two kilos of caviar."). The wretched caviar is worth over £100, says Dicky. We've run a small party on one tin; the second is given to Alan Pars; the third is being consumed at school by Dicky and his fellow-toffs and his housemaster; and the fourth is in our freezer…'

(The caviar had not been sent to our house, but needed to be collected. When Pippa and I visited London for an exhibition, we afterwards went to Kensington, and found the Iranian Embassy guarded by a van with snarling dogs in front. I rang the bell and was confronted by armed men in uniform. It seemed absurd to say 'I believe you have something for my husband in your fridge'; but after some hesitation someone was sent down into the basement for this heavy package, and we stepped outside with relief. We returned home in an overcrowded train with our clanking burden.)

A handsome book on Persian Architecture arrived from the Iranian Ambassador next Christmas, too. But the great scheme for Robbie to organize a school of international studies in Tehran never came to anything.

—◆—

Legal Practice Increases

1973-74

Any international arbitration, from its inception to conclusion, can become a lengthy process. *The Beagle Channel* case spanned almost ten years, beginning on 11th December 1967 with the formal request for proceedings to be initiated by HM Government, followed by an agreement by Argentina and Chile, 'overcoming their differences of view,' to submit their case to arbitration (the *Compromiso* or formal Agreement) on 22nd July 1971. The Memorials (bulky documents presenting arguments accompanied by maps and other supporting material) were deposited on 2nd July 1973; the Counter-Memorials a year later; Replies on 1st July 1975; a visit by members of the Court to the 'disputed region' in March 1976; the deposit by both Argentina and Chile of 'a number of additional documents' on 29th July; Oral Proceedings opening on 7th September; the 'Final Statements' from both sides in November 1976; and finally the *Dispositif* – the Award, or Judgment, delivered on 18th February 1977.

Robbie was involved throughout, and it is no wonder that during those years so much of his time had to be spent in Geneva, where the Argentine team had set up their office. But there was a great deal more going on at the same time.

———

Apart from the periods of sabbatical leave to which he was entitled, university teaching was never neglected; he made contributions to academic journals and continued his editorship of the *British Yearbook of International Law*. In term-time his absences from Cambridge occurred as far as possible at weekends.

A major article[205] published in the *Jubilee Book 1923-1973* of The Hague Academy of International Law is a resumé of all the academy lectures delivered over that period. It must have been a huge undertaking to read through every

---

[205] 'Fifty Years of Hague Academy Lectures on Public International Law' (1973), p.297 of *Collected Writings*.

volume of the *Recueil* – 'a unique record of the development of international law during the last half-century', for most of that time written entirely in French. While noting that often the name of a lecturer can signal in advance what his theme – his hobby-horse – is likely to be, Robbie approves the general hardening of approach towards 'lawyer's law ... the backbone of the whole corpus.'

'... in all [the lectures] form a contribution to the science and development of international law of outstanding power and quality. In recent years there has been a tendency to question the value of formal lectures, to suggest that the seminar method with its "dialogue", as the modish jargon has it, is superior. Doubtless these more discursive methods have their place in training a novitiate; but these ephemeral occasions, however titillating at the time, can seldom if ever make a permanent contribution to the stature of the subject, comparable to many of these straight lectures prepared for publication, as well as delivery to a particular audience.'

He traces the impact of events during the late '30s, in particular the Spanish Civil War. He notes that on the resumption of the courses after the Second World War, the establishment of the United Nations and many other international organisations had increased the complexity of the subject; and the law of international organisation and institutions had, indeed, begun to be studied as a branch of international law in its own right, developing 'remarkably elaborated and perceptive thinking on particular problems', making it 'a more teachable subject and, as Maitland sagely observed, taught law is tough law'. The contributions of Islam, of Hinduism, and of Buddhism to international law were each given a full course, too. He comments on how –

'... recent courses have been invaded by the latest "challenge", namely the concern about the environment, pollution, conservation, over-population, the so-called "energy-crisis" and the rest of the dialectical armoury of learned Jeremiahs whose baleful prophesies add a shrill note of impending doom to the close of the *Recueil's* first fifty years. It seems a pity that in discussing the balance of population and food, the desire to present this as a new awareness vouchsafed to a prescient few, results in less than justice being done to the work of the Rev. Thomas Robert Malthus[206] nearly 200 years earlier...'

---

[206] RYJ could not resist making this reference to a former Fellow of Jesus College, Cambridge.

The problems of changing population and climate, and the transformation of transport and communications through advances in science were not really dismissed, however. He would in the coming years be in the forefront of the scholars addressing these very matters.

A final comment in this article was, for him, an important one:

'It is astonishing how very few women are to be found in the list of lecturers. The selective few are certainly of great distinction. But it ought to be possible to find many more who could give courses well up to the best standards…'

Another piece of work published in the *Collected Writings* is Robbie's contribution to a Max Planck Symposium in 1974 on *Judicial Settlement of International Disputes,* about the role of the International Court of Justice. In it he recognises some of the Court's limitations, and suggests an extension of its powers. This, of course, is of special interest in the light of his later career.

As the year approached its end, Robbie spent several days in discussions on Artificial Islands with a German, Gunther Jaenike, and a Dutchman, Boucher. And even on Boxing Day another problem, an important Oil negotiation, claimed his attention. The family just had to accept that Muslim countries (in this case, Libya) don't stop for Christmas. But we did fit in a party for more of the college fellows – hoping to establish peace and goodwill after the Mastership election.

There were plenty of social events: a dinner given by Pars to introduce the new Master and his wife; the wedding of Robbie's godson Simon Fisher at a Roman Catholic church in Chelsea, and a dinner the same evening in the Master's Lodge at Pembroke, given by Tony and Miriam Camps[207]. We went, too, to hear Richard Marlow[208] conduct Bach's *Matthew Passion* in Ely Cathedral. A

---

[207] Both distinguished people: Professor W.A. Camps, Master of Pembroke, was a classical scholar, and Miriam, an American, served in the US Department of State and became involved in the Organisation for European Economic Co-operation and Development, among other activities.

[208] Director of Music at Trinity College, Marlow composed church music, and many recordings were made of the college choir and his own organ recitals.

Vice-Chancellor's dinner was particularly memorable. Our host was Master of Sidney Sussex, J.W. Linnett, and it turned out to be an all-star cast: not the usual gathering made up entirely of dons, but a mixture of interesting arty people – David Willcocks (Director of Music at King's), Michael Jaffé (Director of the Fitzwilliam Museum), Lucy Boston (children's author), Nan Youngman (artist), a sculptor called Gillespie and a young stage director called Richard Eyre.

Work on the *Beagle* case took Robbie to Geneva so frequently that one free spell provided an opportunity for us to visit my Swiss cousins. He telephoned Uncle Fritz[209] (charmed to find this octogenarian speaking fluent Edwardian English) and a short family holiday was arranged. We first went to St Gallen, home of Fritz Saxer and my cousin Vreni – and a place that appealed strongly to Robbie. Then we all travelled on the Rhaetische Bahn down to the Engadin. As the train spiralled in darkness through the mountainside Uncle Fritz demonstrated its turning motion by dangling his penknife on a string and swinging it like a pendulum. He was a natural teacher whose career had been as a schoolmaster (Head of a *Gymnasium*) but also awarded an honorary doctorate in recognition of his distinguished work in mapping the geology of Switzerland.

Our stay was in an old farmhouse in Guarda. It was early April, with the first wild crocuses breaking through, the air so clear, so still. And there, in the Lower Engadin, we attended a church service and tried to join in hymns sung in Romansch. Here, too, Robbie met more of my relatives, my cousin Marta and her husband Rüdi (a professor of economics at Schaffhausen). While appreciating their hospitality and delighting in our surroundings, some family idiosyncrasies (such as Rüdi's insistence that bread needed to become stale before it was fit to eat – in spite of the delectable aroma of that morning's baking) would never be forgotten.

Robbie himself had by now few remaining relatives and kept in touch with them fitfully. But he had been fond of his cousin Annie, and when he heard that after a few years of widowhood she was to marry again he felt that we should attend the wedding. That excursion to Lowestoft became something of a farce as what had seemed plentiful time shrank in traffic delays. Once in Lowestoft, after wild sorties along wrong streets,

---

[209] Friedrich Saxer, widower of my aunt Chriss (née Bennett), father of my three cousins.

'…Robbie nearly ran down a traffic cop and implored him for directions, which he gave with good humour – we turned right too soon, and looped back through a garage forecourt – we followed a minicar with white ribbons, but that was going to a grand hotel reception with a dazzling young bride – we broke into a line of traffic and got furiously honked at by someone, then suddenly saw a parking gap and were honked at again (we smiled and waved in apology, but it was ill received) – but there we were at the South Methodist Church.

'I plonked on my hat, and scrabbled in the back for my gloves but only succeeded in impaling myself on a needle which Joey, inevitably, had left (doing patchwork on the journey). We charged up some steps, Robbie throwing himself at what turned out to be a glass wall and not a door … and at last we were inside, with the first hymn getting under way. We had thought only a small group of friends would be there, but the church was packed. Red-faced wind-blown Jenningses, amid fuss and whispering, got passed down the aisle and at last crammed ourselves in a half-filled pew. Blood oozed onto my hymn-book from Joey's needle-stab … We were glad to meet another Jennings relative, a cousin Roy who, totally deaf and with an equally deaf wife, has brought up two strapping sons. He and she are tremendously nice…'

Annie's new husband was a slightly pompous lay preacher, who made an overlong speech at the reception. We hoped they would be happy together, but soon lost touch.

———

The children's growing independence brought new anxieties, although we both felt great pride in their exploits. Dick was now learning to drive ('Oh gosh! Our nerves and our gearboxes!') and soon tried rock-climbing and took his first flights in a glider. He and a schoolfriend, Jeremy McCallum, ended their final term at The Leys with a fund-raising[210] cycle ride of 577 miles across to Snowdon and back, with some wretchedly uncomfortable nights on the way. But, like his father, he had revelled in the fine scenery they passed through. Then, before taking off to their universities, he and two friends took advantage of student Interrail tickets and went off on a Grand Tour through the

---

[210] For the Muscular Dystrophy Group, having been moved by a talk at school.

Netherlands, Germany, Switzerland and France, making the most of various contacts on their way.

———

By now it had become possible to make regular telephone calls from Geneva, and so Robbie's letters describing his activities abroad dried up. Once back at home he tended to look 'pretty tired and preoccupied' as he pressed on with work on the Argentine Counter-Memorial. Still, the girls and I did join him in Geneva again for the wonderful *Fête de Genève*, with its noisy dazzle of fireworks and fairground entertainments, and the *Corso Fleuri* procession, viewed from a high window of the Argentine team's office; also a Sunday spent with our friend Sami Shubber over the French border, at Annecy.

At Arment House that summer we received my other ancient uncle, Donald Miller, who had driven over from Bassenthwaite. A highlight of his stay was a clamber up to Hardknott Roman Fort, with sunshine and clouds racing over Upper Eskdale – a view that he tried to capture in his sketch book.

Then it was back to the new academic year. Robbie and took Dick to Oxford, to see him installed at Christ Church, in Peckwater Quad. The young freshman was probably less well off than most of his contemporaries, since Harold Wilson's Labour Government was in power at that time, and taxation squeezed high earners 'until the pips squeaked'. And now that he was earning some large fees, Robbie found himself 'caught between the upper and the nether millstone'– heavily taxed because of his income and then, for the same reason, having to pay all the university fees. But Dick, in spite of his limited parental allowance, was soon revelling in his new crowded social and intellectual life.

In late October Robbie had meetings in Jersey, and took the girls and me with him as a mini-break to 'set us up' for the winter with a burst of sunshine and fresh air, intended particularly to make me fighting-fit for an operation I was about to undergo.

———

At the end of the month I went into Addenbrooke's[211] for a hysterectomy. The weeks that followed must have been particularly stressful for Robbie, for his work was unremitting and he was fearful of a possible psychological effect of

---

[211] 'Old' Addenbrooke's, later transformed into the Judge Institute of Business Management.

the operation.[212] My recovery was going well until an infection delayed my homecoming; but with patient support from the family I was able to deal with much of my usual activities. On Christmas Eve I had just completed a number of tasks and lain down to rest, when the telephone went –

'… It was Robbie: "I've got the High Commissioner for Bangladesh here in college, and I'd like to give him a cup of tea before he drives back to London; but there's nowhere open in Cambridge …" So quickly we prepared tea and mince pies. He was a *very* nice man. It was interesting to hear him talking about John Stonehouse[213] (quite frankly, as an attractive man who was rather a menace in his business schemes and proposals for "helping" Bangladesh) and then to realize that he had not heard the morning's news and still supposed that Stonehouse was drowned. We had to convince him that he was in safe keeping in Australia! Anyway, that was an interesting encounter, and there is the possibility that it may lead to Robbie's going out to Bangladesh sometime next year – among all his other fascinating advisory jobs and all the teaching that will again be in full swing…'

It was a quiet Christmas. Robbie had spent his money-gift from Grandad on a saw, and was 'having a very happy time with it, putting up shelves everywhere.'

---

[212]   He had confided to me his belief that a change in personality had occurred to his mother – once outgoing and cheerful, later anxious and withdrawn – after a hysterectomy.

[213]   Stonehouse, who had been a member of the Cabinet in an earlier government, had been under investigation for fraud when, in November 1974, he faked his own suicide by drowning in Australia. On Christmas Eve that year he was recognised and arrested.

Work Proliferates

1975-76

And so Robbie was now involved with Bangladesh, for whom he prepared an Opinion. Because he could not undertake to fly out to Dacca at short notice, two men came over to consult him in Cambridge, and then London, instead. In the meantime Ambassador Barbosa wanted him to join the Argentine team in Geneva again. It was all work he enjoyed; but soon the university term would claim his attention.

He did find time, though, for an unusual treat:

> '… he was invited by one of his ex-pupils [Tommy Langton] who is at the top of Lloyd's, to one of their luncheons… – the company (a dozen or so) was distinguished, the menu relatively unpretentious but everything served (in a splendid Adam room) in exquisite style, and by 2.30 the Lloyds men were off back to work (having abstained from their excellent wine). They ended by being asked to sign the visitors' book, wherein the last guest had had a page to herself – *Elizabeth R.*'

He attended, too, the funeral of Stanley Mitchell, our former neighbour at Claremont who came from Idle and who, following Robbie's pioneering example, had progressed from Belle Vue School to Cambridge.

In early May I reported to my father –

> 'Robbie had a few days in Geneva again – Bangladeshis at 8.30 am, Argentines at 9.30 – working and meeting people non-stop – and on Monday took off again from Heathrow straight on to Manchester, where he gave a talk and was entertained. In the meantime another case had been brewing up, so he went up to London on Wednesday all day, back at 8 pm; and yesterday, after lecturing, again to London and back at 8 pm. He felt, he confessed unaccountably tired in the evening, but thought it silly to go early to bed … and today has a very full programme, ending at about 10.30 pm.

[A South African ex-pupil, John Dugard[214] was in Cambridge.] 'This is the man who is wanting Robbie to visit Witwatersrand University – at the invitation of the students, of mixed races. We would like to do this (the family is included in the invitation) and I feel it would be a beneficial break for R – who just *can't* stop working but would find refreshment in the change and promised excursion to a safari park. But I doubt whether it's possible. A practising lawyer just daren't take a few weeks completely off, lest he lose his practice altogether…'

And, although urged to go, and sympathising in the university's rejection of *apartheid*, it of course was not possible. '… There is a case coming up in which Robbie is to advise the Foreign Office, and he has to be available for that.'

So now Robbie's comings and goings became even more dizzying, with the *Beagle* case in the final throes of its written pleading. On one trip he had gone to Geneva expecting 'a fortnight's work' –

'… But he was not fully recovered from a very heavy cold; and, as I later found out, he developed a temperature on the way to Heathrow. He forged ahead, though, and on arrival got to bed. The Hotel d'Angleterre know him very well by now, and they looked after him well (including sending up roses) – as did the Argentine team. So – since there is nothing else to do in bed, says Robbie – he worked a 10-hour day for his four 'fluey days, to such good effect that he completed all the stuff they had for him. They then sent him home to me … to recuperate (and partly to give themselves time to catch up). So he had a quiet*ish* weekend, and just after 7 am on Tuesday was off to Geneva again. He got back about 9 pm last night looking happy and suntanned, and cycled off to college this morning. He has a busy weekend in Cambridge, then must be off to Geneva again from Tues.-Thurs; then London, then The Hague; and home in time for another busy Cambridge weekend.'

The other family members were at full stretch, too – Dick sending us amusing accounts of his second year at Oxford as it drew towards its end, including Eights Week bump supper celebrations and an Oxford Union

---

214 John Dugard's career took him from Witwatersrand to become Director of the Lauterpacht Institute of International Law; then Professor at the University of Leiden; and to the International Law Commission.

debate on the European Referendum. For me the Cambridge May Week ended with CUMS performances of Bach's *Mass in B Minor* both in King's and at the Snape Maltings. Next door, Idwen Banister was developing Alzheimer's syndrome, and her close neighbours had to come to the rescue now and then.

—

A notable event that summer of 1975 was the death, at 90, of Lord McNair. At his Memorial Service in the chapel of Gonville & Caius College, two judges of the International Court gave addresses – the current President, Manfred Lachs, and the British Judge, Sir Humphrey Waldock, whom we entertained to lunch beforehand.

Robbie's article on McNair for the *Cambridge Law Journal*[215] expresses his deep respect for his mentor, and also his own similar attitude towards the practice and teaching of international law. He would pay further tribute when he delivered the first McNair Memorial Lecture a year later at the 1976 ILA conference in Madrid. In *The Discipline of International Law*[216], he was able to quote from a personal letter from Arnold McNair on a theme dear to both of them:

'Of the many activities that I have had I do not think that anything has given me more real satisfaction than giving a lecture or taking a class *for which I have had time for adequate preparation*. My mother was a teacher in Scotland before she married, and I have always rated the *art* of teaching very high. I call it an art because I am very sceptical about the scientific training of teachers, though it is a necessary safeguard for the public because some teachers who would otherwise be a menace can by training become tolerable.'

When Clive Parry produced a Bibliography of McNair's writings, Robbie was asked to provide the brief Introduction. It ends by mentioning in particular

'…just one of [the minor writings] which this writer remembers with affection because, while he was still an undergraduate, it shed light for him on the hitherto dark pages of the *Polemis* case. The article carries the arresting

---

215 *Collected Writings* Vol. II p.1307
216 *Collected Writings* Vol. I p.314

title: "This Polemis Business". This seems to epitomise the McNair approach: urbane; slyly humorous; gently sardonic; an almost architectural sense of the structure and elements of the law; a refusal ever to seek safety and refuge in jargon and obscurity; definitive.'

That summer of 1975, as in his first Long Vacation, Dick had chosen to work as a farmer's boy for Trumpington Farms, spending long days out on the nearby fields driving a tractor and lugging great irrigation pipes about. Pippa was earning some pocket-money at Heffers bookshop, and we had Joey's French exchange friend with us.

Robbie went off to spend eight days in Germany for the *Institut* meeting at Wiesbaden. It was an attractive place, and the customary Sunday outing should have been a delight – a boat trip on the Rhine – when

'…They sipped wines from various vineyards and admired the views; but the day was darkened for them all by their coming upon a tragedy at the start – an upturned rowing-boat from which two children had been drowned, and which their accompanying police-launch efficiently took charge of. His final day was spent, actually, at Heidelberg, where a friend, Dr Gunter Jaenike, and wife entertained him and another couple to sumptuous meals.'

Later he had more talks with visiting Argentine diplomats before escaping to Arment House. And Dick, after energetic walks there, took a week-long course in gliding at Perranporth, ending with a solo flight.

Robbie's next visit to Geneva got off to a bad start. He and Mr Robb, the driver, had become such friends that they, chatting animatedly, set off in the car to Heathrow without realising that Robbie's suitcase, containing papers as well as clothes, was left behind in the hall. After leaving at 4.45 pm, they did not get back, crestfallen, until 11 pm … and set off once more at 7 am next morning to catch a less convenient flight. But his meetings went well; he spent a pleasant weekend with Sami and Suzie Shubber; with a series of meetings afterwards of the International Committee on European Migration which proved particularly interesting and introduced him to some important people from Italy, France, Egypt and Venezuela.

And there was more variety, right up to Christmas – one being a lecture[217] at Chatham House given by Sir Michael Palliser, Permanent Under-Secretary at the Foreign Office.

Dick, in his final year at Oxford, was beginning to think about what might succeed his PPE course, and so was attending some law lectures out of interest. It led to his later move to Jesus College, Cambridge for Part I of the Law Tripos (and also to an invitation to Robbie to be Edward Burn's[218] guest at a Christ Church Gaudy). One Saturday Mike Ely[219] and Jeremy Carver came to lunch, conferring afterwards with Robbie about the ongoing *Buttes Gas & Oil* dispute with Hammer, or perhaps the new *Tunisia/Libya* boundary case, another major undertaking.

We now heard from Rosamund that she had found accommodation at Nether Wasdale, close to Rosalind's cottage, and would be leaving Arment House. This was a relief, though it presented some fresh problems as the place really needed an occupant. But her departure lifted a cloud of faint resentment on both sides, and our relations became easier. With the removal of her furniture, we needed to start afresh, collecting chairs, beds and tables on a few shopping expeditions to sales and junk shops in Cambridge, all to be somehow transported to Eskdale. Mr Robb provided the solution. One Sunday he arrived very early with a large hired van into which everything was packed. He then drove Robbie all the way there and back in the one day – steep hills, hairpin bends and all. Lean and muscular, he did most of the carrying upstairs of beds, and together they got all the stuff, mostly flat-packed, into the right rooms. There was just time to eat the lunch I had provided and to take in the fine view before their 300-mile return journey; but Mr Robb always said afterwards what fun that day had been.

Next time Dick and a friend went up for a climbing holiday at Arment, they first had to assemble some of the furniture they found there. Robbie,

---

217   This was organised by the David Davies Institute, on whose executive committee Robbie served.

218   Edward Burn was Law Tutor and Student of Christ Church, later Professor at City University, London.

219   Northcutt Ely, of the Watergate Building, Washington DC, was a lawyer with expertise on seabed mining for oil and other valuable resources.

meanwhile, worked in Geneva with the Argentine team, and later spent a few days conferring with colleagues on the *English Channel* case in Jersey. We met the Bailiff, the Attorney-General and the Greffier[220] and their wives, all very friendly.

At last the whole family travelled up to Eskdale, to a house that was entirely our own. It was a busy stay: 'all five of us,' I wrote, 'have been washing, polishing, hammering, plastering, painting and generally trying to improve Arment House,' with one or two real walks before it was time to leave.

That summer Robbie was so engrossed both in the *Beagle Channel* and the *English Channel* case which was due to be heard soon after, that I saw little of him. Then at short notice, with the Oral Hearing of the *Beagle* case starting straight after, he was off for his first visit to Tunisia for one day of intensive work. I commented afterwards –

'I suppose as a man of nearly-63, he ought by rights to have been feeling whacked, but he was stimulated and regretful that I had not been able to share his latest adventures…

[Ringing from Geneva] He told me that, although it was the time of Ramadan, his hosts ['important oil chaps'] gave him the most concentrated dose of Tunis life possible in one evening. People end their fast at nightfall, and so the Kasbah, where they went, was particularly animated. And he was driven to Carthage. Most exciting!'

And for Dick there had come a summons of a different kind:

'… there was a telegraph boy on a motorbike (we'd almost forgotten they still exist) with a wire for 'Jennings' from Geneva. But this one was for Dicky. "Come soonest with black shoes and white shirts" – an invitation from Robbie's usual hotel, who will take him on as a waiter!'

Actually, he did not go 'soonest', but once back from his Arment stay, was given a lift by a friend's uncle who was driving to Rome. And at the Hotel

---

220   The Channel Islands keep to some of their original Norman French for legal matters. The Bailiwick of Jersey is a Dependency of the British Crown, which appoints the Bailiff (President of the States Assembly and head of judiciary) and Greffier (Registrar of the Crown Court).

d'Angleterre, dressed in a blue uniform suit, he found his role was not to be a waiter but a *chasseur*, running errands for hotel residents and acting as hall porter in the evenings. It was hard work – 'room poky, food appalling' – but a very good training in the sort of French needed in banks, shops and everyday conversation.

When Robbie next returned to Geneva, he was at first a little hesitant about staying as usual at the hotel lest it embarrass Dick. In the event, father and son took some meals out together, Dick read newspapers in his father's room in the evening, and they enjoyed each other's company. They were entertained, too, by Sami Shubber and by an Indian Old Leysian friend of Dick's. Altogether, our *chasseur* worked for seven weeks at the hotel, with one or two memorable short breaks in the mountains.

At the end of August Robbie took me with him to Madrid for the ILA conference, where he delivered the first McNair Memorial Lecture, greatly praised: Richard Wilberforce's comment in a letter afterwards was 'I wish we could organise a star performance like that at all our Conferences'. Our two-day stay was just enough to allow us time to see the Prado and the Royal Palace.

Before setting off for his next journey, Robbie wrote to my father about his decision to become an underwriting member at Lloyd's. It would be a relatively small commitment, but – apart from our house – just about all he could manage. He confessed:

'… And of course there *are* risks – not least at present with the whole future so uncertain. It may be then that I am rather foolish to plunge, especially when approaching retirement.

'On the other hand, with things so very uncertain one almost feels that just another risk is neither here nor there. And also I have reached the time when I would enjoy a new, quite different interest. The syndicate who have invited me is a cautious one. They always themselves reinsure for catastrophe risks but do not do that class of insurance themselves. In the worst ever year for Lloyd's – Hurricane Betsy in 1965 – the average loss per name at Lloyd's for that year was £7,000, and Langton's highest loss was £2,000 …

'The other thing that attracts me about this group is that they are all old friends of mine.'

And that was a significant point. *Langton Underwriting Agents Limited* was run by Tommy and 'Bungie' Langton among others, both brothers having been pupils of his at Jesus. Tommy, who came up before the war, was one of the small group Robbie had taught while still himself at Downing, and Jeremy/ Bungie had joined the college after the war. Both were great oarsmen and very good company. An advantage of the proposed scheme was that Robbie would be relieved, to a large extent, of having to decide how to invest his capital.

It would be a few years later, when he had been made a Judge of the ICJ, that he became concerned lest being a 'name' at Lloyd's was incompatible with his new position. As it turned out, his withdrawal was complete just before claims arising from the *Torrey Canyon* disaster drained so many accounts.

At home, I was typing 'yet again' the McNair Memorial Lecture, this time for publication. 'It's as well Robbie is at a safe distance now, otherwise he would *still* be improving it and messing up this typescript!' In the days before the use of computers his perfectionism meant repeated efforts liable to be returned with afterthoughts, additions and rearrangements of paragraphs signified with a variety of symbols, all to be typed afresh from the beginning.

Why was the Whewell Professor called to advise the Channel Islands, Sharjah, Bangladesh and so many others? His explanation, to his unbelieving and amused daughters, was 'You see, I'm very *trendy*'. He had indeed built up considerable expertise on coastal disputes.

Two of the other Cambridge international lawyers at that time were trendy, too. Eli Lauterpacht, advising the Chile team, had been down to the Beagle Channel and had taken the opportunity to tease Robbie. Two envelopes had arrived in the post, one marked *Isla Nueva 18 March 72* and the other *Isla Picton 18 March 72*. Inside, each contained a small sheet of paper with a scrawled message: 'Greetings from Chile / Eli'.

Now at last, in late September 1976 the second bout of Oral Hearings were under way. I went to join him in Geneva for a weekend which turned out to be typical of many over the coming years:

'Robbie had supposed it would coincide with a lull when he, (who had had *no* free time except an hour's outing with friends in their car during his four-week slog) could escape and enjoy things with me. In fact that happened only partially. It turned out that he was due to address the Court again on the Monday and Tuesday, and that the Argentines wanted several points presented quite differently from the prepared texts. So he worked all Saturday, Sunday and Monday mornings, and from 3-7.30 on Sat. and 4-8 pm on Sun; and I bade him goodbye at 1.50 on Monday before catching my 'plane back at 5.45! Still, it *then* turned out that he was free on Tuesday evening – and he came home for a week's break. That "break" consists of catching up with accumulated correspondence, university and college meetings, and a trip to London tomorrow for talks at the Foreign Office (with a French Memorial to read and digest in preparation)… He relaxes, as far as he can, in his own way. The gramophone was playing merrily yesterday evening, he came for a walk with the dog, made silly jokes at supper, and unwound over the *Hi-Fi News*.'

Pippa received a postcard on her birthday (27ᵗʰ September) with his own description of his activities –

'I open our case in Court on Friday & have just been through my speech for the umpteenth time for this is the 4ᵗʰ draft & it still seems to me to be capable of improvement. Monday I shall be in Court but probably not speaking myself again till Thursday…

'I have not had time even to go for little walks this last week – just work & sleep. But my French is improving no end with a long stay. Today I managed to buy a new watch strap in French without the man offering to speak English. And I find I can do simple telephone calls like refusing invitations!'

The Oral Hearings of the *Beagle Channel*[221] case officially came to an end on 23ʳᵈ October 1976 in the International Labour Organisation buildings in Geneva. But the case, I wrote, was 'giving one last twitch – a sort of postscript exchange of opinions on a few fresh ideas which had cropped up in the Argentine "final" reply'. And when he finally got home on a Sunday afternoon, he then spent the Monday in Oxford examining a D.Phil candidate… 'Even if he did take a break, he says, what on earth would he *do*?' I became resigned to a husband who feared that if he allowed himself to unwind, he might never wind up again.

---

[221] The arbitration court consisted of 5 judges: Dillard (US), Fitzmaurice (UK), Gros (France), Onyeama (Nigeria) and Petrén (Sweden).

There was no chance of that. In the final weeks of 1976 we again attended a David Davies lecture, this time delivered by the Rt. Hon. George Thomson, talking about his four years as first Commissioner for Britain to the Economic Community. At dinner afterwards in the River Room at the Savoy were several guests met before – Lord Home, 'so nice and gawky and humble', with well-darned socks and NHS specs just like my own; Lord Wilberforce and his wife Yvette, who sat next to Robbie and told him in detail about her great mauling by an enraged elephant in Ceylon a few years before; Sir Francis Vallatt; Lord Caccia; and Lord Noel-Baker, who was my neighbour and dazzled me with his recollections. Typically, Robbie and I passed the train journey home in proof-reading for the British Yearbook of International Law.

On Christmas Eve Robbie was busy with representatives of Rio Tinto Zinc, providing him with yet another task on which work was postponed until Boxing Day. Meantime, this year's Christmas treat to ourselves was our first (small) colour television set.

At the turn of the year we went up to Arment House – a labour-intensive undertaking as usual. Since Robbie's driving licence had expired, he entrusted Dick with driving, taking us over the steep passes ('Unsuitable for traffic in winter conditions') where a few skiers were enjoying the snowy tops: five people, a dog and lots of luggage; one house to leave clean and tidy; another to be warmed up and have its beds made. Evenings were spent around a log fire in the snug parlour. Our stay could be for six days only because of the demands of Robbie's work; so we left, tantalisingly, on a brilliantly fine and frosty day, ideal for skating on one of the tarns ... and on our return there were 17 pairs of woollen socks for me to hand-wash.

When the *Dispositif* (or Award) on the Beagle Channel was announced on 2nd May 1977, it ruled that all three islands, Lennox, Picton and Nueva, belonged to Chile, and a new clear boundary line was established. That should have concluded the matter. But, unlike almost every other arbitration, one party refused to accept the ruling. The Argentine junta, a year later, threatened military action against Chile, and the matter was referred to the Vatican for mediation. After some six years of study, the papal decision supported that of the original Arbitration Tribunal, and was accepted.

Yet More Cases

1977

There was certainly no danger of Robbie unwinding. He was straight into work on the *Franco-British Continental Shelf Delimitation* case.[222] It meant spending weeks away again, this time with Derek Bowett acting as counsel with him. I told my father that he had no time to write me letters …

'… So he rings up each Sunday. He sounds cheerful – his stamina amazes me: they are working till past midnight each day. Yesterday (Sunday) it was bed at 2 am and up early to work again. He will himself be addressing the Court on Tuesday, Wednesday and possibly Thursday; and it's just possible that he may be able to get home for a slight rest next weekend. He and the others in the working team … get themselves snack lunches in their hotel and go out for an evening meal.

[On 23rd February I wrote] 'Robbie rang up a few minutes ago – 11 o'clock by his time, 10 pm by ours – and said that the French, the stinkers, had given notice that on Friday they would reply to the English reply to the French reply to the first English reply … and so, instead of coming home that day, he would have to stay to give *them* a reply on Monday morning. But that really will be the end of this arbitration … The French "stinkers" were, of course, also charming …'

By late March 1977 Robbie was turning his attention again to Sharjah, the small emirate on the Persian Gulf which was now in a boundary dispute with its neighbour Dubai – with his friend Derek Bowett this time on the opposing side. Once again the process of arbitration would take some years. And now, tantalisingly –

---

[222] I refer to this as the *English Channel* case.

'... Robbie has to consider very seriously a pressing invitation from the University of Witwatersrand, where the students (white and black) nominated him as visiting lecturer some years ago. [The proposal was for six weeks at the university, with two extra spent on a trip to the Cape and the chance of a safari.] He had had to put it off for two summers because of other work; and this time, he feels, he ought to go. The three children all have their own plans for the summer (Dicky farming, Pippa working full-time at Heffers; Joey off to France for August) and *say* I could go with Robbie. I should be thrilled to share the adventure ...'

But it was not really going to be possible that year. We found that Derek Bowett was later invited to take Robbie's place; but he, with three children of exactly the same ages as ours and a busy practice, also had to say 'No'.

Our spring break at Arment House allowed just one really intoxicating walk with the girls:

'... up Yewbarrow, the tough craggy height which looks across Wastwater to the Scafell group of mountains, and has from its long ridge-walk a wonderful variety of revelations all around. Robbie, with a heavy cold, nearly gave up on a steep scrambly bit ("Age does tell on you", he complained – he used to be up Yewbarrow between tea and supper in his younger days); but fortunately he got up and enjoyed it all. And I think the break has helped dispel some of his tiredness (although a *little* opinion on Dubai got written while there!)'

Leaving Pippa behind, our drive home involved a large diversion into Shropshire as we delivered Joey to join her friend Tamsin for a week's stay in the Geach family's retreat, which turned out not to be the imagined dear little stone cottage but a long red tin hut standing alone on a hillside. Her stay there exposed her to a quite different donnish family, whose parents were both professors of philosophy,[223] and the upbringing of their large family was notoriously unconventional. It was good to find that Joey had enjoyed her rather strange experience:

'... The effect of frequent theological discussion, a constant barrage of bookishness, and a strongly carnivorous and grimy version of "the simple life"

---

[223] Peter Geach was teaching Philosophy at the University of Leeds at the time. Elizabeth Anscombe, his wife, a disciple of Wittgenstein, was Professor of Philosophy at Cambridge.

for a week seems to be a more articulate and self-confident Joey, ravenously hungry for everything except meat! Her role was largely a Caliban one, chopping wood endlessly for the great fire kept in an open hearth; but she did go riding three times too, and interest in horses is revived.'

Soon after, Robbie and I attended a banquet at the Mansion House. We had been invited by…

'… the Master of the Worshipful Company of Solicitors of the City of London, a relatively new (post-war) livery company. The Master, George Clark, was at Jesus just before and after the war, and was taught by a rather raw and diffident Robbie in his last year. He had asked the Bursar, Derek Taunt (contemporary as an undergraduate) for the College Grace to be spoken at the banquet… We knew precious few people there – and there were a vast number. All white ties and tails, and decorations – the Lord Mayor, Sheriff and such particularly grand; great stately rooms with chandeliers, the dining hall really enormous and high, with a string quintet playing like mad (but almost inaudibly,) on a distant gallery; six speeches … The bit I enjoyed most was the passing-around of the Loving Cup. Robbie thinks of hygiene and has reservations; but it is such a charming ceremony that it's worth the germs. It is a custom which I think has now finally died out in Cambridge, though it dates back to King Edward the Martyr and the manner of it has to do with protecting the drinker from attack while he is actually taking his turn. "When a guest receives the Loving Cup, he turns to the neighbour who will drink after him and they bow to each other. The latter removes the cover from the cup, holding it while the bearer of the cup drinks and wipes the rim with the napkin. The cover is then replaced, the two bow to each other again, and the cup changes hands. The same procedure continues round the table, each guest who has drunk remaining standing, back to back with the next drinker, and resuming his seat only when the cup cover is replaced." It is all very stately and nice. The cups, of course, were fabulous great things of silver and silver-gilt.'

It was either on that occasion or when we later attended an actual Lord Mayor's Banquet that I found Robbie failing to bow to me. 'If I bend forward, the woman behind me will fall over', he muttered. She had been drinking heavily from the succession of wines and was leaning against him.

June 1977: Dick taking his Final Schools, Pippa her A Levels, Prince Philip made Chancellor of Cambridge University[224] and, surpassing all, the Queen's Silver Jubilee. Robbie and I attended the great tea party for the new Chancellor at Trinity –

> '—some 800 guests, many in scarlet gowns of course. He is marvellously friendly and interested, even though any more ordinary mortal would have been fagged out by the week's events. He told someone he was feeling "a bit like Walter Mitty" with the many changes of role and costume, though: one day an Admiral of the Fleet, another academic Chancellor, then sitting astride a horse as a Colonel!'

Grantchester made a great effort for the Jubilee, with a pageant arranged by 25 groups (leaving few villagers on the roadside to watch). Robbie joined us for the hog roast and the sports held on the Meadows when, after the children's races, there was a tug-of-war competition between men and women. So many women joined in that the rope broke – and Robbie caught a blurred photograph of us all falling on our backs.

At Jesus there was an innovation – a dinner for Fellows and Staff. (No longer was the status of *College Servant,* essential to the wellbeing of these ancient institutions, recognised as an honourable one, but was now, apparently, considered demeaning.) Times were changing: already in 1976 the college's first woman Fellow, Lisa Jardine,[225] had been installed. She, and the women undergraduates who were admitted a few years later, were welcomed by Robbie.

And in that summer of 1977 I became a beekeeper – something that would involve many curious, and sometimes painful, episodes over the following 20 years as I learnt much of its fascinating art. Robbie firmly left it all to me, though he once or twice assisted when I had to take a swarm high up in a tree: he, in protective clothing, standing at the bottom of the ladder with a long pruning-pole hooked over the branch above, waiting for me to get my skep into place and shout – at which he jerked his pole. The great dollop of bees would fall into the skep – and he would quickly withdraw indoors.

---

224   Prince Philip, Duke of Edinburgh, served as an active Chancellor until the year of the Queen's Diamond Jubilee.

225   Lisa Jardine was the daughter of Jacob Bronowski, himself a famous Jesuan.

On the second of our escapes to Eskdale in the vacation, we were joined one day by our new friends, the Cottrells. Jean and Alan were staying in a cottage in Borrowdale belonging to an Old Jesuan, Alan Hill,[226] and drove through heavy rain for tea, seeing little of Eskdale's scenery. After they left, of course the sky cleared, and Robbie and I walked up onto Burn Moor in glorious evening sunshine. This time we left the house clean and tidy for the next visitors, Father Barnabus Lindars[227] and his sister.

—

In between those breaks Robbie was immersed in his various advisory tasks: off to Rotterdam in a small 'executive jet' for a seven-hour meeting in The Hague on Shell business; more consultations; more typing for me; another trip to Tunis; and at the end of September yet another visit to Jersey – this time probably to discuss the ruling given by the Court of Arbitration on the continental shelf delimitation earlier that year. (The *English Channel* case was to reach its final conclusion in March 1978, clearing up some technical details.)

It was now that a quite different project was suggested in a letter from Judge Hardy Dillard[228], who, when presiding over the *Beagle* arbitration tribunal, had been so impressed by Robbie's performance that he had urged the University of Virginia to invite him there as a Visiting Lecturer. Together with the invitation, he enclosed a copy of his recommendation:

'On the personal level let me say [Dillard wrote] that of all the outstanding advocates who have appeared before the International Court of Justice in the last seven years and the numerous advocates who argued before our Tribunal in the Beagle Channel Case, I would put him at the very top of all, the more so because of his personality and his capacity to communicate in a way that I am sure will appeal to our students and faculty.'

It was a huge compliment; but that visit could not, alas, be fitted into an already over-busy life.

---

[226]   Alan Hill, a well-known publisher at Heinemann.
[227]   The Rev. Prof. Barnabus Lindars, Anglican Franciscan and biblical scholar, was Dean of Jesus College at the time.
[228]   Judge Hardy Dillard, of the ICJ, had been a member of the Arbitration Tribunal for the *Beagle* case. Before joining the International Court he had been Professor of International Law at Virginia.

The new academic year meant that Dick, buying the necessary B.A. gown and college tie, would start on a year at Jesus studying Law for Part I of the Cambridge Tripos; and Pippa was to read History at Leeds.

We drove Pippa up to her Hall of Residence, a typical northern grand house at Adel, on the outskirts of Leeds. But Robbie could not help feeling anxious lest that move from south to north might be for her the sort of culture-shock that he had experienced in reverse as a northern freshman at Downing many years before. The horror of his first year came back to him vividly, and the day after our journey he sat down and wrote to her:

'… Coming back yesterday … I was thinking of how you must be feeling, and of my first arrival in Cambridge. Yours in Leeds was, I can assure you, a great improvement on that!

'In those days there were men at the station, to meet students, with little hand carts. And for a tip they carried the luggage thus to one's lodgings. I was in lodgings at 14 Mawson Road, between Mill Road and the station. I had the little bay-windowed front room to myself, and a bedroom I suppose. The front room, which was filthy dirty and smelt of dirt and messy cooking from the kitchen, remains vividly in my memory. The bedroom, oddly enough, I cannot recollect at all.

'The loo was out at the back, through the kitchen. On the way through the kitchen one had to pass bearded Mr D., who sat in the only armchair staring at nothing any time of day the pub across the road was not open. Any time the pub was open, Mr D. was not at home.

'Mrs D., quite soon in term, would cringe and wheedle till she got the whole term's rent out of me in advance. Once she resorted to a stratagem that I only tumbled to much later (I was *incredibly* green and frightened and submissive). She told me her daughter was very ill in bed and she couldn't afford to get a doctor. I paid the rent. Shortly after, I heard a furious daughter charge downstairs and out of the door shouting, "It's ridiculous, Mother, I won't stay in my room a minute longer; I'm going out whatever you say!"

'Do you know, I stuck that awful squalor for a whole year because I hadn't the nerve to complain. I remember one particular moment of shame when a Methodist "group" met in my room (the Methodists were the saving of my sanity, I must say – marvellous friendship provided for all) and one of the girls banged my sofa, with clouds of dust coming out, and said "That's dirt". That was the parson's daughter, Marie Hamon. If I'd had any sense I would have asked her to go and interview my landlady for me, which she would have done willingly and effectively!

'Poor Mrs D.! I'm afraid she *did* have an awful life, getting pennies here and there and Mr D. drinking it all across the road. I am afraid I might have been her last undergraduate. At the end of the year (*how* I loathed Cambridge you can imagine after my spotless home in Yorkshire!), I asked my old-Etonian tutor, Hyde Charnock Whalley-Tooker no less, whether I could change lodgings. He said "What is wrong, then, with the old?" And I, no doubt scarlet with shame (because in Yorkshire dirt was *the* sin against the Holy Ghost), said "They're not very clean". His eyebrows shot up, and he said "Ah! That, Jennings, is rather a serious fault, is it not?" He said no more, but I'm sure she must have been struck off the list. At least the interview with my tutor was the beginning of a restoration of my faith in the "south". They were not *all* dirty. And, at any rate an old-Etonian felt that dirtiness was "rather serious".

'Oh, but the misery! I would get a Heffers calendar (free to all undergraduates then) and cross out the days, and count, and count, the days remaining for my return to Idle. And yet also the then hidden joy! The beginnings, so very slight but yet important for me, of independence, and meeting different sorts of people and finding they did not entirely dislike me …'

This outpouring continued for several more pages, with recommendations that Pippa should look at the beautiful Adel church nearby, get out into the country beyond, and stop on her walk to the university campus to buy the delicious curd tarts sold by Silvio's, the baker's shop.

This was followed by more letters at regular intervals, full of reminiscences and gossip. On 14th October he reported:

'… I have been pretty busy of late. The term is well under way and at the same time I have had other jobs to do. I was at Coward Chance yesterday, and Jeremy Carver was anxious to know how you are getting on.

'This year, amongst the graduates who have come to do international law as a special subject or for research, we have several Americans, some Canadians (both sexes), *three* from Iceland (if you count one wife who is *really* a musician), some Africans (Ghana and Cameroons), an Italian girl from near

Padua, a Turk from Istanbul, 3 Germans from West Germany, a Sudanese, an Egyptian and an Englishman! It is very nice to feel that young people from so many countries want to come here to study international law. Oh, I forgot! There is also a Belgian, and a Dutchman and a Spaniard.

'Yesterday in Coward Chance I saw a wonderful new machine which was "typing" – if that is the word – one of my Opinions. The first typist types on a machine that transfers the letters … to a magnetic card … The card is then put with others in this machine which "types" it (actually it *squirts* ink!) perfectly at the rate of one page in 14 seconds. Moreover this machine is controlled by a computer [with all the magic of "justifying" and so on]. How it does that and yet also observes the paragraphs, spacing between headings etc. passes my imagination. But I saw it doing it.

'I delivered 170 pages of Opinion to them yesterday, with quite a lot of corrections and alterations. [Next day] 8 copies, printed and bound, were delivered to the people who wanted them … Tomorrow it will be on its way to Canada for a cabinet meeting on Monday…'

Three days later he wrote:

'… I am very, very pleased that you have taken to Leeds. It was, after all, my University (& indeed I might have been Vice Chancellor of it if the question hadn't arisen just as we moved to Grantchester – and anyway it is not quite Mummy's cup of tea, entertaining all week!)

———

'Examinations/Continuous Assessment – mainly a matter of temperament. *I* would choose the examination every time. That is because (a) I would not like the *continuous* pressure and tension of the other system (b) the short answer written to a time-limit is a better test. Long essays are difficult to make really good until you *are* good and that is logically at the end of your training; (c) I, at least, thrive on the tension of the big occasion. I feel sick and feel like running away. But I always do better once it starts than I possibly could in a routine thing. It may well be that you are much the same and will show up better on the big occasion than from day to day.

'Anyway, you can get the best of both worlds. Your work throughout the year must make some impression even subconscious on your potential examiners, even if you are not on that particular assembly line, and yet you have *another* chance in the written examination to confirm or improve upon that impression…'

The following week, hearing that Pippa was joining the university choir to sing *Messiah* evoked more memories, of the many performances of that work in Bradford by two great rivals, *The Old Choral Society* and the *Bradford Festival Choral Society* (which now had a '*very* promising young conductor, Richard Hickox[229]) when many in the audience either followed the score or knew it from memory.

'As a very little boy, I got sufficient thrill out of the Idle Chapel Messiahs, with organ accompaniment (probably a guest organist, though. The Wesleyans and Baptists had rival Messiahs, and there was always dispute about which was the best. But it was much the same people singing in the "augmented" choir anyway. Men who never darkened the door of the chapel on any other occasion would turn up to "help" with the choir (not having been to any rehearsals!) The old hands rather took pride in holding their scores down at their sides to show they knew it anyway. The chapel would be packed out, with forms in the aisles. And the great thing in the choruses would be to make the roof collapse if possible.

'I remember – I must have looked a wild-eyed little boy in my excitement – watching Wilfred Knutton, the captain of Idle Cricket 2nd XI & a good slow bowler, with his big chest stuck out, his copy down at his side, belting out the Hallelujah Chorus from the basses. And then there would be plump, dapper little Reggie Goldsborough on the tenor side, always a bit early and a bit sharp. And there was Herbert Saville joining in – a rather good tenor. But he wouldn't go into the choir (he had come out after some obscure row before my time), so *that* tenor part came loud and clear from two pews behind! You see one knew all about "surround sound" even in those days.

'The soloists engaged for the occasion would be mainly from the north round-about. Struggling would-be artists who were glad of £3.3.0 for the afternoon. But of course if you were lucky, they could be the unknown up-and-coming, and very good indeed. For instance, I first heard Kathleen Ferrier in Idle Wesleyan Chapel, before any but a few locals had even heard the name.

---

[229] Richard Hickox, CBE 1948-2008, achieved great success as an orchestral conductor, with many acclaimed recordings.

———

'Last night we had a dinner in College to celebrate the 30th anniversary of the founding of "The Club". I had to make a speech proposing the health of the "founder Members". I was not quite a F.M., having been elected very soon after its foundation.

'It was pleasant to see some of my old pupils again. Professor Peter Mathias from Oxford, now Professor (they *all* seem to be Professors now) Alan Weir, now in the chair of mathematics in Sussex, Bob Heller, now a financial pundit who talks on the radio about economics from time to time, and of course Mike Marshall who used to be at Ball's Grove [in Grantchester] you remember.

'I told them about Joey's effort at a constitution for a good club – "Rool 2: do not start larfing and being stupid in meatings". Still a very good rule for *any* club. That brought the house down and it was some time before I could continue!'

———

'On Thursday I saw a Dr Moreno from El Salvador (just N. of Panama in the thin neck of Central America) who wanted to consult about a border dispute with Honduras. They have already had a little war over it, but decided they weren't getting anywhere that way. An enormous jolly, pompous man, who had a quiet little chap from their Embassy trailing behind him picking the bits up (literally, because at the Garden House, where they took me for lunch, Moreno left a clutch of pound notes on the sofa when he got up). They had had some time to spare before coming to my rooms, having arrived in Cambridge early. So Moreno had gone to Ryder & Amis, bought a Jesus College tie, changed in the shop, and arrived at the Porters' Lodge to greet an astonished and nonplussed Mr West [Head Porter] wearing his Jesus tie! I suppose he thought it was a sort of compliment to me.

'Anyway, the long and short of it is that I may have to go to El Salvador sometime – very hot and sticky (well within the tropics) but it could well be beautiful. We shall see. I gather that it was one of my Argentine friends who told them to come to me...'

He did not go to El Salvador; he was suddenly summoned to Canada, and his next letter tells of that rushed visit.

'13 Nov. 1977

'Well, I had my Canada adventure. I didn't do them much good, I'm afraid and I returned with a depressing feeling of failure as far as the work went. It is a mistake, I decided, to attempt to go straight into a conference from the airport, suffering from a 9-hour time difference. One feels impossibly sleepy and tired. Then when one gets to bed it is by one's internal clock time to get up, so one can't sleep, one keeps getting up, looking at the clock and wanting breakfast terribly at about midnight.

'But the trip itself was exciting and I wouldn't have missed it for anything. The journey out to Ottawa was 1.15 pm from London, arriving Montreal at 3.15 pm! By the way, that was my first flight in a Jumbo (Boeing 747) and I liked it – lots more room and no feeling of enclosure. It was British Airways, in which the service is a little officious but very good. [He found Montreal dark, foggy and pouring with rain.]

'From Montreal to Ottawa, what a contrast in mode of conveyance! Instead of waiting for the Air Canada jet, I elected to take the local service – a tiny twin propeller de Haviland "Otter", to carry eight passengers. Very, very noisy. The pilots, in shirt sleeves, did not bother to shut their compartment door, so one could watch the whole operation. So we flew quite low in the fog to Ottawa – about 100 miles.

'At Ottawa I was met and whisked through the driving rain to a quite nice but very large hotel called "Chateau Laurier" (Ottawa is still quite a lot French-speaking – Montreal, of course, is in Quebec Province and speaks French entirely; but nearly everyone also speaks English.) [After a 'club sandwich' and beer, he went to bed.] 'In the morning, breakfast in my room at 6.50 am and picked up by government car at 7.35. We picked up the leader of our delegation, Ambassador Cadieux, a French-speaking Canadian from Montreal, and very, very impressive. Then to airport to meet rest of delegation – 4 of us in all.

'I should explain that this was a delegation from the central, federal government in Ottawa, to the government of the Province of British Columbia. You see Canada is, like the USA, a Federal system comprised of separate States or Provinces, each of which has a large measure of sovereignty and independence. The Federal Govt. is responsible for external relations, but it must get the agreement of the Provinces in most important matters. And the situation is delicate because the French separatists threaten (with the help of France) to break away from the Federation altogether. (The French have never forgiven the conquest of Quebec by Wolfe.) 'Of course not all French

Canadians want to break away. Ambassador Cadieux took a much more realistic view. But it is not unlike Scottish nationalism and the devolution problem.

'However, we got a DC9 jet from Ottawa, still in rain and fog, so there was no view. The route was over the Great Lakes ... and first to a short stop at Winnipeg. Here it was not raining but it *had* been snowing. After Winnipeg, the prairies of Saskatchewan, sprinkled with the first snow. And then the Rockies – but fog and rain again and not even a glimpse.

'This journey added another 3 hours of time difference, so we landed at Vancouver (rain and fog!) at about 1 pm local time, but having in fact flown for over 6 hours.

'Then by another jet over 80 miles of island-studded sea to Vancouver Island – fog and rain, but even so very beautiful indeed, with wonderful green fields and forests, mountains, rivers and sea.

'Then taxi for 12 miles to the capital City of Victoria – i.e. the capital of the entire vast Province of British Columbia, which includes most of the Rockies and out to these islands in the blue Pacific (*really* blue – much bluer than the Mediterranean).

'Victoria curious but nice place. *Very* British in an old-fashioned way. Stayed in famous hotel called the "Empress", where they serve muffins for tea every afternoon, and the great wide corridors have pictures of members of the Royal Family including all the Victoria relations. The City had photographs of our present Queen everywhere. Beautiful harbour just by hotel, with seagulls to wake one in the morning with their cries, and old-fashioned steamer hooters.

'After the meeting in the huge and very impressive government buildings, we had dinner all together at the "Union Club" – *very* English again. The sweet was apple pie and cheese!

'British Columbia is *extremely* attractive. The country is superb, and they have water, sea, oil, timber – everything.

'It was nice to see banks with open counters, instead of assistants in cages. Very civilized!

'In the afternoon it was time to start back, so bus to airport and then jet (fog and rain!). The 80 miles or so over the sea to the mainland at Vancouver.

'By this time I had with me Professor McCrae of the University of British Columbia, who is now visiting in Cambridge (the one with the kids at our party in the summer). We had a couple of hours to spare at Vancouver. So we hired a car and he drove me to the University (superb position out on a headland at "English Bay", with forest all round it) and then a look at the City. But couldn't see any mountains. Raining harder than ever!

'And so to UK by "direct" route, i.e. over Hudson's Bay, Greenland and Iceland, then north coast of Ireland, Solway, and Manchester, Birmingham, Heathrow. Jumbo again but now Air Canada – very good. And Mr Robb waiting.

'I *like* Canada. Everything works. And all the people seem so friendly and helpful. If you got into difficulties I am sure somebody would rush up and help. And all so cheerful too. Quite sold on it!

'Of course, British Columbia is the place. In the east they have this terrible long winter, with snow for 5 months, and temperatures of up to 30° of frost. But BC is mild, with super summers. Must be incredibly beautiful when the sun is shining. Even in rain and fog, it was beautiful.

'Well, there it is! All in 3 days! I've been pretty well sleeping ever since.'

I told my father about his return home after this experience: –

'He arrived home at lunchtime on Friday, and was later with me at the Inauguration of the new University [West Road] Concert Hall by Prince Philip, which went off very pleasantly, with most accomplished music-making by university musicians. I was worried at his driving home in the gale after a very late meeting that same evening … but he got home safely. Sleepiness made itself felt over the weekend, though; so we all enjoyed a good fire in the sitting room and some television.'

Lawyers – some young students, some eminent – were constantly turning up to be entertained at the house; but at the end of November 1977 it was an attractive family with five young children (two boys and triplet girls) who came to tea. I wrote:

'The father is a Foreign Office lawyer [Frank Berman[230]] who was here to give a particularly good talk to the International Law Club, and they had all come for the weekend to see Cambridge. It was such fun to have well-behaved,

---

[230] Later Sir Franklin Berman, Chief Legal Adviser to the Foreign Office, and the author of a generous article about Robbie for the New Oxford Dictionary of National Biography.

high-spirited children on our hearth gazing into the fire (which they never had at home), eating lots and lots of tea, and rushing around the house after a self-possessed but mischievous Leo!'

And then we all enjoyed a thoroughly good family Christmas.

The Trendy Professor

1978-81

Interwoven with Robbie's many professional commitments were occasional distractions. Our children survived their various adventures, but there was concern about Mrs Banister, our aged neighbour, whose increasing dementia called for tactful assistance. One Sunday, having accepted our invitation to lunch, she failed to appear at our house but could be seen through her window to be expecting us at her own, having laid her dining table with silver, fine glasses, lit candles and all. What to do? It was Robbie who solved the dilemma. He led a procession of the five Jenningses each carrying dishes of hot food to her door. Having eaten at her table, we all thanked her for her hospitality and took away the crockery for washing-up.

Other social events were less bizarre. Sir Alan Cottrell had become the latest university Vice Chancellor, and we greatly enjoyed a dinner in the Master's Lodge with, as was usual on such occasions, interesting guests – Sir Duncan Wilson, Master of Corpus Christi College and former British Ambassador in Moscow, James Meade, recently awarded a Nobel Prize, and so on. This evening our hostess, Jean Cottrell, was rather more than usually agitated, for they were summoned to Sandringham next day. Prince Philip, as new Chancellor, wanted to learn more about the university from Alan, and so they were to stay the night. ("No other guests: just family." Phew!).

In return for Pippa's long newsy letters from Leeds, Robbie chatted about his own doings in January 1978:

'Last night we had a "Club" meeting in college addressed by a distinguished former pupil of mine, Sam Brittan, who writes the economics commentaries in the *Financial Times*. Brilliant paper – witty, amusing, really dense with fact and observation, entitled "Inflation & Democracy". Very instructive to be told what *really* happens, instead of what the politicians (of any party) think happens…

'On Monday and Tuesday I had Jeremy Carver + a couple of Tunisians. There was Ambassador Slim Bengazi – elderly, little English (French or

Arabic), very nice, highly intelligent, noted scholar of Muslim history; and Professor Belaid ("ah-id" pronounce), their Prof. of International Law – not a practising Muslim, very sophisticated, French-educated in Paris, *very* good lawyer, very cultured. Mummy & I gave them a dinner party in College on Tuesday – very nice but a bit wasted. The excellent claret much appreciated by Belaid, but Bengazi had water!

'You will see from the papers that there is trouble in Tunis – I fear it could interfere with our attempts to get our case before the International Court of Justice.

'Oh, and did I mention to you that I went to The Hague last week for just one night? It was one of the Shell meetings – this time with the Dutch end, called "Royal Dutch Shell"… My, is Holland dear, now! But I brought back some Droste chocolates and some Hopjes sweets…

'Also I had a pleasant meeting at the Airport with Federico Mirré (the Argentine who has been to our house several times). He was in London privately (*incognito* as he said). The only chance of a meeting was at London Airport, so I got there a bit early and he nobly came out from the City, and we had ½ -hour together over a beer. He was looking very well.

'You may have seen in the papers that Argentina has *rejected* the Award in the Beagle Channel case. Of course I'm not officially involved now – but I see them from time to time at the Embassy, and I tell them my ideas, and they still send me their confidential papers. The man at the Embassy in London even took the trouble to ring me up and tell me about the rejection before it actually happened, so that I would know it was coming.

'Well, it's a pity in a way – but I do sympathise with them. The Award was very one-sided. Anyway I can never feel *not* involved with whatever Argentina does. I don't know why it appeals to me so much – for they are in many ways a mad lot, who always do the wrong thing or something stupid. But I love 'em all, and there it is!

[He explains why he would not himself be able to meet her train at Huntingdon, because of] a dinner in College for Gardner Smith's 90th birthday. Well done, that man! We all thought he would want a simple lunch. Not at all. He wants a slap-up dinner with everybody in black tie and gowns! …'

Robbie always formed an attachment to each place he was involved in, and the sort of descriptive chat that Pippa received and preserved was what we enjoyed at home.

Easter at Arment House was typical, as I reported:

'The weather has been the sort which must have been terribly trying for people holidaying in tents and guest-houses. We can always find plenty to do indoors – though letter-writing has been almost impossible for the past week, when cold weather kept us all in the main kitchen where the Rayburn is. There, with six people, a sprawling dog and drying clothes hanging from the beams, it was rather too congested; especially when the six needed to be fed, and the other five were all spreading books and papers about. Robbie is reading proofs or other matter; Dicky had law textbooks and files of notes; Pippa lots of volumes on medieval history and political theory; Joey her revision for O Level geography, biology, classics; and Liz[231] rather gruesome textbooks on physiology!

'… on Good Friday we drove to the head of Wasdale … and walked up Sty Head pass, and then a bit further up through snow to Sprinkling Tarn – a heavenly spot. Spectacular views on every side, with climbers ascending with ice-axes, clouds drifting across the tops, and shafts of brilliant light on snow and crag … and – mortification of flesh and spirit for Good Friday! – I had brought up my camera but failed to load its film in!'

Another day Robbie was tied to the house waiting for a telephone engineer (and so spent the time at work on *Oppenheim*) while the rest of us did a splendid walk over to the Duddon valley. Dick left before the rest of us and drove Liz back to Cambridge.

'He afterwards told us how he got a shock later, when listening to the wireless, to hear that "A Cambridge professor and his wife were found dead in bed in their country cottage, with their two children unconscious in another room, from fumes coming from their stove". Since, when he left, we had been fussing about our Rayburn fumes which Robbie and I, sleeping immediately above, suffered from particularly, his heart gave a lurch … he then heard that the tragedy had occurred in Wales.'

And in fact I had climbed onto the roof that day and cleaned the chimney by shoving a pliable ashplant down, and then up from below.

---

[231] Liz Jopling (later Sim), an old schoolfriend of Pippa's, was training as an Occupational Therapist.

On 28th April, 1978 I reported that

'Robbie is on his way to Sharjah … [His] expedition is largely for a formal opening of proceedings between Sharjah and Dubai, in the Gulf: an oil dispute, which will be heard at length in the autumn.'

And on 6th May he wrote to Pippa that 'the family seem to think you would like a blow-by-blow account of the trip':

'Well, it began typically enough. At 9.30 a.m. Mr Robb appeared in a splendid, new bright-red Rover. And we had a pleasant journey to Heathrow, where I met Jeremy Carver, whom you know,[232] and "Mike" Ely, a very tough 70-year-old US Attorney. The flight (Gulf Air) was a 12.25 take-off [and actually left, after repairs and some strong complaints from Jeremy, after 3 pm] … The flight is 8½ hours, so we arrived at Dubai (after one stop at Dohar) at 4 in the morning local time. There we were met by the driver (in Arab dress and headgear) of the manager of the Crescent Petroleum Company. [Slight confusion because Robbie, in his enthusiasm to help with the luggage, snatched up some stranger's brief case and suitcase and added them to their own pile.] Ever-resourceful Jeremy took it back through the armed guards (not easy), found the owner (who had not missed it!) and was back with us within 5 minutes, ready for the 30-minute journey north to neighbouring Sharjah, where we were soon very comfortably installed in the Holiday Inn, where the manager (very young man) was ready to welcome us at 4.30 a.m!

'Up at 10 a.m. – nice breakfast of hot coffee and toast in the Coffee Room… Then to the offices of Crescent Petroleum to meet Hamid Jafar, the young (ex-Cambridge, Iraqi, engineer) manager. I have known him for a long time. The weather was a pleasant surprise. It had been very hot the previous week (106ºF), and this had created turbulence and much cloud from the steaming sea. So it was overcast, humid, but relatively cool (about 88º to 92º). That sounds hot, even so. But one expects it there …

'After some pow-wow, Hamid took us in his Mercedes 350* [R's footnote: *Only the ruling family are allowed Rolls Royces in Sharjah. But that does not apply abroad. Jaffar has a Rolls, a BMW and a Mini at his house in Eaton

---

[232]   … and whose skill in fixing or anticipating trouble was a huge help for years.

Square, Belgravia, for his use in London!] along the sea-front. I said, "Where are we going?" and he said, "To a rather nice restaurant along here". A joke! It turned out to be his home – a nice house on the sea; but only temporary because he is building a new, rather larger house in land granted to him by the Ruler.

'The first thing I noticed was B & O quadraphonic amplifier, B & O cassette deck, B & O turntable with the automatic device for raising and lowering the pick-up which "senses" whether it is a "78" or a record, and a Revox tape machine![233]

'The lunch was superb, served by two Arabs in spotless freshly-laundered and starched white linen suits. It was good meat cooked in various sauces and tasting delicious, garnished with Lebanese garnishes (the wife is from Beirut); and finally superb fresh fruit including mangoes straight from Bombay (which is not far away). Very light but excellent.

'After lunch we first looked at some local fishing boats being built in the old way with wood and pegs, the whole done by hand. You must have seen pictures of the local shape for ships which has been the same for centuries: a sharp prow with a huge stem rising 10 feet or so from deck level, and a stern with the deck rising towards an after-cabin, so that the whole ship has a very intriguing change of aspect towards the rear-end… All the planking, by the way, was being hand-sawn and hewn from tree trunks!

'The rest of the afternoon we spent exploring the boundary zone of the coastal area near the fishing port, trying to identify land-marks (a well, and two houses, one now demolished). Not easy because Dubai is (illegally, we say) building new houses and offices right across the area.

'But this exploration took us into the midst of a community of men making fishing pots, I suppose you would call them: rather like a very large lobster-pot but made of thin wire. Scores of men were doing this in an area of sand, with ramshackle shelters to give them some protection from the sun. They seemed to live in one of our ancient "houses" – really a walled compound, with various camps and huts in odd corners of the common compound.

'The method of making these nets was fascinating. Each man had an enormous bundle of long, straight, thin steel wire. He had scooped in the sand a large, bowl shaped, hollow. Then he somehow wove the wire into

---

[233] – All of which must have made RYJ drool with envy, being the very latest hi-fi equipment.

a mesh following the shape of the bowl, and then continued it above the bowl in the same curve which the bowl-shape had set, so that in the end he was himself totally enclosed in a steel wire mesh which he had built around himself. How to get out? He would then make a sort of door, by pushing some of the wire to make an opening, weaving the dislodged wire to form a very strong frame to the opening, through which he was able to emerge from his own net, and also through which the fish would enter the trap. Like this: *(diagram)*. The wire was very thin. But the woven mesh trap was very rigid and strong. *How* it was woven it is impossible to say because the men's hands worked so fast that one only saw the mesh grow rapidly out of those lengths of straight wire. A very remarkable skill. They were mostly very young men at this work.

Sunday – The first job was to see the Ruler, His Highness Sheikh Sultan al Quasimi. The Quasimi (pronounced Kassimi) family has ruled over Sharjah since antiquity and probably beyond. Every so often a Ruler is deposed or more often assassinated. But some member of the same family – the ruling family – is chosen to succeed. Not necessarily the eldest at all. A family council decides who must do the job, and the people can make representations. The present ruler is a young man (his elder brother Sheikh Saqur (Sakra) didn't want it).

'So, to the Government Building for our "appointment" at 9.45 a.m. Armed guards everywhere but everybody full of smiles. Eventually ushered into the large room where the Ruler was receiving in "private" audience. Anything less private it is difficult to imagine. The room was full of people waiting to have a word, as well as ministers and also other members of the family. We were introduced to H.H. and also to the oldest member of the family – a most impressive and handsome old man with a splendid, still quite black, pointed beard. They were all in Arab dress, of course. White robes to the ankle, sandals, the headgear and white scarves.

'The ruler then took 4 people to a far table at the other end of the room and listened to what they wanted. Long, animated conversation, each making fluent, intense speeches at the Ruler, pleading, cajoling, arguing. All in Arabic, of course. Eventually all that party except one left, and the remaining one drew a printed prospectus and plans from his robes and went through it item by item with the Ruler, who paid great attention. I have no idea what it was he was selling!

'Meanwhile we sat at the other end, talking to our neighbours, all sitting on couches facing each other, so general conversation was possible. And a man in, not Arab dress but a white suit (the evident mark of a servant to wear a western suit!) plied us with revolting coffee in those little cups without handles … One *must* take a little. The servant will go on filling it for ever, until you shake it in the hand, which means "I've had enough," then he takes it, fills it, and hands it to someone else (no washing up!) The coffee is awful – but there is also sweet tea in tiny glass cups, quite nice, and those cups *are* washed up, because it is not part of an ancient courtesy rite.

'After some 2 hours or more thus waiting about, the young Arab with the prospectus went, with great ceremony, shaking hands with everybody, including us. Then the Ruler came to us, and sat with us (his English is perfect – he read agriculture at an American University). First, pleasant small-talk about the health of his wife and children. Then Ely launched into what struck me as a rather clumsy account of what we wanted (to give the *federal* government in Abu Dhabi a push, to get our Arbitration Court established). But in a short time Hamid Jafar had come to squat on the floor by the Ruler and now looking up into his face, smiling and cajoling, and speaking in rapid Arabic.

'Meanwhile the Ruler had handed me, from his pocket, a cigarette from an ordinary packet of Players, which I was smoking, feeling that to refuse might have been thought discourteous.

'Well, a plot was soon hatched. We gathered the Court of Arbitration was sitting in the hotel at Abu Dhabi (next State but one, 150 miles towards the head of the Gulf) being ignored totally by the Federal Government there, and that they were wondering whether to forget it and go home (which our opponent, Sheikh Rashid of Dubai, the old scoundrel, wanted to happen; and he knows very well that nothing discourages Europeans so much as hanging about in hotels waiting for things that never happen).

'The Court was to be told that they would be received that afternoon by our Ruler. Meantime he rang the Federal Minister and told him in the sweetest possible way to get cracking. We were to wait about in case we were wanted. So we just sat around in another office – the office of the local Judge, guarded by a nice old Bedouin (desert nomad) with a machine gun across his knees.

'About 3.30 p.m. we were summoned again to the Royal presence, and found the Court (a French man, John Simpson from the Foreign Office, retired, and Ken Simmonds from London University) sitting on the edge of the sofa, smiling empty, uncomfortable smiles, and desperately trying to think of something to say.

'We were most solemnly "introduced" to these three (we had known them all for years, of course) as the Ruler's legal team for the arbitration. So we sat with them all, drank more foul coffee, and tried to look like experienced Arabists well used to the Royal presence. And indeed, this being well on in the afternoon, we were beginning to feel like experienced members of the Court.

'The Ruler spoke very shrewdly and said all the right things to each of the Court (he is a *very* able man). And then we took our leave, and so back to the hotel for our "lunch" at something like 4.30 p.m.

'It gives one a good idea of life in a medieval Court – for that is what it is. The Ruler decides *everything* – even to details. And he does it just by saying yes or no. But he will listen to *anybody*. The poorest widow in the country has a complete right to audience with the Ruler and can, and does, put her grievance in the strongest terms. And he will do what he can for her.

Monday – By car to Abu Dhabi – a richer oil State, with enough money to keep greenery and trees everywhere by constant watering. Stayed at Abu Dhabi Hilton – a very expensive luxury hotel with slow, sulky service, and rather a comedown from Sharjah, which is already the place "we" feel we belong to.

'Found one of the Judges by telephone. "Happened" to meet him in the Bar, where he told us of their fresh woes. They were being ignored again and could not declare the Court in business till they did get some word from the Federal Minister. (All the Emirates are in a new, very experimental federation for some purposes, especially foreign affairs and inter-Emirate disputes.) So Jeremy rang the Sharjah Judge, who went straight to see the Ruler again, who forthwith got on the blower to the Federal Minister. Whilst we were having supper in the coffee room, the Court filed in, looking pleased but exhausted, having seen the Prime Minister, the Foreign Minister, the Education Minister – in fact the entire cabinet. (This because thanks to our intervention, the Foreign Minister *had* to do something at last, but he was determined not to be solely responsible, so he had summoned the entire cabinet from their siestas, to spread the load!) Still, it was becoming impressive: what we could do with the help of our Ruler! When he spoke, things happened even in Abu Dhabi.

Tuesday Formal opening of the Court in a room at the Hotel (which Jeremy booked because the Court was looking helpless again!). There was the opposing team (Sir Frank Layfield, QC, and a Junior called FitzGerald and some English solicitors from Dubai). The French President, Cahier, was excellent, as we thought he would be (he had been Registrar in the Beagle case and I knew him *very* well, accordingly). And we agreed a time-table which would make a formal hearing in Abu Dhabi just after Christmas, with exchange of written pleadings meantime.

'And so back to Sharjah. Dined at the Holiday Inn with the Jafars. More fresh mangoes!

Wednesday – wanted to explore the desert. Turned up at the Judge's office to go with him on an expedition at 9.30 a.m. sharp. He was sorry but too busy. (He *was* busy.) So waited in his waiting room 2½ hours. Meanwhile Jeremy and Hamid trying to see Ruler again about new crisis. Starting at 9.30 they saw him at 2.30! Ely and I gave up all hopes of desert and returned to hotel; after, however, having a very friendly informal chat with Sheikh Saqur, the Ruler's older brother: splendid-looking man who is very able and the idol of the Bedouin. He has a team of racing camels!

'4 p.m. Judge suddenly appeared in Land-Rover with his armed Bedouin bodyguard, and we all piled in and went off to the desert – *very* rough ride, holding on to the rails even along the tracks, let alone the pure cross-country. We were guided from one place to another by the old Bedouin who clearly knew every inch of this desert.

'Surprised by the beauty of the desert. Low scrub in the sand gives quite a variety of plant life. There are birds and insects. And grazing camels and goats.

'Then there is the interesting question of scale. The desert is immense in area; but the changes of elevation – in this desert anyway – are very slight. So the landmarks (which we were studying so as to follow older descriptions of the frontier) are quite insignificant features which, in the desert, acquire great significance. For example, one ancient, lone tree was one of them. And one needs some very elementary Arabic. Ud = tall tree. Hadib = a small hill, or rise, with low scrub (*not* trees). So we had to look for a Hadib al Zana (hadib where ammunition was hidden). Our opponents have invented (we say) a new one. But we think we do know the right one. For it has a hollow on top of the hill, so nobody in the surrounding desert could see you hiding or getting ammunition. Lots of Urqub (Arcoob), which is a different kind of hill, without scrub and with a steep side so that it is difficult to walk up the sand. But remember this "hill" might be 15 feet at the most. Looking around at first you would say there are no hills. Until the Bedouin points it out – in strange Arabic dialect but with such eloquent gesture that one can understand, once you have learned those names like hadis, arqub etc. for different kinds of hills. Then there is a nadir, i.e. the name for a girl's bosom, so that kind of hill is easy enough. Then there is a tawi = a well; but bida is a well with some superstructure.

'At one point we were fortunate. The Judge was thirsty, so we were directed by his Bedou to a Bedouin encampment. Normally, I gather, you would keep well away. They are suspicious of all strangers and always have guns. But we had a Bedou with us after all. It was a ramshackle palisade with tented shelters inside, a tawi, a fenced lemon tree, lots of goats, some tiny hens and cocks, and seven or eight camels, kept as cows and milked. There were two wizened men (brothers), their women (veiled but gaudily dressed, vociferous and looking altogether plumper than the men: the desert men are very thin and angular and lithe); and also the most handsome children (3) I have ever seen. Really startlingly beautiful.

'The camels are really funny. Very cynical faces. They stare at you with obvious dislike. The male one told us in no uncertain terms what he thought of us in a quite remarkably eloquent series of grunts, growls, complaints and – well, just obvious swearing of the most shocking kind. They are really fascinating. I think even Leo would meet his match with a camel. Surprisingly small and thin, they are. They "graze" on the desert! The hens seem to exist by picking nits off the camel. One old cow camel was lying with neck outstretched on the sand, looking utterly content, whilst a tiny hen went systematically finding her dinner in various parts of the camel's hide.

'Back to town in the sunset – when the desert is magical. Altogether a very satisfying trip. Our own Bedouin still in the back of the Land-Rover, with his machine gun across his knees.

'Entertained the Jafars to drinks in the Bar, then a local English solicitor to dinner and to bed about 11.30 p.m. Called at 2 a.m. to be driven to Dubai to board a Singapore Airlines flight to London … Arrived at [Heathrow] about 10 a.m. to find Mr Robb waiting with yellow Rover!

'Looking forward to the Arment trip.

Love, Daddy

'PS – Geography! Sharjah is part of Trucial Oman, Oman being the peninsula that nearly closes the eastern end of the Persian Gulf. Called Trucial because of the truce the British imposed in the 1830s onwards. Hitherto there was constant war between the Quasini and Dubai, and both existed on piracy. This was the infamous "pirate coast". Even the Admiralty Sailing Directions gave no details here and warned navigators to keep clear of the Oman coast.'

That was quite an exciting letter for an undergraduate to receive. My own summary for my father ended:

'… Well, Robbie got back safely on the Thursday morning and went straight to a long Faculty meeting that afternoon, and then entertained Frank Berman, a Foreign Office friend, at the Ascension Day Feast at Trinity that evening. We had Frank here for the night …'

It never stopped … just over a week later he was off for a weekend of meetings in Jersey.

When my Swiss cousin Vreni came to stay for a few days in May, she was plunged into our Cambridge life in all its variety. She was still with us when we gave a party for Grantchester friends, several of whom could chat about their links with Switzerland – altogether a lively gathering. But for her, the earnest Moral Re-armer, the question afterwards was, 'What did you *intend* with this party?' Her experiences of our world were unlike her world, and left her a little bemused.

At the end of May Robbie collected Pippa from Leeds and took her for a few days at Arment to climb Scafell Pike one day, and Great Gable on another. Back in Cambridge, he gave some extra supervision to undergraduates[234] [on a Sunday], then brought six young men out for drinks (typical, and always remembered gratefully by former pupils).

Dick's final Long Vacation included a week spent with a group of young men, all from Christ Church, escorting American debutantes experiencing 'the Season'. Attending Ascot races in a Moss Bros topper and morning coat was rather different from tractor-driving on a farm.

---

[234] As professor, he was no longer responsible for supervising undergraduates, but was happy to help them.

For Robbie, the vacation was largely dedicated to his various cases. Once we got away, in late July, he sat out rainy days listening to a Test Match in the car in the Arment yard, where it was possible to get crackly radio reception. When the weather relented we yielded to a determined Joey and joined her in climbing Scafell Pike. Conditions were ideal, and the whole day a joy … except that by the end, the parents, after 3,000 ft ascent and more than 16 miles distance, felt quite tired; but Joey added two more to fetch the milk.

Even at remote Arment House, though, Robbie was not spared from work, and one afternoon we were unable to get out for a walk as a Canadian Foreign Office man, Lorne Clark, was calling. As it turned out, less than an hour of talk, followed by a cup of tea, seemed to suffice before he went off again by hired car to Manchester airport. It had been important to consult the oracle in person; and once home, Robbie produced a long Opinion for Canada on their *Gulf of Maine* fisheries case.

Robbie's thankyou letter to my father for his birthday present that year ended:

> 'No, I haven't been doing a lot of travelling lately, other than to London. They are trying to get me to go to El Salvador, but I can't say I am too keen. Very hot and steamy I should think. And none too stable politically.'

Nor could he possibly fit this extra task into days already filled with university teaching, the Sharjah/Dubai and Tunisia/Libya disputes as well as advising the Canadians. What he had squeezed in, though, was a one-day visit to Arment House at a weekend when, taking Pippa up to Leeds at the beginning of term, they indulged in a roundabout route to let them join in the Eskdale Show – revelling in the hound trails, fell racing, the competition for the best dressed huntsman and best hunting song as well as the sheep-judging.

He did go to Tunis just before Christmas, and I accompanied him. At Heathrow I found to my horror that my passport had expired. The official at the control post warned that although I could board the plane I might be refused entry. But the resourceful Jeremy Carver, when we arrived, grinned and said 'Don't worry'. At Tunis airport, where the passport-officers seemed to take a long time inspecting each book before stamping it, he had gone ahead and quickly explained my problem to the genial Professor Belaid, who was able to persuade an official to stamp my passport after a firm promise that I would go to the Consul in the morning for a new one. This I did.

Then, in those few days, I absorbed a huge impression of this place as the delightful young Mme Belaid drove the lawyers' wives around and walked us through the Medina and part of the wonderful *souk,* with its strange offerings, bright colours and sounds:

'… the Arab voices, the feet and handcarts, the beating of metal – loud deep strokes as a coppersmith shaped a huge cooking-pan, sharp high tappings as intricate patterns were formed on coffee-pots and trays, the wail of Arab music from transistors here and there, the hawking-and-spitting, the shrill singing of a canary in a cage, the sizzle of cooking … There were stalls with unattractive-looking minerals, seed-heads and stringy bits of bark, to be used as traditional cosmetics by the Moslem women (like stage ghosts in their white draperies) – colouring for the hair, bark to clean the teeth…'

Thanks to my incompetence, the British Embassy had become aware of Robbie and Jeremy's presence, and so the Ambassador invited us to dinner. His residence was a fabulous building, a 19th-century enlargement of the old Caliph's palace. As we passed through its gates, before us was a theatrical façade: symmetrically-curving staircases rising from a forecourt with fountain to a deep balcony (from which, one felt, a Mozartian aria should have been delivered). We were welcomed and found ourselves in a room at once exotically Tunisian and Englishly domestic, with a huge Christmas tree and very English comfort beneath portraits of bygone royalty. Other rooms had handpainted tiles in intricate patterns, and ceilings of pierced plasterwork. (It was a posting that His Excellency was enjoying, for in addition to the wonder-house they had 22 acres of fruit trees, poultry and vegetables.) Surrounded by both Islamic and British splendour, I was amused to find our after-dinner conversation accompanied by the very faint wheedling sound of a television set – political harangue followed by domestic farce and then, most incongruous of all, a documentary about the River Thames, with Eights Week, Swan Upping, Morris Dancing, Eton Wall Game and Winston Churchill's funeral.

The Jenningses and René-Jean Dupuy and his wife were taken next afternoon to the ruins of Carthage, and to Sidi Bou Said; and I had some hours in the Bardo Museum as well, with its wonderful range of antiquities. But our hosts wanted to impress us with magnificent meals, which took an age to serve: a prolonged luncheon delayed our excursion to the east coast so that it was late as our car tore along a narrow road through arid country, where people were returning home from their fields with laden donkeys or mule-carts or the occasional camel, and encounters with opposing cars meant a test of nerves – *Beep-beep-BEEP* – until one car swerved off the track to make way for the other. We paused at Nabeul, and at last reached Hammamet, where I could just run down to the sea's edge as the sun sank below the horizon. Disappointed, we were guided into the *souk* and a most elegant dress shop,[235] far beyond our means. Embarrassed, we expressed admiration and tried to leave. But 'Mesdames, you are each to choose something,' urged Mr Rourou (President of the Tunisian oil company); and at his insistence each of the ladies had to take home a beautiful *burnous*. This was my own first experience of the social side of what had of course been a serious consultation for the lawyers.

When we started for the airport at 8 am, Jeremy had already been to the market and was carrying, besides the soft parcel containing a *burnous* for his wife, a large bag of oranges and dates, fresh and succulent. M. & Mme Rourou saw us off, and we were home just in time for a very happy family Christmas.

Robbie and the children went off to Arment House, leaving me to give some support to our increasingly frail old neighbour. But after two days of freezing cold and pouring rain up north, they returned to snow at home and tobogganing on the meadows. The family had been invited to a New Year party in the Headmaster's house at the Leys School, with Scottish dancing. We all joined in the rumbustious fun except a reluctant Robbie, and Joey wrote to Grandad…

'… it wasn't until after midnight that Daddy made his debut. It was hilarious, if you can imagine Daddy, totally lost, making brave attempts, hopping up and down, with all the wrong partners. Eventually Rob [our hosts' son] volunteered to stand and dance behind him, guiding him like a puppet through the steps!'

And thus Professor R.Y. Jennings saw in New Year 1979.

---

[235] The shop, we found, was patronised by Princess Grace of Monaco, Sophia Loren, Mme Pompidou, and Greta Garbo among others.

Early in January, Robbie went again to Sharjah, and I wrote to my father –

'… They had worked hard for their 10 days there (on until 2 a.m. on at least one occasion), and then he had to adjust to the five hours' time-change. [He] had some more traveller's tales to tell. His most notable experience this time was flying by helicopter, which he tremendously enjoyed. He had to wear intercom headphones to give directions to the pilot, using a chart and compass. The Arab sitting behind thought he knew the desert better and so insisted on his own vague directions being followed, with the result that they became quite lost. Still, in a helicopter – no problem: spotting a Bedouin camp, they simply dropped down on the sand-dunes and asked the way!'

Once back, he spent a day in London giving (as he told Pippa…)

'…three lectures to a thing called a "Government-lawyers' course", run by the Ministry of Overseas Development – mostly young legal officers, civil servants, legal advisers and such, from Commonwealth countries: India, Singapore, etc. Even Nepal had 3 of them! …'

And Pippa's description of the way the old ladies in the streets around her new lodgings swept their 'flags' every morning evoked more of his memories of growing up in just such a place, and the Sunday routine of his pious Jennings grandparents – 9.30 am Sunday School, chapel service at 10.30, Sunday School at 2.30, chapel at 6 pm … and 'family prayers' with Bible readings after supper. '*That* was the day of rest!'

In February Dick took his Law Society examinations. The candidates – all 4,000 of them – had to sit in great chilly halls in Alexandra Palace, squatting huddled on the concrete corridor-floors to eat sandwiches between papers. Although not confident about the results, he was due to start as an Articled Clerk with Coward Chance a few days later, and would actually receive a wage.

It was on 25th February 1979 that Robbie wrote a heartfelt letter to Pippa, with 'melancholy news'. Leo – always regarded by him as a *noble* cat – had died. The second page of this detailed account of his demise is blurred with tears, which might be his own or Pippa's. But Cambridge termtime rolled on with its usual varied entertainments, which I described:

'1. An evening piano recital in the Master's Lodge at Jesus. Not only an enjoyable performance of a wide range of pieces – but the pianist was Otto Frisch,[236] a highly distinguished physicist now aged 74. We know him slightly as a Fellow of Trinity. His talents include the drawing of quick portrait-sketches of those about him at dinners or meetings!

'2. A feast in the Hall at Jesus – an opportunity to meet college friends and a fine occasion.

'3. Lunch with the Master of Caius [Wade] – a gathering of ?10 of us, the chief guest being a High Court Judge, Patrick Browne. Again, nice company and good conversation.

'4. Last night: a dinner at Trinity (16 of us) in honour of an American friend and one-time pupil of Robbie's, Dick Baxter, to mark his giving up his Chair of International Law at Harvard to become the new American judge at the International Court at the Hague. Perhaps the nicest occasion of all.'

(At one Trinity Ladies' Night dinner Otto Frisch had scribbled a portrait of Robbie on the back of an envelope, a clever likeness that we preserved.)

Dick Baxter[237] was someone with whom Robbie felt a warm rapport. He had been admitted to Jesus College for advanced legal study after spending years as an officer in the US army and would go on to become Professor of International Law at Harvard, so that his election to the ICJ was entry into a 'third career'. The *Harvard Law School Bulletin,* reporting this, said that when a Fulbright award had brought him to Cambridge in 1951 his supervisor had been 'the late Sir Hersch Lauterpacht … "the one hero in [his] life"… Another major influence on Baxter was Professor R.Y. Jennings … a Fellow of Jesus College and a well-known international lawyer'. Now, at Robbie's suggestion, he was made an Honorary Fellow of the college.

Then, writing of these events to Pippa, Robbie went on to say:

---

236 Professor O.R. Frisch, an Austrian Jewish émigré, was one of the most remarkable of Trinity's many brilliant Fellows. He had in 1940 designed the first theoretical mechanism for the detonation of an atomic bomb, and went on to further outstanding scientific achievements. His father had been a painter, his mother a concert pianist, and had passed on talents in both arts.

237 Richard R. Baxter had reached the highest positions in American International Law, after a military career. His time at The Hague turned out to be tragically short, allowing him to sit on only two contentious cases, for he was diagnosed with leukaemia and died in his second year.

'… Rather exciting: the big case between Canada and the USA about their sea frontiers is actually to be taken to Court, and it looks as if I might be the leading counsel for Canada. That would be nice, because it really will be a most important case, and it would be hard work but rather thrilling. Trouble is that I have the Tunisian case as well, not to mention the Sharjah one, and I shall need to be lucky with the timing not to find some incompatibility. Still, I am going in for them all and assuming I shall be lucky! The Canadian case is not wholly in the bag yet, but they rang me from Ottawa on Friday, and promised to come and see me at the end of the month.'

Next time he had two consecutive days at Coward Chance working on the Sharjah case he spent the night in great comfort at the Savoy (at the Ruler's expense). It enabled him to attend a great dinner at Lincoln's Inn in honour of Lord Denning's 80th birthday – a most enjoyable occasion, at which he, as now an Honorary Bencher, sat at the top table. He told Pippa there had been –

'… two speeches of about 40 minutes each: one by this year's Treasurer, Sir David Renton; and of course one by Lord Denning. Magnificent for a man of 80, with little in the way of notes, with some jokes and some serious parts, telling us about the great Lincoln's Inn members of the past, such as Sir Thomas More, Lord Mansfield and so on; and, looking at the students, we had "just as fine material coming on today!" All in the sing-song, lilting, Hampshire accent – for his family were quite poor country people. (One brother was killed in the 1st World War, one became an Admiral, one became a prominent surgeon, and this one the Master of the Rolls) …

'One of the Hon. Benchers (like me, that is) there, was Margaret Thatcher. Very nice, I must say. When you see her face lively with talk, it is much nicer than the impression one sometimes gets from photographs, when she can look a little stiff…'

On his next trip to the Gulf he and Jeremy Carver flew in Concorde[238] to Bahrain, a flight paid for by the Ruler of Sharjah. They stayed the night

---

[238] – a thrill 'just for once to have flown at 1,400 mph!' that he was anxious to share with me sometime. But many years later, when we travelled together to Washington DC, it turned out not to be possible.

in Bahrain and next day, after some talks there, flew more sedately down to Sharjah. This time, he wrote to Pippa:

'Desert was beautiful & exciting – tho' we also saw its more angry mood in a sandstorm – rather frightening, when visibility comes down to nill & *everything* is full of sand …

'Have now been actually within the palisade of a desert Bedouin camp, and received in a 'burasti' hut (made of knitted palm fronds), to drink ceremonial coffee. Only 3 cups which were just splashed in a bowl and handed on. But courtesy is more important than hygiene.

'Then we had a Bedouin meal. Oh, what agony! Servant (?slave) brought in a mat, and placed upon it an enormous tray filled with rice, spices, cooked mutton and chicken. And everybody squatted round and took scraps of it in the right hand. No implements. No plates. Bones &c you just spit onto the mat, any-old-where. No alcohol, of course: just water. All tasted rather spiced and horrid. Much belching. There *were* the eyes of the sheep. My neighbour had one like an oyster. And at the climax, one realised the skull of the sheep was in this mess, and the chief took a chicken bone and cleared out the sheep's brain, handing round spots of it in his hand. I was very nearly sick at one point, but managed to pass it off as a cough, and somehow by a great effort, to swallow. But one could not conceivably offend them. They are so nice, gentle, and full of marvellous smiles. And so clean! Their dish-dashas and long cloaks are beautifully laundered.

'At one very nice oasis, with palms and a good view all round, one of our Bedou, old Sultan, squatted on the sand and started singing a strange, wailing song. I was told he was just singing about a good place to rest.

'Well, it was really a great experience. And a great privilege to be with some of the only remaining really primitive people in the world. I can see how Lawrence of Arabia was converted to their ways. Even the feast one might get used to! But it is not easy. Even Jeremy went pale!

'Mind you, there was also super fruit – great piled dishes of it – wonderful oranges, and bananas and dates. So that part was O.K.'

This adventure ended with them rising at 2.30 am and driving to Dubai for a 9-hour flight to Heathrow (and in his sleepiness leaving his scarf and spectacles on board). Once home, he chaired a meeting which went on until 11 pm… A snatched visit to Arment House was managed between work on the *Sharjah/Dubai* Memorial and other consultations, with his essential teaching fulfilled as usual.

That year we heard Prince Philip deliver the Rede Lecture, which I described for my father:

'This is the university's chief public lecture, and he responded to the invitation with characteristic energy and thoroughness – an hour of fast-delivered good sense on 'Philosophy, Politics and Administration'. I saw his arrival, too – a perfect descent by the royal red helicopter on the Jesus soccer field, H.R.H. piloting ...'

And the day after, at the Honorary Degrees ceremony in the Senate House Robbie was interested in one graduand in particular, Sir Peter Kent, the geologist with whom he had worked on the English Channel case. But besides Kent there were Cardinal Hume and Lord Todd (biochemist and recent Master of Christ's). In addition, halfway through one of the orations a strange figure in a wheelchair was pushed in through the side doors. It was Pevsner,[239] dressed in his scarlet doctor's robe but no collar or tie, brought in by a man in morning dress and accompanied by another in full academic rig. The old man was shaky but seemingly able to enjoy his honour – though not able to attend the junketing afterwards. The procession, as last year (but only for these two years, while Sir Alan Cottrell is Vice-Chancellor) then walked all through Cambridge to Jesus College, where they were this year [1979] greeted by trumpeters up in the Chimney Tower. There was champagne in the Master's Garden, followed by luncheon for 220 in a grand marquee. Then the indefatigable Chancellor, with his great appetite for involvement in the University, moved on to visit various labs and the new Robinson College, and to a garden party at Fitzwilliam. Lady Cottrell was left feeling a little wistful now that the last of the many exciting events they had had the responsibility of arranging for the Prince was ended (though he was to continue to use the upper suite of bedrooms in the Jesus Lodge for his visits to Cambridge) as the Vice-Chancellorship was now to pass on to the Master of St Catharine's. So a few of us retired to the sittingroom for a cosy chat over a sip of claret left over from the previous night's dinner. ... And as we left, 16 pieces of luggage, all labelled 'Duke of Edinburgh,' were leaving by shiny Range Rover for Sandringham.

---

[239] Sir Nickolaus Pevsner, famous for his great series of architectural guides to the counties of England.

With the frivolities of May Week over, Robbie was back to his practice, going to Nice to confer with Dupuy and the Tunisians for two days. Straight after, he was driven by Eli Lauterpacht to Oxford for the funeral of Professor Dan O'Connor, the Chichele Professor of International Law, who had just died:

'… It is a terrible loss [I wrote] – he was a man of seemingly inexhaustible energy, aged only 54, and leaves a very nice wife and five children. His achievement in published writings alone is monumental…'

But Robbie had found it 'a happy day' – his first experience of a full Roman Catholic Requiem Mass, with a warm family gathering afterwards. And three weeks later, just back from a two-day visit to Tunis, he went again with Eli and Derek Bowett to attend O'Connor's memorial service in All Souls.

Now an enjoyable lunch with Basil Markesinis[240] brought…

'… another set of engagements to fit into the jigsaw-puzzle of [R's] diary (while, if possible, retaining the chance of a week or so at Arment in August)… At the end … out came the diaries – and into Robbie's crowded programme goes a visit to Holland next spring for some lectures, besides meetings in Greece this September. His health is good, but he *is* fearful lest tiredness reduces the quality of his work.

'Next day the task was to chat with Canadians. There was an evening reception in Neville's Court at Trinity, with lots and lots of Canadian diplomats and academics (over here for a special law course)… But the opening session had apparently been introduced with a speech in which the great legal minds of Cambridge had been extolled, with a roll-call starting with Erasmus and ending with R.Y. Jennings! We missed that.'

The Long Vacation was full, as ever, and Trinity Ladies Night was presided over by the 90-year-old Tresillian Nicholas.[241] We managed three days at Arment, but a second visit was delayed by Robbie having to produce a longish

---

[240] Sir Basil Markesinis was at this time a law Fellow of Trinity, but – immensely active – went on to become Clifford Chance Professor of Comparative Law at Oxford, with a Fellowship at Brasenose.

[241] Tresillian Nicholas, a geologist, as Bursar of Trinity had managed the development of college land near Felixstowe which became a great port for container-ships, and transformed the college's financial situation. He lived to be 102 and was active almost to the end.

Opinion for Venezuela (offshore oil drilling complications). Once there, we had Tom and John Tyson (sons of our earlier builder) re-roofing the big barn across the yard, cutting and boring holes in heavy thick slates and carrying them aloft with no thought of safety precautions.

By early September a heavy cold infection threw Robbie's programme into disarray, and he had to cancel his attendance at the *Institut* conference in Athens, and could not obey an urgent summons to Tunis, nor another to The Hague.

In the meantime there had been a momentous event at home: Joey had acquired a kitten. It was just the wrong time to introduce a new animal. But we were all besotted, and named her 'Folly.' 'She is enchanting [I wrote] ... a prodigy of intelligence and zip. Life is transformed by this little flibbertigibbet darting about ... and it's all total folly!' After a few months we realised that Folly was a *he*, with great agility and hunting skills.

Pippa's 21st birthday was celebrated at the end of September; but on Robbie's own birthday he had to leave for Paris for talks with Dupuy and Virally, and then go on to Tunis. Once back, I heard that it had not been an enviable trip: hard continuous work, and cooler and rainier than in England. Soon after, he was in London at the Canadian High Commission, working in a special office reserved for him... Later I made a note in my diary:

> '11th Dec. 1979 – 4 Americans to talk to Robbie, arrived in huge embassy car. Shut in sittingroom discussing Iranian problems – American hostages, and freezing of assets.'

On 20th December I did accompany Robbie on a four-day trip to Tunis. The team now included Frances Meadows,[242] a very capable young assistant solicitor from Coward Chance, and Georges and Rosemary Abi-Saab. Georges, Egyptian, was like Frances an ex-pupil of Robbie's, and his wife was French-Swiss. We stayed in the vast suite in the Hilton hotel, where at dinner a huge trolley was rolled in...

> '... with ice on which was heaped a glorious variety of fish, all brilliantly fresh. (The Mediterranean fish are celebrated in the Roman mosaics, which have scenes of Neptune surrounded by all the pink, blue, grey creatures with fins, shells, tentacles ...) The meal was accompanied by a Hungarian band –

---

[242] Frances Meadows had studied international law at Newnham, and would (1995-98) become First Secretary at the ICJ. From 2003 she has been a freelance translator.

fiddle, cello and cembalo, and we had to endure the attentions of the violinist who hovered over one's head, hoping for a tip.

'The men had come for work, and were kept hard at it. I spent Friday morning with three French ladies (wives of the men involved in the case), and we first had our car take us to Sidi bou Said…'

I found it a great help to have Rosemary Abi-Saab with me as we wandered in the souk, since she was fluent in both English and Arabic. At one point we paused by a small mosque to see

'a crowd of men cross-legged in a courtyard, listening to a long speech (more a political harangue than a sermon, I gathered). Apparently religious fervour is growing generally, and makes the government nervous in a country where they have a vast number of young educated unemployed.'

Not sharing the expensive tastes of Mesdames Dupuy, Virally and Abi-Saab, I asked the young driver at my disposal to take me to the Bardo Museum for another look at the marvellous antiquities I had seen before; then along the coast, to stand among Roman walls being eroded by the waves, and on to a Roman amphitheatre.

Inevitably, the men's work went on late and delayed dinner. After tedious standing about with drinks,

'… By the time we actually moved into the dining room it was 10 pm. It was a night club place, on the 20th floor of the Hotel Africa. Seating the 30 or so of us took ages, and the food was less attractive than the previous night's. I had Professor Virally on my left, and found him most pleasant. But conversation was killed absolutely when the entertainment started. First it was a singer, accompanied by electronic organ and double bass and percussion: just loud and bad. At last he (husky and white-suited) and then she (bleached and frizzed hair, and shrill voice) finished, and one hoped for some respite. But then came an Egyptian band. Egyptan music is awful anyway, all wailing and jangling. But done in force (2 violinists, an electronic cembalo-thing, a singer, an accordion, a tambourine and an African drum – with a piercing flute and louder drum as extras) straight into microphones and heavily amplified, it was murder. One of the loudspeakers was by my ear, and by the end of the evening that ear was deaf. This hullabaloo accompanied a belly-dancer, twirling and quivering under coloured lights. It grew hotter and hotter. Professor Virally, during a slight lull, managed to bawl: "Even Dante never thought of this!" ... [Later] a whole troupe of dancers ... all highly energetic, in ingenious and colourful costumes – although at least half the girls were topless. Just the thing to entertain elderly professors and their wives ... We got to bed at 1.10 am, and rose at 6.30 am to catch the plane home.'

– Home to find the house already decorated by Joey and friend, leaving me just one day to complete the final cooking (and Father Christmassing) before bed... and a good Christmas.

Early in 1980 Robbie had a brief visit to Paris, for just a three-hour meeting – probably the Hague Academy curatorium – and stayed in an attractive old-fashioned small hotel on the Left Bank, enjoying the chance of walking about on his own in very cold but dry and bright weather.

Soon after, he flew to Ottawa – 'cold (18 degrees of frost) but very pleasant – everyone, as it seemed, out on the frozen river and canal, skating and tobogganing'. It was after this consultation with the Canadian team that he was entrusted with highly confidential papers on the *Gulf of Maine* dispute for which a safe was installed at home, bolted to the concrete floor of the cupboard under the stairs. (We used it to keep our own valuables, too, but Robbie felt honour-bound to remind the Canadians to remove it once his involvement in the case was finished.)

Our Cambridge life this term included two notable events. The first was dinner with 'a bearded barrister', Bill Ballantyne,[243] and his wife after he and Robbie had conferred about the Persian Gulf area. The other was a college talk given by Peter Hurford. Hurford had been one of Robbie's more unusual pupils: advised by his father that his principal subject, Music, could never be relied upon for a living, he had taken Part II of the Tripos in Law. He spoke about his later career – 'for over 20 years Organist of St Alban's Cathedral, and now just making the last of his 23 gramophone records of the complete organ works of Bach!'

I asked my husband to help me when I conducted a small group of Grantchester schoolchildren around Jesus College. After they had seen the

243 Professor William Ballantyne, a lawyer specialising in the Arab Emirates.

264

hall, the chapel and the cloisters I took them up to the Ghost Room. One boy, already unnerved by his climb up 40 steep stairs, nearly had hysterics when a wailing figure in white erupted from the inner room, flapping its arms ... and had to be calmed as he realised that it was only Robbie in the long surplice worn by dons for some services in the college chapel. The other children entered into the Ghost Room fantasy with glee. Incidentally, one had to move about that room with care, for there were papers stacked in heaps not only on the table but on the floor: documents and writings concerning the different cases on hand, as well as the seemingly interminable *Oppenheim.*

———

Robbie described his next visit to Tunisia for Pippa –

'10 March, 1980 ... I never had a chance to tell you about our last visit to Tunis, which was "different"! Tunisia is in a rather precarious situation, poor things. Bourguiba, the old President and great unifying power, who founded their independence, is old and ill and can only work a little each day. And now the Prime Minister is also ill. And Libya, under Gadaffi, would like to take Tunisia over. You will remember there was a raid on a desert township, said to have been engineered by Libya. And there is trouble in the university, probably financed from rich Libya.

'So the Tunisians are certain (may well be right) that the Libyans would go to any lengths to seize the pleadings we are preparing for the Hague Court, and so gain an advantage (though I can't quite see Derek Bowett, as a Libyan counsel, accepting material got by a spy without rejecting it as a double-plant by me!).

'Anyway, the result was that, instead of the usual sedate lift to the Tunis Hilton from the airport, we were whisked at high speed 20 kms out to a charming seaside hotel at the Baie des Singes. I had a suite with a balcony on the sea, and generally felt that security had improved matters. But the hotel was surrounded by evil-looking thugs who were there to guard us (or, more likely, our papers). There were always two in the entrance hall of the hotel, ready to pounce on anyone who asked for us. And there were about 10 of them round the hotel.

'Carver had the worst of it. He could not be found a room in the hotel proper and was put in a bungalow down by the beach (meant for families in the summer – rather nice, with tiny private swimming pool just outside the sitting room). They were specially bothered about the isolation of this place, and the first night he was kept awake all night by these types pacing up and down and even peering through windows.

'Being a Carver,[244] he dealt with the problem. The next night he collected them all up and stood them in line, and addressed them like an officer addressing troops, saying he must sleep tonight, and would they please patrol very quietly? They did!

'… Of course, it was all incredibly amateur. They seemed not to notice that, besides the door into the corridor, which they watched 24-hours a day, there was a French window onto my balcony, which I kept open to let in one of the hotel cats I made friends with the first day.

'Another bonus of the security was that we were taken back to the hotel by a different route every day, so one learned quite a lot of geography. We are hoping the situation [on our next visit] will again demand that we be whisked out to some nice lonely holiday hotel by the sea, with a good kitchen! Of course they never thought to stop me from ringing Mummy to say where we were and what the telephone number was! Talk about Dad's Army!

'Of course, the *really* nice part was at the airport when we left for home. We went to the VIP lounge, and when the plane was ready, we were escorted past the queue of people who had been standing there for ½ hour, to a special bus, and only when we were safely planted in the best seats in the aircraft, did they fetch the "ordinary" people. But as Carver said, after watching the faces of the people who had to wait for us to pass up before them: "Good job none of *them* had a knife!"'

In between this and another major trip abroad there was the writing of another long Opinion for Canada; a three-day visit to Arment House with Joey, at her half-term; and the celebration of her 18th birthday, an occasion when the whole family were assembled – something now increasingly rare but always relished.

Then, to resume Robbie's description:

'My other trip was Ottawa … Could not be more different. Real winter this time. Snow and icicles everywhere. Ottawa River (at least as big as Thames) solid ice. Temperatures between -14C [6.8ºF] and -5 ("mild", they said). But

---

244   He was a nephew of Field-Marshall the Lord Carver.

you know, I never once felt cold. Less humidity, I suppose. There was one day when it snowed steadily all day and all night. But the rest of the time was beautiful sunshine, and the snow and ice looked super in the sun. And the country, with its little homesteads, is so vast and untamed, even just outside the city. And the people so friendly and helpful, whether French-speaking Quebecers, or the English-speaking ones from Ontario (the boundary river flows through Ottawa). And then there is the Rideau Canal. Seven miles of it, right through the residential part of the city, with nice houses on its banks (like Holland). And that is the place to skate. The whole town seems to skate at weekends. You see whole families, with a baby in a pram on sled runners – just spending hours on this super-ice.

'The hotel also was very good indeed … Vast Victorian Scottish baronial building, with turrets and towers like the scene in a German fairy tale, a copper roof all over those towers and the lot…

'One evening I gave a talk, followed by discussion, to the local branch of the International Law Association. It was a talk after dinner – 45 minutes then ½ hour of questions. Was delighted to see so many old friends there, including some former pupils. Apparently the biggest turn-out they had had for a long time…

'Whether that case will in fact come on, I don't know. It depends upon the US Senate ratifying the Treaty. And nothing is likely to happen before the Presidential election. So that *could* be the last time in Canada. If so, I shall be rather sad. I have made some nice friends there.

'Reasonable journey home. It's tiresome having to sit up all night… Of course the first part – the 100 miles from Ottawa to Montreal – is in a 20-seater Dakota, propeller aircraft. Very funny. And very noisy. Yet rather fun. And this time really rather nice because I found myself sitting next a most *beautiful* Swedish girl who had been visiting friends and was on her way back via Copenhagen. Of course I made sure that she found just where to go for her plane in Montreal! Nice girl, actually, as well as stunning…'

[His journey back to Heathrow, in a Jumbo Jet, was smooth and fast.] 'The only thing was, I had to get up and go and ask them, long after take-off, to turn their wretched Musak off. But they did, so that was all right …'

This case, the *Delimitation of the Maritime Boundary in the Gulf of Maine area*, would be heard before a Chamber[245] of the ICJ in 1984, by which time Robbie could take no part. But he did enjoy returning to Canada once or twice in later years.

———

Basil Markesinis' lunch had introduced Robbie to Professor Deelen, from the University of Tilburg in The Netherlands, who now arranged a two-day visit during which he was to give four lectures there. The Deelens' hospitality was wonderful; we stayed at their home in Breda, and saw a little of Dordrecht, Willemstad and a remarkable church designed as St Peter's (Rome) in miniature. For Robbie it was less of a holiday than for me – and indeed, he was straight back to work on the Tunisian case on his return. And more commitments loomed ahead.

This intense activity was made possible by a bout of sabbatical leave, intended to free him from his Cambridge teaching responsibilities. As it was, several graduate pupils begged for attention and were not disappointed.

At Easter we received Joey's French friend Sophie, and at the end of her stay it was Robbie who nobly took her to Heathrow to catch her plane to Paris, leaving the house at 6.30 am. and then waiting for three hours before catching his own plane to Geneva for hours of hard work there.

Then, after a brief visit to Arment House, normal life was resumed, with another request for advice concerning something to do with business assets in Iran. I told my father of the day when Robbie

'...had to be in London at the Tunisian Embassy; and, coming away from there – as it is No.23 Prince's Gate – he saw a long black bundle being brought down from the window of the burnt-out Iranian Embassy.'

He had witnessed the aftermath of the Iranian Embassy Siege (30 April–5 May 1980) which had ended when SAS men broke into 16 Prince's Gate to release all but one of the hostages trapped there.

Later in May he travelled with Derek Bowett to Venezuela for a week of consultations. They were taken by air inland to see the country beyond Caracas itself, and came home impressed with their glimpse of the grandeur of that wild hinterland.

---

[245] The Chamber consisted of Judges Ago, Gros, Mosler, Schwebel and (*ad hoc*) Maxwell Cohen.

His next trip to The Hague with the team working on the Tunisian case reveals a Robbie momentarily abandoning diplomacy for confrontation:

'That particular engagement was exhausting before it ever started, as the leading Tunisian lawyer has political ambitions and his machievellian manoeuvring involved, at one point, the cutting-out of the English solicitor, Jeremy Carver … "No Carver, no Jennings," said Robbie … "And so say all of us," said the French lawyers … "A mistake: please forget," came from Tunis … and so, after these emotion-draining offs and ons, the meeting finally took place.'

May Week, 1980, with the usual densely-packed succession of events, included two dinners given by Heads of Houses – the first at Jesus, where we met the composer/conductor, Pierre Boulez, who was to receive an Honorary Degree next day; and the second at Queens':

'That was a very nice occasion: the most beautiful of all the Lodges in Cambridge, and our hosts and most of the guests good friends of ours. The chief guests were the Honorable Paul Martin, retiring Canadian High Commissioner (here to take an Honorary Degree) and wife. Some consternation was caused when he said "Our Minister for Foreign Affairs and the Deputy High Commissioner are just following", and the poor President [Derek Bowett] and wife Betty realised they had two extra uninvited guests. It meant that the sherry-sipping was protracted while downstairs the kitchen staff coped with the crisis; but all went beautifully, though we were rather tightly packed – 18 instead of 16 – at table!'

We snatched a three-day visit to Arment between days filled with Robbie's meetings in Cambridge and giving the opening address at a conference in London. It was a shame to miss the Ruby Wedding celebration of Russell and Vera Walton, at whose wartime wedding Robbie had been Best Man, since loyalty to old friends was so important; but it simply could not be fitted in.

Among all the goings-on there was an event Robbie was not going to miss. On 17th July Pippa took her degree at Leeds, and our souvenir photograph shows him wearing his Yorkshire Cricket Club tie and glowing with pride. That day left us pretty tired, but it was worth it. We set off at 7am and once there were on our feet standing about or climbing flights of concrete steps and walking along the long corridors of a civic university. But the actual graduation ceremony was taken by the Chancellor herself – the Duchess of Kent, looking beautiful in a robe of olive-green silk with lots of gold, its train borne by a small page in tricorne hat. She and Lord Boyle, the Vice-Chancellor, made speeches and congratulated each graduand.

For our Silver Wedding on 4th August that year, the children had produced imaginative gifts. I had called on our old friend Angela Taunt to buy one of her paintings[246] for Robbie, but found it hard to choose from those in her studio. Seeing me dithering, she very generously *gave* a lovely drawing of Littondale as her own present. Both that and the painting I eventually bought are treasured still.

For nine days that August, Robbie was engaged in a new and rather unlikely task in Geneva at the World Health Organisation, where he was advising his old pupil Dr Sami Shubber on drafting legislation to control the marketing of baby food (breast-milk substitute). In 1998 Shubber would publish a book, *The WHO International Code of Marketing of Breast-milk Substitutes: History and Analysis* with a Foreword by Robbie; and the second edition (2011) was dedicated 'To the memory of Sir Robert Jennings, the inspiring leader ...' Shubber explains that it had been at the stage when the Third Draft of the International Code was being prepared, that the Whewell Professor [RYJ] and Mr Heyward of UNICEF joined the drafting group. Later, 'the final touches of [that] text were added on 5-6 October 1980, in the rooms of Professor Jennings, at Jesus College ...' Later still, Robbie had contributed a clarifying statement in place of one which might allow misinterpretation: his habit of expressing his thoughts so lucidly must have been particularly valuable. His Foreword summarizes the problem they were addressing:

'The social and medical problem that this joint endeavour has been concerned with can be stated simply. It is well established that natural breast feeding is generally medically safer, psychologically superior and a good deal cheaper than the use of manufactured breast milk substitutes; though these substitutes also have their uses in certain exceptional cases where natural feeding is for

---

[246] Angela exhibited under her maiden name, Angela Verren. She owed much of her development as a professional artist to a close association with Ben Nicholson.

one reason or another not expedient or not possible. In a developed and relatively well-off society there is probably much to be said for leaving this kind of choice for the individual to make, with the help of such advice as they choose to seek. A complication arises, however, in developing and poor countries when, for instance, commission-driven salesmen are tempted – and one can only hope not instructed – to offer free, or "special offer" samples of their product, well aware that, after this "free" or very cheap use for a time, the mother's own milk will dry up so that even in their poverty they become easy victims of "the market".

'It was to rescue these mothers and their babies that WHO and UNICEF entered upon this joint endeavour …'

After comprehensive consultations and revisions, the full Code was issued. But it has not yet become fully effective. As Shubber writes:

'Unfortunately, the implementation of the Code at the national level is not very encouraging. Thirty years after the adoption of the Code, only some thirty Members States [i.e. of the UN] have adopted it in full or substantially. There is an absolute need to have a proper legal instrument regulating the marketing practices covered by the Code, in both developed and developing countries…'

Nevertheless, it amused Robbie, never a boaster, in old age to remark with pride to startled listeners that he was 'a world expert on the breastfeeding of babies'.

—

In September I again joined Robbie and Jeremy Carver in Tunisia, this time in a pleasant hotel at a seaside resort, together with the wives of other counsel and advisers. They included Pierre-Marie Dupuy, son of René-Jean Dupuy, and his German wife Oota with two young children, as well as Christiane Dupuy and Danielle Virally. As before, the ladies made small excursions; and as before, our stay culminated in a grand dinner, this time given by Ambassador Bouziri in his home. By midnight the protracted meal had ended and the French guests thought of the early plane they must catch next morning; but we were all obliged to stay and admire the twirling and wiggling of a belly-dancer, her fourth performance that evening, before we could leave.

Real life resumed: Dick and Pippa got safely back from a great cycling trip around France; Robbie took part in a conference at Madingley Hall; we enjoyed another of Markesinis' dinner parties; and then we took Pippa up to Durham, where – to the surprise of her tutor, she had chosen to take the PGCE in preparation for teaching in a primary rather than secondary school.

Final Academic Year

1980-81

It was, for Robbie, a melancholy prospect to be entering upon his final year of teaching, the activity he most valued. The university statutes laid down a retirement age of 65, which might be extended by two years but no further; and his 67th birthday came on 19th October 1980, just into the Michaelmas Term.

That allowed him one final year of teaching – at least, mostly teaching. The other commitments continued, with scarcely any cracks between. During one of those cracks he took part in a BBC discussion. In a letter to Pippa I wrote:

'Daddy refused to listen to *Talking about Law*, so he ate his supper in solitary state by the sittingroom fire while Dick, Joey and I listened avidly in the kitchen. (Several bits of "Robert Jennings," and contributions by Eli and Derek B. and others familiar to me.)'

He was reluctant to take part in this sort of performance, feeling that his contribution was bound to be superficial.

By late November the *Dubai/Sharjah Border Arbitration* hearing began. It was an intimidating prospect to be for the first time 'leader' in in a big arbitration – with his friend and successor-designate[247] Derek Bowett leading on the other side. After delivering a lecture from 10-11 am, he was off to Kensington to work with the Sharjah team for some weeks.

The hearings were presided over by Professor Philippe Cahier of the University of Geneva. On Robbie's side were Judge Yusri Dweik, the agent, and Northcutt Ely as counsel, with Jeremy Carver described as 'adviser to the Emirate of Sharjah'. The Dubai team had, together with their agent, Sir Frank Layfield, Derek Bowett and William Hicks. After a fortnight he was able to come home and relax for a few days. I commented that…

'…the actual Oral Hearing of a big case is such an exhausting affair: in court all day either speechifying or listening intently, and then up most of the night

---

[247] As Whewell Professor

drafting the perfect counter-arguments. (They have a couple of typists who have tapped all night, too.) Still, he feels they should have made a strong case, so the excitement brings satisfaction.'

On 19th December Robbie arrived home late in the evening, 'white and reeling with exhaustion,' and next day I noted in my diary 'R remarkably bright again – he spent the day putting up new bookshelves in study...' And then we were into the season of Christmas parties with university and village friends. On the 28th we drove up to Arment House, taking Folly the cat with us as well as Rags. There, as Joey wrote to Grandad, 'everyone's sitting around the Rayburn with silly smiles on their faces reading the books they gave to other people for Christmas ... Folly is upstairs on the double bed'. We did some repairs and decorating, took one good walk, had our neighbours in for tea and local news ... and on 2nd January 1981 drove home in torrential rain ... back in time for another Grantchester party, this time given by fairly new neighbours, the Goodharts[248] an especially pleasant occasion (and which turned out to be a significant one for Pippa, who noticed particularly the middle Goodhart son, Michael).

———

Robbie was soon back to his various duties. Early in January he was off to Paris for a meeting of the Bureau of the *Institut;* then seeing pupils and lecturing; and then by executive jet to Geneva (possibly for the still active *Buttes Gas & Oil* case), hoping to be back in time for college dinner followed by a Society meeting.[249]

We fitted in various social occasions – Eli Lauterpacht and Cathy's party to show off their newborn son; another to preview an exhibition of Cockerell Bindings at the Fitzwilliam Museum; and a Subscription Concert at which we heard the young Andras Schiff in a deeply impressive performance.[250] And so on – an Evening Talk by Vivian Fisher on 18th Century Cambridge; another, to The Club, by Erskine Hill[251] on Shakespeare's Historical Plays.

---

248   Dr Charles Goodhart was a zoologist Fellow of Gonville & Caius

249   A meeting of all the college fellows.

250   We heard many promising young musicians in this series, organised by Pat Jaffé, wife of the Director of the Fitzwilliam – among them, Nigel Kennedy.

251   Erskine Hill, Fellow of Jesus College, later moved to Pembroke College, Cambridge and became Professor of Literary History.

At home we entertained overnight the current Legal Adviser to the Foreign Office, Sir Ian Sinclair and his wife Barbara, when he gave a talk to the International Law Club. Robbie of course already knew Ian, and we always found them both good companions at conferences. In one of the many letters of condolence I received after Robbie's death, Ian would write:

'Robbie was in fact one of the chief influences in my life in encouraging my interest in, and dedication to, the study of international law. I had already at the age of 13, in September 1939, made an internal vow that if I survived the war (which seemed unlikely at that time) I would devote the remainder of my life to the study and practical application of public international law. Fortunately, and with Robbie's help, together with others such as Hersch Lauterpacht, Eric Beckett and Gerald Fitzmaurice, I was able to keep that silent internal vow – although, when I look around at the world of 2004, I am not sure that I have been all that successful!'

After giving some lectures in Geneva (not completely written at the time of departure, but no doubt fully assembled in time for delivery) Robbie was back for his final Lent Term of teaching commitments in Cambridge. A notable visitor calling at that time for a consultation was Carlyle Maw.[252] Our entertainment of him and his wife included a guided tour around Jesus College.

Meantime, work with the Tunisians continued; and Frances Meadows, the young Newnham graduate from Coward Chance assisting Jeremy Carver, would years later recall what her own experience had been like:

'I was two years qualified in 1979 when I went to work for Jeremy, who immediately gave me a section of a pleading to draft and dispatched me off to Cambridge several times to work on it with Robbie, who fed me beer and sandwiches in his lovely room in Jesus and paid me the supreme compliment of saying he could always use my drafting. And at intervals he would appear in London in our office annexe wearing his duffle coat and college scarf, and be scooped up by Alison [Jeremy's faithful secretary] and fed coffee. He managed to be revered and loved at the same time.

---

[252] US Under Secretary of State for International Security Affairs 1974-76, later specialising in the Law of the Sea.

'When we were at drafting meetings in Tunis we used to find RYJ in his hotel room surrounded by the entire cat population of whichever resort it was, often unable to move from the chair…'

In late March that Tunis case[253] had a preliminary hearing before the International Court, since Malta was to 'intervene' between the chief protagonists. It meant that besides the preparation of pleadings, Robbie was obliged to buy a wig (a periwig in a japanned box inscribed with his name). I explained that –

'Previously, he had addressed only small arbitration courts (the way most international disputes are tried, with only three judges). This time he wore silk gown, bands and wig to address 17 judges of 17 nationalities[254] … and we have some interesting photos to prove it!'

When he next met the Tunisian team he was, I wrote, 'acclaimed as a hero. That pleading at the International Court was a complete victory'.

While away for a visit to Arment House in April he could not quite escape thoughts about Tunisia, even when building walls. And a telephone call from Strasbourg warned him of the date for a brief appearance he was to make as a Judge *ad hoc* at the Court of Human Rights. It is not surprising to find that, writing to Pippa on 2nd May, Robbie confessed:

'I really have rather *too* much work just now, even for me, and feel just a bit oppressed by it. Next week I have to run (as "Director") a high-powered seminar on commercial arbitration, at the Inn on the Park Hotel, in London. There will be over 100 experts from all over the world, so I must be on my toes. The week after I am in a big case[255] in the House of Lords (with and led by Brian Davenport, the Willmer son-in-law![256]) Then LL.B. examination in Cambridge. Then British Judge in a Human Rights case in the Court at

---

253 *Tunisia/Libyan Arab Jamahiriya* continental shelf dispute, with Malta intervening.

254 In addition to the permanent court of 15 judges, the two states in a dispute are permitted to nominate extra *ad hoc* judges to ensure impartiality.

255 The *I Congreso del Partido* case concerned a dispute between Cuba and Chile over state immunity.

256 Brian Davenport, QC, was married to a daughter of our Grantchester neighbour Professor Nevill Willmer.

Strasbourg; then another H.L. case with Anthony Evans, which will last 10 days or so of talking; then prepare for Tunis/Libya in the International Court in September/October; not to mention Dijon Conference in August and another big case involving many millions on a breached contract with the Gulf States, in which I am supposed to deliver an opinion. Too much! And that case between Sharjah and Dubai that nearly killed me before Christmas – the Ruler of Sharjah hasn't paid a penny for all that work and I doubt whether he now will do so!'

And indeed the year 1981 would continue to be crammed with incident.

As Trinity Term teaching gave way to Tripos exams Robbie delivered his last lecture as Whewell Professor, and received an ovation at the end. He then gave two hours of supervision before being whisked off to London for the opening session of that high-powered seminar on commercial arbitration. By chance I was there at the seminar's opening dinner, and wrote afterwards:

'… At the end Richard Wilberforce made an introductory speech with his splendid cogency and humour, followed by an address by Robbie Jennings. I listened (sitting with my back to him) with great interest, as I had typed the speech the day before. There were a number of additions, all improvements; and he put it over to the very best effect. He *is* a good lecturer and an effective barrister, because he delivers with great attention to timing and voice-control, and so holds people's attention and compels them to follow the argument. (I am, of course, somewhat prejudiced in his favour!)'

'…On the Friday, after the second full day of all this high-powered discussion, he whizzed home by hired car and, with the chauffeur standing by chatting with me for a moment, rushed upstairs and changed into a dinner-jacket for a college feast. It was a long affair [the Rustat Feast] and bed was at about 11.30 … but at 1am we were woken from deep sleep by the telephone. Admiringly, I heard Robbie find pencil and paper to take a note, and courteously promise someone to… "think about it and let [him] know later". It was a call from Vancouver, evidently with the 8 or 9-hour time-difference overlooked!

'When Robbie went back to London on Monday, it was with heaps of luggage – papers and books, and the fancy-dress for his appearance at the House of Lords case… I have just seen the suit, although not the total ensemble: the jacket has 16 buttons, none of which fasten, and the waistcoat some 10 or 11 more. They are mostly hidden by the silk gown, anyway. And, after all that, the judges sitting in the House of Lords wear their everyday modern clothes!'

I began my next letter to my father and sister, on 25th May, with a disclosure:

'Robbie has been nominated as the British candidate for one of the seats about to be vacated at the International Court of Justice. This is itself an honour which pleases him, for the body of four (Lord Wilberforce, Sir Francis Vallatt, Sir Ian Sinclair and – ? – I forget who) might well have put forward a senior Foreign Office name. The present Judges at the World Court would all, I think, welcome him (and Sir Humphrey Waldock, at present President, would like to have Robbie as his successor), but even though there is strong support among lawyers, the actual election of the 15 judges of the court is subject to political bargaining among power blocks – and so results can be unexpected. The election takes place at the United Nations in New York in September (in both the Security Council and the General Assembly); so at present one can't go further than say that Robbie is the British nominee.

'… Apart from that, the *I Congreso* case came to the end of its hearing … and Robbie is back here doing last bits of teaching and is hard at work on other cases. He did, however, feel moved to take me out for a little celebration dinner on Thursday evening…'

To Pippa he conveyed the news of his nomination for the ICJ in typical style:

'… That is *only* nomination, Pip; it does not in the least follow these days that the British name will be elected … But there is a chance. And anyway it is nice to have the confidence of the UK bigwigs. It had been expected that they would stick to the establishment and choose Sir Francis Vallat, who used to be at the FCO.

'I am specially proud of the fact that I know that Lord Wilberforce – easily the ablest Judge we have – worked for me. He is a man I have always looked up to and greatly admired – both as a man and an intellect. Also it seems that Sir Ian Sinclair of the FCO was for me – he it was who wrote the most warm congratulations.

'Well, we'll see. It would mean a change and some relief from the big pressures of these big cases in the ICJ and the House of Lords (tho' I enjoy it!). And it is the no.1 job for international lawyers. And, let's face it, it would provide a large, tax-free salary for 9 years with a good pension and a widow's pension! However, I'm not counting any chickens yet.

'Jeremy Carver and his office have been beside themselves with delight! Nice of them!

———

'And now – perhaps even more exciting! We have – on trial – two of the first examples of the *new* Quad electrostatic speakers. They are incredible! Really astonishingly true and untiring. We are listening to the *Messiah* now. Superb, easy, true sound. And a British invention again. They are still made at Huntingdon …

'University Audio know me so well. They did not even take them into the shop from their packing cases, but sent them straight out here… "to see what I thought of them!"

'But they *are* a good shop for me. This afternoon I must have jogged something on the amplifier when I was changing it for the new speakers. So I rang up and young Martin came with a new amplifier and took the other away. They will mend it and sell it and I keep this. Cost = one glass of sherry!'

That was totally genuine, on both sides. He had made real friends with the people in University Audio, and they – shrewdly but in response to his eager fascination with Hi-fi – knew that he was unlikely to resist buying this new apparatus.

———

Early in June he drove over to Oxford for the funeral of Beattie, Lady Waldock. Her death was a shock which touched Robbie, for he had always found her immensely charming; and for Humphrey, he knew, the loss was devastating.

May Week ended, as usual, with entertainments of all sorts. This year they included a curious party given by a former Chaplain of Jesus College, James Owen, now Vicar of Little St Mary's – a contrast to the farewell party we had attended the evening before for the current Chaplain, James Attwell.[257] Owen

---

[257] The Very Rev. James Attwell rose to be Dean of Winchester.

was a High Church Tory character. His gathering, all crammed into a tiny narrow garden backing onto the river, were a Trollopean mixture of clerics (including the Bishop of Ely) and dons, many in dandyish summer rig with boaters (our host in a cream suit of wild silk, with carnation). Next day some former pupils of Robbie's called on us at Grantchester – the Deputy Attorney General of India[258], Milon Banerjee and his wife Anita, Professor of Economics, with their son Debal who would in due course study law at Jesus College.

On 22 June he began a gruelling spell in London for the House of Lords hearings of the *Buttes Gas & Oil* v *Occidental* case. I described his experience:

'…Since the leading counsel on his (*Buttes*) side is so very expert – Sir Anthony Evans – Robbie had felt it best to leave all the talking to him. But then he was asked to prepare to speak. So he went up to London early on Sunday afternoon, a prepared speech in his case, and spent that evening discussing and rewriting. On Monday it was all Evans, so R. was up till midnight re-drafting; and the same happened on Tuesday and Wednesday – Robbie "sitting on the edge of his seat" and then having to rethink his own speech all over again. But this morning (Thursday) he is to give the first short speech, and after that can relax a little!'

It was a familiar pattern: extreme stress, leaving him thoroughly tired. A performance of *HMS Pinafore* by the nearly-defunct D'Oyley Carte Company, intended as refreshment, was lame and disappointing. But we did get off for a few days at Arment House.

———

That summer there was an event which affected Robbie in many ways:

'We are in rather a state of shock over another sudden death [I wrote on 18th August], that of Sir Humphrey Waldock, the President of the International Court. His wife's death in May had been a severe blow, but we were expecting to see him next week in Dijon, and Robbie to pleading before him a week or two later. The news came by telephone yesterday … and today came a friendly letter from Humphrey himself … So there is a sudden alteration in all sorts of arrangements, as well as the loss of a friend.'

---

258 Banerji was later Attorney-General.

Grandpa Thomas Yewdall & Grandma Jennings
(born Annie Harland) with their family.
Arthur, Robbie's father, top right.

Grandpa Bob
Brotherton

Grandma Brotherton
(born Ann Schofield)

Hawthorn
Cottage

Arthur Jennings, Robbie's father

Edith Jennings, Robbie's mother

On holiday in Morecambe: Arthur J, 'Aunt
Minnie' Brotherton, Robbie & Edith J

Proud Robbie, aged c13,
with Leghorn cock

Downing College 2nd boat, with Robbie, cox, centre front c1934

The Downing undergraduate

Southampton: the small figure waving from the deck of the QM is Robbie 1936

Robbie has a shoeshine at Fort Sumter, Charleston, S Carolina

Major RY Jennings, Intelligence Corps

Robbie as one of Grantham's
crew-members

Clive Parry,
another member of the crew

Robbie on Clothilde with
Jim Grantham

Arthur & Edith Jennings meet their
grandson Richard (Dick) 1956

Wedding of Professor & Mrs RY
Jennings, Littleham, Devon 1955

A visit to Grantchester: Robbie with
small son by the millpond, spring 1957

Robbie with Dick and Pippa
on a country outing

Alfordsway, Robbie's home from 1961, shown here as he finally knew it in the 2000s

Some notable figures extracted from a group photograph of the
Master & Fellows of Jesus College, 1959

Glanville Williams Alan Sharpe David Daiches Shackleton Bailey Moses Finlay Bernard Towers
Thurston Dart Tony Roberts Robbie Jennings AHM Jones. Alan Percival Derek Taunt
Rev Percy Gardner Smith Alan Pars EMW Tillyard (Master), Sir Claude Elliott Bill Thorpe

A meeting of the Hague Academy Committee, c1960.
Left to right: 2 Oda, 3 RYJ,4 Panhuys (Chair), 5 R-J Dupuy, 6 Boutros Ghali

Holiday in Borrowdale, 1965: Robbie with Joey on Catbells

Arment House, acquired in 1971

The front and yard of Arment House

Robbie enjoying the view
at Arment House

On Argentine vessel exploring the Beagle Channel, 1972
Robbie, 4th from right.

In Sharjah, 1975, searching the desert
for a boundary point

Sharjah/Dubai arbitration, 1981.
Sharjah team: RYJ, Jeremy Carver,
Yusri Dweik, agent, Northcutt Ely

Queen's Counsel: Robbie on the day he 'took silk'

Tunisia/Libya boundary dispute before ICJ: Robbie with Slim Benghazi, agent

Joey, Pippa & Dick Jennings in the snow, Christmas 1981

The Whewell Professor as many knew him, in the Ghost Room, Jesus College

Robbie's initiation at the International Court, 1982, with Judges Mbaye (Senegal) & El Khani (Syria)

Audience with Pope John-Paul II in the Vatican, 1982 (8th centenary of St Francis)

On the 40th anniversary of the ICJ in 1985, the judges and wives meet His Holiness individually

Robbie listens intently to a student 'counsel' at a Telders moot

Robbie making his 'solemn declaration' for a second term of office, 1991,
with Judges Tarassov (Russia) and Kooimans (Netherlands)

British woman is world's most senior judge

Robbie's successor at the ICJ: Dame Rosalyn Higgins (from *The Daily Telegraph*)

Robbie at home, recovering from flu with Sorrel as company

40th wedding anniversary, 1995 – a gathering of grandchildren at Leicester

Christine   Robbie
Polly   Philip   Annie
Lizzie Susie Mary Thomas Tabitha

Grandpa Robbie on his 90th birthday, with all the family (Annie absent on a school trip)

Adults standing: Jill & Dick Jennings, Andrew Eddleston, Michael & Pippa Goodhart, Joey Eddleston
[Next line] Standing: Mary, Philip & Alice, Lizzie, Thomas, Susie
[Bottom] Sitting: Tabitha, Christine, Robbie, Polly

At his 90th birthday dinner given by the Law Faculty, 2003,
Robbie chats with Professor Sir David Williams, Vice Chancellor

The very last photo, taken by Peter Edwards
in the garden at Alfordsway

Robbie's grave in the churchyard at Grantchester

Our departure for the *Institut* meeting at Dijon was delayed by three days so that we might attend Waldock's funeral.

'We were so glad to have been present: that funeral was a marvellously fitting one. It was in a most beautiful old village church, Old Marston, close to Oxford, very small and simple. The coffin stood there draped in a huge United Nations flag; and besides members of Humphrey's family (his son came over from Vancouver, his daughter from an American university with her husband and children) and close Oxford friends, there were the Vice-President of the International Court (a Nigerian[259]) and other dignitaries – judges, Foreign Office, United Nations. A superb address, and an appropriate reading from the Book of Wisdom (about being made "judge over all the nations"). And after the service in church, the hearse took the coffin very slowly down the lane, about ¼ mile, with the long procession of people walking after, to the burial-ground. Robbie had been there in May for the very touching service for Beattie, Humphrey's beloved wife, in the same place.'

For him, I added, 'the emotion of the funeral was a strain'.

The very next morning, at 5.45 am, we left for Dijon, with Pippa as companion. Soon I found what this sort of multi-national gathering was like for wives:

'Attending a conference of this sort as a hanger-on is a mixed experience. Long, long hours of tedium, standing about while speeches are made in French and English; a bewildering number of people to meet and be pleasant to and try to remember with terrible names like 'M. et Mme. Diez de Velasco Vallejo', 'M. Abdullah El-Erian', 'M. Seidl-Hohenveldern', 'M. et Mme. Uichi Takano', 'M. Krzystof Skubiszewski', &c., &c. – about 150 of them. (Van Hecke of Belgium must not be confused with Van Heusen of America or Baron Von der Heidte of Germany!) …'

We hoped to be able to miss the final grand banquet, which Robbie knew from experience was an ordeal. But it was not to be: Waldock's sudden death had created a crisis, since he was to have been the next President of the *Institut*.

---

[259] Taslim Elias, judge from 1976 to 1991, who would succeed Waldock as President of the Court.

Robbie would now have to take his place, and in two years' time it would be ourselves having to organize the conference – not only the programme of meetings but accommodation, outings, persuading local bigwigs to provide entertainment … And attendance at the banquet was now obligatory.

After several outings, the Dijon conference's Sunday excursion had been to a place which enchanted us all, the Abbey de Fontenay, a huge Cistercian monastery, actually founded by St Bernard in 1118 AD. Pippa recognised it from her medieval history course, and Robbie, wandering among these great deserted stone buildings set among trees and with a stream and a pond full of trout, 'felt strongly drawn to the meditative and austere life'. But our luncheon there was not austere at all – a joyful al fresco meal at long tables: casks of wine from which jugfuls were drawn; a buffet of cold salad; hot ham encased in pastry borne in and displayed by the chefs; cheeses; gateaux and tarts, and then fruit. We were then taken to a small archaeological museum where we had to see the Vase of Vix – a huge bronze bowl from the 5th century BC, impressive indeed … but many of the international lawyers discovered a little patisserie nearby, where they could cool themselves with coke or ice cream cornets.

On the coach my neighbour was a Russian, Professor Grigory Tunkin, a tiny man with gleaming gold teeth. He spoke good English, and we got on well. I was chatting, I found, with someone who had once been the chief legal adviser for foreign affairs to Khruschev, and possibly Stalin as well.

For Robbie the conference was of course a serious matter with one meeting following another. At the end we found that such a gathering of international lawyers was, understandably, liable to attract outsiders with grievances that they hoped might be resolved:

'At the conference centre (a very modern town hall) we found a mass of Iranian students holding a demonstration. They were hoping that the Institut could assist in the overthrow of the Khomeini regime. A number of police were in control – we had been to a reception at the Préfecture the evening before – and so our demonstrators sat in polite rows holding their placards and giving pamphlets explaining their cause. Later, I heard, the Secretary-General of the Institut made them a speech, saying that the lawyers did indeed support human rights, but had no intention of doing anything to intervene in an internal dispute between nationals and their own government. A further pamphlet, expressing thanks, was then given by the demonstrators.'

The final banquet was indeed exhausting, being preceded by receptions from 6 to 8.30 pm – wearisome standing until at last the local dignitaries arrived. The election of Robbie as President was formally announced, and my hand was kissed several times by gentlemen offering their 'felicitations' to 'Madame la Presidente'. When at last we got home next day we supped on what Pippa had been craving for days – baked beans on toast.

Robbie had just three days at home, catching up with correspondence and chucking out stuff from his now-ended academic days, before going to Geneva as an adviser to the I.L.O. From there he went straight to The Hague for the final concentrated preparations before the *Tunisia/Libya* oral hearings. It was going to be a long haul, during which he would return home for weekends.

On 14th September I joined him at the Kurhaus in Scheveningen – now (instead of a proposed demolition) with many more bedrooms of reduced size, but still having much of its former grandeur. Jeremy Carver was there too, and his secretary Alison from Coward Chance. She, together with her word-processor and other up-to-date gadgetry, heaps of files and reference-books, were installed in one of the bedrooms, from where one might hear the humming and tapping of the machine.

My own time with Robbie came in fits and snatches, a pattern typical of what I could expect for years afterwards (and indeed had long ago become accustomed to). His meetings became protracted, or he might be rewriting parts of his address to the Court as Alison retyped it, the other lawyers and the geologists still checking that their addresses would fit together as a consistent and effective argument. So I would take myself off to the Mauritshuis or read a paperback, and eventually we supped with Jeremy at a small café on the seafront.

On Wednesday 16th September 1981, I had my first impression of the ICJ.

'[Robbie] was awake and at work at 6.15 am, going through his address yet again. We breakfasted in our room, he dressed in his "conjuror's outfit", and we all went in Jeremy's car to the Peace Palace. Alison and I had to be as inconspicuous and undistracting as possible, so we walked around the ground floor of the building to keep out of the way. It is all huge and of stupendous grandeur, in the Edwardian manner: every window has stained glass to convey the sense of international brotherhood, of progress and aspiration and so forth; all the stonework, woodwork, brasswork is moulded and elaborated … and when it was nearly time to go into the Great Hall of Justice, a couple of the geologists were straying about having fun identifying the various marbles and other minerals!'

Now I was able to witness that extraordinary scene: the long, elevated bench with the row of judges in dark gowns and lace *jabots* beneath a row of tremendous stained-glass windows[260] depicting *the Evolution of the Peace Ideal*. Facing them were representatives of the parties to the dispute; and on one side a cubicle where linguists were translating everything spoken into French or English, the two languages employed in the Court. On this occasion:

'… "our" side had one English Q.C. [RYJ] in wig and black gown, and three French advocates in scarlet gowns (with trimmings of white fur) and jabots. The Libyan team were even more colourful: two Q.Cs, one scarlet Frenchman, and one Italian in a handsome blue gown with gold tassels.[261] '[The judges] enter slowly, and sit looking impassive. But as the hearing gets under way, (and, I like to think, in response to the persuasiveness of Robbie's delivery) they show their interest in the argument; and presently the long row of figures reminds one of a Last Supper, with the draped forms beginning to lean towards each other in groups and with signs of animation appearing. Robbie spoke for 2¼ hours, feeling very hot in his layers of black clothing, and his voice beginning to show strain by the end. It was a very strong performance, presenting an outline of the Tunisian case which was to be argued in more detail later from the various points of view – juridical, historical and by the geologists. The dispute is over a continental shelf boundary line, and depends largely upon "geomorphology" – the exact formation beneath the shallow sea. I became so interested that I have been getting reports on the subsequent speeches from Robbie …'

For, leaving a very tired husband behind to continue his labours, I returned to Grantchester. His weekend breaks allowed me just enough time to provide him with clean white collarless shirts for the next stint (their winged collars being sent for professional laundering).

---

[260] The windows, given as the British contribution to the Great Hall of Justice, were designed by Douglas Strachan.

[261] Virally, Dupuy (father and son), French, for Tunisia; Bowett and Vallat (English), Colliard (French) and Malintoppi (Italian) for Libya. There were also the agents, counsel and advisers on both sides in everyday suits.

On 15th October he came home for a slightly longer spell, and next day 'sported the oak' of his college room in order to concentrate on composing the address he was to give at Humphrey Waldock's memorial service. (A gap in the readily-available information about Humphrey's career had been filled thanks to Charles Wilson,[262] who had spent the war years on secret wartime work for the Admiralty under Waldock's direction.) On the Saturday we joined Ian and Christine Brownlie[263] at All Souls before moving into the University Church. There, before a packed congregation, Robbie delivered his tribute from its high pulpit[264] – an appreciation of a greatly-admired international lawyer and friend.

In that address Robbie revealed that it had been those years of intensive work during the war which had turned Waldock from his former speciality in the English law of mortgages to public international law:

'… And what better way could there be of becoming an international lawyer, than through the exigencies of practical situations of grave importance where often an irreversible answer had to be given within hours? …'

[And he spoke of Humphrey Waldock's willingness to listen to a point of view opposing his own long-held conviction] –

'… I well remember him telling me in his room at All Souls, how he had come to the conclusion that the orthodox view on the effect of reservations to treaties, which he had himself defended for years, was no longer tenable and must be abandoned. That was the beginning of a break-through in the development of the law of treaties. This willingness to think again – and then yet again if necessary or useful, was one of his great strengths.'

On our next visit to The Hague we were invited to dinner by Hugh Thirlway, an administrator and translator at the ICJ and a quite exceptional

---

262 Professor C.H. Wilson, Fellow of Jesus, economic historian.
263 Brownlie, previously a Professor at the LSE, succeeded Waldock in the Chichele Chair of International Law at Oxford, becoming a Fellow of All Souls. He was later knighted.
264 The text is included in *Collected Papers*, Vol. II, p.1395.

character. He and his wife were both Cambridge graduates: Hugh had read first Greek and then Law, becoming fluent in French while doing a year's research at a French university. The fact that his wife had read Geology was some help to him when translating the complicated arguments exchanged in the current case, about the formation of the seabed. Their house was in a street not far from the Peace Palace, tall and narrow with the typical precipitous Dutch staircase and we gathered upstairs in a comfortable room with a fire. Evidence of their large family appeared mostly in the dining room downstairs, which was crammed with musical instruments: Thirlway himself played the bassoon, piano, harpsichord and flute and was both conductor and composer. One learnt to look out for a large black rabbit on the staircase. Another guest that evening was Derek Bowett. Conversation flowed until midnight, and we learnt a little about life in The Hague for English exiles.

Jeremy Carver's wife, Anthea, had come over for the final session, and Hugh beckoned her to tiptoe out with me during the tedious summing-up speeches, to show us the two rooms adjoining the Great Hall whose walls were hung with portraits of former Presidents of the Court. I wrote that:

'At the end of the hearing there is an end-of-term sense of relief, everyone smiling. They have been at it for nearly seven weeks, and all have had enough. Robbie and I waited for Judge André Gros[265] (France) who very kindly took us to lunch at his hotel. He is a dear. He has a deep affection for England (having served here with the Free French army during the war as well as studying in London earlier), and with his excellent accent he had read the lesson – the Beatitudes – at Humphrey Waldock's memorial service in Oxford. This lunch would not have been possible a day earlier, for the judges are very correct in avoiding any sign of partiality towards counsel, and always balance their entertaining with representatives of both sides being present. We had him to ourselves, though, and besides being an attentive host, his talk gradually moved on to conveying a good deal about the character of the Court. He is himself just at the end of a double stint (18 years) as a judge, and was passing on some of the sort of hints Robbie could have expected to have heard from Humphrey Waldock. Being no longer in the role of counsel, Robbie was now

---

[265] Described as 'definitely one of the major figures in the Court's history', Gros was a Judge from 1964-84.

a friend probably about to start on a nine-year term as judge himself; and Gros was being simply kind and wise.'

An invitation from the Lachses had provided an excuse to release us from the tremendous final dinner party the Tunisians were holding. Even when we found the Lachs dinner had been cancelled, Robbie could not face a long evening with the Tunisian team; so, 'feeling rather furtive', we went by tram to eat a 'nice ordinary little meal' at an Italian restaurant at Scheveningen, and on our return found the Tunisians still standing around in the foyer of the Bel Air waiting for their party to get under way. Next day, too, we spent quietly, 'Robbie reading through his Strasbourg papers as well as resting', and descended from our room to have lunch at the Pavilion Restaurant in the nearby Gemeente Museum garden, afterwards going inside to look at 'pottery, pewter, silver and musical instruments, the last including a stunning collection of gongs and drums from the former Dutch East Indies'.

Then it was time for a fairly uncomfortable flight to Strasbourg, arriving in the dark at its little airport – '*cottagey* in style, with the high steeply-sloping tiled roof of the district'. We got to bed at about midnight, and were delighted with the warm welcome early next morning when:

'A beaming middle-aged lady came in with "Bonjour, monsieur, dame" and set before us a trayful of cheery blue-and-white crockery with huge dishlike cups. Lots of coffee and milk, super croissants, warm toast, and rolls. Honey and strawberry jam in real little pots. And two bunches of sweet little black grapes!

'Robbie went off before 9 am, and we did not meet again until about 8 pm...'

I had been warned by Peggy Wortley, wife of the Manchester Professor of International Law, that while friends might envy one's travels, life as a camp-follower might be largely spent waiting in boring hotel rooms or on street corners. Still, I did manage to explore this fascinating city and absorb a sense of its dual identity, standing between the Vosges and the Black Forest. At one point I became thoroughly lost, confused between the churches of St Pierre le Vieux, St Pierre le Jeune Catholique and St Pierre le Jeune Protestante –

recovering my sense of direction only when I glimpsed the cathedral spire. That cathedral I inspected in some detail and found much to admire – but its Catholic gloom gave Robbie the horrors when he looked inside.

Robbie's service as a Judge of the Court of Human Rights lasted for just two days. That court, part of the Council of Europe organisation (not the European Union), has many judges from its member states at any one time, but in 1981, since the retirement of Sir Gerald Fitzmaurice, had none from the United Kingdom. As a case was to be heard concerning a British national ('X') who was challenging the legality of his detention in a mental hospital, a British judge *ad hoc* – R.Y. Jennings – was appointed to ensure full representation. It was a case which troubled Robbie slightly, since it seemed clear that the young man was mentally unstable. Yet the law as it stood must be applied, and that gave him his release (which, as it later turned out, left him free to inflict injury on someone). Still, Robbie had played his part in giving the 'correct' ruling during those two days. And on one evening we were pressed to join the Irish Judge Walsh in his hotel bedroom to drink some whiskey [*sic*]– Irish Paddy's Whiskey – before dinner. As we sipped we listened to his many tales. At dinner we joined the President of the Court, a charming Dutchman called Wiarda[266] and his wife.

The Court's judgment would be delivered in September 1982. On this visit there was just time for Robbie to go wandering with me to see something of this city crammed with historical relics and sheer charm. Working our way back from the covered bridge and high old half-timbered houses beside the waterways, we found ourselves in Martin Luther Street, where we looked inside St Thomas's Church. Its original Catholic identity had been changed to Protestant, with a severe high pulpit, and its former altar moved in front of the transept, with a huge open bible set on it and vases of flowers on each side. The pews, enclosed with little doors, all faced the pulpit. But in this spartan setting was an astounding mass of sculpture high on the east wall, full of congested symbolism to commemorate a heroic 15th century Marshall. But even stranger for us was to find two black cases with glass tops, one containing an Austrian Count who had been killed in 1636, the other a girl of 12, both withered almost to skeletons, still dressed in their original clothes.

---

[266]   Judge Gerardus Wiarda, an international lawyer, had served on the Netherlands Supreme Court before moving to the European Court of Human Rights. Robbie developed a real affection for him and his wife.

Altogether, Strasbourg provided an interesting experience. Woken on the Sunday morning by the gloomy tolling of church bells, we returned home to the welcoming girls and animals. Three days later, Robbie was off to New York.

This time, his visit was an introduction to the United Nations headquarters, to present himself as a candidate for a vacancy at the International Court of Justice. He was modest and hated self-promotion, but the Foreign Office wanted him to accompany the British delegation attending the General Assembly when the Legal Adviser, Sir Arthur Watts, could introduce him to various delegates and show him something of the great organisation in action. Once there he found, of course, that a good many people – officials within the UN, or representatives of nations from around the world – were old pupils of his, and many more were familiar with his work. It turned out to be an interesting week.

And it was during that week that a telegram arrived from the Chairman of the Board of Buttes Gas and Oil Co:

'PLEASE ACCEPT MY PERSONAL CONGRATULATIONS ON THE SUCCESSFUL RESOLUTION OF THE OCCIDENTAL PETROLEUM LITIGATION. THAT YOU PREVAILED IN THIS MOST COMPLEX MATTER IS TESTIMONY TO YOUR EXTRAORDINARY LEGAL ACUMEN.'

News came, too, of the Dubai and Sharjah border dispute, which was less of a triumph but a reasonable compromise. The Award given by the arbitration tribunal in December 1981 would alter the boundary to allow both sides room for development – 'Sharjah to develop its industrial zone and Dubai city to expand to the northeast'.[267] In the 3½ years since it was set up the tribunal had had to look at evidence going back as far as 1810, and study the areas occupied by wandering tribes. The tribunal's settlement 'removes one of the inter-emirate disputes which block the adoption of a permanent UAE constitution...'

And then, on 6th November 1981, we were woken by a telephone call. It was Rachel Lauterpacht, the first to give us the news (which she had heard in the

---

267 Taken from a MEED report by Michael Petrie-Ritchie.

small hours, on the BBC World Service) of Robbie's election to the Court. His own first remark to me after putting the receiver down was, 'Now we can have a car with your initials on it!' (The registration number for our principal car during his term of office would be CDJ 18, standing for *Corps Diplomatique Juridique* – matching my full name, Christine Dorothy Jennings.) He seemed to take the news calmly; but I knew just how excited he was to be following a great succession of British judges – Lord McNair, Sir Hersch Lauterpacht, Sir Gerald Fitzmaurice and Sir Humphrey Waldock. I realised, too, the reorganisation of our lifestyle that this was going to entail.

On 30th November I wrote:

> 'There have been plenty of little events to keep us occupied in the last weeks. Robbie has heaps of nice letters and telegrams to acknowledge. We are still in a state of limbo as regards the new appointment, though. Apart from being asked for measurements for the judicial gown, nothing has happened as yet: he goes to The Hague for his installation on February 8th.[268]
>
> 'In the meantime, Robbie has the International Law Association taking him to London occasionally, and is doing some teaching of undergraduates (supervisions in college) for love, besides plenty of other work…'

Family life carried on. Dick had spent a wonderfully action-packed fortnight in California by simply turning up at Heathrow with a rucksack and taking a 'standby' ticket to San Francisco and then, with a hired car, exploring Yosemite National Park and miles of wild coastline. At home, Joey was taking her driving test.

—

The letters and telegrams of congratulation on Robbie's election to the ICJ were heartening, especially in their range: from Lords Carrington, Denning, Hailsham and Wilberforce to old Jesus College pupils and former colleagues, and even the girls in the travel agency he had used. There were those who rejoiced with him at his elevation but were sorry that they could no longer call on him for advice. And a confidential letter from Sir Ian Sinclair disclosed the actual votes cast in the UN ballots by both the Security Council and the General Assembly, which were reassuring.

---

[268] – though in fact it took place on 23rd February 1982

One evening during those weeks of limbo, Robbie invited to supper two of the Jesus fellows who shared his enthusiasm for gramophone records. One was the elderly Bill Thorpe (whose research on the song of chaffinches had entailed the slowed-down replay of recordings of their song), and the other the young Roy Howat (at that time a Research Fellow in Music, already giving recitals of Debussy's piano works). A happy evening, with Robbie showing off his precious Quad electrostatic loudspeakers playing Bill's record of Schumann, Roy's of Gershwin and his own of a Hoffnung festival concert.

A very good Christmas this year included snow, church, splendid turkey, walks, and log fire. Up in Eskdale people were snowed-in for a fortnight, and our Arment House lonning was filled with drifts up to 8ft deep; but we stayed snug and enjoyed the little parties among Grantchester neighbours.

On 31ˢᵗ December Robbie's knighthood was announced in the newspapers – and there were telephone calls and telegrams (including one from '*Philip*'[269]). In the following days there was another outpouring of congratulations. Counting the letters and telegrams from all over the world received during those weeks, I find 285 were saved in a large box.

The Honours List was a shock for the children. The letter from 10 Downing Street intimating the submission of Robbie's name, 'that H.M. may be graciously pleased to approve' his nomination for a knighthood and asking for assurance 'that this would be agreeable to you', had come back in November. He had of course consulted me, and I found the prospect terrifying: I knew that my uncle, Dr G.M. Bennett, had turned down his offer of a knighthood and accepted instead a C.B., he and his wife having socialist sympathies and being very private people. But as the British judge at the ICJ it was proper for Robbie to accept the title, and I must just do so too. We happened to live in a village with four or five titled residents at any one time, which made it easier.

---

[269]   Duke of Edinburgh, Chancellor of the University of Cambridge.

H.E. Judge Sir Robert Jennings

1982-83

There were letters to write during those first days of the New Year 1982, acknowledging the kind messages and in some cases having to explain Robbie's new situation. Aunt Kitty (now aged 100) and cousins Muriel and Geoff Womersley had spotted the announcement of the knighthood, as did his old friends Russell and Vera Walton – all supposing that a gentle retirement lay ahead. Once told that in fact Robbie was embarking on a new and demanding career, Russell immediately responded to 'the splendid news of your appointment to the Hague Court':

'... I cannot think of anything more fitting to crown your remarkable career ... The prestige will be modestly carried, I'm sure, but none the less enormous ...

'As you say, it is monstrous that the papers do not carry information about such nationally important appointments ...'

(*The Times* seldom mentions the International Court of Justice, although the International Criminal Court and the International Criminal Tribunal for the Former Yugoslavia provide 'stories' which attract its attention.)

The multi-talented Hugh Thirlway could not resist offering his own *Forensic Fable*, in the style of those by 'O' (Theo Mathew, published in the 1920s):

'The Eminent International Lawyer and the Knighthood

'There was once an International Lawyer of Unquestioned Eminence and Immense Learning. While Deeply Read in the works of Bynkershoek, Vittoria, Pufendorf and Grotius, he was no less at home with the Modern Italian School and the Tortuous Phraseology in the pages of the *American Journal*: he was furthermore reputed to have read the UNCLOS Draft Convention on the Law of the Sea, from Beginning to End, not once but Several Times, and to have understood the Greater Part of it. For many years he had held the Professorship of Public International Law at one of the two Universities; and when he Travelled Abroad, as he frequently did in order to make his Services available to the numerous Governments who Begged for his Assistance in matters of State Succession, the Exhaustion of Local Remedies, Diplomatic Immunity, or the Right to Control the Collection of Fixed Species, namely Sponges, with Tridents on Banks outside the Limits of Territorial Waters, he was Universally known by the Title of "Professor" in regions where the Inner Significance of such Marks of Learning as "QC" or "Ll.B." would have been lost upon the Unenlightened Foreigner. At the peak of his career, when he had been elected both to a Judgeship of the International Court of Justice and to the Presidency of the Institut de Droit International, in an Unguarded Moment he accepted the offer of a Knighthood in the New Year Honours. Did this additional Title of Honour increase the Splendour and Satisfaction of his Life? It did not. The Ignorant Continentals who had deferred to the Professor, either knew nothing of Knights, supposed that his First Christian Name was "Sir", and equated him with a Mere Tourist; or, if Better Informed, took him for a Television Interviewer, the Chairman of a Nationalised Industry, or a Trade Unionist MP who had Unaccountably Failed to secure a Life Peerage. At the same time, he was so regularly Overcharged in all Transactions on account of his Knighthood that he and his wife were obliged to Travel under the Pseudonym of "Mr and Mrs Smith", an Appellation which prompted the Deepest Suspicion of Hotel Receptionists.

Moral: A Good Title does not Always Ensure Quiet Enjoyment'

It was the first of Hugh's many parodies we would enjoy over the following years.

More explanations were needed over the following years: – No, Robbie's work was not in Strasbourg, Luxembourg or Brussels but The Hague; the International Court of Justice was the 'principal judicial organ of the United Nations'; it was composed of 15 judges, each from a different country; its principal cases were of disputes between States … and so on.[270] There was even a need to convince disbelievers of the existence of international law.

---

[270] The UN Department of Public Information publishes an excellent booklet, *The International Court of Justice,* answering questions about the purpose and organisation of the court, and explaining its difference from the older-established but still functioning Permanent Court of Arbitration.

For the first weeks of 1982 we had no answers to friends' enquiries about life in The Hague. Robbie was not inactive, of course: early in January he spent a day in Paris, presiding over a meeting of the Bureau of the *Institut*, and towards the end of the month both Pippa and I accompanied him to Jersey, where he was to be given a fitting farewell after his fourteen years of advising and acting as counsel for the States in their delimitation dispute with France.

That Jersey visit was memorable. After a splendid dinner in his honour, Robbie was presented with a fine lithograph[271] of *Grosnez Castle by Moonlight*. Next day we presented ourselves for dinner at the Greffier's home. It was an occasion to welcome the new Governor (they serve for five years), an ex-marine General, Sir Peter Whiteley: very nice indeed. The other guests were the Deputy Bailiff and his wife, an Irish doctor. Earlier that day, though, we had taken a walk up on the wild northwest headland known as 'Les Landes' to see the ruined archway of Grosnez for ourselves, and in mist had become lost in squelchy bog, where Robbie had fallen and hurt his hand. He, with increasing age, found it rather a trial to have several big dinners on the trot. And on this occasion, at the end of the lavish second course he fainted. The Bailiff's doctor-wife took his wrist and said 'There's no pulse at all', which terrified Pippa and me. But it turned out not to be what we feared. While the rest of the company continued the meal (the Governor telling a tale of one of his own fainting exploits on parade which set people laughing), Robbie spent the rest of the evening on the sofa. Next morning, with his arm in a sling, he had his last meeting with the Jersey lawyers, all by now good friends. And we sent a bunch of flowers to thank and comfort our hostess of the previous evening.

While the state of limbo continued, Robbie continued to teach a few undergraduates at Jesus, simply for love. He had, too, quite a heavy load with the *Institut* and – more – with the ILA, and pressed on with work on *Oppenheim* as well. Although not yet required to appear at the Court, he had already been given papers to read concerning the first matter he would be dealing with as a judge, an 'Advisory Opinion'[272].

---

[271] – c1840 by Le Capelain, a celebrated Jersey artist.

[272] *Application for Review of Judgment No.273 of the UNAT.* An Advisory Opinion differs from the 'Contentious' cases which are the usual business of the International Court, resolving disputes between States. The UN, or one of its organs, will have requested legal advice to support a difficult decision to be made within its own organisation.

At last, on 23rd February 1982, we (Sir Robert, wife and two daughters, all unnaturally smartly dressed) were off early to Buckingham Palace for the investiture. Suitably awed by lifeguards standing rigidly to attention with raised swords at the entrance and up the grand staircase, the long gallery hung with royal portraits and the vast stateroom, we womenfolk were directed to our seats by Guards officers who clinked slightly as they walked – Robbie, meanwhile, receiving his instructions elsewhere. As we sat on raised benches facing the dais, above us a military band played an amusing medley of popular music. Each stage of the ceremony was perfectly organised – the Yeomen of the Guard marching to take their places, their officer giving orders by rapping his ornate staff on the floor, and the two smart little Gurkhas in pillbox hats who accompanied the Queen and stood guard immediately behind her.

Fortunately, Robbie was just the third person on that immense list. Before him was a General receiving a knighthood of a special order; then came a slightly unusual K.B.E., being the Master of Selwyn College, Cambridge, Owen Chadwick (brother of Henry, Dean of Christ Church in Dicky's time there). He, being 'the *Rev.* Professor', was not dubbed but merely given the insignia, and would not be addressed by his title.

Then Robbie. No mishaps – the Queen chatted for a moment most charmingly. He was simply announced as "Sir Robert Jennings." "You are a Professor, aren't you? What is your subject?" – So Robbie told her that he had just retired from the Chair of International Law and was now to serve as a Judge at the International Court. "That's at The Hague, isn't it?" … not much conversation, but thoroughly on the spot. One saw her showing that same sort of interest in people on and on through the long list, especially to those who were disabled. (One such was a young, very brilliant, Professor[273] from Cambridge who received the CBE. I wrote –

> 'He is terribly stricken with a wasting disease, and can barely communicate – his wife can still understand his speech, and with the help of special machinery he can type his calculations. His young son took the wheelchair up, and the Queen bent right down and spoke for some time to them.'

---

[273] This was Stephen Hawking, Lucasian Professor of Mathematics, later made a Companion of Honour.

... And so the list continued, and after more than an hour one of those elderly Yeomen who had been standing to attention suddenly staggered and leaned heavily on his pike for support. Immediately, two attendants were by his side (no fuss, no sound: the Queen carrying on exactly as before), so that when he finally collapsed, he was removed with no disturbance ...

We found that Mr Robb had arrived, bringing Dick to join us (though between them they altered the setting on my camera so that the hoped-for photo of our hero failed). We all then walked down the Mall to the Oxford & Cambridge Club for a celebratory lunch, and found both the Chadwick and the Lewis[274] families opening bottles of champagne in its Ladies' Dining Room too: a very happy and convivial gathering altogether. Once home and changed back to tweeds, we walked the dog and tossed our Shrove Tuesday pancakes for supper, and packed for next day.

———

So at 6.20 a.m. next day we were off to Stansted airport, a quite modest set of buildings with parking (50p for an unlimited period), immediately in front. Thanks to the Foreign Office, we now found ourselves received as VIPs and offered coffee. Most of the other passengers on that flight were huge tough Texans in baseball caps or Stetsons – oilmen from Houston on their way to an oil rig. From Schiphol a driver from the Peace Palace conveyed us to The Hague.

Robbie would not go straight to the Court that morning, since judgment was just then being delivered on the *Tunisia/Libya* case for which he had been counsel. We were given lunch, though, by Judge Nagendra Singh (Indian) to meet the Acting President,[275] Judge Taslim Elias (Nigerian). Sitting next to the very quiet, dark-skinned Elias, I tried to open a conversation by asking whether he had been to England – and found that he had spent six years at Oxford, one at Cambridge, and one at London University; moreover, his son had entered Magdalen College, Oxford at the age of 16 and got a First! Altogether a very impressive man.

A new wing had recently been added to the Peace Palace, a beautifully-designed building in which judges' offices were arranged in pairs, each with

<hr/>

274 The newly-honoured Sir Jack Lewis was Master of Robinson College and later made Baron Lewis of Newnham

275 Judge Elias, formerly Deputy President, had to take on the Presidency on the death of Waldock.

a secretary's office in between. In the main building we found the small post office from where mail was dispatched with special Peace Palace stamps[276], and explored the gardens more thoroughly. More importantly, Robbie could learn from the judges he already knew some details of their judgment on the *Tunisia/Libya* case. That, alas for Tunisia, favoured Libya on the whole; but now he heard about the dissenting opinions and the difficult and prolonged meetings that had led to the final Award. He found that if his initial proposals for Tunisia's arguments had been followed they would have fared much better. … And as I listened, I realised that much of what I was hearing must not be disclosed.

On the 25th the new judges made their 'solemn declaration' in the Great Hall of Justice, where an audience composed of diplomats and ICJ staff were assembled. It did not take long: all the judges filed in, in their full black gowns and lace jabots; the President introduced each new member of the Court with a short *curriculum vitae,* after which they read aloud a short statement, undertaking to give honourable and impartial judgment. This was followed by a reception, with multiple handshakes and bows and a determined effort to memorise names. Back in Robbie's room it was easy to catch the name of the secretary he was to share with Judge Schwebel: she was Angie Brown – young, beautiful, capable and even from Yorkshire.

Robbie's background never left him, and he was delighted to receive from a Mrs Patricia Popple of Idle a copy of *Thorp Methodist Chapel Magazine* which had an article headed 'Local Lad Makes Good'. Someone had got the news about him and was recalling his and his family's connections with the chapel. It prompted him to respond with a piece for them about his own memories of the chapel and Sunday School which had been such an influence in his boyhood.

He became, too, one of the guests of honour that year at Trinity's Commemoration Feast, along with Lord Lane (Lord Chief Justice), Mr Nott, (Minister of Defence), the Head of the Anglican Order of St Francis and editor of the works of Isaac Newton, and Mr C.R. Milne, who had marked his father A.A. Milne's centenary by giving the manuscripts of *Winnie the Pooh* and *The House at Pooh Corner* to the college library. Although not yet allowed to dine in hall, the Master's wife gave the wives dinner in the Lodge, after which we went up to the Combination Room and took turns to peep down upon the men

---

[276] These stamps, being so exclusive, are valued by philatelists.

feasting below[277] – made possible by opening one of the panels overlooking the High Table, quite unnoticed by those in the hall.

———

At the end of March we were back in The Hague, where Robbie now had work to do and I passed much of the time exploring the area, finding that most people had an understanding of English and my inability to speak Dutch did not matter much. We got on well with them – their rumbustious sense of fun and sometimes disconcerting directness seemed to Robbie very similar to his own North Country temperament.

Now the British Ambassador, Philip Mansfield[278], gave a dinner in Robbie's honour at his residence on a narrow street, and I described that event for my father:

'...we went to the entrance – an odd one, in the side of an archway which leads into a courtyard, across which is a great church – a 19th-century Jesuit one. On pressing the bell, you stand and wait for a while – not for a footman to open the door but for a television camera to inspect you, a voice to speak and be responded to; after which the door automatically opens. At the top of the steps another door (with glass, through which you can be seen) eventually jerks itself open too. And then you are welcomed by Dutch police and Embassy staff. These extreme security precautions have been in operation since the last British Ambassador was gunned-down at his own entrance. The present ambassador finds the restrictions on his movements irksome: he cannot walk along the pavements, although his wife may move about fairly normally.

'Once inside, all that is forgotten. We pass through a magnificent high room with a fire burning and great bowls of flowers, into another even larger. There are H.E. and Mrs Mansfield – we have met them before: dignified but breezy and fun. (It turns out that he is a Yorkshireman and she was at Oxford in my time.) When all the guests are assembled, we number about 16 or 18. The others are from the diplomatic or legal communities, some Dutch, all English-speaking (they include the Irish Ambassador and wife, the

---

[277]   This was, of course, 1982. Things have changed since then, and the Trinity arrangement was relatively kind to wives. I heard that at King's the custom was for the poor things to sit in the gallery eating sandwiches and drinking lemonade while their husbands guzzled and drank wine.

[278]   – Later Sir Philip Mansfield, KCMG. The Ambassador's Residence at that time was in Westeinde.

Canadian Ambassador and wife, and an Englishman on the embassy staff, Colin Budd[279], Robbie's contemporary as a QC, and his Dutch wife).

'For dinner we moved into a third grand room, and sat at two circular tables – Robbie at Mrs Mansfield's right hand at one, I beside H.E. at the other. A delicious meal, superbly served by the liveried butler and footman. It made one smug to be British, as the plates appeared with their tremendous coats-of-arms, and such fine royal portraits hung about (not *all* royal – there's an excellent Oliver Cromwell among them). Interesting, cheerful, easy conversation. I asked about the building. It doesn't actually belong to the British Government, although it has been our ambassador's residence for over a century; it is rented from the Jesuits. But it *is* one of the finest residences, having been built as such in 1750 for Spain: hence its rococo style and the layout of its reception rooms. Altogether a thoroughly enjoyable evening.'

This was the first of many such evenings, not all quite so relaxed. For me, hating to search the shops for suitable clothes, it was a relief to find in Cambridge a sympathetic American woman, Sarah Fermi,[280] ready to design and make for me several evening dresses. Mincing about in 'suitable' shoes was always agony, especially on the small uneven paving-stones of a city built over sandy subsoil.

One day, skipping one of the plentiful embassy receptions, we took a jaunt by tram to Delft, a jaunt we were often to repeat.

'... As we walked through narrow streets and over little canal-bridges, we could hear the sound of a street organ. By the time we had reached it, its own raucous pipings and bangings were mixed with the clumsy janglings from above – the Nieuwe Kerk doing its quarter-hour carillon. Confusion of noise and colour and movement – it was fun to sit in the pale sun at an outside table in the marketplace and watch the crowds as we ate a *halve uitsmijter* (half 'outsmighter' – an egg on ham on bread). There were stallholders bawling their wares, people of all shapes and sizes on foot or bikes, huge black hairy dogs, and so on. After, we looked around that big church – very bare and tidy compared with an English one, with its great height all shaped in brick and covered in timber vaulting...'

---

279   Colin Budd was to become Ambassador to the Netherlands in 2001.

280   Sarah's husband was the scientist son of Ernino Fermi, nuclear physicist.

These few days provided many impressions, and more advice for Robbie about managing life in The Hague. And we got to know Mr Pronk, whose duties combined the work of chauffeur with that of court usher, announcing the entry of the file of judges to the Great Hall by knocking his staff on the floor and shouting 'La Court!' – at which everyone would rise to their feet.

A nine-day spell at Arment House in April included a climb, with Dick, from Wasdale (with sweaters on and off as we became exposed to ice, snow and wind, or to warm sun and shelter) up Scafell Pike by way of Piers Ghyll and down by horrible steep scree. And during this transition period Robbie was also given a number of congratulatory dinners by Shell; by Jesus College; and by the Law Faculty.

Pippa had now acquired a tiny one-up-one-down house on Castle Hill from where she could walk to work each morning at Heffers, where her enthusiasm was soon recognised by promotion to Manager of the Children's Bookshop. She loved the work, and it would turn out to be a good foundation for her later career as a children's author.

When Robbie returned to The Hague I noted (11th May) that he and his friend Ruda, the Argentine judge, 'met in sorrow' and were talking over the Falklands situation. (Robbie had become aware of Argentina's dream of claiming the Falkland Islands on his visits to the country, and he had indeed brought home a set of *Malvinas* stamps for Dick's collection.) By now the Falklands war had begun, triggered by the Argentine invasion a month before. 'Sadness over Falklands Islands crisis deepens with news of Argentine cruiser sunk', and then of the British *Sheffield,* were diary entries too. The situation was felt by international lawyers at the ICJ and by those advising the British Foreign Office to be a grievous breakdown in diplomacy.

The weeks of uncertainty about his first real involvement in the Court were ended when Robbie was recruited onto its Drafting Committee, a rare honour for a newcomer and a considerable responsibility. It meant that from now on he must often be in The Hague, the demands of the Court ruling our diaries. The children's growing independence made their time with us more precious, too: the entries in Robbie's pocket diary, mostly just abbreviated notes of appointments, always stressed the importance of occasions when he could jot down 'Family *all together*'.

To be invited into a Dutch home was always a treat; and that July we dined with Klaus Cuperus[281] and his wife Iek at their very pleasant house beside a waterway on the outskirts of Rotterdam. They were a warm and friendly couple, and I noticed on the wall a delightful portrait of a fair-haired young girl. That, we were told, was of Iek and had been painted by Han Van Meegeren[282] before he started making money by forgeries.

Robbie's regular dining companion in The Hague in those early days was Roberto Ago, the Italian judge. Ago, who hated the chill grey Netherlands and revealed that he had a 'complicated' life, never in his 16 years as a judge attempted to get an apartment in The Hague. He had a Machievellian streak, so these meals together were spent in discussion and intrigue about the current ICJ case. He would address me with gallantry: 'Ah, Christina! How well you are looking! What is that lovely necklace?' – kiss-kiss (no notice taken of my embarrassed reply that the necklace was of wooden beads and came from an Oxfam shop). I was in fact an irrelevance: what mattered were the fascinating intricacies of the case and the manipulation of his colleagues. Yet we were both charmed by him: Robbie had a deep respect for his ability as well as affection.

On 13th July 1982 the UN Secretary-General, Perez de Cuellar[283] and his wife visited the Court and were entertained to dinner. Next morning we found them sharing the VIP lounge at Schipol with us, and chatted less formally. They were to be the guests of honour at a lunch at 10 Downing Street next day, where we met them again. I described the event for my father:

'… Talked to Denis Healey,[284] Sir Anthony Parsons,[285] Rhodes James,[286] John

---

[281] Klaus Cuperus was a prominent member of the International Law Association. I have guessed the spelling of his wife's name – pronounced *Eek*.

[282] Van Meegeren's forgeries of Dutch paintings of the 'Golden Age' were so successful that when a fake Vermeer was found among Goering's possessions at the end of the war, he was arrested as a 'collaborator'. He had to paint another example, under surveillance, to prove his innocence of that charge.

[283] Javier Perez de Cuellar had succeeded Kurt Waldheim as Secretary-General in January 1982.

[284] Denis Healey, at that time Shadow Foreign Secretary. Later Baron Healey.

[285] Sir Anthony Parsons, UK Permanent Representative to the UN, then special adviser to the Prime Minister on foreign affairs.

[286] Robert Rhodes James, MP for Cambridge, had worked at the UN under Kurt Waldheim.

& Elnora Ferguson,[287] &c. Sat between Humphrey Atkins[288] and Terence Higgins.[289] R & I spent ¾ hour in Nat. Gallery after…'

This was our only visit to Number Ten – astonished to find how much bigger it seems inside than out, impressed by all the portraits of recent Prime Ministers up the staircase, slightly chilled by Margaret Thatcher but warmed by the affable Denis.

Robbie returned to The Hague for the Award of the court's Advisory Opinion. It had been a curious introduction to the work of the court – examining an appeal against the ruling of the UN Administrative Tribunal[290] about a former UN staff member – and quite unlike the resolution of disputes between States which was the Court's main purpose. (I seem to remember that the applicant, a British national, was actually stalking Robbie while deliberations were in progress.)

In August we attended the International Law Association's biennial conference, this year held at Montreal. It was a huge gathering – some 800 people from more than 40 countries. Robbie, as 'Director of Studies', had a good deal of responsibility, attending as many of the sessions as possible and also doing a brief interview for local radio.

It was good to meet a number of friends there and make new ones, and we very much liked what we saw of Montreal in our walks around. The Inaugural Ceremony was delayed because of the late arrival of Perez de Cuellar, and not all of the social programme was to our taste. The private entertaining, though, we did enjoy: meals with Blair Hankey[291] and with a prosperous paper manufacturer, Mr Colcas, and his wife at their lovely house; drinks with the

---

[287] John & Elnora Ferguson were already known to us, since he was a nephew of our neighbour Idwen Banister. A Chair of Global Ethics at Birmingham University seems to be named after him.

[288] Humphrey Atkins was Lord Privy Seal, and Government spokesman in the Commons on Foreign & Commwealth Affairs who, with Lord Carrington, resigned over the Falklands war. He became Baron Colmbrook.

[289] Terence Higgins, PC, was a senior Conservative, later made Baron. Married to Rosalyn (later Dame) Higgins, at that time teaching at the LSE but later to succeed RYJ at the ICJ.

[290] Later abolished.

[291] Hankey was prominent in the Canadian Foreign Ministry.

Bloomfields in their lavishly-furnished apartment high in a great skyscraper; and later a walk to a gloomy bare apartment block to sup with John Hurley[292] and his mother, who had cooked pecan pie in Robbie's honour.

The formal occasions included a reception in the Hotel de Ville, where we signed the visitors' book, and the grand excursion to Quebec, where we saw the Parliament building and a little of Laval University. Back in Montreal I sat in on part of a conference session on State Immunity at McGill University and, among the mostly good speeches noted evidence of political bias from the Russians and supporters. Lunch, with 'Judge' Maxwell Cohen[293] presiding, was at the Faculty Club. Throughout we enjoyed the company of the Wilberforces, Wilfred Jenks and his wife, the Fox Bassett family,[294] Klaus and Iek Cuperus, Ian Sinclair and Jeremy Carver, who could always find somewhere for a really relaxed light meal.

On our final day, with no commitments, we walked up Mont Real, where we saw Mounties and squirrels and simply sat for a while. Waffles with maple syrup for breakfast, and the first signs of autumnal colouring in the woods added to our liking for Canada.

That summer Robbie had some relatively quiet weeks for relaxation with family, besides his work on editing the *British Yearbook of International Law* and *Oppenheim*. One of his American former pupils, Delbert Smith, was in Cambridge and as usual made contact. Currently working with NASA,[295] he wanted to discuss some possible projects with Robbie – a mini-seminar on Space Law being one.

And in mid-September came a shock: the sudden death of Sir Gerald Fitzmaurice, the revered 'Fitz', whose funeral at Gray's Inn Robbie attended. He made, too, a second brief visit to Strasbourg a few days later for the delivery of judgment on that curious case at the Court of Human Rights.

In October I told my father about Robbie's most recent task:

'…This was in the University Church (and a year ago he was giving an oration
for Sir Humphrey Waldock, similarly, from the pulpit of the *Oxford* University

---

292   John Hurley, a former pupil of Robbie's had shown us many interesting corners of the city.
293   Professor Maxwell Cohen had served on one case as an *ad hoc* judge.
294   Nigel Fox-Bassett was a partner of Coward Chance, later to become senior partner of Clifford Chance.
295   Dr Delbert Smith later became Senior Telecommunications Counsel at Jones Day.

Church) for Professor Clive Parry, a friend of 45 years; an "original", as Robbie said, a man of genius and warmth with a sharp streak of mischief. The preparation of that address[296] took a great deal of time and care; and it came over superbly. Alas, he has to do yet another, for a very different character (Sir Gerald Fitzmaurice) in St Margaret's, Westminster, in a few weeks' time.

'Robbie also gave a talk to the Union Society about the International Court the other day. That, too, was greatly appreciated, and repeat performances are called for. He is certainly not idle, even when here in England! Among other things, there are preparations in train for next summer's meeting of the Institut de Droit International in Cambridge.'

Those three memorial addresses – for Humphrey Waldock, Clive Parry and Gerald Fitzmaurice – expressed the respect and affection he felt for each of them. But they were very different characters, and Robbie was good at perceiving idiosyncrasies. Speaking of Waldock, on 17th October 1981, he had said:

'He could never be satisfied with doing something really quite well, or even very well. It had to be the complete, professional job, and done with a tenacity and thoroughness that even most professionals can only admire from a distance…' [He then spoke of HW's impressive efficiency during the war, in Military Branch I.] '…So it was a wonderful thing for international law when in 1947 he was elected to the Chichele Chair, and these great gifts of mind and character were dedicated to its teaching and study at Oxford…' [Then, more searchingly…] '… the severity which enabled Waldock to accomplish so much was almost all directed at himself, and in relation to his own work. For behind that tenacity, there was a man who was gentle, quiet, even a little shy, and diffident of offering an opinion on any question which he had not thoroughly examined; he was always easily approachable, especially by students, to whom he gave so generously of his time and ideas.'

Then a year later, on 16th October 1982, about his old friend Clive Parry:

'Clive Parry, for all his prodigious output [the *British Digest of International Law* especially, but much more], was no hermit scholar. He was a fine teacher.

---

[296] The text appears in RYJ's *Collected Papers*, p.1400.

As a lecturer he was uneven, depending very much upon mood and occasion. One could never be quite sure when his sense of fun and even mischief would come to the top … [A particular example is quoted, of a spontaneous outpouring, when he…] was stimulated to talk off-the-cuff for 50 minutes on … how to use the law library. It was far and away the best, completest, clearest and most stimulating talk on how to set about serious study of the law that I had ever heard or am ever likely to hear. I think all of us felt, when he had finished, that the only thing to do was to tip-toe quietly to the library and start work. It was a momentary exasperation that had sparked off his genius. For genius he certainly had …'

'He was happy in his lot, for he regarded being a don as the most desirable of all the professions … mercurial and unpredictable and sometimes exasperating, but always lovable …'

I am unable to find the text of his address from the pulpit of St Margaret's, Westminster on 26th November 1982 at Fitzmaurice's memorial service, complementing those given by Judge Manfred Lachs and Sir Francis Vallat. Lachs would have spoken about Fitzmaurice's work at the International Court and Vallat about his Foreign Office work, while Robbie's approach was more personal, remembering Fitz as President of the arbitration court on the *Beagle Channel* case and as scholar and Legal Adviser. Both the Fitzmaurice sons had studied Law at Cambridge (Maurice at Jesus College) and so he knew something of the family background. But it was not just as lawyer that he admired Fitz: it was as a truly cultured man with an impressive breadth of reading, and ability in both music and art. When Fitzmaurice was to receive an honorary LL.D. at Cambridge, the Public Orator of the University (at that time Patrick Wilkinson of King's) asked for Robbie's assistance in composing his oration, spoken in Latin. In a long article published in his *Collected Writings,*[297] Robbie quotes a little of the English translation:

'You would guess rightly that he has an enthusiasm for mathematics. But he also has an enthusiasm for literature, especially poetry, feeling as he does that law no less than literature depends upon elegance of phrasing…'

---

[297] Written in 1984 for the *BYIL*, the article (64pp) appears in Vol.2, p 1313. It presents a close examination of Fitzmaurice's published work.

And in his Foreword to Professor Merrill's book on Fitzmaurice, Robbie was able to reveal the deeply human side, referring to his –

'... "politically incorrect" and unpopular stand ... in the *South-West Africa* cases of 1962 and 1966; which was somewhat unjustly to cost Fitzmaurice the Presidency of the Court, to his great but quietly borne pain.

'It was a sad incident. For Fitzmaurice, his conclusions in those two cases were compelled by an honestly reasoned view of the material and the arguments presented to the Court, although – and this needs to be said – it was with very great reluctance that he felt thus compelled. In a letter to the present writer in January 1963 he tells how "this case" (the first S-W Africa case was decided in December 1962) had been "for me a major cause of worry and heart-searching"; and how he felt "guilty" at having disagreed "both (a) with what Arnold *has* said in a previous case; (b) with what Hersch *would* almost certainly have said in the present case (although I think he alone could have found the reasons that might have convinced me that this was right). [And he goes on] If you add to this my utter lack of sympathy with S-African racial policies you will be able to imagine what intense mental travail I have endured over this case."'

Robbie fully understood. He himself was to speak of the *anguish* involved in making a judgment that went against one's instinctive response.

———

In those last months of 1982 the Court was engaged with the *Tunisian/Libyan* dispute and the *Gulf of Maine* case, in both of which Robbie, having been involved as counsel, could play no part. He had plenty to do, though, and kept up a regular routine of going into college to deal with correspondence, writing articles, editing the *British Yearbook* and receiving the many former pupils and foreign visitors who valued his advice. (At some point at around this time the labour of writing the new *Oppenheim* was largely handed over to Arthur Watts.)

Besides this daily ascent to the Ghost Room to work, college life itself remained dear to him. He lunched at Jesus or Trinity, and browsed over newspapers in the Combination Room afterwards. And conversation on high table was not merely gossip: among the fellowship were experts in every discipline, so he might quiz a physicist about the technicalities of his beloved hi-fi equipment, or discuss music, economics, ancient history. At Trinity a particular friend was the Professor of German, Denis Greene, with whom for years he kept up a jocular sparring relationship. It was all stimulating, and made sure that he never became enclosed in a strictly legal world.

The children and I benefitted from these connections, too. When Joey, now at the Bath Academy of Art, had to write a mini-dissertation on some aspect of modern art for her degree, I asked Leslie Martin[298] if I might bring her to meet him. At his lovely home at Shelford he showed her paintings, sketches and small sculptures by the very people she was studying – Ben Nicholson, Barbara Hepworth, Naum Gabo, Henry Moore, Brancusi – and reminisced about that group. It was a magical session of two hours or more, and typical of the privilege we enjoyed in this academic world.

Robbie always encouraged me in my own forms of mental exercise, choral singing and taking part in the Cambridge Reading Circle. That October the Learned Ladies (the C.R.C.) had a departure from their customary meetings. Rachel Lauterpacht, instead of reading a paper to members, arranged a recital to which husbands were also invited. Marni, Lady Hodgkin, received us in the great drawing-room of the Master's Lodge at Trinity, where Rachel's niece Diana Ambache (piano) and her partner Jeremy Polmear (oboe) played: a memorable evening. Although marriage to Hersch had brought Rachel's own professional aspirations as a pianist to an end, she could be proud of her niece's success.

We did go to The Hague in early November for a dinner given by the Pakistan Ambassador, Dr Hyder. It was the first of many foreign embassy dinners and receptions we were to attend over the following years, and a particularly agreeable occasion. Dr Hyder was a beautiful woman, and someone with whom Robbie felt a rapport whenever they met. Our surroundings, formerly the Chinese Embassy, were of course grand; the meal was of Pakistani dishes, cleverly spiced. And conversation was easy with our neighbours that evening: H.E. Slim Benghazi, the Tunisian Ambassador already well known to Robbie; the Editor of The Hague's leading newspaper; the Austrian Ambassador; the Turkish Ambassador – herself a very attractive woman, seemingly in her 30s,

---

[298] By then, Sir Leslie Martin had retired from the Chair of Architecture, but retained his connection with Jesus College as an Honorary Fellow. He had been one of the early members of the Seven and Five Society, and co-edited, with Ben Nicholson and Naum Gabo, the magazine *Circle*.

whose husband stayed in Ankara as a career-diplomat ... and a stately lady, Mistress of the Queen's Robes, Mme Bischoff van Heemskerck.

Now he was fully engaged with the work of the Court, I was seeing little of Robbie, except at weekends. Yet just before Christmas 1982 we made together an extraordinary visit to Italy. A letter in Italian, received on his birthday, had asked him to attend, as President of the *Institut*, the celebrations taking place in December to mark the 8th centenary of the birth of St Francis of Assisi. It seemed that he was invited as a recipient of a Nobel Peace Prize (the prize having been awarded to the *Institut* rather than to an individual), and would be presented to the Pope. It was not until the end of November that a message announced that we were expected in Rome the very next week; and even at that late stage information was scrappy. Still rather mystified by this invitation, Robbie asked his efficient secretary, Angie, to telephone the office in Rome and ask for further details; and in response a bare itinerary was sent. So we went, and once it was over I typed a long account[299] of our adventure.

Francesco Ieri E ... Oggi
St Francis Yesterday & Today

'It seems that the committee running these celebrations must have found themselves with lots of funds left over after the initial festivities; hence the rather hurried arrangements for the 'Nobel' events... so we knew very little when we set off.

'To emphasize the theme of Peace, dear to St Francis, the Committee were linking a series of events to the Nobel Peace Prize. They had invited Mother Theresa, Henry Kissinger and Perez-Esquivel to come – all individual laureates. The first two declined, though the third (an Argentine, a heroic dissident and Human Rights worker) was there. The other eight were representatives of organisations which had been awarded Peace Prizes. In Robbie's case, it was the *Institut de Droit International*, which had received it in 1904.

'Four wives came, and so altogether we were a group of about a dozen, treated as "celebrities" for these four or five days. One might have had delusions of grandeur, being so heavily guarded night and day (but thoughts

---

299   The version below is greatly reduced.

of St Francis ensure that one is mindful of humility). It must have been fears of the Red Brigade and of the Mafia which made it necessary for every journey to be in a set of tight-together government cars, lights flashing and sirens wailing to break through the traffic. Neither of the two principal organisers spoke English, so we only found out what was happening by begging our nice Pia [young Italian woman accompanying us] to find out and translate. The life of a celebrity, one now understands, is pretty exhausting: either standing about shaking hands or listening to speeches in bewilderment, or breaking-off from something really interesting and being rushed away! Rome was warm – we could not turn off the heating in our room at night; and Assisi was cold. Meals were good but unfamiliar, and desperately late …

Personalities

Perez Esquivel. Robbie got to know him more than I did. A man of passionate conviction, understandably socialist in outlook – he had endured the ugliest manifestations of a capitalist dictatorship; yet a gentle and shining character. His wife, Amanda, looked rather S. American-Indian, with her broad face and small eyes, curly brown hair and engaging dimples. We could only smile more and more warmly day by day, and finally embrace as I said, "Adios," and she "Goodbye."

Annette Wallis. A model of the earnest Quaker – to Robbie it seemed almost to the point of naivety in some respects. I thought her so open-minded and intelligent that she was probably more astute in worldly matters than he supposed. Very nice indeed: very easy for me to feel rapport – she is much the sort of person one knows from a nonconformist, fairly intellectual upbringing, and our interests coincided.

Senora Sciuto, of Amnesty International. She looked a pretty hard cookie, with her too-blonde hair, her fur coat and spindly high heels and cigarettes. But I liked her more and more. She is French, married to an Italian, and speaks good English as she spends 1 week in 4 in London for her work. She needs to be tough, for that job. But she was moved by Assisi; she has a sense of humour; she is a pretty warm-hearted person, utterly committed to her work. Lives on Lake Maggiore.

Francis Wolf, I.L.O. Robbie knows him fairly well (a member of the *Institut*). A great diplomat: when ideas are in conflict, his way of seizing and holding a hand, and his irresistible clownish smile, ease the tension a lot. French from Alsace, lives and works in Geneva.

Kadry, of the UN agency for refugees [UNHCR]. An Iraqi, who kept quiet but seemed very nice – quite impressive as a person with his shafts of quiet wisdom. Lives and works in Rome.

De La Mata, International Red Cross – arrived just for the last day, with his stunningly glamorous wife. Large lugubrious eyes … I got no further!

The UNICEF man, and the representative of the International Bureau for Peace, did not turn up (unless they were there, momentarily, among the confusing entourage whom we never quite identified).

Professor La Rotunda. The Major-domo, controlling our movements. Exceedingly nervous, no doubt desperate to please his government masters (and the new government was sworn in only on the Tuesday of our visit). Relaxed at the very last meal together.

Senator Mezzapesa. Fat, genial. Made speeches everywhere – eloquent but fairly platitudinous.

Mystery Man. We never got his name: a rather handsome though baggy-eyed man who smoked cigarettes endlessly. He and a middle-aged-arty lady seemed in charge of publicity. Among the undercurrents complicating the whole programme, the mutual dislike between him and La Rotunda was one of the fiercer. Robbie found him good as a television-director; and I noticed him directing what looked like some interesting shots in the Basilica and in the Vatican. He arranged for us all to have posters with the signatures of every member of the group.'

This adventure began on Monday, 6th December, when we were welcomed at Leonardo da Vinci airport by 'a very nice efficient woman,' Pia Scambelluri, a law librarian with excellent English. As we and our fellow-passenger, Annette Wallis, were driven into Rome, Pia gave a commentary. It was my first visit to Italy, and Robbie's to Rome, and just as the guidebook says, 'packed with interest at every turn'. After resting for a while in our fine room, Robbie and I ventured out – past the carabinieri with machine-guns, on duty day and night guarding our floor of the hotel – for a short walk, and were deeply impressed by our surroundings … all tantalising, for by now we had seen a more detailed programme of events for the coming days which left little chance for us to wander.

Dinner was very late, very good but heavy. I had on my left a bespectacled balding-ginger-haired Senator of Assisi, who spoke little English, but we managed a little conversation. At the beginning of the meal there were short speeches, with the presentation of St Francis medallions to each Nobel representative.

We did not sleep well in our overheated room, and next morning... 'Robbie woke feeling, and looking, thoroughly peaky.' Nevertheless, we took part in the first planned event of the day, a visit to the Campidoglio, the centre of Rome's municipal government –

'...The weather was greyish. There, we first walked around the rather chilly piazza, then up steps and into rooms which were stuffy and overheated, where we were left standing about. I got Robbie to sit down, and felt worried about him; but he managed to cope well with a little ceremony (televised – the exchange of speeches, the presentation of another medallion and a huge lithograph of an olive tree, the picture which appears, enlarged, on the posters announcing all the St Francis commemorative events). The medallion turned out to be in celebration of Garibaldi's victories, irrelevant but pleasant enough.

'Then – the Mayor having urged us to treat his great residence as our own home – we passed through a sitting room and his study, onto a small balcony with a breathtaking view. We were right over the Roman Forum (below us were the dungeons where Saint Peter had been imprisoned) and though the light was dim, I took a set of photos of all the great buildings and ruins around.

'But after that, as Robbie was looking unwell, we decided to excuse ourselves from the next part of the programme, *The Treasures of the Kremlin*, an exhibition which the group were rushed through; the church of St Francis in Ripo, which again they had no time to view properly; and lunch, big and prolonged and best avoided. As it turned out, our escape was not swift: a huge demonstration (with some Communist banners) was slowly marching along, causing a total traffic-jam. It took 40 minutes to complete the journey of 5 minutes – a wearisome effort for our driver, who tried one way after another to get through, but which took us around with close views of the Colosseum and other parts not normally on the route.

'So we rested, drank water and ate a sandwich. And an hour late, the cars at last appeared and we were picked up for the journey to Assisi.

'What a journey! It was raining, and we were late. Carabinieri on motorbikes and 2 police cars escorted our motorcade of five Mercedes at top speed through the traffic, through red lights, sirens warbling ... It is a long way, and the cars kept close together at speed all the way, for two hours or more.

'The view was of "nothing in particular" according to nice loquacious Pia, but of interest to us – hills, woods, rivers, and always towns or villages perched on hilltops, their churches and castles silhouetted in the haze. We were happy to notice little things – the Roman pines with their flat tops, the slender cypresses, the olives and vines… And although it was such poor weather, the dimness made a poetic dreamy series of tone-washes of the landscape, showing up those hilltop silhouettes.

'Assisi at last, in the dark. Up the hill, and first the Sanctuary of San Damiano. Our visit was brief – a short pause at each part of this tiny complex, filled with associations with both St Francis and St Clare. Masses of roses by the altar, otherwise everything left bare. It was here that a young friar approached us at the end, saying that he was from the Lebanon, and would we do anything we could for the people of his country? (The Friends for Peace organisation does run a school and other projects there.) A bearded studentish young man also seized the opportunity to press upon the Nobel representatives a petition for help for his own country, Nicaragua.

'Up the hill further, and to the Basilica. There, in the lower church, was a special service, with a quite large congregation of people from round about, besides some of the community. A choir sang plainsong from behind the altar for the service; and then they – the Cantori of Assisi (quite renowned, we heard) – stood on the altar steps to perform a series of unaccompanied pieces – the best, I thought, by Victoria and Palestrina. There were Franciscan pieces deriving from old folk tunes (my guess,) and Carl Orff's setting of the Canticle of the Creatures. A splendid soprano soloist, dark, slim, vivid; the friar conducting in his own unorthodox but expressive way; at the end, two Negro Spirituals sung in English, which came out rather engagingly – "Marry hed a buybee," and so on. Unfortunately there was the beastly television apparatus, with lumpish men messing about with lights, cables and gadgets throughout.

'After that, we were conducted through a door into the private part of the monastery, and into the great refectory. A huge hall, high and empty except for the tables all round the walls. This meal – although by the end we were all cool, and I shivering – was a delight. You sit on a bench built into the wall, and before you is a stack of plates; a knife, fork and spoon laid on them; bottles of water and wine. Under the napkin is the first course, the "antipasto" of thin cold meats; then the other food is brought by friars or young seminaries. It was nice plainly-cooked food, which you take yourself. (They must need to eat fast off their cold plates, in the coldest depth of winter!) We had an American Franciscan, Father Claudio, beside us, happy to talk about it all. They were all glad to receive us, we heard, partly because it gave them this particularly good meal: supper was usually broth, bread and wine. All the friars were so cheerful and serene: grace ended with "Bon appétit!"

'At last, dreadfully cold, we hurried through the rain to the very nice old-fashioned hotel close by (Hotel Subasio). While I warmed-up in bed, Robbie had to go downstairs for a special consultation between the Nobel people. I was worried that this was keeping him so late when he really needed more rest; but when, at about 11.20 pm, he came up he was not too exhausted. Their discussion had clearly been stimulating. It seemed that all the Nobel people were expected to make a united pronouncement to the Pope on Friday. If the spokesman was to be Perez-Esquivel, he declared his willingness but was unprepared to read out a statement prepared by an Italian professor, who had ready something which Robbie described, in a resigned way, as "unexceptionable", but which nobody thought of much value. Esquivel was the one individual Peace Prize man, a charismatic figure of great interest to the Italians, who have a strong connection in Argentina. He would have spoken in Spanish (he has neither Italian nor English) and would have stressed his antipathy for Capitalism. After discussion it was agreed that if the Italian professor could produce a shorter version of his statement, the members of the group who were representing institutions might well be prepared to give their assent.

'*Wednesday 8ᵗʰ·* We were woken in our nice bedroom by the booming of the great bell from the monastery. Another, higher and faster, followed after about 10 minutes. Down we went to breakfast in the vaulted basement – attractive, like all we saw there. Upstairs again, I opened the shutters and found the view from our little balcony, although only dimly lit, breathtaking. The hotel on that side looks right out over the Umbrian plain.[300]

'Just half an hour or so in which to take another quick look at the Basilica. There, fortunately, Father Claudio came to show us around. He was the ideal

---

[300] After our return home I found that my uncle Donald Miller had stayed at that same hotel and sketched that wide view, as well as several other parts of Assisi.

guide, with a torch to illuminate details of frescoes and all the information we needed. So we were greatly privileged yet again.

'The cars bore us upwards, through the narrow streets. Awful to have such a procession in such a place; but for us, a delight. Every view was exciting – such ancient, higgledy-piggledy yet enduring houses, up and up, with the castle at the top. There we stopped just long enough for a few photographs … and down we went again.

'I had caught sight of some men in bright costume in the little old square, and thought it must be for a local festival – perhaps to celebrate the Immaculate Conception. But we found it was for us! For those who had earned Peace Prizes, anyway. A fanfare from their long trumpets greeted us; we went up into the town hall; and first entered a large cold hall decorated with local heraldry. Here the eight trumpeters, four on each side, played again. There followed a long programme of speeches, welcoming the Nobel delegates and speaking of St Francis and modern work for peace. Nearly two hours of speeches in Italian, translated by Pia – one, admirably fluent and impassioned, in Spanish by Esquivel. More fanfares; we moved out, and into the Council Chamber. Yet another fanfare – our trumpeters, each with one red leg and one blue, might have stepped off playing cards or out of a *quattrocento* painting. There followed a ceremony – the presentation of the Freedom of the City of Assisi.

'After that, we moved into the Mayor's chamber, a lovely smaller room with mementoes of Assisi's links with other places (such as San Francisco) and organisations (the UN, &c.). Here, each delegate was given a medallion of St Francis and two beautifully-wrapped parcels (books about Giotto, Lorenzetto and – in Italian – St Francis). The windows were opened onto another marvellous view – across the square to the Temple of Minerva, and up the hill to the "Rocca" … all intensely interesting and romantic.

'Down the hill again – to the Basilica of Santa Maria degli Angeli, a great baroque church containing the dear little ancient church, the "Porziuncola" where St Francis used to worship as a boy. And to one side is a little sort of shrine which is the spot (then an open place) where St Francis died.

'At the monastery attached (not now completely a monastery, but an inexpensive guest house) we ate a very good and convivial lunch – again in an attractive refectory, sitting at tables around the edge, when I sat next to Professor La Rotunda and managed a little conversation in bad French and he taught me how to eat tagliatelli on a fork.

'Out in the rain, "Avanti! Presto, presto!" we had to leave Assisi rapidly, missing a planned last event, since (ironically) a peace demonstration was on its way and would have jammed or confused our programme. But there was one last stop, to see "the hovel" at Rivotorto. This was again a large church (? 19th century) with a crowded service in progress. We crept in to see, near the west end, the little stone building with a very simple slab-altar supported on a single thick column, the place where Francis had sheltered when he first took his vow of poverty.

'Then the cars took us back to Rome. Rain, mist, gloom. No gloom in our mood: we all felt tired, but talked a good deal (about the Society of Friends, about the Falklands dispute and international law, and all sorts). And the countryside is beautiful.

'After a very light supper with Annette Wallis[301], Pia came and took us for a walk. Such was our enthusiasm, and hers, that it became a mighty trudge of about two hours. A marvellous extra: we were so glad that the evening's threatened dinner was cancelled and that we had this freedom. So, in the romantic gloom of sparsely-lit streets (although the celebrated sights are floodlit) we saw the Spanish Steps, the Trevi fountain, Piazza Navona and much else. We talked a good deal as we explored – some of it on the subject of peace and justice. Robbie threw out one of his provocative, illiberal-sounding remarks; and immediately he and Annette were in animated discussion. ("All great truths are ambiguous", as R's friend A.P., a great teacher in the English Faculty at Cambridge, used to say.) They were going at it ding-dong, and it was comical to see their astonishment when we had at last stopped and shushed them to realize that we had reached the Pantheon. There, looming above, was the largest nearly-intact Roman building in the world!

Thursday 9th A wearisome ceremony in the morning. We had to be conveyed again to the Campidoglio, and there sit in the front row of a large hall. There was a certain amount of pomp: two enormously tall guards with high helmets with horsetails on top, and police in white helmets – two men flanking the banner of Rome, with SPQR on it, and two women flanking the banner of Assisi. Various dignitaries arrived, and one shook hands without being

---

301   We were to find that a few years after our quite intimate association with Annette during this gathering, Pippa and her husband moved to a house in Leicester close to hers and had their own pleasant relationship with the Wallises.

quite sure with whom … At last the session started. It was the first of a series, all lectures on the dissemination of the ideas of St Francis in Europe. We, on high upright chairs, sat through four speeches in Italian. As boredom set in (the Amnesty International lady, Signora Sciuto, would mutter "That's another finished – I am *fed up*") I examined the florid paintings of ridiculous horse-borne heroes, and watched the police gradually sag and sway. At last it was over. Coming out, a short old man briefly shook hands: the President of the Republic.

'Then the red carpets were rolled up and we were left hanging about … until, suddenly, action yet again. Off in the cars through the rain, quite a distance to somewhere on the far side of the Tiber, just beyond the Mussolini stadium and the oldest narrow bridge.

'This was a marvellous place. First, in the wet garden one saw an old chapel. Beyond that was another old building, now a house, in which we were received. A lovely old room with a big fireplace, and off it a circular study. This was part of an ancient tower – some 2,000 years old. (The place is called La Torro Marcellus, or something of the sort – the name of an early Emperor.) The bigger room had been added in the ?15th century, when this became a retreat for short weekends for the Pope; and at that time Charles V, the Holy Roman Emperor, visited the little house and its lovely gardens. The antiquity was evident – scraps of carved or inscribed stone set in walls, some retrieved quite recently when the house was restored by wealthy Americans and by the present owners, the Centre for the Study of Human Evolution, who were our hosts. The hospitality was warm, though we were all in a tight scrum, first in the tower-room, then down in a basement diningroom. Our delicious lunch had to be eaten standing up; and following Robbie's example, I abstained from some of the meal. Talking, talking (some of it about the Centre's strange theories about controlling Man's destiny by deliberately influencing the two hemispheres of the brain) we grew rather weary and were relieved when at last, with a dash through the rain, our cars set off again.

'After a short rest, lying flat and looking at the map to see where we had been, we were off to an exhibition. Two more speeches in Italian for the opening, and handshakes and some conversation with a splendid Monsignor, Nuncio from the Holy See to the State of Italy. The theme of the exhibition was "The image of St Francis in the Counter-Reformation", all drawings and paintings from the turn of the XVI-XVII centuries. Included were some magnificent paintings – by Caravaggio, Carpaccio and others.

From this period a quite different concept of Francis emerges – not Giotto's humble little man with the love of animals, but the figure with swirling robes, elegantly gesturing hands, upturned eyes, accompanied by a radiantly fleshly Madonna, or agonising over a skull. Again, too little time to linger over what did interest; all too much time when we were obliged to sit or stand fast submitting to what did not!

'Back in the hotel, Robbie gave a short speech for television, recorded in a corner of the lounge, and helped by a sympathetic producer.

'Our evening meal was again a free time, and we, together with Annette and Pia, chose a nice simple meal: green salad, grilled sole and poached pear. By the end, though, the anxiety about the exact wording of the group's statement to the Pope was giving rise to earnest discussion again. The representatives now decided to make their own statement, carefully worded to contain more substance than the bland one concocted for them (which, to their indignation, they heard had already been forwarded – without consent or signatures – to the Vatican); and that Robbie should be spokesman. This clearly needed prolonged discussion over the drafting, which in the event went on nearly till midnight; and so the wives, plus Annette Wallis (who said she would abide by Robbie's choice of words, since they had already talked fully on the matter) went off, rather late, to a recital.

'This was on our original programme, and we were glad to have gone. It was in a large modern building, the Bibliotheca Nationale, and was again on the theme of St Francis. A man read (excellently) extracts from the legends, from Dante, and finally the Canticle of Brother Sun. And the choir was the same Cantori of Assisi …

'Friday 10ᵗʰ

[After an interesting morning stroll together, we prepared for our audience with the Pope. Everyone wore sober black, the women in mantillas.]

'… A last flurry about that wretched statement for the Pope. The text (slipped under our door in the night, after Pia had worked to get it typed so terribly late) was demanded from Robbie, and pocketed by La Rotunda. Difficult to find out what was happening (neither La Rotunda nor Mezzapesi, the men chiefly in charge of the whole programme, speaks English); then it is found that no statement is to be given after all. Senator Mezzapesi is to introduce the Nobel people, and that is that. The Senator's speech is wrung out of La R., and seems, when translated, harmless. The delegates are not pleased but have to accept the situation. (But surely, I was thinking, there will be *some* opportunity to communicate the right sort of message to John Paul II?)

'Well, it all worked out very happily in the end. The string of cars this time made the journey right into the Vatican, past Swiss guards, past formal gardens and through massive arches to the large inner courtyard. Two large mahogany lifts carry people up; and then there is a walk through about five rooms, including the great stateroom. Ceilings are decorated with frescoes or elaborate panelling, but the walls are bare except for a single great religious work of art on each one. The small audience room has brown walls, four marvellous carved figures of the apostles and a carved relief of a mitre above a very austere raised throne. We sat – as directed by Prof. La Rotunda – on rows of chairs. The television people (just four of them this time, in decent clothes) first filmed us sitting there, looking as if listening enthralled to the Pope – in fact sitting quietly staring at his empty seat! Then we just waited for quite a while; a troop of monsignors or cardinals passed through the back of the room, probably at the end of a meeting.

'Then the Pope entered – just as one expected: genial, dignified. The Senator made a speech of introduction, and His Holiness listened in a pose which suggested both ease and attention. He was looking at all of us, as well as listening. Then came his own address. After all the anxiety, here was the Pope himself saying everything that the others had hoped to express, speaking in careful French (a choice of language which all could understand). Esquivel, when presented, handed to the Pope his own personal statement. Robbie had just time to speak in appreciation and to add a word or two about his own concern for justice. Annette and the others could say just a little, too. I simply smiled and gave a quick curtsey: "Glad to meet you", he said. A rough-and-ready group was photographed. He beamed at us all, and as he left bade us "Bon Noel". Everyone felt pleased.

'Our cars drove us then to the Piazza del Populi, where to our surprise we all went into a large café for "an aperitif". It was already about 2 pm or later. Then off again, to the Altar of Peace, the *Ara Pacis*, a sculptured monument dedicated to the peace that Augustus wished to usher in with his reign (from 13 to 9 BC). It is a magnificent huge mausoleum, now protected by an enclosure of glass – and here, after much standing about, Robbie was interviewed, live, on television.

'Curiously, this was one of the moments when the whole thing made sense. Although we were standing chatting "naturally" for the television cameras, and the situation was in many ways contrived, there was, amidst the television apparatus, a monitoring screen. There, we who were no longer being filmed could see the programme that was going out. It was cleverly produced, linking various events and places to make a visually interesting programme and bring together the Franciscan ideas of creating peace. So we saw a few moments of our papal audience; this morning's ceremony in Oslo when two new Nobel Peace Prizes were conferred; shots of the Altar of Peace with ourselves looking about; an interview with Mother Theresa in India; and live interviews with Esquivel, with Robbie and with Senator Mezzapesi, all broken up with tracking shots across the marvellous carved frieze surrounding the Altar. The interviewer's questions kept to the topic of St Francis and his relevance to the Nobel organisation.

'This, amidst wonderful surroundings, all came to an end at about 3.30 pm, and at last we were off to lunch, driven upwards, past the observatory, to a restaurant with a fine view down upon the great city. It was a very good and relaxed meal, and we were by then hungry enough to do it justice – almost. Just three short speeches to end things off.'

We gathered again informally in the evening to receive photographs from the Vatican and watch the television news. We supped on a bowlful of soup, with water. Next morning all the glamour and the tension came to an end. We had a good flight in clear weather and arrived 'back to cold England', and a good traditional Christmas all together.

Although Robbie's introduction to the work of an International Court judge had so far been low-key, it had been a remarkable year.

Not Just a Judge

1983

The work of the International Court is largely hidden from public view. The British media, indeed, show little interest in its activities. But Robbie was now fully involved with all the mysteries of the Peace Palace. As the official booklet explains:

'In addition to the public sittings, which represent the visible part of their work, Members of the Court participate in a large number of internal meetings of all kinds: deliberations, sittings devoted to the reading of draft decisions, administrative meetings and committee meetings.'

One new contentious case was now under consideration by the Court: *Libyan Arab Jamahiriya/Malta*. Each of the parties had submitted their Memorials – bulky documents presenting their case in great detail, often supplemented with maps and marine charts – which every judge had to read. Robbie could do some of that reading at home, but for more thorough research he needed the resources of the Court's library. He also valued the informal contacts with his colleagues – a tap on the door, a chat in a corridor or a discussion over lunch – which helped to develop their collective decisions eventually to be refined into the formal Award.

It was necessarily a long process. He found it all interesting, and as someone fascinated by relations with people of different backgrounds, enjoyable. In his own words:

'The judges are from many different parts of the world ... from different cultures, and not least from very different legal systems. The layman's question is always the same: how do you manage to have a coherent and useful deliberation in those circumstances? ... The answer is that in practice the problem hardly arises ... International law is a language which transcends different tongues, cultures, races and religions.'[302]

---

[302] This passage, extracted from his address, as President of the Court, to the UN General Assembly in October 1992, is quoted in the official *Questions and answers* handbook about the ICJ issued by the UN.

A major distraction during those early months of 1983 was the responsibility imposed on Robbie, through Waldock's death, by the Presidency of the *Institut*. He must organise the great biennial conference that was to take place this year in Cambridge. He had experience of administration and was good at it; but these conferences were grand affairs, and expensive. The British government (at that time Conservative, under Margaret Thatcher) could not be expected to provide the funds needed, and so first came the distasteful task of sending begging letters to the major solicitors' firms, barristers' chambers and any likely big businesses. Once sufficient funds were promised, he engaged a team of helpers, first of whom was his secretary, Angie.[303] Some of the younger members of the Law Faculty were recruited, together with a few of Cambridge's professional event-organisers and guides. I was made responsible for overseeing the social events for ladies, as well as the final great Sunday excursion.

All this had to be fitted into his irregular comings-and-goings to The Hague and other activities. And on one of his precious weekends at home I got him to clarify for me some points of international law and the function of the World Court, in preparation for a paper I was to give to the Learned Ladies – something he did with patience and good humour.

In March we were introduced to a glamorous side of our years at The Hague when all the members of the International Court were invited to a banquet given by HM Queen Beatrix at her palace, *Huis den Bosch,* the 'House in the Woods'. It was a very great privilege, for the royal family had not long been in residence[304] and the palace was newly restored.

As was usual for diplomatic events, we were provided in advance with a list of everyone to be present; and on this occasion there were also helpful instructions about protocol – how to greet the Queen (ladies not to curtsey, but to shake hands with a slight bow, murmuring 'Majesteit' or 'Your Majesty' – and ending 'It is not proper to tip the footmen'). I wrote to my father:

---

[303]   Angela Norbury, née Brown, his secretary at the ICJ during his first years there.

[304]   Queen Beatrix's accession was in 1981, on her mother Juliana's abdication from the throne. The Huis den Bosch, which had been damaged during the Germans' occupation of the Netherlands and afterwards made habitable, had undergone thorough renovation by the new Queen.

'... So we did our best to get everything exactly right. – The Indian,[305] for instance, had chosen to wear national costume, his nice high-collared black frock-coat; but that left a difficult question of conscience about headgear, which for a Hindu should never be removed when addressing a person respectfully. With our encouragement, he wore his damask cap throughout the evening.

' [After a drive through woods and pauses to be checked by guards]...the final approach was along a drive with lovely little lanterns hung on slanting poles on each side; and there we were, with the glorious footmen in livery to help us, and two imposing guards in period costume standing rigidly at each side of the door. So then, just as we had been told – first to the Japanese Room, where we received cards marked with our places at table; then to the "White Dining Room", where members of the Royal Household greeted us and made conversation for a while; then to the "Blue Drawing Room", where H.M. Queen Beatrix, H.R.H. Princess Margriet and her husband all shook hands and there was further standing about chatting; then into the "Oranjezaal", a stupendous great high room (conceived, apparently, as a mausoleum in memory of Stadholder Frederik-Hendrik, the man who had started the building in c1646 but died within a year). Here, at a great horseshoe of tables, we took our places – 56 of us. There was music playing all the time, and I looked about for the small string band. I never did see it (it was high on a balcony above our heads; and those who did look up saw also the three young princes staring down for a while!) but was sufficiently impressed by the gigantic flower-arrangements (all produced in the royal greenhouses, I heard) and the wall-paintings, allegorical presentations of Prince Frederik-Hendrik in his glory. We ate off Sèvres porcelain which had been presented to Queen Juliana and Prince Bernhard on a state visit to France, and the pudding spoons and forks were silver-gilt with ceramic handles. My neighbour on the right was Vice-Admiral Roest, Chief of the Military House, who had tactfully adorned himself with the sash of a British order (presented at their State Visit to Britain last November) because he knew he was to sit next to me, and a German medal, because he knew he would have the wife of the German Judge on the other side! On my left was Judge Roberto Ago, the Italian, wearing the magnificent green sash of an Italian order.

'In conversation with the Admiral I found that the Household had been doing a little homework, just as we had. It was remarkably easy to talk with

---

[305]   HE Judge Nagendra Singh

these stately people, and with Princesss Margriet the conversation turned to children's books. When, after the dinner, our turn came to chat with the Queen, it was astonishing – her first remark was, "Oh, you must tell me all about your bees". Response – open mouths! ("It must have been because you were such a bore about the bees when we met the Mistress of the Queen's Robes at that embassy dinner", said Robbie afterwards.) She was interested and interesting, and full of fun.

'Next day, in *The Times*, we read about "Another Palace Intruder"[306] – the young man who had got into a utility room that same evening and been caught by security guards. This was something we were quite unaware of at the time.'

There were to be other diversions that year. Robbie had accepted an invitation from Antonio Cassese[307] to lecture at the University of Florence, and from Francesco Francioni at the University of Siena. Those lectures needed preparation, though he did find time for some vigorous gardening, and also a secret visit to Pippa's little house to instal hi-fi equipment while she was away skiing with Dick, as a 'nice surprise' for her return. And we did manage an Easter break at Arment House.

There, we were joined for a few days by Barbara Grant and her daughter Charlotte.[308] It was Barbara's first husband A.P. Rossiter who had introduced Robbie to Rosamund and Rosalind and the fells around Wasdale; and so it was to the churchyard at Wasdale Head that we took her, to see A.P.'s memorial stone there. Barbara was by now severely arthritic, so our fellside walks were gentle. We took her for tea with Rosalind, herself bent with age, and heard that Rosamund had died a fortnight earlier. It was an afternoon rich with memories and humorous tales, relished by us all.

After a three-day visit to The Hague for a Grotius conference, we set off for Florence, a little uncertainly since Robbie was developing a cold.

---

[306] A reference to a recent episode at Buckingham Palace.

[307] Cassese, addressed by friends as Nino, was at that time Professor at the University of Florence, specialising in Private International Law. He would later be the first President of the International Criminal Tribunal for the former Yugoslavia, and later of the Special Tribunal for Lebanon.

[308] Charlotte Grant, daughter of Barbara's second marriage, would later become a Research Fellow at Jesus.

We just hoped that Italian sunshine would quickly dispel it. And as I wrote afterwards:

> 'Well, it *was* a help. Although not at all well, he did manage to give all seven lectures. One was at the University of Siena, and the other six at the University of Florence. A microphone was provided, and all the talks were tape-recorded. (They now have a strange record of what I should scarcely recognize as my husband's voice, in *basso profundo*!) The students were all very appreciative, and he has warm invitations to return – something we would most gladly do if the opportunity comes.
>
> 'So it was a successful visit in many ways. We were both entranced by Tuscany in springtime…'

While Robbie had completed his task with honour, we had missed a good deal in that place so rich in promises because he needed to rest whenever possible. Still, there was much that we did enjoy there together. The Pensione Monna Lisa, which presented just an obscure doorway onto a narrow street, turned out to offer inside a cool entrance hall with antique furniture, a lofty bedroom and a delightful courtyard garden. Nino and Sylvia Cassese conducted us around the nearby streets to a *trattoria* which became our regular eating-place, choosing strange but delicious food from its mystifying menu. At Siena we were astonished, as English visitors must always be, by a sudden view of the Piazza del Campo and the marvels around, seen both in daylight and starlight. After Siena we were taken by the Casseses to their country retreat, a renovated farmhouse. It provided a short break and an altogether delightful one – walking down a slope through an olive grove to a small lake; supping together by a great log fire, and sleeping in an adjoining cabin open to a great view across the valley. Returning to Florence, the Casseses gave us dinner with old friends, the Bowetts – Derek having come to give a lecture himself at the university. In the following days I sat in on two or three of the lectures ('about 30 students, attentive and nice') and we did make a brief visit to the Uffizi.

A special privilege was to be admitted to the *Villa I Tatti*, the former home of the art collector Bernard Berenson. Nino Cassese took us up there and we were finally accepted after a strict scrutiny of our credentials – Robbie as a member of Harvard, I a fairly convincing student of Italian Renaissance art (having attended

Sir Kenneth Clark's[309] Slade Lectures at Oxford) and allowed to look around the rooms full of treasures. Robbie's tolerance of religious images was limited, though, and the most wonderful and memorable part was our walk through the gardens spreading down that high hillside, especially a tunnel of wisteria through which iridescent beetles darted: altogether a restorative experience.

It was a tired Robbie who returned to Grantchester, still troubled by fever and sinus pain. He needed more rest, and even on 4th May spent some time in bed 'so as to be fit for evening talk to college law society', and next day I had to help him 'into full evening dress for Grand Night at Gray's Inn'. A fortnight later, his health at last restored, he went to The Hague, and from there telephoned me with a 'bizarre proposal' from Steve Schwebel[310] that we should buy his house in Celebestraat – 'Something to think about'.

We did think, but it did not take long to reject the idea, since we needed a far more modest residence in The Hague than the Schwebels, who had settled there with their two daughters for longer periods than we contemplated. What, then, did we actually need? Home, for Robbie, was at Grantchester, close enough for commuting; and we decided that for us a quite small place, preferably in the historic centre of the city rather than its quiet but rather stuffy outskirts, would suit our intermittent residence in The Hague.

In Cambridge that summer, while we were preoccupied with *Institut* conference arrangements, there were plenty of other events. Among them was an innovation – a *Conversazione* held by the Friends of the University Library. Robbie had joined Frank Thistlethwaite,[311] the Librarian, in setting up this 'Friends' organisation to provide support for the Library. It meant a violation of the great Reading Room's customary hush with animated conversation. And when the event happened one year at Midsummer, we were lucky enough to be taken to the top of the library tower at midnight to view a panorama of dimly-lit Cambridge college buildings and distant countryside.

Dick was by now specialising in commercial law, and his work for Guinness occasionally took him off on trips abroad – to Zürich, to Brussels, and once

---

[309] Sir Kenneth Clark was by this time Lord Clark, ennobled after the success of his television series, *Civilization.*

[310] HE Judge Stephen Schwebel, American, formerly academic and Deputy Legal Adviser for UN Legal Affairs.

[311] – Later Sir Frank Thistlethwaite, first Vice-Chancellor of the University of East Anglia.

even Sydney, Australia. Pippa, living and working close by, was often with us, and had joined the bell-ringers at Trumpington Church. All three children would take their friends for spells at Arment House. That summer, too, the funeral of my father brought together many members of the extended family at my niece's house in Kent, where Robbie could chat with her husband Bunny Tubbs, someone for whom he had a great affection.

Poor old Arment House, when we got there, was in need of attention – high grass and weeds everywhere, a wasps' nest against the kitchen window, and sparse water reserves. After setting things to rights (Robbie making a point of washing in the rusty trickle from the water-butt in the yard, and drinking bottled water) we drove to Wasdale and climbed Kirkfell, a steep ascent rewarded with views to the Solway Firth and the Isle of Man; then an equally steep descent towards Pillar, and down by Black Sail Pass. Next day Robbie found himself so tired that he left it to me to drive all the way home.

We never did take holidays the easy way! And we returned to the final intensive arrangements for the *Institut* conference.

At last Robbie's secretary Angie arrived, to cope with last-minute hitches and keep things running smoothly. She spent a sightseeing weekend with us before establishing herself in Wesley House for her work; and on 24th August the conference began. Next day I scribbled a card to Joey: –

> 'We are in the thick of our Institut meeting, and – touch wood – it is all going very well. Daddy gave a super speech at the opening session (some of it in well-rehearsed French) and I am coping with the terrifying ladies. We are so *tired* in the evenings!'

So it went on: from the grand *Ouverture Solenelle* in the Senate House, the group photograph on the steps outside and the reception in the Regent House, the members' sessions proceeded day by day. A memorable evening reception was held in the Wren Library at Trinity, arranged by the Lauterpachts. There were individual dinner parties, including one we gave in the Alcock Room at Jesus College. The 'ladies' (including male spouses or companions) were shown the Fitzwilliam Museum, Anglesey Abbey and the Pepys Library at Magdalene College. A distinctly provincial reception given by the Mayor and Corporation of the City in the Guildhall may have left some Institut members bemused: a former Mayor (a postman) to whom I tried to explain the relevance of international law, and the current Mayor, a beaming lady who worked as a secretary in the Law Faculty, must have seemed very different from the professional Burgomasters of continental cities.

But the Sunday outing to Hatfield House[312] was, to our relief, a great success. In perfect weather the whole group were conveyed to the perfect Tudor great house. There was much to see inside, and splendid grounds in which to wander. The place's association with the 3rd Marquis of Salisbury, a great Foreign Secretary of his time, was recalled; an exhibition of Shakespearian costumes appealed to some; and a good buffet luncheon, with fruit cup or wine served by 'wenches' in Tudor costume in the Old Palace enhanced the general bonhomie.

There was just the final banquet. Distinguished guests included the Lord Chancellor, Lord Mackay of Clashfern, and Richard and Yvette Wilberforce. And despite last-minute anxieties, all went well. The great hall at Trinity, with its huge Holbein portrait of Henry VIII looming over high table, provided a glamorous setting for our foreign visitors, and for Mackay it was a homecoming.

———

Once the conference was over and wound down, we had the Thirlways out to supper at Grantchester. After making plum chutney and extracting honey from my hives, Robbie and I returned to Arment House, this time with pieces of timber to make a new wicket gate. It was a familiar experience: 'Arrived in rain. Usual feeling of "why do we do it?"' Robbie did his carpentry and I scraped, washed and painted bedroom walls, did some gardening, gathered blackberries to mix with apples from Grantchester to made a large pie, read detective stories while it rained outside; rejoiced in our one really fine day; and for our final evening ate out – 'Supper at the Burn Moor Inn – walked home in dense darkness and torrential rain!'

Normal life was resumed, with Robbie reading all the complex material to be mastered for the ICJ's current case, pressing on with *Oppenheim*, and now writing the 19-page entry on International Law for the *Encyclopedia of Public International Law* published by the Max Planck Institute in 1984. It was during this period that he reached his 70th birthday, celebrated with Pippa very quietly that evening with home-cooked tea and supper.

---

312   Hatfield House is the seat of the Marquess of Salisbury, of the Cecil family.

It was later that month that a distraught Robbie telephoned Pippa and me (away in Eskdale at the time) to tell us of Rags' death. Treatment by the vet had been in vain, and he was now buried in the garden. As a Yorkshireman Robbie seldom showed his emotions (deepfelt though they were) over human relationships, but was utterly sentimental with cats, dogs, horses and other creatures. We were left now with just Folly the cat, who entertained and infuriated us for a good many more years.

After a Grotius colloquium in Geneva, Robbie spent a longer spell in The Hague that November as the *Libya/Malta Continental Shelf* case drew closer to its conclusion. We now needed to consider more urgently our need for a small home there. The first two places Robbie saw involved curious incidents: one was a flat overlooking the great wide Lange Voorhout which he found it difficult to look at it seriously since he was distracted by a great display of horses and soldiers and carriages outside, as the Queen conducted her Trooping of the Colour (or its Dutch equivalent). More attractive was a tiny house, where they had been urged to come early, since the owner was giving a lunch party. Robbie was very taken with it … and then found that it was the home of an old pupil-friend (Christopher Pinto[313]) with whom *he* was to have lunch! Feeling rather bewildered, we were now wondering whether to rent a small attic flat for a while before making our decision.

Back in Cambridge, we enjoyed the Jesus College Advent Carol Service, the choir singing magnificently and now enlarged with women's voices for some pieces – the occasion even more memorable when I suddenly recognized the startlingly handsome young man opposite me, who rose for the second lesson, 'read by a First Year Undergraduate'. It was H.R.H. Prince Edward.

Even when he was in England I often saw so little of Robbie that we occasionally met for a snack lunch in the University Regent House if I was in the town, and now and then he would extract Pippa from the Children's Bookshop for lunch and a chat there. One of the agreeable college events at the Christmas season was the Tenants' Luncheon, when farmers and wives came from land near and far that had been Jesus College property since its foundation, and some even from the endowment of the Priory of St Radegund that had preceded it.

[313] M.C.W. Pinto, from Sri Lanka, was a member of the UN International Law Commission among other appointments.

Each New Year we would attend the Epiphany Service in Trinity College Chapel, to boost the congregation in support of Richard Marlow's excellent choir, since it was broadcast live at a time when no undergraduates were in residence. Robbie got on well with the slightly reclusive Marlow, admiring his performances and his own distinctive choral compositions and adding his recordings with the Trinity choir to his CD collection.

Residence in The Hague

1984

Robbie's search for a *pied à terre* in The Hague was assisted by by Ann van Lynden,[314] who found a nice women agent to show us both the Pinto house and then, as an alternative, some newly-built flats in *Houtweg* – a quiet but very central street with some handsome buildings on either side of a canal, the façade of the new set of apartments fitting in quite well. We found that just two of these remained unsold, one at roof-level with a separate bedroom, the other lower down offering just a studio-flat. It was the second, a large bare room, south-facing, which appealed to us both. … But was a big decision, and took some time.

In the meantime we drove over, one Sunday, with David and Sally Williams[315] to Buckinghamshire for a memorable lunch given by the Slynns at their house at Egginton, not far from Woburn – a marvellous building (1696), full of lovely things. We found Sir Gordon Slynn[316] and his French wife Odile had other guests, Lord Hailsham[317] and Deborah Lavin.[318] Hailsham, that extravagant personality, was by now quite old but was in cracking form, entertaining us with his mimicry of the Northern Irish accents, distinguishing Roman Catholic from Protestant. With so much good talk, we didn't leave until late in the afternoon.

---

[314] Ann (English by birth) was the wife of the Dutch diplomat Baron van Lynden, who was at that time President of the Carnegie Foundation, in charge of the Peace Palace premises.

[315] David Williams was Rouse Ball Professor of English Law and President of Wolfson College.

[316] Later Lord Slynn of Hadley. At this time he was Advocate General at the European Court in Luxembourg.

[317] Quintin Hogg, Baron Hailsham of St Marylebone, had been Lord Chancellor 1979-87.

[318] Deborah Lavin, a South African academic historian, at this time teaching at Durham University and President of Trevelyan College. She had for a while taught at the University of Belfast.

On 9th March I joined Robbie in The Hague, where he was busy with his own and others' deliberation notes. On the Sunday this time we tried a service at the English Church. The 1930s building was filled to bursting, with lots of beaming welcomes from everyone. But it was overwarm – not just in manner – and used a modern form of service that felt alien to us. What we were to adopt instead was occasional attendance at the great *Kloosterkerk* on the Lange Voorhout, originally built by Dominicans at the end of the 14th century but now a great, spare, lofty Protestant building. Once a month its Sunday morning service was a *Cantatadienst*, with the Bach cantata for that day performed by a small choir, chamber orchestra and soloists; and although the eloquent preaching from the pulpit baffled us almost entirely, we could join in the congregational singing, sung so slowly that it was a great help in learning to pronounce the Dutch language. We were to find, too, that Queen Beatrix came to these services. The congregation filled the main body of the church and its gallery, but a part of one of the front pews would remain unoccupied until just before the service began – when, unobtrusively, the Queen and a Lady-in-waiting would move in from a doorway close by. After the service a cluster of people might linger outside and clap politely as she emerged after a chat with the musicians, and stepped into her Ford car to be driven home.

We were constantly extending our experience of the city's life and our circle of acquaintances, growing increasingly comfortable with our Dutch neighbours, whose directness and humour had similarities to those of a Yorkshireman. We became accustomed, too, to a semi-diplomatic life, with receptions and dinners attended by people of all nationalities.

One day, after being given lunch by Judge Nagendra Singh at the Harbour Restaurant at Scheveningen (and feeling relieved to arrive back intact after being driven by him[319]) we were driven more skilfully by Mr Pronk to Utrecht, where Robbie had been invited by Professor Martin Bos[320] to give an after-dinner lecture to his law students. It was a good evening: dinner beside a canal, then Robbie's provocative talk, ending with lively discussion and a late return.

During a weekend in Grantchester thoughts of that studio flat on Houtweg were gently marinating, though scarcely spoken. And on the Monday morning

---

[319]   At home in India, Singh – a Maharaja – had a driver. In The Hague he airily announced that, being unable to remember whether to keep to the right or left, he simply went down the middle of the road!

[320]   Dr Maarten Bos was in his final year as Professor of Public International Law at Utrecht. He had, as President of the ILA, organised its memorable conference in The Hague in 1972.

Robbie phoned his decision to buy. By the end of the week he had signed documents and already made choices of tiles and fitments, while I began a search for furnishings. We ended with modern furniture, though draping the huge windows with William Morris curtains, matching their rich blue, pink and buff colour-scheme to the two Persion rugs. Important, of course, was the incorporation of yet another set of hi-fi equipment. Here, Robbie could play Handel's organ concertos played by his former pupil Peter Hurford or *Messiah* at full blast without disturbing the neighbours, since those Houtweg apartments were built of solid concrete and nothing could be heard through the walls.

In those early months of 1984 the *Libya/Malta Continental Shelf* included an intervention by Italy, so Robbie gave a dinner for three friends appearing for the Oral Hearings – Sir Francis Vallat, Michel Virally and Eli Lauterpacht with their wives, observing the rule of impartiality as our guests were correctly balanced: counsel for, respectively, Libya, Italy and Malta.

Having acquired a flat in The Hague, Robbie was confronted with the loss of his accommodation in college –

'26th March. Robbie heard from John Adkins, President of the college, that his "Ghost Room" must be given up for a younger teaching fellow. Sad, but inevitable!'

For him, as for the other Fellows who had reached the age of 70, the eviction presented a problem. As a lawyer he possessed many shelves of law reports and other volumes relating to his work. So did Professor Glanville Williams; and Vivian Fisher, a historian, also had a considerable library in his college rooms. It meant giving away much of the stuff no longer strictly relevant, and dispatching some to his office at the Peace Palace. More came to Grantchester, to be stuffed into his study or along new shelving in one of the bedrooms.

His furniture in the Ghost Room was all large: leather armchairs and sofa, a grand mahogany table and matching chairs, besides an oak wardrobe and a chunky oak bookcase too big for either Alfordsway or our new flat. As it turned out, two people were glad to accept these pieces – Dick for his own flat at Camberwell, and my brother Tony for his holiday-home in the Cotswolds. We had to get strong men from the local builders' firm to heave and manoeuvre these things down the steep staircase of 'Cow Lane' and – temporarily removing a barrier – out into Cloister Court.

Life was unpredictable. After a week or two at home, with occasional meetings in Cambridge or London, our next stay at Arment House was interrupted when he was suddenly recalled to the Court 'because of the situation in Central America, where the U.S. is involved with the laying of mines in Nicaraguan sea-approaches, to the danger of international shipping' (my own description at the time). It meant he must cancel the series of lectures at Siena he was to have given in May.

He came home for the Easter family weekend, then was back to The Hague again. And now the Court was dealing with the opening proceedings of a truly contentious case. On 1st May he rang '– weary and rather depressed. He says discussions on *Nicaragua/US*[321] "tense"'. But on the 7th May his telephone call was 'cheerful, as Nicaragua judgment is done', although this was just the first stage, imposing 'interim measures.'

In Cambridge there were some notable events that summer. HM the Queen and HRH Prince Philip, as parents of that first-year undergraduate Prince Edward, made a visit to the college. Fellows and wives stood in a line around the college hall. In came Her Majesty, Prince Philip and Prince Edward, accompanied by the Lord Lieutenant, the Vice-Chancellor, the Bishop of Ely &c. In turn we were greeted by the Queen and her husband – she starting on one side, he on the other. As she proceeded there were deferential murmurs, bobbed curtseys and slight bows; his progress evoked some livelier sounds, with outbreaks of laughter. Students, staff and children were assembled outside, and we all watched the stately Rolls-Royce depart.

One May Week party was a celebration of Robin Orr's[322] 75th birthday, with George Guest and Professor Frederick Rimmer[323] as prominent guests. Another was at Heffers bookshop, launching a book about the Cambridge

---

[321] *Military and Paramilitary Activities in and against Nicaragua* dispute between Nicaragua and the USA was a particularly difficult case, eventually 'removed' in 1991.

[322] This was the same Robin Orr whom Robbie had known doing secret intelligence work at Mednemham during their war service. He was now Professor (retired) of Music at Cambridge, after a career as teacher and conductor, partly in his native Scotland. He continued to compose until his death at 98.

[323] George Guest had succeeded Orr as Director of Music at St John's; Rimmer had succeeded him as Professor, and organist, at the University of Glasgow.

University Press's 400-year history written by the University Publisher, Michael Black, a Jesuan and one-time resident of Grantchester – and a chance to chat with Reuben Heffer who had for so long managed that shop. Then there was the annual Old Boys' tea at Jesus, when a number of Robbie's former pupils crowded around him; a small concert in the Master's Lodge given by members of The Club; and James Owen's summer party, after which this year Robbie joined Hisashi Owada for dinner at the Garden House Hotel. Owada, briefly visiting Cambridge, had been one of his most brilliant LL.B. pupils and they liked to keep in touch. He was at this stage a Japanese diplomat in increasingly senior posts.

Next day we attended the Honorary Degree ceremony in the University Senate House and the luncheon afterwards at Downing College, the Vice-Chancellor at that time being the college's Master, Sir John Butterfield.[324] Downing's vast classical court made a splendid setting, and on this occasion the graduands included a grand old man of literature, the blind Jorge Luis Borges; the scientist Tjalling Koopmans; the theologian Hans Küng; and the singer Dame Janet Baker. The proceedings ended when HRH the Chancellor rose, removed his magnificent gown, and then walked over to a red helicopter standing on the lawn. A young man carrying a small suitcase had quietly arrived and climbed in. Then Prince Philip took the controls and they rose in the air, to head off towards London. (And in next day's Court Circular I noticed that his passenger, Prince Edward, had taken part in a military ceremony that afternoon.) For years that distinctive red helicopter would be seen passing over our garden, piloted by the royal Chancellor on his way to some University event.

But, as I ended a letter to Joey describing these glories –

'Oh, yes. Among the various excitements of this week: Daddy found dry rot breaking out in the kitchen doorway last Sunday morning. He took action as promptly as he could – tore out the rotted wood and had a go with your blowlamp. When the builder's foreman arrived early on Monday morning he was amused. "Proper little vandal when you get going, aren't you?" he said.'

While workmen attended to the damage, we ended that week with our usual visit to Fen Ditton for the final 'bumps' – the May Races, when college

---

[324] Sir John Butterfield was an eminent medical researcher, and in 1988 became Baron Butterfield of Stechford.

boats chase each other along the Cam. That evening we were at the University Library's *conversazione,* and chatted with Walter Hamilton,[325] who told us a story about his exact contemporary as undergraduate at Trinity, the art historian and spy Anthony Blunt (recently deceased). After graduating they had both competed for a Trinity prize fellowship, and it was Hamilton who had been successful. A postcard arrived from Blunt:

> 'Oh blest communion, fellowship divine,
> We feebly struggle, *they* in glory shine.
> Anthony.'

Our large empty room at Houtweg waited to be made properly habitable. It was difficult to get things in the right order: we first took delivery of the Danish dining table and chairs, several weeks before the carpet (British, and made of Herdwick wool) could be expected, likewise the Liberty curtains. The bed and wardrobe were to take another 6 weeks, having been ordered from Germany.

So when Pippa came at the end of July, we all stayed at the Promenade Hotel. She saw the flat 'looking nice but bare' and had a taste of the dizzy social life we seemed to be leading, sharing a delightful evening at the British Ambassador's residence to hear a recital with dinner afterwards. She shared, too, our usual trip by tram to Scheveningen, then to Delft to look at its two great churches, gasping at the tomb of William of Orange in the New Church and pausing by the stone slab marking Vermeer's burial in the Old. And she came with us to a party given by the Odas at their own very nice new apartment, at which Mrs Oda, having at that time little English, entertained her guests by playing the piano – alarming me by appointing me page-turner. Somehow I followed all the rapid runs and twiddles and pounded chords, to Robbie's, Pippa's and my own relief.

We then had a ten-day spell at Arment House.

Robbie found that at first working at home in his study was unnatural: it was more difficult to discipline himself to attend to things there than after

---

[325] Walter Hamilton, a classicist, had recently retired from the Mastership of Magdalene College.

the short journey to college for the purpose. This summer he was writing his long article on Fitzmaurice and also 'happily putting pine shelving together' for more of his books. The Fitzmaurice piece was an impressive article for the *British Yearbook of International Law*, an exemplary tribute to a man he greatly admired. As with his obituary notices, it is not just informative, examining his subject's published writings with scrupulously fair judgment, but reveals a deep perception of the character of the man. One of Fitzmaurice's book reviews,[326] for instance, had seemed an aberration:

'... The review is sardonic in tone, and quite unlike the author's usual urbane preference for understatement and elaborately courteous respect for other views and writings. It is sprinkled with literary references, all of them calculated to add pungency. In fact it is obvious that Fitzmaurice had been exasperated by the book. So it is interesting to ask why this man, ordinarily the very model of serene detachment, was so angered by the thesis of the three distinguished authors.

'There need be little doubt, of course, that Fitzmaurice was, not unreasonably, infuriated by the sociological argot in which the book is – apparently designedly and even in the learned author's view necessarily – written: "a highly esoteric private language – we do not say jargon ...", observes Fitzmaurice. For one who had pre-eminently a sense of style, the ungainly pomposities of his "private language", as well as its perverse opacity, must have hurt...'

Robbie himself shared Fitz's rage, and aimed to express himself with the same precise elegance. Simple prose was often more trouble to write than jargon; but it was far more effective.

———

Joey came with us when in September we crossed by the Harwich-Hook car ferry, our small car filled with stuff for Houtweg. By now the flat was *almost* completely furnished, but not quite; and some improvisation was needed:

'We all had to sleep on the floor for our five nights there – it was tantalising to have notice, on the final afternoon, of the arrival in Holland of our German-made bed!'

---

[326] *The Interpretation of Agreements and World Public Order* by McDougal, Lasswell and Miller.

Arment House had taught us to cope with its often spartan conditions, but sleeping on a thin camping mattress of foam plastic on a carpeted concrete floor was particularly hard for a septuagenarian. Yet we somehow managed, and once back home we drove Joey down to Wiltshire to spend her next academic year in a cottage at Biddestone.

We felt we should mark that other momentous transition, so on 28ᵗʰ September we held 'a strange – quite pleasant – little ceremony in the Ghost Room'. Robbie invited the new occupant, Dr Peter Nolan,[327] and his wife to mark the handover with sherry. As the room was now empty except for two upright chairs, when John Adkins gate-crashed the little party three people had to sit on the floor.

Back again in The Hague, we once more spent the first night on the floor, and ate from a very odd mixture of china until the new set arrived. When our bed finally came and was installed together with the wardrobe alongside, there was a bad moment. Our immediate neighbour Mr Wynaents[328] appeared, angrily complaining of the smudge-marks on a staircase wall made by delivery men in carrying it up. Robbie found that Wynaents was President of the Residents' Association, and that he (RYJ) had signed a document promising to observe the rules of the Houtweg complex. So he had – but since they were in Dutch he had not understood the undertaking that major pieces of furniture should be brought in only through the windows, and that workmen should on no account be permitted to use the lift. Oh dear. Abject apologies. Efforts were made to remove the offensive smudges on the paintwork.

It was only after seeing removal men at work on Dutch streets that we fully realised why our windows were so large. A neat mechanical hoist could be deployed to lift even a grand piano into an upper window; and this was the reason why the old houses along the canals often tilt slightly forwards and have a beam with a pulley for raising furniture. Anyway, a week later the Van Lyndens gave an informal party for us to meet our Houtweg neighbours; and once our big room looked sufficiently welcoming, we in turn invited them in and found them both forgiving and extremely friendly.

---

[327] Peter Nolan, at that time Lecturer in Economics, later became Sinyi Professor of Chinese Management at the Judge Institute of Management Studies. He tells me how much he loved that room during his own 30-year tenancy, even though he had actually sensed a ghostly presence.

[328] Henry Wynaents, Dutch diplomat, later to be their Ambassador in Paris.

We were to go to an Embassy Ball for the first and only time during Robbie's years at The Hague. Sir Philip Mansfield was about to retire as Ambassador, and the British Government had decided that the Residence he and his predecessors for 140 years had occupied was to be given up. That *Huis van Assendelft* in Westeinde, built in the 17th-century (and with a resident ghost) had immense style. But it actually belonged to the Jesuits whose church stood in its courtyard, and there were serious drawbacks to its continuing use by a British Ambassador. Not only was the entrance from a narrow street in what was now a less salubrious part of the city, but a former Ambassador, Sir Richard Sykes (1977-79) had in fact been shot dead by IRA gunmen on its doorstep, and maintaining security was difficult. And now in 1984 the Jesuits were demanding a higher rent.

The Mansfields decided that the end should be marked with a bang rather than a whimper by inviting fellow diplomats to a final event in its ballroom. The day before I noted our growing nervousness, particularly as Robbie was to be seated beside Princess Margriet and opposite to Princess Anne. Would he have to offer to dance with one or other princess, he who had never learned to dance? In the end, of course, we thoroughly enjoyed the evening. I remember chatting with Princess Anne (who was combining this event with another for the Save the Children Fund in The Hague) and spinning to an old-fashioned waltz around that amazing Rococo ballroom, partnered by a Dutch baron. We got home to bed at 1.45 am.

Next day there was a long sitting in the Great Hall of Justice for the reading, in French, of the *Gulf of Maine* Award. And then we brought Roberto Ago to Houtweg for supper. He was quite probably shocked at the modesty of our little home, but, gracious as ever, declared himself charmed. (I had cheated by bringing in dishes from the nearby *traiteur* restaurant and small grocers.)

Someone with a better kitchen and greater love of cooking was Frances Meadows, who treated us to a leisurely Sunday lunch with good conversation, and was to give Robbie many meals in the following years.

———

Sir Philip Mansfield's departure was marked by another very special occasion, to which we were invited: lunch with Queen Beatrix at the *Huis den Bosch*. I described for Joey our stately reception on arrival: –

'... we go in to be greeted by members of the Royal Household, three of whom we know already. – A lovely room, of course, and everyone friendly and courteous but constrained: everything is arranged to go exactly according to protocol. We stand at the window and watch the arrival of the British Ambassador. It is his occasion, to mark his retirement, and we are enormously privileged to have been nominated by him as the only other British couple to be invited. The Mansfields arrive in style: on this special day they are brought with an escort of six motorcyclist-guards in tight formation in front, and a great police Mercedes behind.

'Once we are all assembled, the other guests being the Dutch Minister of Finance and his wife, a Judge-Professor (van Wassenaar, my dancing partner at the ball) and his wife, and an art-historian specializing in portraits. (He is a sort of Sir Anthony Blunt figure [F. van Kretchmar], and I was very sorry not to have the chance to talk to him.) Together with the Royal Household, the lunch party numbers 18. Once we are all assembled, the doors open to a further room where Her Majesty and Prince Claus are waiting. We are presented in turn, and are standing in a circle, with the Mansfields, facing the Queen. Queen Beatrix then makes a speech – very expert, fluent, friendly, saying that it is usual to confer a decoration upon a departing Ambassador, but that as Sir Philip has done so much for relationships between the two countries he has received his already ... After which Philip makes his own speech, thanking warmly, reminding the Queen of his country's and his own personal links with the Netherlands, &c ... That done, we spend some 20 minutes or so chatting informally (deftly moved about by the Master of the Household and Mistress of the Robes, so that we meet everyone).

'Then lunch – a walk through several marvellous rooms to the dining room, which is decorated with an elaborate plaster ceiling and breathtaking grisaille tromp d'oeil pieces on the walls. (They are famous: they give the illusion of stone bas-reliefs.) The Queen sits at the centre of the table with Sir Philip on her right and Daddy on her left. Opposite her is Prince Claus, with Elinor Mansfield on his right and me on his left. He talked for a long time with Elinor, and when the Queen saw this she included me in some of her own conversation with Philip – about the "trade union" of Crown Princes the young royals of her generation had once formed as a sort of joke, and so on. When I did have Prince Claus's attention we had a nice conversation. He loves wild places, and told me about a happy stay he had spent in Scotland with a friend 'who has a large estate north of Inverness', walking between hunting-shelters, rough little cottages on the moors. They walked about 15 miles each day, mostly in rain, and took turns to cook meals on a calor-gas stove in the evenings. Their eldest son, Prince Willem-Alexander, is at Atlantic College in Wales, and he and Queen Beatrix go to visit him about once a month and love to eat at little Welsh restaurants in the country around the school …

'All very nice indeed …'

When Robbie and I returned to our simple flat we sat for a while opposite each other, still rather dazed, marvelling that we, such ordinary people, should have been allowed such an extraordinary experience.

By the end of that stay I felt that Houtweg had become a proper small home, where I could leave Robbie to carry on with his work. He was certainly hard at it, and tired after long sessions with the court, first working on the parties' Memorials, and then hearing the oral pleadings of the *Nicaragua/US* case. I had attended the opening session in the Great Hall of Justice and tried to sketch the scene, fascinated by the resemblance of that long bench of judges, leaning this way and that, listening intently or scribbling notes, to depictions of the Last Supper. But I never stayed for long.

The Work of the Court

Afuller description of Robbie's place of work and its procedures seems now to be needed.

The International Court, together with the senior body, the Permanent Court of Arbitration, is housed in the Peace Palace. This great edifice, designed to impress, took six years to build and was opened in 1913. Andrew Carnegie, the Scottish industrialist and philanthropist, had made the whole project possible by setting up the Carnegie Foundation, which controls the whole complex of buildings in perpetuity. As with the *Palais des Nations* in Geneva, countries sympathetic with its aims made their contributions, enhancing the grandeur of the Palace: there is, for instance, a breathtaking jasper urn donated by Tsar Nicholas II of Russia; spectacular ceramic jars and wall-tiles from the Netherlands; exquisite silk tapestries from Japan; and the vast stained-glass windows of the Great Hall of Justice from Great Britain. The building itself is the outcome of an international competition among leading architects, and was designed by a Frenchman, Louis Marie Cordonnier. (It is fascinating to see the rival designs from which this was selected, many rather more handsome to modern eyes, embodying different concepts of how such a building should look and function.)

For the open sessions of the International Court, members of the public are admitted to the Great Hall of Justice. There, humbled by its height and slightly oppressed by the symbolic messages contained in every image around, they sit on upright chairs and wait for the stately entry of the file of judges, who sit in line at a raised table in front of them. To their right is a glass-fronted cubicle where the translators work, ensuring that all the proceedings may be heard in both English and French.[329]

But that is as far as the public are permitted to go. They do not see the parts where most of the work is done: the Judges' individual offices, the many

---

[329] At the UN Headquarters in New York, speeches are available by simultaneous translation into five languages.

rooms (some high up in the building) where the Registrar and the multitude concerned with administration have their rooms; the library; the subterranean Refectorium where refreshment is served.[330] Most significantly, they are probably unaware of the Deliberation Room in the new wing, where the judges gather for their formal discussion, seated at a horseshoe-shaped table with the President at its centre.

Guided tours take place regularly for fee-paying visitors, to raise money for the Carnegie Trust's expenses in maintaining all these premises. They are shown the more spectacular parts of the building – both the Great Hall and the Small Hall of Justice, the wonderful Japanese Room and the 'Ferdinand Bol Room', rooms intended for the Permanent Court of Arbitration and the ICJ's predecessor, the Permanent Court of International Justice[331], and now scarcely in regular use.

By the end of the Second World War, with the creation of the United Nations, it had become clear that an enlarged and more fully representative Court must replace the former PCIJ; and in 1946 the present International Court of Justice, the 'principal judicial organ of the United Nations', was inaugurated. The Court's Statute is made up of 70 Articles, laying down exactly how it is organised and how it should conduct the 'judicial settlement of disputes'. (It should be understood that the ICJ is concerned with the resolution of disputes between *States* and not *individuals*. The International Criminal Court [the ICC], founded in July 2002, has a quite distinct function[332] and is not a part of the UN.)

It was in this setting and in this organisation that Robbie had embarked on his new career.

———

Most members of the Court at that time (the early 1980s) were likely to have been affected by the Second World War, some with particularly painful memories. It meant that conversation was conducted with a certain delicacy as we grew aware of these shadows in the background; but all these men were colleagues now dedicated to Peace and Justice – the emblems displayed all around.

---

[330] More recently, a private diningroom has been provided in the new wing for ICJ members and staff.

[331] The Permanent Court of International Justice was set up by the League of Nations in 1922, and established Rules of Procedure which form the framework of the present Court.

[332] The ICC operates under the Statute of Rome, with 123 states agreeing to its jurisdiction.

Robbie became close to Shigeru Oda (former Professor at Tohoku University, Japan) whom he had known already for some years, but never, I think, questioned him about his war service.[333] The German judge, Hermann Mosler, is described[334] as having done his principal work at the Max Planck Institute and at the European Court of Human Rights, and his early career, from 1937 spent as research fellow at the Kaiser Wilhelm Institute in Berlin, had been conducted '*under politically complicated circumstances*'. (Mosler made clear his repugnance for the Nazi movement.) There was the Polish Judge Manfred Lachs who served the court for 26 years and whose brilliance was always acknowledged; yet he must have needed his skill as 'a natural conciliator' to survive the changing circumstances imposed by his masters behind the Iron Curtain. The Russian Judge Morozov's impressive career (including USSR Deputy Representative to the Security Council) gave him great authority; but, unlike Lachs, he seemed remote and humourless, and Robbie felt wary of his political allegiance. Another, who seemed at first baffling but turned out to be genial, was the Chinese Judge Ni, who had been a Member of the National Committee of the Chinese People's Consultative Council during the period 1959-1984.

All 15 members of the Court came, necessarily, from different parts of the world, bringing with them their accumulated experiences. Yet instead of Babel, just two languages – English and French – were spoken and, as Robbie found, there was little to disturb their common purpose. He wrote:

'… In a society of States much divided by ideologies, by religion, by poverty and wealth, by power and weakness, by size, by history and by geography, it is well never to lose sight of the fact that the one vocabulary of ideas that they have in common is public international law…'[335]

He already knew several of the judges through the *Institut* and the Hague Academy, and had a deep respect for the President, Judge Elias, a Nigerian. The other African, Kéba Mbaye of Senegal, was a strikingly handsome man

---

[333] There were rumours that he had been given the horrifying task of training *kamikaze* pilots.

[334] In *The International Court of Justice, 1946-1996*, by Arthur Eyffinger, written to celebrate the half-centenary of the ICJ, there is a section called *The Judges*, pp. 258-340. The author provides a skilful description of each judge, with a summary of his (or her, in the sole case of Judge Rosalyn Higgins) career.

[335] This comes from the concluding passage of RYJ's long article about Fitzmaurice.

(who had, among other distinctions, served on the Olympic committee), a francophone. From the Middle East there was the Syrian, El-Khani; and from South America the Brazilian Sette-Camara and the Argentinian Ruda. Guy Ladreit de Lacharrière, from France, was a supremely able man who died after just five years at the court.

The whole composition of the bench at the time of Robbie's installation was as follows:

Roberto Ago (Italy)	Mohammed Bedjaoui* (Algeria)
Taslim Olawale Elias (Nigeria)	Abdallah Fikri El-Khani (Syria)
Guy Ladreit de Lacharrière (France)	Manfred Lachs (Poland)
Kéba Mbaye* (Senegal)	Platon Dmitrievich Morozov (USSR)
Hermann Mosler (Germany)	Nagendra Singh (India)
Shigeru Oda (Japan)	José Maria Ruda (Argentina)
Stephen M. Schwebel (USA)	José Sette-Camara (Brazil)
& Robert Yewdall Jennings* (UK)	
(new members' names are marked with *)	

As judges retired, having completed their terms of office (or in three cases, died before completion) new faces appeared – 15 of them during Robbie's 13 years as judge. Among those new members were men from Venezuela, Norway, Hungary, Sierra Leone, Madagascar, Guyana and Sri Lanka. It was truly a World Court, made up of colleagues who came to know and respect each other. The Registrar at the time of Robbie's installation was Santiago Torres Bernardez, from Spain, who was succeeded by Eduardo Valencia-Ospina, from Colombia. The Principal Legal Secretary, Philippe Couvreur, was from Belgium.

One judge whose final term was extended by the completion of the *Gulf of Maine* case was the genial André Gros. Although not popular with everyone there, he had a warm regard for Robbie (and indeed for Britain). He told us of his own wartime experiences, of escaping from the Pétain regime in Paris and, by stages, travelling from Spain to Portugal and across to Brazil before at last reaching Britain, where he served with the Free French and became prominent in diplomatic work at the end of the war.[336] Judge Jens Evensen, who joined

---

[336] It was Gros who wrote, confidentially, to Robbie in 1993 warning of Lachs' allegiance to the Communist Party, having spent 2 years in the USSR after the war.

the Court in 1985, had been a leader in the Norwegian Resistance Movement ... and so on.

———

A talk Robbie gave (I think at the L.S.E.) in about 1988 – *The International Court of Justice from the Inside* – first describes the court's procedure in some detail, and ends with an impression of the final stage of a case as experienced from the bench. Rather than attempting a summary of my own, I will quote from the talk itself:

> [*Concerning the distinction between 'legal' and 'political' disputes*] –
> '... by the time a dispute has been put, if indeed it can be put at all, into the form of quite specific particular issues of fact or law, on which the parties are divided, and that are justiciable, i.e. put into a form apt for an adversarial court procedure, the "dispute" has undergone a change in its nature if only by the selection of some elements and the discarding of others. This may be a good thing or sometimes not so good in all the circumstances. Deciding that is a political decision. But it is no mere change of form. A court of law is simply unable to deal at all with a dispute unless and until that dispute has been reduced – and I use that word *reduced* advisedly – to the form of a specific legal or factual issue or group of issues on which the parties take differing views. Every court of law anywhere insists upon some form of "submissions" – roughly the "statement of claim" of English law – in its procedures. Pleadings are directed to this end. This is why the Rules of the International Court of Justice require the addition of formal "submissions"; the drafting of those submissions, as experienced counsel well know, is the day of truth for many arguments which till then had seemed cogent and even powerful; and may indeed still be so outside a court of law, but not when proposed to be subjected to public confrontation with a cogently argued opposing view, before a *third* party for decision by the application of rules of law.'
>
> ...
>
> [*He gives examples of the type of cases recently before the Court which illustrate the political importance of their outcome*] 'sea boundaries, limiting a nation's access to fish or oil, and the exercise of military or commercial power, will usually affect whole economies; a case between Italy and the U.S. at present before

the Court[337] could, we were told in the presentation, be very important for the international movement of investment and know-how generally; the political implications of any case about the relations of the Sandinista Government of Nicaragua and the Contra forces could hardly be exaggerated.'

…

[*Describing the 'process of decision*] '…what happens after the public hearings of argument are concluded, and the Court has retired behind the firmly closed doors of its so-called "deliberation room". Obviously the deliberation, as with most courts, must be private… [The Rules state that…] "The Registrar, or his deputy, and other members of the staff of the Registry as may be required shall be present. No other person shall be present except by permission of the Court." Such staff members, e.g. translators, will have been required to make a solemn declaration before the Court to perform their duties, "in all loyalty, discretion and good conscience…"'

…

[*Describing the peculiar demands of conducting a meeting of 15, or even occasionally 17, judges*] 'Obviously what one is going to get is not a conversation but a series of more or less formal speeches, called, with only occasional exceptions, in the order in which Judges have signified to the President their desire to speak. You will appreciate at once that if one wishes to criticize what Judge A has just been saying, and with which you may profoundly disagree, you may, even if you hurry onto the list by catching the President's eye (and he may be looking in the other direction, whether by chance or advisedly) not be called upon until after Judges B,C,D and E have made more or less long speeches on perhaps quite other matters; by which time your criticisms of A may have lost their freshness. So, the timing of one's signifying one's desire to speak is itself a decision calling for skill and experience; and one soon learns not to rush in, but to wait a while. The whole thing calls for formality and elaborate courtesy. A deliberation with a neat, logical and continuous pattern is really hardly possible to achieve. But it must be remembered that you have here 15 people who are constantly working together, and know each other extremely well. And there is a great deal of informal talk in each others' rooms. Accordingly, there *is* usually a progression in the deliberation and a feel of where the preponderant opinion lies does gradually emerge. In any event there is really no other way of doing it if, so to speak, the main forms

---

[337] This must refer to the *Elettronica Sicula S.p.A (ELSI)* case, between the USA and Italy.

of civilization and the principal legal systems of the world are to be heard on each important issue.'

———

'Well, now we are in a position to see how the Court, in its internal practice and procedures, sets about attempting to be a reasonable approximation to a world court, and to speak with the authority of a world court in rather exceptionally difficult circumstances; or, in practical terms, how it seeks to ensure that the representatives of the different forms of civilization and legal systems all take a full part in the process of decision. Assuming, therefore, that the probably two, possibly three, stages of written pleadings – both documents, and arguments, and submissions – in many volumes – have been submitted and studied by the Court and the parties; and that probably two rounds of oral proceedings lasting some weeks are over, with of course a written *verbatim* record; and that the rival arguments and submissions are now at last in their final form (for in fact they will both have changed, possibly markedly, from the effect of confrontation in argument – one learns to examine carefully the at first glance seemingly tedious repetition of arguments, for probably an important difference – a different emphasis – a quiet omission – will be apparent) what will the Court now do behind its closed doors?

'First there is what is conveniently called the Article 3 deliberation, at which the President will present a paper stating the list of issues and questions that have to be decided (with references to pleadings and to the records of oral argument); this will be discussed and additions or deletions proposed; judges may give their preliminary views on the case; or, more often, refrain from even an appearance of commitment at this stage.

'Then comes the Article 4 stage, in which "each judge prepares a written note which is distributed to other judges". Judges have secretaries – usually one between two judges – to file and type, but they do not have "clerks" – both tradition and the budget have between them prevented any such development – so each really does his own research for the Note, whether in the enormous mass of pleadings, or in the Reports and books in the library. Some weeks are allowed for this. I have never seen a Note much under some 30 pages; 70 or 80 is normal; well over 100 pages are sometimes to be seen. The task at this stage consists not only of writing one's own Note but the formidable task of reading, with some care, 14 other such Notes (made available only in exchange for one's own Note!).

'For every one of 15-17 Judges to research and write separately and independently (there are of course informal discussions in small groups; or, like a barristers' chambers, at tea time…) is not a very rapid or efficient way of disposing of a case. Each Note, moreover, has to be translated into the other Court language, French or English. Quite a number of Judges can readily read either language; but Francophiles tend "on principle" to insist on having a translation, even though they may secretly read the English original and sometimes demand correction of the translation!

'There is some danger that a Judge will be so convinced by his own Note he will get locked into it and become reluctant to contemplate a different view. But the system does ensure that each Judge individually works at the case, reads the materials, and forms a view. It does, therefore, serve the idea of a world court…

'Then follows the most important deliberation stage – the Article 5 deliberation – which will probably last through several days, meeting morning and afternoon. Now *all* the Judges are required to "*declare* their views". Moreover … they are not called upon in the order of their signifying their desire to speak, but "in inverse order of seniority". Thus the newer Judges are not permitted to wait and see which way the wind is blowing before declaring their views. By the same token, the more senior Judges are required to wait patiently before giving the Court the benefit of their accumulated wisdom.

'Having declared his view – maybe half an hour, maybe an hour or more – each Judge is then questioned on his views by his colleagues, and the questioning can be telling and even mischievous.

'The President will, of course, speak last; and in the nature of things, his statement will be not only a statement of his views but a summing-up of the main tendencies of the deliberation. And it will have appeared, probably quite clearly, in which set of views the majority of the Court lies; and of course the Court will eventually decide by majority.

[*There is still a long way to go, for we come now to the* Drafting Committee, *of which Robbie had personal experience.*] 'Then obviously comes the time for actual drafting. This cannot be done by the whole Court, and so, for the first and probably only time in this procedure, resort is had to a committee: the very important drafting committee. This consists normally of three persons. The President, if he is part of the majority view, will be a member. The other two … are elected by secret ballot – though there will no doubt have been informal discussions beforehand. And the choice will not be all that difficult.

During the Article V deliberation it will have become pretty clear where the majority opinion is going to lie. It is a working committee, so you want Judges who are at home in drafting either in French or English. You want people known to have drafting experience – it is not an easy assignment. And you want judges who are in the mental and physical state to face some weeks of very hard application, and the patience to deal with the quite difficult problems that will surely arise; and the temperament needed to face many meetings discussing drafts, re-writing, and perhaps abandoning, with a good grace and rapidly, one's own cherished, ingenious and obviously sound solutions.'

...

[*And the labour continues: the First Reading of the prepared draft, with scrutiny and criticism by fellow Judges. Then those who have strong views not in accord with the majority may write* Separate *or* Dissenting Opinions *to be appended to the eventual Judgment/Award. And then there is the Second Reading and Final Vote.*]

'Between the first and the second readings, the drafting committee will have been extremely busy carrying out the wishes of the Court that appeared in the first reading: answering the more important criticisms in separate opinions or dissents, removing the target in cases where separate opinions have destroyed part of the draft judgment. The resulting amended draft, in which all changes are keyed for quick identification, is then circulated for the *Second Reading*, which is relatively speedy: the draft is taken page by page instead of paragraph by paragraph; and the pages are not read aloud, unless some serious problem arises …

'The final vote is then taken, either at the end of the Second Reading, or after a suitable interval if things still remain to be done to the draft. The voting is "Yes" or "No" on each separate issue. Abstention is not permitted. And nowadays, unlike the former practice, the names of Judges voting "Yes" or "No" are listed in the report, so it is not possible for any Judge now to be anonymous in the voting. It is fair to say that anyone who supposes that the final lists could be guessed from the geographical or political background of the Judges will often be disappointed. The lists yield many surprises; which is as it should be.'

[All *this has been behind the scenes; but now comes the moment when the Court returns to view in the Great Hall of Justice, for the* Reading Out.]

'The voting over, the Court is now ready to return to the public gaze for the formal reading out of the judgment by the President, in the full Court, and in the presence of the parties' agents and counsel, and such members of the public or The Hague diplomatic corps as suppose they might have some interest in the matter. This reading out is presumably a remnant of the days before quick duplication was possible; but nearly all higher courts everywhere seem to regard it as being still a good way of giving judgment. The parties are supplied with printed copies of the judgment, and can be seen turning to the end to consult the terms of the *dispositif,* whilst the President in his reading is still busy with the facts. The reading, not always very skilfully done, can take a tedious two or three hours or even a good deal more. Members of the public creep away after a half hour or so, trying to look as if they had just remembered an urgent appointment elsewhere. The judges, however, are kept amused by watching how counsels' eyebrows shoot up in incredulity at the seeming rejection of a favourite argument; or just occasionally at the acceptance of one.

'An adequate but hardly fascinating summary is meanwhile supplied to the press; and one then waits in trepidation to see what new standards of total misapprehension of issue and decision the media will manage to achieve; with one or two exceptions, amongst which must certainly be counted the Law Reports of the London *Times* which, after many years of refusing to notice the International Court of Justice at all, now reports it excellently.[338]

. . .

'*Conclusion*

'I have tried briefly to describe the ways by which the Court sets about its very difficult role of speaking and acting with the authority proper to a world court in a world which has deeply differing ideas about what is just. I have set before you the ideal situation, which our rules in a measure force upon us. And judges, like everybody else, are subject to human frailty. Often our deliberations reach a very high standard of intellectual and moral integrity; sometimes one is thankful that the proceedings are held in strict privacy. Yet our rules of internal procedure are designed with the object in view of speaking with a collective voice, as a world court should be able to do. And I have tried to show how even dissenting judges take a full part, up to the last comma, in the decision from which they dissent. In that sense the decision is *always* the decision of the whole Court. Indeed, our last two decisions were unanimous – quite a triumph for fifteen judges chosen under Article

---

[338] That was in 1988. The newspaper seems have reverted to its old neglect for some years now.

9. In fact, I believe that it is at present a pretty good court, that it performs an extremely difficult task – much more so than the task of, say, the EEC Court[339], where there are not those big differences of culture and civilization – and I wish more people knew about it; for awareness of the law is after all the main sanction of law anywhere.'

This text does not appear in *The Collected Writings of Sir Robert Jennings*[340]. The talk was, after all, a fairly private and informal one. But it does give an idea of the labour entailed in each case which comes before the ICJ; and during Robbie's time as judge the number of cases increased considerably. It was no sinecure for one's retirement. He was not allowed to be an 'idle' man, even though that upbringing in Idle remained within him to the end.

———

[339] (Now the EU Court)

[340] An article which appeared in the *BYIL* in 1997 was published too late for inclusion in his *Collected Writings. The Role of the International Court of Justice* is another important account, owing much to his own experience both as judge and as counsel appearing before the Court.

Either Side of the North Sea

1985

Maintaining his commitments in both England and the Netherlands was quite demanding for a septuagenarian, but he carried the burden remarkably well. I seemed to be constantly driving him down to Stansted for or from a flight to Schiphol.

A college event on 28th January was the death of Alan Pars, the aged bachelor maths don who had been Robbie's best man at our wedding. On that day 'R called on Gardner-Smith, who observed that now at last (97 next Sunday) he is Senior Fellow!' On 1st February I noted that Robbie, finding himself an executor, was anxious to know the contents of Alan's will. But on the 3rd, he was obliged to return to The Hague and was unable to get back for the funeral on the 9th. I went, through falling snow, to the college chapel. The slow tolling of the chapel bell was followed by the bare funeral service, the interment to follow at Acton. Tea in the Alcock Room followed, where I talked to 'Howard [head gardener], West [head porter], Muriel Brittain, James Owen [former college chaplain], and nice Acton neighbours. The view as I crossed Chapel Court was memorable – driving snow, with gowned figures flapping like bats as they hurried for shelter. It took me 80 minutes to drive home through the blizzard. And next evening, when Robbie rang, he asked me to open the sealed envelope with Pars's Will.

We found that Alan Pars's main bequest[341] was to Jesus College. (He had hoped that there would be enough to pay for a swimming pool for the college, but this, entailing so much maintenance as well as building expense, could not be carried out.) His 'chattels', though, were bequeathed to the two executors, Robbie and a mathematician Fellow of Queens' College, Dr Maxwell. We knew that the house at Acton had been burgled some years before, with the loss of just a few select items, two elaborate Meissen groups of figures and one or two Turner watercolours. 'Ah,' Pars had said, grieving, 'I had meant them to

---

[341] Alan Pars [Dr L.A. Pars] had no surviving relatives.

go to you'. What remained that might be of interest we did not at that stage know.

—

It had been the day after Pars's death that we drove up to Hull for the inaugural Josephine Onoh Lecture at the University. Miss Onoh, a Nigerian graduate student in international law at Hull, had been killed in an air crash, and in her memory her family had provided a fund for annual lectures and prizes. It was fitting that the first lecture was was to be delivered by HE Judge Taslim Elias, since he was not only the current President of the ICJ and a distinguished scholar, but also from Nigeria.

Although this was not Robbie's own part of Yorkshire, we found much to enjoy there: not the hotel, nor the austere university buildings (though we were later to see the library and the impressive Ferens Gallery). But the people we met were totally friendly: the University Chancellor was our friend Lord Wilberforce, and Robbie was happy to chat with the crowd of graduate students of all nationalities, mostly African. Lunch and dinner were lavish.

—

At the Court at this time there were two cases on which Robbie was working (a third, the *Burkino Fasso/Mali* frontier dispute, was opening before a Chamber of just five judges and did not include him). There was the continental shelf dispute between Libya and Malta still to be settled, and the far more contentious matter of *Nicaragua/US* concerning the alleged support by the United States for the 'Contra' uprising against the government of Nicaragua. That dispute dragged on, the US withdrawing its participation but the court nevertheless finding for Nicaragua; and eventually, in September 1991, it would be dropped altogether without formal resolution. But the drafting of statements along the way was a challenge to Robbie and his colleagues on the Drafting Committee. (It was, too, a case which Robbie later described as having broken the mould of disputes being submitted to the World Court, which until then had been 'between States members of the same political bloc.'[342])

It was as well that our pleasant room at Houtweg provided a regular place for work and relaxation in the evenings, for his spells in The Hague

---

[342] This phrase is quoted from an article by Philippe Sands.

were now more prolonged. From early February to early June 1985 he spent 85 days there, mostly solo. I no longer received letters describing his days away from home, for he had developed the habit of telephoning almost every evening, when I would be ready for the daily exchange of news and family gossip which meant so much to us both. I would hear a little about the progress of the current case, but more about the friends with whom he was dining. Anxious that he should remember to eat sensibly, I would ask how he was coping on the occasions when he stayed in. 'Oh, I've made myself supper,' he would say proudly. 'I got half a melon and some Parma ham from Mr Westerman.' Mr Westerman's small grocery around the corner was a godsend: it was stacked with cheeses ('oude Gouda' was a favourite), hams and all manner of food and drink; you could get a *brodje* made up – a split roll with your filling of choice – and so I could be confident that my husband would not actually starve. And whenever I joined him in the flat, my first task was always to wash everything and stock up the refrigerator so that he could survive alone for his next spell.

At the Peace Palace we found that the Refectorium (a crypt-like structure with Art Nouveau decoration), though an agreeable place to sit and chat, offered thoroughly disagreeable food. If possible, one ate a salad or *brodje* at a nearby café. But it was pleasant to stroll around the Peace Palace gardens, laid out in what was claimed to be 'English style', with its rosebeds and long pool where huge carp swam among the water-lilies, and stately black swans floated together with moorhens and exotic ducks.

Since one of the judges' diplomatic privileges allowed them to buy a car in the Netherlands free of tax and with a discount, we took the opportunity to look at more expensive makes than we might consider at home, and got a BMW with the CDJ numberplate. Next time I was in the Netherlands Robbie drove me to Kijkduin for a bracing walk along its beach and I drove back, timidly. Then at the weekend we drove eastwards towards Apeldoorn and found the great national park at Hoge Veluwe looking marvellous, with thin snow on the ground. We viewed the Kroller Müller collection and were thrilled by its Van Goghs – I, heart in mouth, driving all the way back. Next day, after a *cantatadienst* at the Klosterkerk with a splendid performance of *Jesu, meine Freude* and a long and incomprehensible sermon, we drove through Wassenaar to Katwijk and Nordwijk for another fierce walk in a sharp north wind along the beach. But lunch with Manfred Lachs was mainly to discuss *Libya/Malta*, the case currently being considered.

There was another treat during that visit, though. Our loyal *au pair* from the 1950s, 'Tiddle', now aged 50, gave us dinner in Amsterdam followed by a concert at the famous Concertgebouw: a great evening.

Another, for Robbie, was to dine with the new British Ambassador, Sir John Margetson. The new Ambassador's Residence was a large free-standing house built at about the turn of the 19th-20th centuries: a quite grand building with a good garden, in an area not far from the Peace Palace and close to a number of other diplomatic residences.

One Saturday was spent as a participant in an international 'moot', an event which appealed to Robbie's love of teaching, sitting with Lachs and a professor from Leuven in judgment while pairs of opposing teams contested a fictional dispute. The competitors were law students from five or six different countries, and it was quite an ordeal for them, since they must speak in English and might be interrupted by sharp questions from the judges, all within a strict time limit. An ordeal for the judges themselves as well, since they too had had to master beforehand the details of a complicated case between 'Ruritania' and 'Utopia'.

This must have been Robbie's first *Telders Moot*, named in memory of a Leiden law professor whose protests at the eviction of Jews by the occupying Germans during the Second World War had led to his imprisonment and eventual death in the Bergen-Belsen concentration camp just before the war's end. Robbie would take part year after year, as the number of competing teams increased and the event developed its own social programme. We were always impressed by the high standard of these aspiring international lawyers and the good humour during those Telders gatherings.

After the Easter break at home, it was Dick's turn to see our apartment in The Hague. In May he joined us there, and we contrived to cram in as many gastronomic and cultural delights as possible into one weekend. Our studio flat had a sort of promontory – a deep bay window – with a door to a narrow balcony. It allowed us to drag the sofa, extended lengthways, into this space and use a Japanese screen to separate it from the main area with our own bed. For a member of the family, it became a tiny guest room. So Dick's stay included a walk around our nearby streets and the Hof Vijver; a tram-ride to Delft to see the great churches and – that day – competing brass bands parading in the market square. At the other end of the tramline we walked along Scheveningen seafront, where – that day – young farmers from Friesland on huge cart-horses tilted with lances at small targets, while windsurfers and sand yachts tried their skills too.

On the Sunday we returned to the Kroller-Müller Museum, finding its lovely setting in rolling woodland at its best in spring sunshine, so we explored its paths on the white bicycles available for visitors.

After taking him to Schiphol for an early flight next morning, Robbie and I called at Keukenhof on the way back. Having only vaguely heard of it, this great showplace of the Dutch bulb-growing industry now thrilled us. Scarcely any other visitors were about at that hour, as we walked through changing vistas of tulips under pale green beech trees, pools of colour enhanced by shafts of light through a dreamy mist...

Back in The Hague and smartened up, we were at the Peace Palace in time for the arrival of His Holiness Pope John Paul II, with a retinue of cardinals and bishops. All the judges and wives were 'presented' in turn by the President, Nagendra Singh. The Pope said a few words to each of us, giving every man a medallion and every wife a pearl rosary. After he left the room, the Registrar remarked, 'Do you realise that he spoke in *eight* different languages as he met this group?' Then, in the Great Hall of Justice, the Pope spoke on the subject of Peace to an audience which included HM Queen Beatrix. For this papal visit there was intense security all around, since there had been noisy demonstrations in the streets in protest at his reception in this strongly Protestant country.

We were at a rather formal dinner that evening given by the Schwebels in honour of HE Mme Ruda[343], prolonged by short speeches. A less pretentious meal next day was very welcome, when Roberto Ago chose for us food from his own region at the 'La Liguria' restaurant.

Unlike Roberto, who had a certain disdain for the Dutch way of life, we found The Hague (a place despised by people of Amsterdam as being too dull) full of interest, with the Lange Voorhout used for all manner of events – becoming at different seasons a fairground, a horse show, a sculpture exhibition, an antiques market or a flower festival. And on the great open field nearby, the Malieveld, one might find a circus, with elephants grazing on its grass. It had at one end a curiously uneven area; and an exhibition about the city's war years under German occupation revealed that this had been one of the launch sites for the V1 'buzz bomb'[344]. Further down towards the Central

---

[343] The wife of Judge Jose-Maria Ruda was herself a diplomat of some distinction.

[344] Detecting the sites where these V 1 'doodlebugs' and their successors, the V 2 rockets, were launched had been part of the intelligence work at Mednemham.

Station was a small enclosed royal park for two herds of deer, fallow and roe, besides rabbits, waterfowl and herons.

Robbie especially appreciated a privilege available to members of the Court, honorary membership of the *Haagsche Club* where he could call in each Wednesday lunchtime for a bowl of soup and a glass of *jenever* gin, or attend the monthly dinner served in its premises on the Lange Voorhout. The regular members were mostly elderly and patrician, and they always included him in their conversation by speaking English.

Among the diplomatic dinner-parties that May was one given by the Consul for Jordan in honour of the retiring Syrian judge, El-Khani, largely an Arab occasion. Our host, Rabbani, had arrived in the Netherlands as a poor Palestinian refugee and was now immensely rich, living in some grandeur in Wassenaar. He had invited the ICJ judges; security guards were deployed; the meal was splendid, and fine wines served but not taken by his Mohammedan guests. We were presented, on leaving, with an illustrated catalogue of the old Dutch paintings on his walls.

It was on this occasion that I found myself seated next to the formidable Judge Morozov. Afterwards, an astonished Robbie said he had seen the Russian in animated conversation with me: how had that been achieved? By luck I had mentioned that I had been reading the biography of Arthur Ransome, best known as a children's author, and had been interested to find that he had worked as Foreign Correspondent to the *Manchester Guardian* during the Russian Revolution of 1917 and had later married Trotsky's secretary, sharing with her a love of sailing a small boat on the Baltic. Ah – Morozov, too, had his own yacht on the Baltic and was a passionate sailor! And after this, Robbie was to find him a far warmer character.

At home, finding another patch of dry rot in the hall, Robbie was determined to dig deep, right below the existing foundations of both hall and staircase, and called in a small firm of builders who took ages over the chaotically organised work, while they created mayhem elsewhere as well. The banging, drilling and dust would have been quite unendurable if he had not liked the workmen – the senior one big and taciturn, the other small and a chatterbox with a great whooping laugh, who was from Bradford … and for Robbie, a Yorkshireman from Bradford could be forgiven anything.

New contacts of all kinds were constantly being made – at a Chilean reception for international lawyers and Antarctic Survey people; at lunch with benchers and judges in the Middle Temple hall; at another of Basil Markesinis' lunches. And it was that summer that Robbie was caught up for a few days in a curious new interest: advising his old pupil Sami Shubber about possible legislation by the World Health Organisation to control the advertising of breast-milk substitutes in Third World countries.

Another preoccupation was the selection of 'chattels' from the late Alan Pars's house at Acton. On 9th August we took Dr & Mrs Maxwell with us for a thorough exploration – a depressing experience, knowing that we could raid all this furniture but feeling no inclination to do so. Eventually Dr Maxwell said he would like to have the good Broadwood upright piano, and we took a small cane-seated chair for our hall. I had spotted, too, a framed sampler of embroidery done by Alan's sister Dora – exquisitely fine needlework which, in its dark corner, might easily have been overlooked. We came away, feeling sad. A few days later we drove down again to take a look at Pars's papers and photos. Then, remembering that as this was 'Liberty Hall', where Pars had so loved entertaining (young men particularly) we looked in the kitchen cupboards and found good crockery and glassware that would contribute to the three households being set up by our children at that time, while leaving plenty for the housekeeper and for the Salvation Army.

Our youngsters were now aged 29, 27 and 24, and we had begun to wonder which, if any, of the friends they had introduced at home were to become settled relationships. They were all leading full lives and could feel sure that Robbie was a supportive, never interfering, father.

We did attend this year's *Institut* conference in Helsinki, where as usual we mingled with old friends and met new. Some noted at the time were Tunkin (Russian), Briggs, McDougal, Schachter, Stevenson (American), Abi-Saab (Egyptian), Wolf (Alsace), Mosler (German), Lachs (Polish) and the Finnish Broms. Robbie had embarked on this visit in a mood of prejudice: Scandinavian countries, he was convinced, were boring. But the performance by a Finnish children's string orchestra at the opening ceremony alerted him to a culture that was far from boring. And as we walked about the city and took a boat trip he grew more interested. As we learnt a little of the country's history, we could appreciate the grandiose architecture that linked it to St Petersburg, while feeling more naturally drawn to the open market with its stalls of flowers, berries, vegetables, herbs, fungi and wooden implements. It was from a stall heaped with wares from Lapland that he bought a pale, soft-furred reindeer skin to drape over our sofa at home. On the all-day excursion, after a long drive northwards in relentless rain, we looked around Hameenlinna castle, an art museum and glass factory, but also – sheer delight – a small old church full of wall-paintings of 1530 showing little sign of their age.

Once all the closing formalities were done, there followed our real treat. A former pupil of Robbie's, Ruth Donner (née Goldstein), was a lecturer at the University of Helsinki, where her husband Kim was Professor of Geology.[345] They took us to their country home, some 60 miles northwards, near Hyvinkaa. There we spent a blissful five days in their old, spreading, red timber house in the woods. The building had in former times been a school, so its rooms were wonderfully spacious. Those days were passed wandering in the forest with their daughter Julia in search of fungi and berries, or taking our own quiet walks amidst the trees. We read several books and ate delicious meals prepared by Ruth and her two girls; and we learnt more about the countryside around – Kim pointing out the large bats hanging from the edge of the roof along the house-front, and calling us out to hear strange cries as a mass of Siberian cranes descended to a small lake, from where they took off next morning on their migration southwards.

Robbie, wearing a big sweater lent by Kim rather than his habitual jacket, relished this tranquil interlude. For us both it was an immense privilege; and for Ruth it meant closer contact with her revered professor, a contact maintained by correspondence over later years.

———

There was no pause in our tangle of commitments. Robbie's at The Hague were important and demanding; those at home often fun. It happened that the current Lord Mayor of London was a Jesuan, Alan Traill, and so the annual Jesus College Old Boys Dinner was held in the Mansion House, with all its customary pomp and ceremony.

Jesus College itself was growing more grandiose in style. Now a new custom was established: Fellows' wives were invited to a 'President's Evening'

---

[345] Professor Joakim Donner, Professor of Geology & Paleontology, had spent some years in Cambridge doing research on the Quaternary period.

at the beginning of each term, when they might actually dine in hall before proceeding upstairs for a talk given by one of the Fellows. The very first of these occasions was simply a gathering for postprandial dessert. Since Robbie was abroad, I missed the dinner and arrived in Upper Hall just for the dessert, to find only the President's wife and one other there waiting for the well-fed to join us. John Fairhurst, the Manciple, had been asked to set out the dessert 'prettily', and so had arranged a resplendent long table in the centre, looking rather like the catafalque for the funeral of the Duke of Wellington in the crypt of St Paul's. It had crimson frills around, and ornate dishes arranged with heaps of exotic fruit or rich chocolates or nuts, and all surmounted with the famous Death[346] Silver, decked with extravagant flowers. We peeped under the frills to find how it was contrived, and found it was constructed of beer crates. One hardly dared to eat anything.

Robbie was back from The Hague, where besides his work at the court he had lectured to about 90 visiting Canadians, in time for his birthday and also for the college's memorial service for Gardner-Smith[347] on the same day: a tribute to one who had matriculated at Jesus in 1906, been Dean, Steward and President, and loved by generations of college men.

We drove up to Eskdale, but this time Robbie had a task to perform *en route*. His secretary Angie Norbury (née Brown) was marrying again, and had asked him to pronounce grace before the wedding breakfast. This he did – wondering what the assembled relatives and guests up in Bramhope, near Leeds, made of the long Latin Jesus College grace. Still, it was a thoroughly cheerful occasion, with lavish Yorkshire hospitality continuing late into the evening at the family home with a generous supper and disco music. Our brief stay at Arment House was a contrast, though Wasdale provided 'beautiful shifting lights, mostly sombre, with snow-showers sweeping across Gable and Scafell'.

Back at home, there was not only Sami Shubber wanting to consult Robbie about the regulations for marketing breast milk substitutes; an afternoon was spent closetted with Alan Redfern and Martin Hunter, discussing their

---

[346] Mr D'eath (as he liked to spell his name) had bequeathed to the college his set of fabulously over-ornamented silverware in gratitude for the personal intervention of H.A. ('Black') Morgan, Senior Tutor and later Master of Jesus, when his house and family were threatened in the 'Death Riot' of 1875, after he, as Mayor, had just opened the new Corn Exchange building.

[347] The Jesus College *Annual Report* for 1985 has an obituary of this remarkable Jesuan, well worth reading (available as 'The Rev. P. Gardner-Smith' on the internet).

forthcoming book on *International Arbitration*.[348] And that term he gave members of The Club a lively talk about the ICJ and the rôle of Judge. After three nights in Geneva, helping Sami once more, and then eleven days in The Hague, he joined the whole family for Christmas at home.

It was at one seasonal party that year that Robbie met yet another Idle man of distinction. Our hostess was the painter Joan Day, who lived at Chapel House – a house consisting of two old dwellings, one with a pigeon-loft, linked together with Grantchester's former Baptist Chapel, now her studio. Among her guests was Jim Holt (later Sir James Holt), Professor of medieval History and Master of Fitzwilliam. As soon as they were introduced, he and Robbie were at it hammer and tongs: "*Woodbine Terrace… Thackley Thick'Eads… Idle Wesleyans… cricket…*" I left them to it, and after about an hour Joan Day prised them apart. Robbie had certainly been excited by the link with his beloved Idle.

Another party stirred memories of the time when the now-retired Professor of Music, our host Robin Orr, had been working in military intelligence with Robbie. We had recently been to a performance of a short opera by him, played in tandem with one by Ethel Smyth.

---

[348] *Redfern & Hunter on International Arbitration*, still in print, is regarded as an essential authority on the subject.

A Spreading Reputation

1986-87

The second Onoh Lecture at Hull University was delivered by Robbie himself. He spoke on *International Courts and International Politics*,[349] and I wrote to Joey that it had gone well, 'though he kept leaving it behind absent-mindedly, so it was a relief to get it and him delivered at the right place and time'. His subject was one with which I think he became increasingly concerned during his first years of experience at the ICJ. It was a topic on which he found the guidance provided by... 'the Kelsen and Lauterpacht school of thought', while correct, was incomplete since it ruled that judgment should be exclusively on the basis of legal points. In discussing awareness of the political aspects of a situation, he quoted the more subtle approach of Lauterpacht's successor at the Court, Sir Gerald Fitzmaurice:

'... justice is very seldom achieved by directly aiming at it: rather it is a by-product of the application of legal rules and principles, a consequence of the general order, certainty and stability introduced into human and international relationships through the regular and systematic application of known legal rules and principles, even if these rules and principles are not always perfect and do not always achieve ideal results in every case.'

After the lecture we met the father of the late Josephine Onoh, an impressive figure in his robes as tribal chief.

Once home, Robbie was off to The Hague for its new session. I joined him there in April for several events, one being a dinner given by the President of the Supreme Court Charles Moons who, with his wife, became one of our warmest Dutch friends. Another was the Telders Moot, to which this year Philippe Sands[350] had brought an English team to compete for the first

---

[349] See p.466 of *Collected Writings*.

[350] Philippe Sands had studied under Robbie as a student at Corpus Christi College, Cambridge. He is currently Professor of International Law at University College, London.

time. Our Sunday was spent in some typically pleasant diversions: a morning strolling around the semi-wild park, Zorgvliet,[351] now rich with birdsong and spring flowers; a champagne brunch at the Hotel des Indes with tinkling pop music or Bach in the background; and the afternoon spent at a 'cello recital in the *Diligentia*, a small concert hall on the Lange Voorhout.

The Court's regular business was interrupted on the Tuesday for a celebration of its 40th Anniversary in a gracious speech from HM Queen Beatrix – someone with a genuine interest in the ICJ, having herself studied Law at the University of Leiden. (It was, too, the occasion when the multi-talented Hugh Thirlway conducted an *ad hoc* orchestra performing one of his own compositions.) The next day was *Koninginnedag*, the Queen's official birthday,[352] when the quiet streets were decorated with festive orange banners and Dutch flags.

Robbie shuttled to and fro. He was with me in Sussex for the funeral of my revered uncle, but had to be back at the Court for long, gruelling meetings, regretfully cancelling a planned visit to Siena to lecture. But in The Hague he enjoyed a dinner given by the British Ambassador for Sir Geoffrey Howe (Foreign Secretary at the time), a man he liked and respected.

His return to Cambridge on 12th June was just in time to attend that evening a more-than-usually significant event at Cranmer Road: the formal opening of the Lauterpacht Research Centre for International Law by the University Chancellor, HRH Prince Philip. There followed one day amid a final flurry – marquee, flowers, catering deliveries – of wedding-preparations.

On the 14th Pippa and Michael were married in Grantchester Church, and all went well. The sun shone, the church looked lovely, we had an excellent organist, Geraint Bowen[353] of Jesus College … and both bride and groom were serene. Robbie, excited and happy, enjoyed the reception in our garden – a throng of oddly-assorted people, relatives and friends, formal and informal, morning suits and cotton dresses, some on chairs and others relaxing on the grass surrounded by a froth of cow parsley … It was Sami Shubber who proposed the toast to bride and groom – an Arab, as he said, at home in our 'tent' whose religion (Shia Muslim), like our own, included the commandment

---

351   It was a 5-hectare (12 acre) section of Zorgvliet's parkland that had provided the site for the Peace Palace, but this secluded place beside the road to Scheveningen remains.

352   It is the custom for the Queen (and now the King) to celebrate this day each year by visiting a different part of the Kingdom, sometimes a quite obscure village. Everywhere the display of *orange* banners, etc. honours the House of Orange.

353   Geraint Bowen is now organist and director of music at Hereford Cathedral.

'Love thy neighbour', fulfilled quite literally by these newly-weds. After their departure, the bell-ringers at Trumpington Church gave a vigorous quarter-peal as a special tribute to Pippa.

Joey's course at Corsham was completed that summer, and she began to practice her craft as a potter, first in the Lake District and then in Somerset. And Dick's increasing earnings allowed him to travel with friends more widely than before.

At Jesus College the retirement of Sir Alan Cottrell as Master was succeeded by the appointment of Colin Renfrew[354]. Robbie's attachment to his three colleges and the Law Faculty remained active, and he fitted in frequent social events and meetings still.

But Arment House, Robbie's dream of a retirement retreat, was still tantalisingly out of reach for us most of the time, although our friends and the childrens' were happy to stay there for short holidays – for our own three children, indeed, it was the setting for much of their courtship. During 1986 Robbie and I had three spells there – at Easter, a week early in August, and five days in September, all times of deep refreshment for him, mending walls or scything bracken amidst a great silence broken by only wind, falling water, bleating of sheep or mewing of buzzards.

It was just before one of these trips northwards that we were both in London and took the opportunity to visit the Design Centre where, Robbie had read, some pianos were on show, made by an enterprising pair of English craftsmen, *Laurence & Nash*. This appealed to him particularly because their workshop was in a former woollen mill at Otley in Wharfedale. Thus it was that on our way northwards we stopped there and climbed the stone steps up to the mill's top floor to find the partners at work – Alastair Laurence adjusting the mechanism, while his colleague Nash was shaping the woodwork of a grand piano. Finding that the instrument's bright green iron frame was actually cast in Shipley, close to Idle, enhanced its attraction; and when Laurence showed us a framed photograph of four generations of his family who had all, like himself, trained and perfected their skills with Broadwood, the instrument's quality[355]

---

[354] Colin Renfrew, Disney Professor of Archaeology, came from St John's College. In 1991 he was made Baron Renfrew of Kaimsthorn.

[355] Laurence & Nash ceased to work as a team a few years later. The quality of these instruments had, however, persuaded the BBC to commission several for their studios, and in 2008 Dr Alastair Laurence acquired Broadwood & Sons. He and his son are experts in restoration and conservation.

was guaranteed. So Robbie commissioned an upright piano, persuading himself that it would allow us a little more space in our sitting room at home, while Dick could accommodate the old 'baby grand' in his own house.

That year's ILA conference was in Heidelberg. Robbie first needed to deal with correspondence in his office at the Peace Palace before completing the journey by train – his preference so that I might enjoy the *Rheingold Express*, then in its final year. It was indeed a thrill to ride along the Rhine valley, with its steep vineyards, hilltop castles and the Lorelei. Heidelberg itself was of course full of interest, especially a great commemorative exhibition of the treasures of its *Bibliotheca Palatina*. We dined at the home of Karl Doehring, and walked the Philosopher's Way; and took a memorable expedition to Schloss Schwetzingen, with its formal gardens and rococo theatre, culminating in a banquet.

Dinners and receptions were often dutiful; but in October we were in London for what I noted as a 'stupendous evening': a dinner given by the French Ambassador in honour of their current Minister for Culture, Jack Lang.[356] Lang, a brilliant character, being both a lawyer and immersed in the arts, had prompted his host to invite guests from a wide spectrum. Thus it was that before the meal we met a flamboyant figure, large, dark– eyebrowed, indulging in glass after glass of pink champagne – Robert Maxwell of the publishing empire; a film distributor, Kenneth Rive, who could not believe how seldom we went to a cinema; and several lawyers. And at our circular table for dinner were Peter Maxwell Davies, Colin Thubron, Sir David Lean ... a friendly company and a dazzling one.

Another of Robbie's identities was, of course, as an honorary Bencher of Lincoln's Inn, and we were glad to attend Matins one Sunday in the Inn's old chapel where John Donne had once preached, followed by a lecture and then lunch with other senior members.

A few days later Robbie was the guest of Pippa's father-in-law, Charles Goodhart, at a college feast at Caius. The Goodharts had become close friends with whom we often shared meals. Charles had served as Senior Tutor of Caius and as Senior Proctor of the University. Although an occasionally cantankerous character, he was an outstanding teacher of zoology, with many unexpected areas of knowledge as well, (some gathered during his time as a prisoner-of-

---

356 Robbie's quasi-diplomatic status led to various interesting invitations, even in England.

war, when he had taught himself Russian). Robbie admired him and very much enjoyed their wide-ranging conversations together.

The Lauterpacht Centre was developing into an important addition to the University. It was there that we met Abba Eban, a brilliant and powerful figure in the creation of the State of Israel, and other significant figures. Eli Lauterpacht, in founding the Research Centre in memory of his father, could draw upon his many connections in the legal and diplomatic world to provide stimulating lectures and contacts. Robbie himself would take part in the Centre's Friday lunch meetings to meet young researchers and give an occasional talk.

By the end of the year our three children were all moving forward to new stages: Dick, now formally engaged to Jillian Nethaway, moved up to York for a more responsible position with Rowntree Mackintosh. Pippa and Michael were settled in Leicester, but were also about to launch on a change of direction as Michael left the work he had been doing and took a long break – one that enabled him to take Pippa to the wilds of Kenya on a five-week trek, as well as a spell at Arment House, before joining a firm of architects offering a more interesting variety of work. Joey, in Somerset with Andrew Eddleston ('Egg'), both working potters, contrived a home together in a former schoolroom.

In the midst of it all, I wrote that Robbie 'was forging ahead with *Oppenheim* (which is going well and nears completion)'. I was over-optimistic: in fact, completion would take several more years, and there were always substantial articles – five published in 1987 – and lectures to be composed as well.

In May he returned from a long spell of work in The Hague to attend the marriage of the Donners' daughter Julia to Peter Lindqvist, a Norwegian mathematician.[357] They were married in the Cambridge Registrar's Office, a very simple ceremony and our first experience of a civic wedding. A small reception afterwards in the Thirkell Room at Clare (Kim Donner's college) followed and the bride's mother, Ruth, came to lunch with us two days later, to collect the many photos I had taken of the occasion. She talked earnestly with Robbie about international law, and revealed that notices were already posted in the University of Helsinki announcing his lectures there in August – another commitment to be fitted in.

---

[357] Professor Peter Lindqvist of the University of Trondheim.

Every few years the Dutch Foreign Ministry would arrange an excursion for members of the Court. This time we were taken by boat to Loevestein Castle, an ancient fortress at the junction of the rivers Maas and Waal, now preserved as a museum of medieval life. The place had a special significance for our group, since it was here that Hugo Grotius, 'the father of international law', had been imprisoned as a political dissident in the early 17th century. We passed over a wooden bridge into a great tower-chamber, where the story of Grotius' principled conflict with the Stadtholder, Prince Maurice of Nassau, and escape from the castle in a book-chest, was recounted. A photograph of the judges[358] shows them standing in front of a bronze plaque commemorating Grotius' incarceration there.

Later excursions were to introduce us to other places of particular significance. One that we regretted missing – genuinely busy, but not until later fully appreciating its importance – was a day spent examining the 'waterworks'. On that trip we would have learnt about engineering marvels crucial to the country's very existence – the 'Delta works' system of flood control, and the draining of the Zuidersee to create a vast new area of farmland.

Dick and Jill were married on 20th June in Grantchester Church, and once again we were largely responsible for arrangements, since Jill's mother lived in Galway in the far west of Ireland, and the couple themselves were now up in North Yorkshire. Once again our garden made a good setting. Jo Nethaway brought with her on the 'plane from Ireland a cake modelled on their church there; relatives and friends gathered from far and wide; and the newly-weds took off for a honeymoon in Tuscany.

On 9th July we were back in Hull, this time for Robbie to receive an Honorary LL.D. The degree-giving ceremony, presided over by Lord Wilberforce as University Chancellor, combined the award of general degrees with those for the honorary graduands, each praised in the customary oration. For Robbie it was Professor Paul Fairest who spoke. Fairest, a Yorkshireman, had while at Cambridge taken a PhD in International Law (though was not now teaching that speciality) and so had attended Robbie's lectures and seminars. His encomium was generous, and I liked his description of Robbie

---

[358]   The photograph captioned 'Members of the ICJ assembled in Loevestein Castle to pay homage to Hugo Grotius in May 1987' appears on p.13 of the great book by Arthur Eyffinger, *The International Court of Justice 1946-1996*. Those present were (left to right) Ago, Tarassov, Jennings, Schwebel, Nagendra Singh, Ni and Sette Camara.

as 'Mr Valiant-for-Truth', a reference to *Pilgrim's Progress* especially apt for a nonconformist.

Dinner afterwards was, of course, generous too, and very enjoyable. I sat next to a newly-honoured man of the theatre, Sir Anthony Quayle – very good company. On my other side was a distinguished engineer, P.G. Davey, who in a speech of thanks remarked that this had been the first academic honour that he had received in person, since he had not dared to appear at the Senate House at Cambridge ... and later disclosed to me just why this had been so. He had been a ring-leader in the unforgettable May Week prank of 1958, when Cambridge had woken to find an Austin Seven van perched on the roof of the Senate House. How had it been done? Its removal had caused a great deal of trouble; and it was a treat to hear just how he, with a group of fellow-engineers, had carried off this coup.[359]

As always, Arment House needed attention. On this summer's visit we had the local builders, Tom and John Tyson, there to restore the roof of the barn across the yard from the house. The exposed roof could have been 200 years or more in age, with its riven timbers and wooden fixing-pegs, thought Tommy. My photographs of the brothers at work show them shaping and punching holes in each individual massive slate before carrying a load of them under one arm up a long ladder and along the sloping roof: no hard hats, no scaffolding, no concern about health and safety.

It was on this visit that I wanted to prove to Robbie that the small white speck just visible in a picture-postcard view of Eskdale taken from the Roman fort on Hardknott really *was* Arment House. We drove up to that astonishing place (*Mediobogdum*, built AD 120-138, 'one of the loneliest outposts of the Roman Empire') with its wide and wild views; and there, sure enough, Arment House could be seen in the distance, with a glimpse of the sea far beyond. Before our journey home there were a few walks and chats with old friends, including the aged Rosalind. And this time, after calling *en route* on one of Robbie's last remaining cousins at Bingley, we were able to spend a night at Leicester with Pippa and Michael.

---

[359] His Caius College rooms were on the top floor, across the passage from the Senate House. By carefully contrived stages the van, minus its engine, had been transferred and reassembled on the roof.

On the 12th August we flew to Helsinki. A description of that visit, compressed onto a picture-postcard to Pippa, told how –

'Daddy gave his 3 lectures the day after arriving at midnight and was brilliant; and we then dined with the British Ambassador too. After that he gave a seminar, then we were brought up here to Ahdenkallia, the Donners' lovely country home. Here we revel once more in food & books & talk & wanders which are all very much to our taste. Lucky us! … The weather turned fine yesterday, so Daddy & I had a blissful walk [to the 'crane swamp' and back through woods and fields, sheer delight] … and then in the evening a curiously tedious supper-party to go to …' [And it was as well that I did not name our hosts at that final party.]

There followed two months spent at Grantchester, though not in idleness. Robbie contributed an article for the *Festschrift* in honour of Roberto Ago as well as other pieces; there was a lecture to write for his forthcoming visit to the University of the Saarland; correspondence with colleagues and former pupils; and, whenever possible, the rather wearisome *Oppenheim*.

Proceedings at The Hague were all the time taking their course. On the morning after his 74th birthday we had to be up at 4.45 am for him to be present at a reception for the President of El Salvador[360], followed next day by another for the Vice-President of Peru.

Back in Cambridge we were at one of those college occasions that particularly delighted him. I described it for Pippa –

'… Then dinner at Trinity. The college was honouring Mollie Butler,[361] whom they have just made an honorary member of High Table. She has just had her 80th birthday, but looks about 65 and is in very good form (and has of course just had her first book published, "August & Rab"). 'Dining and then

---

[360]   One of the cases before the Court at that time was a frontier dispute between Honduras and El Salvador.

[361]   Mollie was the wife of the current Master, Lord Butler – 'Rab'. Both she and Rab had previously been married to members of the Courtauld family, and when widowed came together in a formidable partnership, 'an emotional Indian summer for both of them' as described in her *Times* obituary. While in Cambridge she became a member of the Learned Ladies. She lived to be 101.

"combining" at Trinity is fun. Yummy food, naturally. But the conversation, half intellectual, half schoolboy teasing, is *really* fun.

'Around me were conversations about excavations at Babylon [Professor Oates] and what it is like to stay in Baghdad at present – with other chat about living in Iran, Syria and Turkey; increasingly wild but erudite pronouncements about Family Life in France, Italy & England by Tony Weir. He is a brilliant lawyer who has become over the years almost unrecognisably gross: a bachelor who indulges his greed and his cattiness with no restraint. As the four decanters circulate around the table in the combination room he fills all three of the glasses before him and quaffs them in between mouthfuls of grapes and asks questions in his rasping voice such as, "Do you ever silently scream?" His elderly little neighbour, pretty tight herself, wriggles in affirmation; next to her on the other side is a formidable mathematician … who disdains to wear a tie [probably Professor Ian Cassells]. I have never seen him look so happy – he is scribbling on the back of an envelope, for the delectation of the handsome but heavy-browed woman beside him, mathematical problems and their solutions. "Ah *yes!*" she enthuses. Beside me is Theo Redpath, the wine merchant and father of Ophelia, whose picture now hangs in our Houtweg flat. Theo is really a classicist who turned to teaching English. His conversation ranges widely. Then he is challenged by Tony Weir to write a poem. No, it need not be a long one since the evening is nearly over. A sonnet? No, we say, a haiku. Theo rummages for paper, and eventually writes his brilliant haiku on a paper napkin. I wish I could quite remember it – it starts "I love your blue dress" – and is so successful that he stuffs the napkin into his pocket to take home for his wife. At the end of the table is Andrew Huxley, flanked by Mollie Butler and Marni Hodgkin[362], all talking animatedly; on Mollie's other side is Patrick Duff[363]. He is now nearly blind, has no teeth, and is a rumpled heap of gown and not-quite-buttoned shirt and straggly white hair. The waiters put food before him ready chopped-up and put implements into his hands. They help heave him to his feet and set him pointing in the right direction with his walking-frame … "right a bit now, sir". But he is alert and interested in everything. A mere 86 or so; Tresillian Nicholas moves about and chats as always, now 99 …

'And so on. A remarkable place, Trinity.'

---

[362] Marni Hodgkin (another Learned Lady) was the wife of Sir Alan Hodgkin, later Master of Trinity, who shared a Nobel prize with Andrew Huxley.

[363] Patrick Duff was Regius Professor of Civil Law.

Soon we were at a rather more formal dinner in London – Ladies' Night at Lincoln's Inn. After two courses half of the company moved, so that we sat between fresh neighbours. I found myself with an agreeable Bencher on my right and the Treasurer[364] on my left, someone rather somnolent and not eager to talk. At last he roused himself to his duty, and asked 'Where do you live?' 'In a village called Grantchester, near Cambridge.' Pause. 'Archer lives there,' he said. 'Yes', I replied, 'I know him slightly' – after which I received no more attention. I peered at his place-card. He was Mr Justice Caulfield, the judge who had presided over Jeffrey Archer's notorious libel case and did not wish to be reminded of it.

Early in November we travelled together to Saarbrücken, Robbie having been invited by Professor Georg Ress to deliver a lecture to the European Institute at the University of the Saarland. On the way we called at The Hague for him to attend a Rules Committee consultation, and for his new secretary, Doreen Bloemendal, to produce an improved typescript of the lecture. Doreen, like Angie, was English, but was married to a Dutchman and mother of three sons – a wonderfully capable person, for whom Robbie developed a warm trust.

Ress had proposed a title for this lecture – *The Place of Jurisdictional Immunity of States in International and Municipal Law* – which at first Robbie felt unqualified to address. Yet he accepted the challenge, and I reported to Joey:

'Friday 6th was Daddy's lecture. I went to hear it. There was a full and attentive audience, and quite a lot of discussion afterwards. Characteristically, Daddy had agreed to speak on a subject which is not his own usual speciality, giving "provocative" views as an "amateur" – but very thoroughly prepared and of great value as a basis for discussion. Prof. Ress and colleagues seemed a little startled; but when they play through their tape-recording and read the article which will follow, they will see just what he was driving at.

'So: some huge platefuls of good food and a glass of beer in the dons' refectory, then we turned to the Resses' programme for the rest of the day. The country around the University was steep woods in their autumn glory, with deer wandering about. It would have been lovely just to walk there for a while …

---

[364] The office of Treasurer, held for one year, is equivalent to Master of the Society.

371

'But no. Off we went in his big Audi, for the promised drive through Lorraine. Not far beyond the French frontier, though, it grew misty – mistier – quite dense fog. On we went with nothing to see on either side. We stopped at Metz, a smallish old town, with grand classical buildings laid out amidst medieval ones. The cathedral is one of the loftiest gothic buildings … impressive, even in the gloom of a foggy afternoon. A small 16th-century organ high above us (built to resemble a "swallow's nest", according to the guide) played melancholy-plangent music as we gazed at the many windows…'

We journeyed on through ever-denser mist, to Nancy. And what made that excursion forever memorable was our arrival. Georg had set a CD playing; and thus it was that our entry into *Place Stanislas,* a gleaming vision through dense fog of spotlit golden gateways and statuary, was accompanied by a brass fanfare from Handel's *Music for the Royal Fireworks.* Our host was insistent in his hospitality and took us to a very fine restaurant where Robbie was pressed to eat, late in the evening, *paté de foie gras* and other rich food. Ress himself, a big man, ate with relish and drank copiously; but it meant that our return journey through barely-penetrable gloom became quite frightening until he, realising that he was nearly falling asleep, let his wife Ulli bring us safely home. They were marvellously kind, and became warm friends.

Back to The Hague for the opening session of the *El Salvador/Honduras* frontier dispute, which kept Robbie, as a member of the Chamber dealing with this case, fully occupied for some weeks, and would provide work for several years.

Still Busy

1988-89

Our life was irregular, but Robbie had learnt to take its irregularity in his stride, finding the sheer variety of demands upon his intellect and stamina quite stimulating.

It was in January 1988 that he first met an Australian protégé of O'Connell and Brownlie, James Crawford[365], in Cambridge to deliver that year's Lauterpacht Lecture. But besides new introductions, it was to be a year of funerals and memorial services for old friends and colleagues. There were Jack Hamson (Professor of Comparative Law) of Trinity; Sandy Cockerell (bookbinder) of Grantchester; Raymond Williams (socialist English don) of Jesus; Miss Suckling (one-time secretary working for the Law Faculty, Mayor of Cambridge 1983-84) and Alan Barker (Headmaster of the Leys School, one-time Research Fellow at Jesus). Advancing age inevitably brought more and more losses.

His age brought more requests, too, for articles for *Festschrifts*, the tributes to respected colleagues marking major anniversaries – a continental tradition that Robbie found taxing. It meant selecting an original topic and devoting his customary care to its composition... only for it to become virtually lost among many such volumes of mixed writings. During the years 1987-89 he contributed articles to *Festschrifts* for Roberto Ago, Richard Wilberforce, Gerardus Wiarda, Karl Doehring and Shabtai Rosenne.

The children's lives were moving on. Dick's job with Rowntree's came to an end with the firm's takeover by Nestlé, so in due course he joined a large solicitors' firm in Leeds. Joey and Andrew/Egg had moved into a small house in a village south of Bath, Peasedown St John[366]. And the last months of 1988 would also bring the birth of our first two grandchildren.

---

[365] This is likely to have been Robbie's first actual meeting with James, who was already an Associate of the *Institut de Droit International* and would later succeed Derek Bowett as Whewell Professor. After that he was, in 2015, to join the ICJ as Australian judge.

[366] An undistinguished village, it was largely composed of terraces of miners' cottages built during a short period between the wars. Coal mining had ceased, and these cottages provided relatively inexpensive accommodation in an otherwise prosperous area.

———

I described for Pippa the momentous arrival, early in February, of –

> '…the most ginormous pantechnicon with THE PIANO. It is in the diningroom now, looking well and sounding far too good for the likes of us. But the best thing, as far as Daddy was concerned, was the gang of three lovely blokes from Blubberhouses. They were splendid, and looked well in their dark maroon aprons. They stayed for coffee and cake, and it was "better than a tonic", said Daddy.
>
> 'When the house is empty but for me, I'll have a little tinkle. Same for Daddy.'

And I ended with tiny sketches of the two 'secret pianists' glancing furtively over their shoulders. (We were neither of us good enough to play publicly.)

———

The new session of the International Court that year was launched with several events. The British Lord Chancellor, Lord Mackay of Clashfern, came to perform the unveiling of a circular cloisonné plaque of the United Nations emblem, a gift to the Peace Palace from the current President of the Court, Nagendra Singh. And next day, members of the Court and wives were received at the Nordeinde Palace for another banquet given by the Queen, this time in the company of Dutch professors of international law as well as the Royal Household.

While still in The Hague we went to lunch with the Fitzmaurices. Maurice Fitzmaurice, elder son of the late Sir Gerald, was working in The Hague, and his wife Malgosia[367] was teaching in the University of Amsterdam. A convivial pair, their informal lunch-parties always included some lively young international lawyers whom Robbie was delighted to meet; and he would admire and encourage Malgosia's own career.

At the Court in April Robbie was involved in the delivery of an Opinion on what I noted as 'the P.L.O. matter.'[368] Then we were off to Geneva, where

---

[367] Malgosia is now Professor of International Law at Queen Mary's College, University of London.

[368] The US Secretary of State had applied to the UN for permission to eject representatives of the PLO that he considered to be a threat to American security. This was referred to the ICJ for an Advisory Opinion as to its compliance with a Section of a UN Agreement of 1947. The matter was dealt with by the Court in just over one month.

he found unexpectedly that he must introduce the Guggenheim Colloquium. Once home, he gave a talk at Oxford. In May we heard that year's Rede Lecture in the Senate House, given by Roy Jenkins,[369] on 'An Oxford view of Cambridge', and met the lecturer at dinner afterwards at Corpus Christi College, where the Master, Michael McCrum, was the current Vice-Chancellor. It was an easy occasion: Jenkins was good company, as were Baroness (Mary) Warnock, Harry Hinsley, Christopher Andrew,[370] Haroon Ahmed, Colin Renfrew and others.

Our next crossing to The Hague was *en route* to Cologne for the Institute of Air & Space Law Colloquium, addressing *Environmental Aspects in Outer Space*. I listened, with Robbie, to two speakers – scientists – outlining the problems of the pollution of outer space, and the discussion afterwards. In the evening we were taken to the European Centre for Space Research, for 'confusingly short and varied glimpses of scientific work in progress' (including a crawl into a space capsule), followed by a crowded reception. Next morning there were three speakers on Space Law, and we joined Günther Jaenicke for lunch. Then (as I recorded in my small diary) there was 'a session on "customary law" with R. making provocative observations', followed by Marcia Williams (from Argentina) and other speakers. Robbie's address[371] is included in his *Collected Writings*. Having earlier in his career been considered an authority on Air Law, he was still keen to learn; and he felt that a colloquium such as this, with international lawyers listening to and exchanging views with scientists actively engaged in work of international significance was of the utmost value and importance. An article written some eight years later in tribute to Skubiszewski, *International Lawyers and the Progressive Development of International Law*[372], would give expression to his growing impatience with the *Institut*:

'...which, in its Reports and Resolutions, seems not to have seen any need to involve, officially at least, any others than international lawyers in [their] work.

'... international lawyers can at least speak to, and try to involve in their work, students of international relations, diplomatic historians, geographers

---

[369] Lord Jenkins of Hillhead had now retired from his distinguished career as a politician, and had become Chancellor (in succession to Harold Macmillan) of Oxford University.

[370] Both Harry Hinsley and Christopher Andrew were authorities on secret intelligence work.

[371] *Customary Law and General Principles of Law as Sources of Space Law*, pp.1187-91.

[372] See *Collected Writings* p.783.

and geologists, cartographers and hydrographers… International lawyers have many organizations where they discuss with each other; but there is relatively little in the way of organizations or even conferences where international lawyers can speak to experts in other disciplines about international legal problems. Here… some of the more venerable associations of international lawyers have something to learn from the younger International Institute of Space Law.'

Later that year I joined Robbie in a reciprocal visit. Members of the European Court having already visited the International Court, the ICJ were invited to see how they did things in Luxembourg. It was a smallish group who accepted their invitation: the current President (Ruda), Lachs, Elias and his wife, Schwebel and ourselves, accompanied by Mr Wittewijn and Mrs El Erian (officials of the Carnegie Foundation).

The European Court is housed in a building of striking architecture among glass-box-neighbours, and inside we found…

'…a great contrast to the Peace Palace: all modern, with a few works of art (Rodin sculpture, a Dutch tall geometric thing in brash colours, good German abstract, a Henry Moore, tapestries from Belgium and France, notably a stunning Lurçat …).

'We heard part of a case – a matter of "dumping" freezers and refrigerators manufactured in E. Germany, Jugoslavia and the USSR at prices with which EEC firms could not compete. Counsel, speaking eloquently in measured English, was a Belgian. The Chamber, under the presidency of an Italian judge aged 82, was of 4 or 5; on the far left the Advocate-General (Sir Gordon Slynn), on the right the Assistant Registrar, a youngish woman – all in crimson silk gowns.'

Another contrast to the ICJ was the provision of a great rank of cubicles for translators – not just English and French but all the languages of the EEC, including Irish.

Judge Oda joined the group on the second day, when more comparisons between the two courts could be discussed (the women, meanwhile, with their own programme). Then as evening drew on we were all driven some miles to the Golf Club, close to the airport. There, as we chatted over drinks, we were amused to see Oda, having arrived early, just completing a round of solo golf before joining everyone for dinner. He, a very keen golfer, liked to mention that he had played against Prince Claus a few times.

Robbie's next spell at home included taking part in a programme, *International Assignment*, on Radio 4. But this was not something he felt comfortable with, fearing that he might be caught saying something foolish and irretrievable under such conditions. Philippe Sands, Christopher Greenwood and others seemed happier to perform.

Once he was back on his own in our Houtweg flat we as usual kept in touch with regular evening telephone chat. On 9th June I was surprised to have a second call. 'I thought you might like to know,' he said, 'that I now have my arm in a sling.' Shock, horror! I had provided a store of easy meals for his suppers, and he had tried to open one in a can with a ring-pull and had gashed an artery in his left hand. It must have been a bad moment, since our flat was so totally soundproof and secure that one could not easily summon help. But he had torn off lots of kitchen paper, pressed it to his hand, made his way across to the telephone and rung Dr Feenstra, who lived just along the street. And the doctor, at home having his supper, when Robbie managed to walk there, put him straight into his sports car, always parked outside. They were soon at the hospital, where Feenstra gave a special whistle-call ... and his son, a young surgeon, appeared almost immediately. Robbie was stitched and bandaged, and quickly delivered home. Next time I arrived at Houtweg I had to remove from the carpet a track of blood-stains from the kitchen area to the telephone.

―

Before we made our longed-for journey up to Eskdale that July, Robbie announced, 'I've got an unbirthday present for you'; and instead of the usual piece of hi-fi equipment he produced something called a Turkish Scythe. It had been recommended by Bill Wade, but with its long aluminium handle and short blade it looked rather flimsy until we tried it (within minutes of our arrival), and found it so deadly-sharp that we were mowing the grass almost as close as a machine. So between bouts of rain we got a good amount of gardening done. A typical Arment holiday! Especially a delightful walk up to Stony Tarn – which was so elusive that we got thoroughly lost, after Eel Tarn skirting squelchy bits and following little tracks through heather and bracken and over rocks until it at last appeared, and then, clambering down, were dive-bombed by an indignant tern who was guarding a nearby nest.

We spent a night on our homeward journey at Kirkby Lonsdale, and so had time next day to stop a little further on to inspect more thoroughly the church and churchyard of Kirkby Malham, to try again to verify Aunt Liza's tales of family burials there. And this time, just as we were about to give up, we found a large raised slab on which could be read the name *John Brotherton.* One could see that he had died in 1841, aged 96, and that his wife had also lived to a great age. As it happened, the Vicar appeared just as we were leaving, and asked whether we were driving further up the valley to Malham, since there was someone who needed a lift there. We had not intended to go in that direction, but were of course happy to pick her up, and on the way told her of our discovery. We had not been able to decipher all the inscription, and told her that it seemed to read *John Brotherton of High Tren—*. 'Oh, that'll be High Trenhouse, where I live!' she said. We learnt that she was the wife of a farmer whose home was high on the moor above Malham Cove. Subsequent research has confirmed that it was indeed in that remote place that Robbie's ancestors had survived through so many seasons.[373]

In September 1988 there was a celebration of the 75th anniversary of the Carnegie Foundation and the opening of the Peace Palace, the main event being attended by the UN Secretary-General, Perez de Cuellar with his wife, and HM Queen Beatrix and HRH Prince Claus. As a result, a great number of Kurds were staging a demonstration at the gates, and the place was surrounded by tight security. This event – with long speeches in the Great Hall of Justice followed by a reception – included the unveiling of a splendid new gift to the Peace Palace, a large silver model of a galleon under full sail.

Next day, with Judges Lachs and Evensen, we watched de Cuellar receive an honorary degree from the University of Leiden. The ceremony took place in the Grote Kerk – a marvellous building, fine organ playing, a procession of university dons in black gowns and velvet bonnets and long speeches, the best being by Professor Schermers.

The Dutch Foreign Ministry took the ICJ members this year to Haarlem. It was a shame that only five judges had accepted their invitation, for we were received with great kindness at all the places we visited – the Law Court,

---

[373] The days of hardship are over: the farmstead has been developed as a conference centre, and its main barn converted into self-catering comfortable accommodation.

newly refurbished; the Town Hall, with many splendours; the church; and the Frans Hals Museum. I noted that its Grote Kerk was 'light, high, grand; organ breathtaking – short recital to demonstrate its glories.' Seeing that organ[374] alone was for Robbie a great thrill.

---

*[From the beginning of the new academic year, October 1988, Robbie's own small engagement diaries have survived. His entries are mostly cryptic, rarely including description except for our spells at Arment House. Other indications of his sense of importance are the notes of the births of grandchildren; the occasions such as Christmas when he stresses '**All together**' and the jotted details of CDs that he intends to buy. Sketchy as these entries are, they indicate what went on during his periods working alone in The Hague.]*

Robbie's life seemed at times impossibly complicated. There were events in Cambridge that he after all was unable to attend because of the demands of the Court; and conversely, he was not always able to attend every social event in The Hague. Both lives were equally valued.

By now his to-and-fro commuting was largely by *Suckling Airways*. This little firm (Mr & Mrs Suckling almost unaided at first) had just moved to Marshall's Airport at Cambridge, operating at first just one flight a day to Schiphol. As word spread around, though, it was able to fly both morning and evening, enabling business men to hop across the North Sea to Amsterdam and back in a day. Increasingly Robbie found that its services suited him and were far more convenient than the KLM flights from Stansted. The tiny Dornier, piloted by Mr Suckling, carried about 14 passengers. It was unpressurized, rather cramped and noisy, but we could get to Marshall's Airport from Grantchester in about 20 minutes, park free of charge, and check-in just 15 minutes before take-off. The flight was at 9,000 feet, so one was glad to accept an offered boiled sweet to ease the pain in the ears when rising or descending. Its little meals were quite appetising, having been cooked in a nearby homely kitchen; and at the airport Mrs Suckling would greet us charmingly, with the offer of a cup of coffee. At the Schiphol end,

---

[374] The organ of St Bavo Church had, at the time of its building in the 1730s, been the largest in the world. The 10-year-old Mozart had tried its keyboards, and later Handel and Mendlessohn gave performances on it. And Peter Hurford, Robbie's former pupil, would also give recitals here.

the nice VIP girls who looked after us found our arrival in such a small plane at an obscure part of the airfield rather undignified ... but it had made a huge difference to Robbie's life.

Something else increasingly valued appears in his diary each month: '*maan diner*' at the *Haagsche Club*. Introduced at his first arrival by Baron van Lynden, he had quickly made friends, finding that one or two of its members were neighbours in Houtweg. Membership, even temporary, was very special. This club had been founded in 1748 (partly by British military officers stationed in the city and bored with lack of action at the time), and its premises were a large but inconspicuous house on the Lange Voorhout. It was thoroughly old-fashioned: ladies were excluded, its rooms furnished in slightly shabby grandeur, with shelves of leatherbound books recording the great patrician families of the Netherlands from whom its members were largely drawn. On the first Wednesday of each month members gathered for a good dinner (the *maan diner* only vaguely heard of) and on other Wednesdays they might drop in at lunchtime for soup and *genever*, the potent Dutch gin served in tiny glasses. The main entertainment was conversation, which Robbie relished: these distinguished elderly men had many wonderful tales to tell, generally in excellent English. In the late 1990s one notable younger member was introduced, the Crown Prince Willem-Alexander.

It all widened his understanding of Dutch history and traditions, and its links with our own. We found it fascinating to follow the William-&-Mary influences, the maritime trade, the similarities and contrasts in our imperial legacies and the supremacy of Protestant over Roman Catholic churches in its northern provinces.

—

October 1988 had some momentous events. On the 7th our first grandchild, Anna Goodhart, was born; but it was not until the day after Robbie's, own 75th birthday that we were able to go to Leicester to see the baby. It was the beginning of a doting relationship with grandchildren – eventually nine of them, each strongly individual.

Characteristically, his diary entry for 25th November is simply 'Saarbrücken for doctorate.' That short ceremony was introduced with music by Handel. Robbie made a fitting speech, followed by the other graduand, André Tunc[375].

---

375 André Tunc, Professor of Comparative Law at the University of Paris.

A reception afterwards was an opportunity to chat with students; and at dinner we were pleased to find that Hermann Mosler had come for the occasion.

But more importantly (to RYJ) he was immersed in the deliberations, amendments and drafting of successive versions of the Chamber's judgment on a case known by the acronym *ELSI*.[376] The judges, moreover, could not attend to one case exclusively after another, but often several at once. While working on *ELSI* there were other matters before the Court – the *Nicaragua/Honduras* dispute, and a new case between Denmark and Norway, the *Maritime Delimitation in the Area between Greenland and Jan Mayen* concerning 'fishing zones and continental shelf areas not defined between the East Coast of Greenland and the Norwegian island of Jan Mayen.'[377]

In early December we attended the installation of the new High Sheriff for Cambridgeshire in the University Church. He was Michael Marshall,[378] looking splendid in velvet, lace and breeches, embarking on a year's service in this largely ceremonial post, just as his father had some years before. Both were Jesus College men (Michael himself one of Robbie's tutorial pupils) and so the formalities were followed by an enjoyable luncheon in college.

But a succession of other events in Cambridge was interrupted on 11th December by the shocking news of Judge Nagendra Singh's sudden death, and so Robbie returned to The Hague for the 'lying in state' in the Japanese Room. This custom is observed for every judge who dies in office: the coffin, draped in the UN flag and flanked by military guards in ceremonial uniform, lies on display while members of the diplomatic corps file past, signing the book and offering their condolences to the widow – impressive, yet for the widow and her family this long gloomy observance an ordeal.

He stayed working at the Court for final readings, culminating in the delivery of the Judgment on the *Nicaragua v Honduras* case. Then he rejoined home life for Christmas, this year spent with Pippa's young family, together with Paddywack the dog and with Joey and Andrew too. On 27th December we heard of the safe delivery of Dick and Jill's first child, Elizabeth (Lizzie).

---

[376] This was a US/Italy dispute concerning *Elettronica Sicula S.p.A.* (One of the registry staff was inspired to write the libretto of two acts of a pastiche opera concerning the heroine Elsi.)

[377] That description is from the press release from the ICJ. In dispute was 'an area of some 72,000 square kilometres to which both parties laid claim'.

[378] Michael followed his father and grandfather as head of *Marshall's of Cambridge,* a major firm embracing garages throughout the region, Marshall's Airport and innovative aero-engineering. His own knighthood would be conferred in 2010.

And for my birthday that year I found that Robbie had bought tickets for a performance at Covent Garden of Handel's *Semele*, an extravagance we thoroughly enjoyed … though horrified at the price of the sandwich eaten in the interval!

Until the ICJ began its new session in February 1989, Robbie was immersed in home and college life – including a striking first exhibition of pictures by Ophelia Redpath, daughter of our Trinity friend; a memorial service for Percy Bullock, the long-serving Jesus College boatman, when a packed college chapel resounded to the singing of its old rowing men; supper with Peter Laslett[379] and his wife at their house, one of the most notable examples of modern architecture in Cambridge; and another, informally, with the Huxleys in the Master's Lodge at Trinity. Robbie went up to London twice, once to have lunch with Arthur Watts, probably to confer about *Oppenheim*. The second was for a meeting in Lord Goff's room in the House of Lords – likely to have been prompted by the death of Judge Singh, since Goff chaired the PCA British Group's small Nominating Committee responsible for choosing its chosen candidate for election to the new vacancy at the ICJ.

After a short break to admire our new grandchild in Yorkshire, Robbie was again in The Hague, working with the Chamber on the complex *ELSI* case. During that spell he attended a formal dinner at the Italian Embassy in honour of Roberto Ago, and an informal one given by Judge Ni Zhengyu and his daughter. Ni, now aged 82, had felt he needed a companion during his residence in The Hague, and since his wife was reluctant to leave their home in China, his daughter, known when abroad as Nancy (an equivalent sound to her actual name), had been required to leave her young family and her work as an engineer to perform this service. We enjoyed their company.

In March, back in England, Robbie had an intensive teaching engagement at the LSE. His diary lists the events:

---

[379] Peter Laslett, Fellow of Trinity, Reader in Politics & the History of Social Structure, had a wide-ranging career. He had worked at Bletchley Park during the 2nd World War; took part in the establishment of the Open University; and founded the University of the Third Age.

8th Lecture; reception; dinner
9th Ros Higgins & Peter Duffy (Human Rights) – morning
    3 pm Ros H on S.D.
    5 pm Birnie on Whales
10th 11 am my seminar
    3-4 pm Res. Students mtg
    5.35 pm Liverpool St

That tells little about his own contribution. But later, when the LSE awarded him an Honorary Fellowship, the eulogy delivered by Rosalyn Higgins gave a fuller impression of those few days:

'We have reason to believe that Sir Robert has maintained an affection for the School. Some five years ago he accepted our invitation to spend three days with us as a Suntory Fellow. He gave generously of his time and showed patient and apparently genuine interest in the teaching of international law in the School. His visit caused a great excitement among the students. Every seat, and all the passages and steps in the New Theatre were filled for his lecture. He attended all the teaching in international law over those days, and talked with all the doctoral students in international law. His accessibility and attentiveness were greatly appreciated.'

That affection and interest were genuine: Robbie loved to be with bright young people.

———

A happy Easter break at Arment House was spent this time with Pippa, Mick and 5-month-old Annie as company. Robbie's diary entries record our walks and the weather – one day '*sunny & bonny. Saw Harry*[380] *again*' – before the homeward journey, this time with a break at the Devonshire Arms Hotel at Bolton Bridge on the way. This was a luxury, allowing us to wander along to Bolton Priory; and its close association with the Duke of Devonshire evoked the intriguing memory of Robbie's Aunt Liza – another of her tales – hinting

---

[380] Harry Harrington, based at Wha House further up Eskdale, farmed the National Trust land that bordered our own territory. We gave him grazing rights over our small fields. The family always loved keeping in touch with the seasonal work going on.

that there was possibly an illegitimate connection of the Brothertons with that great family. Was not Uncle Artie christened 'Arthur *Cavendish* Brotherton?' And had not some female forebear worked as a servant at Holker Hall? Unresolved mystery.

After his contact with young people at that spring's Telders Moot, he welcomed another bright youngster at home – Jared Blumenfeld, who spent some hours consulting him about his future education and possible career. Jared, the son of our Grantchester neighbours Helaine (sculptor) and Yorick (writer) would choose to study international law and settle in the U.S. where his parents came from[381], and to develop an impressive career.

And so it continued. While at home in June 1989, a visit of the young Goodharts was the occasion for an important discussion, for Michael was to design and oversee the complete rebuilding of Robbie's study. That part of the house, a projection with thin walls and a flat concrete roof, had always been unsatisfactory and was now beginning to leak. A contract was signed for Frank and John Offord, father and son (our neighbours in the Bridle Way) of *Offord & Camp, builders,* to pull down the old study and build a better one. Starting on 29th June, it was to be completed by 11th November. Robbie's desk and other furniture were meanwhile crammed into the dining room and there was general disturbance as lorries brought building materials. One of my photographs of this operation shows the moment when a mini-JCB started digging the deep foundations, with a slightly dismayed Robbie wondering whether the whole project might be a dreadful mistake!

———

Among events when we were next in The Hague was dinner with the Indian ambassador, to be introduced to their new judge, Raghunandran Swarup Pathak.

'It was slightly confusing [I wrote to Joey], because the first Indian lady one met – very beautiful and impressive – was the judge's wife; then a fierce elderly lady; and only later did I realize that the handsome but modest third lady was our actual hostess. The fierce one was her mother-in-law, and as Daddy explained afterwards, even the wife of Her Excellency has to defer to mother-in-law in India, letting her rule the roost. – Anyway, an interesting

---

[381]   Jared Blumenfeld is currently Administrator for EPA's Pacific Southwest Region, a position of great importance in conserving the ecosystem there.

evening, with the sort of food we (but not all the guests) enjoy, and in a large house in 8 acres of wooded garden…'

Crossing on the *St Nicholas* from The Hook to Harwich, we returned for a Jesus College garden party to celebrate the 80th birthday of Laurence Picken; dinner with Sami Shubber, celebrating 20 years of friendship; and an excellent one-man performance in the garden of the Old Vicarage, Grantchester, of *Rupert Brooke*.

Then up to an unusually arid Arment House, where three days later a wet blustery night brought the sight of Birker Force in spate. That stay also brought an unexpected diversion – the arrival of a car in the yard, from which emerged a hefty shaven-headed man. It was rare for strangers to notice the entrance to our lonning, even rarer for them to venture past the gates up its rutted slope. Our visitor introduced himself: he was a Mr Walsh, whose childhood had been spent at Arment House. It had been during the war years, when his father was the tenant farmer. He had happy memories of that time: hard work, a few cows in the byre, poultry in the chicken-loft, sheep gathered and dipped in the enclosure still there, a horse or two, oats and root vegetables grown and harvested by sharing a tractor with a neighbour down the valley. They had been almost self-sufficient and were not troubled by food-rationing. In those days the well had provided just enough water for both family and livestock. But it had been a spartan life, which came to an end when Mrs Whattam-Ward, the owner, had decided to live at Arment House herself and ended the tenancy. He, needing steady work allowing him to marry and raise a family, had become a plumber at Bootle… and we met his wife and children, waiting in the car. Once they had gone, I wrote down as much as I could remember of his tales about those years when Arment House had been a just-viable working farm.

This time our homeward break came near Newark, when we turned off the A1 to call at Ossington House for lunch with Robbie's retired lawyer friend, Daan Goedhuis[382] and his wife. It made an ideal stopping-place on journeys up and down the A1, and for years, even after Daan's death, Pamela Goedhuis would always provide a warm welcome.

---

[382] Professor Daniel Goedhuis (1905-1995) of Leyden University held the world's first Chair of Air & Space Law. As Robbie wrote in his *Times* obituary, he had also been 'a dashing equestrian good enough to be in a winning Dutch Cavalry team in the Olympics … [and] a notably successful professional diplomat…' He was also head of IATA.

In September the *Institut* conference took us to northern Spain, to Santiago de Compostella, where we stayed in the magnificent Hotel de Los Reyes Catolicos. Robbie had meetings to attend of the *Commission des Travaux*, but there was plenty of shared experience. A guided tour around the great cathedral concluded with a demonstration of the *Botafumeiro* – the enormous censer which is set swinging across its transept by eight men pulling ropes, and which, pouring smoke, sweeps past at terrifying speed. For Robbie, that was the greatest thrill of the conference.

I was taken by the ageing Viennese Stephan Verosta by hired car up the north-west coast to Cape Finisterre, revelling in views of rocky inlets and farmland as well as small churches. We were fascinated by the profoundly Celtic character of Galicia, and, together with Barbara Sinclair, who was familiar with both Cornish and Western Scottish customs, learnt more about it in the local museum. Members of the conference were also taken to La Coruna, and on an all-day major outing south-west to Cambados, La Toxa and Pontevedre naval college, where we were carried out to sea on a well-equipped white cruiser once owned by General Franco. Although the heavy set meals and speeches were tiring, we did enjoy the Galician music and dancing – much of it raucous folk music played on bagpipes by students in the cathedral forecourt.

For Robbie the real value of *Institut* conferences lay as always in the opportunities for informal chat with colleagues – the Agos, the Abi-Saabs, the Schwebels, Rosalyn & Terry Higgins, Frances Meadows, the ancient de La Pradelle and others encountered only at these events… but by the end, weary of socialising, we skipped some meals and explored quietly together, finding the wonderful market (full of the fruit and vegetables I had been craving) and climbing up the streets for a panoramic view.

In Cambridge, as the Long Vacation rolled on, Robbie gave a 'little talk' to the United Nations Association. And Gardner Smith's widow, Elizabeth, invited all the surviving friends of her late husband to lunch. This became an annual event, with the number of aged Jesuans dwindling as the years went by. Fourteen of us were gathered this time, helping ourselves to a buffet lunch and sitting around small tables. At each course we moved about so that we all met – Leslie Brown, the retired Bishop and Archbishop (of Uganda), 'Pushy' Clark, retired Archdeacon, Sir Arthur Marshall and so on… all with memories of 'Perks' and fond of their hostess, 'Buffy'.

We made a visit, too, to Joey and Egg to see the terraced cottage, incompletely but colourfully furnished, in which they had settled, and their work as potters. With them we spent a blissful afternoon at Stourhead, where autumn tints were setting in. Then Robbie was off to Holland, to lecture at Leiden and to join those receiving visitors to the Peace Palace from Erasmus University.

He returned on 1ˢᵗ October, the beginning of the new academic year, to be honoured by Jesus College with a special dinner to mark his 50 years as a Fellow.

Straight back in The Hague, on the 3ʳᵈ he heard Adolfo Suarez, Prime Minister of Spain, address the court. The following day was the Oral Hearing on an '*ECOSOC case*' and consequent deliberations for two more days. Very probably both Suarez and Goedhuis (with whom he had dined the evening before) were interested in this matter, for the Court was to give an Advisory Opinion on the interpretation of a section of Article VI of the UN Charter, presumably for the benefit of the UN's Economic & Social Council (ECOSOC.)

Although his next spell at home provided a longer than usual respite from other engagements it was not easy to get on with correspondence and serious writing, with his desk in a diningroom still crowded with furniture and books while various workmen were completing the new study. He was glad to escape to college for lunch, or to enjoy faculty gossip at that term's Luncheon Club gathering.

He went to London for Gerald Draper's[383] memorial service in the Guards Chapel; again for an engagement noted as 'Longmans 12 noon FCO'[384] and again for an ILA dinner. And on the weekend of the 19ᵗʰ October our whole family gathered to celebrate not only his birthday, but the completion of the new study. Michael Goodhart could be proud: it was a huge improvement, fitting the original building very happily.

I find an entry in my own little diary for 9ᵗʰ October: –

'R talks to Arthur Watts and says he is definitely going for another term. Do I want to veto it? I am terrified, as always; but say "OK, go on."'

---

[383] Colonel Gerald Draper, at the end of a varied career, became Professor of Humanitarian Law at the University of Sussex and an authority on War Crimes.

[384] This was, almost certainly, another consultation with Sir Arthur Watts (at that time Legal Adviser to the FCO), with whom he was collaborating on *Oppenheim*. But (see final paragraph) they evidently had something else to discuss.

And Still More

1989-1990

Any hope that at the completion of his nine-year term as Judge we might settle down to something like a normal life was dashed. After shuttling to and from The Hague nearly 20 times a year, it was a shock for me to find that his name was to go forward as a candidate for the Court once again. One or two surviving letters reveal that the possibility had already been discussed before September 1989, as far back as January – and indeed one other British aspirant had hastily withdrawn his own candidacy when he heard of it. Success was, of course, far from certain. The Foreign & Commonwealth Office were strongly in favour, having learnt he was likely to be elected President of the Court; and it was they who suggested that he might step down after those three years of service.

There had evidently been a good deal of behind-the-scene discussion at the ICJ already about who should follow Jose-Maria Ruda (successor to the late Nagendra Singh) as President. One ambitious judge had apparently started canvassing for support for himself; but there was an unwritten convention that the presidency should rotate between regions of the globe, and since recent presidents – Elias, Lachs, Singh and Ruda – were from Africa, N.Europe, India and South America, it was now W.Europe's turn again. A letter written to Robbie by a candid member of the Court with an indecipherable signature reveals his colleagues' thoughts on the matter: that although Judge Ago's ability and experience were highly respected, he was not likely to comply with the rule of residence in The Hague. Robbie was both English-speaking and 'quiet' – dependable – and so more suitable.

That was all assuming that Robbie's name would go forward, and it was for the British Nominating Committee, rather than the Foreign Office, to propose their preferred candidate, after which the actual election must again be made by the UN General Assembly and Security Council. At the time of election Robbie would be 77 and certainly not wanting to continue for a further full nine years.

But all that was in the future, with a year still to run. In late October 1989 I shared with Robbie the Dutch Foreign Ministry's jaunt for members of the Court.

This year it was to Utrecht, where the judges spent the morning at the university. After lunch at the *Fundatie Verhout* given by the impressive woman Burgomeister, we all visited the great cathedral. That was followed by the *National Museum van Speelklok tot Pierement,* full of mechanical musical devices. Its Director had a sense of humour. In conducting us around, he teased Oda by asking him to turn the handle of a primitive barrel organ – calling it 'the first computer, invented long before the Japanese developed theirs' as it played hymn tunes from a perforated drum. Marvelling at one mechanical instrument after another, we finally gathered around a mighty street organ. I was asked to turn its heavy handle, but was soon beginning to flag… whereupon he called on Gilbert Guillaume, the French judge, to relieve me; and thus it was that Guillaume found himself playing a loud rendering of *Rule Britannia!*

After weeks in The Hague, Robbie returned home to deliver the annual F.A. Mann Lecture in the Great Hall of Lincoln's Inn. His title was *An International Lawyer Takes Stock*[385] – a survey of developments in international law from the time of his own first attendance at McNair's lectures in 1932 to the date of delivery. This lecture does not merely list historical events but displays his own readiness to welcome and adjust to major shifts at a time of 'rapid and still accelerating change'. In it, he recollects – without revealing the name of the 'much revered international lawyer' – the far-sightedness of Wilfred Jenks:

'In 1955, the late Wilfred Jenks submitted to me, as then an editor of *ICLQ,* one of the first legal articles to speculate on the need for a law for outer space, and the resources of the moon and other celestial bodies. A much revered international lawyer [Hersch Lauterpacht] who had also seen the manuscript pleaded with me not to risk such reputation as I might have by publishing what he regarded as fanciful nonsense: "He talks about the moon!" he said. I did publish the article, not from superior wisdom but because I hesitated to say "No" to Wilfred Jenks.

'Two years later the Sputnik was launched. By its orbit the hitherto universally accepted rule of sovereignty over airspace *usque ad caelum* was changed virtually in a matter of hours…'

---

[385] The F.A. Mann Lecture can be found on p.354 of his *Collected Writings.*

And he speaks of the wide range of expertise called for in dealing with some of the cases brought before the International Court:

'...The International Court of Justice – in theory – applies and knows only international law and, governed still by what is essentially a 1920s Statute, it still deals only with States. But in the recent *ELSI* case ... a chamber of the Court found itself having to learn a great deal about Italian bankruptcy laws, Italian administrative law, about municipal law notions of property, and even about accounting methods for the valuation of assets.'

– which indicates the demanding range of work he was regularly engaged in at The Hague. It was remarkable that – deprived of a proper study at home during the months of preparation – he had been able to write a lecture such as this.

The turn of the year 1989-90 allowed a little time for relaxation at home. Robbie had been to his favourite shop for family presents that Christmas: we now had our first colour television, a set of cordless telephones, and I was given a video-camera with which to record the young grandchildren.

In late January 1990 we were at the Memorial Service for Tresillian Nicholas, who had at last died aged nearly 102. Trinity College chapel was packed; the beautiful singing included the Russian *Kontakion*; the Alberni Quartet played; Dr Lynem spoke on 'Grandpa'; and Bradfield (his successor as college bursar) spoke about his work for the college. Tress's death had been followed, next day, by that of Rachel Lauterpacht – a mere 89 years old, but also leaving a great gap.

At Jesus, Lodge dinners now meant the likelihood of being introduced by the Master, Colin Renfrew (a strong Conservative[386]) to prominent members of the Cabinet. At one dinner we found the chief guest was the Rt Hon. Michael Howard, the new Minister for Employment; and on a later occasion we would meet Kenneth Clarke (current Education Secretary). A contrast was a hugely enjoyable evening at Derek and Betty Bowett's house – a fish-&-chip supper, true to their Lancashire origins. After lots of chat, we left with Betty calling 'Tara, love!' to a delighted Robbie.

---

[386] He would the following year take his place in the House of Lords as Lord Renfrew of Kaimsthorn.

In The Hague his social commitments were different again: 'tea with Sir Ti Liang Wang, Chief Justice of Hong Kong' (probably diplomatic) was soon followed by 'van Lynden's funeral' – marking the end of another friendship. And a small ceremony was held at the Peace Palace for 'Nigerian presentation of bust of Elias'. Taslim Elias, who had served as judge for 15 years and became President on the death of Waldock, was so dark of face that he would have been difficult to portray in the customary painting. The portrait in bronze is an effective likeness.

By now a maritime dispute between *Guinea-Bissau and Senegal* had reached the stage of Oral Hearings, and Robbie was busy with the Drafting Committee and the Rules Committee. But a family weekend in March called for a triumphant entry in his diary – '… JOEY ENGAGED'.

A later weekend that month was especially interesting. He had been asked by Francesco Francioni[387] to attend a meeting of the Advisory Committee of the Siena Centre for International Peace Studies. It included 'a colloquium with about 15 distinguished colleagues from Italy and other parts of the world on the subject of *International Responsibility for Environmental Harm Resulting from Industrial Activities*' at which Robbie should chair one session. Tuscany in early spring was tempting; and it turned out that the event would take place in an old monastery a few miles from Siena.

We went, and found the place was indeed special. While our husbands were engaged in the colloquium, the elderly Luciana Ago explained to me the methods of cultivation used in the monastery's large enclosed garden. On the Friday evening an excellent dinner was served. By the Saturday evening there was just a simple meal before almost everyone left. Since our own transport home had been arranged for the Sunday, we were staying overnight and were promised a tray of breakfast next morning. Next morning there was no tray. The porter at the gate spoke no English, knew nothing about arrangements and was totally unhelpful. We drank a little unpleasantly-chlorinated water from a plastic cup in our stately bedroom, and wandered in the garden. By late morning the pangs of hunger were growing, so we set off down the road towards the hamlet further down the hill. Delicious aromas were wafting from farmhouses, but there was no inn: their cooking was to provide a hearty Sunday meal for the men in hunting gear that we saw shooting birds. Then

---

387 Professor Francesco Francioni of the University of Siena was also Director of the International Peace Studies Centre.

a car approached and drew up. Its occupants, two young people from the colloquium, offered a lift to Siena. But by now it was too late: our luggage was back at the monastery, from where we were soon to be driven to Pisa. Our experience so far that day had been a properly monastic one, and so we promised ourselves a good meal at the airport. There, the *Ristorante* was closed for the Sabbath, but after much queuing we procured pieces of dry Madiera cake from a stall in the foyer. On the evening flight home there was a mean, stale meal that deserved rejection; but we ate it.

Pippa, Mick and the toddler Annie joined us at Arment House for Easter, a very happy stay – this time recorded by my new video-camera. Thus it is that we can still see and hear Annie surrounded by bleating newborn lambs, and an afternoon spent at Muncaster Mill, its great wheel turned by rushing water, the chuff-chuffing of the approaching and receding train along the Ravenglass & Eskdale Railway, a strong-willed goat, varied poultry wandering and pecking amidst daffodils – and Robbie himself exchanging crows with the two handsome cocks.

He had eight days' work in The Hague before returning in time for Joey's wedding on 16th June. The couple had chosen to be married at the Registry Office at Bath rather than our village church – an arrangement that their conventional relatives found quite acceptable on the day. The brief ceremony was conducted with due gravity; Joey looked lovely in a dress of her own design; the reception, in the sunny garden of an old building[388] was informal, with young people sitting on the grass while gentle guitar music was played. Pippa and Jill were visibly pregnant once more, and the two little cousins, Annie and Lizzie, were both cuddled by Grandpa Robbie.

A very different weekend soon followed. Professor Patricia Birnie had invited Robbie to present degrees and diplomas at the first award ceremony to be held at The Institute of Maritime Law (IMLI) in Malta. Pat Birnie, well-known to Robbie through his connection with the LSE and the International Maritime Organisation, was the founding Director of the brand-new Institute, whose first students had now completed their course of studies.

---

[388] The Old Parsonage, recently turned into a guest house.

Malta was, for me, a revelation: an island composed of pale limestone, with all its buildings of the same material. Warmly welcomed by Professor David Attard and Pat Birnie herself to the newly-built Institute, we were impressed by the simple elegance of its courtyard and the evident enthusiasm of its multinational students. I found myself on the front row of the hall next to the President of Malta and other dignitaries as Robbie addressed the graduands and handed them their degree certificates. They chatted with him afterwards, and we were then taken to the President's palace to sign its visitors' book.

After that we were given a pleasantly informal afternoon at the home of Dr Fenech, head of Malta's senior law firm. Later he drove us to Mdina and the north and eastern side of the island, stopping at St Paul's Bay to look at an archaeological site and reflect on *The Acts of the Apostles*. As dusk fell, we passed a festive gathering setting off fireworks. Next morning, Pat Birnie took us in her own car to see a little of the southern end of the island and the Grand Harbour at Valletta. We lunched with Attard at his splendid club, and learned more about the island's history and customs. And then – having absorbed a remarkable amount in that brief visit – we flew home in a much-delayed small plane.

That to-and-fro life meant that Robbie missed various cricket matches and other Cambridge enticements that summer, though in the Netherlands we managed to see two major Van Gogh exhibitions, both impressive.

Our summer break at Arment House was brief, but particularly memorable for the visitors who joined us for a couple of days. They were Shigeru and Noriko Oda, who were touring England at the time. Oda, by now a good friend, had never forgotten his earlier visit in 1966, when he had consulted Robbie at Windermere rather than tear him away from our family holiday. That glimpse of the Lake District had made a good impression, and now he wanted his wife to share it. Arment House, we felt, might be too primitive for our Japanese guests, since conversations could be heard from one room to the next; so it was a relief to find how pleased they had been with the village inn. We took them to Wasdale, at its very best that morning[389], and to Tim's Tarn in Eskdale. And by the 20th we were back home, welcoming them again for tea in our garden and boasting that our grandson Thomas Jennings had been born that very day.

---

389 A photograph of the two judges standing together by Wastwater is included in Oda's biography.

Robbie's diary notes from 6th-8th September '*[Hague] Academy Colloquium (with Sinclair and Watts – E. European problems)*'. Sinclair and Watts were, of course, the previous and current Legal Advisers to the British Foreign Office, and the early stages of the break-up of Yugoslavia at that time involved many problems for international lawyers.

Events that autumn included the birth of our 4th grandchild, Mary Goodhart.

On the 21st October my journey up to Yorkshire for the christening of Thomas was slightly delayed when I found that Robbie had driven off to Harwich, leaving behind his case full of essential papers. I tore down the zigzag road through Grantchester and finally caught up with him (flashing lights until he stopped) two miles further on.

In The Hague, meanwhile, judgment on the *El Salvador/Honduras* case was delayed by an intervention from Nicaragua, and another – *Libya/Chad* – was opening. I joined Robbie there in time to share the Court's trip to Leiden arranged by the Foreign Ministry. That allowed us one day in which to clean the Houtweg flat, do a little desperate shopping, and pack; and on the 31st October we flew to New York.

It was my first visit to America, and I felt very nervous and doubtful about it. New York surely meant gangsters, jazz, and vulgarity of all sorts – though Robbie knew there was much that I was bound to enjoy. In any case my misgivings were beside the point, since he was to make this trip as a candidate for re-election to the ICJ bench, and the Foreign Office wanted him to make a good impression on those who would be voting at the election. Sir Arthur Watts was there to introduce him to all the right people at the United Nations headquarters.

Arthur was a wonderful companion at the meals we shared. He was a perfect diplomat, the exemplary English gentleman – ex-Guards-officer, restrained, a dry sense of humour – and he briefed Robbie before guiding him through the series of meetings during our nine days there. As for my actual impressions of New York – after that *Wow!* moment as we drove from the airport and first saw the Manhattan skyline – I was excited and enthralled by everything. From the British Mission office we went to be photographed and issued with identity cards for admission to the UN building, after which one was remarkably free to walk about inside. But Robbie had many people to meet, and I was not wanted. So I went exploring on foot.

I found the Rockefeller Plaza, where people were practising their skating to music on an open-air rink; walked on to the Metropolitan Museum; wandered a little in Central Park (and was fiercely warned, later, not to venture too far); and procured bus tokens from a machine in the lower region of Grand Central Station. When Robbie reappeared for dinner we had plenty to tell each other.

On the Saturday he was free to come with me to the superb Frick Collection. Then, as tourists, we rode around Central Park in an old Amish buggy amid trees beginning to shed autumnal leaves, and with health-conscious New Yorkers exercising along its paths. That evening we went down to Washington Square to be given dinner by Ted Meron[390] and his wife Monique. The concern of our taxi driver to see us safely inside their building gave a suggestion of the caution needed in certain areas of the city. But once inside, I was surprised to find that their upstairs apartment seemed comfortably old-fashioned, to the extent of even having a log fire.

On the Sunday we were joined by Jeremy Carver, also in holiday mood, teasing Robbie about his prehistoric impressions of America as the raw lad from Idle in 1936. Since the New York Marathon had that day caused some streets to be closed, Jeremy proposed a trip around Manhattan on a Circle Line ship – an excellent way of understanding the isolation of the central city, and even sailing out and around Ellis Island and the Statue of Liberty. Not only that: we then took the lifts up to the top of the south tower of the World Trade Centre.

On the Monday evening we retired to our room at the *Intercontinental,* hearing as usual street noises including distant alarms – whoops and screams and wailings. But a lot seemed to be coming our way, so we looked down onto Lexington Avenue, where indeed something was happening at the Marriott Hotel opposite. Ambulance after ambulance arrived, and police cars as well. A man ran fast across the road towards our side and out of sight. Others dashed out; stretchers were unloaded and carried into the hotel; and soon two of the six ambulances were moved along the street to where that first man had run. Then from the hotel emerged stretchers – two bearing figures half-undressed and bandaged, one covered. The ones up the street were loaded too, and went screaming away. By this time we were pretty sure there must have

---

390 Theodor Meron, Professor of International Criminal Law at New York University.

been a shooting. The Marriott Hotel entrance became the stage for television interviews and flash photographs.

Next morning the drama was on the front page of the *New York Times* and took up a good deal of space inside. We had witnessed the aftermath of the assassination of Rabbi Meir Kahane, an anti-Arab agitator, at a meeting in the Marriott hotel. He was shot dead by an Arab, and two others had been wounded in the disturbance. The assassin had run across the street and tried to compel a taxi-driver, at gunpoint, to drive him away. But the taxi was outside a large Post Office guarded by a policeman so when attacked, the policeman, protected by a bulletproof vest, had shot back and seriously wounded him.

Even though we had seen very little, it was sobering to read on subsequent days how this episode had repercussions in Israel and was of long-ranging significance. And I found that New York could indeed be a dangerous place.

On the Wednesday evening we were both driven northwards through the 'heartbreak-area' at the northern end of Central Park, pausing to look at the Cathedral of St John the Divine, still incomplete and with an atmosphere of crushing gloom, on our way to Columbia University, where Robbie was to give a talk hosted by Professor Oscar Schachter to their international law students. In writing later to our children, I described the evening:

'Columbia, a rich university by British standards, has much which is drab and scruffy. The main campus is probably handsome; but it is severely guarded and so we were admitted only to the Law Faculty Building. Here although we did peep at a great lecture hall, our chief impression was of dropped litter, lavatories out of order, and professors' rooms like prison cells. R gave his talk in a room lined with portraits – good ones – and spoke for 40 minutes, answering questions for a good while afterwards. The more wide-awake of his audience loved the provocative remarks, and stayed to talk. We then, in a group of 12, went to the Faculty Club for dinner.'

Next day he spoke at New York University.

'The Law Faculty Building here was a contrast to Columbia. A recent benefactor had paid for the refurbishment of the club building, with wonderful glowing woodwork, Persian rugs and portraits, looking well cared-for. Lunch was at several tables, and was delicious – beautifully served and chosen… This gracious setting must affect the people there. They were all well-dressed and gave a feeling of relaxed good humour. R spoke for about 15 minutes, and responded to questions for another 20 or so.

'At the end of that we were shown other highlights of their buildings, the chief being the sumptuous library, now extended by tunnelling beneath the road and the university buildings opposite…'

Later, inside the UN buildings, we thought of exercising our privilege as 'delegates' to hear a debate. Robbie took me to Room 7, where the Security Council were discussing the Iraq-Kuwait crisis. But warned by reproachful glances, we withdrew in embarrassment when a little oriental lady tiptoed round and whispered that it was a *closed* meeting. So we explored the basement, where one could post letters or cards with special stamps and have them franked with the UN postmark.

That evening we were entertained to dinner at an Indonesian restaurant by James Crawford – 'a very lively-minded Australian international lawyer' I noted – and someone destined to play an important part in the Cambridge Law Faculty later.

As an opportunity to spend a little time with a favourite pupil of Robbie's who was just about to leave New York, we presented ourselves early next morning at…

'…a grand apartment on Park Avenue. This was the residence of the Japanese Ambassador, where we were invited for breakfast as the only possible way of meeting Hisashi Owada, an old pupil of Daddy's who is very important now – Deputy Foreign Minister – in their government, and was returning to Tokyo later in the day.

'The apartment was vast, with very select – quite sparse – pieces of furniture and pictures, some 18th century European, some Japanese. Moving into the dining room, we found the long table was laid for four of us – Owada, Sir Arthur Watts, and ourselves; and the Ambassador sat on my right, sipping a glass of orange juice while we worked our way through grapefruit, exquisitely cooked & served omelette & grilled bacon, a delicious side-salad, and toast. That was as much as I could manage, but I was amazed to see R consuming a whole bowlful of yoghurt! He is prepared to make any sacrifice in the cause of diplomatic duty.'

We arrived home next day; and on 15th November – marked in Robbie's diary simply as 'ICJ elections' – the not-unexpected vote of the General Assembly and Security Council of the UN told us that we would be back in The Hague in 1991.

There was one more major event that year. On 21st November we flew to Rome,[391] invited by Roberto Ago, who showed us some of the city's marvels and gave us lunch at his club,[392] a place full of exuberant murals and plasterwork.

From the rococo splendour of Roberto's club we moved to the *Sapienza University*, where he was still Professor Emeritus. After giving a lecture, Robbie was to receive an Honorary Doctorate. The ceremony took place in a vast hall built during the Mussolini era, where I joined a sparse audience and was fascinated by bizarre aspects of this grandiose occasion. There were just two graduands, Robbie and a German professor of law, the first and only academics to be honoured in this way since before the war. The German, with white hair and cherubic face, seemed a nice old gentleman, yet we heard later that he had been a Nazi supporter. All the university dignitaries looked splendid, and Robbie himself was similarly decked in voluminous crimson silk and wore a curious biretta with a fluffy red pompom on top. There were orations in Italian and gracious responses from the new doctors in German and English. And all this Tiepolo tableau was set before a huge mural loaded with fascist symbolism. As Robbie disrobed afterwards, one professor hanging up his gorgeous vestments wryly murmured '*Sic transit gloria mundi!*'

Before leaving Rome next day we were driven to Ago's home. It was a house he had designed himself. Its north-facing entrance opened into a high gallery, hung with choice pictures; and the wide windows of the reception rooms beyond looked southwards onto a great view. We felt privileged to be welcomed there, and by the whole family – all except for dear Luciana, who had died a fortnight earlier. Stepping down from one small terrace to another of her garden, I noticed a few flower-pots and a trowel, signs of the work she had so recently been doing there. We heard that just a fortnight before her

---

[391] It was during this visit that the news came by telephone from Paris of Margaret Thatcher's downfall. I think it was Gaetano Orangio-Ruiz who was present and saw her, shocked and trembling, hear of her party's withdrawal of support. He joined us in Rome later.

[392] I think this was the Old Chess Club, wealthy and exclusive.

death she had fulfilled a wish to see the newly restored Michelangelo frescoes in the Sistine Chapel. Suddenly faint, she had been allowed to lie down – and thus, she had quipped, had a better view than anyone else!

Roberto's children were a gifted group, and a vivacious daughter-in-law, Loretta Malintoppi, had followed her father[393] as an international lawyer and would appear as counsel before the ICJ before long. One sensed an emotional undercurrent as the family remembered Luciana, the sweetly dignified mother, knowing that her passing would lead to uncertainty over the future of this home. (Roberto's affection and pride in everything represented by this gathering was deep-felt, yet nevertheless torn by a resistless attraction to his mistress, living in Geneva.)

Another curious and colourful event we enjoyed was in London: the Swan Feast of the Vintners' Company.[394] Our host, the Master Vintner Jeremy ('Bunjie') Langton, like his older brother Tommy, was a Jesuan, and so the Master of Jesus, Colin Renfrew, and his wife Jane were among the other guests. We sat on a balcony overlooking the splendid hall and between courses were entertained with a succession of rituals, including the display of a swan on a platter and military pipes and drums. And yes, we did eat swan: just a speck, in one of those courses.

Robbie was again in The Hague at the beginning of December, but was home in time for the christening of baby Mary Goodhart in Grantchester church. It was the season of festivities, and Arthur Watts arrived to spend a night with us. He was attending a Downing College feast, but realised when unpacking that he had failed to bring the trousers matching his dinner-jacket. It was one of those occasions when one is grateful for candlelight, for he went in imperfectly-fitting trousers borrowed from Robbie.

And Christmas, that year, was spent very happily with Pippa's young family in Leicester.

---

[393] Professor Malintoppi, Loretta's father, was assisting Roberto Ago, his former teacher, with preparatory work on his ICJ cases.

[394] The Vintners and the Dyers share the privilege of conducting a 'swan upping', to gather and mark their mute swans on the Thames. All others are owned by the Crown.

President of the International Court

1991

A fter a quiet time at home, on 28ᵗʰ January we were again in Saarbrücken, this time for Robbie to give a major lecture at the Europa Institute, with Ress presiding. 'Very full; went v. well', I noted. The title of this talk, *Judicial Reasoning at an International Court*,[395] had been set by his hosts, and he began it by stressing that cases heard before an international court differ in many ways from those before a municipal court…

'… For in many of those cases, there is a degree of complexity greater in degree, almost indeed in kind, than is found in the kind of situation that normally comes before the domestic court. Take for example the case pending at present before a Chamber of the International Court between El Salvador and Honduras (Nicaragua intervening), which involves six separate sections of land-frontier, and also the legal status of the Gulf of Fonseca, as also of islands in the Gulf and maritime areas outside the Gulf. Now, quite apart from the many questions involved, as soon as one begins to think of the question of boundaries and sovereignty in that part of the world, immediately one is involved also with the principle of *uti possidetis juris*, which in this *El Salvador/Honduras* case takes one straight back to 1821, which was the date of the independence of these countries and thus a primary critical date. And since this legal principle refers to the position in 1821, it also takes one further back to inquire into Spanish colonial times in earlier centuries. So one has to investigate a very large tranche of diplomatic history of considerable complication; because it is not only a question of establishing facts but also a question of interpreting a large number of documents of some antiquity.'

I quote this because, as in his earlier comments about the range of information, in more than one language, that needed to be mastered for the *ELSI* case, it is

---

[395] This talk does not appear in the published *Collected Writings*.

an indication of the tasks he was regularly undertaking during his years at the Court.

The ICJ came to life again in February. Robbie returned to The Hague, first working with the Court's Rules Committee and having 'lunch with Valencia'. That was probably significant: Eduardo Valencia-Ospina,[396] a Colombian, was Registrar of the ICJ, and the harmonious relationship he and Robbie established was to make a great contribution to the success of the following three years. It might have seemed an unlikely friendship: Eduardo the big, burly, outgoing, art-collecting homosexual, and Robbie the Yorkshireman whose sense of pride took the form of 'never letting on' except in subtle irony. But they shared both a passion for justice and a love of music.

A gathering of all the members of the Court and staff in the Small Hall of Justice bade farewell to the retiring President, José Maria Ruda, and that evening the departing Rudas and their successors were entertained to dinner by Steve and Louise Schwebel. Andrés Aguilar-Mawdsley, from Venezuela, was to be the new Latin-American judge, and, like his predecessor, would be greatly admired by Robbie.

Next day the new ICJ session began, and on the 7th Robbie was unanimously elected President. On the 8th, the day of the opening public session of the Court, he took his place at the centre of the long table in the Great Hall of Justice for the first time and conducted the formal ceremony at which he delivered an obituary of Colliard[397] and introduced the new judges as they were sworn in, 'v. clearly and with dignity' (note by proud wife). A new case was announced: *Nauru/Australia*[398].

As President, Robbie now moved to a new set of rooms overlooking the Peace Palace gardens. It had a spacious reception room furnished with his desk, a table large enough for small meetings, and an area for entertaining visitors to coffee, as well as a sizeable office for Doreen. In addition, there was a small room with a bed where he might lie down and rest (but never, I think, did). Steve Schwebel was strongly in favour of the President being provided with a dignified Residence; but the Carnegie Foundation would never have found

---

[396]   Eduardo Valencia-Ospina would follow his work as Registrar of the ICJ with years on the International Law Commission and as its Special Rapporteur on the Protection of Persons in the Event of Disaster.

[397]   Claude Albert Colliard, noted international lawyer who had appeared as advocate in several cases before the ICJ.

[398]   *Nauru v Australia: Certain phosphate lands in Nauru.*

the money for this, and since the President's term of office was just three years it would have meant an extra upheaval in his living arrangements. Instead, an entertainment allowance was provided which allowed him to give occasional receptions or dinners in one of The Hague's excellent restaurants.

By the end of that day the temperature had fallen to -10° C and snow was falling. But Suckling Air's small Dornier flew us back to Cambridge safely.

Despite having spent a little time talking over his new duties with Ruda, Robbie was not, I think, quite prepared for the reality of his new role. During his first week or so he found how difficult it was to work in his grand room uninterrupted. There were endless diplomatic duties: not only a buffet supper at the Czech Embassy, but people kept calling on him – 'courtesy calls'. These included someone from the US Department of State; the Director-General of ISNAR;[399] the Ambassador of Oman; the Head of Protocol, Limburg Stirum; the Iranian judge; the Japanese Ambassador; Bob Petrouwski (a former pupil). On the 28th February Robbie jotted, among all these names, 'GULF WAR ENDED. KUWAIT LIBERATED.'

He came home on 1st March pretty tired, and was confined to bed for six days with a bad infection. Barely recovered, he gave a talk to the United Nations Association members at Saffron Walden on the 14th – noted by me as 'a cracking good talk (c1¾ hrs with answers) despite thin voice and deafness'.

On 20th March we returned to The Hague, where early next morning Robbie was attended to by an ENT surgeon to be fit for the dinner that evening given by Queen Beatrix for the visiting President of the Czech Republic, Vaclav Havel. We were for the next three years to be conveyed everywhere in the President's big limousine whose driver, Jacques van der Meer, was disappointed that Robbie would allow him to flaunt its UN flag only for these formal occasions. This occasion was at the Nordeinde Palace and our first experience of having to lead the diplomatic corps in stepping forward to be greeted by the Queen and the visiting Head of State – something we would be obliged to do repeatedly during Robbie's time as President.[400] At table, Robbie sat between

---

[399] ISNAR – the International Service for National Agricultural Research, an agency closed in 2004.

[400] In the Netherlands the President of the ICJ takes precedence over the entire diplomatic corps.

the Queen and Mme Havel, and I was on Prince Claus' left. The Prince was, as before, friendly and interesting in conversation. The Havels, I noted, were 'nice, unassuming and weary'. They were at the end of a round of state visits; and when Robbie asked Mme. Havel whether she enjoyed living in a palace, 'Enjoy is not the word' was her reply.

While Robbie returned home for an Easter break, Judge Oda (Vice-President) received the agents of Iran and the U.S. concerning the *Aerial Incident of 3 July 1988.*[401] That spell of sunshine, with Joey and Egg doing some vigorous gardening for us, dispelled the last of his infection, and he was back to work on the first hearings in the *Guinea-Bissau/Senegal*[402] case; and the day after, preliminary discussion noted as 'Portugal/Australia,' about a forthcoming case concerning East Timor. Then it was *'G/B v Senegal'* again, and – by way of distraction – the Telders final at the weekend. In addition there was administrative work to be discussed and a provisional agenda agreed… and so on.

I joined him again for the dinner given by Prime Minister Ruud Lubbers for the President of Tanzania. This took place in the Binnenhof, the great complex of historic government buildings at the centre of the city: red carpet and hussars, but slightly less formal than for royal banquets. We dined, though, in a glorious room, the *Treveszaal*,[403] and were surrounded with baroque decorations. Senior members of the Dutch cabinet and one or two academics were there; we met and chatted with President Mwinyi, and the company consisted of senior members of the Dutch cabinet and a few academics. I, like Robbie, needed to pay attention and try to learn the names and faces of all these people, for we would be meeting them again.

And indeed, it happened the very next evening. After a friendly lunch given by Guillaume to introduce another new judge, Christopher Weeramantry from Sri Lanka, our evening engagement took us to the *Catshuis*,[404] the official home of the Foreign Minister van den Broek, who was giving a farewell dinner for Judge Ruda. The Odas were there – Mrs Oda in her beautiful national dress[405]

---

[401] Missiles fired from an American warship in the Persian Gulf had destroyed an Iranian airbus, killing all 290 passengers and crew.

[402] *Maritime Delimitation between Guinea-Bissau and Senegal.*

[403] '… which Daniel Marot remodelled and redecorated in 1696 in the Louis XIV style.'

[404] *Het Catshuis* is not a house full of cats, but one named after Jacob Cats, a 17th-century statesman who built this handsome residence in the Sorgvliet garden.

[405] Noriko Oda needed assistance from ladies at the Japanese Embassy in dressing traditionally.

– together with the Stirum van Limburgs and the Kooimans. The atmosphere was one of elegance and ease.

Early in the Court's year, there were other introductions to be made – to Mohammed Shahubuddeen, the judge from Guyana, and the Mbayes (from Senegal), who had to delay their eating until moonrise because they were observing Ramadan. That was followed by lunch with Steve Schwebel to meet Mary-Ellen O'Connell, one of Robbie's brightest former pupils.[406] And Frances Meadows, another of those ex-pupils now working in the Registry, gave us a happy evening in her fine new flat with Robbie's former secretary Angie, glamorous as ever, now once again single and about to take up a new job in Vienna.

During that spell, besides another dinner given by the Prime Minister for the visiting President of Chile, we dined with the British Ambassador, who was entertaining the current British Minister for Agriculture & Fisheries. The 'Minister for Ag & Fish' greeted us effusively with hugs, for she was Baroness Trumpington, Jean Barker, formerly Headmaster's wife at The Leys School. It was a lively evening.

And so it was to continue, sustained by Robbie's heavy use of those convenient Suckling Air flights to snatch weekends at home as often as possible – allowing just enough time for the laundering of his clothes. I, who found shopping for clothes a misery, was relieved to discover a rather unusual dressmaker,[407] a sympathetic American who enjoyed designing and making for me slightly theatrical evening dresses.

Robbie was of course spared the what-to-wear panic, and for him the provision of new suits was resolved most happily. A London tailor, Mr L.G. Wilkinson, would call at The Hague from time to time, taking orders from diplomats and judges while he stayed at the Hotel des Indes, having arrived in an open Bentley equipped with large cases of samples so that measurements and fittings could be made on the spot. These trips suited him as much as it did his customers, since he loved opera and regularly included Vienna, Salzburg and Bayreuth on his rounds, attending opera performances and picking up orders from Fischer-Dieskau and others. To the end of his days Robbie would

---

[406] M-E O'Connell was currently teaching at the University of Indiana. She is now Robert & Marion Short Professor of Law and Research Professor of International Dispute Resolution at the University of Notre Dame.

[407] Sara Fermi, who enjoyed the challenge of contriving individual garments. Her scientist husband was the son of Enrico Fermi, the distinguished Nobel laureate physicist.

wear suits, tweed jackets and overcoats made by Wilkinson; and the firm, now in its sixth generation, continues still.

That year, on 24ᵗʰ May, we drove to a quiet cul-de-sac off the Milton Road in Cambridge for a nice little ceremony, when Robbie was invited to unveil a carved name-plaque, *Robert Jennings Close*. Here the apartment-buildings had been provided by the King Street Housing Association whose first Chairman he had been, and one grateful resident showed us around her own flat.

———

Our next royal banquet, given for the President of Venezuela, took place in Queen Beatrix's Amsterdam palace with customary grandeur, and was followed next day by the Prime Minister's lunch in the *Ridderzaal*. That same evening the Venezuelan President reciprocated with a very grand reception in the *Rijksmuseum* back in Amsterdam. One could hardly beat that vast hall, hung with masterpieces all round, as a setting; but the hours of standing left us exhausted.

Robbie's engagements continued unremittingly: receiving the Agents of Finland and Denmark to discuss their forthcoming case (*Passage through the Great Belt*); lunch with Nicolas Valticos;[408] entertaining representatives of Italy, Japan, Jordan; pondering details on maps with a cartographer … I heard about these encounters when he phoned home each evening, and also his impression – simply as effective advocacy – of the submissions he had heard that day in court. Always there was admiration for Bowett's performance: 'Derek was quite the best …'

For a man of his age, the workload might have seemed unbearable. Yet it was all fascinating, and I think he knew how well his accumulated experience fitted him for it. Often I felt my own support inadequate, yet he had chosen to keep his Grantchester life and college connections in Cambridge active. And it was all made possible by his capable secretary Doreen, who managed his appointments and typed his work; and who, realising that he needed some help with our small apartment at Houtweg, now introduced a Scotswoman married to a Dutchman to clean it regularly for us.

———

---

[408] Nicolas Valticos, senior official of the ILO, included President of the Hague Academy and Secretary of the *Institut* among his appointments. At this time he was serving as Judge *ad hoc*.

My own next visit to The Hague was in July for a luncheon given by the head of the Carnegie Foundation for that year's Academy lecturers. It was held in the Ferdinand Bol Room, [409] that grand room in the Peace Palace whose walls displayed Bol's paintings. We always wondered how the judges of the earlier Permanent Court of International Justice had been able to concentrate on their deliberations with a voluptuous Venus and lurid biblical figures looming over them; but historic photos show that they did indeed meet there.

And that evening we were in the *Treveszaal* at Prime Minister Lubbers' dinner for the Prime Minister of Japan. My neighbour was Jacques Delors, [410] at that time regarded with great suspicion by Margaret Thatcher's government; but I found him, though weary from a recent G7 summit, good company and with warm memories of his student years in England. And to Robbie's delight, Hisashi Owada was there too.

After days of heavy (but eventually triumphant) work reaching unanimous accord with his colleagues, Robbie was glad to relax on the Sunday. We found Arthur Watts (in The Hague for a few days' work) was wandering like ourselves among stalls of antiques in the Corte Voorhout. So we all went by tram to Delft and rode around the streets in a wagon drawn by two heavy horses, which was fun – the clip-clop over cobbles accelerating each time it approached a humped bridge over a canal.

In late July Robbie was in Cambridge for the Law Faculty's celebration of Sir David Williams' knighthood and his appointment, after serving the usual two-year term as Vice-Chancellor as a Head of House (President of Wolfson College), to be the University's first full-time Vice-Chancellor under its new statutes.

And now, for the first time that year, we were free for some real holiday, begun in Leicester, where Pippa had gathered the whole family (Robbie's diary – '*Perfect day*') on our wedding anniversary. Next day we drove up to Arment House for one of those stays that yielded just one properly fine day. On our way home we visited Dick's little family, now living at Birstwith in Nidderdale. In Grantchester Robbie was relieved, on hearing of Judge Elias's death, that Bernard Noble, Vice-Registrar of the Court, would undertake to go to Nigeria himself for the funeral.

---

[409] Ferdinand Bol was considered to be Rembrandt's best pupil

[410] Jacques Delors was a long-serving President of the European Commission

The 1991 *Institut* conference was held at Basle, in Switzerland. Robbie had some tasks to attend to at the Peace Palace on the way there, seeing the agents of Chad and Libya and then dealing with some proof-reading of *Oppenheim*. (I, meanwhile, watched on CNN television the Supreme Soviet in Moscow making 'momentous changes to the USSR'.)

That conference included a very pleasant variety of outings and private dinners; and the great Sunday excursion took us all to Lucerne, where we embarked for a gentle cruise in hazy sunshine all around the lake. But at its end, we received a shock – for news had arrived of a drama that day at the Peace Palace. A group of tourists being conducted around the building by a guide had, when assembled in the great Japanese Room, drawn guns and demanded to meet the President of the International Court. The frightened guide had called the officer in charge of security, Mr Koch, who explained that the President was not available. Nor was the Vice-President, also away floating on Lake Lucerne, nor the Registrar who was in New York. At length the group, who turned out to be Kurdish protesters, had been made to leave. There was nothing more to be done, and so we carried on with our excursion.

That took us from Brunnen up to the Abbey of Einsiedeln, a place huge and heavy with baroque decoration, not exactly to our taste. Robbie was so taken, though, with our guide – a tall monk who answered our questions with a humorous glint in his eye – that he was almost persuaded, he confessed, to become a Catholic! After a long, long, hot return journey via Zürich we were glad to have a quiet supper with Roberto Ago and Francis Mann.[411]

After seeing just a little more of that attractive place, we left before the the end of the conference; and back in The Hague we heard from Mr Koch further details of the 'armed occupation' of the Peace Palace. For all Robbie's sympathy for the Kurds (and Croats and other protesters who appealed to the Court) there was nothing the President of the ICJ could have done for them. The Court's purpose is the peaceful settlement of disputes between States which are presented in legal terms. It cannot take action on behalf of one or other party.

Finding that despite a recent change in the Polish government, Skubiszewski[412] was still Foreign Minister, Robbie received his formal visit to

---

[411] F.A. Mann, a German Jewish émigré from a distinguished family of lawyers, was principally a solicitor with the firm of Herbert Smith. Unusually, he combined casework in common law with important writings on private and public international law.

[412] Krzystof Skubiszewski had taught international law at Poznan University and was a member of the Hague Academy curatorium, who would later serve as an *ad hoc* judge of the ICJ.

the Court on 3rd September and attended the dinner given by van den Broek in his honour.

In mid-September we went to New York, this time staying in the Harvard Club – 'extremely decorous and sober' with its décor of dark crimson. All around its vast halls were the heads of slain beasts: moose, deer of all sorts, elephant (greenish, with spread ears and extended trunk) and warthog; and along the corridors and bedrooms were framed photographs of long-ago teams of sportsmen. Although the effect was slightly surreal, it was a privilege to be allowed into this astonishing oasis of calm amid the outside tumult of the city streets.

It was hot (93° F) and humid, like a steam-bath. We sat in on the opening session of the UN General Assembly, watching from the side as seven new members were admitted – most dramatically the three Baltic States, Latvia, Estonia and Lithuania which had recently become independent. (Those ranks of delegates representing member states, all arranged in alphabetical order, brought home a recognition that each one had just one vote in the General Assembly, whether its population was 10,000 or 10,000,000,000; yet a speech given from its rostrum might carry worldwide influence.) For the following days Robbie had a full series of engagements, calling on the Secretary-General and attending a meeting of the 5th (Finance and Administration) Committee.

Eduardo Valencia showed us a nearly-completed film on the Law of the Sea, and took us up to his office high in the UN building. Looking down, we commented on the narrow island visible below in the East River. That was Roosevelt Island, and Eduardo told us of the day some years before when he had suddenly noticed a group of men at its tip, firing a rocket at the UN Headquarters building. Fortunately the missile fell short; but since then, that end of the island is kept bare, and forbidden to intruders.

We lunched that day with Sir David Hannay, the British Ambassador to the UN, a most pleasant occasion. (I was particularly interested in the choice of modern British paintings on the walls of the residence.) Then, on the Saturday, we took again the Circle Line trip around Manhattan, enjoying crystal-clear weather and an excellent commentary. Sunday was touristy too: queueing to ascend by lift to the 102nd floor observatory at the top of the Empire State Building. Then we took a bus up to the Metropolitan Museum where we moved from one gallery to another until 'exhausted, we went out to

Central Park, where hundreds of people (a crowd of 250,000) were walking to a Billy Graham meeting; also cyclists, roller-skaters, &c...'

The next day was more serious: the Assembly was addressed by successive Heads of State or representatives. We heard speakers from Brazil, Iceland, El Salvador and New Zealand, followed by President Bush[413] ('good clear speech, excellent delivery'). Listening to these speeches I was seated beside Mme de Cuellar and Barbara Bush, both pleasant and friendly. But because of the President's visit, security was more intense than usual and I was only able to get out of the building by way of the basement tunnel.

On the Tuesday there were more speeches to the General Assembly: South Korea, Netherlands (van den Broek) and the Soviet Union. Robbie attended the Secretary General's luncheon for Heads of State and met the King of Swaziland, Prince Sihanouk of Cambodia and others. With a free afternoon, we visited a less well-known part of the Metropolitan Museum at the northern tip of Manhattan, The Cloisters. It was thoroughly rewarding, full of medieval treasures of all kinds gathered – we hoped legally – from all over Europe. The drive there through the different ethnic areas of the city was of interest, too.

On our final day we heard more speeches to the General Assembly – Gensche of Germany, a Chinese delegate, and then Douglas Hurd, current Foreign Secretary of the UK ('excellent'). Lunch, given by Eduardo at his '21 Club' – full of hunting prints, I seem to remember – was in honour of the Fleischhaurs. Carl-August Fleischhaur was Under Secretary-General for Legal Affairs at the UN, and would in 1994 become a Judge of the ICJ.

After just three days at home, Robbie was back at The Hague working on the Drafting Committee for the *Guinea-Bissau/Senegal* judgment; next day looking at the Memorials for a new case between Bahrain and Qatar; the day after receiving the Turkish Ambassador and attending a dinner at the Swiss embassy... and the day after that (4th October) flying back midday to Stansted and going up to London for a Lincoln's Inn dinner.

On Sunday 6th October he was back to The Hague again, where his diary records the circulation of the preliminary draft on *Guinea-Bissau/Senegal*; a visit from Mrs Elias, followed by a late evening concert at Delft; and 'Spain', presumably a courtesy call. The following weekend at home included plenty of family: my brother Tony (over from New Zealand after a gap of three or four years) breezing in for lunch, then the arrival of Dick's little family. On Saturday,

---

413   This was George Bush Snr.

Robbie's 78th birthday, the rest of our family arrived and were joined by Charles and Diana Goodhart: 14 for birthday tea in the kitchen, present-giving in the sitting room, slight rumpus with tired children... Quieter evening by fire.

On Saturday 2nd November he was home for Charles Wilson's Memorial Service in Jesus College Chapel. Charles was already a college Fellow when Robbie had arrived at Jesus in 1939, and so their friendship had been a long one. He was a brilliant economic historian, always amusing company, a nearly professional-standard string-player, and had for some years been Bursar of the college. His book *Holland and Britain* was of particular interest to Robbie. Charles's married life had been erratic: his first wife Angela, mother of Elizabeth who became an expert on antiques, was displaced by the Czech, Alena, whose son adopted his surname; and his final years were spent in Australia with a third wife. But he was remembered with affection:

> 'Chapel full for Charles' service: Alan Sharpe read Tennyson, Simon Phipps said prayers, choir sang ... and an outstanding tribute by Maurice Cowling, who was meticulously frank. Elizabeth Wilson there, embodying both parents. Stanislaw, Alena's son, read from Ecclesiastes. Met Barry Till[414] among others.'

And then on 4th November we returned to New York, staying this time at the UN Plaza Hotel with an amazing view, from its 36th floor, of the Empire State and Chrysler buildings besides the UN building and the East River.

On this visit Robbie had a challenging task to carry out, and needed to prepare himself for it. He and Eduardo, the ICJ Registrar, had decided that as the General Assembly had little knowledge or appreciation of the work of the Court, he should deliver for them the first of what would become an Annual Report. He must, the first day, be left in peace for time to think and make small amendments to his text for the morrow. That evening we presented ourselves at the American Mission headquarters, where we underwent fierce scrutiny before being admitted to a reception on the 12th floor. 'R approached by many, so much hand-shaking and talking. Then, exhausted, small supper in bar and earlyish bed.'

---

[414] The Very Rev. Barry Till, a Jesus man, had returned to the college as Chaplain and Tutor for some years. He moved on to become Dean of Hong Kong cathedral, and then became Principal of Morley College, London. There he succeeded in extending the college's membership and its range of adult education.

He did not sleep well. But on 8th November 1991 I nervously watched as he stepped up to the green marble rostrum, a lonely figure in that vast hall.

'R spoke for ½ hour, very effectively. Speakers from Mexico, Spain and Sierre Leone followed and endorsed what R and Sec-Gen had proposed – advisory role to extend ICJ's present activities. Lunch in Delegates' Dining room; Afro-Asian seminar afterwards.'

Perez de Cuellar had been especially keen that the agencies of the UN should make use of the Court's service in providing Advisory Opinions on uncertain points of international law. It was not that there was a dearth of activity at the ICJ in these days. As Robbie pointed out in his Statement:

'After decades of underuse, the Court now has a full docket of important cases, with Parties ranging from Scandinavia to Australia and from Central America to the Gulf. Perhaps I might give the Assembly a brief rundown of the present list of cases, in order to give some idea of the topics and of the Parties involved.

'First, the Court will give its Judgment early next week in a case between Guinea-Bissau and Senegal on whether an arbitration award of 1989, concerning their dispute over the maritime boundary, is or is not binding.

'Second, beginning next week will be the oral proceedings in a case brought by Nauru against Australia regarding the mining of Nauru's phosphate resources during the period of trusteeship.

'Third, progressing at the same time – for gone are the days of taking one case at a time – is the case between El Salvador and Honduras, with Nicaragua as intervener, brought before a Chamber of the Court, concerning six portions of the land frontier, the legal position of the waters of the Gulf of Fonseca, and questions about islands in the Gulf. This dispute, going back a very long time indeed, has at least once led to armed hostilities.

'Fourth, a new case introduced by Guinea-Bissau against Senegal seeks to bring the substance of the question of their maritime boundary before the Court.

'Fifth, there is the case brought by Finland against Denmark complaining that a suspension bridge that Denmark proposes to build over the Great Belt will, if completed, be in breach of rights of passage for drilling rigs and drilling ships that pass through those waters from Finland to the North Sea. The Court has already adjudged an application for interim measures of protection in this case and will probably be holding hearings on the substance of the matter next year.

'Sixth, there is a case between Denmark and Norway over the delimitation of the maritime boundary between Greenland and Jan Mayen in which a very large area of sea and shelf is involved.

'Seventh, the Islamic Republic of Iran has brought a case against the United States concerning the shooting down of Iranian Flight 655 in the Gulf on 3 July 1988.

'Eighth, the well-known case of territorial dispute between the Libyan Arab Jamahiriya and Chad, which has at times been the cause of armed hostilities, now comes before the Court as a result of action by both Parties.

'Ninth, Portugal has recently brought a case against Australia concerning the continental shelf off East Timor, Portugal complaining of Australian dealings with Indonesia over that maritime area.

'Tenth, there is an application by Qatar against Bahrain regarding the maritime boundary in the Gulf.

'Eleventh, the case concerning border and transborder armed actions brought by Nicaragua against Honduras remains on the list but proceedings have been suspended at the request of both Parties.'

He had a good deal more to say about the role of the Court, and to clarify some misapprehensions about its purpose. But the passage quoted does emphasize how fully occupied Robbie himself had been during his first year as President.

Our return to The Hague next day gave no respite, either. Robbie, as the more experienced traveller, managed to sleep during our 5-hour overnight flight to Schiphol though I did not. Once at Houtweg, we pulled down our bed and rested for three hours before changing and being taken to the Ridderzaal. There was high security all over The Hague – helicopters overhead and even police boats patrolling the canals – for President Bush, who was taking part in G7 discussions in the city. The talks ran late, which meant that all the diplomatic corps assembled to meet him at 11.30 am were kept waiting for an extra hour. I, standing so long with a glass of rather acid orange juice to sip, found myself growing faint. Fortunately, after sitting and breathing deeply for a while, I managed to step forward for the formal greeting of the President, the Queen and other dignitaries. But food, I knew, would be my undoing; so, making slight gestures with knife and fork but eating nothing, I found I could chat with my neighbours in a fairly normal manner. Robbie was placed at the central table with the great ones and was very impressed with Bush's interest in the Court and his courtesy. (Bush had even, I later heard, asked one of his staff to keep a discreet eye on me to make sure that I was all right.)

We took that Sunday very quietly… for on Monday Robbie was opening the Oral Hearings on the *Nauru/Australia* case and prefacing them with a short tribute to the late Judge Elias. While I returned home, he dined with Judge Weeramantry; and next day had to read out the *Guinea Bissau/Senegal* judgment, in French. He then had three more days work at the Peace Palace before his weekend break.

The moment he arrived home we were both driven to London for a Foreign Office dinner in honour of Arthur Watts, hosted by his successor as Legal Adviser, Frank Berman:[415] a very pleasant occasion held in the Oxford & Cambridge Club, where we spent the night and were able to fit in a National Gallery exhibition before returning to Cambridge. A week at home (which included dinner with our Bridle Way neighbours, Kenneth and Jane Berrill[416]) was followed by another spell in The Hague to conduct the deliberations on the *El Salvador/Honduras* case. And then he arrived home on the Friday in time for a college feast at Caius as the guest of Bill Wade,[417] his old friend from the Law Faculty.

Robbie's last crossing to Holland that year was by air, and he returned by ferry 'with CDJ 27'. This was the powerful BMW that he kept until the end of his time as judge. (I grew used to driving both this beast and my own Honda Civic, changing from right-hand to left-hand controls and from gear-changing to manual. For the journey up to the Lake District our custom for years had been to toss an old penny before starting: the loser would do the tedious drive up the A1 and the winner had the more interesting drive across the Pennines and up to Eskdale.)

And now he had a whole month free for Christmas and the New Year.

———

[415] Sir Franklin Berman QC served in the Diplomatic Corps; became Legal Adviser to the FCO 1988-99; then Visiting Professor of International Law at Oxford and Fellow of Wadham. It was he who wrote the entry about Robbie for the New Oxford Dictionary of Biography.

[416] Sir Kenneth Berrill's career had taken him from being an economics don and Bursar first of St Catharine's and then of King's College, Cambridge to becoming Chief Economic Adviser to the Treasury, among many senior appointments.

[417] Sir William Wade, Professor of Constitutional Law and Master of Gonville & Caius College.

Second Year as President

1992-93

Although free of commitments at the Peace Palace, January 1992 was not uneventful.

On 8th January Robbie was in London for the Memorial Service for Francis Mann in the hall of Gray's Inn: a farewell to a greatly-respected lawyer he had known for many years, and with whom we had spent that evening of intimate warmth such a short time before at the *Institut* meeting at Basle. On the 10th we were welcoming a quite different character to tea at Grantchester, Judge Bola Ajibola, larger than life, exuberant with stories and laughter, in his brightly-coloured Nigerian robes and embroidered cap.[418] He always arrived bearing some gift – perhaps smoked eel or raw herring from the airport shop.

On the 13th we were at a dinner at Lancaster House given by the Foreign Secretary, Douglas Hurd, for the new Secretary-General of the UN, Boutros Boutros-Ghali – a stately occasion, graced by HRH Princess Anne and the Prime Minister. Next day was more demanding, as he addressed members of the Royal Institute of International Affairs at Chatham House on '*An Expanding Court.*'[419]

… And after that we had to get ourselves ready for a visit to Japan.

We set off on the 18th, and found that from the moment we stepped into the First Class section of the Japanese Airways plane we were in a different culture. Off came our jackets, to be replaced with cotton kimonos for comfort overnight. The flight took us over northern Siberia (or so I guessed, peering downwards as dawn rushed towards us on a landscape of barren ruggedness, with just a rare etched line of a river flowing northwards and a very rare hint of human activity, a rectangular enclosure that might have been a military

---

[418] The splendour of his attire reflected his status as a tribal Prince.

[419] The text of *An Expanding Court* appears in the *Collected Papers*, pp554-566

installation). Towards the end we were offered breakfast: European or Japanese? Oh, Japanese of course we bravely said, and a trayful of delights was set before us, to be tackled with chopsticks. Clumsily, I managed to convey rice, pickled cherries and less easily identified titbits to my mouth, ending with a large dollop of brown goo ... which turned out to be horseradish! It was the first of many startling experiences.

We were enormously impressed by the thoroughness of our hosts' hospitality throughout this visit. In advance at The Hague, Robbie had been consulted by the Japanese Ambassador, who enquired about our preferences and particular interests. Thus it was that, once installed in a spacious suite at the New Otoni Hotel in Tokyo, one of our first visits was to the headquarters of SONY, to fulfil Robbie's passion for 'hi-fi'. There we were shown the very latest developments in their recording technology both in sound and (for my benefit) video-cameras. We were then conducted through Asakusa, a large open area of enticing shops decorated for the New Year, leading to the great temple complex of Senso-ji. Wherever we went, throughout our stay, a wonderful guide and interpreter was by our side to explain everything. He was Mr Iida, seemingly available day and night, assiduously consulting his notes to make sure nothing was missed in our planned itinerary.

It was on that first day, I think, that we called at the Foreign Ministry to make contact with our actual host, Hisashi Owada, now Vice-Minister for Foreign Affairs. With Shigeru Oda we were taken to the Tokyo Tower, from which to survey the great city – a less than inspiring view, in rather dim light. And then on that first day Robbie had to sing for his supper, giving a two-hour interview for the Japanese *Jurist* magazine.

Next day he was guest of honour at the Supreme Court, both observing its procedure and meeting the judges at a luncheon. I, in the meantime, was conveyed to several small museums and, with Noriko Oda, given a lesson in *ikebana* – flower-arranging, Japanese style: quite different from the sweet disorder of my usual displays for our village church, for here each 'element' of the arrangement was to be added in accordance with rigid rules. Everything was perfect, everyone behaved with the utmost courtesy; and though I would never have chosen to see an exhibition of ceremonial swords, I could only admire its exquisite craftsmanship. That evening we were honoured guests at a formal dinner given by the Foreign Minister, where Robbie coped with chopsticks better than I did, and I was glad to have the gentle Owada by my side to guide me through the multitude of strange dishes.

Wednesday morning was spent at the National Museum among its impressive collections of paintings and artefacts, then for a while wandering in the Ginza district of extravagant department stores and souvenir shops, choosing just a few small gifts for our grandchildren. We arrived for lunch at the British Ambassador's Residence, finding an entire compound of embassy buildings (unusual in that densely-packed city) and our hosts[420] most agreeable. And that evening we enjoyed a theatrical experience never to be forgotten – a *Kabuki* performance. From the gramophone record of a *Noh* play that Robbie had brought home from his 1964 visit we were already familiar with the other-worldly sounds of high wailing flutes and tapping drums, so it was fascinating to both hear these sounds and watch the musicians producing them. *Kabuki* is a more popular type of entertainment than *Noh,* with every part (even simpering women) played by men groomed from birth in that tradition. At moments it recalled Shakespeare's clowns or even pantomime, yet with a compelling formality that was utterly Japanese.

The prepared programme for our stay, making quite sure that we missed none of the best sights the city could offer, had prescribed an early-morning visit next day to the fish market. 'No thank you,' Robbie had to say, since he was unsure whether we had the stamina to present ourselves at 6 am for this experience, considering that the following item on the agenda was our audience with the Emperor and Empress. (It was a shame, for we understood that we were missing one of the great sights, the arrival of freshly-caught fish from the docks and the swift processing and auctioning of the day's catch.) But we needed to feel fresh and composed for the coming event.

At the Imperial Palace we entered a vast reception hall. From there we were taken along a glazed passage running across a quintessential Japanese garden: on one side gravel, a well-placed stone, a delicate tree; on the other a few miniature pines and a trickling stream. We waited awhile in an antechamber, sipping green tea. Then we moved on towards a flight of stairs leading to closed double doors. We paused. The doors opened and we ascended, to be welcomed into an enormous bare room – Matsu-no-Ma (Pine Chamber) in which two sets of upright chairs had been arranged. Robbie was conducted to one, where he would sit opposite His Imperial Majesty Emperor Akihito, with Shigeru Oda slightly behind and to one side, and an interpreter close by the Emperor. I was taken some distance

---

420 HE Sir John & Lady Whitehead.

to a similar set, so that I sat opposite Empress Michiko, with Noriko Oda slightly behind me. (We hoped, desperately, that our bows had been of an appropriate degree, and that we were not breaking rules of etiquette, since remaining beside the doorway was an official of the Imperial Household, stately and severe.)

Robbie told me afterwards that his half-hour conversation with the Emperor had been rather hard work, since it was conducted very formally through the interpreter despite the Emperor's good knowledge of English. There were questions about the International Court and its current activities, and although there were smiles from the Emperor, little feeling of real contact. My own experience was different. An old friend from Robbie's Argentine days[421] had called on us the evening before, and told us that his wife had found the Empress 'an angel'. So did I: there were few moments when she needed the assistance of her interpreter, and our conversation flowed quite naturally. She was interested when I mentioned Benjamin Britten's 'church parables', influenced by *Noh* plays; we chatted about what we had already seen in Japan; and she spoke about her husband's annual New Year ceremony at which poems are presented on a theme set by him (which that year had been 'wind'). I was growing increasingly uncomfortable about poor Mrs Oda being left out of the conversation, and so – with a glance at the official by the door – the Empress invited her to draw her chair a little closer. Our half-hour passed pleasantly. On leaving, after deep bows, we retreated down the stairs, but then turned to see the imperial couple still standing in the doorway. We bowed even more deeply, and the doors closed.

Now we were taken to the railway station, to board an express train to Sendai. Once more, the degree of perfectionism impressed us. As the train opened its doors, several maids in pink uniforms entered and swept up every speck of litter before standing in line and giving synchronised bows. During the journey, hot towels were offered at intervals to freshen our hands. There were large flower displays at the stations (so uniform in colour and pattern that they might as well have been plastic). At Sendai – the northern city where Oda was emeritus Professor of International Law at its Tohoku University – we were shown their splendid new museum. I became aware, with a slight feeling of horror, that this stage of our programme had been arranged partly with my own interests in mind. In the consultation in the Netherlands it had been mentioned that I had recently

---

421   Ernesto de la Guardia, now Argentine Ambassador to Japan.

read a book[422] based on the pilgrimage made by the poet Matsuo Basho in the 17th century. Thus it was supposed that I was a scholar of Japanese literature, *haiku* in particular. The relevant professor accompanied us as we examined the relics displayed in the museum and then drove further to a place where we left the car and, under the night sky, climbed a frosty hillside to a wooden enclosure sheltering a high stone. Men with notebooks and cameras gathered round, and there were expectant looks directed at me … Help! Gathering my wits, I realised that this must be the famous Tsobu stone that Basho had trekked to see. I stretched a hand and touched it reverently, saying how wonderful it was to think of Basho having been here some 300 years before. They smiled. And next day's Sendai newspaper had a photograph and description of this moment! (The gifts the professor gave me, of valuable facsimiles of early printed poems, I was able to pass on to a Grantchester friend who was an actual Japanese scholar, Carmen Blacker.[423])

We were very tired. Oda stayed for dinner with us at the hotel; and, though we were expected to revel in the chance of relaxing in the hot spring water of an open pool under the stars, we declined that experience and went to bed. Next morning brought the delight of breakfast eaten beside a stunning view of Matsushima Bay (so beautiful that even Basho had been almost tongue-tied). We were now to be guided by a lady, Mrs Aichi, across a scarlet wooden bridge to one of the many rocky islets in the bay. There we admired ancient tombstones carved into a cliff-face and enjoyed the stillness. After that there was a monastery to see, and more antiquities. (To protect us from the deep chill, the thoughtful Mrs Aichi had provided woollen scarves, and warm socks for our shoeless walk about the monastery.)

But now it was Robbie's turn to be interviewed, seriously, for a piece which would appear in the next day's newspaper. Then, returning to Sendai, we called in at the Odas' apartment – a very special privilege, for few foreigners are invited into private homes in Japan. It was, with its matting floor and sparse furnishing, of course very simple except for Noriko's grand piano. We moved then to the Sendai City Museum (Robbie trying on a replica *samurai* helmet) and from there were driven to the airport for a flight to Osaka. (On that plane

---

[422]   *On the Narrow Road to the Deep North* by Lesley Downer, a young English woman fascinated by traditional Japanese poetry. Her title is taken from Basho's own name for his series of haikus.

[423]   Dr Carmen Blacker, a most distinguished Japanese scholar, was most grateful for these papers.

I noticed that we, alone of all its 200 or so passengers, did not have black hair.) And from Osaka we were driven to Kyoto, to the Miyako Hotel set on a hillside. By now Robbie was very tired indeed: too intensive a programme, combined with jetlag, combined to make him uncharacteristically tetchy all of a sudden. We were conducted along corridors to our suite. It was in the section of the hotel designed as an ideal *riyokan*, in accordance with a wish I had expressed to stay in a simple country inn. Robbie's immediate response was indignant: 'But where are the beds? I need to lie down!' Indeed this calm and spacious room had no hint of where we might sleep ... and to our eternal gratitude Yumiko Owada, who was there to dine with us that evening, understood the situation. Instead of yet another strange Japanese meal, sitting on the floor (for neither of us could fold our legs in the proper manner before those low tables) she took us to the hotel's restaurant with European-height tables and chairs and ordered grilled steak for Robbie. It made all the difference; and when we returned to our room, lo! there were futon beds spread on the floor. Robbie grumbled a little, but settled to sleep. He woke in the night, complaining that I must have left a tap on in the bathroom because there was the sound of trickling water, but after checking and finding the taps properly turned off, he lay down again and slept. I, having also woken, discovered that our wonderful room (recently occupied by HRH Prince Charles) overlooked a steep rocky garden, with a little pool which overflowed in a thin stream. Silhouetted against a moonlit sky was one of those bristling pine branches and a slender bamboo. I lay there in perfect contentment; and I think the following night Robbie did too.

Now, on the Saturday, Hisashi Owada was free to join us, and we had a day of privileged sightseeing. At the Myoushin-ji Temple we were received by the 88-year-old abbot, who cheerfully told us how he rose each day at 3 am to carry out his duties. We walked along an open passage where a line of kneeling figures was practising the art of meditation as they gazed at an area of raked gravel and a blank wall – and were touched on the shoulder with a long pole by a disciplinarian monk if they showed signs of losing their concentration upon nothingness. This was Zen Buddhism; and we felt the appeal of the strangely carefree effect evident in the abbot's demeanour. We came away with examples of the old man's wonderful brush-drawings and calligraphy.

That was one temple. Another was Saiho-ji, or Koke-dera, the Moss Temple – a place of utter tranquillity: tall trees, pools, and rocks set in green velvet. In its simple building we were handed thin slips of wood on which to write a prayer. We each took a brush and wrote a word or two, then dropped these tokens into a slot (I think for burning). Afterwards we found our thoughts had been the same: the hope for the safe birth of our next grandchild, Joey's baby.

While the men spent the afternoon with the Law Faculty of the University, I was taken with Yumiko and Noriko to the Temple of 1000 Buddhas, 'Kannon' statues: certainly impressive but quite dreadful and totally alien. The next temple we visited was more soothing, with a friendly abbot. Then we called at a ceramics-shop, where a master potter demonstrated the making of a teapot. I had seen Joey and Egg, both potters, at work, but the fine porcelain moulded on a wheel by this man was of a different order. He worked fast, with utter assurance, shaping the vessel and adding its handle and spout… and then, taking a length of wire, sliced it in half to show the fineness of his work. Although tempted, I dared not buy more than one item because of the difficulty of fitting it into our luggage.

Our dinner that evening was once more an extraordinary experience, hosted by Professor Tabata with a group of international lawyers. We were entertained by two elderly *geishas*. Unlike the demure girls in elaborate kimonos who had served us at previous meals, these two had undergone the full training in their youth, and could provide amusing chatter or music (but alas, we did not hear them playing the *shamisen*). Robbie hugely enjoyed the way they joked and grew increasingly tiddly as the evening wore on. He brought away the card given to him by the older lady, who had fished it out from her bosom.

Our last day brought more delights. We were taken to the Textile Centre, which we found full of unexpected interest. There were craftsmen and women at work on the intricate weaving of silk for fabric and hangings of the finest quality. To produce this, the weaver's fingernails were grown and the tips cut like narrow combs to catch the fine threads of silk. We marvelled – and even more so when we were introduced to the Director. His father, we found, had created the tapestries of the Japanese Room in the Peace Palace, *Hundred flowers and hundred birds in late spring and early summer*, one of the building's greatest treasures. And here, indeed, were the designs preserved still. After that we watched a fashion parade of the latest gorgeous kimonos.

Then we moved to Nijo-jo Castle, home of earlier emperors and stupendous in its decorations. And then to Kinkaku-ji Temple, where as we wandered in I was so interested in the little streamers of prayers hanging from trees that suddenly seeing the temple itself – the Golden Pavilion – was a revelation. We viewed it across water, its surroundings laid out with sensitivity towards the placing of stones and trees to produce perfect harmony.

That same spirit was present in the small garden surrounding the restaurant where we ate lunch. And we were then privileged to be taken to the Urasenke Teahouse where, sitting on the floor, one received a small vessel (hardly a cup) of green tea served with great ceremony by the Grand Tea Master XV and his assistant. There was some guidance about the Way of Tao – and I hoped my awkward gestures and remarks had broken no rules.

Our final temple was, I think, the great Kiyomizu Temple, a scarlet pavilion of many tiers set on a steep hillside, where people caught streams of pure water for sacred ablutions. And then, deeply grateful to the Owadas, the Odas and many discreet helpers, we returned home.

A week later, Robbie was off to The Hague to resume his various and intensive duties there before returning to Cambridge to hear Arthur Watts' Lauterpacht Lecture on *International Law and the Antarctic Treaty System*. Arthur's work on that treaty and his clarity as a lecturer were greatly admired.

To-and-fro life resumed next day, and in The Hague this time one dinner was given by Jose-Maria Ruda, now President of the Iran-USA Claims Tribunal. After Robbie's next weekend at home (diary note: '*Folly to vet*') he was back on duty on 2nd March, when he noted '*Folly died*' (the tragic words surrounded by a black line) … and on the opposite page, '*Jo gave birth 3 pm*'. Folly, athletic and teasing, had been a favourite cat and was sorely missed. And Joey's baby was Tabitha Rose Eddleston, our fifth grandchild. (I drove down to Somerset a fortnight later to meet the new baby, stopping on the way to give a talk about the International Court at my old school – relying heavily on Robbie's patient explanations beforehand.)

A new and fascinating case was now before the Court, the *Passage Through The Great Belt,* concerning Denmark's proposal to build a major bridge spanning the waterway through which tall oil rigs from Finland might find their passage blocked, a case which kept Robbie occupied until his Easter break. On a day when my diary had tentatively noted, 'R to address conference of ILA at Cairo?' he was instead at home entertaining Judge Weeramantry to tea. It may have been the moment when Weeramantry discussed a book he was writing about the Lord's Prayer[424] and its universal relevance – a project that interested Robbie, who in due course read the typescript before publication.

---

[424]   *The Lord's Prayer: Bridge to a Better World* by C.G. Weeramantry.

During that home spell he also fitted in several university events, including an evening with The Club at which he gave an after-dinner talk about the ICJ, enjoyed his Luncheon Club, and gave a speech cryptically noted as '*Bar: Anglo-Dutch 9-11 speech + American postgraduates*'.

———

'*To Charles Goodhart to look at Caius portraits*' is Robbie's diary entry for 30th April. Its significance is that, having found that a President of the ICJ was expected to present a portrait of himself to the Peace Palace, he needed first to find and commission a suitable artist. Charles's college, Gonville & Caius, had in recent years acquired a number of good portraits, and it was a great help to see them before making a choice. We were particularly struck by those done by an Anglo-Indian, Paul Gopal-Chowdhury, who had been their Artist in Residence for a while. His portrait of a particularly difficult subject, Stephen Hawking,[425] and a brilliant conversation piece of a group of Fellows enjoying dessert in their combination room, impressed us both. So he became our choice.

Now we both received vaccinations against yellow fever and polio followed by typhoid and cholera two days later.[426] Though feeling a little poorly afterwards, we drove up to Yorkshire to spend a few very happy days with Dick's family. Once home, I noted, '*Sky television interview for R, 10.15-11 am, mostly in study but ending in sunny garden*'.

Robbie must have arranged for Oda to take his place at a '*dinner with Mayor, Lubbers & Mugabe*' while he, as Charles Goodhart's guest, was enjoying a Drosier Feast at Caius. Next day he was at the memorial service in St John's College chapel for a Law Faculty colleague, John Hall, who had taken his own life – a grievous loss of a gifted and sensitive man.

We met our chosen portrait-painter on 18th May. Driving him from Cambridge station, I told him a little about Robbie and the sort of image we had in mind. Artist and subject got on well, and he immediately made some quick pencil sketches besides discussing the terms of the commission. He appeared again at the end of the week, having lunch with us and taking a series of photographs of Robbie. 'Don't worry', he said, 'it will be a good

---

[425]   Stephen Hawking, Lucasian Professor of Mathematics was a Fellow of Caius.

[426]   These were to protect us during attendance at the UN Conference on Sustainable Development at Rio de Janeiro in June… quite unnecessary, as it turned out.

likeness,' and in due course, when the portraits were delivered – two copies, one for the ICJ and a slightly smaller one for the family – we were very pleased with them.[427]

On the 25th May Robbie was off to The Hague for a day or two with *ACBAQ* (the Advisory Committee on Budgetary and Administrative Questions, whose members came from the UN General Assembly) and work on the *Nauru/Australia* dispute. There followed meetings with the Agents from Finland and Denmark to discuss their forthcoming case concerning the *Great Belt* project …

… And after that our diaries say '*Fly to Rio*', but we did not go. The UN Conference on the Environment and Development (the 'Earth Summit', involving thousands of delegates, journalists and representatives of NGOs) was a momentous event. Yet, even having endured all those inoculations for tropical diseases, Robbie found himself unable to face that exhausting double journey and crowded meetings while his commitments in The Hague were so heavy. He had, however, prepared a statement,[428] and Eduardo Valencia-Ospina was willing to deliver it in his stead. (Robbie was, in fact, ahead of many distinguished contemporaries in his concern for the need for the regulation of environmental problems, and would provide the Preface to Philippe Sands' book, *Principles of Environmental Law*.)

I joined him in The Hague a little later for a royal banquet in the Nordeinde Palace for the visiting President of Surinam. The day after that we dined with Roberto Ago (now aged 86 but in good form), who revealed his plan 'to marry Mrs N. and travel with her to the UN in October'. One Saturday we spent the afternoon in Amsterdam at a mini-conference on *Minorities,* arranged by Malgosia Fitzmaurice, at which Robbie was to make the concluding speech. It was hot, and he was weary after a heavy week. Yet, as I noted, 'adrenalin flowed, and he gave an excellent off-the-cuff address'. He enjoyed the reception afterwards in the impressive Bourse building designed by Berlage. I was always amazed at his ability, in his late 70s, to come alive and respond to a young audience even when tired. But then – excusing himself from what was bound to be a very late dinner – he was able to get back to our flat in time to watch part of an England v Pakistan Test Match on television before bed. Sunday

---

[427] Not long after this Gopal-Chowdhury seems to have given up portraiture in favour of semi-mystical paintings deriving from his Indian background.

[428] *The Role of the International Court of Justice in the Development of International Environment Protection Law* appears on pp 567-573 of his *Collected Writings*.

allowed some typical relaxation, walking along the seafront at Scheveningen, ('a dazzling display of kites in a clear blue sky') and then, on impulse, getting Frances Meadows to join us for 'brunch' at the Hotel des Indes and wander around the flea market in the Lange Vorhout. While I returned home, he stayed on for a further fortnight which included a royal luncheon for the President of Benin, and the delivery of judgment on the *Nauru/Australia* case.

———

Back in England at last, he saw a consultant about his eyesight. He was developing glaucoma, which would soon need attention. But on 15th July he attended a symposium on International Economic Crime arranged by Barry Rider[429] and gave the after-dinner speech.

An oddity in Robbie's diary on one of his home weekends is the entry: *"Armistice Day" farce at church'*. We had been asked to come to church on that July day wearing heavy sombre clothing. Then, as the normal service ended, we had to sing 'Oh God, our help in ages past' as a television crew using a track-mounted camera moved down the aisle filming the congregation, who afterwards gathered around the War Memorial for the final moments of our regular Remembrance Sunday service (filmed from a high cherry-picker to hide the summer foliage all around). This false image of Grantchester remembering its war dead was shown on television in November, to Robbie's rage.

Later that summer Paul Gopal-Chowdhury came with his two portraits of Robbie. We approved: the likeness was good, his style was broad yet perceptive, and the 'family' version less stern than that for the Peace Palace. Four days later another artist appeared. This was Peter Edwards, who had been commissioned by Jesus College to produce a portrait in time for Robbie's 80th birthday. He arrived after lunch, worked all afternoon in the study, and dined with Robbie in college. Next day he set up his easel in the sitting-room, painting Robbie as he watched a televised Test Match. But the match was not going well for England, and it shows in the resulting sketch portrait, which was discarded (although now hung in Dick's house). We were getting to know and like this young man, who lunched with us in the garden and supped with us at the University Centre. On the third day he worked again, with Robbie this time sitting in the study, his back to the windows, his hands folded in typical manner as he rested

---

429   Professor Barry Rider, Fellow (later Fellow-Commoner) of Jesus College, has organised a series of annual symposiums on International Economic Crime since 1982.

his elbows on the desk. Then he left to drive home to Oswestry with the two unfinished canvases.

August allowed a little more family time, with a great family gathering at Pippa's house at Leicester, and a particularly happy spell at Arment House with Joey's little family for our one visit that year.

A tea party at the beginning of October was notable. It was given by James Crawford at the attractive cottage in Whittlesford where he and his wife Patricia[430] had recently settled. The other guests were Derek and Betty Bowett, making it a gathering of three successive Whewell Professors.

When we travelled to New York for the UN meetings later that month it was with Roberto Ago and his new wife, Hanke. 'Roberto,' I noted, 'looked dapper,' and first impressions of the outgoing and talkative Hanke were favourable.

The programme was much as before. Robbie addressed the General Assembly on the first morning and had lunch with the Secretary-General, Boutros-Ghali, afterwards. His full report on the work of the Court was given to the Sixth Committee next day, when he himself hosted a luncheon. Next day Roberto was giving an address to the Afro-Asian group, and we then joined a big gathering for lunch in the Delegates' dining room. The UN building was full of familiar faces: as Robbie was to say, when asked about his 'disciples' by Antonio Cassese,[431] they came from all over the place:

'… Not only Cambridge, but also from when I used to lecture to the many, many foreign students we used to get, especially from the Commonwealth, at the Inns of Court where I used to give regular courses of lectures. So many of them I meet now are Lord Chief Justices or Attorney-Generals, or Ministers of Justice, or even Prime Ministers, who say "Do you remember that I came to your lectures at the Inns of Court School of Law years ago?"'

With the Agos we looked at a major Matisse exhibition, and then went to the Met. Opera House for Verdi's *Falstaff* – a new experience for both wives.

---

[430] With Patricia, James's second wife, two young daughters were adopted. After some years there was a parting, and he married again. His third wife is Joanna Gomula, herself now a Professor and mother of his son James. In 2014 he married for a fourth time.

[431] *Five Masters of International Law* p.163.

At the weekend there was a concert celebrating UN Day in the great General Assembly hall, transformed for the purpose – a wonderful performance given by the Spanish National Orchestra under de Burgos, followed by a reception ('frightful scrum') and a tiny supper in our room.

On the Sunday Robbie proposed a small adventure for the two of us. Our hotel room overlooked a small helipad beside the UN Headquarters building used mainly for quick flights to JFK Airport, but also offering sightseeing trips by helicopter; and so up we went for an aerial view of Manhattan, showing that densely-packed narrow island below with, in its centre, the rectangular oasis of Central Park.

The week went on: more lunches, including one given by Frank Berman for British delegates at which we met Michael Wood.[432] On our return to The Hague we attended an interesting event, the celebration in the Grote Kerk of Queen Beatrix's half-jubilee (12½ years) as monarch: not a religious service but a ceremony with a good deal of pomp. For us it was particularly notable for our brief chat afterwards with Princess Juliana[433] and Prince Bernhardt. Although old and a little vague, the former Queen expressed her interest in the International Court.

———

The demands of the Court eased off during November, allowing a little more time with our young families. We even watched television one morning (normally unthinkable) to see a story written by Pippa presented on a children's programme. And among Robbie's activities were a talk to the college law society and visits to London – one for an 'Oppenheim lunch'.

The next time I joined him in The Hague we fitted in a private excursion to see more of the Netherlands. Our driver, Jacques van der Meer, had suggested that he might take us to see more distant provinces. It was now early December, and our trip was in pouring rain all day. But setting off early, he drove us by minor roads northwards to the thoroughly watery village of Giethoorn and to Urk, both in the newly-created province of Flevoland; then on to Stavoren and Hindeloopen in Friesland – once major ports, now with

---

[432] As Sir Michael Wood, he would succeed Sir Franklin Berman as Chief Legal Adviser to the FCO 1999-2006.

[433] As Queen Juliana of the Netherlands she had succeeded her mother Queen Wilhelmina, who had abdicated in 1948. Juliana herself abdicated (resuming the title 'Princess') in 1980 in favour of her eldest daughter Beatrix, who herself was to abdicate in 2013.

fishing and pleasure boats only, a transformation that had come about by the building in the 1930s of a great dam blocking off the Zuiderzee to make the inland lake of the IJselmeer and gradually create rich farmland from drained areas. We drove back along that dam, the 32-km Afsluitdijk, in the dark. I had taken some rainy photographs; we had eaten an enormous lunch of fish and bought an example of Hindeloopen craftwork; and we were pleased with these experiences.

Once back at home, Peter Edwards arrived with two versions of his more successful portrait of Robbie and also one of me (which Robbie liked, and bought). The frames provided by his local workshop in Oswestry were rather disappointing and though we sighed and accepted them, the college demanded something better. Peter took their canvas back with him and returned with a new frame – which turned out to be a large, heavy and very original construction he had made himself. After recovering from the shock, we liked it; but the college later replaced it with something more conventional to be hung on a college wall opposite the splendid portrait of Steve Fairbairn, the famous rowing coach.[434]

The Christmas recess included fun in the village: a crowded buffet supper down at The Old Vicarage given by Jeffrey and Mary Archer[435] after the Carol Service; another musical party by our new neighbours, Ann Keith and Jeremy Wong; and later another by more Grantchester neighbours, Helaine and Yorick Blumenfeld,[436] where we were shown Helaine's latest work in her newly-enlarged studio. Christmas Day was spent with Pippa's family, and Joey, Egg and Tabitha came to us for the New Year. As always, it was the family visits that were for Robbie best of all.

---

434 The portrait is currently – 2016 – hung in the room of Michael Waibel, Law Fellow and international lawyer.

435 Dame Mary Archer (as she later became) was at that time our church choirmistress.

436 Helaine Blumenfeld's sculptures were becoming internationally famous by this time.

Oppenheim

1992 had seen the publication, at last, of the 9th edition of *Oppenheim's International Law* Vol. 1: *PEACE*, edited by Sir Robert Jennings and Sir Arthur Watts (1333pp).

This great textbook was originally written by Lassa Oppenheim,[437] whose first edition of Volume I was published in 1905. Successive revisions had been made over the years, the 4th, (greatly enlarged) jointly by McNair and Lauterpacht, and the following four by Lauterpacht alone. The 8th Edition, of 1955, incorporated so much material by Hersch Lauterpacht that there was little of Oppenheim's original text left. Lauterpacht died in 1960, leaving his notes in preparation for a 9th Edition which would have become more of a total rewriting than a 'revision'.

By that time there was a clear need for this new and definitive edition, and Robbie was asked to undertake it. Hersch's notes were passed to him, but he felt that rather than use them as they stood he should be more radical still: the whole subject encompassed by the title *Peace* had expanded so greatly that it must be approached afresh. The publisher was Longman. Their 1966 contract made it clear that Robbie could not expect any great financial reward for the great task ahead, since the copyright was still to a large extent derived from Oppenheim. Although Lassa Oppenheim had died long since, his widow had inherited the copyright; on her death it had passed to her daughter, on whose death it went to her widower; and now, although he (Geoffrey Hudson) too had died, there was a Mrs Tomoko Hudson, his relict from a later marriage, who could still claim a share of the copyright. It was an unavoidable complication: the great textbook was known as *Oppenheim* and its successor must bear that name if it was to attract sales.

Robbie's work on the book has been mentioned at intervals in this biography. It was largely drudgery, calling for careful organisation and

---

437   L.F.L. Oppenheim (1858-1919) was a German lawyer who settled in England, taught at the L.S.E., and then became Whewell Professor of International Law at the University of Cambridge.

sheer hard work. He had no regular secretarial assistance when he began, so produced foolscap sheets largely handwritten (sometimes typed by himself) to be copied more tidily by a professional typist. It is difficult now to recall exactly who did what. There was the charming Danish lady, Mrs Jansen, who had typed for Hersch and who laboured on the text for some time. She was the widow of an eminent orchestral conductor and knew many of the great musicians of the early 20th century; but she was slow. My own sister was a highly efficient secretary with her own agency down in Kent, and so packets of manuscript would be posted to her for typing. But mailing this precious stuff to an office on Romney Marsh was not ideal, and the typist had to decipher often unrecognisable words, obscure technical terms in scribbly writing. I think there was a young woman working at Jesus College who did some typing for him for a while. And then, once my children were old enough to make it possible, I myself worked on many pages. It was only when he was at the ICJ and had the services of a secretary (shared, for the first nine years, with Judge Schwebel) that there was more regular assistance; and it was only once she – and we, at home – had mastered a computer that the task became a little easier. For in the earlier stages, one had needed to estimate the space needed at the bottom of a page for the insertion of footnotes – complicated and sometimes lengthy – when judging when to break off from the main text; and any mistake called for careful rubbing-out and retyping of top and carbon copies.

It was after Robbie had been working on *Oppenheim* for many years, fitting it into his other activities, that he recruited Arthur Watts to join him. Longman's then drew up a fresh contract, and their collaboration began. It was a remarkably effective one: two busy international lawyers sharing the work by each taking sections and, on completion, passing them to the other for scrutiny. Part of their success came about because they had a great respect for each other and yet were at ease in pointing out possible improvements. Arthur had been to Haileybury and Sandhurst, and it showed; yet they both were Downing men, had a similar sense of humour, and shared a passion for cricket. (No-one else would be able to claim, as Watts could, to have organised a cricket match in Antarctica at -12°C, as captain of the Beardmore Casuals, narrowly defeated by the Gondwanaland Occasionals!)

Because their collaboration took place before the adoption of communication by email, a great bundle of their correspondence in the later years has survived. An important letter from Francis Dodds, Literature and Law Publisher, *Longman Academic*, addressed to 'Mrs Hudson, Sir Robert, Sir

Arthur and Mr Lauterpacht' in April 1990, summarizes the situation at that point:

'1.1 Arrangements for a new Ninth Edition of *Volume One* of *Oppenheim's International Law* were set up in 1966 under the editorship of Sir Robert Jennings. He was to edit the text of the Eighth Edition, incorporating into it existing material for the Ninth prepared by Sir Hersch Lauterpacht before his death. In 1975 the arrangement was adjusted, but not fundamentally altered, to bring in Sir Arthur Watts as Sir Robert's co-editor.

1.2 For various reasons, not least the interminable delays over the new Convention on the International Law of the Sea, which was not signed until 1982 (by which time both editors were deeply involved in other compelling professional commitments) Sir Robert and Sir Arthur were unable to complete the new Ninth edition in the time expected. Work appeared to have stalled on the new version; and in due course, when the last copies sold out, the old Eighth Edition of *Oppenheim* was put formally out of print – the rate of continuing sale (unsurprisingly for an unrevised work first published in 1955) was insufficient to sustain a further printing of so large a book.

1.3 There matters rested, and it was generally assumed that the project had lapsed, though it was in nobody's interest formally to cancel it unless and until the parties involved felt it desirable to set up a Ninth Edition afresh under new auspices. Longman was therefore more than somewhat astonished – though very gratified! – to receive out of the blue a letter from Sir Robert and Sir Arthur towards the end of 1989 announcing that, far from being dead, the project for a new Ninth Edition was still very much alive, and that they were, against every expectation, in the final stages of producing the text. They had been working at it steadily during the long years of silence, but had preferred to say nothing of progress in the meantime in case they proved unable to complete the task.

1.4 That is exciting news, and we are sure that all the parties involved will share our anxiety that the world should indeed see the Ninth Edition of the book after so long, and under such distinguished editorial control....'
    [... And so, for five more pages, the letter discusses the need for an entirely new contract. In this] 'messy situation ... I am afraid there is no way

any publisher today – whether it be Longman or anyone else – could make any commercial headway at all with a project so inflexibly tied down to the facts of economic life of 86 years ago! … It seems to us, therefore, that the 1966 contractual arrangements (with their 1904 constraints) are so utterly adrift from the 1990 text, and the economic context into which it is arriving, that the sensible thing is to set up new purpose-built arrangements to cover the situation as it now is.'

Many complications had to be dealt with: the proportion of original text that was now out of copyright, the considerable rewriting that Lauterpacht had prepared, the major – virtually total – rewriting by the two most recent 'editors', and the tiresome survival of a Mrs Hudson who had inherited what remained of the Oppenheim estate. Later correspondence resolved the question of Hersch Lauterpacht's contribution: it was agreed that those sections of the text had been entirely rewritten by Jennings and Watts, and that Lauterpacht's own proposed rewriting had already been published in his *Collected Papers*.[438] The new contract was signed in June 1991. Even without allowing any residual royalties to the Lauterpacht estate, the new editors were to receive a very modest amount, Arthur slightly more than Robbie.

There followed a determined race to the finish, fitted around Robbie's very full workload at the Court and Arthur's own heavy workload as Chief Legal Adviser to the FCO. There had, for instance, been a remark by Arthur in August 1990 that…

'Iraq has unfortunately mucked up my plans, and I am not as far forward as I had hoped to be… I hope to put in some work … in some spare time in New Zealand (where I go after Australia) and will try to let you have something during September.'

In January 1990 he wrote to Lord Blakenham, chairman of Pearson Publishing, in support of an appeal by Eli Lauterpacht for funds allowing his Research Centre to appoint a Research Assistant 'whose principal task would be to provide assistance for future editions of *Oppenheim*…

---

[438] *International Law; the collected papers of Sir Hersch Lauterpacht*, Vols I-IV, 1970-78, edited by Sir Elihu Lauterpacht. C.U.P.

'...a large part of the problem has been keeping track of the vast amount of material which is available these days. Once one waits for more than about a year or two the task of catching up with past material greatly increases, since in the time taken during that catching up, yet more material has become available. It becomes an almost never-ending process trying to keep up...

'... Having had the experience of working, with Sir Robert Jennings, on the 9th edition, I know how valuable a Research Assistant would have been ...'

The final editorial arrangements about book production seem to have been carried through principally by Arthur Watts, but always while consulting Robbie.

It was with a great sense of relief that, their task completed, we went to London on 18th May 1992 to find that Longmans had prepared a very nice launch party, with Francis Vallatt, Ian Sinclair, Frank Berman, Gordon Slynn and other distinguished international lawyers present. On the table was a book-shaped cake lying ready to be cut, and a photographer caught the moment when Robbie and Arthur, Tweedledum & Tweedledee, hands together, clasped the knife. In due course there were reviews, although it took time for its bulk to be absorbed and any praise, of course, was for its usefulness to practioners. By December Rosalyn Higgins, after reading substantial parts of it, wrote to Robbie, 'It is *splendid*, and all that the expectant users had hoped for...'

A 25-page review entitled *Lassa Oppenheim's Nine Lives* appeared, however, in *The Yale Journal of International Law* of Winter 1994. It was by Professor Michael Reisman, whose searching comments included a comparison of the succession editions of the work.

'The decisive factor in the First Edition's success... was the coherence of an explicit theory...' [McNair's 4th Edition relied on and discussed more than 400 cases in Vol. 1, while Oppenheim had listed only 54. In Jennings & Watt's edition] 'the editors fail to apply the distinction between what scholars now call "hard law" – legal formulations that are attended by the requisite political force to make them effective – and "soft law" – legal formulations for which political support is intermittent, quite thin, or simply nonexistent. ... As a result, the picture that emerges – one of a consistently strong system – fails to catch the reality of international law.'

Reisman acknowledges, nevertheless, that the authors had 'set out to create an English-style legal treatise in a field whose research is far more challenging than any in municipal law. There is no doubt that they have achieved their objective brilliantly.'

That was Volume One disposed of – actually in two tomes. There remained a need for a revision of Vol. II dealing with *War*, and even a new Vol. III on *International Organisations*. On 3rd June 1992 Arthur Watts, having discussed the matter with Robbie, wrote to the publishers about *OPPENHEIM: THE FUTURE*, with their first suggestions about who might undertake the work.

At that point he thought that Robbie and he might take on Vol. II. 'But Robbie would prefer not to be as directly involved in this work as he was with Vol. I, in which case we might develop the "Consulting Editor" idea …' As a substantive co-editor he proposed Christopher Greenwood, 'a Fellow of Magdalene College Cambridge, and already something of a specialist in this area'; and it is indeed Greenwood who, probably using the framework proposed by Watts, is working on that section covering *War*. In November 2017 Rosalyn Higgins and her co-authors published *Oppenheim International Law, United Nations.*

Rosalyn had in 1997 asked Robbie to comment on her own scheme. He replied:

'Let me say something about your question whether there is any need for another volume on international organization, especially after the publication of [Leyden professor] Henry Schermer's important work. I think the answer is very straightforward: there is no need for another *similar* treatment. But Henry's book is redolent of his own personality and attitudes; and there is surely any amount of room for something different. The Higgins volume will speak for Higgins; and I cannot believe it will be like Henry's.

'What I would like to see would be something not only different from Henry's, but very different. I would like it to get right away from the immensely learned and sincere but innocent Kelsen/Lauterpacht tradition – to which Henry really belongs, the idea that international law is sacred and all we want is more of the same, invented by dedicated Professors – to the healthier realist tradition of Charles de Visscher and James Brierly. (I well remember Hersch's strong dislike of *Theory and Reality*, which he regarded as a kind of treachery to the subject.) We all agree that this is to be a practitioner's book. But a practioner needs to know what the thing is really like, and what are its limitations and weaknesses, as well as what it is *supposed* to be.

'Recent events, for example, have shown all too clearly that the UN system is inadequate, clumsy, easily subject to ill-informed political pressures, and generally pretty useless when it comes to dealing with a situation like former Yugoslavia, or Rwanda. What we need is a critical analysis of the existing institutions which not only describes what we have but also points out where it is lacking and what can and might be done about it and indeed whether anything can be done, eg why has Article 47 of the Charter never been implemented and (a) is there any chance that it might still be? and (b) if it were implemented, would it help solve the difficulty over making military decisions, or had we better forget about it?

'It is surely … time that the Hague Yugoslav Tribunal were subjected to a critical cost-benefit analysis. There they are, with just over 4 times the staff of the ICJ, and an expensive prison full of ordinary Dutch prisoners because it would otherwise be empty, and all they have accomplished so far is to convict one wretched Serb of lowly rank. The inadequacy of this politically correct tribunal in face of the situation on the ground makes one wish that Gilbert were still writing his operas. It is not lack of money or will or ability. It is just the inadequacy of much of the stock international lawyer thinking that seeks to deal with a complicated situation involving intense hatred, much of it stemming, it seems now to be conveniently forgotten, from the behaviour of Croat and Bosnian Muslim SS battalions during the 2ⁿᵈ World War – to deal with it by yet another stock adversarial adjudication operating against a few individuals picked from the many hundreds of guilty on all sides; but of course a system with cosy jobs for international lawyers. The so-called Rwanda tribunal will hardly bear a mention; which might explain the conspiracy of silence about this egregious farce?

'Now of course we cannot contemplate a new *Oppenheim* in the forthright language I use among ourselves but, if we are to have a book for the *practitioner* the new volume should warn him of the grave shortcomings and inadequacies of present international organisation…'

The ineffectiveness of this tribunal and the later International Criminal Court enraged him. He would fulminate in private over what he felt were these misconceived organisations. The United Nations, for all its manifest weaknesses, must be made to work, yet too often its proposed remedies were unrealistic. As he had said in the extended interview with Antonio Cassese in 1994:

> '...I find some difficulty about an international criminal law because, in the case of common crimes like murder, it raises questions about the relationship to municipal law and courts that need a lot more thinking about. Moreover, practice in Nuremberg and Tokyo and so on has always been to bring it down to the individual. And yet, in spite of what was said at Nuremberg, it is a fact that criminal acts are sanctioned, if not committed, by what Nuremberg called "abstract entities". It is all very well bringing it down to the individual, but I am loath to let off some of the "abstract entities" all the same. *Many breaches of human rights are committed by faceless bureaucracies, i.e. "abstract entities".*'

Cassese, in the many pages devoted to Robbie in his *Five Masters of International Law*, never once mentions the Ninth Edition of *Oppenheim*. But of course those many years of labour had produced merely a tool for the practitioner. Evidence of the 'scholarship' Cassese was looking for would appear in 1998 with the publication of Robbie's *Collected Writings*, edited by Georges Abi-Saab. And curiously, Robbie himself quite failed to include *Oppenheim* in the list of his publications in *Who's Who*.

Oppenheim Vol. I, crushingly expensive as it was, did sell and was translated into Chinese. It continues to sell, mainly to libraries. There are other books on international law intended as comprehensive instruction for students of the subject; but, being different in scope, they do not compete with *Oppenheim*.

Final year as President of the ICJ

1993

By now Robbie was fully into the swing of his duties as President, though it scarcely made his task any easier.

He was back in The Hague early in the New Year for a 24-day spell of diplomatic receptions and dinners and those short formal interviews with ambassadors. More importantly, there were the labours entailed in the proceedings of the Court: administrative committees, oral hearings, and the writing and reading of successive notes at each stage of deliberation. He was engaged in every case, and each one was complex. They would not necessarily lead to a judgment, for occasionally the process might lead to the parties themselves agreeing to a settlement, as had happened the previous September, when at the last minute Denmark and Finland withdrew their case concerning the *Great Belt* bridge which had threatened obstruction to the passage of tall sea-going oil rigs.

I doubt whether anyone other than his wife would be able to decipher the cryptic daily entries in his *Cambridge Pocket Diary*. For example:

'Friday 8 January:*Pk Lane lunch – Ajibola   Q.B. Agents 3.30   curatorium Joanna Thuransky 5 pm   Residentie Orchestra 8.15*'.

'*Q.B. Agents*' would have concerned the dispute between Qatar and Bahrain. '*Curatorium*' is probably the curatorium of the *Institut de Droit International,* but might mean the committee overseeing The Hague Academy. '*Joanna Thuransky*' was the charming and enthusiastic young lecturer from Leiden who would consult him about arrangements for the next Telders Moot. And lunches with fellow judges were of course a regular way of developing the 'collegiality' that contributed to the success of his term as President. There was evidently a concert that evening as well.

In the midst of these activities came news of the death of Judge Manfred Lachs. Malgosia Fitzmaurice, his step-daughter, had warned Robbie at the turn of the year that Lachs was gravely ill, and he had died on 14th January. That was followed next day by the customary 'lying in state' in the grandeur of the Japanese Room, where Robbie stood for 1½ hours by the coffin, receiving members of the diplomatic corps.

It was the Vice-President Shigeru Oda and the Deputy Registrar who went to Warsaw for the funeral of Judge Lachs, while Robbie met representatives from Leiden University making arrangements for the memorial gathering that would be held there later. On the 29th his diary notes *Art. 3 Deliberation* – which meant that the Court must consider a replacement for their deceased colleague, someone from the same region (not necessarily the same country, but in this case from Eastern Europe) to complete his term of office. And that was to be Judge Herczegh, from Czechoslovakia.

In Cambridge an old friend, Alan Percival, was celebrating his 80th birthday. He and Robbie had shared many experiences – their pre-war year in the US and their many years as Fellows of Jesus College (Robbie as Senior Tutor and President, Alan as Tutor, Bursar and President); and their ages matched.

Age brought with it the possibility of a *Festschrift*. One afternoon Malgosia Fitzmaurice and Vaughan Lowe[439] called for tea to discuss the scheme they had in mind for one in Robbie's honour – not to be the usual collection of articles on random topics but a more cohesive volume whose theme would be the International Court of Justice, and its publication timed to celebrate the Court's fiftieth anniversary in 1996. Since Vaughan was to write the Introduction, he came and spent an afternoon talking with me about Robbie. The result was a remarkably sympathetic verbal portrait: he had immediately understood the importance of Robbie's Methodist background and deep attachment to his northern countryside.

During that home spell we also attended the university's first William and Mary Lecture, given by Ruud Lubbers, the Dutch Prime Minister. The Senate House was suitably set up and there was a good audience. Then, embarrassingly, the amplification system broke down as Lubbers was speaking, so that his excellent lecture came in deafening bursts between sections that were barely audible. Shame on Cambridge, home of advanced science! Lubbers was entertained afterwards at Gonville & Caius.

---

[439] Professor Vaughan Lowe, QC, was at this time Reader in International Law at Cambridge and a Fellow of Corpus Christi College. He later became Chichele Professor at Oxford.

Back in Holland in late February, the memorial event for Manfred Lachs was held in the university hall at Leiden – equivalent of Cambridge's Senate House – when, besides some words from Malgosia, addresses were given by a Leiden professor, another by Robbie and the last, a more personal recollection, by Kooijmans.[440]

Our experience of Netherlands culture was slightly extended by a visit to Rotterdam at the weekend – but on such a bitterly cold day that we needed to stay indoors, and simply went into the Boymans-van Beuningen Museum, where among Dutch and Flemish paintings we tried to distinguish between the various Breugels. Before returning home, we attended the Prime Minister's luncheon for the visiting President of Israel. Queen Beatrix was there, and I was surprised to find myself called by her Lady in Waiting to join their group. The wife of the President (Chaim Herzog) had asked to speak to me because I had known her aunt, Rachel Lauterpacht, well.

We were back in Cambridge to hear the Inaugural Lecture given by Derek Bowett's successor in the Whewell Chair of International Law, James Crawford, and afterwards to share a splendid buffet supper at the Crawfords' house at Whittlesford.

On 10th March Robbie reverted to his rôle as teacher. First we flew to Dublin, where he lectured to an ILA audience on 'Solving international conflicts through law', hosted by the genial Judge Brian Walsh who had been so friendly in Strasbourg; and after a convivial evening with his group, we had another memorable encounter next morning when we called on the Irish President, Mary Robinson, at her residence in Phoenix Park. We were both deeply impressed by our conversation with her – a lawyer-politician who, among many other achievements, had made an imaginative effort towards conciliation among their Northern Irish neighbours by inviting groups of women from there, Catholic and Protestant together, for relaxed weekends away from the bitter dissension that ruined their relationships at home. She has since become a renowned advocate for Human Rights internationally.

---

[440] Peter Kooijmans would serve as Judge of the ICJ 1997-2006, and had a distinguished career as Professor at the Free University of Amsterdam and as Foreign Minister in the Dutch Government.

We then took a train to Galway, Robbie having been invited by Dennis Driscoll[441] to speak to his students at the University there. We spent three nights in the cottage-annexe to the Driscolls' house, surrounded by a green landscape of quiet small fields, drystone walls and tiny cottages. Robbie of course enjoyed his sessions with Driscoll's students; but besides his academic work, we had not far away some family friends to meet. Jo Nethaway, mother of Dick's wife Jill, had settled in a cottage at Moycullen, and entertained us to lunch and a walk in the woods with her lively small dog. Next day – after 'R talked for 1½ hours for students (drawing questions mostly) – it was Jill's brother John who took us northwards by car for an impression of Connemara – alas, in characteristically damp conditions though well worthwhile. And as our final glimpse of the West of Ireland, we drove a tiny hired car down to Shannon airport by way of County Clare.

On 19th March Robbie returned to The Hague and, before going out to the Haagsche Club's annual dinner, rang me 'with news of imminent Bosnian application to ICJ for Interim Measures against Yugoslavia.' It was going to be a busy session: he was seeing the Agents from Chad and Libya to discuss procedure for the hearing of their dispute, and the deliberations on the *Denmark/Norway* case were continuing.

But the *Bosnia/Yugoslavia*[442] case was urgent, and Robbie was determined that the Court should show that in an exceptional situation its usual measured pace could be speeded up. That autumn, in his Statement to the UN General Assembly, he would be able to report:

'Twice during this last year the Court has had to deal with complicated and lengthy requests for interim measures of protection in the case brought by Bosnia and Herzegovina against Yugoslavia (Serbia and Montenegro) concerning the Genocide Convention. Such requests for interim measures, according to the Court's rules, "have priority over all other cases". These two separate requests were such requests, and the Court dealt with them immediately and with dispatch: the first was handled in some three weeks,

---

441 Professor Dennis Driscoll was at that time Dean of the Law School at the University of Galway.

442 The full title of that case is *Bosnia and Herzegovina v. Yugoslavia (Serbia and Montenegro)*.

and the second in only a little longer time – that period including in both instances time for an oral hearing in which both parties were heard and for the study of several lengthy written observations.'

He was justifiably proud of this achievement. It had kept them all at full stretch, even over weekends. In my diary I noted, with some anxiety –

'Saturday 3 April: An exhausting day for Robbie. Morning spent in Great Hall of Justice, hearing and adjudicating Finnish v. German teams in Moot. Afternoon, the real Court in deliberation over "Interim Measures" to be brought against Serbia.'

On the Sunday, 'R working all day'; on Monday, 'R with drafting committee for Bosnia/Serbia case'. On the 7th, 'ICJ announced Order on *Bosnia/Serbia*. Shown briefly on BBC news.' And a report, with a photograph of RYJ, appeared on the 9th in the *New York Times*.

Home for the Easter weekend; another busy week with deliberations, and the delivery of a lecture in Amsterdam. Then on his next weekend at home there were two events. One was noted as 'Ian Edwards with furniture', a special treat. In his *Hi-Fi News* Robbie had spotted an advertisement for individually-made storage cabinets for CDs and sheet music. The attraction was that these, like our piano, were made in the West Riding of Yorkshire. We had called on the cabinet-maker on one of our journeys north, and Robbie had been instantly charmed by him. His workshop was an old Methodist chapel in Harrogate, and Edwards himself turned out to be a gnome-like enthusiast who arrived on a bike, his trousers tucked into his socks and a knitted bobble-hat on his head. The 'furniture' did not disappoint, and the two pieces fitted well into Robbie's study. The second event that Saturday was a concert given in King's College Chapel in memory of a friend, Peter le Huray, musicologist, sung by the choirs of King's, St John's, Trinity and Peter's own college, St Catharine's.

Robbie returned to his tasks on the early plane next Monday, and I joined him a few days later for a dinner (an enormous affair for all the Honorary Consuls in the Netherlands) given by Kooijmans. On the annual *Koninginnedag* which followed, we took a blissful wander in the woods, full of wild flowers, at Sorgvliet. The Lange Vorhout was lively, spread with pots of geraniums and other flowers for sale, while as part of the *kermis* the Korte Vorhout became a fairground, with fireworks in the evening. Next day, Saturday, Jacques was eager for another excursion. This time he drove us southwards:

'... over Haringvliet, through Goeree-Overflakkee, then to Duiseland (coffee at Bruinisse); Zierikzee – fine – Browershaven (lunch excellent.) Walcheren – Domburg (spoilt by tourists); Middleburg (fine), Vlissingen (old town OK). Home via Bergen op Zoom (splendid, but awful pop concert in marketplace)...'

It was interesting to find that even Jacques was defeated by the dialect spoken in Zeeland. Early on the Monday morning he took us to *Keukenhof*, arriving just as the great garden opened, so that we could walk among its drifts of spring flowers in a lovely gentle light, and admire the vivid fields of tulips before coachloads of other sightseers arrived.

That little break was welcome, but Robbie had more work to do with the drafting committee and the inevitable diplomatic occasions. One was a crowded reception in the City Hall bidding farewell to Michael Jenkins, the retiring British Ambassador; next day a more intimate one in the Odas' new apartment, at which I was recruited once again to turn pages for Noriko's thunderous performance of Scarlatti and Chopin. The next was a luncheon in the *Treveszaal* – all baroque splendour and beautiful flower arrangements – given by Prime Minister Lubbers for the King and Queen of Belgium. It entailed a wearisome hour of standing before the meal, and long speeches. In the evening we had 3½ more hours of standing at a crowded buffet supper, at the end of which our legs were giving way. But I noted that 'King Baudouin seems v. gracious and good'; and we had tasted strawberry beer, which was a new experience.

Robbie spent most of May in The Hague, apart from a one-day journey to Paris for the prize-giving ceremony of the Hague Curatorium. Among the visitors to his office one diary-entry is worth remarking: '*Gorbachov and Lubbers 4 pm*'. On his next weekend at home we dined in the Master's Lodge at Jesus, where the Renfrews were entertaining two rich ladies expected to make generous donations to the college.

After his next brief spell in The Hague, Robbie returned to work in his study at home. He needed to be in Cambridge for a very special occasion on 10th June, marked in his diary simply by outlining the printed words *Congregation of the Regent House (Honorary Degrees) 11.30.*[443] In his own hand is '9.30 Jes. Lodge'.

---

[443] A modest note of his own Honorary LL.D.

441

But first, on the evening of the 9th, there were drinks in the Fellows' Garden and a fine dinner in Upper Hall in his honour at which Peter Edward's portrait was unveiled. Joey, the senior Goodharts and Jeremy Carver were all present as guests. I have, on several small cards, Robbie's notes for his speech of thanks, with his recollections of the career that had brought him to this moment. He wanted particularly to dispel some popular misconceptions: it was one of the...

'...frustrations of age that remembered history was so different from the myths and views of history invented by those with present vested interest in seeing the past in a certain way... E.g. that pre-war and even in the '50s, Oxford & Cambridge were difficult to get into unless [you were from] public school, or very rich or both. Not my experience...'

... and he recalled his own admission to the supposedly exclusive university, and how the...

'...Fellows at Jesus [were] even less in keeping with the myth. In the 1950s the Master, Senior Tutor, Bursar, Steward and all the Tutors were from grammar schools or less. C.H. Dodd, CH, was from Wrexham Grammar School; the Dean, Gardner-Smith, from another. ...Public School dominance in more recent times when Shirley Williams clobbered our Grammar Schools and so removed the Public Schools' only serious competitors.'

This was followed by recollections of some stalwart college 'servants' (as they were still known) of the past: Captain Austin, the formidable Head Porter; Jeeves, the Manciple, a 'Sir Humphrey' figure; Robinson, Miller, Lenoir... And the physical changes to the college – the fire in First Court which had led to the creation of a library in place of A and B Staircases; the demolition of Small Hall, 'Victorian mock-gothic at its most exuberant'; alterations to the layout of the gardens, and more. It all went down well.

And then, on the 10th, came that 'tremendously exciting day', as I noted in my diary. It was indeed exciting. While Robbie went to be escorted from college to the Senate House, Dick, Joey and I arrived to take our places. The bells of Great St Mary's were pealing, and inside a small orchestra and the combined choirs of King's and St John's provided lively music from the gallery. Before the ceremony I met the Chancellor (HRH the Duke of Edinburgh), together with the nine honorary graduands. They included the Chief Rabbi Jonathan Sacks, and James Watson (who, with Francis Crick, had worked out the structure of DNA); and there was the novelist Iris Murdoch. She looked rather lost, so I asked whether her husband was here. 'No', she said. In fact Professor John Bayley was not far away, but a hint of her later dementia was already evident.

The Public Orator, James Diggle, had the task of presenting these nine people in turn with a neat encomium in Latin: not easy, particularly with advanced science. In Robbie's case he included a quip about his love, as a Yorkshireman, of cricket. And he contrived to render a parody of Gilbert and Sullivan –

'The Court's the true embodiment
Of everything that excellent:
It has no kind of fault or tort,
And he, my Lords, embodies the Court.'

– into a Latin jogtrot metre which gave just the same comic impression.

While enjoying all this, both Robbie and I were preoccupied with an anxiety: was Pippa all right? A boy or a girl? For we knew that Pippa's baby was due to be delivered by caesarean section at 10 o'clock that very morning, and wanted news.

Amid the clamour of church bells and gawping tourists, the university procession made its way along King's Parade to King's College for the Honorary Degree Luncheon. Robbie and I slipped into the Porters' Lodge and asked whether any message had been received; but no. Tents had been set up on the lawn, where we first joined the great throng chatting with drinks, and then moved to our places for the meal. Halfway through, there was a welcome interruption: a silver salver appeared before Robbie, with a note:

[A telephone message from Mick] 'You have a beautiful Granddaughter Susanna Joy born 10.09 am. Pippa and Baby are doing fine.'

In his relief and delight Robbie could not at first think what to do. But his neighbour, the Provost's wife, suggested that he might get up and show the scrap of paper to me, which he did. There were smiles all around, and quite probably Prince Philip was told of this birth occurring on his own 72nd birthday.[444] That

---

[444] When, 19 years later, Susie (Susanna) went to St James' Palace to collect her Duke of Edinburgh Award, she hoped to receive it from Prince Philip himself. It was, though, the Earl of Wessex who made the presentation.

evening a great party was given in the Wren Library by the Law Faculty and Eli Lauterpacht's Research Centre in honour of the new LL.D. We came home 'V. tired and hot, but happy'.

The whole episode meant so much to Robbie that he kept all the mementoes and the letters of congratulation. And two days later we drove to Leicester to see our new grandchild and her mother.

Next day, of course, he was back in The Hague; back for the Oral Hearings of the boundary dispute between Libya and Chad, and that same afternoon delivered the judgment on the case between Denmark and Norway.[445]

Two days later we attended the third of the banquets given by HM Queen Beatrix for members of the ICJ; and this time Robbie, as President, had been invited to suggest which members of Dutch society we would prefer to meet. Given this opportunity, he said that we were interested in the Arts (as was the Queen herself, we knew). And so, in the Paleis Noordeinde, we found 22 prominent figures from the Dutch art world, together with their consorts: musicians; artists; the architect who had designed the extension to the Peace Palace; actors and television folk. It was a particularly enjoyable evening.

On it went, this hard-working and varied life in The Hague through the rest of June and most of July. I joined him there again for a dinner on the 23rd given by 'ASIL/Neth. ILA' (as noted in Robbie's diary), a gathering of Dutch members of the International Law Association linked with the American Society of International Law at which Robbie was to receive a rare honour – the Manley O. Hudson Gold Medal, awarded annually in recognition of outstanding work. In his short speech of thanks Robbie could recall the guidance he had been given by Manley Hudson himself during his year at Harvard. That guidance had been limited by Hudson's election to the Permanent Court of International Justice, but the encouragement he had given to the young Englishman was significant.

Now, since Robbie's secretary, Doreen, was to be away on holiday we came home together, hoping to get off northwards for our own break.

---

[445] The two cases were *Libyan Arab Jamahiriya/Chad* and *Maritime Delimitation in the Area between Greenland and Jan Mayan.*

Relaxation was not easy, though. 'R. received notice of Bosnian Muslims bringing application for interim measures to ICJ. – Telephone calls all day', I noted. For the next few days, 'Stuck in Grantchester because of constant consultations by telephone about Bosnian case...' and so it was not until 5th August that, after some delay while Robbie conferred by telephone with the Deputy Registrar, we at last drove up to Arment House. We spent five whole days there, four of them in rain. But he was content to stay indoors listening to a Test Match commentary (just audible on a portable radio held close to the ear) and reading a Dick Francis thriller. On the fifth day we had sunshine, and went down the valley to enjoy Muncaster and Ravenglass. As rain set in again next day, we cleaned the house and drove to Birstwith to spend a night with Dick's family – pleased as always to be with our youngsters. Soon after, we were off to Leicester for the christening of baby Susie, baptised with water from the River Jordan brought by Charles and Diana Goodhart from their recent visit to the Holy Land.

On the 23rd August Robbie returned to The Hague for Bosnian hearings. On the 27th the *Institut* was starting its biennial conference in Milan, but work with the drafting committee on the urgent Bosnian case took precedence and we did not travel until the 30th. Robbie had been made a *rapporteur* for the conference, and so the morning of the 1st September was spent in discussion of his report. It meant that he saw little of Milan, though I was able to go up onto the roof of the *Duomo* and stand amidst its stunning statuary. After just a few meals with friends – the Weils, and Arthur Watts – we were back to The Hague on the 2nd. Robbie's discipline meant that others involved in the Bosnia deliberations[446] had to return too, while the rest of the *Institut* members went off on a jaunt to Bergamo, and later to an operatic performance at Verona.

After days spent on those deliberations, on 13th September Robbie could jot down the words '*reading out*' – the Court imposing, for the second time, 'interim measures' intended to restrain the bloodshed in Bosnia. While the United Nations had made no effective intervention, Robbie was determined that the Court, at least, should respond to the crisis as promptly as possible.

Now he was free to come home, though on the 21st we returned to The Hague for just one night in order to attend the Dutch State Opening of Parliament, something we had not managed before.

---

[446] Steve Schwebel, Eli Lauterpacht and Mohammed Shahabuddeen had to return to duty.

'Robbie and I dressed up (he in morning coat, I with hat) and were conveyed with due pomposity (UN flag on car) to the Ridderzaal. Long speech in Dutch from HM Queen Beatrix; brass music; and afterwards the wonderful procession of bands, mounted cavalry and carriages – the Queen in her gold state coach with 4 mighty horses. Great crowds lined the route, including children from all provinces, people in regional dress, veterans, &c. Military rather poor in drill but magnificent in costume.'

After a few days at home we were back to attend a royal dinner for the President of Mexico.

(The cost of all these to-and-fro journeys, apart from just two each year, was paid for by Robbie. Our house in Grantchester was such an essential retreat that he felt the expense worthwhile. The UN paid for his annual visits to its headquarters in New York.)

On 1st October we crossed the Atlantic again, but this time not directly to New York. Stephen and Louise Schwebel had invited us to visit their country retreat in Vermont, and so we flew first to Boston, then to Lebanon in New Hampshire, and from there were taken to Cady Brook Farm, near Woodstock. Robbie had longed to show me something of the New England he had known during his year at Harvard, and I found this small sample of New York's great hinterland a wonderful experience. The vast stretches of woodland around were changing into their autumn colours, and I marvelled at the quietness of the little townships – though their names seemed disconcerting, taken as they were from familiar but dissimilar places in England or other countries.

Robbie delighted in this visit, too, and recorded it in his diary:

3 Oct 'Beautiful a.m. at Cady Brook Farm. Walks in woods. Then car excursion to *Stratford* (famous church), *Norwich* for lunch, then to *Hanover*, New Hampshire, to see Dartmouth Univ. – superb library and campus. Ice cream at Ben & Jerry's, then back to Vermont by ?Quechee (super shops with furniture and glass). Very wet at Norwich. Otherwise pleasant but colder.

4 Oct Fine morning (dangerous news fr. Moscow). Inspected remarkable house of rich friends of Schwebel! Mooched around Woodstock. Dinner with

5 guests p.m. – 2 Peabodys (the super house) + 2 Martins (insurance) + Prof. from Vermont Environmental Law School.

5 Oct Super frosty, sunny morning. Car at 10.45 to White River Junction Airport. Delta Express to La Guardia, NY. Met by Larry Johnson. Nice simple supper at Hotel.'

It was all very different from our own rural retreat. Steve's 350-acre estate included hillside, woodland and a pond, and the new-built timber house was beautifully appointed. Louise had furnished it in the style of her homeland, Sweden, and there was a smaller house for their daughters as well. Everything was bright and fresh.

In New York I again was the hanger-on, trying to occupy myself while Robbie met other delegates much of the time. I swam in the hotel swimming-pool on the 27th floor (a strange experience to be afloat with a view of the Chrysler Building through the windows), increasing the number of lengths day by day. On the 7th I sat in on the General Assembly to hear speeches from Isebegovic of Bosnia, and the Libyan foreign minister. That evening, after a sightseeing bus trip, I joined Robbie at 'a rather boring reception'. Boring it may have been, but there were some wonderful robes, since our host was the Kenyan ambassador.

I listened to a meeting of the Sixth Committee at which Robbie and Steve Schwebel led a discussion on the functions of the ICJ ('both excellent'), and ate a buffet supper on that stifling hot evening in the overcrowded flat of the Chairman of the Committee. On the Saturday Robbie and I visited the Metropolitan Museum's new extension, and there met the entire Schwebel family and found that the Odas had come earlier. That evening we dined with the Secretary-General:

'… very friendly welcome: elegant but not too elaborate. Boutros-Ghalis' own bronzes, [Egyptian] ink-cases and drawings all very fine, and supplemented by splendid paintings (Matisse, &c) on loan from Met. I was on Boutros' right, with Steve S. on my right. Out into pleasant riverside garden…'

Because of fierce security, the windows of the dining room were of bullet-proof glass, but Boutros chose to open them on that warm evening. As we strolled in the garden we were aware of guards disapproving of our exposure. Yet how could a Secretary-General live any sort of normal life without some risk?

The Sunday was brilliantly fine and cool, allowing us to walk about more freely. And Monday 11th turned out to be Columbus Day, when we watched with delight a parade of bands along Fifth Avenue – noisy, colourful and including flag-tossing Italians in medieval costume. Robbie then had meetings to attend, and we met again at a great evening reception at the Hungarian Embassy. Torrential rain all next day kept us inside, reading:

'… That evening, though, we took a taxi through rain to Carnegie Hall. Amazed to find Odas right beside us. Peter Serkin played Bach partitas and Goldberg Variations, later rather sniffed at ("too dry and intellectual") by NY Times. But we thought it splendid – warm, fluent, well-articulated.'

A few more cultural experiences enriched that visit. Robbie had hosted a luncheon for the UN legal office, and a dinner at our hotel for Ted Meron who was trying to persuade him to return in the New Year to talk to his students at New York University.

On our final day we took our places in the General Assembly hall promptly at 10 am, but found nothing happened until 50 minutes later. Then at last Robbie gave his address, and was followed by the representatives of Denmark, Australia, Mexico and Sierre Leone, 'all supportive'. And we lunched with the British Ambassador, Sir David Hannay, at his residence before flying home.

There was little relaxation in the days that followed, although some memorable occasions. Robbie's birthday on 19th October was his 80th, and it called for celebration. First, on the 18th, Jesus College gave a dinner to which I was invited, at which his health was drunk. Next evening – his actual birthday – he was making another speech of thanks after a dinner in his honour at Downing, and the following evening there was a reception for him at the Lauterpacht Research Centre.

Then came the birthday weekend with the family. By the Friday afternoon they were all assembled. On Saturday we had the great family luncheon in the Riverside Restaurant at the University Centre, where the five older cousins could clamber onto a wide window-seat and gaze happily down upon a scene of cattle grazing on Laundress Green and people walking, cycling and running along the path beside punts and swans on the Cam. Baby Susie lay contentedly in her carrier.

At home, Grandpa was presented with a special present from his three children, a 'gazebo'. They had planned it all carefully: a little summer-house whose position at the far end of the garden was the focal point of a minor vista. It was coloured deep red and black (Jesus College colours), had slabs of Yorkshire stone set in front, and white roses planted on either side. Pippa, our aspiring children's author, had written a little fantasy about it which Michael had illustrated: a lovely and amusing picture-book to be treasured. And there were cake, champagne and fireworks as well.

November included a meeting of the UN Committee for Refugees. Among the names noted in Robbie's diary, 'Cassese' appears on the 18th and 19th – signifying, I think, sessions spent with Nino on the extended interview later to be published in *Five Masters of International Law*,[447] the book that appeared after Cassese's death.

At the end of the month we dined with the Danish Ambassador, a particularly agreeable character who liked, he said, to spot Robbie's bright red scarf as he walked past to the Peace Palace each morning. At his residence we were struck by an intriguing piece of apparatus – a *Beosound*, a compact and elegant CD-and-radio-player made by the Danish firm of Bang & Olufsen. It was not long before Robbie bought one for himself.

I was with Robbie, too, for the state visit of the President of Argentina, Carlos Menem, admiring as always Queen Beatrix's ability to deliver a warm and seemingly spontaneous after-dinner speech of welcome to her guest. Robbie's diary also mentions a discussion about Chemical Weapons included in his busy schedule. In Cambridge in early December we both enjoyed Sir Arthur Marshall's 90th birthday luncheon in Jesus College hall. Marshall, now made an Honorary Fellow of the college, was still amazingly active, having founded a great business with garages all round East Anglia and, most impressively, Marshall's Airport from which we regularly flew, and the advanced engineering works on the same site.

Hearing that on the feast of St Nicholas *Sinta Klaas* was himself to arrive at Scheveningen, we decided this was another Dutch custom we shouldn't miss, so despite the cold, we went. And it *was* cold, a biting wind coming straight down the North Sea to the exposed harbour walls where stood hundreds of young families. Sure enough, a white ship was moored there, its painted port of origin seemingly Madrid (which, come to think of it, was a

---

[447] *Five Masters of International Law: (Dupuy, Jiménez de Arechega, Jennings, Henkin & Schachter)* pub. Hart 2011.

little odd). And the white-bearded Sinta Klaas, in bishop's mitre and robes, emerged and moved among the families. With him was *Swarte Piet,* 'Black Peter', with a big book. His assistants had baskets of sweets to toss to good children; but first their names must be checked in the book to see whether they had been naughty. It was worth being there, to hear the gentle singing of traditional children's carols which spread quite spontaneously around the crowds. Later, warm in our flat, we read that Sinta Klaas had arrived that same day in one place riding a camel, in another descending by helicopter. Miraculous indeed.

But that experience probably intensified the severity of the cold Robbie then developed. It meant that he came home and delegated several responsibilities to Oda, his Vice-President – among them discussion with Yasser Arafat about a form of agreement between the PLO and Israel. Unable to return to The Hague until halfway through January 1994, he was kept in contact with proceedings at the Court, and on one occasion Hugh Thirlway called with papers for him to deal with at Grantchester. Another caller was Vera Gowlland-Debbas,[448] a former pupil.

In The Hague on 16ᵗʰ January 1994 – a Sunday – his diary notes: 'To see [Madeleine] Albright[449] of USA 10.30 am in my office', renewing an acquaintance made at the UN Headquarters in New York. (Next day there were several others, notably the 'Agents in Oil Platform case' [*Islamic Republic of Iran/US*] for which the Court would shortly impose time limits). Mrs Albright must have been making arrangements for the impending visit of the UN Secretary-General, who on the 19ᵗʰ delivered a lecture at the Grote Kerk. 'Court's day with Boutros' followed, with Robbie hosting a luncheon at the Witte Club and attending a royal banquet that evening.

Soon the Court's year came to an end. On 3ʳᵈ February Robbie read out the Judgment that brought the *Libya/Chad* territorial dispute to a triumphant conclusion. And that evening there was a party for the judges who had reached the end of their tenure and were leaving the Court.

---

448 Mrs Gowlland-Debbas became Professor at the Institute of International & Development Studies at Geneva.

449 Mrs Albright was at this time the US Ambassador to the UN. She later became Secretary of State.

I had arrived for this and the succeeding events: first a dinner given by the Australian Ambassador and then, next day, one of Malgosia Fitzmaurice's Sunday lunches, this time in honour of Krzysztof Skubiszewski ('Skubi', as we called him) who, having retired as Foreign Minister of Poland, was to preside over the Iran-US Claims Tribunal. We already knew Skubi as a member of the *Institut* curatorium, and enjoyed his company.

Next day, 7 February 1993, Robbie's diary notes: *'New P. (new Ct.)'* – the formal installation of his successor, Mohammed Bedjaoui of Algeria, as President, with Schwebel as Vice-President. The incoming judges were Fleischhaur from Germany; Koroma from Sierra Leone; Shi Jinyong from the People's Republic of China; and Vereshchetin from Russia. Three days later Robbie's own effects were transferred from the President's office to a smaller one, and we returned home.

Although a genuinely modest man, Robbie had just enough vanity (or gratitude) to cause him to preserve the kind letters from well-wishers at significant moments in his life. There had been the congratulations on his election to the Court, and on his becoming its President. There were letters marking his 80th birthday and now some more as he stepped down from the Presidency. One, which I am sure made him smile, was from a star-struck Indian who had at a conference…

> '…shared some moments… in the sunshine of your immaculate wisdom. It was as if the cup of the Peace Palace was filled to the brim with the wisdom and learning of the ancients and the moderns and the theme for their action was to strive, to seek, to find and not to yield, a solution or varied solutions to the problems of the homo sapiens race bent on creating new modes of self destruction. The stream of knowledge that flowed from the lips of the wise was succour to many and to the merely thirsty, a manifold quench.
>
> 'Your towering presence and your words of profound rationality and sagacity were not only a boon to those who basked in the glory of your transplendency but were in effect, shafts of light in the tunnels of darkness of the politics of human error…'

In reply to Cassese's question, in one of his interview-sessions, about his contribution to the work of the Court, Robbie's own estimate was characteristically down-to-earth:

'… I would like to think that my major contribution was being President for three years at the time when the Court was so extremely busy, and surviving. We did become a very good club, and towards the end we had that decision of 16:1 [in the *Chad/Libya* judgment[450]]. I enjoyed the work partly because I think it was almost a reversion to my first period as a don when I was in university politics, and was chairman of one or two important committees. It's not the done thing to pretend to like committees, but I did like committees, and being President at the ICJ was a bit the same sort of thing; I found it wasn't altogether strange, though there was a different set-up, with different nationalities and different people and so on. But I found I could manage it and I enjoyed it very much. I like to think of that as a major contribution; and of course I've done a lot of drafting one way or another.'

A greatly-admired friend, Prosper Weil,[451] rated his performance more highly:

'…Robbie Jennings is one of the greatest – maybe the greatest – lawyer of our times.'

And Sir Frank Berman, at this time Foreign Office Legal Adviser, wrote in March 1994 with congratulations, ending:

'I hope that you take great satisfaction from the part you have been able to play, as President, in laying the ground-work for the future. I doubt if I have ever seen decisive authority exercised with such gentleness, courtesy and modesty, but underpinned by the utmost intellectual rigour. In our times, only one other similar figure comes to mind, that of Richard Wilberforce. I trust you will take it as the highest compliment if I couple your name with his, both in respect of the quality of the example set and the affection in which the exemplar is held.'

Lord Wilberforce was indeed one of Robbie's heroes.

---

450 By a vote of 16:1 the Court had allotted the disputed territory, then occupied by Libyan troops, to Chad, and in consequence the Libyan troops were withdrawn under UN supervision.

451 Prosper Weil, Professor at Pantheon-Assas University in Paris, was a member of the *Institut* and appeared as counsel in several cases before the ICJ. The quoted remark comes from a private letter to Professor Barbara Kwiatowska, disclosed to Robbie.

Still at the Court

1994-1995

In agreeing to stand again for membership of the Court and be made President, Robbie had resolved not to serve the full nine years of his second term – something probably already discussed with the Registrar and even informally with Boutros Ghali. He had made the decision because he felt that continuing to the age of 86 risked a falling-off in the quality of his performance.

First, although not prepared to stay for a further six years, he needed to complete his part in two important cases and provide background support for his successor. Those cases were *Qatar/Bahrain* (judgment 1.7.94) and *Portugal/Australia (East Timor)* (judgment 30.6.95).[452]

With responsibilities at the Court now less demanding, he still took a prominent place on Drafting Committees and shared much of the social life in The Hague. Malgosia Fitzmaurice recruited him to give occasional lectures in Amsterdam; he played his part as usual in judging the Telders Moots, and at the Haagsche Club he was no longer regarded as merely the foreigner allowed honorary and temporary membership but a fully contributing member. During the year 1994 he made 21 visits to The Hague, and 10 more in 1995 up to the time of his retirement from the ICJ. His to-and-fro life continued, his spells of solitary life in the Houtweg flat relieved by weekends at home. On a Friday evening I would arrive at Marshall's Airport to wait at a wire-netting fence and listen for the distinctive Dornier sound, then watch the plane land. Usually the first Suckling Air passenger to emerge would be the familiar small figure carrying a cabin-case. We would wave, and soon he was on his way home to Grantchester.

---

[452] *Libya/Chad* was a frontier dispute; *Qatar/Bahrain* maritime delimitation; *Portugal/Australia* likewise the delimitation of the shallow waters of the continental shelf known as the 'Timor Gap'. Such cases were arising because of rivalries in the exploitation of hydrocarbon resources.

In February1994 he made a quick visit to Edinburgh to give a lecture there.

But now that the pressure of work really had eased we actually took a small holiday, joining Joey, Egg and little Tabitha in late April, to drive with them down to Dorset for three nights in a converted farm building near the coast. It was a most happy time, with a visit to Lyme Regis and Seatown ('dramatic shingle and big surf') little walks and games. The Sunday was perfect for everybody. In spring sunshine we visited Parnham House, at that time owned by the furniture-maker John Makepeace – an intensely romantic 16th-century house and garden, used also as a college and display-gallery for craftsmen in wood. Robbie had a great feeling (a frustrated longing to make things in wood himself) for the skill and elegance of Makepeace's work, and he bought several books in the subject while there.

Next morning we were first at Abbotsbury, surrounded by a multitude of nesting swans; then called at the great tithe barn filled with 'rural bygones' and with wonderful poultry pecking around – always a delight for him. Along the coast again we looked for ammonites and gathered pebbles. Our final morning was spent with the potter Richard Batterham. Joey and Egg, as potters themselves, discussed technique with him, and we bought jars and bowls; and in Robbie's diary it was noted as a 'glorious day.'

There were soon more 'glorious days' when we stayed with the young Goodharts for the weekend. On the Friday evening Robbie gave a lecture at the University of Leicester and we dined with the Vice-Chancellor.[453] Besides playing with the children and taking a good walk with Paddywack the dog, we were given something new and absorbing to read in typescript – Pippa's first children's novel. Called *Flow*,[454] it told of the adventures of a boy and his dog in a Lake District setting. The book itself was published a week later, and Heffers Children's Bookshop filled one of its windows with copies.

We were proud parents. At this time Dick moved from Hammond Suddards to another law firm in Leeds, Ford & Warren; and with a growing reputation in his branch of commercial law, he was addressing seminars on the subject.

---

[453] This may also have been the occasion inaugurating the Robert Jennings Chair of International Law at Leicester, with Malcolm Shaw as its first Professor.

[454] In later editions the title is *A Dog Called Flow*.

It was, I think, in the summer of 1994 that Robbie sent his formal notice of resignation from the ICJ to the UN Secretary-General, indicating that a successor would need to be elected for the remainder of that nine-year term. Arthur Eyffinger's book about the International Court explains the process:

> 'The system of nomination of Judges of the ICJ is an intriguing one. In a way it is an anomaly and virtually outdated; it can only be explained in historical terms. It is a reminder, and this cannot be sufficiently emphasized, that the ICJ, by following in many respects the intellectual wake of the Permanent Court of International Justice, is perhaps as much the brainchild of the Hague Peace Conferences as it is of the League [of Nations] and the United Nations.
>
> '… The crucial feature of this procedure is the idea of *indirect* nomination, that is to say not by Governments directly but through so-called National Groups…'

The members of those groups are enlisted from among those already available to serve on the Permanent Court of Arbitration; and it was as a potential arbitration judge that Robbie was himself one of the British Group which would shortly be choosing which name should go forward for election as successor when he vacated his own appointment. The UK, as a member of the UN Security Council, was always likely to have a British judge at the International Court, but that was not a certainty. We were, however, a country well provided with strong candidates for the post.

Since any resignations of judges up to this point had occurred only through illness or incapacity, Robbie's decision – generally accepted with understanding – gave rise, he found, to one writer's suspicion of a devious plot. Fortunately he was able to disabuse the author and prevent publication, when in 1997 he was asked to make clear just how his resignation had come about. Dr Sam Muller, at that time a legal officer for UNRWA in Gaza, was submitting an article about the ICJ for publication in the *International and Comparative Law Quarterly* and wished to check the truth of a certain matter – 'the practice of a national judge resigning early so that a substitute judge may be slipped in for the remainder of the term and hence gain a track record before the next general election'. He refers to this as the 'early resignation strategy'.

Robbie recognised the rather dangerous assumptions that may have developed as a result of his own resignation, and responded (in some indignation) with a clarifying statement:

'I think you are reading too much into my resignation from the ICJ. There was no "strategy". First you have to remember that the British National Group of the PCA act as a wholly independent body. They will normally wish to be aware of opinion in governmental circles, but they can and do make their own decisions independently. The normal understanding for UK judges is that, if elected at a general election they will serve for 9 years and then it will be somebody else's turn. That would have applied to me, of course; had it not been that the members of the group had been told (I think by one of my colleagues on the Court) that, if I were elected for a second term, I had a reasonable chance of being elected President. On this possibility – which turned out to be right, of course, but who knows what may happen in a secret ballot – they nominated me for a second term. The understanding, unspoken but obvious, was that I would serve my three years as President and perhaps a little more as a help to the new President, but then resign to make room for another. As I was already 83 [actually just short of 82] when I did resign you will appreciate that it was normal and expected, and no strategy was involved (the compulsory resignation date for UK Judges is I think 75!). And perhaps I should add that the decision about when to resign was mine alone.

'There was one innovatory element of which I can perhaps boast. The Statute of the Court makes resignation difficult by providing that the resignation shall be notified to the Secretary General of the UN, which notification makes the place vacant: i.e. starts the whole business of holding an election. Obviously drafted when mail would take a fortnight to arrive, this makes notice of resignation at a date in the future very difficult; which of course is highly inconvenient. I wanted to be able to give notice of resignation at a future date which would be convenient for me and for the Court, which depended partly at least on the state of the list of cases. I did therefore write giving notice of irrevocable resignation on my chosen date. In doing this I had very good advice from my colleagues on the Court and nobody else. The S/G found it in accord with the Statute to accept this notice as effective…

'The attitude of the Board of Editors of the *ICLQ* frightens me; it frightens me that they should read into a perfectly normal resignation at the age of [*sic*] 83 some sort of election strategy. It rather confirms my ambition sometime to write a long study on "The great harm done to international law by international lawyers". I am particularly angry about the phrase you at any rate put into their mouths about an "early resignation strategy followed by a state": absolutely not this state, as the Editorial Board ought to know. It is a matter for decision by the judge himself or herself alone, and the nomination of a new candidate is a decision of the PCA group. Even in my time on the PCA we took at least one decision that was not the line the FCO would have chosen…'

As an innovation and likely precedent, Robbie's retirement brought a comment from Shabtai Rosenne,[455] who was at that time writing his book on *The Law and Practice of the International Court.* Rosenne 'had difficulty' not over the actual retirement, but about the manner in which notice had been given to the Secretary-General and the process of electing a successor. This, he felt, should be addressed by an amendment of the court's Statutes.

In The Hague for the oral hearings of the *Qatar/Bahrain* case, Robbie also played host to the group of eight British judges making a visit to the Court when the current Lord Chancellor[456] delivered a lecture. And that May he himself lectured in Amsterdam, meeting some of Malgosia Fitzmaurice's pupils. Her buffet lunches, and those given by Frances Meadows, often introduced him to lively young international lawyers; and he loved to keep in touch with former pupils such as Mary Ellen O'Connell,[457] who called to chat with him at this time as well.

New undertakings appear in his diary. The name *Guggenheim*[458] denotes an annual competition for the best thesis on a topic in international law. As an examiner, Robbie had the task of reading a number of very heavy tomes – not exactly entertaining, though occasionally revealing an exciting new talent. And '*Dinner for J.C.'s gang, St John's*' indicates, I think, some enterprise for which Jeremy Carver hoped to recruit him, such as an ILA colloquium or the Commonwealth Fellowship committee.

He made trips to London that summer for a lunch at the Old Bailey, a meeting of the National Group, and lunch a few days later with Frank Berman at the Oxford & Cambridge Club. Two days after that we were together in

---

[455] – in a private letter of 18 July 1995.

[456] The Rt. Hon Lord Mackay of Clashfern.

[457] Currently Robert & Marion Short Professor of Law and Research Professor of International Dispute Resolution at the University of Notre Dame.

[458] Paul Guggenheim, 1899-1997, a founder of the Graduate Institute of International Studies at Geneva, was a friend of Hersch Lauterpacht and had taught at The Hague as well as serving as Judge *ad hoc* at the ICJ on one case.

London for an event held in the Royalty Theatre – the London School of Economics' degree-giving ceremony at which Honorary Fellowships were conferred upon a select few. On this occasion Robbie himself was presented by his former Cambridge pupil, Professor Rosalyn Higgins, with an oration recalling his early association with the LSE as assistant lecturer, and a perceptive *resumé* of his subsequent career. We had enjoyed a celebratory dinner the previous evening, when Robbie sat beside Sir Peter Parker (famous particularly as Chairman of British Rail for some years) who, like him, had served in military intelligence in India during the war. My own opposite neighbour was Mary Wesley, the novelist.

Writing to Joey in these stiflingly hot days, I reported:

'Things happen almost every day. Daddy has airily taken on another arbitration case (presiding over a court of three judges to rule on an international dispute not to be taken to the ICJ), so the telephone rings with calls from Bangladesh and Washington and – just now – The Hague...'

Even though he was preparing for 'retirement,' Robbie, as a member of the Permanent Court of Arbitration, could not say no to an interesting case (and the fee to be earned). New names crop up among the appointments in his diary – Kamal Hossain and Don Wallace; and the case in question, noted by him as a dispute between *Ghana & Applicant,* must be that described as...

'...between an African State and two foreign investors. The tribunal consisted of Sir Robert Jennings, President, Dr Kamal Hossain, and Prof. Don Wallace. In November 1996... proceedings were suspended.'[459]

Similarly, in the same report one finds:

'(20) ... Three separate but related proceedings ... Asian State and three European enterprises. Tribunal: Sir Robert Jennings, President, Dr Kamal Hossain, and Sir Roger Parker. The parties agreed on a settlement.'

I think he must have considered these fairly minor matters that would not distract him from the work he was still doing at the ICJ.

---

[459]   PCA Report, 1996, p.9 : (18) UNCITRAL Arbitration Rules.

On our next weekend visit to Leicester Pippa had a new typescript for us to read, her second children's novel, *Ginny's Egg*. A longer journey the following weekend took us up to Birstwith to be with Dick's family, and a fortnight later we had the Eddleston family for a weekend stay at Grantchester.

Eight days of real holiday at Arment House at the end of August evoked the word 'perfect' once or twice in Robbie's diary, and on one day:

'Remarkable a.m. – sun, clouds, illuminated rain, new scenes every second.
P.m. sun, then thunder, rain, followed by fine and bright.'

And we again broke the final leg of our journey for lunch with Robbie's Dutch lawyer friend, Daan Goedhuis, who welcomed him warmly. Daan had married the widow of the last in line of a great family, the Denisons of Ossington Hall. That grand Hall had been demolished thirty years earlier, but the house he and his wife occupied was itself impressive and richly furnished. After lunch Pamela Goedhuis walked us through the great gateway into the now-desolate estate, where the last remaining building was its chapel, 'the church in the woods', full of memorials to the Denison family and of great interest. And, although Daan was to die the following year, Pamela would continue to entertain us to lunch whenever we journeyed northward, eternally grateful to Robbie for the wonderful obituary of her husband he had written for *The Times*.

It had been a shock, back in July, to hear of the sudden death of José Maria Ruda, the Argentine judge who years before had appointed Robbie to be counsel in the *Beagle Channel* case and so launched his career as an advocate. Robbie attended the memorial meeting in The Hague in September for this greatly-admired friend. But that was followed a fortnight later by another shock at the death of Judge Tarassov, the man who had taken Robbie aside at the start of his term as President and warned him that he was 'talking too much'. Typically, Robbie had been grateful for his candour and adjusted his style accordingly. He went again to The Hague to join in the grim observance of Tarassov's lying-in-state in the Peace Palace.

Another one-night visit was for a dinner given by Mrs Van Loon, Lady in Waiting to Queen Beatrix, at her home in Amsterdam – one of the finest houses on the *Keisersgracht*. Such treats were now rarer, and our Cambridge life was resuming its importance for Robbie. The link with his first college was strengthened when he was made President of the Downing College Association. He was asked, too, to speak to young international lawyers at the Lauterpacht Research Centre, and made a habit of attending the lunchtime talks there. In his diary entries appear hints of other developments: a lunch in Cambridge with Vaughan Lowe and Malgosia Fitzmaurice, another in London with Frank Berman and Rosalyn Higgins.

What was certainly important was the birth of two more grandchildren in October, Joey's second daughter Polly Eddleston on the 3rd, and Dick's third child Philip Jennings on the 8th.

We were in The Hague from 17-20ᵗʰ October, when Robbie was briefly in charge of the Court as Acting President – a spell including his birthday, which was celebrated, first by Jacques taking us, as long promised, to Maastricht: a long journey (260 km,) for just a few hours' wander, but a place we found attractive. That evening Nino Cassese gave us a special dinner, with Oranjio-Ruiz as fellow-guest. And while there, Cassese[460] may have gathered more material for his *Five Masters of International Law.*

Nino's scheme was to ask each of his five 'Masters' – Dupuy, Arechega, Jennings, Henkin and Schachter – the same set of questions, and it resulted in a fascinating volume. His conversations reflect the outlook of both interviewer and his subjects: his own tendency more purely scholarly and positivist, others' – Robbie's particularly – rather more pragmatic and flexible. And in probing more intimately their attitude to life, none of them seemed to suffer the anguish suggested by Freud. He found, for instance, that they had little need of palliatives to alleviate 'the miseries of life': even Jiménez de Aréchaga, who had suffered tragedies in his family life, was sustained by a passion for his legal work. As for Robbie, the response was robust:

[Cassese]*So you don't agree with Freud that life is unbearable …*

'No, I think he was a silly old fool when he said that. I don't think life is unbearable at all. I think it's marvellous and much to be enjoyed by sensible people, and being miserable about it is no help at all. I don't regard my many activities other than being an international lawyer as a catalogue of palliatives or comforts. I regard them as important aspects of living a full life. Music,

---

460   Antonio Cassese would be in The Hague a good deal during these years. After six years as Professor at the European University Institute in Florence, he was now the first President of the International Criminal Tribunal for the former Yugoslavia.

for example, I would regard in many ways as vastly superior to international law as an intellectual discipline and an imaginative discipline. I can't do more than respectfully enjoy it from a distance, because I haven't got that demon, if you like, I haven't got the gift…'

What are the other activities you enjoy?

'Well, I'd put music very, very high; that's grown with me rather. Again I have no great accomplishment: well, I'm rather like Christine, we have a piano and we both play it if there's nobody else within a hundred yards, and quite enjoy making the attempt. We don't seek to inflict it on others. So that it's mainly going to concerts or listening to the "gramophone" – I still like to call it that. But I also have an enthusiastic attachment to "hi-fi" and take all the magazines… Christine knows (I am getting too near Freud for my comfort) that when I am tired or a bit depressed I find some reason to talk to my friends in the local hi-fi shop, and probably get them to talk about some apparatus which they know that I probably will not buy, but they are very kind, and I do buy from time to time…

'The hi-fi satisfies, I suppose, the remains of feelings at Cambridge that I wished I knew more about physics and about electricity and sound, and science generally.

Other things, Nino… Well, very important to me all along… is walking, and especially walking in… the English Lake District, where we now own an old farmhouse… Walking the fells, a bit of mountaineering: I used to enjoy it enormously as a young man, when I liked especially walking alone. I rather resented company, and I'd spend the whole day walking the mountains quite alone. The little of it I can now manage I still enjoy; and fortunately, so does Christine. And now I am grateful for the company.

'Reading, of course… And apart from that, well, I think one of my great joys is the college scene in Cambridge, where you have this intellectual companionship of people from different disciplines living in the college, each teaching and talking about his or her own thing… This intellectual society I've always found a tremendous joy, not a palliative but a great stimulus… For this stimulating and delightful company there is no retirement age. (And, one should not forget to mention, one finds this sort of refreshment in the International Court of Justice too.)'

There were many more valuable revelations in his interview and, as a reviewer commented in the *Journal of International Criminal Justice,* Cassese's book 'emphasizes and praises the human qualities of the interviewees, which were also his own, such as simplicity, affability, gentleness, urbanity, *esprit de finesse* and witty irony'.

The final months of 1994 were filled with the usual mixture of events – work in The Hague, including the Standing Committee of the Permanent Court of Arbitration; in England, Shahabuddin's notable Lauterpacht Lecture, a dinner with members of his 13 Old Square chambers, a weekend visit to Birstwith, the college Audit Feast, a Christmas party at the FCO...

That winter was bitterly cold; but on 5th January 1995 Robbie made a short visit to an equally cold Hague (*4" snow. Roads awful a.m.*) to work with the Drafting Committee and to call on Bette Schifman, chief administrator at the Permanent Court of Arbitration. The PCA, although largely inactive for years, had still, as the senior body, retained the grandest offices in the Peace Palace, and Robbie would spend a good deal of time in those lofty dark-panelled rooms in the coming years.

On 17th January we made a two-day visit to New York, where he lectured at New York University.

> '... R nervous about lecture, revising and re-reading until last moment. But it went well, with big audience including many senior people. Nice dinner (I between Ted Meron and Philippe Sands) followed by questions, which R answered splendidly.'

This was the Hauser Lecture,[461] and his title was *Some reflections on the implications of Humanitarian Law for International Law generally*. Even at 81 he could never feel entirely confident about a big occasion, but his text, carefully prepared, reveals great breadth and clarity. Next morning we walked down to the Pierpoint Morgan Museum to enjoy an exhibition of master drawings. Elizabeth Wilmshurst,[462] legal adviser to the UK mission to the UN, joined us for lunch at the Harvard Club.

---

[461] The lecture was reprinted in RYJ's *Collected Writings*, pp1233-1250.

[462] Professor Elizabeth Wilmshurst, CMG, is now Distinguished Fellow of the Royal Institute of International Affairs, Chatham House, and Visiting Professor at University College, London.

Two days later, Robbie was back to The Hague for intensive work. Judgment was given on the *Qatar/Bahrain* dispute, and there were hearings on *E. Timor*. With breaks at weekends, he continued working at the Court until the end of February, when I joined him for a very special occasion. The Haagsche Club, celebrating its 250th anniversary, had invited wives to dine there for the very first time. It was a buffet dinner, with circular tables for eight, at which our neighbours of course spoke perfect English. We made friends with the Chamberlain of the Queen's Household, who also ran several hotels and had set up the Centre Parcs holiday camps: a jolly companion. Next day, at a major exhibition of Mondrian's work, Robbie earnestly followed the evolution of the artist's sketches of an apple tree and a windmill into total abstraction. On the Sunday, after a *Cantatadienst* in the crowded Kloosterkerk, we heard the news of the death of Roberto Ago.

Robbie had engagements that prevented his travelling to his old friend's funeral, but we learnt a good deal about poor Roberto's lonely final weeks from Nicolas Valticos and the Abi-Saabs, who had visited him in hospital in Geneva. It seems that his wife had not managed to do so and the situation for his family in Rome was not good. Ago's term as a member of the Court was cut short at 87, with three years still to run. It had been, I think, partly with him in mind that Robbie had resolved to leave before reaching such an advanced age.

But although Robbie was now aged 81, he still had energy enough for another trip to New York in March, staying at the Knickerbocker Club, an elegant neo-Georgian building overlooking Central Park whose style resembled that of an aristocratic huntin'-and-shootin' great house, with delightfully quirky features.

Robbie's business this time was once more at New York University, where Rita Hauser was setting up her Global Law School, in which he was to be involved for some years. There was also a short conference at the UN Headquarters where, as usual, he was entertained by delegates – the Ambassadors of Japan, Spain and Germany. On the Sunday we found our way to a flat in Tribeca for lunch with Philippe Sands and his young wife; then an afternoon of wandering around 'the Village' with Ted Meron, followed by a very friendly supper with Elizabeth Wilmshurst. Finding himself free on our final afternoon, Robbie added yet another experience of New York's minor thrills by taking me on the

59th Street cable-car across the East River to Roosevelt Island and back. And we dined, that evening, with Hisashi Owada.

The following day we flew to Toronto, where Robbie spoke to the Bar Association and we enjoyed their hospitality. There was just time for a glimpse around the huge department store with the romantic name *Hudson Bay Trading Co.* and a walk down to the lakeside; but not, alas, to see the Niagara Falls.

Next day we moved to Ottawa, where we were welcomed by former pupils of Robbie's, Frank and Nancy Iacobucci. Nancy drove us around, most memorably to watch enormous chunks of melting ice crashing over the Rideau Falls. Frank, now a Judge of the Supreme Court, showed us around its buildings. We spent just one night in the city, but it allowed us to accept an invitation to lunch next day with Maxwell Cohen[463] and his wife in his club. We were enjoying the special club ambience and the company of our generous hosts when, just halfway through the meal, Max mentioned that it was his 85th birthday. So that made it a very special occasion.

We returned home that evening. Soon Robbie was back for a week in The Hague. There, he took part in the final session of a Telders Moot; he lunched, on the Sunday, with a former pupil, Lal Vohrah[464] and his wife; and had meetings at the Permanent Court of Arbitration.

The Dutch Foreign Ministry's excursion for members of the Court was this time to Amsterdam. The weather was perfect and the programme well-devised. We went to the Maritime Museum, had drinks and lunched at the Burgomeister's house (delighted to find an enchanting springtime garden hidden behind), cruised the canals and ended at the Van Loon house for tea. The only flaw was the annoyance of finding our viewing of the Maritime Museum delayed by a rather smug Dutch lawyer addressing us at great length about the wisdom of his country's leniency on the use of recreational drugs.

---

[463] Max liked to be called 'Judge Cohen', having served *ad hoc* on the Gulf of Maine case at the ICJ. He was Professor Emeritus and former Dean of the Faculty of Law at McGill University.

[464] Judge Lal Chandra Vohrah served at The Hague on the Tribunal for the Former Yugoslavia. He is a Malaysian, and his wife Paula is English. In 1966 he came to Jesus College, Cambridge, to read for the LL.M. in International Law under Robbie.

Robbie's only real disability by now was his dimming eyesight; and that meant that as soon as his duties at the Court were over he would need to undergo surgery for glaucoma and the removal of cataracts. In the meantime, though, his activities continued in all their variety. In May we were in London to hear Guillaume deliver the Wilberforce Lecture at Lincoln's Inn, followed by a dinner for distinguished members of his audience including Wilberforce himself. Next morning we were off to Geneva, where on the 13th Robbie gave the opening lecture in a conference at its Institute of International Law, followed by Georges Abi-Saab, Lucius Caflisch and others.

Home on the 14th and to The Hague on the 15th, to lecture in Amsterdam next day, and also work on the draft judgment for the *E. Timor* case. I joined him for the weekend, and on the Monday we were in Amsterdam for one of the most remarkable of the many state occasions we attended – a dinner given by the Dutch Prime Minister, Mr Kok, for the visiting German Chancellor, Helmut Kohl. The great man was entertained in the Rijksmuseum, its main gallery filled with circular tables, each named after one of the Dutch 'Golden Age' masters. Around us were all those famous paintings, with the greatest of all, Rembrandt's *Night Watch*, highlighted as the focal point. It was in front of this huge masterpiece that Kohl was photographed with the Queen.

Back in Cambridge there was a memorial service for another Fellow of Jesus, G. I. Jones – *Ritual Murder Jones*. At a time when the college had several Fellows named Jones, Robbie had differentiated them by nicknames. Gwilym Jones was an anthropologist, expert in African tribal customs; *Potato Jones*, F.G.W. Jones, had researched eelworm infestation of potato crops; *Dictionary Jones*, Trevor Jones, was German scholar and lexicographer; and *Roman Jones* was A.H.M. Jones, highly esteemed Professor of Ancient History.

From 4th-7th June Robbie was in The Hague and then Cologne, for a meeting with Professor Bockstiegel. Then next day at Grantchester we had a visitor, Bill Foster, the University of Leicester's Public Orator who was hoping to gather a personal impression of the man he was shortly to present for an Honorary Degree. While Robbie's academic and judicial CV could be easily found in *Who's Who*, his actual personality revealed itself instantly when the two men struck a great rapport over cricket and other shared tastes as we gave him lunch at the Green Man.

There followed an intensive series of engagements. In Cambridge, the college marked Glanville Williams' Hon. Litt.D,[465] and the Law Faculty the retirement of Turpin, Prichard and Steiner. Over in The Hague we began our farewells with a party for our Dutch friends.

On 26th June we were in London for the celebration of the 50th anniversary of the United Nations, held in Westminster Hall. I described the event:

'It was all tremendously grand and carried out with meticulous discipline. Music by a Guards band set the tone at first, until exactly at 9.45 a line of heraldic figures marched across and took their places on a high ledge under the great stained-glass window. They were the State Trumpeters, who announced the start of proceedings with a fanfare.

'In, slowly, came the Archbishop of Canterbury preceded by a high cross and stately clergy. Then came 50 British peacekeeping soldiers in their blue berets. Then, far more colourfully, the Yeomen of the Guard and the Gentlemen-at-Arms (high helmets with drooping plumes and fearsome pikes). Then H.M. the Queen, Prince Philip and Prince Charles, who sat on thrones facing us on a high dais. And there were the Lord Chancellor, the Speaker of the House of Commons, and many very recognisable members of the Government. An orchestra and choir had also filed in. In the seats directly behind us were Guards officers, swords and helmets awkwardly balanced on their knees.

'So we had a speech from the Queen; a longer (and good, well delivered) speech from John Major; a performance of the "Charter for Peace" – the Atlantic Charter set to music by a composer, Howard Blake, whom we later met and chatted with; prayers led by the Speaker's Chaplain; and a special prayer read by Perez de Cuellar, the former Secretary-General of the UN...

'Finally, while the choir were perfoming *Zadok the Priest*, we and others from two rows of seats were taken out to a coach and driven to Buckingham Palace, a lady from the Foreign Office advising us how to acknowledge the Queen's greeting... how, in case we may have forgotten, to curtsey... There, the Royals were lined-up just inside the Music Room, and my small ordeal of arthritic curtsey was quickly over. The Queen was cheerful and animated, and knew about Robbie's retirement.

'It was rather wonderful to be in these lovely rooms, overlooking the garden. An Air Force officer (equerry?) chatted pleasantly, before we moved on to find

---

465   Glanville had already been awarded the LL.D.

other people. There was the Chief Rabbi (Jonathan Sacks), who remembered meeting R when they both received honorary degrees at Cambridge. There were Perez de Cuellar and his wife, who also recognised us. There was a now-portly figure, in cheerful humour, whom Daddy accosted since we had met him at our one luncheon in Number Ten – Denis Healey. Recalling that they had common origins in Bradford, Healey fell into Yorkshire dialect, as did Robbie; and on hearing that Dicky lived up in Nidderdale, he exclaimed "*Loocky boogger!*" There was Tony Blair, with eager smiles – he knew R's book on the *Acquisition of Territory* from his law studies at Oxford (good mark!). An aged sweet-faced man with wispy white hair was given particular attention by the Queen, who bent down to his wheelchair – and a murmur from nearby identified him: Gladwyn. As Glydwyn Jebb, he had been, briefly, acting Secretary-General at the opening sessions of the UN and our first Permanent Representative in the 1950s. There was Petrovsky, a very nice Russian UN official, and (I think) Sonny Ramphal, Commonwealth Secretary... a lot of interesting people. One small and thin elderly lady to whom the Queen had been attentive was standing alone, and so we enquired what her connection with this event was. "I am Ernest Bevin's daughter" she said; and we recalled how greatly Bevin had been loved and respected at the Foreign Office in the late '40s. Who else (while I'm name-dropping?). Geoffrey Howe, hurrying after his wife and with no time to chat; Lord Mackay of Clashfern, on the staircase on the way out. And in further rooms, to which the double doors were later opened, the UN military people were gathered for the Queen and Princes to move through...

'We walked out through the splendid gilded gates, and then through a corner of Green Park and along to Pall Mall; and rounded off a very special morning with a delicious lunch at the Oxford & Cambridge Club.'

Back in The Hague on the 29th, the main farewells began. Robbie attended a lunch given in his honour by the Nicaraguan Ambassador (magnanimously forgiving his Dissenting Opinion on a point in one of the Court's decisions favouring Nicaragua in the course of their case against the U.S.A.). That evening we went to the British Ambassador's residence for the very fine dinner arranged by Sir David Miers, the current Ambassador, in Robbie's honour. Those invited were all well known to Robbie: three other members of the International Court, the head of the Permanent Court of Arbitration, the President of the Haagsche Club, Mrs van Loon-Labouchere (the Queen's Mistress of the Bedchamber), Baroness van Lynden (English widow of the former Head of the Carnegie Trust), the Australian Sir Ninian Stevens (*ad hoc* Judge at the ICJ and member of the new International Criminal Court), plus wives in three cases, and – a nice surprise – Philip Allot, Cambridge law lecturer and Fellow of Trinity, an old pupil and admirer. Our host made only a very short speech, and so Robbie's response was brief, too.

Next day, Friday 30th June, was Robbie's final appearance as Judge of the ICJ. The business of the day was the reading of the Judgment on the *East Timor* case – a dispute between Australia and Portugal. It was preceded by two obituaries, first that of Roberto Ago. Hanka, his second wife, was there to hear President Bedjaoui's fulsome speech. Next was a tribute to Mme Bastid, the only woman so far to have sat in the Court (as an *ad hoc* judge on one case), a renowned jurist and formidable lady, whose two daughters were present.

From speaking French, Bedjaoui changed to English to read the text of the Judgment – seeming to take forever, for his delivery was a work of art involving gestures, pauses and many variations in voice. (One gathered that the Portuguese had failed.) Finally, reverting to his natural French tongue, he made a long and generous speech in honour of Robbie Jennings.

This rather exhausting session was followed immediately by a big farewell reception in Robbie's honour in the Small Hall of Justice. Gathered were the other judges, the staff of the court, the Permanent Court of Arbitration and Hague Academy people, and the ambassadors and counsel who had attended the hearing… most of whom wanted to speak to him. Then Bedjaoui made another graceful speech, to which R. replied; and finally there was the presentation of the gift which all departing judges receive – a silver tray engraved with the signatures of all his fellow judges.

After, there was yet another farewell meal, a nice luncheon in a quiet restaurant given by Shigeru Oda, Robbie's loyal Vice President and old friend, for about 10 of us. Lastly, in Robbie's office, there were more presents to unwrap, one from Doreen Bloemendaal his devoted secretary, who though English and determined not to get 'emotional', became moist-eyed.

By the time we reached Grantchester that evening we were pretty tired. I had already put another lot of clothes out in readiness for our next adventure, and feeling too weary to make a selection, bunged the whole lot into a suitcase.

Thanks to my 81-year-old husband's astonishing stamina, we were able to carry on: from the ancient Westminster Hall to Buckingham Palace on 26th June, and from the Peace Palace on 30th we took an early flight on 1st July to Florence, and on to three *palazzi* in Siena.

We had been invited by Professor Grotanelli di Santi, current President of the *Monte dei Paschi di Siena*, the oldest bank in the world – he, and his English wife Ann, being already known to us from previous visits to Siena. Our fellow guests were Mr Coleby, a financier, and his wife, who was afflicted with Huntingdon's Disease[466] but was determined to join in every activity while she could, despite her advancing disability.

Our arrival was on the eve of the *Palio*, the traditional horse-race which is held twice each summer: a contest symbolising the rivalry between the many *Contrada*, or parishes, of the city. There was evidence of that fierce and brilliant rivalry even on our first walk through the streets – the silk flags fluttering above, each bearing a different emblem. And the *campo* itself was already prepared, its perimeter packed with a deep layer of tufa, sandy soil to protect the horses' hooves. All the high buildings around this great sloping piazza were hung with banners, too. Simply seeing this was not enough, though. We were conducted again through those streets to the *Palazza Sansedoni,* to watch a 'trial run' of the next day's race from a high window. Since it was only a trial, some riders simply practised the start, others taking the deadly San Martino bend – a notoriously dangerous corner, padded with mattresses – at speed. And it gave us an impression of what was to come, as Sicilian jockeys mastered the spirited horses they had been allotted.

After that glimpse, we found ourselves made honorary members of the *Drago* Contrada, and walked that evening to the monastery of San Domenico, to share in their great feast. There (wearing green silk scarves displaying the Drago, or dragon) we sat at long tables set around the cloisters, where polite youngsters served us food.

Next morning we were shown around the grand rooms, full of interesting treasures, of the bank itself; and then we walked to another palazzo belonging to the bank which has become the *Accademia Musicale*, with its own highly decorated concert hall.

After lunch we walked again to the *Palazzo Salimbeni*, the bank, to a balcony overlooking its own small *piazza*. And there a series of groups in rich costumes arrived to perform a flag-throwing display. They were dazzling in their skill and grace, and impressed upon viewers emblem after emblem of each contrada –

---

[466] Huntingdon's Disease is a genetic disorder which typically manifests itself in the 40s. Rosemary Coleby had been athletic in her younger years, and feared that her daughter might have inherited the disease.

flags of Aquila (eagle), Bruco (caterpillar), Chioccilla (snail), Civetta (owl), Giraffa, Istrice (which sounds like ostrich but is really porcupine), Leocorno (unicorn) … and so on. Then, as these groups moved away to repeat their display at many stations around the town, we walked down to the great building overlooking the Campo again, the *Palazzo Sansedoni*. This time we mounted to a higher level, where a window had been reserved for the four English in a bare room with just a chair or two, but with velvet-covered padding to the window-sill from which we gazed at a stupendous scene: the great *Campo* now filling with spectators at the centre and around the perimeter, and the immensely tall tower of the *Palazzo Pubblico* opposite us, looming over all.

At last the proceedings began. A deafening boom from a cannon marked the moment, followed by a tolling of the bell in the campanile on the tower – a regular tolling that was to continue for more than two hours. First came the band, twelve drummers followed by eighteen trumpeters, playing a harsh and monotonous short tune over and over again, marching slowly around the Campo and then settling in a stand before the City Hall. Then came a procession of all the dignatories of Siena itself and its surrounding region, with their own banners. Then again the contrade groups tossing their flags. When this is at last complete there are still horsemen wearing heraldic helmets signifiying contrade now defunct, and dignified figures from six of the noble families of the city. Finally there is a concerted display of flag-waving by ensigns of all the contrade, in line before the City Hall.

All this has taken two hours, but is so compulsive, so perfectly done, so colourful, so replete with historic significance that our moments of rest were spent studying the guidebook with its explanations.

But then the tolling stopped, and the drumming; no more harsh brass-playing. By now the crowd numbers some 60,000 and no more are allowed into the centre. In come the racehorses, and each jockey is handed a whip, a whip with which to thwack at his rivals. It is a ruthless business! The start involved some fidgeting and manoeuvring as the horses were lined-up in their allotted positions, the tenth horse staying behind the other nine, to join the rest at a gallop. So it was a shock, after all the slow build-up, when suddenly they were away, careering round that terrifying corner. Three times around the circuit: a jockey comes off, but somersaults to safety, and a horse takes a spectacular tumble but even he and his rider miraculously leap up and run again. The whole race takes only about a minute and a quarter. And it is a clean win (although just how clean only the jockeys really know) for Onda, the Wave Contrada whose flag is wavy blue-and-white with a dolphin. Immediately the rejoicing began: processions with blue and white flags would march the streets that evening and for days to come.

It left us feeling dazed, exultant, withers-wrung, as we descended to the grander floor for a buffet supper at which the race, filmed in close-up, played on a television screen again and again.

The Colebys left next morning, but we were able to spend another day, first revisiting the Duomo, and then walking and learning more of the city's history from Professor Francesco Francioni – that attractive man, tall, tawny-haired and bearded, originally from the rival city of Florence but content to attach himself to Siena.

Thanks to Ann Grotanelli, I was able to trace an old schoolfriend I had not met for 50 years, who I knew was now living near Siena. We were driven out into the countryside, trying to follow directions to an old farmhouse 'with a bust of Rossini on the balcony'. At last we found it. My old friend, Signora Lisa Benaim Sarfatti, was now white-haired but welcoming, and we were given tea. She and Robbie got on well together, and we were enchanted with the late-summer landscape around us. (We were to meet her again several times in Cambridge, where she had a cousin, John Rosselli, and friends known well to us.) Our evening ended with supper generously provided at the Grotanelli's own country house, itself with an enchanting view culminating in a distant silhouette of the towers of Siena.

Those two days had been a tremendous experience.

The last events of that month were noted in Robbie's small diary:

July 6 Guildhall : LSE centenary
8 Downing Ass. Lunch
10 Ceased to be a Judge
12 Election to UK vacancy …

After attending the LSE's centenary dinner in Guildhall, he was renewing his connection with Downing College, both at its Old Boys' Association and, on the 10th, a farewell dinner for Peter Mathias as Master. And it was on that day that Robbie took his fountain-pen and wrote extra clearly, '*Ceased to be a Judge*'.

... *But Not Quite Retired*

1995-96

At last, I thought, we might take life more gently. But 'Don't ask me to stop', Robbie said, 'or I shall conk out.' So I did not suggest such a thing; and although the end of his years as full-time Judge of the International Court brought a change of focus, it was not to be the end of his legal work.

First, on 12th July, there was that 'Election to UK vacancy'. As a member of the British Group he had taken part in choosing who should be nominated for election to the vacant seat. It had not been easy, for of several very strong candidates all but one would be disappointed. The group's eventual choice was Rosalyn Higgins, who if approved would become the first woman judge.[467] She was duly elected to complete Robbie's nine-year term, and would then be re-elected for another nine years and made President for the final three.

Just one of the original candidates failed to express satisfaction at this choice, and it was to grieve Robbie. Derek Bowett was so bitterly disappointed that he wrote a short letter saying so. We knew that Derek, having injured his back in an accident at home, would have found the demands of a seven-year term at The Hague (including the physical torment of sitting for hours while concentrating on complex arguments) a great strain. He had already achieved so much: the Whewell Chair, President[468] of Queens' College and membership of the International Law Commission, and was greatly respected. Feeling hurt, Robbie and he – two proud Northerners – never managed to repair the rift.

But already a new honour awaited Robbie. Two days after his retirement from the Court we were off once more to Leicester and dined that evening with the university's Vice Chancellor, Dr Edwards. Next day Robbie received an

---

[467]   – apart from Mme Bastid, who had briefly served as *ad hoc* judge on one case.

[468]   Head of House of his college, Queens. Later to become Sir Derek Bowett, QC, he was from Lancashire; and Robbie was of course from Yorkshire.

Honorary LL.D., introduced by his new friend Bill Foster the Public Orator, who did not fail to mention his love of cricket. We were to be at Leicester again for our Ruby Wedding on 4th August, when Pippa arranged a great family gathering in celebration. With Dick's family from N. Yorkshire and Joey's from Somerset feasting and playing silly games in the garden, it was just the sort of 'all together' occasion that Robbie loved.

With more freedom to plan events, it was now possible to turn his attention to two important matters. One was the medical attention needed to stabilize his eyesight and the other was a major improvement of our Grantchester house.

But first he fitted in some work on a commercial arbitration, officially described as *Asian State-owned enterprise – three European enterprises* (noted in Robbie's diary as *FARE v RNAC*[469]) which entailed meetings with the other members of the tribunal in London and The Hague before, on the 14th, he went into Addenbrooke's for the successful glaucoma operation.

Now *Offord & Camp* set to work, and the disruption of demolition and extension-building began – an ambitious scheme designed by our son-in-law architect, Michael Goodhart. As the diningroom's outer wall was destroyed we shifted ourselves and our furniture elsewhere and prepared to endure banging, drilling, lorries and dust for months to come. The men themselves were no trouble, since we knew some of them already and were interested in the various skills needed for each task. But life was far from peaceful as they created a large well-lit extension, with a curved roof of copper beneath an enlarged master bedroom with its own projecting central window. There was more knocking-down and transformation of the back entrance, too, and work on the front porch. Although not fully completed until May 1996, by Christmas we were able to entertain the Goodhart and Eddleston families in our handsome new dining room. Thanks to Michael, everything had proceeded with great efficiency.

All that work was the background to other events during those months and we could not think of visiting our beloved Arment House. Nor could we attend the biennial *Institut* conference, held that year in Lisbon. On 10th September I could comment to Joey 'Daddy keeps going, of course. He was advising 4 Japanese yesterday about sea-boundary problems between Japan and Korea'. And then there was a 'Treaty meeting, SPTL'[470] followed by a day

---

[469]   This was a contract dispute, one of the parties being the *Royal Nepal Airlines Corporation*.

[470]   The Society of Public Teachers of Law is now named the Society of Legal Scholars.

in London for a preliminary meeting on the *FARE/RNAC* arbitration, and more consultations.

By the end of that month we were able to snatch a weekend in Somerset with Joey's family: a joyful interlude when we visited Laycock Abbey, and then Stowe on the way home, in autumn richness.

October brought more activities. Robbie lectured at the LSE, and next day gave the lunchtime talk at the Lauterpacht Research Centre on 'The ICJ after 50 years'. On the 9th he was in London again, this time to the Museum of Mankind for the launch of Philippe Sands' important book on Environmental Law[471] for which he had contributed the Introduction.

Then in late October we had an entirely new experience, joining a group of young aspiring Lincoln's Inn barristers for a weekend at Cumberland Lodge[472] in Windsor Great Park, where they would hear talks by eminent Benchers and meet them over meals. Many were from the Commonwealth, and Robbie was happy to chat with them, though we withdrew to bed rather than prolong the evening with their rowdy sing-song. Instead, we rose early to go outside for a quick frosty walk. Then after listening to two more lectures, we crept off again for another walk.

'...Absolutely lovely: maple trees turning red, Spanish chestnuts shedding nuts, two separate small lakes, ancient oaks, riders taking their horses along wonderful tracks...'

We left after Saturday lunch, rather regretfully. If we had stayed we would have attended Matins in the Chapel Royal '... but Daddy was committed to a full day's work in London (in Jeremy Carver's office) on Sunday, with his co-arbitrators from Dacca and Washington...'

Typical: even at the age of 82 one task followed another relentlessly, never allowing time for the sort of breaks our friends were able to indulge in.

———

Jesus College now had women fellows,[473] and Robbie found that the young Law Fellow Mika Oldham shared his love of cats. We needed little persuasion to accept

---

[471] *Principles of International Environmental Law,* Manchester University Press, 1995.

[472] This 17th-century stately building, once owned by the Crown, was given by George VI to a charitable trust for residential conferences on social matters.

[473] The first woman Fellow of Jesus College was Lisa Jardine, elected in 1976.

two of her enchanting pure-bred Abyssinian kittens, to come to Grantchester as soon as our building work was complete. They were not used to country surroundings, so needed a gentle introduction; and alas, Prawn, the pale buff-coloured male was so nervous that he never quite settled, running off one night to be knocked down by a car. His sister Sorrel, though, became an imperious beauty with whom Robbie would walk around the garden's '*peripatos*' each day.

———

Returning from one of his Hague visits to the PCA headquarters in November with a developing cold, Robbie felt reluctant to go to London next day but the Fitzmaurices picked him and drove him to Queen Mary College, where, stimulated as always by a young audience, 'the lecture and questions – 1½ hours – went brilliantly' in spite of tiredness.

Dick's family came for a brief visit in December, when, as I reported, we woke to…

'…Freezing fog, so garden a dim fairyland. Children drawing, me cooking. Great joy to have them all and to get to know bright little Philip a little more; but after lunch we urged them to go (visibility c30 yards). Yet they had a good journey – home in 3 hours… We would have loved to have kept them longer.' Next day, though…

'In evening, heard from Dick that they had had a frightening time with Philip. He nearly died from allergy to peanuts – Jill having given him peanut butter. A dash to the doctor for antihistamine and adrenalin, then emergency treatment at Harrogate Hospital. Now recovered and cheerful.'

I could scarcely believe Dick's quiet voice on the telephone that evening saying, 'I think you should know that we nearly lost Philip today'. But it was true, and it would affect their lives for years to come. Purely by accident, the 14-month-old Philip had been handed a sandwich filled with peanut butter, which he seemed to enjoy until his watchful mother noticed a fearful change as he went into anaphylactic shock. Her prompt response, and that of a doctor who by chance was available, had saved Philip's life; but after an eight-mile journey by ambulance to the hospital at Harrogate, there had been only about 'two minutes to spare'.

Philip's extreme allergy would soon prompt that family's move into a large house with a very large garden in Malton, a small market town with its own hospital. Their new home, a former Youth Hostel, was dilapidated, needing a gradual transformation, room by room; and after a year or two all three (later four) children used one of its huge reception rooms as their school. Later still, in 2004, Dick would leave the firm of Ford & Warren and, instead of commuting to Leeds, set up *R.D.Y. Jennings & Co* at home in an office approached by the servants' staircase.

Robbie's diary entry on 12th September 1995 had been 'SOLD Houtweg 80'. It had been easily arranged: after a professional valuation there was fortunately no need to offer the flat for sale on the open market, since our immediate neighbour Mr Wynaents was happy to buy it as an annexe to his own larger apartment for guests or young family members. Some of our Houtweg furniture could also be disposed of very amicably: Frances Meadows, who shared Robbie's taste in music and was furnishing a country retreat in France, could take the hi-fi apparatus, and Doreen's teenage sons were glad of some pieces, too. But the rest – arriving in large packing-cases just as Christmas preparations were under way – now had to be accommodated at home. Somehow all was ready for Christmas. The five small Goodhart and Eddleston cousins played happily together, and we all enjoyed frosty walks.

By the beginning of 1996 life was back to normal, Robbie's diary noting a visit from 'Miss Wing Kay Po of Hong Kong', a young Jesus graduate student preparing an article for the *Hongkong Standard,* who asked his opinion about the possibility of Britain bringing proceedings against China at the ICJ concerning Hong Kong.

At the end of February we were in Hull for that year's Josephine Onoh Lecture, chaired by Robbie and delivered by Ian Brownlie. This time we took the opportunity to explore Hull's attractons – and found one or two. In its great parish church we spotted a familiar emblem, Bishop Alcock's *rebus* of a cock perched on an orb, and found that the founder of Jesus College had been Vicar there back in the 15th century. Worth seeing, too, was the Ferens Gallery, whose collection included a large portrait of Bobby Moore by our friend Peter Edwards.

Early in March, instead of attending meetings of the Hauser Trust in New York, we were present at the formal opening of the Jesus College

Quincentennial Library by HM the Queen. It was for Her Majesty just one of five engagements in Cambridge on that bright but bitterly cold day; but it marked the creation of a major addition to the college's facilities.

On 14th April we went to The Hague for a series of events relating to the fiftieth anniversary of the International Court. No longer having a flat of our own, it was wonderful to be able to stay in the Haagsche Club (although I, as ever, was to be excluded from its reception rooms downstairs). Here we slept in a vast bedroom with heavy antique Dutch furniture; washed in a fantastically domed great bathroom; and were served by Ben, the butler, with two boiled eggs apiece for breakfast in another huge room overlooking the Lange Voorhout.

After a luncheon in Robbie's honour at the British Ambassador's residence which included several old friends – Rosalyn Higgins, Frank Berman and Ian Sinclair – that same afternoon a large group gathered in the Peace Palace entrance hall for the formal presentation by Vaughan Lowe and Malgosia Fitzmaurice of their own tribute, the book they had edited: *Fifty Years of the International Court of Justice*.[474] Most generously, Rosalyn and Terry Higgins gave a splendid buffet supper in their flat afterwards.

Fifty Years of the International Court of Justice was indeed a wonderful tribute. Its compilation had not been kept secret from Robbie, who had been consulted by its editors from the first. Knowing that he used to sigh over the custom of inviting scholars to write articles for a *Festschrift* with no indication of any connecting topic (meaning that often valuable articles were lost among a random collection in a huge and expensive book that was largely ephemeral), they had resolved to make Robbie's volume more substantial. This, therefore, was to be a book with a single theme; and the Court's 50th anniversary provided one. 34 international lawyers, all well known to Robbie, wrote chapters (and 'many others would have wished to contribute …' as Lowe remarked in his Preface), all together providing 'a compendium of the Court's practice covering the principal areas and themes of its activity over the past 50 years.'[475] It was an important book over which its editors had taken immense pains.

---

[474] *Fifty Years of the International Court of Justice*, edited by Vaughan Lowe & Malgosia Fitzmaurice, Grotius Publications, Cambridge University Press, 640pp.

[475] Iain Scobbie, Senior Lecturer at the University of Glasgow, in his review of the book for the *Leiden Journal of International Law*, 1997.

Already back in November 1994 Vaughan had written to me, asking for my comments on the Introduction he had written. I replied saying it was 'magnificent,' and that I had only one quibble – the omission of any reference to *Oppenheim*, that *magnum opus* that was always somehow overlooked; and he, with due apologies, set the matter right with a generous reference. A presentation copy was prepared with an *RYJ* monogram (designed by our son) embossed on its leather binding. On 20th February 1996 both Vaughan and Malgosia had called at Grantchester to give Robbie a copy of the book in its regular binding, so that he could read it and prepare his speech of thanks for the great day.

Although its cover gives no hint of its subtitle, *Essays in Honour of Sir Robert Jennings,* the Introduction is indeed a magnificent piece of work. In his résumé of Robbie's life and work Vaughan Lowe (perhaps drawing on his own background as a Welshman) perceives the significance of that early upbringing among Wesleyan Methodists and northern hills. He senses, too, Robbie's awareness of...

> '...the way in which international law has, during the sixty years of his career in the law, embraced both technological and political changes of a scale that would have been beyond the comprehension of those who crafted the doctrine of international law during the preceding three-and-a-half centuries. Perhaps attracted by the deep mystery of the immaterial regulating the intangible, he sometimes uses the example of the international regulation of radio frequencies as an example of the accommodation of technological change...'

(Robbie's own struggle to master advances in Hi-Fi and his personal computer meant that he was perhaps more open to new developments than some *Institut* members stuck with a pharisaic devotion to ancient texts.)

Vaughan and Malgosia were not the only admirers who wished to make his achievements better known. Georges Abi-Saab had also been active in collecting together Robbie's many articles and lectures which ought not to be neglected and that would lead to another wonderful publication later.

———

While in The Hague, we were able to see several of the exhibitions celebrating the artist Johannes Vermeer in the Mauritshuis and at Delft. That was not Robbie's main purpose that April, though. International lawyers – many old friends from around the world – were assembled for a colloquium on the ICJ[476] which he was to chair on the day before the major event. From the printed record it is evident that for one session considering *The Contributions of the Court to the Resolution of International Tensions* it was Judge Fleischhauer who took the chair so that Robbie – recruited 'at the very last moment' – might lead the discussion and deal with questions raised afterwards. One participant afterwards wrote to him:

> 'What a fascinating meeting that was!... I cannot remember anything like it, where counsel and agents and Judges all mixed together informally and discussed in a professional and collegial manner matters of obvious common concern, with such a positive atmosphere...' [He had sought Robbie's help beforehand in composing his own paper about the 'presentation of a case.]'

Then on 18th April 1996, a solemn ceremony in the Great Hall of Justice marked the International Court's actual 50th anniversary, attended by Queen Beatrix and Prince Claus, both of them lawyers by training and genuinely interested in the ICJ.

We stayed another day for Robbie to sit in judgment for the final session of that year's Telders Moot, and afterwards wandered happily among the spring flowers of Sorgvliet and along familiar streets. As we walked along Houtweg and past our old grocer's shop, Mr Westerman, on whom Robbie had relied for supplies of *oude Gouda* cheese, *boeren ham* and other essentials, spied his old customer through the window and dashed out to shake his hand.

In Cambridge there were some notable events, too. 1996 was the Quincentenary of Jesus College, marked by one of those group photographs of the Master and all the Fellows. Robbie had made a note in his diary, with the word 'scarlet' – a chance to wear his splendid LL.D. gown. But alas, he is missing from that commemorative photograph, having absentmindedly forgotten all about it on the day![477] We did, though, attend the special service in the college chapel,

---

476   This was the ICJ/UNITAR Colloquium with the theme 'Increasing the Effectiveness of the Court.'

477   A series of these photographs, taken with successive Masters at their centre, show how greatly the college had expanded during Robbie's years as a Fellow. From sixteen in 1939 the Fellows now numbered about eighty, including several women.

with a sermon delivered by the Bishop of Ely[478] and music composed for the occasion by Francis Grier. It was good to chat afterwards with two of Robbie's former musician tutorial pupils, Peter Hurford and Richard Lloyd, and to find Barbara Grant among those present. And that evening Robbie did flaunt his 'scarlet' at the Commemoration Feast.

On 10th May we went up to Edinburgh for a short ILA conference hosted by Alan Boyle.[479] Robbie's address gave rise to some lively discussion, one speaker being a Jesuan he already knew, V.V. ('Johnny') Veeder. While there, we explored the city as much as possible in our limited time between sessions, particularly St Giles Cathedral and the National Gallery of Scotland.

Being now Cambridge-based, Robbie was able to join in more academic events. In May he noted a lecture by Bob Hepple; another by Geoff Harcourt;[480] Eli Lauterpacht lecturing at Chatham House; a 'Treaty Committee' meeting; a 'Greenwich Forum' about the Law of the Sea held in the Map Room of the FCO; and a seminar at All Souls conducted by Alan Roberts. He skipped a visit to Geneva for the Guggenheim prize award, and a suggestion in faint pencil that we might fit in a visit to Arment House did not come to pass. Instead, he was working in his study, dealing with correspondence, preparing articles and talks, and working on the *FARE/RNAC* arbitration.

On 18th June we went together to Oxford for the University's *Encaenia* celebrations and spent two very enjoyable days staying in the Principal's Lodgings at Jesus College. It was for Robbie a return to the college which had welcomed him as a member of its High Table while doing his hush-hush work as an Intelligence officer during the war; and for me it was a return to my own university. Our hosts, Peter and Stephanie North, were friends through the *Institut de Droit International*.[481] We found the University's Chancellor, Roy

---

478 The Bishop of Ely is *ex officio* Visitor to the college. At this time he was the Rt Rev Stephen Sykes.

479 Alan Boyle is Professor of Public International Law at Edinburgh University.

480 Professor Geoffrey Harcourt, an Australian economist, shared Robbie's passion for cricket and became a close friend.

481 Dr Peter North, whose subject was Private International Law, was currently President of Jesus and Vice-Chancellor of the University of Oxford. He received a knighthood later.

Jenkins[482] and his wife, Dame Jennifer, were also staying with them. That first evening we attended the Chancellor's Dinner given for honorary graduands in the ancient Founder's Library at New College, at the end of which, 'our host made a speech which seemed typical of Roy Jenkins in comfortable old age: he is portly, very pleased with himself, and enjoys bringing out bursts of Latin – pronounced, I was told, with all the quantities garbled…'

Next day Robbie received an Oxford DCL degree. Pippa, who had been prevented from witnessing his Cambridge LL.D three years ago by the birth of baby Susie, was this time able to be present. The proceedings began with the honorands receiving Lord Crewe's Benefaction – peaches, strawberries and champagne – while their wives and hangers-on (including the Chancellor's small granddaughter Flora, dressed in miniature tailcoat as the page to carry his train) were offered the same indulgence in the President's Lodgings. While the cheerful procession of university dignitaries and honorands made their way to the Divinity School, Pippa and I took our places on a backless bench in the Sheldonian Theatre. Organ music gave way to a fanfare of trumpets as the procession entered and the ceremony began. By the time the Public Orator had introduced each candidate and spoken the tedious Creweian Oration, his auditors were suffering acute back pain.

But then we processed through the gates of All Souls College, to be offered more champagne on its lawn (Pippa, meanwhile, going off to a working lunch with a children's book publisher at the OUP). It was a brilliantly fine day, and among the colourful throng were plenty of old friends – Richard and Yvette Wilberforce, Noel Annan, Robert Goff, Hazel Fox, Frank Berman; and among his fellow honorands Robbie met Amartya Sen,[483] the architect Norman Foster, the novelist Doris Lessing and Lord Habgood.[484] Luncheon was in the Codrington Library, a wonderful setting.

We and the Jenkinses withdrew to rest briefly in Jesus before moving on to the Encaenia Garden Party, held at Magdalen. There Pippa joined us again. It was a gaudy scene, ladies in hats and summer dresses outdone by a glorious

---

[482]   The Rt Hon Baron Jenkins of Hillhead, having formerly served in the Labour cabinet, became one of the 'gang of four' who founded the Social Democratic Party and was now in the House of Lords.

[483]   Economist, later to become Master of Trinity College, Cambridge.

[484]   The recently-retired Archbishop of York, now styled 'the Rt Rev and Rt Hon Baron Habgood PC,' turned out to have settled in Malton, and could sympathise with the allergy-problems of Dick's family since it had occurred in his own.

variety of academic robes, and rich with eccentric personalities. After the people-watching we wandered along Addison's Walk.

The Norths had arranged a dinner party, for which Robbie had been asked to suggest other guests. He had nominated Sir Philip Mansfield, British Ambassador to the Netherlands during our first years in The Hague, and Henry Chadwick[485] whom he had known for some years. In doing so, Robbie had added as an afterthought: 'One I would like very much to be present is my old, sharp and mischievous friend, Hugh Lloyd Jones,[486] former Regius of Greek; but I think he has secreted himself permanently in the United States'. Even without Hugh, the resulting company, ten in all, had a very good evening indeed.

—

A week later it was Robbie's successor at the Court, Rosalyn Higgins (by now Dame Rosalyn) who received an Honorary LL.D. at Cambridge and an Honorary Fellowship of her college, Girton. We attended both the college dinner and the degree ceremony in the Senate House, where Robbie joined in the procession. Comparing and contrasting our two recent experiences, I judged that 'Cambridge beat Oxford very slightly in its ceremony, as the Public Orator's performance was a more polished one and the musical part – the choir of St John's, conducted by Christopher Robinson… was stunning. (But Oxford wins on hospitality!)'

And in July we enjoyed Trinity Ladies' Night as usual. This time, though, we cut short the romantic stroll in the gardens by the river afterwards, since there had been another pressing invitation. At the Old Vicarage, Grantchester, Jeffrey and Mary Archer[487] were celebrating their 30th ('pearl') wedding anniversary with a huge party, and we were urged to join them halfway through. We turned

---

[485] The Rev Professor Henry Chadwick, KBE had been Dean of Christ Church at the time Dick was an undergraduate there. Later he came back to Cambridge as Master of Peterhouse.

[486] During a brilliant career as Greek scholar, Lloyd-Jones moved from Oxford (Christ Church) to Cambridge (C.C.C. and for some years at Jesus) before returning to Oxford as Regius Professor. He was awarded a knighthood. During the war he had served in military intelligence in the Far East.

[487] Jeffrey Archer, Baron Archer of Weston-super-Mare, novelist, and his wife Mary had moved into the Old Vicarage in 1979. His extraordinary career is well known. Now Dame Mary Archer and Chairman of the Science Museum Group, she had first met Robbie when supervising at Trinity.

up just before midnight, were given Krug champagne and rich cake, and went round to the back garden where the band of the Royal Marines were playing as they marched about with a background of 'the most wonderful and stupendous fireworks I have ever seen' set off from beyond the screen of chestnut trees. At that point a few of their guests, including Margaret and Denis Thatcher, withdrew. But there was much more to come – a cabaret (chief performer Mary herself) and dancing. In the vast marquee, hung with pearly-white balloons, Robbie and I sat and watched the Conservatives at play, as John Gummer jived with Gillian Shephard, Kenneth Baker became hyperactive...

'...John Major took to the floor for a while more sedately... half the members of the Government letting their hair down with an abandon which was rather appealing. Outside, one knew, were the security men and the cars waiting to carry them back to London and grim problems of various sorts. Inside, they were cheerful dervishes to deafeningly cheerful music: judges, showbiz people (and Clive James was the liveliest and most inventive dancer of all), Lord Renfrew, Master of Jesus and Professor of Archaeology, the Vicar of Grantchester (John Beer)... all great fun.'

A quite different event was the garden party a fortnight later given by the University Vice Chancellor at his official residence. Sir David Williams, having been President of Wolfson College, was now the first full-time Vice Chancellor ever to be appointed in the University's long history, replacing the tradition of a short tenure by one of the Heads of Houses; and henceforth this handsome house in Latham Road was to be his or her residence.

We missed that year's ILA conference at Helsinki, instead enjoying short visits by our young families and trying to settle in those nervous cats. Robbie always had work on hand, an article or lecture to prepare and constant correspondence.

Then, after a one-night visit to Birstwith, where we played with Dick's three children in their lovely hillside garden, Robbie was off next day to London for the arbitration hearings. What should have been an uninterrupted long session broke off for a weekend when he was escorted home by Philippe Sands, who explained that he had suddenly fainted at an over-rich dinner the evening before, causing alarm. They had taken him to St Thomas' Hospital to be examined, where (confirmed by a further check by our own doctor) no serious trouble was found. But the episode was a hint that despite his continuing stamina, he must learn to be a little careful. Once back at work, the arbitration case was settled and the parties signed their agreement.

After noting successive social events, Robbie's diary records that on 7th October, Annie's birthday made the grandchildren's ages neatly run as 8,7,6,5,4,3,2,1;[488] a magic sequence broken next day by Philip's birthday. Robbie's own 83rd birthday on the 19th was marked pleasantly but quietly, since I was to have a knee replacement at the Evelyn Hospital next day. I stayed there for twelve days, during which he was fed partly in college and by kind friends.

On 20th November he lectured at Queen Mary College; on the 22nd he was again in London for a 'Corfu seminar at the Foreign Office with dinner at Lancaster House;'[489] and on the 26th he was at the Francis Mann Lecture, dining at the Savoy and staying overnight at the Oxford & Cambridge Club. So it went on, one event following another. For him, a particularly special one was a trip to London as the guest of John Mills, a Fellow of Jesus, for the 'Hobbs Lunch' at Lord's. For a lifelong devotee of cricket this was a sort of heaven, and he got himself proposed for membership of the MCC (but the waiting list was so long that when his name eventually came up, it was after his death).

I, in the meantime, was steadily graduating from crutches to walking stick, and managed to take part as usual in the village Carol Service. We went to Leicester for Christmas with Pippa's family, and took a Boxing Day walk – my longest yet – with the children and dog in glorious sunshine and hard frost… only to find, when back at their house, a telephone call from Grantchester saying that there had been a burglary at our own. It could have been much worse: someone had forced open a window in Robbie's study and opened drawers and cupboards mainly to find money, leaving some damage. But it meant that we were obliged to fit more locks and install a burglar alarm.

We had a great *together* day for my birthday – a rumbustious celebration, with six adults and five granddaughters who after lunch dashed around and around the rooms. Robbie always loved whipping up the excitement with noisy music, leaving the poor mothers having to calm things down before bedtime.

So, with weather noted by Robbie as '*V. cold. Record snow in E.England & Midlands,*' the year ended.

---

[488] It was Pippa who had noticed the sequence when she wrote her special story in celebration of his 80th birthday.

[489] This was a Symposium held at the FCO to mark the ICJ's 50th anniversary. Its theme was *Issues arising out of the Corfu Channel Case*, with Robbie as Chairman. Members of the Court attended as well as all the principal British international lawyers.

The Arbitrator & Collected Writings

1997-99

On 14th January 1997 Robbie's diary (growing more cryptic and indecipherable than ever) notes meetings with '*Parties E/Y*'. It is the first suggestion that he might be going to conduct an arbitration of far greater significance than the two commercial ones already disposed of: a dispute concerning the sea boundary between Eritrea and Yemen. This, however, would not get fully under way until late autumn.

There was still plenty to occupy him. At the end of the month he lectured at Nottingham University and took a discussion session afterwards. (He was impressed there by Catherine Redgwell,[490] who had organised it so well, and who played a prominent part in the ILA's Treaty Committee which he was chairing.) There were frequent contributions to the weekly talks at the Lauterpacht Research Centre, too.

In February we spent a few days in The Hague, staying once more in the Haagsche Club. A proud Jacques welcomed us with the huge BMW 7 saloon car now in his charge; and after a meeting of the Telders committee, Robbie enjoyed a chatty lunch with old friends, Doreen Blumendael and Frances Meadows. We were there for the presentation of a *Festschrift* to Skubiszewski and his splendid dinner afterwards for Polish colleagues and others who had contributed to the volume. On the 25th Prince Claus performed the formal opening of an extension to the Peace Palace buildings, designed by the architect responsible for the modern wing opened by Queen Juliana in 1978. It included a pleasant dining room where palatable lunches were served. Along its new corridor I noticed a door labelled *Judge Jennings* – marking an office still reserved for the time when Robbie might be called as *ad hoc* judge to play a part in deliberations over the Lockerbie air crash, with both the UK and USA as parties opposing Libya.

After the formal opening ceremony and reception, Robbie was able to hear more of the latest Court tidings from Eduardo Valencia and be shown

---

[490] Catherine Redgwell is now Chichele Professor at Oxford.

around the new office areas that had been created in the high roof-spaces of the original Peace Palace. Next day we had time for some sentimental wandering along familiar streets, and lunched with judges Rosalyn Higgins, Kooijmans and Guillaume before our flight home.

We both went to hear Robert Goff[491] deliver his Wilberforce Lecture on 'The Future of the Common Law' in the hall of Gray's Inn. The occasion was particularly notable, being Richard Wilberforce's 90th birthday, and we were among those privileged to share the celebratory dinner afterwards. I sat between Lord Mackay of Clashfern, by now quite a friend, and Sam Wilberforce, schoolmaster son of Richard and Yvette, who bore one of that illustrious family names ('Soapy Sam', the Bishop of Oxford who in 1860 had sneered at Huxley and Darwin in a famous debate on evolution). It was altogether a very good evening – recorded in snapshots taken by Yvette, herself always ready with a small camera.

One event followed another: the memorial service for 'Uncle Basil', Sir Basil Neild, held in the Temple Church; a dinner in honour of William Christie, head of Robbie's chambers, 13 Old Square;[492] next evening another with the Cambridge Law Society… and so it went on.

That Easter we had Joey and her children to stay, joined one day for crazy games in the garden by Pippa's family. A huge poplar tree had fallen across our front garden, and the children fashioned its twiggy remnants into a little house. (We were to watch an intrepid tree surgeon bring down its pair some days later.) Meanwhile up north, Dick's family were ending their Easter visit to Arment House with a return, not to Birstwith but to their new home at Malton.

———

We were still constantly receiving visitors from abroad wanting to talk to Robbie. But on 25th April there was a visitation on a rather grander scale. Two large cars drew up at the house, the first carrying the Deputy Foreign Minister of Taiwan and his wife, and a Taiwanese Professor of International Law. We were to be given lunch at the Garden House Hotel – but first they

---

[491] The Rt Hon Lord Goff of Chieveley was by now Senior Law Lord, High Steward of the University of Oxford and would become President of the British Institute of International & Comparative Law – among many other distinctions.

[492] In 2004 13 Old Square merged with 9 Old Square to become known as Maitland Chambers.

had a 'small gift' for us. And now from the second car emerged two men carrying a huge wooden box, which they set down in our entrance hall. It was opened, and our small gift was lifted out: an enormous and handsome spherical black vase, decorated all over with *sgraffito* chrysanthemums. They put it, on its ornamental stand, on a side table in our dining room – where it has stayed ever since, almost immovable. (It is, we were told, a facsimile of a Sung dynasty piece, a wonderful example of craftsmanship.) Our visitors were delightful people, whose mission was to try to persuade Robbie to visit Taiwan. He did think seriously about this, and there was no doubt that they would have made it a special experience. But he had a full diary and felt rather old to be undertaking such a journey. More importantly, there might be awkward political implications in his favouring Taiwan rather than the People's Republic of China. Politely, he declined.

On 1st May we lunched with Charles Brower, and I think it was on this occasion that he sounded Robbie on the possibility of becoming involved in a case concerning Costa Rica – describing the delights of that country's mountainous interior as an inducement. That, too, was not to be. Robbie had plenty to occupy his time already.

But we did this year manage a whole week's stay at Arment House, recorded in some detail in both our diaries: the grounds of Muncaster Castle full of azaleas and rhododendrons in bloom; a good exhibition of local art in the village school at Eskdale Green, followed by a delightful bread-and-cheese-in-the-garden lunch with friends encountered there; next day a favourite walk by the Esk and finally, as Robbie's diary notes, a look at Wasdale 'to see the magic haze lift from the mountains'.

We made another visit to Germany that summer for Robbie to lecture (with no script) and answer students' questions at the University of Saarbrücken. The Doehrings had come from Heidelberg in his honour and we were well entertained by the Resses. Among other social events, Robbie attended as its President the Cranworth Law Society dinner at Downing; Glyndebourne to see *Figaro*; the Law Faculty's buffet dinner; an evening at Jesus to hear Peter Glazebrook talk about the treasures in the college's Old Library; and a Sunday visit to Lincoln's Inn for morning service in its chapel and lunch.

He was slightly involved, too, in a summer course for Canadian lawyers. We were at the opening ceremony of the handsome new extension of the Lauterpacht Centre, performed by the University Chancellor, HRH Prince Philip – another of Eli's organisational triumphs. There was a college dinner to mark the retirement of Lord Renfrew as Master of Jesus; the usual Ladies Night at Trinity; and for Robbie, another Trinity dinner given by the Commonwealth Trust – yet another organisation with which he was now involved at the request of Anil Seal.[493]

Contact with Robbie's remaining relatives was by now sparse, but one day there was a surprise telephone call – a woman's voice with a strong New Zealand accent saying 'Hi! Rachel here, Rachel Jennings…' A bewildered Robbie passed the telephone to me. It transpired that this young woman was a daughter of Keith, who was a son of Roy, the son of Herbert Jennings, Robbie's uncle. No wonder he could not cope immediately! But she was, genuinely, a distant relative, and he certainly had very few. On a Sunday in July she and her partner arrived for lunch – both tall, tanned, athletic and bursting with enthusiasm. They stayed until 6 pm, and then set off in a car with bicycles strapped behind. Over the following years we caught scraps of news of their energetic travels all over the world. It had been a cheering encounter.

Robbie's diary entry on the 29th July – 'Chris to Cley for Peter Ward' – marked a diversion of my own. I drove that day to the Norfolk coast to talk to the former owner of the Old Vicarage, Grantchester,[494] knowing that he, Peter Ward, had over many years gathered a lot of material concerning the Victorian residents of that house, the Widnalls. I brought home a boxful of these archives, and eventually – six years later – published my book about that household.[495] My absorption in this project aroused a mixture of encouragement and exasperation ('*Bloody* Widnall!') from Robbie.

In August, on a blazingly hot day, we drove together down to Broxbourne for the wedding reception of my nephew Jonathan Bennett and his wife Amanda. On arrival Robbie accepted a glass of champagne, standing for sometime in full sunshine. By the time I managed to persuade him to move into the shade and sit down it was too late, for he was fainting. A woman doctor there told

---

[493] Dr Anil Seal, Fellow of Trinity, was a founding member of the School of Historiography, concerned largely with the British Empire.

[494] Peter Ward's father, Dudley Ward, had been a close friend of Rupert Brooke and it was after Brooke's death that the house came into his possession, given by the late poet's mother.

[495] *Widnall: a Capital Contriver: the story of a Victorian household in the village of Grantchester.*

him to stay lying flat even when, to his slight indignation, he was missing the first course of lunch. Once allowed to join the rest of us at table he was his usual self, chatting and enjoying it all. But it had been another warning of a tendency (evident even a few times as a young man) to pass out.

———

A week or so later we went northwards by train to spend two nights with Dick's family and see the astonishing house they now occupied. Its vast reception rooms and some bedrooms were still undecorated, leaving bare walls on which Jill, Lizzie and I could make great fantasy drawings in charcoal. Its 2½-acre garden clearly had potential. And this house, *Derwent Bank*, was to provide not only a home and school for growing children, but also an office for Dick, and pasture for sheep and other creatures as well.

Pippa was becoming a recognised children's author, and in September came over to Cambridge to give a lecture at Homerton College.[496] Joey and Egg were combining their work as potters with other jobs using their creative skills.

By now Robbie was having to contemplate surgery for glaucoma in his second eye. That, and my own need for a hip replacement, were matters to be fitted into his schedule somehow. In the meantime there were more engagements in Cambridge – Robbie giving a speech of welcome to lawyers gathered at Jesus for Barry Rider's annual symposium on International Economic Crime; a meeting of the King Street Housing Association; and the admission of a new Master of Jesus, Professor David Crighton.[497]

There was another important matter before any time could be spared for surgery. On 22ⁿᵈ September Robbie went to the Foreign Office building for the actual opening of proceedings in his third and most important PCA arbitration, the dispute between Eritrea and Yemen – each party presenting Memorials setting out their rival claims, on historical grounds, to the islands lying in the southern end of the Red Sea. (I had for a moment wondered whether there might be an excursion for members of the tribunal to see the disputed territory for themselves, allowing me to accompany Robbie on one of these adventures. But no such visit was contemplated since the Zuqar-Hanish islands were composed entirely of barren rock and inhabited by snakes.)

---

[496] Homerton was a Teachers' Training College still, although would later widen its range.

[497] Crighton, a Fellow of St John's, was Head of the Department of Applied Mathematics and Theoretical Physics.

He was back at the FCO on 2nd October for a seminar held on the 50th anniversary of the International Law Commission, and attended the opening of the new Moot Court at the Cambridge new Law Building by Lord Mackay that same evening.

On the 12th he was off to the Netherlands, this time as a judge *ad hoc* for the opening of the *Lockerbie* case. These preliminary hearings on claims against Libya for compensation by the US and UK for the damage caused by the bombing of Pan-Am Flight 103 kept him there for ten days, and he marked his 84th birthday by giving the Fitzmaurices tea at the Hotel des Indes. While there he also conducted some arbitration business in the PCA office, and dined with friends on several evenings.

He came back on the evening of the 22nd, and two days later was at The Lea Hospital for Mr Moore, the eye surgeon, to operate on his second eye. A few days at home were spent recovering, and always afterwards he had to keep to a regime of eyedrops. On the 29th, besides a check-up visit to Mr Moore, his diary notes 'frustrated robbery'. Two young lads had tricked their way into our kitchen, and it was Robbie who quickly spotted one of them stealing my camera and gave chase, shouting, as they both fled. (The young villains were well known to the police, but too young to be charged.)

We had tried to plan our 'elective' surgery to fit around our complicated commitments with the least inconvenience. Robbie's operation had been a success, and now it was my turn. Since a hip replacement was less of an ordeal than a knee replacement, I would surely be home in 10 days and fully active by Christmas. But not so: as it turned out, Robbie's demanding schedule became far more stressful than usual. Writing to Karl Zemanek[498] enclosing an article he had written, he added a postscript:

'Christine had a bad 5 weeks in hospital – hip replacement but wound picked up one of those virulent hospital infections. V. bad for a time but now home and doing well. But *not* good for my writing!'

Despite all the arrangements I had made beforehand to provide him with regular meals, he was so helpless about such matters that when Pippa came over from Leicester she would find them untouched and uneatable. His own recent operation prevented him from driving, so he had to rely on a taxi for

---

498   Karl Zemanek, Professor of International Law at the University of Vienna.

rides into Cambridge. He visited me when he could, and several times ate lunch at The Evelyn Hospital. One day, though, 'R called 3 pm – had quite forgotten to eat any lunch (writing an article, dealing with man mending central heating) …' He did not quite starve, since Pippa would bring food or take him out to one of the village pubs, and our neighbours took it in turn to invite him to dinner. But he missed the use of his car, and walked for miles on his various errands.

Being Robbie, he wanted to fulfil all his obligations. So while all this was going on, he worked on the *Yemen/Eritrea* dispute, gave lunch to a visiting Taiwanese at the University Centre, went to a BYIL meeting, heard Frank Berman lecture and then attended a black-tie dinner at Jesus for Derek Taunt, dined at Trinity to meet a guest of Peter Laslett; and on 25th November, while I was having my third operation, went to Holland. There, he conducted the tribunal's 'Article 5 deliberation' when the parties exchanged their Counter-Memorials, and was home on the evening of the 27th. There were two more suppers with Grantchester friends, and a feast at Sidney Sussex as John Thornley's guest before I was back at home with him. We were, as always, grateful to the faithful Mr Robb,[499] who had become a family friend.

The year ended as cheerfully as possible. Both Joey's and Pippa's families came for Christmas Day, and they made a special meal for my 70th birthday (when, to my amazement, Dick appeared as well). With their encouragement I took my longest walk so far with crutches. Things were getting better.

———

The first stage of the *Yemen/Eritrea* arbitration (deciding sovereignty over the scattered islands) was proceeding. On Sunday 25th January Robbie was driven to London for meetings of the tribunal, and worked with his colleagues and representatives of the two sides until 7th February. The oral hearings were conducted in the Durbar Conference Room of the Foreign & Commonwealth Office. (A diary entry during that period, 'Sheikh Mohammed at Claridge's Hotel 1 hr Bahrain,' suggests that he was also advising on a case being heard at the ICJ at the time.)

---

[499] Bob Robb was employed by Marshalls of Cambridge as chauffeur for many years. When not driving us in one of their cars (registered as MER 1 and MER 2) he would turn up in his own.

There were just 2½ days at home before he was off again, this time to The Hague for the First Reading and deliberation of the *Lockerbie*[500] case. Home on the evening of Saturday 14th, and next day to London for one of the Fitzmaurices' lunch parties, now in their flat in Soho. But there was no rest after that: on the 17th we were entertaining Judge Charles James (a Bencher of Lincoln's Inn) and his wife; on the 20th Robbie was in London to give a morning lecture at Queen Mary College and spend the afternoon on the tribunal's Second Reading; on Sunday the 22nd, after lunching with friends at a village some miles away, he caught an afternoon flight to The Hague again.

This was an intensive session, combining his work at the ICJ, which gave its judgment on the first stage of the *Lockerbie* case on 27th February, with many hours of work for the PCA on *Yemen/Eritrea*. Back he came on Sunday 1st March, and next day his diary notes: 'Society Mtg (new building)' – a meeting of Jesus College fellows about the new accommodation wing beside the new library – and 'Newton Trust, Old Kitchen 5.30' – one of Trinity College's many charities, I think. On the Friday it is 'Jesus Law Ass. & lecture on "International Litigation"'. My own diary says 'Robbie gave a splendid talk …'

On Sunday there was something different: 'Hussain Majidi & daughter to tea.' Our guests were an interesting Iranian with his gifted daughter, hoping for advice from Robbie, who was of course happy to help as far as possible. But these people were in a difficult situation: Hussain, son of a senior official in the Shah's government, had had to leave Iran on the downfall of that regime. Educated in the US in preparation for a probable senior appointment himself, Hussain had found no possibility of returning to his native country and no family wealth to support him. He was a proud man, so found a new way to earn a living, opening in Cambridge a *Digital Imaging* business, always advancing into the latest technology. (It was because of his firm's high-quality photographic processessing that I had got to know him.) His wife was British, and their daughter – a beautiful girl, with a range of languages as well as a good degree – had trained as a lawyer. Robbie discussed the next stage of her career and probably endorsed her entry into one of the top London firms of solicitors. But there, sadly, she would be kept at demeaning work with little prospect of advancement, and a few years later returned to Cambridge to help her parents in their shop. Racial and gender prejudice seem to have prevailed.

---

[500]   After a number of hearings, this case was removed from the Court's list in September 2003.

So it went on: a mixture of activities that kept Robbie occupied all through the spring and early summer of 1998. At home in his study there was always writing under way, including a contribution to the very first, 'zero', issue of *FORUM*,[501] part-edited by Frances Meadows. For this sample edition he had been asked to write a short piece under the heading *The Bookshelf* on his choice of reading-matter. It begins by mentioning his favourite legal authorities and the need to keep up with the latest publications, but quoting McNair in stressing that the scope of a lawyer's reading should range more widely. He was at that time reading the life of Thomas Cranmer – a man 'very much concerned with international relations and law and [who] was also clearly, for the English language, the greatest draftsman of all'. As for fiction, 'I am at a loss to understand how anyone can get the true flavour of maritime matters and the law of the sea without reading at least some of the historical seagoing novels of Patrick O'Brian'. These choices were characteristic: a deep interest in one of the earliest Fellows[502] of Jesus College, Archbishop Cranmer, and a relish for the detail, verve and humour of adventures at sea. During this year Robbie found he must also contribute to more *Festschrifts*, with serious articles for Judge Christopher Weeramantry, Professor Seidel-Hohenveldern, and Boutros Boutros-Ghali.

As the year progressed there were still outside demands: once more to chair Barry Rider's symposium on International Commercial Fraud in London, and more work at The Hague for *Lockerbie* and *Eritrea/Yemen*.[503] At Cambridge there were other interests: the formal admission of David Crighton as Master of Jesus; the funeral of one of Robbie's more unusual friends, Peter Biles (one-time gamekeeper, chauffeur and latterly a wonderfully candid salesman at University Audio); the launch-party at Heffers of Robin Orr's autobiography (evoking memories of their wartime years in Intelligence); and so on. And after another two-day spell at the PCA, he spent some hours in London at a Clifford Chance 'G8 Conference'.

At Clifford Chance his chief contact was still Jeremy Carver, with whom he had shared those adventures in Tierra del Fuego and Sharjah years before. Jeremy, a solicitor whose Cambridge degree had been in Engineering, was

---

501 *International Law FORUM du Droit International*, The Journal of the International Law Association, pub. Kluwer Law International.

502 Thomas Cranmer is generally referred to as a Fellow, but his position was actually that of graduate Fellow-Commoner.

503 For *E/Y* Robbie relied on the efficient Bette Schifman, Deputy Secretary-General of the PCA.

always more alert to new technological and cultural developments in the world than most international lawyers of the time – an outlook which Robbie, despite a wide gap in their ages, shared. Commenting on suggestions made by Robbie back in March 1997 for the *Institut* which, he said, 'came to me like a breath of fresh air', he wrote in a personal letter:

'You are, of course, totally right to identify the *electronic communications revolution* as of primary importance for the international community; and entirely ignored by international lawyers.'

Jeremy had attended a 'dreadful seminar' at The Hague which revealed the ignorance and even paranoia of senior international lawyers concerning the Internet.

'In practice, the Internet – or, rather, the world wide web – is transforming both the way we work and what we will be delivering to our clients. . . It is not fanciful to see a time – within a decade – when national government, legal regulation and fiscal liquidity – will have been so eroded that the landscape in which we exist will be barely recognisable . . .'

There was more, expressing their exasperation about insistence on 'legal process' in situations where the South African example of a Truth and Reconciliation Commission showed a more humane and effective solution. And Philippe Sands, too, had of course found an ally in Robbie in promoting the development of Environmental Law.

———

At the end of May we indulged in a treat together, being driven down to Sussex for a Glyndebourne performance of *Cosi Fan Tutte*. The drive home in the dark rather took the shine off that lovely experience; so when we made a second visit in June for Handel's *Rodelinda*, we spent the night at a Bed & Breakfast place in Ditchling – partly out of curiosity to see how that house, The White Barn, had been altered since my Uncle Donald had lived there for many years. We were relieved to find it recognisable still, and greatly improved.

Robbie had another intensive bout of work on the arbitration in The Hague in late June; a further one held at Essex Court in London about a week later; and a good deal going on in between.

A particularly significant event at home was the arrival of our first computer on 2nd July. Robbie had recently made his most extravagant purchase from University Audio (a whole new set-up of Quad equipment) with the assistance of a charming salesman there, Colin Parr. Dissatisfied with that job, Parr had now left to start a business of his own in St Ives, hoping to deal in computers as well as hi-fi equipment. Wanting to encourage this new enterprise, it was from him that we acquired our first PC. It meant that at 84 Robbie had to adjust his typing from a word-processor to an inexpertly-installed computer – giving rise to some frustration and fury. (On a later model, having mastered most of its tricks, Robbie once typed the greater part of a long article for the Max Planck Institute. When I called to say that lunch was ready, he touched something… his text disappeared… he panicked, tapping and clicking… and 50 pages, closely argued with supporting footnotes, were gone and we could not retrieve them. But it happened that our church organist[504] at that time was working on his doctoral thesis in advanced mathematics and actually understood how computers worked. I invited him for Sunday lunch – with extra vegetables and stuffing added – and this lean and hungry genius set to work. Some two hours later the text was restored, and we had learnt the hard lesson, to *save* our work or *undo* mistakes instantly). Although he scarcely ventured into the internet and never tried email, Robbie did become adept at writing letters and articles on the computer.

— —

'I hate holidays,' Robbie would say, claiming that to unwind led to the terrible labour of winding-up again; but in July 1998 Pippa invited us to join her family for a week's stay in the Channel Islands on Herm. It was a complete and welcome change. We flew to Guernsey and crossed to Herm by ferry. There, while our baggage was carried up by tractor, we climbed the steep track to Bramble Cottage. A gale blew the first night, and in the island's tiny old chapel next morning we joined the hearty singing, to a harmonium, of 'Eternal Father, strong to save'. The three little Goodhart girls, Annie, Mary and Susie, had a lovely time, including a treasure-hunt covering much of the island set up at dawn by their father; and one day we all went across to the larger island of Sark, where we rode in a horse-drawn cart and ventured across the *Coupee*

---

[504]   Dr Ian Talbot played the organ for our church services, and I at this time was choirmistress. He later used his expertise in a new business, *Cambridge Logic*.

to Little Sark. On the final day, while the young family stayed on one of the beaches trying to catch crabs, Robbie and I walked around the S.E. end of the island looking across to the cliffs of Sark, and I told him how at one of our Trinity dinners my neighbour, Sir James Lighthill,[505] had boasted of having on several occasions swum all around Sark, using his knowledge of tidal flows to make this possible. It was with a chilling shock that we read, three days later, his obituary in *The Times*. Lighthill's death had occurred while undertaking this 9-mile swim for the seventh time on the very day we had been speaking of it.

Robbie had two more visits to The Hague in August, and a brief one in September when the new British Ambassador, H.E. Rosemary Spencer, hosted a recital of 17th century music, followed by dinner. We spent the Saturday revisiting Delft and Scheveningen and dining with Steve Schwebel, but Robbie worked all Sunday in the Peace Palace on *Eritrea/Yemen*. For the rest of the month he noted a two-day UK Government seminar at All Souls, and a Foreign Office seminar held at Selwyn which ended with his giving an after-dinner speech. Finally, he spent one night at The Hague, perhaps to sign important papers at the PCA.

On 9th October the first stage of the *Eritrea/Yemen* Arbitration came to its formal conclusion, with the 'Award handed to Parties', as he noted in his diary. Eke Boustin and Edward Helgesen, two young international lawyers who had assisted him, were with us at Grantchester that day. It was satisfying for them all to know that after detailed consideration of the historical background, the legal implications of petroleum exploration and of fishing rights, sovereignty over the clusters of islands had been agreed by both parties.

E/L, as he referred to it, could now be laid aside for a while. 19th October that year was his 85th birthday, celebrated at home with a visit from Pippa's family and the gift of a bottle of burgundy brought by Christopher Greenwood. And three days later we were in The Hague for the launch of the *Collected Writings of Sir Robert Jennings*, published by Kluwer Law International. Its editor, Georges Abi-Saab, was there with his wife Rosemary, and a number

---

505   Sir James Lighthill, Lucasian Professor of Mathematics at Cambridge and Provost of UCL, had made a particular study of aerodynamics and marine currents. He would calculate the flow of tides and currents to assist his swim around Sark.

of admirers (including Arthur Eyffinger, the ICJ librarian) were gathered in the Peace Palace for the occasion. That book, in two volumes, was important indeed.

Oxford's Public Orator, in presenting Robbie for his honorary DCL, had made one inaccurate statement: 'he is the author of many books'. Not true – Robbie had never been one of those 'hermit scholars' turning out learned tomes; he had been engaged in so many activities – principally teaching – that there was never time nor inclination to do so. Apart from *Oppenheim*, a work which did not allow for originality, there had just been the hardback publication of his Schill Lectures, *The Acquisition of Territory* (1961) and the Hague Academy's printed record of his General Course.[506] His name was by now widely known and revered, yet his many other writings were scattered among a variety of publications and could easily have become quite forgotten.

Robbie's own explanation for the sparsity of his published writing[507] was characteristic in its modesty:

'… It was typical of me why I wrote those books. The first, *The Acquisition of Territory*, was because Ben Wortley, who was a great friend of mine, another Yorkshireman, asked me to go and give the Schill Lectures at Manchester University. Otherwise I might never have written that little book, Nino. The General Course on international law – I suppose it was Fitzmaurice who engineered the invitation through the Curatorium. He gave me some hints, "you know how important it is" and so on, and I just had to do it. And I did it. I've always been a bit like that. If I'd had somebody with a big stick behind me, I would have written more, Nino. Laziness, that's what you must bring out.'

It was Abi-Saab, a former pupil and admirer, who had gathered this material into a single publication. Already by February 1995 he was considering how to present all these essays, writing 'The simplest way is to publish them in their chronological order … [which would be] quite unsatisfactory'. Instead, he suggested they should be sorted into categories. In August '96 he sent Robbie his proposal for their selection and codification. By January '98 he was struggling to write 'a longish intellectual portrait worthy of you' but had difficulty with the language

---

[506] The General Course was issued by the Hague Academy 'for private circulation only.'

[507] In reply to Antonio Cassese, reported in *Five Masters of International Law*, p153,

barrier, being an Egyptian now speaking mainly French. He was 'spending hours consulting dictionaries (both English and French-English for equivalents) on almost every word…' and had finally 'panicked, retreating to a much more modest minimalist design', the 'very humble result' which he now submitted.

But Georges need not have worried about the text of his Foreword, which is excellent. He writes of Robbie combining 'deceptive simplicity' with 'effortless supremacy' knowing, in fact, what concentration of effort it takes to achieve the simplicity, and the years of experience behind that impression of effortlessness. He ends:

'The reader is thus invited to an exciting intellectual journey into the life of international law during the last crucial five or six decades, as chronicled by one of the most perceptive exponents of our discipline.'

The bulkiest part – 264 pages – of the publication is a reprinting of the General Course that Robbie had delivered to the Hague Academy in 1967 which, as Abi-Saab comments, 'reflects the pedagogic style of Sir Robert and conveys some of the flavour of his oral lectures to successive generations of students in Cambridge and elsewhere'. There follow his writings (dating from 1938 to 1997) on a range of topics, ending with his obituaries of admired predecessors – McNair, Fitzmaurice, Waldock and Parry.

Barry Rider, as a young law fellow of Jesus, had for years been glad of Robbie's advice on work he was doing with the FCO to address the problem of international economic crime. It may be that, as well as his readiness to address totally new areas needing international control, Robbie's wartime experience with MI6 had assisted them. It was probably at about this stage that Rider, after studying the less-than-effective efforts so far of INTERPOL and other bodies, submitted his report to the Commonwealth Secretariat's Legal Division with a proposal for the setting up of a specialised intelligence unit within the Commonwealth Secretariat, operating with diplomatic immunity; a proposal which was 'unanimously accepted by ministers and implemented the following year'. Rider later wrote to me:

'One of the reasons why this (potentially very controversial) proposal was accepted … was the support that it received from Robbie. While to most lawyers (even international lawyers) all this would have been high risk heresy, Robbie recognised three things in giving his support for the proposal – firstly, something needed to be done immediately to assist developing countries, and international law was developing in this area too slowly; secondly, many of the issues were extra-legal and whatever developed in terms of domestic or international law (and he was not hopeful it would – other than in a trans-national context) the weakness was likely to be in enforcement – and prevention was even better – particularly in the context of more fragile economies.

'Robbie made these views known on three (I think) occasions in meeting with Mr Kutlu Fuad and his deputy (Jeremy Pope – who was later involved in setting up Transparency International), at a separate meeting at the FCO and at a meeting with the new Attorney General of Hong Kong ... who with the Attorney General of Bermuda led for the UK on this. Given the tremendous respect for Robbie in particular in the Commonwealth and FCO, without his support, albeit expressed informally, the proposals would not have got past the FCO – let alone be presented internationally.'

And now, in October 1998 Rider, as Director, invited us to dine with the Institute of Advanced Legal Studies in Middle Temple.

This particular behind-the-scenes work of Robbie's is something I was scarcely aware of at the time. He was not alone, I am sure, in looking beyond established international law to address the problem of economic crime: Jeremy Carver, in constant touch, became Senior Adviser to Transparency International UK. Robbie recognised the importance of Intellectual Property Law, too. In April 1999 we paid a brief visit to Geneva for a meeting of distinguished delegates at the WIPO[508] headquarters where, as usual, Robbie played a full part and had good relations with everybody.

Nor were these Robbie's only 'incidental' occupations at that time. He was in London for a conference of the Greenwich Forum on *The Law of the Sea: Challenges & Opportunities* at the FCO on 25th November, when he gave an opening address that: 'Set the current situation so perfectly in its historical context, and opened a lot of participants' eyes in the process,'[509] that it stimulated lively discussion at the conclusion of the meeting. The text of

---

[508] WIPO – World Intellectual Property Organisation.
[509] Quoted from the letter of thanks afterwards from Rear Admiral Richard Hill.

his short address (typed on 'clean-on-one-side paper') reveals the clarity with which he summarised the development of the Law of the Sea, ending…

'…A final word about the delegations that formed the conference, [the Third UN Conference on the Law of the Sea, 1982] for so long and saw all its problems and periodic crises and its eventual triumphal success. They were of very mixed skills, not only lawyers but also naval officers, hydrographers, and special interests like the oil and gas industry representatives and many others. It was the mixture of skills that in the end made it work.

'…It is time that the making and developing of international law should be more often seen to be what it is and should be an interdisciplinary subject of study.'

And earlier that November Robbie, while attending a meeting of the Hague Academy, had also signed letters to the agents of Yemen and Eritrea setting in motion Stage Two of their arbitration. Memorials were exchanged the following March; there were meetings in The Hague in June; Oral Hearings in July in the Great Hall of Justice at the Peace Palace; the Parties' written responses to questions from the Tribunal received in August; the Reading and final deliberations in The Hague in September; another brief visit in October; and at last, on 17th December 1999, Robbie could note: 'FCO for Award 11 am'. He was now aged 86.

Stage Two of *Eritrea/Yemen* had been concerned with 'maritime delimitation,' settling the sea-boundary running down the Gulf which was particularly important for fisheries and petroleum exploitation. First the 'historic use of resources' must be considered – which for Eritrea included:

'…fishing, trading, shell and pearl diving, guano and mineral extraction, and all associated activities on land including drying fish, drawing water, religious and burial practices, and building and occupying shelters for sleep and refuge.'

All fascinating matters. For the more technical examination of shorelines and the actual waters of the Gulf, experts in geodesy and hydrography were used; and the arbitrators looked back at precedents such as the *Anglo-Norwegian Fisheries* case of 1959 and the *North Sea Continental Shelf* judgment of 1969 in deciding the 'basepoint co-ordinates' on each side.

The volume (published after Robbie's death) which records the *Eritrea/Yemen* case begins with a Foreword written by Tjaco van den Hout, Secretary-General of the Permanent Court of Arbitration. He praises Robbie's achievements as 'an educator, academic, and member and president of the International Court of Justice', adding:

'...Perhaps less well known is the pivotal role he played in the revitalization of the PCA in the 1990s. He was the first in decades to entrust important international arbitrations, including the Eritrea-Yemen case, to PCA administration, thereby laying the groundwork for subsequent developments. Robbie – as he usually insisted on being called, despite his impressive titles – will long be remembered by the staff of the PCA as a staunch supporter and trusted sounding board.'

The other members of the tribunal had played their part unstintingly, both Rosalyn Higgins and Steve Schwebel being at the same time members of the ICJ. The one deserving special mention in the Foreword was Keith Highet, who had seen the process through to its end while enduring 'an increasingly debilitating illness' from which he died soon after. The loss of Highet was lamented by Robbie, who valued him both as a brilliant lawyer and as a wonderfully gifted and generous man, always entertaining company.

As an Introduction to the volume, its achievement is summarised under the heading '*THE ERITREA-YEMEN ARBITRATION: Its Contribution to International Law*' by Professor Jean-Pierre Queneudec. In conclusion he writes:

'On the whole, the task accomplished by the Tribunal between Eritrea and Yemen was quite remarkable, not only for the reasons given above, but also because, as shown by the two Arbitral Awards... the Tribunal endeavoured to fulfil a pedagogical role towards the two States while taking great care to scrupulously analyze the arguments put forward by each and to readily reveal the grounds on which it deemed it had to retain or, on the contrary, reject them. The solicitude it demonstrated in providing as much explanation as possible has without doubt been crowned with success.'

(The fact that all five members of the tribunal had been professional pedagogues[510] must have contributed to this aspect of the Award.) While its success had brought an end to the conflict which had broken out in 1995 between the two countries, it made possible a later arbitration, conducted under Eli Lauterpacht's presidency, between Eritrea and Ethiopia, intended to end their hostilities which had been raging for some years. This, the *Eritrea-Ethiopia Boundary Commission* delimitation of the border between the two states, completed its work in April 2002, and, after years of difficulty in making their ruling effective, a peace treaty was finally signed in June 2018.

The later months of 1999 were not taken up entirely with this work. A note in Robbie's diary shows that he had been writing an Opinion for Israel, which he signed on 4th November at Clifford Chance. A month later he was conducting a 'PCA seminar' in The Hague. His work on the arbitration had, though, prevented his joining the *Institut's* biennial conference held in late August that year in Berlin.[511]

At the end of the year we managed to spend time with all three of our young families: first, on a weekend at Malton, we made a memorable visit to Rievaulx Abbey, its quietness enhanced by brilliant frost. Christmas was spent once more at Leicester with Pippa's family, sharing the girls' excitement over the gifts and customary rituals. And then Joey's family came to Grantchester, with more fun and games.

---

[510] In addition to RYJ's long academic career, Stephen Schwebel had taught at both Harvard and Johns Hopkins Universities; Dr Ahmed El-Kosheri had been Professor and President of the International University for African Development; Keith Highet had taught in universities in the US, France and Ghana; and Rosalyn Higgins had been Professor at the LSE. All were of immense distinction and experience.

[511] At this meeting one *rapporteur* was another notable Cambridge Professor of [Private] International Law, Kurt Lipstein, who at the age of 90 was returning to Germany for the first time since he had left in 1932.

The Final Years

2000-2004

Robbie and I saw in the new millennium, watching the vexingly lame celebrations (the ceremony in the new Millennium Dome, the fireworks) on television, and stepping outside briefly to see distant flashes and explosions from parties round about. That morning Grantchester church was packed for a special service, greeting the new era with a reading of Tennyson's 'Ring out, wild bells …' and a spirit of high intent.

Although Robbie's diary now noted fewer events of special significance, there was always quiet activity in his study. He had written for *Forum* a short article about 'Kosovo and International Lawyers'[512], setting in its historical context the problem that the recent conflict presented to lawyers. The agony suffered on all sides had certainly disturbed him deeply but the more he thought, the more he came to reject belief in the panacea of 'the peaceful settlement of disputes' in a court of law.

> 'Every legal system must have courts applying the law; but it must equally have means of applying political experience and wisdom. It is not merely, or even mainly, a question of "settling" disputes or even situations. It may be a question of creating a new situation…'

As authority he quotes Brierly who, like McNair, he admired for his readiness to look beyond the confines of prescribed international law. In a note to Gilbert Guillaume he described his own article as

> '… a short diatribe in effect rejecting the Kelsen/Lauterpacht simplistic and tragically inadequate view of international relations (though I do not actually mention them).'

---

[512] *Forum* Vol.1 no.3, 1999. The article was written, as Robbie later noted, 'when the bombing was in its early stages.'

The need for a distinction between *legal* and *political* solutions for threatening international situations was one that he felt that elite body of international lawyers, the *Institut de Droit International*, failed to address and he expressed his frustration in personal letters to colleagues who he felt might sympathise. One such was Karl Zemanek, to whom he had written in June 1997 when preparing an article for Seidl-Hohenveldern's *Festschrift*, warning that:

'...what I have in mind to say ...will be scandalous and may get me drummed out of the *Institut*! I believe more and more that large parts of accepted international law are long outdated, and the whole system needs looking at again. I mean, for example, the dangerous, juridical nonsense comprised in the so-called "right"(!) of self-determination (I think the proponents of that "right" ought to look at the blood on their own hands); the nonsense that Hersch Lauterpacht taught about "non-liquet" (so recently approved by my successor at the Court); the great need for adequate machinery for *political* and administrative decision, as *well* as the general approval for any kind of litigation (jobs for Professors!) the fallacy (H.L. again) that recognition can be brought under the power of Professors of International Law, when it is and always will be and should be a political decision for political reasons; the general tendency to tackle public law questions with private law solutions (the private law analogy fallacy); etc. etc.

'Of course *young* people ought to be doing this questioning; but the ones who might, do it at such a high degree of abstraction (Kennedy, Allott, Kostemienni) that nobody can quite understand what they are trying to say. What we need is a young new Charles de Visscher and a new, young James Brierly.

'Can you contemplate the iconoclasm of an old man, Karl? I don't *want* to shock, but I think a good shock is what I.L. at the moment very much needs...'

The resulting article was '*International Law Reform & Progressive Development*', submitted on 9th December 1997 and received by Zemanek with approval – 'In spite of your protestations it is a splendid piece. I haven't enjoyed anything like it for a long time...' And a letter from Yoram Dinstein[513] showed that he, too, was on Robbie's side.

---

[513] Professor of International Law at Tel Aviv University

In August that year a similar outpouring was dashed off to Professor Michael Reisman of Yale, a candidate for election to the *Institut*. Robbie added:

'…I myself get to like the Institut less and less. There is a smothering climate of mutual congratulation and self-importance. It is a very closed society even of international lawyers. It does not seem to be understood that I.L. is now an interdisciplinary subject – and that if we do not seek to discuss I.L. with intl. economists, intl. trade experts, geographers, hydrographers, sociologists, political and economic historians, *et al*, it is not surprising that they do not discuss these matters with us. But good luck! …I have voted.'

His continued contact with former colleagues and pupils in discussions on the telephone and correspondence (much of it scribbled by hand) often expressed his impatience with the blinkered outlook of so many of the highly-esteemed *Institut* members. And in a note to Vera Gowlland-Debbas accompanying the typescript of an article he had written for the *Festschrift* for Abi-Saab[514] he expresses exasperation at the overindulgence in the writing of 'separate opinions' that may be appended to an agreed Judgment of the International Court – started, he says, by Lauterpacht.

(In spite of his genuine love and admiration for Hersch and his hatred of disloyalty, he found himself increasingly at odds with aspects of the great man's work.) Among colleagues he was simply forthright: his correspondence with Rosalyn Higgins reveals some sharp spats over humanitarian law, their disagreements never spoiling their warm friendship and mutual respect.

Another frank comment in the Gowlland-Debbas letter refers to the long-drawn-out search for a ruling on the extradition from the UK of General Pinochet, Robbie seeming content that the final decision should be made by the UN Secretary-General:

'…the buck has to stop somewhere. And international lawyers always think that it is all right provided the last stage is a court of professors of I.L. But frankly they are the very last people I would trust with a political decision –

---

[514] 'The Pinochet Extradition Case in the English Courts' for *The International Legal System in Quest of Equity and Universality*, edited by L. Boisson de Chazournes and V. Gowlland-Debbas.

the question of compliance with the legal provisions of the Charter – O.K! But not please *anything* that requires political judgment…'

He ends by saying, 'if you really want to understand PINOCHET 3, read Hazel Fox, and Robert Goff's speech!' Goff, as senior Law Lord, had dissented from his colleagues in their judgment approving the extradition, and was relieved to have Robbie's support.

It was Rosalyn Higgins, now at the International Court, who kept him abreast with gossip from there and who referred at this time to his having, 'more horrid stuff from the Iran/US Tribunal… although the ICSID cases sound fun.'

Robbie had been made Appointing Authority for the *Iran/US Claims Tribunal,* work which (as he explained to his accountant) 'is to settle internal disputes of this not exactly easy Tribunal and to make actual appointments when the members of the tribunal are unable to agree', rare but disturbing occasions when he needed to rule over the removal of a member of the tribunal and appoint another in his place: 'horrid'. More to his taste were the requests for advice on odd ICSID[515] cases. And one of these that was certainly 'fun' was the *Loewen Case,*[516] a Mississippi jury trial over a claim for damages against a Vancouver-based funeral home company. It was an example of the way a jury in a largely rural state could be led by an unscrupulous advocate to indulge their prejudices against the 'foreigner'. Robbie, with memories still of driving through the southern US states during his Harvard year, could imagine that situation. There is no doubt he had enjoyed writing his 22pp Opinion, dated 26th October 1998, especially a passage such as:

'The Mississippi case in the court below was doubtless one which Mr Gary for the plaintiffs must regard as one of his greatest triumphs of advocacy of a certain kind. It was a scandalous performance done with great skill, experience and knowingness. From the first moment he made it clear how he was going to play his hand. His two aces were to be (i) the latent prejudice of a small, remote and not at all well-off, African-American community against strangers from a strange land many hundreds of miles to the north of even the north of the United States, and who were moreover "Canadians"; and (ii)

---

[515]   ICSID = International Centre for Settlement of Investment Disputes
[516]   *O'Keefe v Loewen Group, Inc.* Robbie's Opinion may be found on the internet.

the gratifying self-importance it might lend a jury from such a community if they were given to believe from the outset that this was a very special case involving unimaginable sums of money and that their gratifying role in the matter was to realise and experience their potential powers to award damages of such amounts as had hitherto been wholly beyond both their experience and even their most unlikely fantasies…'

(In spite of this blistering piece, the result was still the thoroughly unfair award of $500 million against Robbie's clients, the Canadians.)

He had by now actually reached a more tranquil stage of life, not exactly retirement but with time to breathe between the requests for advice or articles. A gentle routine set in. Breakfast each morning was exactly the same: he was not inclined to talk, so we each took a section of *The Times* and read as we consumed toast and fruit, I filling and refilling his cup without speaking. After walking around the garden with the cat he would withdraw to the study, writing or simply sitting. But the sitting meant, probably, that he was engaged in deep thought – thought that tended to mean stepping back and contemplating a situation *as a whole*. He still accepted mental challenges, being one of the few who read Philip Allott's book *Eunomia (1999)* and its successor *The Health of Nations (2000)* to the end and appreciated their message – the need for a moral reappraisal of international law and social order in general from the deepest philosophical roots. He found Richard Tuck,[517] at Jesus, was on much the same wavelength, and read his *The Rights of War & Peace (1999)*.

On a weekday Robbie, using his pensioner's free bus pass, was likely to eat lunch at Jesus or at Trinity. He had for years enjoyed his membership of Trinity high table – but one day it suddenly struck him that on his retirement as Whewell Professor in 1981 the privilege of a free meal must have lapsed. He wrote to the college steward, apologising for his presumption; and soon a message came back saying that the college council had decided to 'deem him *to have been* a Fellow', a status he had never actually possessed. Trinity, it seemed, liked his company as much as he liked theirs, and so he was welcome to eat with them indefinitely. And he valued the stimulating conversation to be had

---

[517] Richard Tuck resigned his Fellowship at Jesus (and was made Hon. Fellow) to become Professor of Government at Harvard.

there: the keenest scientific minds as well as those on the arts side. It was at Trinity that he got to know the composer Judith Weir during her artist-in-residence year and gave her his collection of classical 78rpm records (including some rarities); where he chatted regularly with Richard Marlow, Director of Music, met Thomas Adès, and regularly exchanged banter with an old friend Dennis Green, Professor of German.

I would prepare coffee in readiness for his arrival home, knowing just when to expect him. If he was late it was generally because he had met a cat in the lane or paused to talk to a horse that waited at a gate to have its nose rubbed. Once seated with his coffee, we would chat. And this was the time each day when, sitting together, I would hear about the high table talk or the work he was doing, and discuss concerns about our children or house maintenance… or (yawn) be told about the latest developments in hi-fi. He, in turn, would hear about my own little discoveries in my research on Victorian Grantchester, or more recent village gossip. It was perfect companionship.

About once a week, instead of lunching in Cambridge, Robbie would take me to one of the village pubs. There was the Green Man, where once, entertaining a group who had come from London with Jeremy Carver, we had all sat at its long table on a dais. Robbie was perilously close to its edge, and (in spite of all those years at college high tables) a particularly good joke set him laughing so much that his chair tipped backwards and over he went onto the lower floor with a terrible crash. To those clustered anxiously over him he wanted only to apologise for any damage he might have caused to the chair… and indeed he was rather proud of his ability to fall without hurting himself.

When the Green Man changed hands and offered only Mexican food, we tried the Rupert Brooke. There, nice Julia stepped towards him saying, in a strong Yorkshire accent, 'What can I do for you, love?' and so of course that immediately became our favourite place. When Julia and her husband were promoted to a grander pub in Surrey we tried the Blue Ball. And there, although they professed not to provide food, Karolyn was easily coaxed into providing delicious sandwiches for us. It was an old-fashioned place for serious beer-drinkers; but we, with our modest half pints, were soon accepted as 'regulars' among the wonderful characters who drank and indulged in banter every day. Our other frequent refreshment was to drive to Wimpole Hall for lunch and a walk in its grounds. (It was there that one of the nice women serving food was so charmed by his resemblance to her own Yorkshire father that she wrote me a long letter of sympathy after his death.)

We had, almost since our arrival in Grantchester, attended the parish church. Although never wishing to be identified as Anglicans, we took our turn at reading the lessons in its services and I had both taught in the Sunday School and was now in charge of the church choir (Robbie disliking the wearing of robes, rather too close to High Church rites for his taste). As he explained in a letter to the Bishop of Huntingdon declining to support an appeal, although 'a reasonably faithful member' of the Grantchester congregation, he remained…

'…as I was brought up, a northern nonconformist of the Wesleyan persuasion [with] absolutely no tendency towards episcopalianism, and I still somewhat shudder when there is talk of "priests."'

His preferred services were Matins and Evensong, using Cranmer's prayerbook. Walking to church – I, having gone ahead on a bike to rehearse the choir – he would join the village's oldest resident, William (Bill) Clamp[518] and sit with him.

The season of Lent was marked for some years with a series of addresses given by members of the congregation, and in 1997 the theme was *Christianity and Freedom*. Robbie, speaking on 'Freedom and the Law', gave a carefully prepared talk, realising that many of those in the congregation might never have thought seriously about the purpose of law at all – let alone international law. So he caught their interest by opening with:

'Five weeks ago [our Vicar] Canon Beer gave us a memorable address about the Ten Commandments… Little children seem somehow to be aware that even to play together one needs rules. I remember our younger daughter as a small child once belonged to a "club" made up of neighbouring little girls. Their *Rool 1* was one that could well be more widely adopted: *Do not start larfing or being stupid in meetings".'*

He then moved on from different aspects of English (Common) Law to International Law, stressing how little we are aware of the effective operation

---

[518] – who, in 2013, would receive a card of congratulations from HM the Queen on reaching his 105th birthday. When he died at last he was buried, as he wished, 'as close as possible to the Professor'.

of most of its rules – passage between nations by sea or air, for instance; and the need for better regulation of other matters – humanitarian, environmental and more:

'…We are in the midst of a new industrial revolution accelerating change by the technological miracle of instant global communication. The changes are bewildering and frightening. But we have to come to terms with the fact that, for all the important matters that we are faced with, only international solutions will do, and states will have to use their sovereign independence to agree to limit that sovereignty and accept an international regime instead. This does not mean that we have to agree to things blindly. Proferred international solutions can, like any others, be bad and sometimes useless. We have to look at each case coldly, objectively and technically, and see whether it will do the job, or not. But just to whinge about loss of sovereignty is today to whistle in the wind.

'So, to go back to our parable, the answer to the lawyer's question "Who is my neighbour?" is that the world is now our neighbour; and that to a degree unthought of even 20 years ago. But the underlying truth was already expressed with perfection in 1624 by an English Divine and Poet, John Donne, when he said:

"No man is an Island, intire of it self; every man is a peece of the continent, a part of the maine."

'Donne was a chaplain of Lincoln's Inn, and knew his lawyers very well. And I think he must have had in mind the tolling of the chapel bell of the Inn when a Bencher died and the clerks were sent by barristers to ask who had died, when he was moved to say:

"And therefore never send to know for whom the bell tolls; It tolls for thee".'

—

On Sundays when he could not face the usual communion service, Robbie would skip church and ring Pippa (at home preparing her own family's good Sunday meal) instead for a chat. Their conversation was wide-ranging, from anecdote to argument, children's exploits to religious matters. He loved following the grandchildren's progress; and when the two elder Goodhart girls promised to become real musicians – Annie on the flute and Mary the trumpet – he helped to pay for good instruments for them, Mary naming her trumpet *Yewdall* in gratitude.

All of them – Dick's and Joey's children as well – to our joy, developed a love of music. He revelled in the individuality of every one of the nine, and they loved their bushy-eyebrowed Grandpa. And it was at about this time that Pippa's three girls devised the set of questions that set off his reminiscences. Nowhere, for him, could ever quite replace that sense of community in old Idle or its closeness to the northern dales, which he enjoyed describing for them. Remembering how we had looked at old photos and heard tales of never-quite-identified relations, we both made albums for the three families in which we set copies of surviving photos of their forebears, with brief captions explaining who these people were and what they were like. Robbie's family came to life vividly in his descriptions!

But this brought home how vague was Robbie's knowledge about his more distant origins; and since the conferment of the status of Knight Bachelor offered the chance to become *armigerous*, he decided to indulge in this minor vanity. At the College of Arms he discussed heraldry with Rouge Pursuivant and acquired a Coat of Arms. (This glorious parchment document with hanging seals arrived in a scarlet leather case, but was kept in its outer cardboard box and tucked away, half-forgotten.[519]) At the same time they were commissioned to draw up a proper 'pedigree' but never completed the task, leaving us with only the product of our own research.

When in August 1997 Robbie had had some correspondence with Professor Michael Reisman of Yale, their discussion was on the issue of 'progressive development' and *non liquet*, and some of Robbie's remarks ('all rather garbled – just as it came out onto the word-processor') are worth quoting:

'… I enjoyed your delicious description of Hersch Lauterpacht as "the leading judicial romantic of this century". That is exactly right, identifying both the strength and weakness; almost the Beethoven of international law, in many ways superb but leading directly to the dreadful Mahler!

… I was quite shocked to find that I must have been giving the wrong impression of my own attitude. Obviously I have been using "progressive

---

[519] The Coat of Arms was used just once, as part of a great display of heraldry of members of the Haagsche Club compiled for some anniversary. Robbie felt quietly proud to be shown alongside such figures as the Crown Prince of the Netherlands, HRH Willem Alexander.

development" carelessly. I think of it as covering the sort of development that is entirely proper for a court. I did, I still think rightly, hold in my 1947 *BY* article on codification that codification without some degree of p.d. is impossible; the very fact of establishing an authentic text is a crucial change in customary law. I did, probably again carelessly, think of "progressive" as indicating a step by step, or to a common lawyer case by case, development. It never occurred to me to think of it as a sort of liberal juridical philosophy. In fact I thoroughly agree with your *own* point of view on this question!

'Equally, I also want to avoid the other extreme of a *Begriffsjurisprudenz.* I always think of the Lotus case as the dramatic illustration of that: a juridically elegant decision that was totally blind to the needs of any mercantile marine and had to be legislated out of existence by the Brussels Convention; but of course still cited by international lawyers with reverence and awe! It is ironic that this egregiously stupid decision, which united shipping employers and employees in opposition to it, was made by the casting vote of a President from a landlocked country!

'… Making a good judgment is I believe an art and not a science.

'More importantly I believe strongly that the ICJ is guilty of using its own precedents in an undisciplined way. It cites passages from earlier judgments too often as statements of general or even universal validity, with qualification by reference to the facts and issues of that particular case. In common law terms it quotes them as if from Holy Writ, and without the discipline of trying to find the *ratio decidendi* of the cited case.

'For that matter I am horrified by the idea promulgated by Lauterpacht and eagerly adopted by Fitzmaurice and Jessup that international law judgments and opinions should be 'exhaustive', discussing every variation and side-point that occurs to an active mind. This is pure professorial indulgence; the professor anxious that no stone should be left unturned in his graduate seminar. But an abuse of the judicial office. I remember McNair, one of H.L.'s staunchest friends and admirers, leafing over page after page of one of H.L.'s judicial opinions, sighing in appalled astonishment and saying to me, "Why on earth does he do this as a judge? What is the point of it?" …

'Finally, one reason I am anxious to keep the work of the judge in its proper place is that, if he is thought to be a proper means of making law in a big way …, this obscures the desperate need for the development of means of true international law legislation or quasi-legislation. I think Lauterpacht and Kelsen and such really thought that an international court with compulsory jurisdiction was the primary need. But even if we got it, it would cover only about 25% of the primary need. We terribly need better machinery not only for political and administrative decision but also for international law *reform*. We sadly lack even theoretical law reformers in our subject. The whole set-up is geared to producing more and more of the same stuff. Yet if there is any lesson to be learned from Yugoslavia it is surely that a lot of core international law needs a good hard fresh look. It is not perhaps surprising that international lawyers should have taken a rather splendid political idea like self-determination and turned it into a so-called "right" of "peoples" (undefined and undefinable). That was very much in the Lauterpacht tradition: let's have more and more international law. But what suffering and violence and poverty and international crime that so-called right has produced! International lawyers, however, never feel guilt about bad international law. They just elaborate it…

… [About *non-liquet*] 'One of my objections to the so-called "doctrine" of *non-liquet* is that it is essentially a misunderstanding, or distortion, of what *n.l.* in the civil law seems to mean: failure of a party to discharge the burden of proof in *a question of fact*. It is wrong to use this for an invented "doctrine" … that a court is obliged to decide a case even if this means inventing law to fill a gap in the law … Surely any healthy community *requires* some gaps in the law. There must be some things we can decide for ourselves. Odd too that it should be the *common lawyers* on the Court who cite a distorted interpretation of a Latin tag from the civil law as being a self-evident (no authority cited except H.L.) part of international law!'

Now for the large part retired, Robbie had time to meditate on the weaknesses that had irked him while in office at the ICJ, and grew increasingly intolerant of them. But although at a less hectic pace, his professional work continued. His advice was sought on various cases – in early 2000 the Canadian Lorne Clark consulted him about an IATA case involving air law; the *The Loewen Claim* took some time; in December 2001 he was consulted by a Washington lawyer, Tom O'Brian, concerning a Hungarian case; and there had been Charles Brower's[520] hint of work. As late as January 2003 he was being consulted by Robert Volterra and Stephen Fietta, prominent public international lawyers, both of whom had studied at Cambridge. There were

---

[520] Charles Brower, American attorney, has served for many years on the *US/Iranian Tribunal* and among many other distinctions, as a Visiting Fellow at Jesus College, Cambridge.

other regular commitments: Robbie was still serving on the Hauser Committee in New York, the Commonwealth Trust committee organised by Anil Seal, the committees selecting young people for Gates awards, and the Leverhulme Trust. As a judge on the panel awarding the annual Guggenheim prize he was still obliged to read the candidates' long theses. And now that his *Eritrea/Yemen* case was over, two of the counsel for Eritrea could come and discuss with him their work on the ensuing *Eritrea/Ethiopia* case. Besides all these, his devoted disciple Sami Shubber (who spoke of Robbie as his 'prophet') had, once the Iraq invasion of Kuwait was defeated, returned to his native country to set up a law firm in Baghdad. In doing so, his prospectus cited Sir Robert Jennings, QC, as Consultant in International Law (though never called upon for assistance).

His meditation about the whole matter to which his life had been dedicated, and his reading of Philip Allott's passionate views in *Eunomia,* had intensified Robbie's pragmatism. He knew he was not quite alone in advocating drastic reform of the whole system of international law; but the conviction had grown, and now he wanted to urge it upon a wider audience.

A text – which seems to be transcribed, inexpertly, from a recording – of the lunchtime speech he had given at an International Maritime Organisation conference in January 1999 shows him taking the opportunity to provoke discussion on this topic.

'… I'm not an expert on the Law of the Sea. Insofar as I am any expert at all, it is in general international law, and that's really what I want to talk about… I was brought up in international law a long time ago admittedly. But I was brought up in the strong culture, which I think prevails even today to some extent, that international law is a splendid thing and the more of it we have, the better. And let us lose no opportunity of making more of it. I think we should be aware that international law has really now outgrown that stage, and we can afford to be more critical …

'… I deplore the present tendency … to forget about the importance of legal history. When I first lectured on international law in Cambridge, I started with a first-year course which was International Relations and the History of International Law. That, of course, is long since abandoned in Cambridge as in other universities in favour of what are called "useful subjects", in other words things that you learn rather better in the office or in chambers. I wish we could look again at this problem because it seems to me that the place of the teaching of the legal history of international law has rather been taken by something else that is really the history of international lawyers [a close study of these distinguished, but dead, lawyers]. Now this, I think, is wrong because in fact, if you're looking at the philosophy of law or the theory of international law, even that needs legal history because all these people that are talked about, Hans Kelsen and the rest, were presented with problems in their own day and they were trying to think out ways of tackling those problems; and it seems to me you can't understand even what they say unless you have some idea of the actual history of international law.

'I would add to that what was said by one of the greatest of legal historians, F.W. Maitland, [that a rule of law was devised to address] a particular problem or set of facts which no longer obtained and hasn't obtained for a very long time. But lawyers have, in the meantime, sought out new theories of why this law is a good one, which historically are a sort of mythology, and therefore it was Maitland's view that you need to know the real truth of the matter to see whether the rule is still useful or not...'

Even as a former President of the International Court, he urged them to recognise the limitations of the Court. Its current busyness was:

'...to a large extent... because governments have begun to realise that this is a most excellent way of dealing with certain kinds of disputes at a certain point in their history that is not, as the public has been rather led to understand, the place for a crisis decision to prevent war and to prevent worse. The Court can't do that. ... Its business is to attract cases as a routine, normal matter, which everybody should do in any civilized society.'

This was an unscripted 15-minute address 'intended to provoke a discussion'. But it had become a favourite theme.

In January 1999, too, a piece (which he had headed '*Editorial*') appeared in a new journal concerned with just this subject, the *European Journal of Law Reform*. Its title is '*Law Reform: a New Idea for International Lawyers*', and his name is given as 'Robert Sir Jennings'. There were surely younger colleagues feeling restless over the inadequacy of that great accumulating bulk of international law to deal with problems never contemplated by its acknowledged masters of past years; and it was they, he said, who must now try to address the situation.

⸻

He was strongly in favour of the ILA's efforts to widen the scope of the subject by keeping up-to-date with emerging problems, promoted in particular by our old friend Jeremy Carver. The ILA's great biennial conference of 2000 was held in London, and he attended its opening ceremony in July in Westminster Hall and, with me, the dinner for c400 members in Guildhall. On such occasions he was always greeted by old pupils and colleagues from around the world. Such friends would come to Grantchester to talk to him, too, still often seeking advice.[521] Friendships were precious, and losses deeply felt.

Sadly, funerals and memorial services were regularly noted in our diaries during these final years – 14 of them in 2000 alone. One, on 23rd March, was of the Master of Jesus, David Crighton, who had been in office for only 2½ years when struck down by cancer. A brilliant mathematician, his passion for music – the music of Wagner particularly – had been expressed in conducting the college orchestra shortly before his death. The funeral was crowded, and we found that our arrival in the college chapel had not been early enough to claim seats in the Fellows' stalls. It meant that Robbie had to perch on one of the stone *sedilia* close to the altar, uncomfortable and chill. At the end of the emotionally-charged service the coffin was carried, as is the tradition for a college master, out into the Master's Garden and then through all the courts, with a sombre black-clad procession following after. It is an impressive ritual but slow, and on this April day, cold. Afterwards we moved with the rest of that great gathering into the college hall for refreshment, still standing. I could sense that Robbie had found the occasion exhausting; and just in time I got him to sit down on one of the chairs set in a line against the wall. As he fainted, I managed to turn him round to lie flat. In such a gathering, fortunately, one can find assistance at the highest level. Nearby were Professor Alastair Crompston, neuroscientist, and Professor Austin Gresham, the 'morbid anatomist'. Both insisted that Robbie should stay flat for at least ten minutes, and accompanied him out to the car afterwards.

[521] These contacts include Michael Zander, Professor of Law at the LSE; Hisashi Owada, now Judge at the ICJ; Rosalyn Higgins, RYJ's successor at the ICJ; Milom Banerji, Attorney General of India, Sami Shubber of the WHO; Ruth Donner from Helsinki University; R.S. Pathak, former Judge at the ICJ and Chief Justice of India; Georges Abi-Saab, of Geneva and Cairo; and many more.

It was a warning that he was not quite as resistant to stress as he had been when younger. A month later he was afflicted with gout, which lingered for a fortnight, and a heavy cold had turned to bronchitis. He was able to keep most of his engagements, and once on his feet in front of an audience seemed as animated as ever; but I grew a little more watchful, and he paced himself more carefully.

———

Another loss at the end of the year was of Dr Charles Goodhart, father of Pippa's husband Michael. Our two families, close neighbours, had become linked not only by this relationship but by the rapport developed with Charles and Diana. Our joint grandchildren could tease away Grandpa Charles's grumpy moments, and it was clear that he delighted in their company. (Grandpa Robbie certainly revelled in comic banter with them: in notes to Annie he would sign himself *Lord of the Fruit Bowl*, and she responded as *Dame Banana*.) The Charles we got to know was not only a generous host but the source of stimulating views and unexpected information. His subject was Zoology, and his pupils appreciative. He had been Senior Tutor of Gonville & Caius and a University Proctor; the experiences of his earlier life[522] had equipped him with several foreign languages and an ability to discuss many topics. Robbie could see the warmth and brilliance in this disappointed man, whose end came some weeks after a massive stroke.

Our own final (9th) grandchild, Alice Jennings, was born in May 2001, and we were glad to make her acquaintance some seven weeks later, when Dick's family came for a weekend.

———

Our days were still varied with callers, some unexpected and colourful. One such was the arrival of a magnificent 1920s Bentley touring car, whose owner explained that he had acquired it from the Barnes family. Robbie was delighted to see it, for he remembered its original owner, Henry Barnes, eccentric law fellow of Jesus before the war, who had adopted the Irish version – O'Bierne – of his name in his later years. A few weeks later we had a handsome Armstrong Siddeley, also in immaculate condition, in the drive; and this belonged to

---

[522] Charles's early education had been in Switzerland; and during the war he had been captured in Italy and while imprisoned in Germany had taught himself Russian.

Professor Kurt Lipstein, already over 90 but who would continue to teach Private International Law at Clare College up to his death at 97. He told us over lunch that the beloved car was named *Nottebohm,* having been bought with the fee he had earned for his one appearance before the ICJ in that case between Lichtenstein and Guatemala in 1953.

In September 2001 Robbie heard that Doreen, his secretary at the Court who had been so reliable and good-humoured, had had a stroke. Rosalyn Higgins, who too had been grateful for her help, sent bulletins suggesting a possible recovery, but she died next month; and Robbie sent flowers – 50 red roses – in sympathy. Rosalyn reported that the funeral was:

'…a splendid send-off. The cortège passed through the Court grounds, and simply everyone was lined up along the pathways. The UN flag flew at half mast. I think it extraordinary that a secretary should have occasioned such an outpouring of grief, affection and respect – but then Doreen *was* extraordinary…'

There were happier events. In 1999 we had decided that our enjoyment of Glyndebourne would be enhanced by the company of our youngsters. Accordingly, Joey had shared the performance of *La Clemenza di Tito,* and Pippa and Michael *The Bartered Bride.* In 2000 they saw with us a grotesque production of *Don Giovanni,* and then it was Joey again for *The Rake's Progress.* (That production was more successful; and because I was unable to go, their companion was Charlotte Grant[523] who, it turned out, was writing a thesis on Hogarth's work.) For our 2001 visit we chose Britten's *A Midsummer Night's Dream*, thoroughly enjoyed by grandchild no.1, Annie, and her mother Pippa. *Fidelio*, later that year, was spoilt by a clumsy production. But *Albert Herring*, next summer, made a splendid introduction for Lizzie (No.2) with her father Dick. In 2003 Pippa brought Mary (No.3) to *Fledermaus*; and in 2004 Jill and Thomas (No.4) shared *Die Zauberflöte* with us. We subscribed, too, to the series of Cambridge recitals given by the Endellion Quartet. The collection of

---

[523]   Dr Charlotte Grant, daughter of our old friend, Barbara, from her second marriage, was currently a Research Fellow of Jesus. She became one of the first to teach at the New College of the Humanities in London. She is married to John Reyntiens, stained-glass craftsman.

CDs steadily grew, while Robbie, fascinated by Hi-Fi, resurrected his maths and physics to understand much of its latest technical advances. He so loved buying apparatus[524] that in September 2002 he ordered a whole new set-up from Bang & Olufsen – more compact and elegant than the former Quad equipment.

But that other sort of modern equipment, the computer, still gave trouble. By now both Robbie and I were engaged in writing. My own project was *Widnall,* the book based on material gathered by Peter Ward[525] about the Old Vicarage's Victorian residents. My researches led to a further visit to Norfolk, accompanied by Robbie. We called on Peter at his old flint cottage at Cley-Next-the-Sea, where, while I made notes and took photos, the two men enjoyed a good chat.

Robbie now had a laptop, but more protracted work was still done on the main computer upstairs, still prone to disasters. On 12th December my diary noted: 'R very busy all week recovering and rewriting work lost on computer'. (Our church organist was to be given many hearty Sunday lunches over these years, and I took to saving Robbie's work at intervals on 'floppy discs'.) In his final two years he had a major project on hand, collaborating with James Crawford on a book about the International Court to be called *International Litigation.* They had agreed the allocation of work: of its 15 chapters, 7 were to be written by Robbie and 2 shared; and Robbie had already prepared outlines of his own chapters. But on 10th January 2004 he lost 50pp of his Introduction, which could not be retrieved. My floppy disc restored some of it, and he set about rewriting once again.

While still occupied with meetings, articles, references for top appointments (sometimes needing to make sensitive distinctions when recommending more than one candidate for the same post) and the adjudication of theses submitted for doctorates or prizes, in June 2002 he responded to a quite different challenge, agreeing to preside over an unfamiliar type of arbitration. This was the investigation of a delicate matter concerning a senior official of the World Bank in Washington DC. It did not specifically involve international law but needed someone of high authority, wisdom and tact. Even at the age of 88 Robbie was a good choice, since all those years of experience as college

---

524 By this stage, all three children had been equipped with good sound systems.

525 Peter Dudley Ward deserves a biography of his own. Like Widnall, he was a 'capital contriver' inventing scientific equipment and, as athlete, had taken part in the 1936 Olympic Games.

tutor, work on administrative committees and more recently presiding over a multinational court fitted him for the task. He wanted, too, to introduce me to Washington, and if possible fly there by Concorde.

We did indeed spend a week in Washington, although the expensive thrill of Concorde was denied us. Under the guidance of Nassib Ziadé, Executive Secretary of the World Bank Administrative Tribunal,[526] Robbie patiently conducted interviews, conferred with Ziadé and his staff, and wrote a report. I was there because he claimed to have reached the age when he needed my support for long distance travel; but to my embarrassment it was I who, having looked forward to seeing Washington's Smithsonian museums and other sights, spent almost all of the time confined to our hotel room, stricken with pain from an acute muscular spasm in my right leg (weakened by the trauma of my hip operation 4½ years before). Pain-killers, massage and a walking-stick made it possible for me to emerge now and then, and everyone was most kind. Steve Schwebel gave us dinner at the Yale Club; Delbert Smith and his wife gave us lunch out at Potomac; Nassib Ziadé took us to the wonderful *1798* restaurant in Georgetown; and his young assistant, Peter Hansen,[527] took us for a jolting drive in his old car, stopping to go inside the breathtaking great railway station and to wander around the folksy outdoor market. By the end of his week there, Robbie had accomplished his task to the Bank's satisfaction. And Peter Hansen, inspired by contact with him, decided to try for a place at Cambridge to take the LL.M degree.

A month later, we had a real holiday. After one of those days of Cambridge entertainment – a very jolly lunch given by Alec Broers,[528] Vice-Chancellor, in honour of Peter Oliver,[529] retiring as High Steward of the University, followed by Trinity Ladies' Night, we set off northwards. There was time to pause again at Kirkby Malham and photograph the inscription on John Brotherton's grave, and to wind our way without haste to Arment House. And this time we were

---

[526] Ziadé, originally from Lebanon, later became Director of Dubai International Arbitration Centre.

[527] Peter C. Hansen was to become head of a 'boutique law firm' in Washington D.C. specialising in African investment law, &c.

[528] Professor Sir Alec Broers was made a Life Peer in 2004.

[529] Baron Oliver of Aylmerton was a Bencher of Lincoln's Inn and member of Robbie's chambers.

not responsible for any of those usual chores: Pippa's family were already installed and had prepared one of the big bedrooms for us, while their three girls cheerfully crammed themselves, wall-to-wall, in the back room. Four carefree days in this beloved place included a drive along Wasdale and a ride on 'Ratty' down to Muncaster, besides simple fooling about with the youngsters. And we stopped once more at Ossington House on the way home, to enjoy lunch with Pamela Goedhuis.

Early that September Martti Koskenniemi[530] came to Grantchester to quiz Robbie about his memories of Hersch Lauterpacht. While the Finnish Koskenniemi was generally regarded as a controversial figure, Robbie liked him and saw him as someone with the energy and vision to break free from the rigid limitations accepted by most of the older academics.

In November we were back in The Hague for a couple of nights when Robbie gave the keynote speech at an ILA seminar at the Peace Palace on *Water Resources*. We managed to creep away from the Small Hall of Justice where the meetings were held, into the ICJ judges' wing. There, he was recognised by two delighted secretaries, and we had a good chat with Rosalyn Higgins (who, in 2006 would herself be made President of the Court).

Early in December we enjoyed one of the Fitzmaurices' buffet lunches, this time in their new London home on the Isle of Dogs, not too far from Queen Mary College. A few days later we were in Oxford as the guests of Robbie's former pupil Vera Gowlland-Debbas[531] for a dinner at All Souls – a fascinating experience, not entirely new for Robbie but nevertheless a great privilege. Vera herself is of course a very serious person, but other slightly more frivolous Fellows talked about the college's devotion to its emblem of a mallard duck (rather like the foolery about the Jesus College cock). We retreated for the night up a steep staircase to a thoroughly unmodernised set of rooms, the authentic Oxford milieu with uneven floor, slightly rickety armchairs, and shelves of books. And breakfast next morning had its quirks: on the table, besides Cooper's Oxford Marmalade, was the most enormous jar of Marmite, its silver lid surmounted by a mallard! We spent a little time wandering those familiar streets and the covered market before leaving.

Two days later we were driven to Matrix Chambers, Gray's Inn, for Robbie to speak at the launch of James Crawford's book on *State Responsibility*. Instead

---

[530]   Koskenniemi is currently Professor of International Law in the University of Helsinki.

[531]   Professor Gowlland-Debbas was at the time a Fellow of All Souls'.

of having to come straight back, we had been invited by Hazel Fox to dine and spend the night at her house in Ladbroke Terrace – a special treat. Her husband Sir Michael Fox[532] was by now nearly totally blind but very sweet, and Hazel managed to combine her warm hospitality with deep discussion with Robbie on shared legal interests.

The year ended with Christmas at home, Joey's family coming for several days and Pippa's joining us on Boxing Day. My 75th birthday, on 30th December, I noted as 'a lovely day – except for news of Dick… crashing their BMW'. The car was a write-off; but mercifully both he and Lizzie, his passenger, were unhurt.

Robbie had passed that car to Dick when he had at last given up driving even the short distance to college. I was relieved that, with fading eyesight, he had made the decision for himself, while otherwise his activities in 2003 continued much as before. There were still callers, some seeking advice – a client of Volterra and Fietta;[533] Lea Brillmeyer, Eli Lauterpacht (both probably concerned with the *Eritrea/Ethiopia* arbitration); and one or two young people uncertain of their best course of legal studies.

My *Widnall* book had reached its final stage, and I enjoyed the process of layout-designing, dealing with the University Printers, and chatting about my hero on local radio. On the Friday after Easter I noted:

> 'Exciting day: Arment borehole (66 metres deep) for water – reported by triumphant Mick. Delivery of WIDNALL (50 copies + leaflets).'
> [Robbie's own entry, in ink, was:]
> 'Widnall books appeared. *Water* at Arment in plenty.'

The water was the more important. Michael Goodhart had overseen the drilling of a borehole which secured a reliable supply for Arment House after all its centuries of dependence on a shallow well. On 16th May *Widnall* was launched at the house where he had lived, the Old Vicarage, Grantchester, with a party kindly given by Mary Archer.[534] After so many months of sighing over

---

[532] Sir Michael Fox, QC was a retired Appeal Court Judge of great distinction.
[533] The partnership became *Volterra Fietta,* a leading international law firm, although Fietta himself set up independently later.
[534] Later awarded the DBE, Mary and her husband Jeffrey Archer (Lord Archer of Weston-Super-Mare) have lived at the Old Vicarage since 1979.

the inconvenience caused by 'bloody Widnall,' Robbie became quite proud of my achievement, I found.

A few days later we were visited by Peter Hansen and his wife Eden, over from Washington DC. After lunch we walked them around the Backs and up to the new Law Faculty Building where, in the Squire Law Library, we found Kurt Lipstein at work. Eden managed to catch a photograph of the two veteran international lawyers greeting each other and that visit strengthened Peter's resolve to come and take a further degree at Cambridge.

———

The US invasion of Iraq in March 2003 was disturbing, with its justification by a dubious claim of the threat of 'weapons of mass destruction'. At a Lauterpacht Research Centre party its new Director, Daniel Bethlehem, punned about 'weapons of maths instruction', but the mood deep down was far from cheerful. Robbie knew Hans Blix, the UN official who had searched for the non-existent weapons, as a former pupil. Writing to Ros Higgins on 5th June he said:

'…Yes, the Philippe & David B. party was delightful and very well organised …

I have been much distressed, not so much by the Iraq war but by international lawyers, especially in this country. The only crucial question was whether it was right and wise to join in the war or not. I'm still not sure, but was much comforted by my Iraqi pupil, Sami Shubber, who just back from Baghdad told me firmly that he was in favour of the war as "the only way out from bondage" for his people.

'But that was a *political* question, and a tricky one. The legal nonsense was enshrined by Clare Short. She had a bad conscience about war. All right. So have we all. BUT *her* conscience would, she said, be at ease if we could get "a second" (i.e. 18th) Resolution from the Security Council, very short and carefully drafted so as to get a majority. Then her conscience would be at ease. How infantile can one get?

'The truth is that she, and many others who should know better, used the legal, international law point in order to avoid being faced with the difficult political question and so having, like Blair, to take a political decision.

'This nonsense was encouraged by academic international lawyers. [X] (who is good on TV because he gives clear, short soundbites and without qualification or doubts) was adamant about the veto and the Security Council – in fact Stalin would have given him a medal…'

He then explained that his 'scrawl' was caused by cataracts, which were to be operated on, privately, by the senior eye surgeon from the clinic at Addenbrooke's where he had experienced well-organised 'expert, prompt and kind attention'.

Three weeks later he was able to report to Rosalyn that the intricate operation had been a success and the eye, apart from some scratchiness from two stitches that would soon dissolve, was 'fine'. What now bothered him was that…

'…the hard drive of our computer has crashed irretrievably, including 17pp already composed for the Max-Planck [volume of Commentary on the ICJ Statute] … I think I will just start again. The 2nd time it's always rather better…

'I have done a book review for the AJIL. I was very pleased with a fax from Stephen Scher … who said he had enjoyed it because it was "quirky, intelligent, probing, concise, and occasionally even funny" – this last being a clear breach of the house style, "which is staider than staid", but he had decided to permit an exception. I must say I rather warmed to Scher…'

The piece is indeed vintage RYJ, very gently indicating that although 'the book … is a perceptive work of integrity and sincerity' it lacked sharpness.

'…The atmosphere is rather that of a learned and highly respectable, and even perhaps a slightly genteel, drawing room discussion by intellectuals and academic lawyers over a cup of tea. This drawing room, however, is peopled mainly, if not entirely, by international lawyers with English as their native language, and they don't seem to read a lot, even about international law, in other languages…'

A few days after our Glyndebourne treat (and a breezy walk up to Beachy Head) with Pippa and Mary, Robbie's diary notes 'Judge & Mrs Landau to tea', our meeting with the venerable Israeli Judge Moshe Landau, who in a long judicial career had presided over the trial of Adolf Eichmann. And two days after his second cataract operation, Robbie enjoyed a lunch party in Trinity for the Malaysian High Commissioner and Foreign Minister. But he cancelled our attendance at the *Institut* conference held that year in Bruges, which would have meant a long and probably tiring stay. Instead, I arranged to take him up to Yorkshire.

That was a real refreshment: I could feel him beginning to purr as soon as we stopped at a country pub in his home county and heard familiar dialect all around. We had a lovely welcome at Dick's home at Malton, where we spent some time in their big garden with the children, and then supped with them before finding our way to the ancient Manor House at Allerton where we were to stay.

Our first excursion, next day, was comically curtailed. Off we went to Scarborough. We 'parked and rode' by bus as far as South Bay, which Robbie remembered from his boyhood. Walking a little way down the slope we could see a fine view across the bay, enhanced by a dramatically threatening sky... and almost at once the rain started. It grew to a deluge, from which the only slight shelter in that exposed area was from a slender footbridge far above. Wetter and wetter we cowered, until a returning bus came into view. We scrambled aboard and returned to the car park, deep in puddles. As the torrent dried up, I drove westwards to Coxwold, the village with a special association for Jesuans through Laurence Sterne.[535] There, although Sterne's Shandy Hall was closed, we admired his church and memorial. We also had an errand in Coxwold – to collect a rather bulky present that Pippa & Mick had ordered for Robbie's impending birthday. It was a small oak table made in the workshop of the 'Mouseman' Robert Thompson, a source of perpetual delight with its rippling adze-cut surface and small carved mouse creeping up one leg.

We drove next day up and across the North York Moors to Whitby. A fine sky, racy sea, interesting harbour; up to the Abbey, then a climb down to the fascinating St Mary's Church; and then, on the way back, tea in a moorland pub ostensibly *Closed* where we received a warm welcome and good chat. Then another lovely evening with Dick's family before returning to our guest house.

Next day's treat was a ride on the North Yorks Railway from Pickering; tea at Helmsley, with fruit cake eaten with Wensleydale cheese and a talkative Yorkshireman as companion; and then dinner for 10 laid on in the old courthouse-cum-dining room at Allerton. There, I was amused when a fellow

---

[535] The author of *Tristram Shandy* was a Jesuan and great-grandson of a former Master of Jesus College, Cambridge. Towards the end of his colourful career he had been 'perpetual curate' of Coxwold, and resided in the house he named Shandy Hall.

guest, opposite, looked at Robbie and said he reminded him of someone whose lectures he had attended at Cambridge … and was stunned and gratified to find that it was indeed Professor R.Y. Jennings!

Returning home next day I felt that that dose of Yorkshire had 'set Robbie up', as he would say. As it happened, it was followed by a memorable lunch, just ourselves with our friend Milo Keynes[536] in his small bachelor house near Midsummer Common. Linked by a shared love of music and occasional contact at Trinity, we liked this rather neglected member of the vast dynasty springing from Darwin and other starry figures. Around us were reminders of that galaxy: pieces of Wedgwood, paintings and wood engravings by Gwen Raverat, photographs and drawings… And in the course of the meal Milo told us of his experience in May 1960, as a newly-qualified surgeon, when he had assisted at the exploratory operation on Hersch Lauterpacht at which advanced cancer was found and the patient's heart had stopped.

College links were maintained. That evening Robbie dined with the Jesus Old Boys, and on successive evenings the following week we were at Downing for a dinner to mark the retirement of Stephen Fleet after a rather brief but hugely popular spell as Master, and then at another to welcome his successor, Barry Everitt. Robbie was now an Honorary Fellow of the college, and had been made President of the Downing Association and the Cranworth Law Society – pleased that his old college was now pre-eminent in law, and happy to be interviewed by a pair of undergraduates in 2002 for a 'profile' in the law society's magazine, *Per Incuriam*. It was a shame that a bout of 'flu prevented his attending the great dinner given for John Hopkins'[537] retirement, especially since his friendship with both John and his wife Cherry had been sustained for so many years.

———

Robbie's own 90th birthday was celebrated several times over. On 17th October 2003 the Law Faculty gave a dinner for him in the Old Hall at Queens'. To be honoured by all these colleagues and former pupils, many coming from far away, was almost overwhelming. In response to their congratulations he spoke

---

[536] WM Keynes MD, FRCS, was third of the four sons of Geoffrey Keynes and great-grandson of Charles Darwin.

[537] John Hopkins, law fellow of Downing and Senior Tutor for many years. His wife Cherry, a fellow of Girton, taught international law and was Robbie's invaluable assistant in editing the BYIL.

seriously about the need for a historical perspective in considering problems of international law. I was puzzled when James Crawford, while congratulating Robbie on his active old age made rather laboured references to Methuselah … and then found that the Faculty's present to him was a Methuselah of champagne!

The birthday itself on the 19th was spent at Leicester, where Pippa had gathered our whole tribe – Jenningses, Goodharts and Eddlestons: ourselves, six children (including in-laws) and nine grandchildren. Robbie of course loved it. Photos record him among this beloved throng, talking about trains with the boys and getting down on all fours to examine Pippa's hens with little Alice.

Next evening, after hall dinner at Trinity he made a brilliant short speech in the Combination Room where the exceptional number taking dessert that evening showed their warm regard for him, too.

But the day after, he developed a fever and his attendance at the Bench's Ladies Night at Lincoln's Inn had to be cancelled, as did the planned luncheon in his honour at Jesus. That was held later, on 16th November in Upper Hall, and Dick[538] was there with us. Robbie's speech – reminiscing about his 64 years as a fellow of the college – was recorded on a CD by John Adkins, and it is wonderful to be able to hear again the typical self-deprecating humour and the roars of laughter in response.

A more spectacular occasion, the luncheon in the Jesus hall to celebrate the 100th birthday of Sir Arthur Marshall,[539] himself an Honorary Fellow and 80 years a member of the college, followed a fortnight later. We enjoyed, too, a magnificent performance in the college chapel of Monteverdi's *Vespers* conducted by Tim Byram-Wigfield, the college's Director of Music who was about to leave Jesus for St George's Chapel, Windsor.

What was to be Robbie's last visit to the Netherlands, on 9-10 December 2003, also went well. He had been asked by John Dugard[540] to take part in the formal disputation undergone by a candidate for his doctorate at Leiden University – a stately and colourful ceremony for which Robbie, as examiner, had to wear his own LL.D. gown and bonnet, after which the unsurprisingly successful candidate threw a noisy beer-drinking party. (The new doctor was Gerard Kreijen, whose thesis would appear as a book[541] the following year with

---

[538]   His year after Oxford spent studying for Part I of the Law Tripos had made Dick a Jesuan, too.

[539]   Sir Arthur Marshall, an aeronautical pioneer, founder of Marshall's Airport and engineering works, Olympic athlete and much more.

[540]   John Dugard was at that time Visiting Professor at the University of Leiden.

[541]   *State Failure, Sovereignty and Effectiveness* by Gerard Kreijen, pub. Nijhoff 2004.

a foreword by Robbie.) Next morning – cold, blue sky, brilliant sunshine – we walked about and, to warm up, drank coffee in a floating café where, with the sound of gossiping Dutch women in the background, we could delight in a canal scene of picturesque houses, a great windmill, and tethered sailing barges. Dugard gave us lunch, and Robbie chose his favourite *uitsmijter*, fried eggs and ham on toast.

Just before Christmas another dose of 'flu set in, and this latest one lasted for weeks. I was anxious (and a little indignant) when his friend Dennis Green came to seek advice about a difficult family problem, just when Robbie's temperature was high and he had a bronchial cough; yet the intense consultation went on and on, with the invalid patiently listening. I think it helped Dennis, and Robbie did not complain.

On 9th January 2004 Downing's deferred 90th-birthday tribute took place, and Robbie was able to respond to the toast in his honour. But next day his work was brought to a halt by that total computer-crash which extinguished the 50pp of his introduction to the book on which he was collaborating with James Crawford. Even a long session by our wizard Ian Talbot, supported by copious refreshment, failed to restore it.

In February a very nice Jesus undergraduate came to tea. She was Catherine Dobson, referred to Robbie by the Senior Tutor, Stephen Siklos, who asked him to help her decide whether to change from her course in Mathematics to Law. Her long chat with him evidently clinched the matter; and she is now a successful barrister and a Bye-Fellow of St Edmund's College.

In March we were at a reception at Trinity for Commonwealth Trust students, where Robbie chatted with youngsters from Mauritius, India, Israel and elsewhere (and failed to notice HRH Prince Charles nearby). I was amused too when, at the end of a dinner at Trinity, Emma Rothschild (herself an eminent economic historian and wife of the current Master, Amartya Sen) introduced him to some starstruck Asian scholars as 'the greatest international lawyer in the world'. After that encounter, Robbie was astonished when I told him what Emma had said.

A Trinity man of great distinction, though not among our usual academic friends, was Sir Francis Pemberton of Trumpington Hall. We always got on well with him and his son Anthony, and were interested in the family's achievements as landowners and farmers for generations. Francis and his wife

Mary had now retired to the top storey of the great house, and it was a treat to be invited to lunch with them there, together with Andrew Huxley and a nice woman friend of theirs. Huxley, now a widower, still had rooms in Trinity and we often sat with him at the monthly dinners in hall when wives were welcomed. He had plenty of tales to tell and curiosities to explain, and we relished his company.

Of our own family we saw the young Goodharts, who lived closest, most frequently. Joey's family had been with us as usual for Christmas; and Dick, *en route* to a business meeting, had managed to spend a few hours with us in April 2004. Later that month, visiting Pippa's family in Leicester, we were taken to the nearby racecourse with a new pavilion designed by Michael, and his firm was providing a buffet lunch. It was a new experience for us to watch immaculately-groomed horses being paraded around and then racing. In defiance of his chapel upbringing, Robbie actually laid a bet of £5 – and won! (and was relieved to lose his ill-gotten gains on the next race). He revelled in the colour and atmosphere.

In late May we attended a lecture given by the Japanese Ambassador ('mostly inaudible; earnest, thorough, full of statistics') largely as a diplomatic courtesy. A large number of Japanese were in Cambridge for a special course of study at the end of which, on 10th June, Robbie received his last and strangest award. This was a Honda Kotaro medal, presented by a representative of Tohoku University in Sendai, where our friend Shigeru Oda was emeritus Professor of International Law. The other recipients were metallurgists or aeronautical engineers, since Honda Kotaro's own fame had been in metallurgy. We met them and heard more about their own achievements at the dinner given in King's College hall afterwards.

People still came out to Grantchester to talk with him. In June we gave tea to Sir Kenneth & Lady Keith, who left a very pleasant impression, confirming Robbie's support for Keith's nomination as New Zealand judge at the ICJ. Then it was an old pupil, Penny Ferreira, specialising in environmental law. She and Robbie became so absorbed in discussion that she had to be sharply summoned away by her hostess in Cambridge for a late supper. Lastly, Peter Hansen was again in Cambridge and called for Robbie's advice about his proposed LL.M. course.[542]

---

[542] When Peter Hansen, his wife and baby arrived in September to start his academic year, his great disappointment was not to have Robbie there as a mentor.

Robbie was known for the accessibility of his writing, and he was always anxious to remove any obscurity. Even when I was still Tutors' Secretary he had sometimes used me as a representative 'general reader' to read through and comment on an opinion or article he was working on, and if I failed to understand a passage he would clarify it. When lecturing, he was acutely aware of his audience and I found that on the rare occasions when I was present he would keep an eye on my reactions – 'I noticed I was losing your attention,' he might say, 'and so I expressed it differently'. And it was in that summer of 2004, not long before his death, that he encountered Peter Glazebrook[543] in Jesus Lane and confided that he was struggling with a piece of writing: it had become *boring*, and he needed to enliven it.

That July provided the usual pleasant events. One was the exhibition of our village friend Joan Day's paintings; another, the grand buffet lunch given by the Archers at the Old Vicarage; a third was an evening reception at the Squire Law Library full of old and young lawyers.

And then there was Glyndebourne. This year it was grandson Thomas's turn to be initiated, and his mother Jill brought him down from Malton to see *Zauberflote*. Our evening stroll around the garden was in gentle rain, but otherwise the experience was as magical as ever.

On Monday 26th July, though, we attended the funeral of Derek Taunt,[544] one of Robbie's nearest contemporaries at Jesus. It was with Derek that Robbie had instituted the annual cricket match between Fellows and Staff and it was Derek, as Bursar, who had founded the King Street Housing Association. His family had taken regular holidays at Arment House, and we had several of his wife Angela's pictures. The funeral at the crematorium, and the crowded gathering afterwards at Kettle's Yard, left Robbie feeling drained. Once home, he sat down and fainted in his armchair.

It was not the first time. I had learnt to be watchful. That evening, though, he revived enough to dine in Jesus. The college had invited Peter Edwards to come and inspect his portrait of Robbie in its new and more conventional

---

[543] P.R. Glazebrook came to Jesus College in 1967 as Fellow and Director of Studies in Law.

[544] Derek Taunt had graduated in mathematics at Jesus, then spent the war years doing vital work at Bletchley Park. He returned to the college in 1947 as a Research Fellow, and Robbie had known him since that time.

frame – hoping he would at least approve of its prominent position.[545] We were delighted to meet Peter again, and lingered, chatting, in the Combination Room afterwards, finally asking whether he would be able to spare the time to come out to Grantchester next day. He did, and after morning coffee we drove him into Downing College to see the re-hanging of another of his portraits and meet again its subject, Peter Mathias. By then it was time for lunch, so we took him to the Blue Ball for beer and sandwiches. While drinking coffee in our garden afterwards I fetched my camera and took a photo of him with Robbie and this prompted him to use his own camera to take the two of us together. The weather was so bright and hot that I had popped a straw hat on Robbie's head. The resulting photos show him looking relaxed and cheerful.

When it was time for Peter to leave, he impulsively kissed Robbie goodbye. As I drove him to the station, I said 'Thank you for giving Robbie such a happy day', for I knew that there was something less pleasant to follow. It was an appointment with a consultant to hear the result of a CT scan made earlier, which revealed a tumour in the bladder – almost sure to be benign, we were told, but needing to be removed. Robbie seemed to take the news calmly … as a Yorkshireman he was not going to 'let on' to any misgivings.

Next day, Wednesday, there was another funeral, this time of Vivienne, wife of Gareth Jones.[546] Vivienne, so bright and animated when we had met her not long before, had died of cancer before her time. The service in Trinity chapel was followed by refreshments in the Master's Lodge, but Robbie soon wanted to leave. Our car was parked in New Court between others, and in reversing out one needed to take care not to hit one of the low granite bollards set around its great central lawn. I had done this manoeuvre before and trusted the car's sensors to warn of an impending collision. But Robbie, anxious to help, gave hand signals from behind as he moved backwards. Suddenly he disappeared from view. I stopped and got out. He was lying on the grass, half-laughing and saying 'Silly me – I forgot where the stone was and tripped over it!'

When two young men attempted to raise him to his feet I saw how one leg was clearly injured and Robbie fainting, so asked them to lay him gently down. And what followed is vividly remembered – a sequence of kind efforts to help, and what must have seemed a slightly surreal tableau for those passing

---

[545]   The portrait had been re-hung to face that of Steve Fairbairn, both in the passage outside the Hall.

[546]   Gareth Jones, Fellow of Trinity and Downing Professor of the Laws of England.

through the court: Robbie on his back on the grass, his head shaded by a colourful umbrella I found in the car, and me sitting on an upright chair with a glass of water thoughtfully provided by the college nurse. An ambulance, summoned by the porter, arrived and paramedics examined and gently lifted Robbie inside. I, determined to stay with him, was about to climb in too when Emma Rothschild approached and asked whether I had any money with me? Not a penny: my small bag held just the keys to the house and the car. So she pressed £15 on me, saying I might need it … and indeed I did, when I eventually left Robbie (being examined in Accident & Emergency) and had to take a taxi back to collect my car.

That evening when I went back to the hospital to see him, we were told by a doctor that his X-ray had shown a clean break in the right femur which could be fixed in an operation next day. I would not be allowed to visit until 2 pm. And when I did so, on Thursday afternoon, I found him in a high airy ward, close to a window overlooking the Gog Magog hills. There had been no operation – the surgeon's list was full for that day – but he had had a good night and morning. Eating lunch, though, had brought on a fit of coughing and he was now feverish, so I sat quietly by or gazed out of that window at a view of ripe cornfields being harvested and an occasional train passing on its way to London. Now and then a faint voice from the bed was saying something as Robbie stared at the ceiling: 'Television … dogs fighting … Downing griffon …' When a nurse appeared and I said he was hallucinating, she replied cheerfully 'Yes: it's the morphine. That's why people take heroin!'

When I got home I found that Joey was on her way. Leaving her family at Arment House, where they had just arrived for their holiday, she was making the tortuous train journey and would walk from Cambridge station. We were glad to get to bed and had just settled down when a call came from Addenbrooke's saying that Robbie had developed pneumonia and one lung had collapsed, so we went at once … and waited a long time but were not able to see him. Next morning he was in a different, more crowded, ward. Pippa came. On Saturday Dick arrived, and Robbie's 'Oh! Oh! Oh!' expressed his joy in having all three children there with him. Later that day Joey and I were called into a side room to be told by a consultant that a further scan had showed Robbie's oesophagus to be ruptured, something that there was no realistic possibility of repairing; also that Robbie himself had clearly said that he did not want 'extreme resuscitation'. What did we feel? After a shocked pause I said 'I confirm that', and Joey agreed. Yet on the Sunday morning, with

Dick and Joey there, Robbie was apparently 'brilliant', even joking until urged to take food (by a fresh doctor who had not read his notes). The resulting setback meant that the only possible treatment was now a regime of palliative care, with water and painkiller delivered by tube, and the family taking turns to maintain a vigil.

The hospital staff did what they could, while we watched over him. It was early on the Tuesday morning that a haunting sound rose from the bed opposite, as a slightly crazed Asian man began the Mohammedan call to prayer … on and on, in a good strong voice. Robbie must, I felt, still be able to hear and recognise that sound, and might even find it comforting. (It stopped abruptly when another patient shouted '*Shurrup!*') When midnight passed the following night I – hoping that the words might be dimly heard – spoke to tell him that it was our 49th wedding anniversary. But the end came later that morning, the 4th August, when Joey was by his side.

After

That final week of Robbie's life, as his body failed stage by stage, had amidst the distress many tragi-comical moments which could have provided material for one of his after-dinner speeches. And there were indeed smiles later when Dick read out to us the second clause of his Will, which I remember had been written years before at the prompting of a solicitor, at first reluctantly and then with relish:

> 'If it be possible and convenient I would be buried in Grantchester Churchyard. I wish the service to be that for the burial of the dead according to the 1662 Book of Common Prayer, and any Bible readings to be from the Authorized Version. Any hymn singing I wish to be of hymns written by Charles Wesley, for thus can one be sure that, in John Wesley's words in the 1770 preface to the *Collection for the use of the people called Methodists*, there is "nothing turgid or bombast, on the one hand, or low and creeping on the other". To find a suitable hymn of Charles Wesley might not be easy because many of the finest of Charles Wesley's hymns are omitted from *Hymns Ancient and Modern;* but if a hymn is found there I hope that the text might be checked against the correct one to be found in the *Methodist Hymn Book* and so avoid the peril of those 'improvements' which John Wesley warned against in his preface ("… but I desire that they would not attempt to mend them – for they really are not able"), and concerning which the authors of *Hymns Ancient and Modern* had the effrontery to boast in their own preface.
>
> 'If burial be found difficult or inconvenient I have no objection to cremation, and if that be my destiny I would ask that the proceedings in the crematorium chapel be confined to the words of committal; and that the customary spineless soft music from their abominable Low-Fi equipment be altogether avoided.'

His wishes were carried out. The funeral service, in Grantchester Church, was conducted by the Rt. Rev. Peter Walker, former Bishop of Ely (a friend of Robbie's for many years) and our Vicar, the Rev. Canon Frank Fisher. Dick, eldest child, and Annie, eldest grandchild, both gave readings; the hymns (carefully checked) were by Charles Wesley; and the burial was in the recently-opened fourth churchyard, with fields around. Those from the village who had known him only as the nice man in a tweed cap who joined them at the bus stop or who sat unobtrusively in church, must have been surprised to find the coffin draped in a light-blue United Nations flag,[547] and to count the 36 wreaths laid out before his grave.

Obituaries appeared in the papers: first an announcement in the *Cambridge Evening News* under the heading 'International Law's Top Man Dies at 90' with a comment by James Crawford on 'the greatest professor of international law Cambridge has produced'. Then *The Times* (Rosalyn Higgins), *The Telegraph* (Christopher Greenwood), *The Guardian* (Franklin Berman & Malcolm Shaw) and *The Independent* (Vaughan Lowe), as well as the piece in the *Downing College Annual Report* (John Hopkins) – all full, perceptive and hearfelt tributes, each catching something of Robbie's particular skills and warm humanity.

Peter Walker's funeral address emphasized how Robbie's dedication to justice was rooted in his early years of Wesleyan Methodism. And it was he who composed, with great care, the final prayers for the Memorial Service held in Great St Mary's Church[548] on 11th December 2004:

'We remember the distinctive marks of character and person which, accompanying incisive intellect, both commanded respect and won for Robert Jennings universal deep affection:

his unaffected modesty:

his generosity in the gift of himself to his pupils, and the high value he set on true collegiality with his fellow Judges in the International Court of Justice;

his passionate concern for the precision of words in the service of mutual understanding;

his respect for differences whilst yet looking always for the ground of agreement;

his resolute firmness of principle once apprehended;

---

547 That flag had been brought over from The Hague by Hugh Thirlway. An enormous one, the size flown from the Peace Palace itself, had been sent beforehand but, being too large for the coffin, was displayed at the reception afterwards.

548 Great St Mary's is the University Church of Cambridge.

his unfailing trust in the cause of the settlement of disputes by mutual agreement, particularly as between nations for the avoidance of the scourge of war and in such a manner that international peace and justice should not be endangered.

And as we remember these, his gifts, let us recall, as their source and the secret of his lightness of step, the firmness of his faith, retained always in the freshness of his inheritance of it, in the GOD of righteousness and mercy of true Christian belief: Giver of the natural world whose creatures were a daily joy to him; and Giver to him of the deep happiness of his family life: the Author of peace and lover of concord, from whom all thoughts of truth and peace proceed ...'

The address for this occasion was given by Rosalyn Higgins – another generous and sensitive appreciation of her predecessor at the International Court.

And that service ended with the *Nunc Dimittis* composed by a former tutorial pupil, Richard Lloyd, who had come over from Hereford to be present. The Jesus College chapel choir sang, and their Director of Music, Daniel Hyde, played organ pieces by Bach. Dick again took part, reading the passage from John Donne's *Meditations* ending '... never send to know for whom the bell tolls; it tolls for thee'.

The chapel bell at Lincoln's Inn had indeed tolled for Robbie's passing, and although I was asked whether a further Memorial Service should take place there, I declined, for both at Grantchester and at the University Church people had gathered from every background. I was immensely touched to be greeted afterwards by so many who had come from a distance:[549] Michael Wood, from the Foreign Office, on his way to meetings at New York; an old lady whom I just in time recognised – the widow of Robbie's old friend Russell Walton, at whose wartime wedding he had served as Best Man; one younger woman who introduced herself as a grateful tenant of Robert Jennings Close ... and so on.

A few months after Robbie's death, his final writings appeared in print. One was his contribution to *The Statute of the International Court of Justice:*

---

[549] Some members of the ICJ who would otherwise have been there felt obliged instead to attend the funeral of HRH Prince Bernhard of the Netherlands, which occurred that day.

a Commentary,[550] for which he had written the General Introduction and the commentary on Article 24 of the Statute. Another was an article in the *Festschrift* published in honour of Gaetano Arangio-Ruiz, *Reflections on the Subsidiary Means for the Determination of Rules of Law.*

The work on which he had been engaged with James Crawford never came to fruition. All that survives is his draft of Chapter 2: *The Essential Characteristics of International Judicial Settlement.*

What can perhaps be regarded as his final words on the need for a more pragmatic approach in devising and applying international law appeared towards the end of 2004, a short piece in *FORUM* with the title *The Imbalance of the International Law System.* In it he expressed his exasperation over the 'legal justification' of the Iraq war in a characteristic passage:

'... Far more questionable than the lack of a second Security Council resolution expressly sanctioning the operation in Iraq was the astonishing response of a "declaration of a war on terrorism". This was the response that might have been expected a hundred years ago or any time before 1946: put volume I [of *Oppenheim*] back on the shelf and take down volume II.[551] But "war" is a technical term of international law, and a "war" on a terrorism that is organised globally in cells located in many jurisdictions and operating spasmodically in others fails to make either legal or military sense. No wonder the military were at first puzzled about what they were supposed to do and where. If they were to seek out and destroy the terrorists, then a sensible place to begin might have been London or New York rather than Baghdad. That the classical law of war is unsuited as a response to global terrorism is clear from the doubts about the position of "non-combatants", the problems of Guanantamo Bay, and a host of other problems that have followed. Terrorism is a problem that the old volume II "war" does not fit...'

There had been no perceptible weakening of Robbie's mind in his last days. A final tribute came in the entry for the *New Oxford Dictionary of National Biography* written by Sir Franklin Berman, published in full even

---

550   *The Statute of the International Court of Justice; a Commentary* published by the OUP, edited by Andreas Zimmermann, Christian Tomuschat & Karin Oellers-Frahm.

551   Volume I of *Oppenheim* deals with the law of Peace. Vol. II was on Disputes, War & Neutrality.

though over-running his allotted word-count. It is, once more, the 'story of the unforeseeable, even improbable, advance to high position and worldwide reputation of a straightforward man of simple origins'; and I am deeply grateful for the care Frank had taken in composing it.[552]

Just a few weeks before his death, I had suddenly asked Robbie: 'Of all you have done over the years, what do you feel was the most important?' And his answer came without hesitation: 'Teaching'. Hence the inscription on his gravestone:

Robert Yewdall
JENNINGS
1913-2004
International lawyer
teacher & judge

---

552 The *ODNB* piece contains one revelation: the remark that (after Robbie's many honours) 'All that failed was the life peerage to which his presidency of the International Court of Justice ought to have entitled him …' I was not aware that his name had been proposed, and feel that Robbie would have had no regrets.

RYJ's Published Writings

Judicial Legislation in International Law, Kentucky Law Journal 1938 pp112-27

The Caroline and McLeod Cases, AJIL 1938 pp82-99

Some International Law Aspects of the Refugee Question, BYIL 1939 pp98-114

International Civil Aviation and the Law, BYIL 1945 pp191-209

Open Towns, BYIL 1945 (note) pp259-64

Government in Commission, BYIL 1946 pp112-41

International Civil Aviation 1945-46, BYIL 1946 (note) pp358-63

The Progressive Development of International Law and its Codification, BYIL 1947 pp301-29

Some Aspects of the International Law of the Air, *Recueil des Cours* 1949 pp5-82

The Commonwealth and International Law, BYIL 1953 pp320-51

The International Court's Advisory Opinion on Voting Procedure, Transactions of Grotius Society 1956

States Antitrust Laws, BYIL 1957 pp146-75

Recent Cases of 'Automatic' Reservations to the Optional Clause, ICLQ 1958 pp349-66

International Laws and Colonial Questions, *Cambridge History of the British Empire*, Vol. III, Chapter 18, 1959 (with H. L.)

The Progress of International Law, BYIL 1958 pp334-55 (inaugural lecture)

Hersch Lauterpacht, ICLQ 1961 (introduction to tributes)

State Contracts in International Law, BYIL 1961 pp156-82

The Acquisition of Territory in International Law, Manchester, Schill Lectures 1961

The State of International Law Today, Public Society of Teachers of Law c1960

The Limits of State Jurisdiction, *Nordisk Tidsskrift* 1962 pp209-229

Note on the Advisory Opinion of 20 July, on Certain Expenses of the United Nations, ICLQ 1962 pp1169-83

Recent Developments in the International Law Commission: its Relations to the Sources of International Law ICLQ 1964 pp385-97

Nullity and Effectiveness in International Law, *Cambridge Essays in International Law* pp64-87 (also ed. 1965)

Chapters on International Law, *The Annual Register* 1957-65

Entry on 'International Law', *Encyclopaedia Britannica* 1963

Rules Governing Contracts between States and Foreign Nations, *Rights and Duties of Foreign Investors Abroad* 1965 pp123-44

Arnold Duncan McNair, Cambridge Law Journal 1965 pp1-2

General Course on Principles of International Law Hague Academy *Recueil des Cours* 1967, Vol. II, *pp324*-605

The Commonwealth and State Succession, *International & Comparative Law of the Commowealth* (ed Robert Wilson)1968

The Limits of Continental Shelf Jurisdiction: Some Possible Implications of the North Sea Judgment ICLQ 1969, pp819-832

The United States Draft Treaty on the International Seabed Area: Basic Principles, ICLQ 1971, pp433-52

The Proper Reach of Territorial Jurisdiction: a Case Study of Divergent Attitudes, Georgia JIL 1972, Supp.2, pp35-42

A Changing International Law of the Sea, Cambridge Law Journal 1972, pp32-49

Clarence Wilfred Jenks, (with H. Waldock) BYIL 1972 pp *xi-xvi*

Report on International Court of Justice Judicial, Max Planck Symposium on Settlement of Disputes 1974, pp35-48

Arnold McNair, CLJ 1975, pp177-81

The Discipline of International Law, ILA 1976, Lord McNair Memorial Lecture

'Glanville': a tribute to Glanville Williams in *Reshaping the Criminal Law* 1978

Treaties as 'Legislation' in *Jus et Societas,* Essays in tribute to Wolfgang Friedman 1979, pp159-68

What is International Law and how do we tell it when we see it? Swiss YBIL 1981, pp59-88

Law-Making and Package Deal *Mélanges offerts a Paul Reuter* 1981, pp347-55

Sir Humphrey Waldock: memorial address, pub. All Souls College 1981, pp178-84

The Identification of International Law in *International Law: Teaching and Practice* (ed. Cheng 1982), pp3-9

Gerald Gray Fitzmaurice, BYIL 1984, pp1-64

International Law entry in *Encyclopedia of International Law,* ed. Bernhardt 1984, pp278-97

Teachings and Teaching in International Law, Essays in Honour of Judge Lachs 1984, pp121-31

A New Look at the Place of Adjudication in Heidelberg Colloquium for Günther Jaenicke 1984, pp67-82

Human Rights and Domestic Law and Courts in honour of Judge Wiarda 1984

Equity and Equitable Principles Swiss YBIL 1986, pp27-38

International Courts and International Politics, Hull University Press: Josephine Onoh Memorial Lecture 1986, pp16

International Force and the International Court of Justice, *The Current Regulation of the Use of* Court of *Force,* ed, Cassese 1986, pp323-35

The Judicial Function and the Rule of Law in International Relations, Essays in honour of Roberto Ago 1987, Vol.III, pp139-51

The Place of Jurisdictional Immunity of States in International and Municipal Law, talk to European Institute, University of Saarland 1987, 20pp

Universal International Law in a Multicultural World in *Liber Amicorum* for Richard Wilberforce 1987, pp39-51

The Judicial Enforcement of International Obligations, Max Planck Institute 1987, pp3-16

Public International Law Today, (Accepting Hon. Doctorate, Univ. of Saarland 1988) pp111-120

Customary Law and General Principles of Law as Sources of Space Law, in *Environmental Aspects of Activities in Outer Space,* ed Böckstiegel 1988, pp149-52

The Internal Judicial Practice of the International Court of Justice, BYIL 1989, pp31-47

The Principles Governing Marine Boundaries in *Festschrift* for Karl Doehring. Max Planck Institute 1989, pp397-408

The Collegiate Responsibility and Authority of International Court of Justice in *International Law at a Time of Perplexity,* essays in honour of Shabtai Rosenne (ed. Dinstein) 1989 pp344-53

An International Lawyer Takes Stock (F.A. Mann Lecture) ICLQ, Vol 39, 1990, pp513-29

The World Court is Necessarily a Regional Court, *Hague Academy Workshop 1990 pp305-16*

Judicial Reasoning at an International Court, Europa Institute, Univ. of Saarland, ed. Ress 1991, 8pp

Les Traités, being Chap.VI of *Droit International: Bilan et Perspectives,* UNESCO, ed. Bedjaoui 1991, pp143-86

Treaties " " English version, in *International Law: Achievements and Prospects,* pp135-77

Chambers of the International Court of Justice and Courts of Arbitration, *Essays in Honour of René-Jean Dupuy* 1991

Judicial Reasoning at an International Court, Europa Institute, Univ. of Saarland 1991 8pp

An Expanding Court in 48 *The World Today*, Royal Insitute of International Affairs 1992, pp44-47

The Role of the International Court of Justice in the Development of Environment Protection Law, *Review of European Community and International Environmental Law* 1992 pp240-44

Oppenheim's International Law Ninth Edition pub. Longman 1992, 2 Vols., total 1419pp ed. Robert Jennings & Arthur Watts

New Problems at the International Court of Justice, Festschrift for Judge Jiménez de Aréchaga c 1993

Reflections on the Term 'Dispute' in *Essays in Honour of Professor Wang Tieya*, ed. Macdonald 1994, pp401-5

International Lawyers and the Progressive Development of International Law in 'Theory of International Law at the Threshold of the 21st Century', *Essays in honour of Krzysztof Skubiszewski* 1964

The International Court of Justice after Fifty Years in *The United Nations at Fifty* AJIL Vol.89 No.3, 1995, pp493-505

The Judiciary, International and National, and the Development of International Law ICLQ Vol. 45, 1996, pp1-12

Hersch Lauterpacht: a Personal Recollection, 2 EJIL 1997, pp301-04

The Proper Work and Purposes of the International Court of Justice ed. A.S. Muller et al. 1997, pp33-45

The Role of the International Court of Justice, BYIL 1998, 63pp

International Law Reform and Progressive Development, *Liber Amicorum* for Prof. Seidl-Hohenveldern, pp325-338

Broader Perspectives in International Law, in *Legal Visions of the 21st Century:* Essays in honour of Judge Christopher Weeramantry 1998, pp 497-507

Advisory Opinions of the International Court, in *Boutros Boutros-Ghali Amicorum Discipulorumque Liber*, 1998, pp531-7

Law Reform: a New Idea for International Lawyers, Editorial in *European Journal of Law Reform* 1999

Kosovo and International Lawyers, *International Law FORUM* 1999 pp.166-170

The Pinochet Extradition Case in the English Courts, in 'The International Legal System in Quest of Equity and Universality', *Liber Amicorum* for Georges Abi-Saab, 2001 pp 677-698

Sovereignty and International Law in *State, Sovereignty, and International Governance* ed. Gerard Kreijen 2002 pp 27-44

The Work of the International Bar in *Man's Inhumanity to Man* ed. L.C. Vohrah *et al.*, pp 443-466, 2003

Commentary on Article 24, *The Statute of the International Court of Justice,* OUP 2004, ed. Andreas Zimmermann *et al* (also General Introduction, pp 3-38)

The Imbalance of the International Law System, *FORUM* Vol. 6, 2004, pp 126-130

... We must rescue international law from being an esoteric cult for a handful of specialists and get it more generally recognized for what it is: a matter of the very gravest concern to everybody ...

[Extracted from Robbie's editorial introduction to
European Journal of Law Reform, 1999]